The Catholic
WITHDRAWN
LIBRARY
Chicago, Ill.

D1599799

Other works by F. E. Peters

GREEK PHILOSOPHICAL TERMS: *A Historical Lexicon*

ARISTOTELES ARABUS: *The Oriental Translation History of the Aristotelian Corpus* (Monograph)

ARISTOTLE AND THE ARABS: *The Aristotelian Tradition in Islam*

THE HARVEST OF HELLENISM: *A History of the Near East from Alexander the Great to the Triumph of Christianity*

ALLAH'S COMMONWEALTH

A HISTORY OF ISLAM
IN THE NEAR EAST
600–1100 A. D.

F. E. PETERS

SIMON AND SCHUSTER · · · NEW YORK

Published by Simon and Schuster
Rockefeller Center, 630 Fifth Avenue
New York, New York 10020
SBN 671-21564-7 Casebound
Library of Congress Catalog Card Number: 73-18733
Designed by Edith Fowler
Manufactured in the United States of America
1 2 3 4 5 6 7 8 9 10

The two maps in this book are reproduced by kind permission of St. Martin's Press, Inc., Macmillan & Co. Ltd., from Philip K. Hitti's History of the Arabs, *© 1970 by Philip K. Hitti, published by St. Martin's Press.*

For Mary,
umm al-kitab,

and Peter Paul

CONTENTS

TABLES

PREFACE

The format of this book is what the Arabs called an "era work," the setting-down of deeds, chiefly those of a political nature, along a chronological line established by the succession of Caliphs, their vassals and their ministers. But I have attempted something more, an excursion into another literary genre known to the Arabs as the "book of refinement." The Arabs' "refinement" (what they called in Arabic *adab*) was a generous term in that it eventually came to embrace the sum of manners and learning appropriate to the Muslim gentleman. And though there is rich material available on the manners of the early Muslim, the emphasis here is upon his literary learning, what the educated Muslim knew and thought about man, the world and Islam. His culture is in his books, a great torrent of them, and some of the most important of them have been opened again here and their contents displayed in the appropriate context.

The only *adab* necessary for the Muslim was, of course, spelled out once and for all in the *Qur'an*. There were many in Islam who went no further, and like a number of their Jewish contemporaries they fashioned out of their own piety and intelligence a scriptural culture which was in no sense intellectually primitive. But, for others in Islam, the *Qur'an* and its talmudic extensions were merely the foundations of a culture that in its upper reaches incorporated ideals and attitudes undreamed of by the Prophet; and the tension that these ideals and attitudes generated within Muslim society constitutes, far more than the interminable struggle for power and priority, the true drama of Islam.

But Islam is not simply an interesting hybrid. Islamic civilization grew out of ground which had been sown many centuries before and what has been called "medieval" Islam, a singularly inappropriate reference to a period in European history and surely not in Islam's own, was, in fact, an authentic renaissance.

The Muslim could and did construe his own religious culture as a climactic rebirth of an earlier revelation given to and perverted by the Jews and Christians. That view will be reflected upon in the pages that follow, but the renaissance that was Islam refers rather to the resurrection of a complex of cultural ideals that long antedated Islam and were fragmented and moribund, if not dead, in the Near East in the seventh century. Islam, for all its uniquely creative qualities, is also a splendidly rising chapter in the history of Hellenism.

The story of Islam is far more than the revival of Hellenism, of course; many others contributed to the evolution of the faith of Muhammad and to the growth of his community from their own political and cultural past. I have tried to do justice to them as well, and the larger purpose of the book is simply to give a detailed and intelligible account of the course of Islam in the Near East at the height of its glories. There is more to be said on many things that occurred then—on Islamic art, for example, and on the social and economic life of the Muslim communities. Their neglect is sorrowfully acknowledged, and with it my own technical inability to provide the kind of totally integrated history that I should have liked.

This is, further, a secular history in that it does not begin with the presumption that Muhammad was indeed the Prophet of Allah; it ignores, as no Muslim can, the divine purpose in history and reduces Islam to a worldly phenomenon subject to the pedestrian laws of secondary causality. One cannot hope to catch the soul of Islam in such fleshly toils; but if the Muslim cannot recognize his faith in these pages, he will, hopefully, see his own past unmarred by anything more deadly than an admiration for Islam and the historian's normal reluctance to transcend worldly thoughts and deeds.

The reader already will have observed that he is going to be asked to deal with a certain number of foreign terms in transliteration. I can make only feeble defense of this custom, and will offer instead the consolation that I have exercised an almost heroic restraint in this regard and have tried to make amends by providing a glossary of such terms at the back. I have further spared him the surrealistic hailstorm of diacritical points and lines obligatory in any "scientific" system of transliteration in favor of something simpler, an apostrophe in place of both *'ayn* and *hamzah*. For place names I have merely consulted a combination of my own preferences and common usage and have settled for the modest goal of spelling the name of a place the same way each time it is mentioned.

Personal names are another matter. The full Arab name is a composite of imposing dimensions and might take the form, for example, of Abu Bakr Muhammad ibn Ja'far al-Kahhal al-Baghdadi Rukn al-Din al-thani, literally, "the father of Bakr, Muhammad, the son of Ja'far, the oculist of Baghdad, surnamed 'The Second Pillar of Religion.' " Happily, not all parts are given or used in each instance, and practice has tended to concentrate, without much consistency, on one or another element in the whole. There is no conceivable way of telling beforehand whether our man might actually be called Abu Bakr or al-Kahhal or Rukn al-Din. Usage is the only reliable determinant and a good index the only salvation.

The Muslim generally dates the events of his history by lunar years from the migration of Muhammad from Mecca to Medina in the year 622 of the Christian era. All dates here, however, are those of the Christian era unless otherwise noted, and there is a chronological table at the end, so that the reader may see the material laid out on a continuous chronological line, if that is useful to him. I have also included a guide to further reading and a few genealogical charts of some of the more complex relationships.

Many hands and many heads went into the making of this book and this is the time and place to offer thanks to some few of them by name: to the editorial staff of Simon and Schuster for taking such good care of the text and its author; to E. P. Fitzsimmons, a long-time friend, whose support in matters historical, philological and social has long since outstripped my ability to thank him in due measure; to Bonnie Jean also; to David Arentz for performing most of my other duties, and better than I, while this book was being written; to Wendy Schonfeld for her willingness to assume many roles; to the staff of the American Research Center in Cairo for their genial assistance during my stay there, and to the Banu Shaw and Pirouzbakhte for the same in Iran; to Beth Uffner as usual; to Boydena Wilson and Linda Pappas for accompanying me in search of *hadith;* to two colleagues from whom I have learned a great deal at every encounter, David Leahy and Seth Benardete; to John Flynn for his long-unacknowledged work on the *Patrologia Graeca;* to my fellow students Michel Mazzaoui, Robert Rehder and Paul Forand for ancient lessons; to Dana Fenton: *ut poesis pictura;* to Jill Claster and Gail Smith for lighting up the end of the ancient world; to my graduate students whom I will not name because I would have to name them all; and finally to New York University for providing a pleasant, stimulating and sympathetic place to work and live.

INTRODUCTION: THE NEAR EAST BEFORE ISLAM

The history of the Arabs did not begin with Islam. For centuries before the appearance of the Prophet, Arab tribes had been moving from their home on the Syrian and Arabian steppes into the pastures, farmlands and towns in the arc of the Fertile Crescent from the Persian Gulf on the east to Sinai on the west. They came as migrants and not as militant invaders—or so we suppose, since there is very little report of them until they are well established in settled areas and begin to play a part in the political history of the Near East. In some cases it was a considerable part. The Nabataean Arabs who settled in the Transjordan and around the head of the Gulf of Aqaba were important entrepreneurs in the rich Near Eastern trade in Hellenistic and early Roman times.

Like the Jewish kingdom of the Hasmonaeans who were their neighbors and rivals, the Arabs of Nabataea were in the end absorbed into the expanding Roman Empire, and in 106 their domains became part of the provinces of Palestina Tertia and Arabia. Farther north other Arab principalities, which were struggling toward autonomy out of the wreckage of the Seleucid kingdom, were likewise urged along the path from Roman clientship to full integration into the provincial system.

Integration inevitably meant assimilation, and though the Arab tribes of the second and third Christian centuries had little political history of their own, individual Arabs passed into the culture of Hellenism and took their place with Spaniards, Africans and Egyptians in the intellectual and political life of the late Greco-Roman *oikoumene*. One of them, Philip, the son of an Arab *shaykh* of the Transjordan, wore the imperial purple when, in 244, the Empire celebrated the millennium of the founding of Rome.

One exception to the Arabs' political anonymity was the oasis city of Palmyra, which sat astride the overland trade route across the Syrian steppe between Damascus and Iraq. There Arab princes still exercised a sovereignty that, like the Nabataeans', was based upon commerce. Palmyrene middlemen organized and guarded the caravans between the middle Euphrates and the borders of Roman Syria. They did it under the watchful eyes of the Romans, of course; but, on at least one occasion it was the Palmyrenes, and not their Roman patrons, who for a brief season held the balance of power in the East.

In 260 the armies of the empire of Iran broke through the frontier, inflicted an enormous defeat upon the Romans in Syria, and returned home with the Roman Emperor Valerian as their captive. In the years that followed Valerian's son Gallienus had no choice but to rely upon the Palmyrenes to defend the Roman East. The Palmyrene *shaykh* 'Udaynath was appointed commander in chief for the East, and in the sequel he richly earned the honor. Palmyrene troops contained the Sasanian Shah and his army and stabilized the frontier.

In the doing opportunity presented itself to 'Udaynath's successors. His widow Zenobia declared herself and her son independent of Rome in 270, she as Augusta and he as Augustus would rule over the Near East in their own name. It was a brief dream, and within two years it was crushed by Roman arms. Palmyra never recovered either its ambitions or its importance; it became just another Roman outpost on the steppe. Its marvelous Greco-Roman public buildings and temples fell into ruin, and it played no part in the history of either the Roman Empire or the Christian Church, which was overtaking Roman, Greek and Arab throughout the Near East.

Despite their Hellenization in architecture, dress, and manner, the Palmyrene Arabs spoke Aramaic, the Semitic lingua franca of the Roman East. They worshiped their own Semitic gods under the oddly hybridized forms that came forth from contact with the Greco-Roman pantheon. Many Arabs did likewise in the third and fourth centuries in their continuing passage from the steppe into the towns along its edges. Others passed more deeply into the Hellenic settlements; they gave up their native Arabic not for Aramaic but for ecumenical Greek, and they traded, at the same time, their Semitic Baals for the new Saviour God, Jesus Christ.

It is only the first group, those Arabs who lived in a semisedentary state outside the frontiers of Hellenism, whose history is in any way visible as the Roman Empire passed into the Byzantine. Some were agriculturalists; others lived by commerce; and still others roamed the steppe in the nomadic style of their remote ancestors. The townsmen who dwelled along the western and eastern edges of the Syrian steppe lived within the political orbit of the Roman and the Sasanian states and served on the fringes of their armies as irregular auxiliaries. Farther out on the steppe was the great uncharted sea of nomads who flowed in small eddies and more deeply running tides between the southern borders of Arabia and the northern edge of the Fertile Crescent where the steppe touched upon the Euphrates.

The Romans and Sasanians were indifferent to their Arab neighbors beyond the frontier; the Arabs were there to be used on occasion, but not to be feared. Rome's problems in the Near East in the fifth century did not include the Arabs, but turned instead upon an issue that meant nothing to the tribes of the steppe and only little more to those Arabs camped for a season in the shadow of the Roman cities of Syria. That issue was the person and nature of Jesus Christ, a complex theological question that had, nonetheless, immense political consequences which no theologian could or would measure in the fifth century.

Byzantine emperors were only sometime theologians, but they could calculate political consequences, and when the Emperor Marcian summoned the bishops of the ecumenical Church to the city of Chalcedon on the Bosporus in 451, it was likely in the hope that they would find a solution to a problem that had already revealed its dangerous potential. The issue at stake, the nature of the God-man Jesus, had been debated for nearly a century. Factions had been formed, alliances joined, and on two earlier occasions judgments had been rendered. At one side of the controversy stood the partisans of Nestorius, the Patriarch of Constantinople (428–431), who had difficulty in reconciling the union of two perfect natures in the single person of Jesus and whose solution to the problem appeared either to weaken the union or to emphasize Jesus' humanity—at what was claimed to be the expense of his divinity.

The problem was indeed one of emphasis, but it had something to do as well with the inadequacies of language. "Union," "person," "nature," and "substance" were all commonplace terms in the language of philosophy, and the theologians of the fifth century were engaged in the painful and difficult task of adapting these highly technical and nuanced concepts to a Scriptural witness that spoke the common tongue of first-century Palestine and knew neither Plato nor Aristotle nor the Stoics. The Christian theologians of the fifth and sixth centuries were coming to know those philosophers, however, and the Christians of Alexandria in particular saw, or thought they saw, the metaphysical direction into which the somewhat haphazard language of Nestorius and his colleagues was heading.[1] Cyril, the Patriarch of Alexandria (412–444), was quickly into the lists against Nestorius' theories of "union," and his views soon prevailed; at a Council summoned at Ephesus in 431, Nestorius and his teaching were declared anathema.[2]

It was not the end of the matter. After Cyril's death others took up what now amounted to a crusade against the Nestorians. Their chief was a certain Eutyches, whose statements about a single divine nature in Christ far outran Cyril's more moderate language. Many were uneasy at the new Monophysite ("single nature") theory. Questions were asked, and theological inquiries were begun, but they aborted in an extraordinary rump Council

---

1. The controversy was affected by nonmetaphysical considerations as well. Nestorius' attitudes were those commonly held at Alexandria's theological rival, Antioch, where theologians like Theodore of Mopsuestia (d. 428) preferred to come to the Gospels from the angle of historical exegesis rather than that of metaphysics; on the subsequent influence of Theodore in Syria, see Chap. IV, pp. 315–317.

2. On the future of the Nestorians, see Chap. IV, pp. 316–319 and Chap. VII, pp. 525–527.

convened in 449 at Ephesus, where Cyril's Patriarchal successor in Alexandria, Dioscorus (444–451), contrived to have Eutyches' positions affirmed by a packed house of his constituents.

This was the background against which the Council convened in Chalcedon in 451. Eutyches' "one divine nature incarnate" or Nestorius' "God-bearing man"? "Union" or "conjunction"? Alexandria or Antioch? The solution came from neither place. The formula finally accepted at Chalcedon was supplied by the Bishop of Rome: "Jesus Christ, at once complete in Godhood and complete in manhood, truly God and truly man . . . one and the same Christ recognized in his two natures, without confusion, without change, without division, without separation." It was, obviously, no solution at all. The Pope's formula adopted at Chalcedon affirmed in philosophical language a position that may have been faithful to the intent of the Gospels but contradicted the philosophers' understanding of their own language. It was nothing more or less than the philosophical description of a miracle.

The Roman Church was happy with the formula—because they did not understand philosophy, the Hellenized Easterners alleged—but few others were, at least until the accession of the Emperor Justin (518–527) and his nephew Justinian (527–565). Both men, who were originally from the Latinized province of Illyricum, in what is now Yugoslavia, were personally convinced Dyophysites ("two nature" partisans), but they had as well an intense interest in reconquering for the "New Rome" of Constantinople the lost lands of the Latin West, a project that would have unlikely prospects without the cooperation of the Pope. The Nestorians were no longer a power in the empire—Eutyches' zealous followers had seen to that—and so the brunt of Justin and Justinian's pro-Latin and pro-Chalcedonian policies was borne by the Monophysites.

The Emperor controlled, or attempted to control, the great Patriarchal Sees like Constantinople, Antioch and Alexandria, and so could insure that they were held by his own "imperial" (Melchite) adherents to the formula of Chalcedon. Beyond those cities his authority ran in shallower channels, however. In the smaller cities and towns out in the hinterland where Hellenism yielded to the vernacular cultures of Syria and Egypt, Melchites and Monophysites fought for the upper hand and, in many instances, for survival.

Byzantine imperial policy in the sixth century frequently sacrificed sectarian considerations for political ones. Violent persecutions alternated with peaceful accords as the emperors attempted to keep their gaze fixed simultaneously upon their own internal problems—Justinian had a major insurrection on his hands in Constantinople in 532 and it was provoked at least in part by his opportunistic pro-Monophysite sentiments during that period[3]—the eastern frontier against the Sasanians, ambitions and projects in the West, and whatever chance or good fortune might offer in the larger arena of geopolitics.

Justin came to the Byzantine throne in 518. His personal convictions were pro-Chalcedon and anti-Monophysite, and it was he who eventually dislodged Severus, the brilliant theologian whose writings were the ideological foundation of the Monophysite movement, from the Patriarchal See of Antioch. Justin replaced him with the ruthless former soldier Ephraem, and the Emperor and his new Patriarch pressed the Monophysites into flight and despair.

Justin could, however, overlook heresy when he chose, and at the same time his agents were relentlessly pursuing Monophysites within the Empire, Justin was raising up allies for himself among the Christian Monophysite powers around the Red Sea. Chief among them was the kingdom of Axum in Abyssinia, whose ruler, the Negus Ezana, had become a Christian in Constantine's day. After Chalcedon the Abyssinians were Monophysites, a fact that interested Justin far less than the possibility that Axum might provide a lever with which to pry open the back door of trade with India and the Far East.

---

3. Constantinople and the other cities of the Empire were dominated by the presence of *demes*, fractious sporting clubs with strong political, social, religious and paramilitary overtones. Two of them, the Blues and the Greens, held pride of place, and there were frequent and bloody fights between them. Pagans, Jews, Samaritans and Manichaeans, all found their place in these factions, and both the membership and the issues at stake varied from city to city.

The long rivalry between Rome and Iran was deeply rooted in commerce. Rome traded vigorously for the raw luxury goods of the East from the days of the early Empire. Much of that trade passed overland, through the hands and customs stations of the Parthians and Sasanians, before it crossed the Mediterranean. There was, however, another route: by sea to South Arabia, thence overland up the western coast of Arabia to depots at Gaza and Damascus. That latter route was controlled by neither the Romans nor the Persians, but was originally exploited, and then long managed, by the Semitic kingdoms located in the southwest corner of Arabia: Ma'in, Qataban, Saba and Hadramawt.

The Arabian overland trade, which began in the first millennium before Christ with the domestication of the camel and depended upon a sophisticated knowledge of the monsoons between the Yemen and India, brought prosperity to those southern kingdoms, the lands known collectively to the ancients as "Araby the Blest" (Arabia Felix). Protected on all sides by a milieu which they had learned to master, the waters of the Red Sea and Indian Ocean and the inhospitable desert and steppe of Arabia, the southern kingdoms enjoyed a mild climate and a well-watered land. Their elaborately irrigated soil produced rich crops of frankincense and myrrh, which fed, at an immense cost, the funeral pyres and temple offerings of the Roman Empire.

By the sixth century the southern Semitic monopoly had been broken; the Ptolemaic and Roman masters of Egypt easily controlled the Red Sea and were now in possession of the secret of the monsoons. Corpses were no longer cremated in the Christian Roman Empire, and the elaborate religious rituals of Roman paganism had yielded to something considerably simpler under Christian auspices. And there was, across the narrow strait of the Bab al-Mandab, the new Christian power of Abyssinia, which had obvious designs on the riches of the "Homerites," as the kingdom of Saba-Himyar was called in Byzantine circles.

There are reports of an Abyssinian invasion of the Yemen about 513, and though the accounts are garbled, they agree on two themes: that Roman traders were somehow mixed up in the business, and that the religious situation in southern Arabia was now complicated by the presence of both Christian missionaries and a strong current of Judaism. A Jew, Yusuf As'ar, surnamed

Dhu Nuwas, now ruled Himyar, and in the second decade of the sixth century he had to face the threat of a second Abyssinian invasion and the not unconnected activity of Christian missionaries in the cities of his realm.

The invasion of 513 was not a permanent occupation of the Yemen, but some Abyssinians did stay behind, particularly in the city of Najran, which was rapidly becoming a Christian center for the whole of southwestern Arabia. Dhu Nuwas found their presence threatening and in 515 attacked Najran and other Christian towns in his kingdom. By then there was a new Negus in Abyssinia, Ella Asbeha, and in 518 a new emperor in Byzantium, Justin. Together they took counsel on another expedition to the Yemen, the Abyssinians to supply the men and the Byzantines the cargo boats.

The planned invasion did not take place until 525. In the meantime Dhu Nuwas, who was now in full alarm, took even stronger measures against Najran. In 523 his troops took the town with a great slaughter of the local Christians. The report of the deed spread rapidly over the Christian *oikoumene*. Early in 524 it came to the ears of Justin's emissaries to the Arab prince of the Banu Lakhm, al-Mundhir. They had sought out Mundhir at his camp city of Hirah to negotiate the release of the generals captured by the *shaykh* on his foray into Syria in 523. He was not there, but they found him at Ramlah, and it was during their stay there that an envoy came from Dhu Nuwas to enlist Mundhir's aid against the inevitable Abyssinian reprisal.

The Christian Negus had necessarily to become involved. A Christian priest had heard the news of Najran at Ramlah at the same time that Justin's envoys did, and he immediately wrote to his superiors in Syria demanding an appeal to the Negus. He suggested, too, that pressure be brought to bear on the Jewish community in Galilee to bring a halt to Dhu Nuwas' activities. The Negus probably did not need much urging; his well-known intentions against the Yemen were likely the provocation for the slaughter which he now set out to avenge.

Ella Asbeha came across the straits in force in 525, and Dhu Nuwas, the last native king of the Yemen, was destroyed. The Negus stayed in the Yemen for seven months, and when he finally withdrew he left behind a native Christian prince and two of his own generals, Abraha and Ariat, to share the rule. The arrangement lasted for nearly ten years. Ariat falls out of the account in the interval, but in 533 Abraha assumed what amounted to sole autonomous rule for himself by removing the local prince and refusing to send tribute to the Negus. Ella Asbeha attempted to reduce his fractious viceroy by force in the following year. He was unsuccessful, and after his death in 536 the next Negus was forced to recognize Abraha as an independent agent.

Shortly after his accession in 527 Justinian made it manifest that his uncle's policies were his own. The Monophysites may have had the sympathies of most of the local population, but the Emperor had his patronage and his armies. From early in his reign Justinian pursued the Monophysites of the East with as much fervor as Justin had, but in 530 the influence of the Augusta Theodora appears to have prevailed and the persecutions began to be relaxed. The Monophysite missionary John of Tella roamed inner Syria in an attempt—successful, it appears—to reconstitute the shattered Monophysite hierarchy. It was then too that Justinian embarked upon a new move in the complex politics of the Red Sea area. He appointed one of his Arab clients, Harith of the Banu Ghassan, Monophysites all, as the supreme commander of the Arab auxiliaries of the Diocese of the Orient and granted him, in the manner of the times, the title of king.

Harith doubtless had his uses. The war against the rulers of Iran was a perennial problem for the Romans and their Byzantine successors from the last centuries of the Roman Republic, and since the accession of the house of Sasan to the throne of the Shahs early in the third Christian century, the fighting had taken on a fierce helplessness wherein both sides were in danger and neither had any expectation of final success. Justinian conducted the war for the Byzantines just as his predecessors had done, but his real concerns and ambitions lay elsewhere. His determination to reconquer for the Empire the lost lands of the European and African West made him vulnerable on his eastern frontier. On the upper Euphrates, the most common invasion route between the two empires, he had constructed heavily fortified positions to guard the eastern approaches, but farther to the south, from the great bend of the Euphrates at Thapsacus to Ailah at the head of the Gulf of Aqaba, the older Roman desert fortifications from the time of Trajan and Diocletian were neglected. In their place Justinian put his trust in his Arab auxiliaries, now organized under the Ghassanid Harith.

Across the Syrian steppe the Shahs did likewise. There were Arab tribes settled on the plains along the west bank of the Euphrates in its middle and lower reaches, and early in the fifth century the Sasanians were drawing on the support of one of them, the Banu Lakhm. The enthronement of Bahram V Gor in 420 in the face of his rivals was accomplished with the help of the Lakhmid *shaykh* Mundhir, and the same Shah had occasion to use his vassal against the Byzantines. Another Lakhmid phylarch, Nu'man II, met his death in battle against Byzantium in 503. He was fighting on behalf of the Shah Kavad, and at his death the Shah immediately intervened to set a successor over his now valuable Arab clients.

When Harith ibn Jabalah received his signal honors from Constantinople in or about 530, the phylarch of the Banu Lakhm was the redoubtable Mundhir III, who shared among the Arabs Alexander the Great's sobriquet of "the double-horned one." For fifty years, according to one of his Byzantine contemporaries, the Lakhmid phylarch "forced Rome to bend the knee." It was al-Mundhir's destructive raids into Byzantine territory between 519 and 529, climaxed by his capture of two Roman field commanders and his penetration to the very gates of Antioch, where he was alleged to have put four hundred Christian nuns to the sword in honor of the Arab Aphrodite, al-'Uzza, that probably prompted Justinian to create his own Arab phylarch system in Syria-Palestine. Its earliest form was the appointment of the Ghassanid Harith as a captain in the Transjordan and of Harith's brother Abu Karib to be chief over the "palm groves," apparently the area to the south and east of Ailah at the head of the Gulf of Aqaba.[4] The latter territory had once been ruled by the

4. And including the sometime customs station on the island of Iotabe. Earlier, about 500, the Byzantines took the island from its Arab masters to open the Red Sea trade to their own merchants. Now, apparently, they were willing to give it back, perhaps because ships were by then putting in at Jiddah, the port of the rising new commercial city of Mecca.

Kindite Arab Harith ibn 'Amr, but in 528 that *shaykh* was captured and killed by al-Mundhir, and the new Ghassanid phylarch Harith, and perhaps Abu Karib as well, led retaliatory raids against al-Mundhir. In the same year Harith further proved his value by helping to put down a Samaritan revolt in Palestine and shortly thereafter was rewarded with the supreme phylarchate.

War broke out between Byzantium and Iran in the summer of 530, and in 531 Justinian sent his envoys to Ella Asbeha in Abyssinia and the Negus' viceroy in the Yemen requesting, "by reason of our common faith," assistance in the war against the Sasanians, specifically by sending an army of Yemenites and their Arab allies against the Sasanians' southern Euphrates flank. Nothing came of the proposal, but Justinian made it again when Abraha had won his independence from the Negus. The year was probably 539, the eve of a new war between Justinian and Khusraw, and to Abraha's capital came envoys not merely of Justinian but of the Shah, the Negus, and of Justinian's two premier phylarchs, Harith and Abu Karib, the sons of Jabalah.

Harith's petitions may have had to do less with the Shah than with his client al-Mundhir. The personal hostility of the two Arab princes, Harith a Christian and Mundhir a pagan, raged unabated across the background of the Roman-Persian wars, oblivious to treaties and accords. In 539 they were quarreling about a sheep walk in the middle of the Syrian steppe, and in 546 Mundhir succeeded in capturing the son of Harith, whom he brutally executed—as a sacrifice to his own gods, it was said. It was not until 554 that the issue between them was finally resolved. The two chiefs clashed in headlong battle near Chalcis in Syria, and the Lakhmid Mundhir was killed.

Abraha, meanwhile, kept his own counsel—perhaps he was still unsure of his own position and strength—but eventually he did as Justinian requested. In 544 Abraha and his Arab allies attacked the tribes of the Ma'add, a confederacy that spread across western Arabia and acknowledged the sovereignty of al-Mundhir. The raid was successful. The Ma'add switched their allegiance to Abraha and accepted his man as their *shaykh*. This was a certain Qays, a Christian and pro-Byzantine prince of the Ma'add, who had earlier been banished from the tribe, likely under Lakhmid pressure, and whose restoration was a consistent goal of Byzantine policy in western Arabia.[5] Abraha's own goal may have been merely to enlarge his power and to spread Christianity among the Arabs of the Hejaz.

At home Justinian's tolerant mood toward the Monophysites lasted no more than six years: in 536 he reverted to his earlier anti-Monophysite stand. Justinian's man in Antioch, Justin's former military commander for the East and now Patriarch of Antioch, Ephraem of Amida, hunted down Monophysites wherever they could be found. The work of John of Tella was partially undone, and so in 542 or 543 the Ghassanid Harith ibn Jabalah led to Constantinople a secret delegation of his coreligionists to request Theodora's aid in restoring their fortunes. She responded by having the Monophysites Jacob Baradai and Theodore consecrated as bishops, the first to serve as bishop of Edessa, the center of Syriac-speaking Christianity, and the second as Metropolitan of Bostra with jurisdiction over the encampments of the Banu Ghassan.

The death of Justinian brought new and more favorable opportunities to the Monophysites. The new Emperor Justin II began his reign in 565 in a conciliatory spirit, and his wife, Sophia, was an avowed Monophysite. The energies of Jacob Baradai (d. 578) reconstituted the Monophysite Church in Syria and Harith was a willing and powerful ally. It was he, for example, who took into his camp and under his protection the exiled Monophysite Patriarch of Alexandria. In 566 Justin II granted amnesty to all the Monophysites without mentioning Chalcedon.

The Monophysites were having their own internal problems, however. There was no agreement among them on who should sit upon the Patriarchal throne in Egypt. The Christians of Nubia had one candidate, the Alexandrians another, and the "Jacobites" of Syria a third. Harith's own candidate was no more pleasing than the others, but both he and his son Mundhir labored hard for unity. Mundhir, who succeeded his father as supreme phylarch in 569, was a leading figure at a Monophysite synod convoked in Constantinople in 580. The parties who met there

---

5. At some unknown later time Qays succeeded or replaced Abu Karib as Byzantine phylarch in southern Palestine.

agreed on a Patriarch for Alexandria, but their candidate won no acceptance back home in Syria and Egypt and the schism lingered on for another thirty-five years. But without the Ghassanids.

In 573 Mundhir ibn Harith discovered by chance that Justin II was plotting his removal. After a few years he was reconciled with the Emperor and resumed his family's traditional wars with the Lakhmids; sometime about 577 he burst into the Lakhmid encampment at Hirah and put it to the torch. When Tiberius succeeded Justin in 578 he took pains to reassure his Arab client. Mundhir was summoned to Constantinople in 580 and was given, as a special sign of imperial favor, the right to wear a royal crown instead of the simple gold chaplet with which his father, Harith, apparently had had to content himself. Al-Mundhir was not reassured, or so it appeared to some. In a battle fought against the Shah in the summer of that same year the phylarch reportedly betrayed the imperial troops to the Persians.

The Byzantine field commander on that occasion was Maurice, and he had his own vassal hunted down and subsidies to the Ghassanids discontinued. Mundhir's son Nu'man then turned the full force of the Ghassanids against his family's former patrons throughout Palestine and Syria. By then Maurice was himself emperor, and it was by his order that first al-Mundhir and then Nu'man were sent into exile in Sicily. In 584 their phylarchate was divided among fifteen different *shaykhs*, whose loyalty could be measured almost exactly by the size of their annual stipends.

Even then the Lakhmids were encountering difficulties in maintaining themselves in power at Hirah, and when Mundhir IV died in 583, the Shah Hormizd IV confronted the phylarch's numerous sons with a single illuminating question, "Who of you can control the Arabs for me?" The one who was thought capable of doing so was Nu'man III; but Nu'man, who was the first of the Lakhmid house to become a Christian, did not have the confidence of Hormizd's successor, Khusraw II, and in 604 he was replaced as phylarch by an Arab of the Banu Tayy', whose powers were strictly limited by the presence of a Sasanian supervisor.

So passed the Arab kings, crowned by their respective sovereigns and honored with titles and cash. They were mute within their own kingdoms, but they were well remembered by their more literary contemporaries, by the Byzantine historians who debated their merits and their orthodoxy and by the Arab poets who enjoyed their patronage. They testify not so much to the growing strength and cohesiveness of the Arabs—there is little sign of that in the sixth and seventh centuries—as to the weakness of the great empires who used them as buffers and allies. The Banu Lakhm stood closer to the throne of the Shahs perhaps, but by reason of their Christianity the Ghassanids presented a complex and aggravating problem to the rulers in Constantinople. Their *shaykhs* tried on occasion to play the role of brokers, but they remained in the end pawns whom the emperor could not trust and so yielded up in the late sixth century.

The Byzantines' other Arabian ally, Abraha, died in 570 in an attempt to further extend his influence over the Arab tribes of western Arabia. His goal on this occasion was Mecca, a city of growing commercial importance that recognized neither Christianity nor Abraha. The Meccans were, as the Yemenites and their own fellow Arabs had once been, worshipers in the primitive Semitic pantheon. Abraha failed because of an outbreak of smallpox in his army or, as the Meccan Muhammad later read the event, by divine intervention. In either case Abraha himself was likely among the victims. His sons ruled in his place for a mere five years. In 575 Sasanian troops came to the Yemen at the request of one of the local princes and installed their own candidate on the throne of Himyar.

Justinian's immediate successors, Justin II, Tiberius and Maurice, had no interest in Byzantium's Red Sea frontier; and Maurice, as has been seen, dismantled the unified Ghassanid phylarchate in Syria-Palestine and preferred to pay his subsidies piecemeal to one or another of the Arab tribes along the southern frontier. But if what the Sasanians were doing in the Yemen—and it was not, it is true, a great deal—was ignored in Constantinople, the three emperors did keep a careful watch on the Shah's forces in upper Mesopotamia and Armenia.

War between Iran and Byzantium was now an endemic disease on both sides, and its successes and failures were more often measured by what was going on at home than by superiority of arms or tactics on the battle line. Khusraw had profited by

Justinian's preoccupation with the West and his successors' with the Avars, while the eastern frontier of Iran demanded constant surveillance by the Shahs. Since the reign of Shapur II (d. 379) the dominant presence there was the Hephthalites, a Hunnic people newly come off the Central Asian steppe and thereafter lodged eastward across the Oxus. They were drawn more closely into Sasanian affairs when Shah Peroz (459–484) invoked their aid to win himself the throne. Once Shah, he continued to demand tribute from his former benefactors. The demand led to war, and in 465 Peroz and his son, the future Shah Kavad, were captured by the Hephthalites. Peroz was released but Kavad was kept as a hostage.

Peroz shepherded his resources and tried the Hephthalites once again in 484. The result was another disaster; the Shah lost his life in it. The Hephthalites were now firmly established in their capital of Balkh on the Oxus, and their authority extended back onto the steppe and across the Hindu Kush into Sinkiang and Afghanistan. Envoys were exchanged with China.

Kavad's prospects (488–531) were not bright. The Hephthalites stood without, and Iran itself was in the grip of a fierce social and religious upheaval provoked by the former Zoroastrian priest Mazdak. Though Mazdak's theology may have been Manichaean in its inspiration, his program of political action called for nothing less than the radical reform of Iranian society. Property and genealogies, the twin props of the class-conscious Sasanian aristocracy, were to be swept away by the wholesale redistribution of land and the sharing of wives in common.

Kavad found Mazdak's communist theories attractive for his own political reasons, but his support of the program in the face of the aristocracy and the clergy briefly lost him his throne in 496. To regain it he had to turn once again to the Hephthalites. It was accomplished in 498, and thereafter the Hephthalites were regular auxiliaries in the Sasanian armies.

Paying off the Hephthalites was a dangerous and galling policy, but it was more than thirty years into his reign before Kavad's son and successor, Khusraw I (531–579), surnamed Anushirvan ("he of the immortal soul"), took action against them. Early in his reign Khusraw sold to Justinian the eastern peace the emperor needed to pursue his western designs. Neither this nor any of the subsequent treaties concluded between the two men lasted very long, however; and just as the peace of 532 freed Justinian's hands for the west, so the treaty signed in 562 gave Khusraw the opportunity to turn to the Hephthalites.

This time he had allies. On the steppe behind the Hephthalites had appeared a new nomadic confederation, a body of Turks known merely from the Chinese sources as the Tü-kueh. The eastern branch of the Tü-kueh rested at Qaraqorum and was a sometime ally and sometime enemy of China; the western branch joined with Khusraw in the years after 562 in sweeping away the Hephthalites. The Sasanians reoccupied Bactria and Balkh, and the western Tü-kueh settled into Sogdia on the other side of the Oxus.

The Tü-kueh quickly proved they could be every bit as dangerous as the departed Hephthalites. Rebuffed by the Shah after their joint military venture, the Turkish *khan* sent emissaries to Justin II, and they found, not entirely unexpectedly, a warm reception. With Justin's encouragement and with promises of serving as middlemen for the lucrative Byzantine trade with the East, the Tü-kueh made several incursions into Khusraw's territory. Justin for his part reopened hostilities on the Mesopotamian frontier in 572. The war was still in progress, without any great advantage to either side, when Khusraw died in 579.

Except for his stunning, if temporary, breakthrough into Syria in 540, Khusraw was no more successful against the Byzantines than his predecessors had been. His destruction of the Hephthalites only served to bring him into collision with the Tü-kueh behind them, and even his prying loose of the Abyssinian hold on the Yemen in 575 could not be long sustained. His true success was within Iran. From the first he sought to conciliate the Iranian aristocracy and to make powerful allies for himself among the Zoroastrian clergy. Kavad had alienated both groups by his support of Mazdakism, but Khusraw did not repeat his father's mistakes. Property was returned to private owners, marriage was encouraged and regulated, and provision was made for regularizing the status of the women and children affected by Mazdak's call to social communism.

Under Khusraw's direction the state was put on a military footing. Previously the powerful barons of the realm supplied feudal levies for the campaign, but now Iran was given a professional standing army, and the entire empire was divided into four great military districts, each under the control of a military governor and his *marzubans* or lieutenants. To pay for his new army and military fortifications Khusraw reformed the haphazard tax methods of his predecessors. He adopted what had been the Roman system since the late third century: a land tax based upon fixed and standardized values of various types of cultivated land and a graduated poll tax on all non-government-employed males.

Khusraw's support within the empire came from the classes most threatened by the Mazdakite reforms, the upper aristocracy and the Zoroastrian clergy. The Shah claimed to have set the "right religion" of Ahura Mazda aright, and it may have been under his auspices that the sacred books of the *Avesta* were put in order and the text itself set down in a new script devised for that purpose. These are essentially conservative measures partly intended to reinforce the backing of the still-powerful clergy, but Khusraw was far from a religious reactionary. It was his boast that he opened Zoroastrianism to the wisdom of the Greeks and Indians, perhaps by reforming the traditional cosmology or perhaps, in the former case, simply by introducing rationalistic elements into Zoroastrian theological discourse.

The Shah prided himself on his urbane and enlightened learning. There came to his court shortly after 529 a group of Hellenic philosophers exiled from Athens by Justinian's closing of the Academy there.[6] Their reception was friendly, but their reaction was not. The formal and class-oriented society of Ctesiphon did not appeal to them, and they returned to the Byzantine Empire after little more than a year. The Shah, they thought, was an *aficionado* of things Hellenic, though not a very sophisticated one.

Their reaction to court life is not surprising. When not in the field the Shah lived in Ctesiphon, a city on the east bank of the Tigris not far south of the site of the future Islamic capital of Baghdad. On the west bank was the earlier Greek city of Seleucia

---

6. See Chap. IV, pp. 294–295.

which had been rebuilt by Ardashir I (228–241) and called after him Veh-Ardashir. This was the home of most of the Christians of the capital, but the Shah himself lived surrounded by his courtiers in a splendid palace built by Khusraw in a suburb of Ctesiphon.

Like his Byzantine contemporary, the Shah was shielded from his subjects by an elaborate court protocol. The grandees of the realm were all represented there, aristocrats of the blood who still dominated Sasanian society, the chief cleric of the realm (*mobadan mobad*), the chief keeper of the sacred fire (*herbadan herbad*), the prime minister, the head of the civilian bureaucracy of the chancery (*diwan*), and, with the increased importance of Khusraw's day, the four major military governors (*spahbads*) of the Empire. Present too, each in his elaborately designated place, was the veritable army of astrologers, musicians, entertainers, grooms and chamberlains, without which court life could not proceed in truly imperial style.

Khusraw's attempt at combining Zoroastrian orthodoxy with a liberal and humane spirit of learning may have proved fatal in the long course. The traditional Zoroastrianism of Iran was a national church supported in these latter days by the Sasanian state. It was a religion of considerable ethical idealism but one whose chief intellectual accomplishment was the elaboration of an intricate mythology. Compared with the faith of the Iranian Jews and Christians, Zoroastrianism must have appeared provincial and naïve. Khusraw probably perceived this and attempted to open the doors to somewhat more stimulating currents of rationalism. But its effects were not always happy. We have the testimony of one man, the royal physician Burzoe, whose learning drove him to a quite un-Mazdaean pessimism and eventually to the kind of asceticism with which both Manichaeans and Christians were challenging the Zoroastrian Church.

Hormizd IV (579–590) succeeded his father without difficulty, but during the eleven years of his reign Khusraw's accomplishments began to crumble. Hormizd could not simultaneously contain, as his father did, the Byzantines in Mesopotamia, the Arabs along the Euphrates, and the Turks pressing against the frontier in the Caucasus and on the Oxus. For a while a brave front was presented by the general Bahram Chobin, but soon he too began to fail. Hormizd lost his patience and his temper and insulted Bahram. Thus was insurrection provoked, and in 590 it cost Hormizd his crown and his life. Hormizd reaped the consequences of Khusraw's firm hand; once that grip was relaxed both the generals and the clergy asserted their own will. In Hormizd's place they crowned his son, Khusraw II Parvez, "the triumphant," a choice that was unacceptable to Bahram who now saw himself as Shah.

Khusraw II (590–628) eventually won his throne, but only with the help of the Byzantine Emperor Maurice, to whose shelter he fled and who exacted as a price for his support the provinces of upper Mesopotamia and eastern Armenia. Bahram and his supporters were run to ground in Azarbayjan by a confederate army of Byzantines, Armenians and Sasanians, and Khusraw returned to Ctesiphon in 591. He was the last major figure of his house to rule in Iran. Over the following years he inflicted upon the Byzantines the most powerful blow they had ever received during the long history of the Persian-Roman wars, and he suffered in return a fatal riposte. The death of Khusraw II was the end of his house; the Muslims found only petty caretakers when they came to the Sasanian Empire.

The Christians had been for three centuries a large and important minority in Iraq and western Iran. They suffered often at the hands of the Shahs, and on other occasions, when reasons of state or more tolerant attitudes prevailed, they received impressive tokens of friendship and esteem. With Khusraw II, the promise implicit in that latter attitude seemed tantalizingly near fulfillment. The Shah had lived inside the Christian Roman Empire. He had two Christian wives: one, Shirin, on whom he obviously doted, was a native Iranian Christian, originally a Nestorian and then a convert to Monophysitism; the other was reportedly Maria, the daughter of Maurice. The Shah himself, some said, became a Christian.

The allegation is almost certainly not true, but Khusraw did show remarkable favor to his Christian subjects. Though still opposed to all attempts at proselytizing among the Mazdaeans, the Shah permitted the Christians to build churches where they wished, and he himself subsidized some of the construction on behalf of Shirin. In the critical year of 590 the Catholicus, or head, of the Nestorian Church was Ishoyabh, who made the mistake of remaining neutral in the conflict between Bahram Chobin and Khusraw. When Khusraw succeeded Ishoyabh prudently withdrew from Veh-Ardashir and took up residence among the newly converted Arab Lakhmids at al-Hirah. He died there in 595, and Khusraw immediately intervened to promote his own candidate to the Catholicate, Sabrisho, a pious ascetic, who supported the Shah until his death in 604. His successor Gregory was also the Shah's man.

Maurice's (582–602) own ecclesiastical policy was relentlessly Chalcedonian. His agent, the Bishop Domitianus of Melitene, came to Syria in 598 and supervised a Monophysite suppression that had no equal in ferocity since the days of Ephraem of Amida at the beginning of the century. Churches and monasteries were expropriated from the Monophysites and handed over to Chalcedonians; at Edessa there was a veritable massacre. At the same time the Melchite Patriarch of Antioch undertook by somewhat gentler means the conversion of the Arab tribes of the frontier who were now, with the Emperor's dismemberment of the Ghassanid phylarchate in 584, left to their own somewhat uncertain political devices. By one account the greater part of them went over to the Melchite persuasion of Chalcedon.

Maurice was overthrown by a military insurrection among the troops on the Danube in 602. In his place they raised to the purple the crude but energetic soldier Phocas, who quickly crushed his opposition in the faction-ridden capital. In the eastern provinces he was less successful, however. It is not always clear what course Phocas was following, Monophysite or Chalcedonian; perhaps he had no strong conviction on either side. What he did care for was power, and the Church was his rival for power; he claimed the right to appoint bishops in all the eastern cities.

The Syrians would not have it so. An ecclesiastical synod was convened at Antioch for an episcopal election. When Phocas was informed he dispatched the general Bonosus who dispersed the gathering and so triggered an insurrection which spread through the eastern provinces as far as Cyrenaica. Anastasius, the Melchite Patriarch of Antioch, lost his life in the affair, murdered, according to one later account, by the Jews. The Jews of Antioch may indeed have been mixed up in the business, but more likely as members of the local political faction that supported Phocas than as warriors in a religious crusade.

All of this likely occurred in 608, when a substantial part of Phocas' eastern provinces was already in the hands of the Sasanians. For Khusraw Parvez the murder of his protector and ally Maurice and the accession of Phocas was the pretext for intervention against the Byzantines. In 603 two Sasanian armies crossed the frontier. One struck deeply into Armenia, and another under Shahrbaraz attacked Byzantine Syria. The frontier fortress of Dara fell, and then in quick order Amida, Harran and Edessa. Phocas had neither the military nor the political strength to sustain the assault. Heraclius, the military governor of Carthage, rose up against him. He struck first at Egypt, where discontent had already reached high levels of violence. Constantinople fed itself from Egypt; the province had to be held, and Phocas sent the faithful Bonosus to hold it. He could not. Alexandria fell to Heraclius' nephew Nicetas in 609. Within a year the rebels had collected enough troops and ships to attack Constantinople itself, and in September of 610 that city too fell. Phocas and Bonosus were destroyed, and the younger Heraclius, the son of the architect of the revolt, was crowned Autocrat of the Romans.[7]

Khusraw found Heraclius no more acceptable than Phocas, and the eastern invasion went on. The Persian army in Armenia at one point reached Chalcedon on the Bosporus, and the other was led every campaigning season into Syria by Shahrbaraz. Apamea was looted, then Antioch and Damascus. In the spring of 614 Shahrbaraz entered Jerusalem after a siege of twenty days. There and elsewhere in the campaigns the Sasanians received the enthusiastic support of the Jews, while the Byzantines may have expended more effort on suppressing their rebellious Jewish subjects than in attempting to stem the Sasanian advance.

The Persian conquest of Syria-Palestine was a novel event in

---

7. A title he later exchanged for that of "king" (*basileus*). Heraclius was the first "Roman"—his family was from Armenia—to have dared assume that ill-omened title in a millennium.

the Near East. Its closest parallel is the Parthian breakthrough into Palestine in the early days of Roman rule there. On that occasion some Jews saw their own political salvation in these Iranian liberators from Roman rule, and now in the seventh century similar expectations appear to have arisen. There was a large and flourishing community of Jews inside the Iranian Empire. Like the Christians, they had their occasional difficulties with the Shahs, but their lot was, by any reckoning, a far happier one than that suffered by the Jews at the hands of the Christian authorities of Syria. In Jerusalem particularly the Jews thought that the appearance of the Sasanians signaled their liberation. When Shahrbaraz withdrew from Jerusalem the Jews occupied or destroyed a number of the Christian churches, imposed conversion on some of the Christian inhabitants, and gave every sign that they intended to reestablish the Temple and a full Jewish liturgical cult in the city.

They badly misread Khusraw's intentions. Accompanying Shahrbaraz's army was the chief treasurer of the realm, the Christian Yazden, a favorite of both the Shah and his Christian wife, and it was probably Yazden who counseled Khusraw's religious policies in the newly conquered territories. In Syria and Mesopotamia, for example, the Chalcedonian clergy recently set down there by Maurice were promptly replaced in the churches and monasteries by Monophysites, not the original possessors of those properties, to be sure, but by "Oriental" Monophysites from within the Sasanian Empire. It was likely Yazden too who supervised the removal of the remnants of the cross of Jesus from the church of the Holy Sepulcher in Jerusalem and had it sent to Ctesiphon. Now in Jerusalem the Jews were forcibly restrained from their designs upon that city. The Christian churches were rebuilt, and the Jews were banished from the Holy City.

Heraclius' first attempts at resistance were feeble and ineffective. He thought to come down from Anatolia with an army, while Nicetas brought another from Egypt into Palestine. His own campaign accomplished nothing, and Nicetas took the brunt of Shahrbaraz's arms near Bostra in the Transjordan. Now the way to Egypt lay open. In 619 the Sasanians entered Alexandria, shortly after Nicetas and the Melchite Patriarch John the

Almoner took ship for Constantinople. Thus, neither Antioch nor Alexandria had "imperial" Patriarchs, and in both places full ecclesiastical authority and in many instances the Byzantine presence pure and simple were represented by Monophysites, in Antioch by Athanasius and in Alexandria by Andronicus, followed in 623 by Benjamin. And now, after nearly a century of schism, the two Monophysite Sees were working in concert. In 616 Athanasius had come to Egypt and with the full knowledge, if not the encouragement, of Nicetas had worked out an accord with his opposite number in Alexandria.

Heraclius did not rest in defeat. He placed the lands he still possessed in Anatolia under the kind of military government introduced earlier into the Sasanian Empire by Khusraw I and then took up the task of building a new army out of the ruins of the old. In 622 he was ready. The subsequent campaigns were fought not in Syria but in Anatolia, Armenia and Azarbayjan; and save for a final desperate attack on Constantinople in 626, the fighting went Heraclius' way from the beginning. Finally in January of 628 Heraclius stood a few miles from Ctesiphon. Khusraw apparently intended to defend his capital, but he never had the opportunity. In the following month he was murdered by his own troops. His son and successor Kavad II bought peace. The frontier would revert to what it had been at the time of Maurice.

There was no going back, however. Heraclius restored the cross of Jesus to Jerusalem with great pomp in the spring of 630, but the moment of triumph was embittered by what this catastrophic war had brought to the eastern provinces: the overt treachery of the Jews and the effective destruction of Chalcedonian orthodoxy. Syria, Egypt and Armenia were all firmly in the control of the Monophysite hierarchy, and it is likely that the bulk of the population were by then members of that same confession. Heraclius had only surrender and reconciliation to choose from. He chose the latter, and a formula upon which his own officially affirmed Chalcedonianism and the Monophysitism of his eastern subjects might agree was put together by Sergius, the Patriarch of Constantinople. It served no useful purpose. There were those who accepted it, the Egyptians, for example, but only under duress;[8] others, Athanasius of Antioch among them, condemned it outright.

There could be no reconciliation, real or otherwise, with the Jews. After a bloody pogrom against the known traitors, Heraclius ordered the forcible conversion of all the Jews of the Empire. This was in 634, when the Muslim armies were already on the road to Syria. They were on the road to Iraq as well, where after Khusraw Parvez's death only anarchy reigned. Five Shahs ruled Iran between 628 and 632, and the last of them, Yazdigird III (632–651) could offer only a doomed resistance to the arms of Islam. The Arabs who once guarded the lower Euphrates for the Shah were now among the invaders.

---

8. Heraclius confided the combined military and ecclesiastical governance of Egypt to Cyrus, an energetic Monophysite hunter in the old style. The Monophysite Patriarch Benjamin seized the point quickly and went underground shortly after Cyrus' arrival. He did not surface again until ten years later, when the Muslim armies came to Egypt.

THE FAMILY OF THE PROPHET

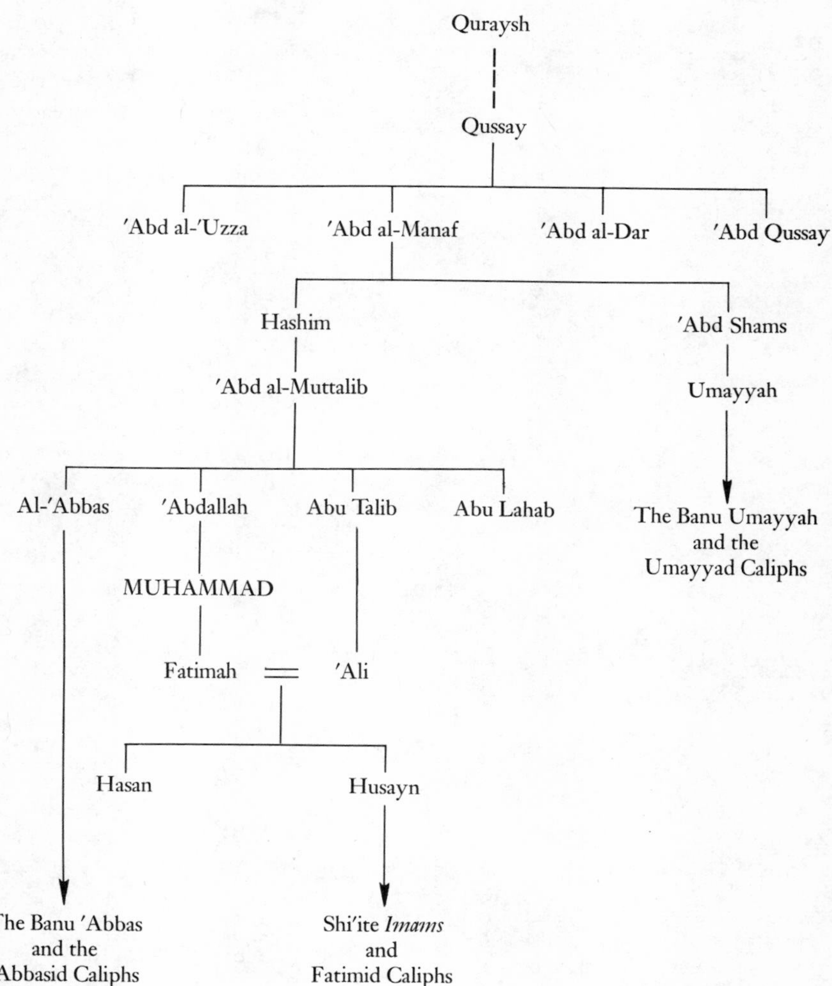

I

THE WORD OF GOD AND THE KINGDOMS OF MEN

In the seventh century of the Christian era God's voice was heard once again in western Arabia. The Semitic High God, whom the Jews called Elohim and the Arabs Allah, He who had concluded a covenant with Abraham and given the tablets of the Law to Moses on Sinai, the Lord and Creator prayed to by Jesus and worshiped by countless Jews and Christians, had now in these latter times chosen a new messenger.

Muhammad was neither a Christian nor a Jew, but a pagan of Mecca who in his fortieth year was startled from his sleep by a supernatural figure that appeared before him and commanded him to "recite." After some initial hesitation the troubled Muhammad did as he was bade. From that moment until his death some twenty-two years later he never ceased to warn and admonish in Allah's name.

Even during his own lifetime Muhammad's "recitations" were gathered up in the *Qur'an*, a Holy Book sent down from heaven for men's salvation. In it they could read Allah's message: it was, quite simply, submission to the will of God; in Arabic, *islam*.

The Prophet and the Book

For one who opens the *Qur'an* in the expectation of finding Muhammad there, only disappointment awaits. The *Qur'an* is not a Gospel; God alone speaks in it. For Muhammad himself one must turn elsewhere, in the first instance to the *Life of the Prophet* compiled out of traditional material by Muhammad ibn Ishaq (d. 767) and preserved for us in the edition of Ibn Hisham (d. 834).

Ibn Ishaq's *Life* is patently biographical in form. Some of the contents are true and some not, but there is some understanding of how the work was put together and where it is worthy of trust.[1] With the *Life* as a guide, one can turn back to the *Qur'an* and attempt to distribute its parts over a chronological framework. The results are not always convincing, but at least certain sections of the *Qur'an* can be attached, as Ibn Ishaq himself attempted to do, to the historical data of the *Life* and so can be used to produce a portrait of Muhammad.

The chief difficulty with this reconstructed life of Muhammad is that, like the portrait in the Gospels, it was fashioned by believers who accepted Muhammad's divine mission and so felt little need of the causal explanations familiar and essential to the secular historian. But if Muhammad's activity elicits little rational analysis from Ibn Ishaq and other Muslim authorities, it is more naïvely unstructured than Jesus' life and betrays no pattern dictated by a prior understanding of what a prophet should be "according to the Scriptures." God's will prevailed, to be sure, but it unfolded through a series of connected events that invite the historian to attempt the inevitable and try to understand the Prophet of God as a man who, in the history of seventh-century Arabia, was subject to the same laws as his contemporaries Heraclius and Khusraw II.

The Mecca of Muhammad was not, of course, Constantinople or Seleucia-Ctesiphon. It was a dusty, suffocatingly hot city located about midway on the long caravan route between Abraha's former domains in the Yemen and the Byzantine depots at Gaza and Damascus.[2] In the century before Muhammad it had become the most important stop on that route. Single caravans

---

1. See Chap. III, pp. 255–257.
2. The entire north-south transit took seventy days by caravan march, thirty days from the Yemen to Mecca, and another forty to the Byzantine frontier.

did not pass from the Yemen to Syria; it was, rather, the Meccans who annually sent their own caravans of a thousand camels to both the northern and the southern termini. Thus it was the Meccans and their paramount tribe of the Quraysh who were the unique entrepreneurs of the Arabian trade, and whatever ambitions the Byzantines and Sasanians may have earlier possessed to expropriate at least some of the control for themselves had gone aglimmering by the beginning of the seventh century.

By the time Muhammad began to preach his message to his fellow Meccans the power struggle in Arabia had entered a new phase. Abraha and the Abyssinians were gone, and the Sasanian presence that succeeded them in the Yemen was brief and ineffective. The Byzantine phylarchates were a shambles; divided and suspicious Arab tribes ruled where once the Ghassanids had sole power. The Banu Lakhm too were scattered, and their place was taken along the Euphrates frontier by other Arab tribes who received nothing from and owed nothing to the last tottering Shahs.

The great power closure on the peninsula in the sixth century had been accompanied by a parallel religious offensive. But now in 600 the wave of Christianity that, no more than half a century earlier, had threatened to overrun Arabia may also have been ebbing. Deprived of Byzantine and Abyssinian support and so no longer a measure of political allegiance, Christianity in Arabia was no more than a personal conviction at the beginning of the seventh century. There may have been those who were so convinced, but their number could not have been great among the notoriously insouciant Bedouin.

This sudden relapse of western Arabia into political obscurity worked to the benefit of Mecca: she now had no serious rivals along the overland trade route. Even at the height of the rivalries a half century earlier Mecca itself stood somewhat apart from the action. It lay just beyond the political grasp of the Byzantines, Sasanians and Abyssinians, who were reaching in its direction. And neither Christianity nor Judaism penetrated the defiant paganism of its ruling tribe, the Quraysh.

If Mecca's commercial eminence was a relatively recent thing, the fortunes of the Quraysh went back somewhat further, to the days of a certain Qusayy (d. c. 450) who led his clansmen in driving out the tribe that earlier controlled the town. He then set to organizing Mecca's other, earlier claim to fame, the pilgrimage to the shrine of the Ka'bah. The Ka'bah was a modest rectangular structure dating back, in one form or another, to the second Christian century, and embedded in it was a black meteoric stone.[3] The shrine was sacred to Allah and was regarded as his "house," but within its precincts there were numerous stone idols of the various deities in the crowded Arab pantheon. The Ka'bah was older than Qusayy and pilgrimages to the site were common enough before his day, but it was Qusayy who had the genius to organize them and place their supervision in his own hands and those of his sons 'Abd Manaf and 'Abd al-Dar.

The pilgrimage trade to Mecca and its Ka'bah made the fortunes of the Quraysh, and the descendants of Qusayy prospered. To his grandsons, 'Abd Shams, Hashim and al-Mutallib, new commercial riches were added with the growth of Mecca as an entrepot for international commerce. By the time the fifth century turned into the sixth the descendants of Hashim, the clan of the Banu Hashim, were not so rich perhaps as they once had been, but others were profiting among the proliferating clans of the Quraysh: the Banu 'Abd al-Dar, who still controlled the Ka'bah; 'Abd Manaf's descendants who had turned to commerce, the Banu Umayyah; and the other great Meccan mercantilists, the Banu Makhzum.

Round about Mecca lay another world, the disintegrating political structures of Byzantium, Iran and the Yemen, and, closer to home, the tribes of tent-dwelling Arabs of the steppe. Gathered in units ranging from the family to huge tribal federations, they ranged their herds across the meager pasture land from the Yemen to the northern bay of the Syrian steppe where it touched the Euphrates. Their milieu was the desert, where history is

---

3. In Muhammad's day the Ka'bah was still made of wood, was unroofed, and reached no higher than a man's head. It burned down sometime before his "call" in 610 and was reconstructed, probably under the direction of a Christian Abyssinian architect, out of the timbers of a ship wrecked on the Red Sea coast. The builder must have had a flair for decor, since there were pictures on the inside when Muhammad entered it in 630. He ordered them all removed with the exception of the portrait of Jesus and his mother.

hypostatized and its record is preserved for us only in those eerily detached "battle days of the Arabs" where tribe struggles against tribe oblivious to time and place, or in the elegant and stylized odes of the Bedouin poets.[4]

The classical ode of the Arabs is poor stuff for history. Its value lies rather in its observation of a society living in what the later Muslim Arabs contemptuously dismissed as "the time of barbarism" (*al-jahiliyah*). What this graceful and illuminating legacy from the pre-Islamic past tells us about Bedouin society is confirmed from other sources. The steppe Arab who lived in a tribal society had a severe code of conduct by which his fitness as a man was judged.[5] He was proud of his own tribe and scornful of others. When his manhood was put to the test in one of the frequent tribal raiding expeditions, he was expected to show courage and skill in the fight. At home among his peers he was called upon to act with honor toward his tribal fellows and with generosity toward his guests.

The tribal code was a secular one. The nomads' obligation toward the gods was satisfied by sacrifice and occasional prayer. Those gods were, moreover, neither paradigms for action nor guarantors of probity. They were simply there. Of much more concern to the Bedouin were the *jinn*, the malevolent *daimones* who haunted the desert landscape. The *jinn* were natural forces, alive, personified and inexplicable. They were everywhere, and they constituted for the desert Arab a more potent and present force than those other heavenly deities whom he knew and accepted.

The other gods of Arabia had their being in the heavens and their shrines in the towns. The female trinity of al-Lat, Manat and al-'Uzza was worshiped from early times at Palmyra and among the Nabataeans. In the seventh century on the eve of

---

4. On the "days of the Arabs" and the classical ode, see Chap. III, pp. 218–224, 251.

5. Or as a woman. The pre-Islamic Arab woman of both the steppe and the town, and even her sister in early Islamic times, knew little of the seclusion later imposed upon Muslim women. They played a lively part in all aspects of society from the commercial to the military. Arab society may indeed still have been in transition from a matrilinear to a patrilinear one.

Islam, al-Lat, the "Lady Goddess" of the sun, and her sisters, the goddesses of fate and the morning star, all had their shrines in the vicinity of Mecca.

The Semitic High God Allah[6] and his various "daughters" worshiped by the Arabs were by no means as spiritualized as their heavenly origins might suggest. Their local manifestations were in rocks and trees and were at a short remove from the crude animism of the desert. Nowhere was it a matter of personal devotion on the part of the worshiper; the only charm of those ladies was that they were somewhat more remote than the obsessively present *jinn.*

On the steppe, the tribe was a social and political unit of great internal coherence characterized by that sense of group solidarity (*'asabiyah*) that Ibn Khaldun (d. 1406), the chief social philosopher among the Arabs, understood was the premise and the strength of Bedouin life. Even as the tribes became sedentary, the older loyalties lingered, not always to the benefit of new commonwealths where, thousands of miles from their native soil, Arab tribes fought endlessly over points of honor vaguely remembered from their desert home.

Members of the tribe shared in the collective responsibility for deeds done and collective glory for deeds done well. A crime against one of them was a crime against all and could be requited only by vendetta. The *jahili* poetry echoes with the most unembarrassed boasting about tribal prowess, while it dismisses with sarcastic contempt all rival claims to valor.

Virtue could be won in the prescribed routines of daily life by a display of wise counsel, generosity and fine speech, but it was only in the war exercises of the nomads that the true test of valor could be met and responded to. There were wars, great bloody frays—wherein the rhetoric ran far more freely than the blood—for the rights to grazing lands, but far more common were the war-gamelike raids, or razzias, conducted more in the name of high-blooded valor than for inflicting real harm or reaping massive gains. There was, surely, booty to be had from the raids; camels and horses could be run off from a rival camp. But not much

---

6. Whose name, *al-ilah*, or Allah, means simply "the God." Al-Lat is the feminine form of the same word.

blood was spilled—the nomadic Arabs, forced to live with a vendetta system, did their best not to trigger its dangerous consequences—and the heroics in the poets must frequently have been of the mock variety.

In war, raiding or hunting, the nomad won his spurs and his place in the pecking order of the tribe. At the top was its elected head, a *shaykh* eminent not so much for his blood lines—all the Bedouin were nobly descended, it appeared—but by his prowess in the martial and social virtues. The *shaykh* was *primus inter pares* simply by virtue of being the manliest, most generous and wisest of all.

The blood members of the tribe were the *shaykh's* associates rather than his subjects. They belonged to the society with fully as much right as he, and their genealogies, their proof of membership in the blood clan, were as long and as pure as his own. Tribal deliberations were open public meetings filled with the elaborate oratory of the Bedouin culture. Outspoken criticism alternated with extravagant praise from the bards, who roamed from tribe to tribe. The poets remained mindful of their own tribal affiliation, but they were condemned by their membership in the ecumenical fellowship of their kind to a life of wandering in the camps of the Bedouin and the courts of the great *shaykhs* of the Banu Ghassan and the Lakhmids.

For any but the poet or the seer life without tribal connection was the equivalent of outlawry. Such a one might claim an honored but limited hospitality from his hosts, but in the end the tribe could assume no responsibility for him. Even the manumitted slave became a stranger to his former owner unless he could claim, or was granted, the fictional tribal membership known as clienthood. As a client (*mawla*) he gained some standing and, more importantly, the protection of the tribe or clan.

The nomadic tribes of the steppe lived off their camel and sheep herds, their horse breeding and their raiding the property of others. It was a tenuous existence at best, but in the minds of the Bedouin infinitely superior to that of the agricultural peasant with his mean plot. The farmer knew neither chivalry nor *'asabiyah;* he was a slave to his garden, his political masters and his gods. All these sat lightly upon the Bedouin who found his fulfillment in the comradeship of dangers shared and challenges met. He had his freedom and his clan, and both are faithfully mirrored in the poetry that was his chief entertainment and his principal legacy.

The Bedouin were somewhat more ambivalent toward the new capitalism of commerce. They understood power and could be enticed into allegiance with it. When the great Meccan caravans headed north to Syria, for example, they were guided and protected by Bedouin outriders serving for pay. The nomads were likewise drawn into the orbit of Mecca by the annual trade fairs and held there in loose alliances that both sides knew could be dissolved for greater gains.

Muhammad was not a steppe Arab but a townsman. According to the traditional reckoning, he was born in 570, the same year that the Meccans thrust back Abraha's advance from the Yemen and so secured their future prosperity. Muhammad did not figure to share in much of that prosperity. His clan, the Banu Hashim, were minor figures among the parent tribe of the Quraysh, and he had the further misfortune of being early orphaned: his father 'Abdallah, "the servant of Allah,"[7] died before Muhammad was born; and his mother died when he was six. His grandfather served as his guardian, and then at the death of 'Abd al-Mutallib in 578, it was his uncle, and the new head of the Banu Hashim, Abu Talib, who assumed responsibility for the child Muhammad. There is no indication that either man shirked his duties, and Abu Talib in particular stood by Muhammad when prudence dictated otherwise. The *Qur'an* dwells, nonetheless, briefly and movingly on the unhappy fate, Muhammad's own, of being orphaned in the clan and family-oriented society of Mecca. Muhammad, who devoted such precise care to legislating for heirs, himself inherited nothing.

The lack of substance in an aggressively capitalist society like Mecca's might have meant a life of disdainful poverty, but at the age of twenty-five Muhammad made a fortunate match with a fairly well-to-do widow. We have little or no idea of what he

---

7. Many of the early Quraysh possessed religious names—'Abd Manaf, "servant of the goddess Manaf," and 'Abd Shams, "servant of the Sun," for example—and 'Abdallah's was of the same type.

was like or what happened to him during adolescence or early manhood—the *Life* is of little value here—except that he was not remarkably unlike his contemporaries and that he was engaged in some not very significant part of Mecca's chief business, trade.

After his marriage to Khadijah, who was near forty at the time, Muhammad's life was more secure; with capital came a sure, if not distinguished, place among his clansmen. In the sequel Khadijah provided far more than financial security. She was the first to accept the truth of his revelation, the premier Muslim after the Prophet himself. She encouraged and supported Muhammad during the first difficult years of his public preaching, and during the twenty-five years of their marriage he took no other wife. Theirs was, by any reasonable standard of judgment, a love match as well as a corporate partnership.[8]

After his marriage silence descends once again upon the life of Muhammad. There are legends in abundance, about his role in rebuilding the Ka'bah, for example, but one of the most popular was the story of his commercial trips to Syria and his encounter with a Christian monk named Bahira near the Byzantine provincial capital of Bostra. There is nothing intrinsically unlikely about either event, the journey or the meeting, but what follows is patently dubious: Bahira predicts, on the basis of his own unadulterated reading of the Christian Scriptures, the prophetic mission of Muhammad.

Later Muslims were deeply engaged in showing that the coming of Muhammad could have been foreseen in the Jewish and Christian Scriptures had not those "Peoples of the Book" tam-

---

8. Khadijah bore Muhammad four daughters: Ruqayyah, who married the future Caliph 'Uthman, but died long before him in 624; Zaynab, who married a Meccan before Muhammad's call and saw her husband captured fighting against the Prophet at Uhud; Umm Kulthum, who married 'Uthman after Ruqayyah's death; and Fatimah, who married Muhammad's cousin and the future Caliph 'Ali. She bore him the Prophet's favorite grandchildren, Hasan and Husayn, and because of her connection with 'Ali, Fatimah gave her name to a dynasty (see Chap. VIII, pp. 595–596) and became a popular figure in Muslim legend.

pered with the texts. The project did not meet with notable success, but here in the legend of Bahira was the lacking validation: Christianity, here represented by Bahira, did indeed know that another Prophet would arise to restore God's purpose.

Bahira may with confidence be relegated to the realm of legend, but the story prompts other considerations. As a man engaged in the Meccan caravan trade Muhammad had ample reason to travel to Syria, the Yemen and even to Iraq.[9] Syria and much of Sasanian Iraq were Christian lands. What and how much did they contribute in the person of this or other nameless Bahiras to the spiritual formation of Muhammad down to the moment of his "call"? Little, apparently. Muhammad certainly knew something about Christianity, but with one notable exception,[10] he was strikingly ignorant of precisely those aspects of Christianity that one or more journeys into Syria might have taught him, Christian institutions and the externals of the Christians' liturgical life.

The Muslim tradition was pleased to think that the Prophet of God was illiterate; the condition would enhance the extraordinary quality of the revelation that fell from his lips. In the strict sense this may not be true; it is difficult to conceive of someone conducting a mercantile business without even the rudimentary ability to read and write. In the larger sense, however, he was illiterate, and precisely in the way that the tradition understood it: Muhammad was not a reader of books, not even, it appears, the Books of the Jews and Christians. Meccan society still possessed an oral culture in that it transacted its spiritual business through the spoken rather than the written word. Its vehicle of acculturation was poetry, and that and much else of permanent value was stored in human memories and not in books.

The evidence is very strong that Muhammad had never read,

---

9. The main line of trade through Mecca ran north and south, but there was branch traffic from Mecca through the central Najd to the Euphrates.

10. Though he does not discuss the subject at length, Muhammad had some experience of the Christian institution of monasticism. See Chap. VI, pp. 415–416.

and had never heard recited, either the Jewish Bible or the Christian Gospels. He understood something of how Jewish revelation had come about, that there was a Law called *Tawrat* that had been sent down to men through Moses, and he apparently concluded that the Gospel (Ar. *Injil;* Gr. *Euangeleion*) was analogous: a Christian Law that had been given to Jesus, who then promulgated it among men for their observance.

In Muhammad's eyes, Jesus ('Isa ibn Mariyam) was a sanctified figure, the offspring of a virgin birth and a "sign" and a "mercy" for mankind. Though gifted with miraculous powers, he was, nonetheless, a man, and this despite the Christians' claim that he was the son of Allah. Like Muhammad, he was both a prophet and a messenger, who was sent to men with a Sacred Book. The *Qur'an* explicitly denies the death of Jesus and explains that it was only a counterfeit that was crucified. The Qur'anic evidence for Jesus' second coming is somewhat obscure, but the later Muslim tradition took up the idea eagerly: Jesus, who is still alive in heaven, will return to signal the Last Days.

Muhammad never lost the conviction that what had been revealed to him was the same as that which had been given to the other "Peoples of the Book." His first serious contact with Jews forced him to modify his position somewhat and to meditate on why those same people were so vehement in their denial of his assumption. It brought him to a new understanding of what it meant to be a Muslim and, after his first violent political reaction, to a more supple notion of Scriptural partnership.

Most of this theological and political contortion of mind arose from Muhammad's experience of the stanchly faithful Jews of Medina, as shall be seen. There was no parallel trial of strength with the Arab Christians. There must have been Christians in and about Mecca, but their number and learning appears to have been negligible. The great Christian tribes were settled farther to the north and the east, and there were Christian cities in the Yemen, but they came into Muhammad's direct line of vision only in the last year or two of his life, when his ideas were more firmly fixed and when he no longer had the same expectations that the "Peoples of the Book" would rush to accept Islam.

Despite the vagueness of the contact, there is a great deal of

Christianity just below the surface of the *Qur'an*. This revelation "in a clear Arabic tongue,"[11] is shot through with Christian religious terms and concepts that came into Arabic through the Christian vernaculars of Syriac and, to a lesser extent, Ethiopic. The very word *Qur'an* is one of them.[12]

Ibn Ishaq's *Life* provides what was to become the classic account of how this *Qur'an* came down to men. "When Muhammad the messenger of God reached the age of forty," it begins, "God sent him in compassion to mankind 'as an announcer and a warner to all men.' " Muhammad, it appears, had the custom of going into an annual solitary retreat of the spirit on the slopes of Mt. Hira just outside of Mecca.[13] It was during the course of one such retreat in the lunar month of Ramadan, in the year 610 of the Christian era by the traditional chronology, that a supernatural figure appeared to him in his sleep.

The account in Ibn Ishaq continues in Muhammad's own words. "Recite!" "I said, 'What shall I recite?' " The command and the selfsame answer were repeated once again. The figure then said:

> "*Recite! In the name of your Lord who created,*
> *Who created men from clotted blood.*
> *Recite! Your Lord is the most beneficent,*
> *Who taught by the pen,*
> *Taught to men what they did not know.*"

In the final collection of one hundred and fourteen such revelations known collectively as *The Recitation* (*al-Qur'an*), these are the first five verses of the ninety-sixth revelation. Each revelation is called a *surah*[14] and is subdivided into verses (*ayah;* pl. *ayat*)

---

11. By which Muhammad meant not "Arabic" as opposed to "Greek" or "Persian," but *'arabiyah*, the pure literary *koine* of the Arab poet. See Chap. III, p. 219.
12. From the Syriac *qeryana* (a "reading," or *lectio* in the liturgical sense). Most such words were probably domesticated in Arabic before Muhammad's lifetime.
13. Ibn Ishaq's source for this tradition claims that it was a not uncommon practice among the Meccan Quraysh.
14. A word of doubtful origins. It is, nonetheless, Muhammad's own term, and he challenged his opponents to produce *surahs* like his.

which, unlike the artificial Biblical "verses," correspond to the true rhythmical divisions of the text.[15] *Surahs* and verses vary markedly in length, but each *surah,* with the somewhat inexplicable exception of the ninth, begins with the formula of Muhammad's own devising: "In the name of Allah, the Compassionate, the Merciful." In twenty-nine of the *surahs* this formula is immediately followed by one to five letters of the Arabic alphabet, a phenomenon whose meaning is totally unknown.[16]

The one hundred and fourteen *surahs* of the *Qur'an* represent, then, the revelations granted to Muhammad over the course of twenty-two years, twelve of them spent in residence at Mecca and the final ten at Medina.[17] In Muhammad's own mind they were "recitations" of the *ipsissima verba* of God, a "book" which had been "sent down" from heaven and in form and content presumably similar to the "books" earlier given to the Prophets of the Jews and Christians. For Muhammad the *Qur'an* was unmistakably Scripture as understood by those two other groups, and it served the same mixed purpose of code of conduct and liturgical text. All three Scriptures, the *Tawrat*, the *Injil*, and the *Qur'an*, were "sent down" from the same heavenly archetype, the "Mother of the Book," preserved on closely guarded tablets in heaven.[18] The Jews and Christians had unfortunately corrupted their versions; the *Qur'an* was intact.

Modern criticism has not surrendered the *Qur'an* to Allah. It regards it rather as the prime document on Muhammad's other-

---

15. In all subsequent citations of the *Qur'an* the first Arabic numeral will refer to the *surah* and the second to the verse or verses.

16. There is additional prefatory material in standard editions of the *Qur'an*, but all of it is the work of compilers and editors; the name of the *surah*—number 96, already cited, is called, for example, "Clotted Blood"—a chronological designation, simply "Mecca" or "Medina," and the number of verses in the *surah*.

17. This is not to say that there were merely one hundred and fourteen revelations. The Muslim tradition asserts, and modern critics agree, that many of the *surahs* are composites and represent more than one revelation.

18. On the debate that later arose on this subject, see Chap. II, pp. 197–199.

wise unreported spiritual life and his evolving religious consciousness. As a document it is attractively authentic; nothing of any substance has been added or subtracted. But before they can serve further, the *surahs* of the *Qur'an* must be laid out along the chronology provided by Ibn Ishaq's *Life*. Earlier Muslim editors had already worked out a rough classification by designating some *surahs* as "Meccan" and others as "Medinan"; but, since the nineteenth century, Western scholars have been attempting to refine further the chronology of the *Qur'an*.

It is a difficult task, since it rests upon internal stylistic considerations of great subtlety, and the results have achieved only a qualified success. The distinction between the earliest *surahs*[19] with their fervent imagery and terse, enthusiastic language and those delivered later at Medina when Muhammad was legislating for a growing community is clear enough. But within those larger divisions the chronology is far more tentative.

Whatever their exact order, Muhammad's "recitations" are the measure of his mature life, the substance of his message,[20] and the foundation of Islam. They began, however, as something quite different. The first vision on Mt. Hira raised only anxiety in the soul of Muhammad. He may have thought that he had seen God,[21] but if Ibn Ishaq may be relied upon in this regard, he was soon instructed otherwise: his vision was neither of God nor of Satan but of the Angel Gabriel.

How did he come to this conclusion? Gabriel was a well-known figure in the Judaeo-Christian tradition but hardly so in the religious consciousness of the pre-Islamic Arabs. In Ibn Ishaq's version of events the distraught Muhammad returned home from Mt. Hira and confided his experience to Khadijah, who in turn consulted her cousin Waraqah. This latter was a convert from paganism to Christianity and a student, it was said,

---

19. Earliest in the chronological sense. In the actual *Qur'an* the *surahs* are roughly arranged in diminishing length, an order that is almost exactly opposite the chronological order of their revelation.

20. Though not its entirety; on the various extra-Qur'anic traditions related of the Prophet and their role in Islam, see Chap. III, pp. 240–243.

21. *Surah* 53 appears to refer to the original vision, and the language there suggests that it was an immediate vision of God.

of the Old and New Testament. It was he who identified the source of the vision as Gabriel and related it to what had earlier happened to other prophets. Muhammad was reassured.

Driven by the divine command to "rise and warn," Muhammad began to communicate the message of Islam to others. Khadijah accepted it from the outset, and then some others—Waraqah notably not among them—in his immediate circle: his former slave, and now his adopted son, Zayd ibn Harithah; his cousin and the son of his guardian Abu Talib, 'Ali; and a man of his own age, though not of the Banu Hashim, Abu Bakr. This was the tiny nucleus that first accepted Islam and thus became Muslims. They submitted to the will of Allah as the unique creator and ultimate judge of the universe: "There is no God but Allah," as the Muslim profession of faith (*shahadah*) later expressed it.

Submission imposed certain moral responsibilities. The new Muslim was required to change his ways from the prevailing code of conduct at Mecca. In turning his mind to the Judgment, he should cease wasting his energies in getting and spending, in oppressing the poor and the weak for the sake of gain. Mercy, generosity and worship were the only appropriate responses in the face of the overwhelming power and majesty of Allah.

As their numbers slowly grew and young men from the various clans of the Quraysh were attracted to the movement—'Uthman ibn Affan of the Banu Umayyah and 'Umar ibn al-Khattab who would one day be Caliphs were among them—the senior members of the Quraysh began to express their disapproval. Their motive, it was once thought, was their fear of the possibility that Muhammad and his Muslims might disrupt the lucrative pilgrimage trade to the Ka'bah in an excess of puritan zeal. By all reports Muhammad was, both before his call and after, a devotee of worship at the "House of Allah" and so gave no sign that he intended to abolish it. Muhammad in fact identified the "lord of the Ka'bah" with the Allah to whose will he and his followers had submitted.

The real reasons for the uneasiness of the Quraysh may have run far deeper. Religion, morality, and norms of social conduct were indiscriminately entwined, in seventh-century Mecca. The code that regulated all three was essentially that of the nomadic Arab, which the Quraysh themselves had once been. They were

Bedouin no longer however. For not much more than a century Mecca was the center of a new urban culture where the nomadic code had perforce to evolve or be dissolved. Like the sixth-pre-Christian-century inhabitants of the new Hellenic *poleis* who struggled to reconcile a code of feudal morality inherited from Homer with a milieu that had little place for kings or martial heroes, the Meccan Quraysh were suffering the pains of moral transition.[22]

Bedouin justice, Bedouin morality, and Bedouin honor evolved in circumstances where intratribal cooperation was a necessary condition for survival and where the relations of one tribe with another were conditioned by the infrequency of their contacts in time and space. As with the Homeric warrior, war was an occasion for honor and glory rather than conquest or slaughter or even livelihood. The Bedouin were excellent scouts and guides, but only dubiously proficient in the tactical warfare conducted by the professional soldiers of the sixth century.

Within Mecca the formerly nomadic Arabs found themselves citizens of what has been called a "mercantile republic," whose unstated and uncodified ideals were those of an aggressively capitalist society. The rough democracy of the Bedouin was yielding to an oligarchy of wealth, wherein men struggled not for honor but for gain. The clan was breaking down in the streets of Mecca and with it the traditional morality. Men still spoke of the "tradition" (*sunnah*) of their fathers, but it was a recollection born of nostalgia and anxiety.

Muhammad had somehow fought clear of the disintegration of the traditional order. The language of his revelations is filled with the commercial images which must have come easily to the tongues of his fellow townsmen, but he was not one of them. By stages that are concealed from us, the moral and social life of Mecca had become obnoxious to Muhammad, but it was on an instant that he found his resolution, not in returning to a dead

---

22. The parallel continued into a later age. The Hellenes developed a new moral code in the sixth and fifth centuries before Christ, but for a long time afterward they paid a cultural lip service to the Homeric ideal. And even after the coming of Islam the Bedouin ideal, which was embalmed, like the Greek, in literature, still claimed its adherents.

Bedouin past with its tribal Achilles, but in an apocalyptic call to reform in root and branch.

It was more likely Muhammad's diagnosis than his solution that terrified the Quraysh. He had read their hearts—was he not one of them?—and proposed something that probably baffled most of them. Some few responded and embraced Muhammad's vision; for the rest, they were moved not to conversion but to anger.

Muhammad's own anger was more fervent than that of his adversaries, or so it appears from the *Qur'an.* He understood with the clarity of one who has seen the truth, while the reaction of the Quraysh seemed more often petty than either fierce or principled. There were taunts and some verbal abuse. Arguments broke out. Some of them were halfheartedly theological—the Quraysh were surely not concerned with the niceties of the resurrection of the body after death—but in one area at least his opponents struck a nerve. For as long as he was in public view Muhammad showed an exceedingly thin skin. Ridicule, parody, or satire drove him to violent and sometimes destructive anger. Now, in the early days he was accused of being a soothsayer, a seer, or someone whose wits were stolen by the *jinn.* On hearing some of his "recitations," they said that these were "old stories," and one insensitive soul named al-Nadr, who had been to Hirah on the Sasanian frontier, followed the Prophet about telling Persian tales and claiming they were better than Muhammad's own.[23]

Al-Nadr may have been referring, with some license, to the considerable number of stories scattered through the *Qur'an.* Some of them are Biblical in their inspiration, like the long *surahs* given over to Jonah (10), Joseph (12) and Abraham (14), while others drew upon the Arabs' own tradition. Among the latter were the parallel stories of the 'Ad and the Thamud, two peoples from Arab antiquity to whom Allah had previously sent prophets. They were treated in the same way that the Meccans were treating Muhammad and as a result their tormentors were visited by a quite exemplary destruction.

---

23. Muhammad had his revenge. The Meccan raconteur of Iranica was captured at the battle of Badr and was promptly silenced by decapitation.

Despite these cautions the harassment of the Muslims continued, and in its course a puzzling event occurred. Sometime about 615 a very large part of the Muslim community migrated across the Red Sea to the Christian kingdom of Abyssinia. 'Uthman was among them, but Muhammad, Zayd, 'Ali and Abu Bakr stayed behind at Mecca. The emigrants eventually returned, some in 622 and the rest in 628, but their motives in going or Muhammad's in sending them remain unclear. Muslims were being edged out of the economic life of the community and, so, simple financial hardship may have been the reason. Did Muhammad have another plan in mind, a military alliance with the Negus perhaps, or was there some schism among the Muslims that only separation could cure? We do not know.

At home a crisis was developing. Pressure was brought to bear upon Abu Talib, Muhammad's guardian and, more appositely in the present context, the head of the Banu Hashim, to withdraw the clan's support and protection from Muhammad. Abu Talib, who never became a Muslim himself, refused to do so, purely on familial grounds. Next, the head of the Banu Makhzum, Abu Jahl, proposed to lay an economic boycott on the entire Banu Hashim. It was not very successful apparently, except that it won the support of one of Abu Talib's brothers, Abu Lahab, who shortly thereafter, at the death of Abu Talib in 619, succeeded to the leadership of the Banu Hashim.[24]

The death in the same year of Abu Talib and of his wife, Khadijah, stripped Muhammad of his two chief psychological supports.[25] There is no sign that he became prey to self-doubt, but he may have been induced into one of his few false moves. Muhammad left Mecca and attempted to raise some support in the nearby town of Ta'if. It was an embarrassing fiasco; and since Abu Lahab had lifted the clan protection from him, the Prophet could not return to Mecca until he could persuade someone else to guarantee his safety. He finally found his man—it must have

---

24. And gained immortality by his opposition to Muhammad; the early *surah* 111 is devoted entirely to a burning condemnation of Abu Lahab and his wife.

25. Though Ibn Ishaq places about the time the famous "night journey"; see Chap. VIII, p. 546.

been a humiliating search—and he returned, with very few prospects, it must have seemed, to his native city.

Then in the pilgrimage (*hajj*) month of 620 an unexpected opportunity presented itself. To Mecca on the *hajj* came six men from the city of Yathrib two hundred and fifty miles to the north. They fell in with Muhammad, heard his message, and expressed interest. They and a few others returned to make the pilgrimage in 621, and on this occasion they formally accepted Islam as it was then constituted. "We pledged that we would give God no associate, that we would not steal, commit fornication, kill our offspring, or slander our neighbors; that we would obey him in all that was right. If we fulfilled our promises, paradise would be ours; if not, God would punish us or forgive us as he pleased." Muhammad sent back to Yathrib with them one of the Meccan Muslims to instruct them in the recitation of the *Qur'an* and the correct observance of Islam.

They may well have needed instruction: the *Qur'an*, at least in its finished version, is not a simple document. The portrait of Allah and his works that unfolds upon its pages is filled with nuances. God is one, without partner or peer. He is compassionate and merciful, yet a severe judge who will call all to justice before his throne on the Last Day. That day and its subsequent punishments and rewards is described in graphic and naturalistic detail in the *Qur'an*. All judgment is Allah's and so too is all power; he creates and sustains. He decrees, and yet man will be judged by his own deeds.

This is Muhammad's theology, which his disciples were now attempting to disseminate in Yathrib. It is simply summed up in the assertion he required of all who accepted Islam: "There is no God but Allah," to which was added the recognition of God's salvational mercy, "and Muhammad is his Prophet." This is the first pillar of Islam, the "bearing witness" (*shahadah*). The other four have to do with regulating man's conduct toward God and man: he must cleanse himself and make prayer (*salat*),[26] particu-

---

26. From the beginning there were prescribed liturgical prayers consisting in recitations from the *Qur'an* and accompanied by a series of standings, kneelings and prostrations. Later the daily number was fixed

larly in the company of his fellow Muslims at noon on Friday; he must pay the alms tithe (*zakat*); he must fast during Ramadan;[27] and once during his lifetime he must make pilgrimage (*hajj*) to the Ka'bah at Mecca.

These are the five principal obligations of the Muslim, but there was much more besides. The *Qur'an* set forth–chiefly after Muhammad's own arrival at Medina–detailed regulations concerning such things as marriage, divorce and inheritance. Wine drinking, the eating of pork and usury were all forbidden. Some legal norms were also prescribed, like the necessity of four witnesses in cases of adultery and the penalties of mutilation for theft.

In 622 the Yathribites returned once again, now with their number swollen to seventy-five. On this occasion they extended their pledge of the previous year to include the political consequences of accepting Islam: they swore they would fight on Muhammad's behalf if necessary. They surely did not intend an attack on Mecca in their pledge, nor is it likely that they envisioned an attack of the Meccans upon themselves. Rather, they seemed to be pledging that they would extend their protection over him in Yathrib, to assume the responsibility *in loco gentis* for his safety in their midst.

What followed was quite extraordinary. During the summer of 622 Muslims began slipping out of Mecca for Yathrib until in September only Abu Bakr, 'Ali and Muhammad himself were left in the city. Late in that month, with 'Ali serving as a decoy, Muhammad accomplished his own stealthy migration (*hijrah*) accompanied only by Abu Bakr. Later Muslims correctly regarded it as a turning point in the history of Islam and marked the beginnings of the Muslim era from that date.[28] And Yathrib in turn came to be known to the Muslims as the "City of the Prophet" (*Madinat al-Nabi*), popularly Medina.

---

at five: at daybreak, noon, mid-afternoon, after sunset and during the early part of the night; but earlier they may have been fewer in number and their exact times not yet set.

27. The fast consists in total abstinence from food, drink, smoking and sexual intercourse from sunrise to sunset during the lunar month.

28. Reckoning from the first day of the lunar year in which the *hijrah* occurred, July 16, 622, of the Christian era.

The final pact compounded between Muhammad and the tribes of Medina is contained in a document called "The Constitution of Medina" and is preserved by Ibn Ishaq in his *Life of the Prophet.* By it Muhammad reconstituted the political life of his adopted city. It was a far different community from the Mecca he had just left. Medina was, in the first instance, an agricultural and not a commercial city, and though it had not progressed as far toward urbanism as Mecca—the Medinese still lived in various fortified compounds scattered over the oasis—it had experienced two costly wars, whose scars it still bore.

The first was the struggle in which the pagan Arab tribes of Aws and Khazraj overthrew the Jewish clans which had previously controlled the oasis. The descendants of those Jews—probably Arabs who had converted to Judaism at some point—still lived in Medina and were apparently prosperous, even though their political power was no longer what it had been. The new rulers of the oasis, the various clans of Aws and Khazraj, had not yet learned, however, to live in peace together. In 618 they were joined by their Jewish dependents in a bloody civil war from which no one emerged victorious.

Muhammad was invited to Medina to solve its internal political problems. That his cure was in the form of a prophetic revelation did not apparently bother the Medinese pagans; their close association with the Jews had already enlightened them, perhaps, in the ways of prophecy. Immediately upon his arrival, Muhammad put down a political foundation. The Muslim "emigrants" (*muhajirun*), a designation soon to become a badge of honor in the Muslim community, were constituted a clan—a small and impoverished clan, to be sure—in the political organization of Medina; Muhammad was recognized as its chief and the equal of the other clan leaders. All the clans would continue to regulate their internal affairs much as before.

This was by way of preliminary. Muhammad's major contribution was the creation of another, totally new body, the "community," or *ummah.* The pagan Medinese had pledged themselves to accept Islam, and so they and the "clan" of the Emigrants formed a new community based on Islam and with Muhammad, the Prophet of Islam, at its head. But the "Constitution of Medina" goes on to suggest something more. It described itself as a covenant between the Muslims from among the Quraysh and the citizens of Yathrib, presumably those who had accepted Islam. The covenant also included "those who followed them, and joined with them, and labored with them. They are one community to the exclusion of all men." The Jews of Medina are explicitly mentioned as part of that "one community," and so Muhammad would serve for them, as he did for the other Muslim clans, as the supreme arbiter of disputes.

This quasi-political understanding of the *ummah* did not last long. In his earlier revelation Muhammad seemed to regard the *ummah* as a religiously or ethnically constituted nation like the Christians and the Jews and the Thamud to whom Allah typically sends a prophet for their salvation. The early Medinan *ummah* was more like a confederation of clans, however, some of them Muslim and some of them not, with a prophet who was its arbitrator but not its unique political head. In that form it barely survived Muhammad's first confrontation with the Medinese Jews.

Muhammad had opposition from the outset. Some few of the pagans rejected his prophethood purely and simply. Others accepted it, or appeared to accept it, but had their doubts about its political consequences. These latter are doubtless the "hypocrites" against which the *Qur'an* occasionally rails, and their leader was 'Abdallah ibn Ubayy, a chief of the Khazraj, whose own political ambitions were blunted by Muhammad's arrival on the scene. This opposition gradually expired as Muhammad's political successes multiplied, but the break with the Jews was far more dramatic and had a more profound effect on Muhammad's own consciousness.

In the first years after his arrival in Medina Muhammad consolidated his position there. Various of the Emigrants were associated, on an individual basis, with Medinese "Helpers" (*Ansar*) for purposes of protection, while for his own part Muhammad, who had already married once after the death of Khadijah, married 'A'ishah, the nine-year-old daughter of Abu Bakr, and arranged for the wedding of his own daughter Fatimah to 'Ali. Politically he adopted a bold stance: he sent out raiding parties to attack some secondary Meccan caravans. The raids were not very successful, and only Emigrants were involved in them, but he had signaled his intentions to the Meccans and the raids themselves added an important new dimension to Islam. They were conducted under the rubric of "striving (*jihad*) in the way of Allah." It was to be a bloody business, this *jihad*, far more so than the honor exercises of the pre-Islamic Arab, but as long as Muhammad's intent held true, the Holy War, which disclaimed any intent but a religious one, was directed outward, toward the non-Muslim.

The notion of war as a religious rather than a purely political activity shows that even at this early stage the concept of the *ummah* as a political confederation of tribes and clans, including non-Muslim, Jewish ones, had inevitably to yield to Muhammad's original understanding of a body whose foundation may be ethnic but whose reason for being is shaped by the divine purposes of salvation. The Jews were just such an *ummah*, and in Medina they were more than just a historical and literary illustration of a theological point; they were a political reality.

Muhammad may have thought that the Medinese Jews would recognize his mission and accept Islam, or perhaps he was willing to compromise because he could not rule the oasis without their cooperation. He was quickly disabused on the first count, at any rate. Tradition relates that in 624 Muhammad abruptly changed the orientation of his prayers from Jerusalem to the Ka'bah at Mecca, and the deed is reflected upon in the *Qur'an* (2:136–147). Most of the Semitic peoples faced in a particular direction during their prayers, the eastern Christians and others toward the East, and the Jews toward Jerusalem. It is uncertain in what direction the Muslims faced while they were still at Mecca, but at Medina Jerusalem served as their orientation point (*qiblah*). Now that was changed, as was the obligation of observing, in Muslim dress, the fast of the Jewish Day of Atonement. For that latter Muhammad substituted the obligation of the month-long fast of Ramadan.[29]

---

29. Two other Jewish practices Muhammad did not abdicate. The obligation of the alms tithe (*zakat*) began at Mecca on a Jewish model, and the custom of the communal mosque prayer and sermon on Friday probably owed something to Jewish Sabbath preparations. He did not, however, intend Friday as a Muslim Sabbath. It was not a day of rest but merely one on which the obligation to common prayer occurred.

From 624 onward, Muhammad appears to have surrendered any hope of the Jews' accepting Islam. It may have been a naïve hope to begin with. He knew nothing of Jewish history or the exact content of Jewish Scriptures; he had fed rather on vague and unsophisticated Biblical legends. The Medinese Jews, on the other hand, though hardly scholarly experts on the subject, must have found it simple enough to give the lie to Muhammad's claims that his own revelations were the same as those given to Moses, a notion that was suggested to him by Waraqah at the very outset of his career. He would learn the same from Christians later in his life, but the challenge at Medina from the Jews was his first and obviously the most painful.

The change of the *qiblah* was Muhammad's symbolic response to the Jewish challenge, and other political responses would follow, but he reacted more deeply on the level of his own theology. About this time there appeared in his mind the twin themes of the Jewish falsification of Scripture and his own mission to restore the "original" religion which the Jews (and the Christians) had distorted. Their most outrageous distortion was, of course, the suppression of those parts of the Book which predicted the coming of Muhammad (2:145–146; 61:6).

Muhammad's new tack at Medina was to dismiss the Jews' version of Scripture and to refer back to an even older form of Judaism. Abraham, he delighted to point out (3:67), was neither a Jew nor a Christian in the traditional sense in that he antedated both the Torah and the Gospels. Abraham was in fact a *muslim*, one who had submitted himself to God, and a *hanif*. *Hanif* may originally have come from a Syriac Christian word for pagan, but the word did not disturb Muhammad. He had found a new concept with which to undercut the Jewish recalcitrants and mockers, and he used it effectively. It was Abraham the monotheist and his son Isma'il, the latter the ancestor of the Arabs, who constructed the original Ka'bah at Mecca as the "House of Allah." Muhammad was merely fulfilling Allah's providential plan and restoring the "religion of Abraham" which the Jews and Christians had perverted to their own ends and which the Quraysh at Mecca simply ignored.

The Quraysh were in Muhammad's mind again in 624. When he received news that the annual caravan was setting out from

Syria on its return to Mecca, he decided on his boldest stroke to date, to attack it en route. His intent soon became an open secret. Abu Sufyan, of the Banu Umayyah, who was in charge of the huge caravan, heard of it while he was still in Syria and sent the news to Abu Jahl and the Quraysh at Mecca. A force of men rushed to arms—a very large investment for a great number of Meccans was at stake—and proceeded northward. Three hundred Muslims, whose number now included Helpers as well as Emigrants, came down from Medina toward the coast, and at the wells of Badr, where the caravan would normally stop, they set up an ambush. Abu Sufyan unaccountably got the caravan past the place without harm, and when news came to the Quraysh approaching from the south that the caravan was safe, indecision set in. Some were for returning to Mecca; their investment was safe and there was little enthusiasm for what had necessarily to be a civil war. Others, Abu Jahl among them, argued for a showdown with Muhammad. The latter view prevailed, and the Quraysh, who were at least double the number of the Muslims, approached Badr, where the issue was joined.

Badr was a Muslim triumph, as total as it was unexpected; the Muslims lost fourteen men and the Quraysh from fifty to seventy, including their leader Abu Jahl.[30] It was an immense psychological victory and there was plentiful booty for the economically distressed Emigrants. This was no mere raid, however. It pitted Muslim against non-Muslim in Holy War, and fathers against sons in civil strife. The Quraysh casualties were extraordinarily high, and since most of them had occurred among the chiefs, the leadership at Mecca was permanently crippled. Those chiefs had never shown themselves either vigorous or united in making cause against Muhammad, and there was even less reason to think that their successors would.

---

30. In Ibn Ishaq's account of the battle there is an interesting sidelight on Muhammad's prophetic role at Medina. When he proposed placing the troops in a certain position, one of the Medinese inquired whether God had ordered it so or whether this was Muhammad's own private opinion. When he was told it was the latter, the Medinese politely suggested another location, and it was his counterproposal that eventually prevailed.

Now secure in Medina, Muhammad turned on the Jews. One of the three major Jewish clans there served as goldsmiths and armorers, and perhaps were involved in some minor commerce as well. On the thinnest of trumped-up charges, Muhammad besieged them in their quarters and in the end evicted them from the oasis. Leaving their property behind, they migrated to Syria, to the considerable benefit, one suspects, of the Emigrants who had come to Medina as traders in an agricultural society and who for four years after the *hijrah* had to live off the Helpers. Now within a few months they had the spoils of Badr and the confiscated places and property of these Jews. The Emigrants, relieved forever of the specter of having to farm for a living, settled into the more comfortable role of merchants of Medina.

The Quraysh had to retaliate for Badr. Muhammad captured a Meccan caravan attempting to squeeze past Medina on its eastern side late in 624, and the news of it probably spurred the elaborate plans for vengeance being hatched at Mecca. An army of some three thousand men under Abu Sufyan the Umayyad finally marched against Medina in March of 625. Muhammad drew up his seven hundred Muslims against the foot of Mt. Uhud north of the city, and the fighting was going well for the Muslims until the Meccan cavalry commander, Khalid ibn Walid, broke the Muslim line. In the confusion it was reported that Muhammad was dead—he was in fact wounded—and the Muslims lost hope. The mountain probably saved them: as they retreated up its slopes the Meccan cavalry could not reach them. Nor did Abu Sufyan follow up his advantage. He had avenged Badr with Muslim blood, and it was enough. The Quraysh withdrew. In a brilliant stroke, Muhammad and his sorely crippled Muslims made as if to pursue them. It was just enough to cause the Quraysh to wonder if they had won the battle at all.

In the following years Muhammad and the Meccans, both of whom recognized the stalemate, attempted to rally the neighboring nomadic tribes to their side. At Medina, Muhammad dislodged the second Jewish clan on the grounds that God had warned him of a Jewish plot against his life. The deed was not beyond possibility; with the rise of Muhammad at Medina, assassination became a frequently invoked political weapon. But it was probably more complex than that. The Medinese "hypocrites" had not fought with Muhammad at Mt. Uhud, and now they may have been cultivating the Jewish clans as a political counterweight to the Prophet. It did not help. The Jews were once again besieged and then expelled without their arms. They went out with full colors displayed, however; their pipers played and their women sang on the road out of Medina, while the Muslims took possession of their vacated date-palm groves.

The remaining Jewish clan must have known what was in store for them, and as at Badr and Uhud it was a military action that provoked the deed. Muhammad resumed his raiding in 626, and one expedition struck deep into the north of Arabia. In March of 627 the Quraysh began their final assault on Medina. This time they came with ten thousand men, including many nomad auxiliaries, and had the financial support of the Jews who were most recently banished from Medina and had taken up residence in the oasis of Khaybar to the north. Muhammad commanded only about a third of his foe's number and had some dubious allies in his rear: the "hypocrites," who were still only lukewarm, and the remaining Jewish clan at Medina, which professed neutrality in the affair. Reportedly on the advice of a Persian convert named Salman, Muhammad had a trench dug across the sole approach to the oasis that might be serviceable to cavalry. It could not have been much of a ditch, but it served its purpose: the Meccan and Bedouin cavalry could not pass.

Out of the stalemate grew defeat for the Quraysh. They could not pasture their horses in the freshly harvested fields and they could not keep hold of their nomad allies. The Quraysh turned around and went home, certain in the knowledge that they could never dislodge Muhammad from Medina. Muhammad now struck out at some of the tribes that had supported the Quraysh. It was on one such occasion that an event with serious future repercussions occurred. At this point Muhammad already had five wives,[31] but Abu Bakr's daughter 'A'ishah was clearly his favorite. That

31. After Uhud, Muhammad promulgated the Qur'anic verse (4:3) which appears to encourage the Muslim to marry more than one wife —"two or three or four." Many of Muhammad's own wives were widows, and it is likely that the injunction had something to do with taking care of the women widowed at Uhud.

fact may have provoked some jealousy, since when 'A'ishah was separated from the raiding party during the night and was brought back in the morning by a young man there was scandalous talk. Muhammad appeared at first to believe it, and 'Ali certainly did. Allah sent a revelation (24:11–20) and 'A'ishah was cleared, but she never forgot 'Ali's treatment of her in the affair.

Muhammad's bloodiest vengeance was reserved for the surviving Jewish clan at Medina, the Banu Qurayzah. They were accused of plotting his betrayal during the "battle of the trench." Perhaps they were, or perhaps neutrality was, under the circumstances, treason enough. For the third time there was a siege of the Jews in their fortified part of the oasis. The Banu Qurayzah had little hope, nor did the intervention of some of their Medinese allies help much. They surrendered unconditionally but were given, nonetheless, the harshest punishment possible: all the adult males were put to the sword and the women and children were sold into slavery. It is perhaps significant that before the end they were offered a way out, if they would admit that "Muhammad is the sent one and he is the one whom we find mentioned in our Scripture." To which they replied, "We will never abandon the Law of the Torah and never change it for another."

The failure of the attack on Medina in 627 marked the end of the Quraysh as surely, if not as spectacularly and savagely, as it did that of the Banu Qurayzah. Their best young men were deserting to the Muslim standard, including their two premier soldiers, 'Amr ibn al-'As and Khalid ibn Walid, who would one day lead Muslim armies to the conquest of Egypt and Syria. Morale was low in Mecca, but there was still some reaction when Muhammad made his next unexpected move. Urged by a dream, he came toward Mecca in 628 with the intention of making a pilgrimage to the Ka'bah. He had with him about a thousand men, somewhat more than a pilgrimage would seem to indicate, but obviously too small for an all-out assault on the city. The Quraysh barred his way, and there was talking but no fighting. An odd agreement was reached. Muhammad undertook to return to Medina on the understanding that he could make the pilgrimage in the following year. He likewise unilaterally promised to extradite any Quraysh minors or clients who defected to his camp. Finally, both sides agreed not to engage in hostilities for ten years but to allow each other a free hand in attracting the nomadic tribes into an alliance.

The body of the Muslims did not know what to make of this, as we do not ourselves. Perhaps they expected Mecca to fall at their feet, while Muhammad was content to take whatever terms he could and bide a season longer. The disappointment swiftly abated, however, when the Prophet shrewdly cast his followers into something new. Those who had gone with him on the abortive pilgrimage to Mecca were almost immediately invited to accompany him on a raid against the rich Jewish oasis of Khaybar seventy-five miles north of Medina. The Jews there, who like those at Medina were ethnically Arabs and not descendants of earlier Jewish settlers, included among their number one of the Jewish clans banished from Medina, and they had openly cooperated with the Quraysh during the siege of Medina in 627. Khaybar fell after some fierce fighting, but this time there was no talk of treachery, or evictions, or executions. The Jews of Khaybar had never been members of the original *ummah,* as the Medinese Jews had been. They were in fact something new: a settlement captured by *jihad.*

Muhammad left the inhabitants of Khaybar where they were; this time he imposed a different kind of arrangement on the defeated. The movable spoils were divided among his troops, the Prophet taking, as usual, a fifth share.[32] The inhabitants kept their land, but henceforward they would have to pay one half of the produce of it into the Muslim treasury, where it would be divided by lots among those who shared in the expedition.[33]

The rest of the earlier Muslim migrants to Abyssinia returned in 628, and in the following year Muhammad performed the pilgrimage to Mecca as agreed. The situation of the Quraysh was deteriorating. Both Abu Lahab and Abu Jahl, his two chief

---

32. A pre-Islamic custom gave a fourth of the spoils to the chief.

33. The later Islamic practice was similar. It left the conquered lands in the possession of their tenants and exacted instead a land tax (*kharaj*) on the property. This income belonged, however, to the community as a whole and not, as here, to assigned lot holders.

opponents, were gone. In their place Muhammad's uncle 'Abbas now headed the Banu Hashim,[34] while the general leadership of the Quraysh was in the hands of Abu Sufyan. Both men were inclined to be conciliatory to Muhammad, and the Prophet for his part had at least partially extended his hand by marrying the sister of 'Abbas and the daughter of Abu Sufyan. Within a year the details of Mecca's capitulation were worked out in private.

In January of 630 Muhammad came to Mecca with ten thousand men and took over his native city against only token resistance. There was little crowing in the hour of triumph. The Prophet entered the precinct of the Ka'bah and ordered the idols there removed. God spoke once more through his lips: "The truth has come and falsehood passed away; truly falsehood is sure to pass away" (17:82). Then, standing at the door of the Ka'bah, Muhammad spoke in his own voice. "There is no God but Allah alone. He has no partner. He has fulfilled his promises and helped his servant. He has put to flight the league against him. O Quraysh, God has destroyed the pride of paganism and its veneration of ancestors. Go now; you are free." He finished and the Meccans in turn swore their allegiance to the Prophet of God.

Muhammad sent his lieutenants into the nearby towns to destroy the idols and shrines there. Among them were those sacred to Manat and al-'Uzza, the two goddesses whom Muhammad had once, during the dark days at Mecca before the *hijrah*, contemplated incorporating into the worship of Islam. "Have you not thought upon al-Lat, al-'Uzza, and the third, the other, Manat?" The *surah* (53:18ff.) originally continued: "These are exalted females whose intercession is to be hoped for." This latter verse is not in the final text of the *Qur'an* but is supplied by later Muslim historians. The Quraysh were delighted on that occasion by what seemed to be a concession on the part of the Prophet,

---

34. It was 'Abbas' descendants who assumed the Caliphate in 750, shortly before the composition of Ibn Ishaq's *Life of the Prophet*, and so 'Abbas' sympathetic role in that work must be viewed with some reserve. The 'Abbasids replaced the Umayyads, the descendants of Abu Sufyan, the other principal in the story at this point, and so his portrait too may have been reworked by Ibn Ishaq.

but Muhammad was shortly given to understand by God (22:51) that the verse in question had been cast into his mind by Satan. God then abrogated the original version and the canonical text of *surah* 53 was made to read: "These are but names that you and your fathers named. God revealed no authority for them."

The third of the goddesses in the "Satanic verses," al-Lat, had her sanctuary in Ta'if, the city of orchards and vineyards fifty miles east of Mecca, where Muhammad had once thought to emigrate. There was no talk of destroying her shrine in 630, not because Muhammad had lost any of his firmness in the face of idol worship, but because the city and its inhabitants were allied with a huge tribal federation of the nomadic Hawazin, who had gathered twenty thousand men in the area with the obvious purpose of destroying at a single blow both Muhammad and the now enfeebled power of Mecca. In the same month that he occupied Mecca, Muhammad marched against the confederates. It was a more difficult struggle than he had perhaps expected, but in the end the nomads were defeated. Ta'if, which was one of the rare walled towns of the Hejaz, was besieged and taken as well. The shrine of al-Lat was promptly destroyed.

Muhammad was now the undisputed master of the Hejaz, and deputations from the surrounding tribes came into Medina, to which he had returned after the defeat of the Hawazin. They came to receive terms and in many cases, if not all, to embrace Islam. By turns superstitious and insouciant, the Bedouin were fearsome allies when enlisted for a cause or profit, but only when the throw was quick and the odds not staggering. For a brief span of time Islam served as both their cause and their profit, and in its name the tribes of the Arabian and Syrian steppe overthrew the feeble ghosts of two empires. In the end Islam held only as many of the Bedouin as it managed to urbanize; the rest returned to their earlier ways, leaving Islam to wrestle with its Arab legacy as best it could.

The Prophet's eye roamed beyond the nomad delegations. From the very beginning he knew something of international politics; the early migration to Abyssinia shows that his thinking was not confined to the Hejaz. During that same Meccan period there came down the *surah* entitled "The Romans": "The Romans have been defeated in the nearer land, but after their defeat they will triumph within a few years. And on that day the Believers will rejoice in the help of God" (30:1–5). The "Romans," of course, were the Byzantines, and Muhammad was glossing for the Muslim community the recent events in Syria, the "nearer land."

The date of the *surah* may be 615 or 616, and what the Prophet was likely referring to was either the Sasanian capture of Jerusalem or the failure of a Byzantine counterattack near Bostra, both in 614. What the later events are, a simultaneous Byzantine and Muslim success, is more difficult to say. By the date of the Muslim victory at Badr in 624 the Byzantines were indeed embarked upon a counteroffensive, but that is only one of many possibilities.

Muhammad was, then, aware of what was happening on the larger stage of Near Eastern politics, and his sympathies appear somehow to lie with the Christian powers—"People of the Book," like the Abyssinians and the Byzantines—as opposed to the Sasanians and the idolaters of Mecca. Muhammad had begun by identifying his teaching with that of the Jews and the Christians; he learned otherwise from the Jews, but he never had such a falling-out with the Christians, and his sense of solidarity with those whom he continued to regard as his coreligionists survived to the end of his life.

One reason for it is that the early Muslim community had no contact with Christian tribes on the scale of its political confrontation with the Jews of Medina. There were Christian tribes in Arabia north of Mecca and spreading into Syria and along the western side of the Euphrates,[35] but Muhammad had little contact with them until after the occupation of Mecca in 630. Even then his dealings were chiefly political and more often ended in alliance than conversion. Some of the larger groups, the Banu Bakr, Kalb and Taghlib, remained Christians well into the Islamic era.

---

35. Those north of Mecca up to the Syrian frontier were likely Monophysites; of those within the Sasanian sphere of influence, some, like the later Lakhmids and Tamim, were Nestorians, while others, the Bakr and the Taghlib, were Monophysites. Muhammad appears to have been unaware of the confessional distinctions involved.

In 630, then, Muhammad saw beyond his immediate triumphs to events in Jerusalem and Iraq. It was in March of that year that Heraclius celebrated his final impressive triumph over the Sasanians by restoring to the Holy City the cross of Jesus which had been carried off to Seleucia-Ctesiphon in 614. And if Muhammad was aware of the fall of Jerusalem, he must have been equally aware of its recapture. Between the two events his own position had changed: he and his community were now Heraclius' rivals in northern Arabia.

That attitude appears as early as 628 when, according to the Muslim historians, Muhammad addressed messages to the rulers of Byzantium, Iran, Egypt, Abyssinia, and a number of Arab dynasts, among them the prince of the Banu Ghassan. That Muhammad may have done so is not improbable, though the documents preserved by the historians do not themselves generate much confidence. The correspondence with Egypt did bring the Prophet his last wife, Mary, a Coptic Christian sent to him as a present and who bore him his last child, a son Ibrahim, who died within a year.

That with the Ghassanid had less happy results. The Prophet's messenger was slain, and Muhammad retaliated with a raid, his first into Byzantine territory. It was an unfortunate project. The Muslims were under the command of the Prophet's adopted son, Zayd ibn Harithah, who was accompanied by 'Ali's brother Ja'far and the redoubtable Khalid ibn Walid. They went as far as the village of Mu'tah in the Transjordan southeast of the Dead Sea. The Arab historians have wildly exaggerated the number of the enemy in claiming that there were a hundred thousand Byzantine troops present with an equal number of Arab auxiliaries. Most of the opposing army was, in fact, made up of Christian Arabs, though there may have been some Byzantine regulars on hand. Whatever their number, they brought disaster upon the Muslims. Zayd ibn Harithah, who was accompanied by 'Ali's brother Ja'far that led the survivors out of a greater slaughter.

Against this background the Prophet planned his great raid against the north in 630, after his victorious return to Medina. It was not greeted with enthusiasm: the season was hot and the Byzantines still had a formidable reputation, confirmed doubtless by what had occurred at Mu'tah two years before. Muhammad assured the laggards that "the fire of Hell is hotter" (9:82), but it took all his powers of persuasion to beat the expedition into shape. There was more foot-dragging on the way north,[36] but the troops finally reached Tabuk not far from Ailah at the head of the Gulf of Aqaba.

There was no fighting, as it turned out; the Byzantine presence had long since disappeared from the region. The entire Aqaba area thus lay open to the Muslims; the Christian ruler of Ailah, likely its bishop, came and offered Muhammad his surrender. In the terms granted to him Muhammad once again expanded the political concept of Islam. In return for payment of a head tax, the people of Ailah, most of them Christians, were granted the protection of the Islamic community. The terms were lighter here than at Khaybar—Ailah had, after all, surrendered without a struggle—and the town was unmistakably being asked to participate in the *ummah*, not now as Muslims, but as a protected minority under a covenant (*dhimmah*) which was to become standard in Islam.[37]

The expedition to Tabuk may have been intended as a riposte to Heraclius' *succès d'estime* at Jerusalem earlier in 630. In the larger arena Tabuk was a very mild ripple, but Muhammad was not yet playing to that arena; his interest was in the Christian Arab tribes in northern Arabia and Syria. They were obviously not embracing Islam, but in the treaty of Ailah they had another model of membership in Muhammad's confederation: protection for tribute but without the necessity of conversion.

A similar model was unfolding on the eastern edge of the steppe over against the Sasanians' Euphrates frontier. There had been new political stirrings on that terrain about the time of the birth of Islam. Tribal relationships were always complicated, or so they appear to us. The Kindah and the Banu Lakhm, for

---

36. And an interesting stop at al-Hijr or Mada'in Salih, where Muhammad and his men could see for themselves the imposing ruins of the tribe of Thamud who were one of the *Qur'an*'s favorite examples of a people visited by Allah's punishment on those who mistreated prophets (27:52; 29:38; etc.).

37. See pp. 84–85.

example, were once the chief powers there, but they were held in fine balance by the other tribes, some of them oasis dwellers in the Najd and the Yamamah, others in nomadic transit into the fringes of the sown. Two of the latter were the Christian tribes of Bakr and Taglib, both originally from central Arabia, where they had been locked in what became for the Arabs a classic blood feud, and now finally migrants into the Iraqi plain west of the Euphrates.

With the disappearance of the Kindite power from Iraq after 530 and the collapse of the Lakhmid phylarchate at Hirah seventy years later, elements of the Bakr became the paramount force in those regions. The Sasanians made at least one attempt at bringing them to heel sometime about 605 and were badly mauled by the Bakr tribes at a place called Dhu al-Qar. It was a portent of Persian weakness as easy to read as Xenophon's expedition in and out of Mesopotamia in the face of the Achaemenians a millennium earlier, and when crisis next beset the Sasanians after the death of Khusraw II Parvez in 628, the Bakr were still ruling the cultivated lands west of the Euphrates. The situation appeared promising for the Arabs of the Banu Bakr, and the conversion to Islam of one of their *shaykhs*, Muthanna ibn Harithah, brought new allies from the Hejaz under the command of the "Sword of Allah," Khalid ibn Walid.

This was in 633, and the Prophet was already a year dead, but it was the fulfillment of the alliances that Muhammad himself had concluded with Christian tribes of the eastern steppe. They were neither Muslims nor "protected minorities" like the Christians of Ailah or the Jews of Khaybar; they were allies in a joint venture against a weakening Sasanian Empire. They presently had no way of knowing that that empire would expire at their touch.

At Muhammad's request, Abu Bakr led the *hajj* to Mecca in 631, but in the following year the Prophet himself was in the lead. It was what came to be known as the "Pilgrimage of Farewell." Its every detail was lovingly cherished and used to establish the precise ritual for all future generations of Muslim pilgrims to the sacred precinct. During it Muhammad delivered what amounted to his farewell address to the *ummah*. The tone was conciliatory and mild—"Every Muslim is a Muslim's brother"—and yet, like the *Qur'an* itself, it is studded with legislative details that illustrate as well as anything the conversion of the enthusiastic and visionary prophet into a legislator.

When the pilgrimage was over, Muhammad returned to Medina and busied himself chiefly with plans for a new expedition into Syria and Palestine. It was perhaps to be another revenge expedition for Mu'tah since Usamah, the young son of Zayd ibn Harithah, was placed in charge. Then quite suddenly in June of 632 Muhammad came down with a fever. He lingered weakly for ten days—Abu Bakr led the prayers during that time—and then the Prophet of God died quietly in 'A'ishah's arms. It was the sixty-second year of his life, twenty-two years after he had first heard the call of Allah, and the ninth year of the new Muslim era.

The Successors

The Prophet of Allah was dead, and there was no expectation that there would be another. His political legacy was a union of the tribes of western Arabia who had acknowledged both his prophethood and his leadership by joining in the revolutionary community that recognized neither tribe nor clan. But if Muhammad had created an *ummah,* he had also, in his progress toward political power, produced a new aristocracy. Privilege and position were regulated by severe custom within a tribal society, but within the new Islamic community the acknowledged merits of the Meccan Emigrants and the Medinese Helpers knew no regulation save the will of the Prophet himself. Now that he was gone, each group fell immediately to asserting its own preeminence.

During his final illness Muhammad had appointed the sixty-year-old Abu Bakr, a very early convert to Islam, an Emigrant, and the father of his favorite wife, 'A'ishah, to lead the community in prayer, and it was he who assumed the role of peacemaker among the contesting parties after the Prophet's death. There was, clearly, no doubt in anyone's mind that Muhammad should have a successor, at least as head of the *ummah,* even though that office was absolutely without precedent. And it was equally clear that there had been no instruction from the dead and heirless Prophet on who that head should be, no public injunction or private arrangement for the transfer of the power that everyone recognized existed.[38]

The Helpers may have soon realized that the powerful Meccan members of the *ummah* would never allow themselves to be ruled by anyone who was not a Quraysh; they proposed, in any case, a system of collegiate rule: an Emigrant, who was presumably a Quraysh, and a Helper would govern jointly. Abu Bakr argued that only a Quraysh would in fact be accepted as the head of the Islamic community. He did not suggest himself as a candidate, but it was he upon whom the office was finally thrust. The Helpers consented, at 'Umar's urging, to accept the authority of this revered Muslim, who was not a major Quraysh *shaykh*, an Umayyad or a Hashimite, but a pious caretaker from a minor clan of that tribe. All those present swore their loyalty by a traditional handclasp, and in June of 632 Abu Bakr became the first "Successor (*khalifah*) of the Prophet of God."

The title was a deception. There could be no "successor" to the Prophet in the sense in which Muhammad had governed the community of Islam. The living voice of God was silenced, and the *ummah* had no expectation that it would ever be heard again until the end of days. The revelation was complete in the *Qur'an*, an injunction and a code, and as yet there were no experts to explicate it nor any authority to do so.

At the accession of Abu Bakr there were only a few kinds of social experience that could properly be termed Islamic: as warrior for the faith, as director of the pilgrimage, and as prayer leader (*imam*) for the community. Abu Bakr had performed all three functions by delegation during the Prophet's lifetime, and so in his following upon the Prophet there was adequate precedent for filling all those roles. They were, however, neither charismatic nor in any sense hereditary; any believer could serve as such.

---

38. In announcing the Prophet's death, Abu Bakr remarked: "If anyone worships Muhammad, let him know Muhammad is dead." Were there really those who did such? The evidence is against it, but it would explain the failure to consult on the succession.

What the Caliphate actually involved was, on the testimony of Abu Bakr's performance in that office, the power to make decisions on behalf of the *ummah*. Two of them were of major consequence for Islam. The first was based on the Prophet's own precedent: the following-through of an expedition to the north of Medina which had been planned by Muhammad and which Abu Bakr put into execution despite the most pressing practical reasons for not doing so. For the second there was no Prophetic precedent, and yet Abu Bakr took it in hand as firmly as the first, the restoration of the unity of the *ummah*.

Abu Bakr had claimed that the Arabs would accept only a Quraysh at their head. It was perhaps a judgment corrupted by the chauvinism of the city Arab; the Bedouin saw things otherwise. Almost immediately after the death of Muhammad they signaled their intention of not paying the Muslim alms tax (*zakat*), which doubtless appeared to them as a form of tribute, and so, in effect, of withdrawing from the *ummah*. Islam probably made little difference to them; what they had formerly recognized was the rise of an irresistible new power in Mecca and Medina, and now that the creator of that power was dead they chose to revert to their own self-interests.

What was self-interest to the tribes of the Najd, Oman and the Yemen was viewed in Medina as apostasy (*riddah*). Abu Bakr reacted with surprising energy against the separatists, and the elderly Caliph even took the field himself in the early campaigning. It was a protracted and bloody struggle, and a new dimension was given the fighting by the fact that some of the dissident tribes had by then possessed themselves of their own prophets.[39] They did not prevail, however, and almost exactly a year after the death of Muhammad the *ummah* was restored through Arabia by force of arms.

---

39. One was a woman of the Christian Tamim and another, Maslamah or Musaylimah, was from the Banu Hanifah, which was also strongly infiltrated by Christianity. Musaylimah, whom Muhammad certainly knew about at the end of his life, may go back to an earlier day. His preserved utterances are not unlike Muhammad's Meccan *surahs*, though he was preaching a far more Christian message than the Prophet of Mecca.

A decision at Constantinople enabled Abu Bakr to put into action the plans for a raid into Palestine that the death of the Prophet had forestalled. In 633 Heraclius decided on grounds of economy to discontinue the annual stipend he paid to the Bedouin tribes of Sinai and the Negev. The payment—the equivalent of thirty pounds of gold, dispensed in produce instead of coin or bullion—was part of the complex defensive system along the Byzantines' eastern frontier. There were some regular troops in Palestine, but most of the burden there was borne by various Arab mercenaries in succession to the once powerful Ghassanids. West of Ailah, however, there were no imperial troops, and the Byzantines' enemy were the Bedouin on both sides of an extremely ill-defined frontier. Up to this point the Bedouin's aims were not political but economic, to raid the pilgrimage and trade routes that radiated east and west and south of Gaza. Many of the towns there were fortified against Bedouin marauders, and for the rest the Byzantines bought off the most dangerous tribes.

The fifteen-year Sasanian occupation of the area must have seriously disrupted those arrangements; Muhammad's raids in 629 and 630 suggest that the Byzantine military control of Palestine and the Transjordan did not extend much south of Mu'tah. The forces of Islam experienced far more severe encounters when they ventured north of Mu'tah, but in 630 they occupied both Tabuk and Ailah without serious resistance. The terms imposed upon Ailah on that occasion were probably the military key to the later Arab expansion. By this treaty the inhabitants of Ailah received a guarantee of "protection" in return for free Muslim access to the wells and roads of the region.

Thus the roads into southern Palestine and Sinai were thrown open to Islam, but for three years that promise could not be redeemed. In the autumn of 633, the same year that Heraclius withheld his stipend from the Sinai Bedouin, Abu Bakr, now once again the head of a unified *ummah*, was ready to pass through the door opened by the Prophet. A large raiding party under 'Amr ibn al-'As was sent through Ailah into the Sinai. They were on the outskirts of Gaza itself before imperial troops could be brought down from Caesarea. It was no help. The Byzantine force was incredibly small—some three hundred men—and in February of 634 it was routed by the Muslims, whose ranks were doubtless swollen by Sinai Bedouin with no attachment to Islam but with a considerable instinct for raiding and looting.

What followed is exceedingly confused in the sources. There was more than one Muslim detachment in southern Palestine, but what does seem reasonably clear is that the initial Arab advance into Byzantine territory took place not in the Transjordan but through the Negev, and when Heraclius finally bestirred himself in the summer of 634 the decisive engagement was fought at Ajnadayn, on the road from Gaza to Jerusalem. The Byzantine forces, which now far outnumbered the Arab invaders and were under the command of the Emperor's brother, were once again put to flight, and all of Syria from Jerusalem north to Damascus was exposed to whatever course the Arabs might choose to follow.

It is not recorded who led the Arabs at Ajnadayn; opinion, however, has a ready answer: Khalid ibn Walid, a warrior who had already figured prominently at Mu'tah and the *riddah* campaign and who had made a recent and stunning appearance in the Syrian theater. In the spring of the previous year, even before 'Amr's transit through Ailah, Abu Bakr had responded to another opportunistic call, this time from Iraq, where the disintegration of the Lakhmid phylarchate in 604 offered the same chance for plunder as the anarchy among the tribes of Sinai. The call came from a recent convert to Islam, Muthanna ibn Harithah, *shaykh* of a tribal confederation of the Banu Bakr in Iraq, and in response the Caliph had sent Khalid with some troopers, newly enlisted in the cause of Islam, across the steppe.

The allied captains captured the Lakhmid capital at Hirah toward the end of 633, but the impetus of the campaign, which almost certainly had no end but booty, was suddenly blunted by the recall of Khalid. We have no idea how the Arab intelligence functioned. Abu Bakr at Medina must have known that Heraclius was preparing a counterstroke; he made the strategic decision to recall Khalid, and sent the orders to Hirah. Khalid responded immediately. He detached five hundred mounted troops from the Iraqi expedition and in April crossed the Syrian desert. Within eighteen days he appeared not in the Transjordan but on the outskirts of Damascus itself. This too was Ghassanid territory, but deep in the Byzantine rear, and Khalid had little trouble with the Emperor's dispirited Arab mercenaries. The "Sword of Allah" then swept down the east bank of the Jordan and joined the main Muslim force at Ajnadayn.

A month after that decisive engagement between the imperial troops and the arms of Islam, Abu Bakr died at Medina and was buried beside the Prophet. Shortly before the end he made his final bequest to Islam: his choice of a successor. He may no longer have feared the apostasy of the tribes, but Abu Bakr had himself been witness to the troubles surrounding his own accession. His Caliphate was a compromise between two parties reaching for power in utterly new circumstances, but this time the succession was left to neither chance nor the will of God. The weakening Abu Bakr consulted among the elders of Islam, Helpers and Emigrants alike, and accepted, not without reservation, their consensual choice: 'Umar ibn al-Khattab, another early convert to Islam and the undisputed leader of the Emigrants. The designation was put in writing and made public (by the future Caliph 'Uthman) before Abu Bakr's death. The people of Medina signaled their obedience.

During the ten years of 'Umar's Caliphate (634–644) the armies of Islam met and defeated the main forces of the Emperor and the Shah: the Byzantine imperial army on the river Yarmuk in the Transjordan in 636 and the Sasanians at Qadisiyah west of Hirah in 637 and at Nihawand near Isfahan in 642. Heraclius withdrew behind his defenses north of the Taurus, but the dispirited Yazdigird III fled for his life in a manner reminiscent of the last of the Achaemenians, Darius III.

After 642 there was still resistance in the Sasanian domains in eastern Iran; it was no longer by or for the Shah, however, but was thrown up by the local dynasts, or *marzubans*, in defense of their own power and privilege. It was one of these, the *marzuban* of Merv, who brought an end to the house of Sasan; the agitated *marzuban* first sheltered, then evicted, and finally murdered Yazdigird III in 651.

Farther west the Arab tide rolled forward against an equally feeble resistance. Damascus fell in 635, Jerusalem and Ascalon in 638; Mesopotamia and Egypt were occupied in 642, and by the following year Arab armies had reached into Armenia and halfway across North Africa.

The undeniable ease of this stunning military conquest, followed at a somewhat slower pace by the Arabization and Islamicization of those same lands, has provoked wonder, theological and scholarly, from that day to this. An equation of their enemies' weaknesses and the Arabs' strengths can be cast up and the results approximate an explanation: the religious disaffection of much of the conquered Byzantine territory before the coming of Islam; civil war and anarchy in Iran; the thin and centralized military cover that the governments relied upon in Syria and Iraq; the loss of the allegiance of the Arab mercenaries by both the Byzantines and Sasanians; the tribal cohesion of the Arab invaders, their *élan,* their superior tactics and their leadership; a high mobility and the powerful motivation of ideology, spoils and glory.

The actual number of the Bedouin armies that came out of Arabia are now perhaps beyond reclaiming. As they appear in the Arab sources, the Byzantine and Sasanian armies are grossly inflated: one hundred and twenty thousand Sasanians at Qadisiyah and Nihawand, and a similar number of Greeks at Ajnadayn and on the Yarmuk, while their heroic Muslim opponents are made to do with a mere ten thousand troopers in Iraq and twenty-four thousand in Syria. But even if the numbers of the government troops are substantially reduced, it remains true that in all their major encounters—and the conquest was achieved by major encounters and not piecemeal possession; after signal victories entire provinces collapsed—the Arabs had fewer troops than their opponents.[40]

What troops the Arabs did possess were probably better equipped and certainly better led than the imperial armies. The Arab trooper was mounted more often than not on camelback and was protected by a mail helmet and round shield. His offensive weapons were a short, Roman-style sword and a lance. He was inured to forced marches, short rations and inclement

---

40. Farther on, across North Africa and Spain, the Arabs found allies, and their troops were considerably reinforced by local Berber tribesmen.

weather.[41] He could move more swiftly, maneuver more easily, and had almost exclusive use of the tactical weapon of surprise.

The Arab commanders were all battle-tested. Khalid and Abu 'Ubaydah in Syria and 'Amr ibn al-'As in Egypt all had begun their careers in the local fighting in the Hejaz and had been blooded, as soldiers and as leaders, in the fierce wars of the *riddah*. The time would come when they would feel the stirrings of their own ambitions, but that was a reflex of the occupation and not of the conquest; in those first breathless years there was not a whisper of treachery.

'Umar played his command part in those stunning military successes,[42] but it was rather by his administrative decisions that he set his permanent stamp upon Islam. The Arab sources date most of them to the famous "day of Jabiya'" when the Caliph went up to Syria to accept the surrender of Jerusalem. Al-Jabiya', the former camp site of the Ghassanids southwest of Damascus, was the first—by accident surely and not by design—of the Arab garrison towns, and it was there in the summer of 638 that the Arab leaders convened to decide matters of strategy and policy.

What occurred in 638 was a division of the spoils. How should the victors profit from the treasures in gold and plate, the occupied land and its agricultural wealth? According to the traditional account, it was 'Umar who in 641 drew up the instrument of distribution, a register (*diwan*) of Muslims who had merited well of Islam. They were ranked in order of their service and sacrifice, from 'A'ishah down through the other wives of the Prophet, his other relatives, Helpers and Emigrants, the veterans of the Hejaz wars and the *riddah*, to the most recently recruited "war-

---

41. The later Arab commanders soon abandoned, however, the practice of fighting in Anatolia north of the Taurus during the winter season, and so with few exceptions the initial conquests from Spain to Khurasan were accomplished in a zone of hot, dry climate not unlike that from which the Arabs had originally come.

42. Not always happily. It was the conservative 'Umar, whose thoughts rarely overleaped his Arabism, who resisted the suggestion of the general Mu'awiyah that the Muslims construct a navy. During Mu'awiyah's own Caliphate, 'Umar's decision was reversed, and the new Muslim fleet won control of most of the eastern Mediterranean.

riors" (*muqatilah*) who joined the *ummah* after Yarmuk and Qadisiyah. An annual pension was prescribed for each, the whole to be paid out of the spoils accruing by law to the common treasury of the *ummah*.

The long-range effect of the institution of the *diwan* was to limit membership in the community in a manner unforeseen by the Prophet and perhaps unintended even by his Caliph. It created a government-sponsored and government-supported meritocracy at the heart of Islam. It distributed the rewards of victory to what had inevitably to become an Arab military caste sanctified by inclusion in the *diwan*. The early Arab Muslims were guaranteed an enormous share in all subsequent booty, while the non-Arab convert to Islam had, at present, no way of being inscribed on that list. In a tribal society he was an outsider who had to rest content with a fictive assimilation to Arab tribalism; he became a "client" (*mawla;* pl. *mawali*), an Arab by adoption, a condition that found him a place in Islam but not on the *diwan* lists.

On a broader scale 'Umar fixed the relationship between the conquering aristocracy, now unmistakably identified as Arab, and their non-Muslim subjects. Following the precedent of the Prophet, the Jews and Christians who now found themselves within a burgeoning Islamic empire were offered a covenant of protection (*dhimmah*), which guaranteed, under certain restrictions, their religious freedom.[43] The terms of that covenant uniformly protected all Christians and Jews as "Peoples of the Book," but they were, nonetheless, the conquered and they were obligated to pay both tax and tribute to the Islamic *ummah*, the amount to be fixed by the treaty of capitulation.[44]

In its widest understanding, conquest by Islam imposed a land tax (*kharaj*) upon the community and a poll tax (*jizyah*) upon its individual members, roughly the same obligations that the former subjects of the Emperor and the Shah had toward their sover-

---

43. A guarantee which did not inhibit 'Umar from clearing all the Christian and Jewish communities from central Arabia.

44. The diversity of the actual capitulation arrangements has been obscured by the later Muslim jurists' penchant for dealing with the Law as if it were a seamless and unvarying garment.

eigns. The difference was merely this: the Arabs undertook neither to occupy, nor to settle into nor indeed to govern, except on the highest levels, these newly conquered territories. The body of Arabs spread over the sprawling and populous lands from Tunis to the Hindu Kush would soon have been swallowed up by the native populations;[45] instead they were set down in those lands within the protective confines of purely Arab encampments (*misr;* pl. *amsar*) where they collected their tribute and garrisoned their armies: Basrah (637) and Kufah (638) in Iraq, Fustat (642) in Egypt and Qayrawan (670) in Tunisia.

The new Arab aristocracy dealt with its subjects through a single agent, generally an *amir*, the military commander of the territory who preserved order, collected the taxes, and supervised the *diwan*. Eventually, with the assimilation of the Arab and non-Arab elements of the population and an increasing number of converts to Islam, the office of the *amir* evolved into that of a provincial governor with considerably wider powers than his purely military prototype. For the Muslim population of the *amsar* he had as his subordinates the other ranks of the military, while the subject populations governed themselves as they or their former dynasts saw fit. As far as the Muslims were concerned, the *amir* was also the chief judicial officer of the territory,[46] while Jews and Christians continued to live under their own canon law as guaranteed by the *dhimmah*.

The Caliph's generally tolerant attitude toward the Christians—reports of repressive measures are probably confusions from the reign of the far more severe 'Umar II—must have reinforced some of the undisguised pleasure that greeted the arrival of Muslim arms in those Christian lands. The Arab conquest of Egypt, for example, had been notoriously assisted by Mono-

---

45. At this point the conquering emigrants out of Arabia constituted, at a very rough estimate, no more than one thirtieth of the population of the occupied territories.

46. Tradition credits 'Umar with having appointed the first Islamic judges (*qadi;* pl. *qudat*), but this appears very unlikely. The *qadi* does not make his appearance until somewhat later, when the Umayyad governors delegated some of their juridical powers to a subordinate. Even then the *amir* continued to function as the chief judge of his territory.

physite Christians—and by the Jews—in open revolt against the Byzantine administration of the province and the "imperial" (Melchite) ecclesiastical authorities there. Almost at the heels of 'Amr ibn al-'As the Monophysite Patriarch Benjamin I, who had been ignominiously chased from his See in 631, returned to a hero's welcome in Alexandria.

The new Muslim masters of Egypt reacted sympathetically at first. Christian monks and clergy were exempted from the poll tax and Chalcedonian churches and property were handed over to the Monophysites. They in turn construed the new Muslim order of things as God's vengeance upon the Emperor Heraclius and his ecclesiastical agents. In Syria the situation was less volatile perhaps, and so Christian enthusiasm was somewhat more restrained. There were, however, no persecutions, and when the Gallic Bishop Arculph passed through Syria in 680 on pilgrimage to Jerusalem he observed that the Christians were still by far the majority in those lands and that relations with the Muslims were harmonious.

In many respects the Muslims of 'Umar's generation appear to have been concerned more with staying clear of their new possessions than with making them their own. They assumed little responsibility toward the new territories save to hold them for Islam. They preferred to leave possession in the hands of their pre-Islamic owners,[47] while they themselves collected their tribute and lived like a somewhat unruly caste of military mandarins, remote from the stains of agriculture and commerce and the corruptive luxuries of the conquered cities.[48]

Such they could not be. The conquered peoples were not

---

47. Except for the Byzantine and Sasanian crown lands. These were not distributed, but were taken over as the common property of all Muslims. If any land was parceled out to the Arabs, it came from estates deserted by their former owners. These too were the common property of Islam, but they were in effect leased to Muslims who paid the traditional alms tax of ten percent on their income.

48. 'Umar's personal simplicity and asceticism is consistently noted in the Arab sources. The fondness of the recollection was in part dictated by a desire to score a touch on his more worldly successors in the Caliphate, but some of it surely goes back to the temperament of the man himself and is reflected in his legislation.

treated like helots and never served as such. Conversion was always an open possibility, and if it did not bring the new Aramaic or Iranian Muslim instant equality with the elite Arab *muqatilah*, it did create a substantial new class whose virtues, military and otherwise, soon subverted 'Umar's intentions. For their part, the Arabs grew weary of their role as a standing army and of life in the camps. The *amsar* turned them from men of the desert and oasis into men of the city who would not settle for garrison living. Kufah, Basrah and Fustat were, in the end, only way stations to Cairo and Baghdad.

In 644, after a Caliphate of ten years, 'Umar was assassinated as he was leading the annual pilgrimage to Mecca. His assailant was a Persian slave bent on revenging some not very consequential personal grudge, but the deed once again confronted the *ummah* with the still unresolved problem of the succession. 'Umar attempted his own solution: while he lingered on close to death, the Caliph appointed a committee of six respected Muslims to chose his successor. 'Ali, the Prophet's cousin and son-in-law, was among them. He had been close to the councils of state from the very beginning, and during the Caliphates of Abu Bakr and 'Umar he lived at Medina in honor and prosperity. 'Ali apparently had never been considered for the Caliphate on those two earlier occasions, but now he came to the fore, together with another son-in-law of the Prophet, 'Uthman ibn Affan, a distinguished early convert and an Umayyad of the Quraysh. 'Ali, like Muhammad himself, was of the somewhat less important Banu Hashim of the Quraysh.

The final decision was left in the hands of the man who had been offered the Caliphate by 'Umar before his appointment of a board of electors, 'Abd al-Rahman ibn 'Awf. His choice rested upon 'Uthman, the wealthy, seventy-year-old Umayyad. It was no more, perhaps, than the selection of the senior member of the elective council, but the mere fact that now the prime candidates for the Caliphate were two eminent Emigrants from among the Quraysh meant that the control of Islam returned to where the control of Mecca had rested before the Prophet, in the hands of the Quraysh. The moment of the Medinese Helpers had passed and would never return.

The Banu Umayyah, the hereditary military arm of the

Quraysh, had come a long way very quickly in Islam. With the notable exception of 'Uthman, who was a very early convert, they had been among the fiercest opponents of Muhammad at Mecca, and it was not until 630 that Abu Sufyan led the bulk of his clan into acceptance of Islam. Despite the scent of what may have appeared to be opportunism, they apparently had the confidence of Muhammad, since two of Abu Sufyan's sons, Yazid and Mu'awiyah, were given positions of trust and first one and then the other rose to be *amir* of Syria.

Now finally power had tipped away from the Banu Hashim to the Banu Umayyah, and 'Uthman (644–656) began to distribute it, in accepted tribal fashion, to his family. His cousin Mu'awiyah was already governor of Syria, one of 'Umar's appointments. The Caliph's foster brother was installed in Egypt in place of its conqueror and first governor, 'Amr ibn al-'As. A cousin, Marwan, served as treasurer in Medina. Other Umayyads were appointed governors of 'Umar's garrison towns of Basrah and Kufah in Iraq. These latter posts were particularly troublesome, and 'Uthman's appointments were doubtless intended to bring the turbulent *amsar* under his own control.

To the east of the Iraqi *amsar* was the Sasanian home province of Fars and beyond that the rich territories of Khurasan and Sijistan. 'Uthman's new governors reorganized their Arab troops and began to raid east of the Tigris. Fars fell easily in 650, and in the following year the Arabs were invited into Khurasan by a local dynast who had made his own choice between the Muslim Arabs approaching from the west and the eastern nomads who saw their own advantage in the total collapse of the enfeebled Sasanian regime in Khurasan. 'Uthman gave his consent, and Arab armies entered Khurasan in 651.

It rested upon the *marzuban* of Nishapur to offer the Muslims their only serious challenge in Khurasan. He failed, and with his surrender the other cities hastened to come to terms. Khurasan thus came into the *Dar al-Islam* by capitulation rather than conquest. When the terms of tribute had been assessed the Arabs withdrew to their camps in Iraq leaving behind them only a holding garrison quartered outside Merv. They had, it appears, no intention of founding *amsar* east of Basrah and Kufah.

In supporting the continuing expansion of the arms of Islam

'Uthman was acting well within the example of his predecessors. Elsewhere, however, he was creating grave difficulties for himself. There were Companions of the Prophet who remembered that the Banu Umayyah had taken up arms against Islam at Uhud in 625. For others the arrogance and self-serving use of power by the Umayyads was subsumed into the larger arrogance of the Quraysh who were converting Islam into a private preserve on the model of pre-Islamic Mecca. And finally there was the matter of the *Qur'an.*

According to some traditions, the first "collections" of the *Qur'an* were due to either Abu Bakr or to 'Umar. The alleged motive was the death of many *Qur'an* "readers" during the war of the *riddah* in 633: as repositories of the oral tradition their decimation would imperil the integrity of the revelation within the community. There is little to sustain the truth of these reports. Even in the Prophet's own day, and particularly after his migration to Medina, parts of the *Qur'an* were dictated to a battery of secretaries including, among others, 'Uthman and Mu'awiyah. Further, it appears likely that those dictated *surahs* were not merely written down but in some sense collected into a book before the Prophet's death in 632.

The "collections" must have multiplied, since by 'Uthman's Caliphate there were different but equally prestigious versions of the *Qur'an* scattered through the Muslim settlements. The differences were beginning to provoke controversy, however, and 'Uthman was persuaded by some of the Companions to commission a single authoritative text. Sometime between 650 and 656 the work was put into the hands of a commission under the direction of one of the Prophet's secretaries, Zayd ibn Thabit.

We are not certain how they went about their task, but the desired text was produced—essentially the one we possess today—and distributed in the major centers with instructions to destroy all other copies. The results were happier in their textual than their political consequences. A canonical text was established,[49] but at the expense of the sensibilities of the local

49. The reconstruction of the various pre-'Uthmanic texts does not suggest that there were any radical differences in the texts of the *Qur'an* circulating before the commission did its work.

tradition, which was supported in this instance by the various "readers" who used no written text at all but were still operating within the tradition of an oral *Qur'an.* A number of such "readers" later show up in the army of 'Ali in his struggles against the Umayyads, and their resentment likely went back to 'Uthman's promulgation of a single written text for all believers.

Dissatisfaction was growing also in the garrison towns, which had to bear the main burden of 'Uthman's rawly opportunistic appointments. It was there too that the ranks of the pure Arabs, who as registered *muqatilah* had an immediate stake in the booty of conquest, were being swelled by increasing numbers of new converts. Finally, in 656, after representations and threats, columns of dissidents from Fustat, Kufah and Basrah marched on Medina. On their arrival they carried their protests to what may have appeared to them a court of higher appeal, the surviving Companions from the elective council that had chosen 'Uthman as Caliph: 'Ali, Zubayr, Talhah and Sa'd ibn abi Waqqas. They in turn carried the complaints to 'Uthman, and 'A'ishah too intervened with the Caliph.

At first it appeared that 'Uthman gave way to their demands and that the insurgents would return to their garrisons. They did not. Instead they laid siege to 'Uthman's house,[50] while 'Ali and the other Companions stood paralyzed with either horror or fear. The siege lasted more than a month and then, when the insurgents, who were being led by a son of Abu Bakr, heard rumors of an Umayyad relief expedition from Syria, they became alarmed, burst in upon the aged Caliph, and assassinated him.

It was an act of far-reaching consequences. It brought 'Ali to the Caliphate and at the same time gave the Umayyads their grounds for removing him. The murder plunged Islam into a round of destructive civil wars, whose echo lingered for centuries, and it thrust the family of 'Ali into a thousand-year preeminence that could hardly have been foreseen in the sad events of 656.

Each of the revered figures who stood as ambivalent spectators

---

50. Actually the house built for Muhammad when he migrated to Medina in 622. The still-modest dwelling served as the Caliphal residence down to the time that 'Ali deserted Medina for Kufah.

in Medina in the summer of 656, 'Ali, Zubayr and Talhah, had his supporters toward the Caliphate among the insurgent troops who had done the deed. It may, however, have been the urging of the other Companions that settled the choice upon 'Ali, a cousin and son-in-law of Muhammad, perhaps the first male to accept Islam from the hands of the Prophet, and a warrior on its behalf in the days before its glory.

It now rested upon 'Ali (656–661) to heal the wounds suffered by the community. Many urged that the murderers of 'Uthman be brought to justice. There may have been some Umayyad special pleading in the insistence on vengeance, but there were others who sincerely felt that the dignity of the Caliphate should be upheld. 'Ali refused to take action and almost immediately a vocal opposition began to manifest itself. The Umayyads among the Quraysh were already slipping out of Medina. Some went to Mu'awiyah in Damascus bearing the bloody shirt of 'Uthman; others moved to Mecca, where they were shortly joined by Talhah and Zubayr.

While 'Ali attempted to remove Mu'awiyah from the governorship of Syria, Talhah, Zubayr and 'A'ishah crossed to Basrah, where the banner of revolt was publicly raised. Fearful of losing the Iraqi garrison towns, 'Ali pursued with troops, and after some fruitless negotiation he defeated his former associates in what has come to be known as the "Battle of the Camel." Zubayr and Talhah lost their lives in the encounter, and 'A'ishah, whose enmity to 'Ali, which went back to the incident of her "infidelity," was well known and who, many charged, stood behind the Companions' opposition to 'Ali, was sent back to Medina by the Caliph. Encouraged by the support that he had received from the Kufans during these last days, 'Ali decided to trade the poisoned atmosphere of Medina for the presumably more friendly climate of Kufah.

Who were 'Ali's supporters in Kufah? The town was a forcing chamber of the mounting social and economic discontent in the *ummah*. 'Umar's *diwan* allocations were distributed by tribes and clans, and so the leaders of those clans that stood high on the register had immense financial and political power. It was a power devoted largely to the preservation of the status quo. But the days of the conquests were already past—the eastern front was largely immobile after 641—and Kufah was filling up with other Arab clans that had not served at either Yarmuk or Qadisiyah and so had only a minimal share in the riches of Islam.

'Uthman, who had no intention of abrogating 'Umar's arrangements, had attempted to alleviate the tensions in Iraq by opening up the eastern front to further expansion. His good intentions had failed, and there were Kufans among the provincial dissidents who finally brought 'Uthman down. 'Ali must have hoped to weld together these Kufan malcontents in a way that was palpably impossible in the Hejaz, where the Helpers and Emigrants canonized by 'Umar's edict held sway, or in Syria, where Mu'awiyah and the Umayyads were firmly in control.

Mu'awiyah was still in Damascus at the head of an army whipped into a thirst for blood vengeance. He had not tendered to 'Ali the usual oath of allegiance, nor had he obeyed the Caliph's orders to lay down his command. 'Ali could not afford to ignore him, and in the spring of 657 he marched northward along the Euphrates with a mixed army of Kufans and Bedouin, Helpers and others who despised Umayyad and Quraysh pretensions, and professional reciters of the *Qur'an* who were still smarting from the measures that 'Uthman had taken against them. At Siffin, near the Euphrates crossing of Raqqah, they were met by the Syrian troopers of Mu'awiyah, among them 'Amr ibn al-'As, the conqueror of Egypt and its former *amir*.

It was reputedly 'Amr who settled what had turned out to be indecisive fighting between the two sides: he suggested that the Syrians attach copies of the *Qur'an* to their lances and ride into battle with the cry "Let the Word of God decide." The tactic worked, only because both the issue and the fighting were confused. Muslim was not as yet accustomed to fighting against Muslim, and no one could have known with surety where justice lay. The armies backed off and 'Ali was forced to accept the challenge to put the matter to the traditional solution of arbitration.

What precisely was the matter? Mu'awiyah had never claimed the Caliphate, nor had 'Ali agreed to vacate it. The issue was simply the death of 'Uthman: whether it was justified by the Caliph's own illegal acts and, so, was not subject to vengeance, as

Mu'awiyah claimed it was. Arrangements were made to select arbitrators who would presumably scan the *Qur'an* as the measure of 'Uthman's deeds, but in the meantime 'Ali was losing important support. There were those who felt that in agreeing to arbitration 'Ali had made not a tactical blunder but a theological error. In their eyes, Mu'awiyah was a rebel against Caliphal authority, not a contestant at law, and so should have been summarily punished. The judgment, they claimed, was in God's hands and the Caliph's and not in those of the arbitrators.

The partisans of this view withdrew from 'Ali's forces and gathered at Nahrawan as plans for the arbitration went forward. There was a preliminary meeting in February of 658 and at it a preliminary judgment apparently went against 'Ali. Before the arbitrators could meet again 'Ali quickly repudiated them and began rearming. His first target was his own dissidents, the "secessionists" (*khawarij*) at Nahrawan. They were unmollified by his pointing out that he had repudiated the arbitration; by his original acceptance he had sinned and must confess it publicly. This 'Ali refused to do and in July, 658, he savagely destroyed the Kharijite forces, though not the movement.

Kharijism was more than an appeal to a theological principle concerning the arbitration; it was a cry for a different kind of Islam, free of the economic inequities consecrated in 'Umar's *diwan* and free of the tribal distinctions and prejudices inherent in the struggle for paramountcy between the Hashimite 'Ali and the Umayyad Mu'awiyah. Ever since the death of the Prophet, the Quraysh had striven to reduce Islam to one of their own possessions. With the deep thrusts of the Arab armies into the East and their occupation of alien empires Islam was no longer such. On the Kharijite view the *ummah* was a community of those who accepted the message of Allah and put it into practice in their lives. Any believer could be Caliph, "even a black slave," as the Kharijites put it.

'Ali may have lost other supporters between Siffin and the final arbitration. There are reports that some of the people who had originally backed his claims refused, at this critical point, to become further enmeshed in what was likely to burst into a full-scale civil war. In their view 'Ali's claims were legitimate, but they would not fight against other Muslims to maintain them.[51]

The arbitrators held another meeting in January of 659. The accounts of it are somewhat tendentious, but it appears to have been seriously proposed that both contestants step aside and a new Caliph be chosen. Neither party, of course, was willing to do so. 'Ali settled in at Kufah, where he was strong, but he did nothing to bolster himself elsewhere; Mu'awiyah, who was now being proclaimed Caliph by his troops, more energetically extended his military power around his foe. There was no need: 'Ali was assassinated by a Kharijite at Kufah in 661. Had he lived, it is doubtful whether he could have withstood Mu'awiyah.

The Kufans reacted by recognizing 'Ali's son Hasan as Caliph. His reign inside the city walls lasted a scant six months; at the approach of the Syrian army Hasan agreed to abdicate. He acknowledged the Caliphate of Mu'awiyah and settled into a comfortable eight-year seclusion at Medina. It was by no means the end, however. The "party of 'Ali" (*Shi'at 'Ali*) resolutely refused to disappear, and one or other of the 'Alids pressed a claim upon the Caliphate, or the "Imamate," as they preferred to call it, until that time in the mid-eighth century when 'Alid political pretensions began to be subsumed into a body of theology and the "party" was transformed into a theological sect.[52]

Mu'awiyah's (661–680) strength lay in Syria, and his Umayyad successors exercised their Caliphate from Damascus and other Syrian towns. Damascus was an old Aramaic city only partially Hellenized during its days as a Greco-Roman administrative center. The Umayyads used it to the same end, and it was here

---

51. Somewhere in this complex of attitudes are the likely origins of the ideologues who were later known collectively in Islam as Mu'tazilites, or "separatists," and whose original "separation" was from the armies of 'Ali after Siffin. See Chap. II, p. 182.

52. By some accounts a theological as opposed to a strictly political view of 'Ali was already beginning to take shape before his Caliphate. The stories center around a certain 'Abdallah ibn Saba', reputedly a Yemenite convert from Judaism, who claimed divine rights for 'Ali and then after 661 denied the Caliph's death. These are positions identified with later "extremist" (*ghulat*) Shi'ism, and whether 'Abdallah or anyone else actually held such in the late seventh century is at best uncertain.

that the official Islamic tax registers were kept, by Greek civil servants in the Greek language. The Holy Cities of Mecca and Medina were left behind, and those other Arab creations, the turbulent garrisons of Basrah, Kufah, Fustat and, after 670, Qayrawan in the new province of Ifriqiyah, lay uneasily beyond the Caliph's immediate control.

The two most troublesome of the *amsar*, the Iraqi Basrah and Kufah, were entrusted to an old partisan of 'Ali, Ziyad, surnamed "son of his father" by reason of being the offspring of a Meccan prostitute. Mu'awiyah won Ziyad over to his side, publicly adopted him, and in 665 appointed him governor of Basrah with effective authority over most of the eastern reaches of the Caliphate. Ziyad's son 'Ubaydallah succeeded him in the same post at his death in 673, and both men, father and son, ruled with a particularly stern hand in Kufah, where 'Alids and Kharijites were equally and effectively subdued by force.

Ziyad's jurisdiction as *amir* of Basrah included the eastern territories of Khurasan and Sijistan where Arab armies continued to campaign from their base at Merv. One of the first of Ziyad's acts was the revision of the Muslim *diwans* of the Iraqi *amsar*, and as part of that reorganization fifty thousand troops were sent eastward to take up their posts in Khurasan. In 674 they provided 'Ubaydallah with the strength necessary for the first major crossing of the Oxus and the reduction, albeit temporary, of Bukhara to tributary status. And they contributed to the rapid Arabization of Khurasan.

There was a new frontier to be considered as well. By the time of Mu'awiyah's self-promotion to the Caliphate, the Muslims had built themselves a respectable fleet in the yards of Tripolis and Alexandria. It now crossed the Mediterranean at will and raided the almost defenseless Byzantine ports. Cyprus was sacked in 648 and then Rhodes and Crete, Sicily, and the cities of Africa. Constantinople's only substantive response came in 655, when a Byzantine fleet with Heraclius' grandson Constans II (641–668) in command intercepted the Arab raiders off the coast of Lycia. It was a disaster for the Byzantines, and the Emperor barely escaped with his life.

In the years that followed, the new Caliph's designs became clear: an assault on Constantinople itself. Constans II knew that it

THE BANU UMAYYAH AND THE UMAYYAD CALIPHS

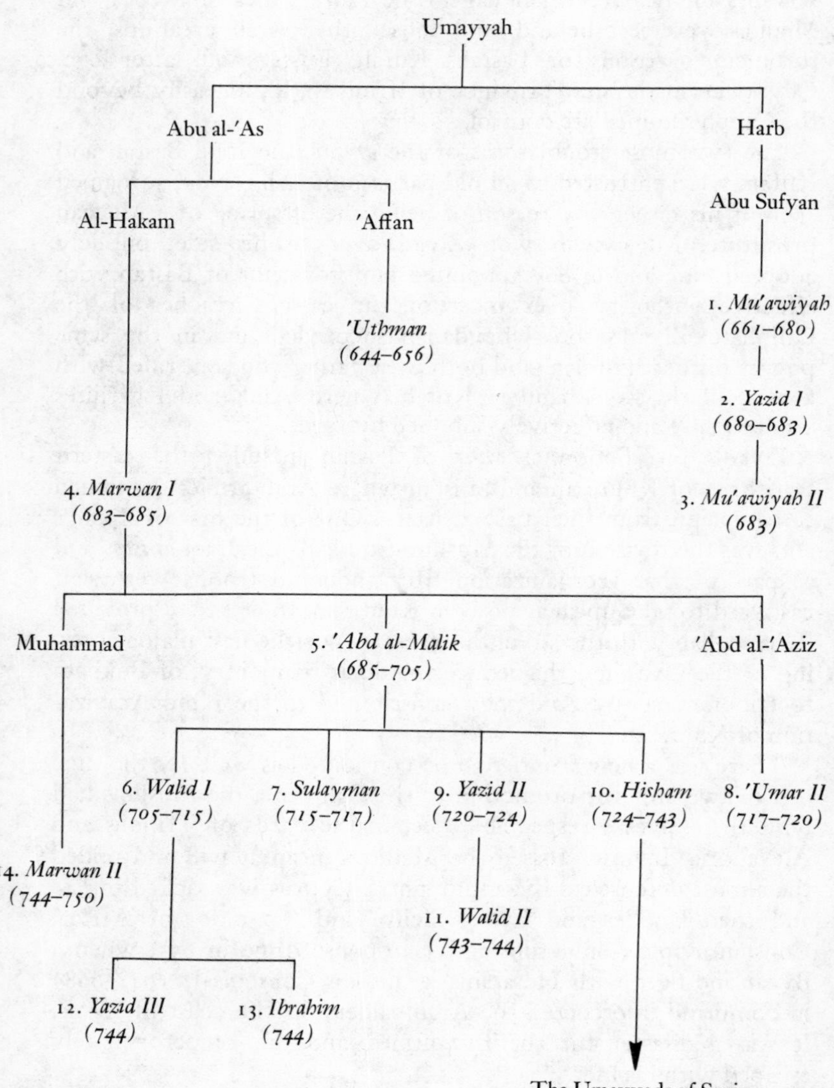

was inevitable, and it must have appeared equally inevitable that it would succeed. Italy and Sicily were likely to be attacked, too, and the Emperor decided that they could be defended even if Constantinople could not. In 663 he moved his government to the West.

Muslim columns raided yearly deep into Anatolia, and the fleet put marines into the port cities of Asia Minor, but it was not until 674 that the Arab armies and fleet stood before the Byzantine capital in force. In the summer of that year a full assault was mounted on the city and was repeated again and again until 677, when the Muslim commanders reluctantly concluded that the capture of the premier city of Christendom was beyond their powers, and so began a painful and bloody withdrawal from Anatolia. On land the Arabs had proved totally incapable of either breeching or scaling the massive city walls, and on the sea they were confronted for the first time with a terrible new weapon, the "Greek fire" that spread under propulsion across water and engulfed its defenseless victim.

Mu'awiyah's gravest miscalculation in a career marked with stunning successes was his decision to promote his son Yazid as his successor in the Caliphate. Just such a bald assertion of the dynastic principle had been put forward by the 'Alids with respect to Hasan ibn 'Ali at Kufah in 661. Hasan was, however, a grandson and favorite of the Prophet; Yazid was a dissolute young man with little to recommend him except for the not unimportant fact that his father was Caliph. For many in Islam it was not important enough. The Companions, many of whom were living in political isolation in Mecca and Medina, were revolted. More pertinently, their revulsion was shared by the ambitious sons of other former Caliphs like Husayn ibn 'Ali, who was now the head of the 'Alids, 'Abd al-Rahman, the son of Abu Bakr, and 'Abdallah, 'Umar's son. Finally there was 'Abdallah, the son of al-Zubayr, a hero of Islam. It was probably Husayn who had the strongest claim upon the office, but it was Ibn al-Zubayr who possessed the sharpest political sense and the greatest ambition for the Caliphate.

Once Yazid (680–683) succeeded his father at Damascus he demanded the allegiance of those other Caliphal scions in Medina. Ibn al-Zubayr and Husayn both slipped away to safer quarters in

Mecca. Husayn eventually allowed himself to be persuaded that his true strength lay in Kufah, the city of his father's downfall. What actually lay in Kufah was 'Ubaydallah ibn Ziyad who, even before the arrival of the unwitting Husayn, had broken the back of 'Alid support there.

Husayn received the bad news en route to Kufah, but he either could not or would not do anything to avert what necessarily was to be a disaster. The event followed at Karbala' north of Kufah on October 10, 680. The small cortege of Husayn was overwhelmed by troops sent out by 'Ubaydallah and the bloody details of what followed are richly preserved in the hagiography of the Shi'ites, for whom the destruction of the pious Husayn was a day never to be forgotten and for whom Karbala' remained a holy name and a holy place.

'Abdallah ibn al-Zubayr was still in Mecca, and now with the return of the women and children from Karbala', Medina broke into open revolt against the Caliph. Yazid's response was the sending of an army to besiege the city, which fell to him in 683. The army was then pressing on against Ibn al-Zubayr in Mecca when news arrived from Damascus that Yazid was dead. Immediately the siege of Mecca was broken off, and since the heir apparent, Mu'awiyah II, was a thirteen-year-old boy, the troops hurried back to Damascus with the expectation that the end was not yet. Barely were they out of sight when Ibn al-Zubayr was acclaimed Caliph at Mecca, and simultaneously at Basrah 'Ubaydallah reached out his hand for the same office. The citizens of Kufah were understandably less than enthusiastic for his candidacy, and when 'Abdallah ibn al-Zubayr began to find support in Iraq, 'Ubaydallah consulted the omens of politics and fled to Damascus.

Within two months Mu'awiyah II was dead (683), and delegations began arriving in Mecca from all over the Caliphate to pledge their allegiance to Ibn al-Zubayr, among them the tribe of the Qays, a branch of the northern group of Arabian Bedouin now resident in Syria. Their submission may have had less to do with 'Abdallah's claims than with their own fierce rivalry with the southern Arab tribe of Kalb, now likewise settled into Syria. Yazid's mother was a Kalbite, and the Banu Kalb were clearly being favored by the Umayyads at the expense, it appeared, of the Qays.

In Damascus the reins were finally and firmly grasped, with some important reinforcement by the now docile 'Ubaydallah ibn Ziyad, by the senior Umayyad, Marwan I (684–685). His first stroke was against the rebellious Qays, who were shattered near Damascus in 684. Quickly Egypt was regained for the house. Another army was dispatched against Ibn al-Zubayr in Mecca, but it had barely made its first contact when Marwan too was dead.

The murder of Husayn was working its leaven in Iraq. Nominally Iraq was in the camp of 'Abdallah ibn al-Zubayr, but sentiment was running high that the first order of business should be the vengeance of Husayn against the Umayyads. A great crowd of "penitents," as they called themselves, gathered at Kufah and their crusading army set out slowly along the Euphrates to deliver a blow against the Umayyads. It was met by 'Ubaydallah, who had meanwhile been commissioned to drive the insurgents from Iraq. The "penitents" were no match for his seasoned troops and the cause of the 'Alids received another bloody check.

In Damascus Marwan's son 'Abd al-Malik (685–705) was proclaimed Caliph at the moment when the leadership of what was left of the Kufan Shi'ites was passing into strange new hands, those of al-Mukhtar. A former Kharijite and at one time a supporter of Ibn al-Zubayr, Mukhtar once again had the Shi'ites in full cry in 685. His efforts succeeded in driving Ibn al-Zubayr's lieutenant out of Kufah, and Mukhtar followed by sending his agents throughout Iraq—Basrah held for Ibn al-Zubayr—preaching vengeance for Husayn and rule for the 'Alids, in particular for 'Ali's surviving son, Muhammad ibn al-Hanafiyah.[53]

The degree of Mukhtar's interest in Muhammad ibn al-Hanafiyah may be doubted. The 'Alid was a theological and political quietist—he later recognized the Caliphate of 'Abd al-Malik—and was, in any event, in the custody of Ibn al-Zubayr.

---

53. Hasan and Husayn were both born to 'Ali by Fatimah, the Prophet's daughter. Muhammad's mother was a woman of the Banu Hanifah.

Mukhtar, on the other hand, may have been exploring, in far more esoteric theological waters, for a Messianic *Imam* with divine powers.[54] Even more potent than his theology was Mukhtar's alliance with the *mawali* of Kufah. Their support gave him the balance of power in the city, and in 686 he formally took possession of the government there. It was the first time that the new non-Arab Muslims made their presence felt in the complex politics of Islam.

Al-Mukhtar's successes came to a sudden and explosive head. An army of his fanatical supporters marched eagerly into northern Mesopotamia and in that same year of 686 met and defeated the Syrian troops of the hated 'Ubaydallah ibn Ziyad. The head of the murderer of Husayn was carried back to Kufah in an orgy of triumph. It was short-lived. Ibn al-Zubayr's brother Mus'ab had by then taken possession of Basrah. It was Kufah, however, that was the administrative heart of Iraq, and without it Ibn al-Zubayr could entertain no realistic hopes for success. The Zubayrids cared nothing for the 'Alids and probably even less for the exotic Shi'ism of Mukhtar. Mus'ab gathered up his forces and marched against Kufah in 687. The city fell to him and with it al-Mukhtar and his hopes of a Messiah.

The position of Ibn al-Zubayr was further complicated by the renewed energies of the Kharijites. These embittered foes of the 'Alids and Umayyads alike were still smarting under the effects of the pogrom leveled against them by 'Ubaydallah ibn Ziyad at Basrah a few years earlier, and so at least some of their number had been willing to come to the assistance of Ibn al-Zubayr during his siege in Mecca. But the death of Yazid had presented the Kharijites with their own opportunities, and by 689 there were insurrectionist Kharijite governments operating in the Hadramawt, the Yemen, Bahrayn, Oman and the Najd. The Najdites, as this latter group was called, were not the extremist Kharijites of Basrah, but represented a new, modified version of the Kharijiyah that was somewhat more flexible in its program once it

---

54. Mukhtar is sometimes connected with the followers of 'Abdallah ibn Saba' (see Note 52 above). On the sect of the Kaysaniyah that grew up in the wake of Mukhtar, see p. 131.

gained the political power the Basrans were still struggling for. Unlike the Kharijites of Basrah, the Najdites did not anathematize all who refused to join their number; they even permitted the Kharijite partisan to dissemble his true beliefs in the name of a prudent self-preservation.

The Najdite relaxation of a severe Kharijism did not include an alliance with Ibn al-Zubayr who remained isolated in Mecca awaiting the inevitable arrival of the Umayyad armies. First 'Abd al-Malik bound the Byzantines to peace by a treaty concluded in 689, and then in the following year he turned to the reconquest of Iraq. Within a year Mus'ab and the Zubayrid forces there were destroyed. 'Abd al-Malik entered into his restored province and immediately sent his new general, the former schoolteacher al-Hajjaj, against Ibn al-Zubayr in Mecca. This time the siege did not fail: after six months of fighting, during which a storm of projectiles was hurled against the city and the Ka'bah itself, the anti-Caliph fell, deserted in the end by all but his most faithful followers.

Ibn al-Zubayr's support had been grounded in the thin soil of the disappointed Arab elite of the Holy Cities, whose claim to rule had already been rendered vain by the evolving history of the Islamic state. The days of the Companions were rapidly running out, and even the traditionalists in Islam, those who accepted the authority of that generation in matters of religion, refused to accord them the right to rule. Power had passed elsewhere, to the Umayyads and their Syrian troops, to new prophets and reformers, or to the ideologues of the Kharijites.

'Abd al-Malik turned to these latter immediately after the fall of Mecca in 692, and within a year the extensive Najd confederation was broken. The Kharijites of Iraq were more stubborn, however. The fiercely repressive measures of the *amir* Ziyad and his son 'Ubaydallah in Iraq between 665 and 684 had driven the Kharijites to either radicalism or compromise. One group, the followers of Nafi' ibn al-Azraq (d. 682), took an increasingly harder line toward those who declined to accept Kharijite authority; the Azraqites hurled excommunication against both their active opponents and those who wished to remain neutral. The toughening of the Azraqis' ideology was accompanied by guerrilla warfare fought through the towns of Iraq by Kharijite irregulars, first against the rump governments of Ibn al-Zubayr and then against the Umayyads.

The war against the Azraqi Kharijites dragged on for four years in Iraq and elsewhere under the direction of al-Hajjaj or his lieutenant Muhallab. The last Azraqi chief perished sometime in 696, and thereafter Kharijite fanatics had to take refuge farther east, in Khurasan and Sijistan. Others of them preferred to modify their views in the light of political realities and continued to live in Basrah and elsewhere at truce with al-Hajjaj and his Umayyad masters.

The revolt of 'Abdallah ibn al-Zubayr was abetted by the scandal of the Meccan pietists at the dissolute character and illegitimate claims of Yazid ibn Mu'awiyah. 'Abd al-Malik, who brought 'Abdallah down, was a far different sort. He had been educated in the same Medinese circles that had fostered Ibn al-Zubayr, and if his piety did not cause him to restrain his troops from the wrecking of Mecca, his reign did mark turnings from some of the earlier Umayyad preoccupations.

Both Mu'awiyah and Yazid had treated their Syrian Christian subjects, whether Arab, Aramaean or Greek, with an easy and friendly tolerance; Christians were a commonplace at court. 'Abd al-Malik did not reverse these attitudes immediately—the Christian poet al-Akhtal of the Monophysite Arab tribe of the Banu Taghlib was in great favor with the Caliph—but shortly after his accession the new Caliph unveiled another aspect of his policy. He began the construction of the magnificent Dome of the Rock on the site of the former Temple precinct in Jerusalem. The Shi'ites later spread the story that 'Abd al-Malik intended to shift the place of Islamic pilgrimage from Mecca, then in possession of Ibn al-Jubayr, to Jerusalem. The Caliph's true purpose was quite otherwise, to erect for the Muslim a rival to the Christians' own churches. Indeed, the circular Dome of the Rock in no way resembled a contemporary mosque, and its interior inscriptions, with their pointed reference to Allah's uniqueness and Jesus' apostleship, make it clear that the Caliph intended to say something to Christian pretensions as well as to Muslim pride.

'Abd al-Malik may have been forced to tread easily with his Christian subjects since he had been forced to buy an expensive peace with the Byzantines to make war on Ibn al-Zubayr. By 699, however, relations with Constantinople had unceremoniously collapsed and the Caliph set in train a series of measures directed toward the systematic Arabization of the Muslim state and the degradation of the Christians within it. Arabic was made the official language of the government bureaus, replacing Greek in Damascus, Coptic in Fustat and, somewhat later, Pahlevi in Kufah.[55] Changes likewise appeared in the coinage. Earlier coins had been imported into the *Dar al-Islam* in exchange for papyrus, counterinscribed and put into circulation for use by Muslims; now the Caliph began to strike his own gold coins with appropriate Islamic devices.

These internal reforms were accompanied by an often savage repression of Christians. There were massacres in Armenia, apparently on religious grounds, and even the Banu Taghlib began to feel the severity of the Caliph and his son al-Walid. The evidence is clearest from Egypt, where the *amir* at the beginning of the eighth century was 'Abd al-Malik's brother—and the father of the future Caliph 'Umar II—'Abd al-'Aziz. Under his governorship the Christians of Egypt were issued identity cards, and sometimes they even were branded or tattooed. On one occasion he ordered the destruction of every Christian cross to be found in the province. Factionalism among Christians, already endemic along the Nile, was encouraged, Christian churches were plundered, and the earlier exemption of monks from the poll tax was rescinded. Conversions to Islam mounted sharply.

Al-Walid (705–715) continued his father's policies on an even more ambitious scale. The Great Mosque in Damascus was his project. There had been both a Christian church and a Muslim mosque within the precincts of an earlier Syrian temple on the site. Walid dislodged the Christians and took over the entire area for his mosque. His too was the al-Aqsa mosque in Jerusalem and the sumptuous new cathedral mosque in Medina, the latter constructed with the help of imported Greek artisans.

---

55. The earlier records had also to be translated. According to one Christian account, 'Abd al-Malik asked the father of John of Damascus (see pp. 117–118), a former official in the *diwan*, to do so, but he refused.

Neither father nor son was engaged in mere Christian-baiting. By all appearances they were searching for an imperial style that would rival the Christians' own and at the same time be peculiarly Islamic. Though some of their successors would look toward Iran for a paradigm, for these early Umayyads of Syria there was only one model for such, the Autocrat of the Romans. The coinage, the reorganization of the *diwans*, the monumental architecture all converged on a repudiation of Constantinople and the simultaneous acceptance of the Byzantines' notion of what an emperor should be.

The breaking of the Kharijites and the fall of Ibn al-Zubayr did not end the Caliph's problems in Iraq. That rested with Hajjaj, the tough-minded young captain who from 694 to 714 exercised what amounted to a viceroyalty over all the eastern provinces of Islam. His first concern was with the Iraqi garrisons. Kufah and Basrah had earlier been built as secure cantonments for the Arab occupiers of Iraq against the native population. Now it was the Arab cities that could not be trusted, and in 702 Hajjaj constructed for his trustworthy Syrian troops his own garrison town at Wasit. Basrah and Kufah he stripped of their military character, though they continued to serve as administrative centers for the East. Further, he resolved to dispatch a strong hand to Khurasan, where the unsupervised Arab troops had been fighting violently among themselves for more than a decade.

Hajjaj's early choices for an eastern command had only indifferent success, but in 705 he found his man, Qutaybah ibn Muslim. The twin pillars of Hajjaj's policy were the centralization of power in the Caliph's—and his own—hands and the extension of the frontiers of the *Dar al-Islam*. In Khurasan the execution of the second was intended to guarantee the first, to turn the Arabs from their destructive internecine feuding by enlisting them in the quest for new booty across the Oxus. Qutaybah was quick to use the first outbreak of local squabbling across the river to lead his mixed force of Arabs and *mawali* into Transoxania.

The Muslims were not the only new presence across the Oxus. Ever since the accession of the T'ang dynasty in 618, and particularly under the Emperor T'ai-tsung (627–649), Chinese forces had been reaching out westward along the east-west overland trade routes. The Chinese had been in Sinkiang, the ancient province of Kashgaria, as early as the Han dynasty in the first century before Christ, and though Hunnic-Turkish pressures forced them out on that occasion, their influence, commercial and other, continued to be felt in Central Asia until their return in the seventh century.

The T'ang reversed a centuries-old flow of Turkish nomads against the northwest frontier of China. The Chinese took the offensive in the seventh century and struck out onto the Mongolian steppe. They reduced their tormentors, the eastern Tü-kueh,[56] and then took the road of conquest westward. Kashgaria had no central government in 630 on the eve of the Chinese reoccupation. Rather it was a series of caravan cities, one linked to another by the rich flow of the east-west trade.[57] The Chinese ruled the easternmost towns; those toward the west were held by various Tü-kueh dynasties. Buddhism was the religion of the region—earlier this had been a major passageway for Buddhism from India to China—and the culture was an interesting mixture of Chinese, Iranian and Indian strains, accompanied, at least as far as the art is concerned, by discernible traces of a lingering Hellenic influence.[58]

The armies of the T'ang occupied the oases across the Tarim basin between 630 and 650, and under T'ai-tsung's successor, Kao-tsung (650–683), the demoralized tribes of the western Tü-kueh north and west of the Pamirs had likewise to accept Chinese

---

56. On the Tü-kueh, see Introduction, p. 30.

57. Sealed off by mountains from the steppe to the north and by the Tibetan plateau to the south, the oval-shaped Tarim river basin is mostly filled by the Taklamakan desert. It was, however, passable to trade along its northern and southern fringes through a series of caravan cities. The southern route, the favorite of Indian travelers who had to pass westward around the Pamirs through Gandhara, Taxila, Balkh and Ferghana on the way to China, began at Kashgar, the first city east of Ferghana, and went through Khotan before arriving at the western gate of China at Tun-huang. The route along the northern fringe of the Taklamakan also began at Kashgar and ended at Tun-huang, but en route it passed through Aksu and Turfan.

58. Our best literary evidence on the area is supplied by the Chinese traveler Huan-tsang, who passed westward through the territory in 629. He took a somewhat different route home in 644.

sovereignty. It was of short duration. During the last twenty years of his reign, Kao-tsung lost much of what he and his father had won. The Tü-kueh rebelled and the newly energized Tibetans burst in upon the Tarim garrisons of the T'ang. Nor could the sudden revival of Turkish power be sustained. The Tü-kueh were demoralized by civil war, and toward the end of the seventh century the Chinese regained their hold on the caravan cities, while on the steppe to the north the Tü-kueh were eventually replaced by new Turkish confederations—in the east by the Uighurs and in the west by the Qarluq.

By 709 Qutaybah had established Muslim power across the Oxus and was in possession of Bukhara, a mixed Turco-Iranian settlement under the political domination of the Turks, in this case the increasingly feeble Tü-kueh. Their *khans* were no match for the Muslim armies, and their calls back across the steppe to their tribal allies at Qaraqorum brought assistance but no real relief. In 712 Samarqand fell to Qutaybah, and the routes leading through the valley of Ferghana and the oases of the Tarim eastward to the borders of China now lay open to the arms of Islam. Qutaybah was preparing to take the first step on that route when his assassination in 715 once again stalled the Arab advance.

Qutaybah's conquests north and east of the Oxus were ephemeral.[59] The *khans* there had more proximate remedies for their weakness than the distant eastern Tü-kueh. No sooner was Qutaybah dead than the Arabs' new vassals in Transoxania either were ousted or rapidly switched their allegiance to a new master, the Chinese. Beyond Qutaybah's unachieved goal of Ferghana lay Kashgar, the first of the Chinese-controlled entrepôts that stretched back across the Tarim basin and the famous silk route to China proper.

The head-on meeting between the Chinese and the Muslim Arabs in Central Asia was still a generation away when Qutaybah was killed by his own troops in 715. His death was the direct

---

59. As was the simultaneous Arab advance into India. Another of Hajjaj's protégés led a Muslim army into the valley of the Indus at the same time that Qutaybah was engaged in Central Asia. On the next, more lasting Muslim drive into India, see Chap. IX, p. 651.

consequence of a shift of power back in Syria. Qutaybah's severe patron and mentor, Hajjaj, had died in 714, and in the following year the Caliph Walid too was dead, succeeded by another of 'Abd al-Malik's sons, Sulayman. Qutaybah calculated that the new Caliph intended changes in the East and cast his hopes into an insurrection. It failed when his own men rose up against him.

Sulayman (715–717) did indeed intend a change of policy: he forcibly repudiated Hajjaj's harsh but effective methods in Iraq. But Sulayman was, nonetheless, as much of an imperialist as his father, and it seems unlikely that he would have interfered with Qutaybah's progress into the East. The war against the Byzantines, which had been postponed because of 'Abd al-Malik's embarrassment by Ibn al-Zubayr, was resumed in spectacular fashion first by Walid and then by Sulayman; and it was the latter who presided over another massive land and sea attack on Constantinople. Like its predecessor of 673–677, the Arab assault in 716–717 failed to take the Byzantine capital. The victories of Walid's reign had been won against the unsettled Justinian II. Sulayman and his brother Maslamah—it was Maslamah who held the actual field command—had to face an aggressive and energetic Leo III. Sulayman was not alive to sustain the bitterness of Maslamah's defeat. That fell to his cousin and chosen successor, 'Umar ibn 'Abd al-Aziz. It was a somewhat odd choice. Sulayman has been remembered, perhaps unjustly, as a profligate womanizer and a gourmand; 'Umar II was remembered as a Muslim saint.

'Umar II (717–720), who was raised not in Syrian court circles, but in the more pious atmosphere of Medina, enjoyed an untarnished reputation in the works of the same 'Abbasid historians who systematically vilified the Banu Umayyah. His too was the only Umayyad tomb to escape violation after the fall of the house; the corpse of his successor Hisham, for example, was exhumed and given an exemplary scourging. 'Umar may indeed have been pious in the style rarely seen in Caliphs since the days of Abu Bakr, but the sanctity of his reputation may have owed as much to political as to religious considerations: he ordered the public *damnatio memoriae* of 'Ali to cease, and he restored to the 'Alids some of their contested property in the Hejaz.

Almost every issue in early Islam appears to the modern historian to be deeply intertwined with both political and theological considerations. We do not know whether contemporary politicians understood them in exactly that way, and indeed the Umayyads had the reputation of consulting only reasons of state. Such was not true of 'Umar, however. During his brief reign he attempted to do justice to Islam as a City of God *and* of Man, to resolve what the Islamic Law prescribed and what *Realpolitik* demanded.

At least from the time of 'Umar I, and in principle from that of the Prophet himself, Islam recognized social and economic distinctions between Muslim and non-Muslim living within the *Dar al-Islam.* From the beginning, the Muslim had certain financial obligations: the payment of a tithe as an alms tax (*zakat*) on his property and the surrender into the coffers of Islam of a fifth of the booty taken in conquest. For the non-Muslim, each one of whom had to pay a poll tax, there was the concordat (*dhimmah*) granting them religious protection and the various contracts and agreements regulating the payment of a stipulated tribute in the form of a land tax.

The issues facing the conscience of 'Umar II were highly complex—if a non-Arab became a convert to Islam, for example, was he obliged thereby to surrender his land in the conquered territory?—but for the Caliph, as for many others, one point was incontrovertible: Islam recognized no classes of Muslims and, so far as the *diwan* registers were concerned, *mawali* should be inscribed and pensioned exactly as the Arab *muqatilah*. Further, as Muslims, they were freed, by 'Umar's express command, of the obnoxious obligations of the poll tax. There remained only the question of the land tax, and here 'Umar held off; new converts to Islam would continue to pay the land tax. 'Umar allowed himself to be persuaded that Islam could not suffer the losses in revenues.

In Egypt, Syria and Iraq, the Arab conquerors had deliberately been discouraged from settling in with the local population by their confinement in the *amsar*. That arrangement served only poorly farther afield, however, and the Berber *mawali* in Ifriqiyah and the Iranian in Khurasan wanted entry into the *diwans*, with the appropriate tax relief, while the Arab *muqatilah* wanted their release to settle into the communities there. The first could be read as the implicit intent of the Islamic Law, and 'Umar may have seen in the egalitarian quality of that law, which was still very much unarticulated at this point, an opportunity to replace the tension-ridden "Commonwealth of the Arabs" of the first 'Umar and the "Commonwealth of the Syrians" of his own Umayyad predecessors with a new "Commonwealth of Muslims." 'Umar died before the policy was fully implemented and before any judgment could be made on its chances for success. It was left to others to construct the "Commonwealth of the Muslims."

'Umar was succeeded by the last son of 'Abd al-Malik, the pleasure-loving Yazid II (720–724),[60] and the last twenty-five years of the Umayyad "kingship," as their enemies called it, were attended by the overt signs of political disintegration. The long reign of Hisham (724–743) was followed by the rapid and ruinous succession of three of his nephews, Walid II (743–744) and within a single year (744) Yazid III and Ibrahim.

Hisham was an intelligent and reform-minded ruler whom circumstances called upon to be a soldier. In the far west of his dominions the Arab armies had at last slowed to a halt in southern France in the face of Charles Martel's Franks (732), while closer to home the Byzantine Emperor Leo III, now at last on the offensive, dealt the Muslims their first serious setback in central Anatolia (740). Across North Africa the Berber tribesmen, who had become Muslims but found little economic advantage in their status as *mawali*, gave expression to their frustration by embracing Kharijism; for three years, between 740 and 743, Hisham had to divert his Syrian troops from other important garrison points to quell Berber uprisings.

---

60. Whose chief influence may have been felt in Byzantine rather than Islamic history. According to a Byzantine historian, Yazid allowed himself to be persuaded by a Jewish occultist that his final illness was due to Christian malevolence and that his continued health could be assured by the destruction of the sacred images in the Christian churches. That was in 723, and three years later the Emperor Leo III began his own campaign against the icons, two events which were inevitably connected in the analyses of the Byzantine opponents of the "Saracen-minded" Leo.

The Berber revolts in the name of an egalitarian Islam were echoed in the eastern provinces. Hajjaj's decision to demilitarize the *amsar* of Basrah and Kufah put the control of Iraq in the hands of the favored Syrians upon whom the regime now totally depended. Beyond Iraq lay the anomaly of Khurasan, garrisoned but not yet settled by restless Arab levies from Iraq. There was no Basrah or Kufah in Khurasan; the Arab troopers living round about, but not in, Merv were intended by the Caliphs to serve as a standing army and not as colonists. Local rule was still effectively in the hands of the Iranian landowners or *dihqans*.

As time passed, many of the Arab tribesmen in Khurasan lost their nomadic ways and with them their appetite for booty excursions into Transoxania. They were pressing for assimilation, while the *dihqans*, who saw in the Arabization of Khurasan the end of their own power, resisted. The Caliphs generally supported the *dihqans* in the name of economic stability, but the pressures from the other side made the Arab possession of Transoxania highly uncertain.

The Caliphs and their *amirs* were well aware that they had rivals for the control of the lands beyond the Oxus. The land and the culture were Iranian, but the paramount military powers there were Turkish, at this time the tribes of the Türgish, who between 724 and 737 succeeded in driving the Arabs from all of their holdings in Sogdia, except Samarqand. Hisham's initial reaction was to send some of his valuable Syrian troops to the frontier, but with the appointment of Ashras ibn 'Abdallah as governor of Khurasan a new tactic was announced, the Islamicization of Transoxania.

Ashras promised and then denied that new converts to Islam would be exempt from the land tax. The Sogdian *dihqans* had apparently succeeded in once again convincing the *amir* that the territory could not bear the loss of such tax revenue, even though no Arab Muslims were called upon to pay the *kharaj*. But beyond the intent of the Islamic Law lay another, more potent fact: wholesale conversion to Islam would inevitably undermine the traditional feudal order in the east and with it the position of the *dihqans* themselves.

In Khurasan Hisham took a far more radical step: he assented to the integration of the Arab troops in the local communities.[61] The standing army was not diminished, but by his new drafts into Khurasan Hisham freed at least some of the veterans to settle into the cities of the province. It seemed a happy solution to the unrest there, but the new Arab citizens of Merv, Nishapur and Balkh now came under the authority of the local Iranian magistrates, a situation that soon led to outrage and agitation among the colonists.

Hisham's political troubles had stretched his Syrian troops to the breaking point, and after his death his successor Walid II was overthrown by those same disgruntled troops. Two of Walid's cousins, Yazid III and Ibrahim, followed within the next ten months, and the total disintegration of Umayyad rule was arrested only by the seizure of power by Marwan II (744–750), a member of a collateral branch of the family who had served his military apprenticeship under Maslamah in the Caucasus[62] and who was serving as governor of the frontier province of Azarbayjan at Walid's death. With the confidence of an experienced campaigner and with the loyal support of his own troops, Marwan marched to Syria and wrested the Caliphate from Ibrahim.

The later Umayyads had grown weary of Damascus. Sulayman had his residence at Ramlah in Palestine, Hisham at Rusafah on the Euphrates and the last of the Umayyads ruled the *Dar al-Islam* from the still markedly pagan city of Harran.[63] Most of the family after 'Abd al-Malik were builders, and there were new palaces[64] and cathedral mosques in a new mixed style. The archi-

---

61. Hisham also undertook the Arabization of Egypt by settling numbers of Qays tribesmen in the Nile valley.

62. Where the expansion of Islam onto the Russian steppe was blocked by the Khazars, a Turkic people settled across the northern approaches to the Caucasus. Drawn by reasons of state to both Islam and Christianity, the *khan* of the Khazars ended by embracing Judaism.

63. On the "Sabianism" of Harran, see Chap. IV, pp. 278–282.

64. Many of which could easily have been mistaken for fortresses. Since these Umayyad "châteaux" were built out on the desert line along the Syrian frontier, it may be that their architectural style was simply a borrowing from the older military constructions of Trajan and Diocletian along the *limes*. It is equally possible that the Umayyads had need of palaces that could also double as fortresses.

tecture and decoration of these palaces owe an obvious debt to the late Hellenic tradition in the East, but from the time of Hisham it is equally obvious that Sasanian models were being consulted as well.[65]

The change in style was due to something more than the whim of the builders. With Hisham and Marwan II there was a distinct turning of the entire superstructure of Islam upon its foundations; and that turning was distinctly toward the East. The Caliphs' power rested as firmly as before upon their Syrian soldiers, but their imperial model was no longer, as it had been for 'Abd al-Malik, the Byzantine Autocrat; now it was the Shah of Iran. That there was no visible representative of that Sasanian style was no obstacle; the resurrection of Iran was by literary and artistic means.

It was during Hisham's reign that the first Arabic translations of Iranian epic and historical material were undertaken. The evidence for that activity is indirect, but more immediate indications of a turning toward Iran are not lacking. Some few pieces are preserved from the correspondence of 'Abd al-Hamid, a *mawla* who served as undersecretary to Hisham and then chief of the chancery for Marwan. In style and content his instructions to the members of the secretariat show that Iranian norms of protocol and court ceremonial were making sensible inroads into the Umayyad administration. 'Abd al-Hamid perished with his patron in 750, but the trend continued and it was one of his students, Ibn al-Muqaffa', who played a similar and even more effective role as Iranian mediator at the court of the early 'Abbasids.[66]

The regard cast here for the first time toward Iran was a response to a new need in Islam. The early Umayyads had ruled with a kind of Homeric simplicity. They were chieftains, not administrators, and they left the effective business of governing in the hands of their *amirs*. If 'Abd al-Malik and Walid attempted

---

65. The mosaics in Walid I's mosque in Damascus, for example, are almost totally Hellenic in their sensibilities, while Hisham's buildings, the desert "palaces" at Khirbat al-Mafjar, north of Jericho, and Qasr al-Hayr, south of Rusafah, show the intrusion of Sasanian elements in both the architectural features and their interior decoration.
66. See Chap. VI, p. 403 and Chap. IX, pp. 644–645.

to adorn their office with something approximating the imperial style, their attempts at executive *mimesis* did not extend into the heart of the Byzantine government, the elaborate and centralized hierarchy of bureaus and offices through which the Autocrat of the Romans exercised his authority.

To add imperial panache to the rudimentary administrative concerns of a tribal *shaykh* was not to solve the problem of government in Islam. The Caliph no less than the provincial *amirs* needed helpers in the work of government, and the latter-day Umayyads began to add them to their entourage. Tradition attests to the presence of poets at their courts, but the appearance of 'Abd al-Hamid, a secretary (*katib*), and his colleagues speaks of something else, the rise of a civil bureaucracy.

It was inevitable that most of the early members of that bureaucracy were either Iranian *mawali* or Christians. The Arab conquerers were mostly Bedouin, who brought no administrative talents to their new domains. They were warriors in lands that had been ruled for centuries not by war lords but by scribes and clerks. If the Caliph stood in need of these latter, as he did in the mid-eighth century, he had to turn elsewhere than to the Muslim Arabs.

There was little to be drawn upon from what remained of the Byzantine civil service. For centuries the emperor had been centralizing his control in Constantinople itself, and what we know of the eastern Byzantine provinces on the eve of Islam suggests that the effects of this policy of centralization, added to religious dissatisfaction and the destructive Persian wars of the seventh century, left the provinces of the Byzantine Near East with only the shadow of an imperial presence. Both justice and the financial administration had lapsed in many places into the hands of the Church, while the government in Constantinople concerned itself almost exclusively, though not very successfully, with maintaining the peace.

The Arabs fell direct heirs, on the other hand, to the Sasanian capital and home provinces in Iraq and western Iran, and with them what was left of the Iranian clerical tradition. The Caliphs had at hand the means to rule like the Shahs. The Umayyads resting in their desert palaces on the strength of their Syrian armies and distracted by the problems of survival were only beginning to understand that possibility when their regime collapsed.

The Failure of the Umayyads

While the last Umayyads were struggling against their enemies abroad and the mounting insurrection at home, their legitimacy was being even more destructively undermined by ideologues whose grievances were neither social nor economic. In legal and religious circles there was growing up a new understanding of the Islamic Law. The expression of that understanding did not reach its canonical form until the beginning of the ninth century, when it corresponded to the stated ideals of the 'Abbasids, the dynasty that supplanted the Umayyads in the Caliphate and, unhappily, wrote the history of that office. The 'Abbasids provided their own publicists, while the all but mute Umayyads were left to the mercies of the remote scholar of modern times.

The Umayyads are portrayed by the 'Abbasid historians as worldlings who seized the Caliphate and converted it into a vehicle for their own aggrandizement and self-glorification, while the 'Abbasids publicly proclaimed their own intent of establishing God's commonwealth on earth. Like the Maccabees who dislodged the Seleucids from Palestine for their godlessness, the 'Abbasids overthrew the Banu Umayyah under the banner of a *Respublica Islamica* and, again like the Maccabees, had difficulty in fulfilling the pious hopes which they themselves had raised.

The issue at stake between the Umayyads and their opponents was not simply a secular versus a theocratic view of Islam. The Umayyads too had their supporters among the pietists and intellectuals. As early as Hasan ibn 'Ali's recognition of Mu'awiyah there were those who chose to view the establishment of the new dynasty not as a capitulation but as the restoration of the unity of the community and the welcome end of the 'Alids' schismatic civil wars.[67] These partisans were concerned not with politics or

---

67. The fall of the Umayyads left this group in a serious political predicament. That they did not, however, totally disappear is attested to by the fact that even in early 'Abbasid Baghdad there was still a

privilege, as were the various tribal supporters of the Umayyads, but with theology in the early Islamic sense of that word. Some traditionalists, like the Medinese, withheld their recognition from the Umayyads because they preferred to remain neutral in the struggle between Mu'awiyah and 'Ali, but the "supporters of custom and the community" (*ahl al-sunnah wa al-jama'ah*), as they were called, valued unity more than neutrality and so recognized the Umayyads as the *de facto* and, so, legitimate rulers of the *ummah*.

The Umayyads found neutrality as useful as outright support. There was, oddly, a neutralist tradition even among the 'Alids, and one of 'Ali's grandsons, Hasan ibn Muhammad ibn al-Hanafiyah, is credited with being the first to formulate the doctrine of *irja'*, the giving-over of judgment concerning the disputants of 656–661 into the hands of Allah: they were all, whatever their sins, true Muslims and not, as the Kharijites asserted, unbelievers. As for the Caliphate, it was possessed by the Umayyads, and since Allah's will achieved what it would, they were legitimate rulers of the community.

Both the partisans of this view, the Murji'ites and the conservatives just described, came to the same practical conclusions regarding the Umayyads, though on different grounds. The Murji'ites were determinists and so recognized in the Umayyads the working of God's will. The *ahl al-sunnah* are better described as traditionalists who had confidence in the infallibility of the Muslim consensus—the Umayyads succeeded in direct descent from the Prophet and had been accepted by the main body of Islam as its rulers.

The Murji'ites were particularly strong in Kufah, where the fall of al-Mukhtar rendered the citizens somewhat more willing

---

lively cult of Mu'awiyah. More seriously, the 'Abbasids found themselves, by reasons of their overthrow of the Umayyads and their early connection with the party of 'Ali, in the position of sinning against both precedent and the community. The 'Abbasids soon freed themselves of the embrace of the 'Alids, but they never quite satisfied the descendants of the conservative supporters of the Umayyads until they made their peace with the latter-day spokesman of that group, Ahmad ibn Hanbal. See Chap. VI, p. 418.

to entertain the Umayyad claims to rule and where Ibn al-Hanafiyah's son's suggestion that Allah was on the side of the victors received a sympathetic hearing. The Kufans' relations with al-Hajjaj were not always happy, however, and it was not until the accession of 'Umar II in 717 that the Murji'ites moved somewhat closer to the throne. They remained strong in Kufah where the jurist Abu Hanifah was reckoned one of their number.

Though they were apparently willing to regard political realities as a function of divine providence, the Murji'ites were not simply determinists. They were unwilling to commit the sinner to the ranks of the infidels in the manner of the Kharijites, but they did take virtue and vice seriously and believed that the Muslim, and the Caliph of the Muslims, had a moral obligation to do good and avoid evil. The Murji'ites did not, however, identify morality with political legitimacy. Nor were they prepared to admit another doctrine that was beginning to appear in some circles, that man was totally responsible for his own acts.

The proponents of the thesis that man determined (*qadara*) his own acts were later lumped under the general designation of Qadariyah. Historically they had their origins in the teachings of a certain Ghaylan al-Dimashqi. Politically Ghaylan remained pro-Umayyad during his early years and so too did his followers, at least down to the time of Marwan. Their support, insofar as it was ideological rather than political, did not, however, rest on the Murji'ite premise that might makes right. The Qadarites judged the *Imam* on his qualifications, and specifically by his knowledge of the *Qur'an* and the *sunnah*. The Qadarites' judgment on the later Umayyads was not favorable, and Ghaylan was executed by Hisham in 743, though more likely for his politics than for his theology.

The Qadarites had other reasons to support the Umayyads. Their membership was predominantly from the Banu Kalb, a Christian Arab tribe domesticated in Syria before the coming of Islam and one of the chief props of Umayyad power. Mu'awiyah's son Yazid had a Kalbite mother and wife, and it was the Banu Kalb who won the lion's share of credit for the defeat of the Syrian supporters of Ibn al-Zubayr at Marj Rahit in 684. Later, under Yazid II and Walid II, the tribe lost some of its political power and consequently some of its enthusiasm for the Umayyads as well.

What is most significant in the present context is that the Banu Kalb were largely Christian in their pre-Islamic days and then, as Muslims, largely Qadarites. The connection is unlikely to have been accidental. We know something of the Christian polemic being directed against Islam in Syria under the Umayyads and the early 'Abbasids. Its two chief sources were John of Damascus, a contemporary of Ghaylan, who died sometime about 750, and the somewhat later Theodore abu Qurrah. Both men taxed their Muslim opponents with a stringent determinism that made man a pawn to the will of God rather than a genuine moral agent. The Christian polemicists held for the moral responsibility of man, as did the Qadarites of Ghaylan.

John was born sometime about 675 into an important Damascene family. His grandfather Mansur had negotiated the surrender of the city to the Muslim invaders in 635 and then continued to serve the occupiers in his previous post of treasurer. John's father, Sergius, worked for the Umayyads in the same capacity, though there may have been some demotion in his office when 'Abd al-Malik decreed the Arabization of the ministries in 700. By that time John was himself enrolled in the Muslim civil service, though he could obviously never aspire to the earlier eminence of his father and grandfather. When 'Umar II removed the Christians totally from the *diwans*, John's administrative career was at an end. He left the city and took up the religious life at the monastery of St. Sabas in Palestine.

From his ordination until his death about 750, John gave himself over to defending his Chalcedonian Christianity against Monophysites, Manichaeans, Muslims and the newly appeared Byzantine Iconoclasts, in a series of treatises in Greek and Arabic. Two major works in Greek were directed toward Islam, an important chapter in the heresiographical section of his *Source of Knowledge*[68] and the *Dialogue Between a Saracen and a Chris-*

68. The chapters "On the Heresies" constituted the second part of this work. On the dialectical and philosophical chapters preceding them, see Chap. IV, pp. 319–320.

tian. John knew a great deal about Islam, from the Muslim oral tradition as well as from the *Qur'an*, but his presentation of that information can hardly be called either accurate or evenhanded. His purpose was not to enlighten the Byzantines on the new religious phenomenon but rather to discredit it.

The *Dialogue* is more pointed than the heresiography. It is a discourse of assertions and responses directed by the Christian toward what must have appeared in the third and fourth decades of the eighth century as critical weaknesses in the Muslim faith: the *Qur'an*'s insistence on the omnipotence of Allah would appear to make God the author of both good and evil and to strip man of both his free will and his responsibility. The Muslim replied by posing a more general problem on the divine causality, and eventually the dispute moved into other areas, to Christ as the uncreated Word of God among others.

There is no sign that a contemporary of John of Damascus like Ghaylan had read the *Dialogue* of his fellow townsman. But the lack of an immediate connection renders no less striking the fact that the points in dispute between Muslim and Christian were identical with those being raised within Islam itself, in this generation of theologians the question of free will and, in the next, the *Qur'an* as the Uncreated Word of God. Striking too is the method of the discourse. The arguments of the early Muslim theologians proceeded in much the same dialectical fashion as those in the *Dialogue*. The method of demonstrative proof set down for the philosopher by Aristotle in his *Posterior Analytics* is equally remote from the pages of John and the procedures of the Muslim divines.

Theodore abu Qurrah, later the Chalcedonian bishop of Harran, was born at Edessa at about the time that John died. He owed, nonetheless, a great deal to his predecessor. He too studied at St. Sabas, where the monastic school was still dominated by the intellectual presence of John. We do not know when Theodore became bishop of Harran, most recently the capital of the dying Umayyad house and one of the last centers of non-Christian Hellenism in the Near East, but he was deposed in 813 and joined the entourage of the Patriarch of Jerusalem. There were journeyings as far abroad as Egypt and Armenia, probably for purposes of disputing with Monophysites, until his death in 820. John, who certainly knew Arabic, preferred to address his audience in Greek; Theodore composed works in Greek, Syriac and Arabic.

Theodore's Syriac treatises, which were directed chiefly against Monophysites, are now lost, but the Greek and Arabic works illustrate an interesting point about contemporary Muslim-Christian polemic. The Arabic works are about subjects of dispute between the two religions, the unity of God and free will, for example; the Greek works are aimed directly against Islam and its Prophet. The polemic was, for all that, somewhat more familiar and more sophisticated than that provoked in John's day. The arguments unfold, albeit dialectically, on more purely intellectualistic grounds; the Muslim—in one work he is called a "master of *logos*" (*ellogimon*), an early Greek translation of *mutakallim*—poses the questions and Theodore himself answers.

The controversial writings of Theodore abu Qurrah reflect, as John's do, common concerns and a theological milieu rather than a precise literary source for early Muslim theology. Both men provide the context in which the thoughts of Ghaylan and others were developing. Theodore's works point explicitly to public disputations between the two sides, and evidence is not lacking that such exercises went back to early Umayyad times in Syria. The Christians' adversaries in John and Theodore are embarrassed by their inability to escape from a position of strict determinism; Ghaylan and the Qadarites may have learned from their opponents in a strictly Muslim setting that other responses were possible, responses similar to the Christians' own position on free will but supported with abundant Qur'anic justification.

There is more in Ghaylan that suggests Christian influences rather than a purely Qur'anic meditation. He made, for example, the love of God part of the formula of faith (he was the earliest Muslim to have done so) and he apparently recognized the role of grace in man's knowledge of God. Our knowledge of Allah, at least in the general sense that we immediately recognize the contingency of the universe, is a priori and is described by Ghaylan as the "working of God." From that generalized knowledge grows a second, acquired knowledge of the uniqueness (*tawhid*) of Allah, his knowledge and his law, a knowledge in brief of the Prophetic message, and it is this latter that constitutes the content of faith (*iman*).

The Qadarite position on human freedom, whether it was expropriated from Christian sources or originated by Ghaylan, was taken up by one of Ghaylan's contemporaries, one who stands, obscurely, at the head of a great many religious and intellectual movements in Islam, Hasan al-Basri (d. 728).[69] Though born in Medina, Hasan spent most of his life in Islam's first intellectual capital of Basrah, where he won a reputation for personal piety and a readiness to have his say on the issues that were beginning to trouble the unity of the *ummah*.

Free will was just such an issue. Its position within the context of Christian-Muslim polemic might seem to qualify it as just another episode in the defense of the faith, but at the beginning of the eighth century it took on, as has been seen, distinctly political overtones: if men were indeed responsible for their actions, then so too were the political leaders of the *Dar al-Islam*, the Umayyads; if, on the other hand, all was preordained by the decree of Allah, then their rule was part of that divine ordinance and must be accepted as such.

Hasan al-Basri entered the dispute with an open letter to the Caliph 'Abd al-Malik in which he stated his unqualified opposition to those who maintained that Allah had preordained all. The letter was argued almost exclusively in Qur'anic terms, that is, as an exegesis of those passages in the *Qur'an* that had been brought forward, on Hasan's own testimony, by the partisans of predestination. The language of the *Qur'an* was, to be sure, ambiguous on the subject, but for all its emphasis on the decree and the determination of Allah, Hasan remained unconvinced that Allah can in any way be held responsible for the evil that men do. In Hasan's exegesis Allah's "decree" is nothing more than a command to do good. Regarding the more difficult "determination" (*qadar*),[70] Allah could, of course, preordain all men to good; but had he done so, they would have merited no reward. Man is,

---

69. On his role in the evolution of Muslim asceticism, see Chap. VI, pp. 417–418.

70. More difficult because *qadar* was used among the pre-Islamic Arabs to express the workings of an impersonal fate, and its fatalistic connotations, now transferred to the will of Allah, continued to cling to the word.

then, responsible for his own actions, particularly for the evil he may do, and that for Hasan was the crucial point in the dispute.

In Hasan al-Basri's formulae man's responsibility is still described in terms of choice, but eventually the question took another, somewhat more sensitive form. Was man, then, a "creator"—a title usually reserved for Allah—with respect to his own acts? Once the question had been posed in that form, the nascent Islamic theology reached the bedrock of the issue of free will and predestination, how to reconcile the omnipotence of God with the power that must apparently be conceded to man to enable him to posit a moral act. Even the Greeks, who came to God without revelation and from the direction of man's deeply experienced sense of freedom of choice, had somehow to weaken the links of causal necessity that bound the universe together so that man could "create" his own acts. The Epicureans in particular had difficulty in reconciling the "openness" of human freedom with a closed system of causality.

In the debates on predestination that overflowed into the generations after Hasan al-Basri, those who followed the positions he espoused were confusingly grouped together under the heading of "Qadarites," a term that would appear to be somewhat more appropriately applied to the defenders of Allah's "determination" (*qadar*). These latter were, in fact, known as "Determinists" (*jabriyah*). The Jabriyah may have arisen from a meditation on the *Qur'an* where there are, as has been noted, texts enough to support that position. Or they too may have been involved in the political debates on the merits of the Umayyads, where a theological "what will be, will be" had obvious political applications.

The niceties of these theological positions did not necessarily lead to a program of political action. Both the Qadariyah and the Jabriyah could, from their opposing points of view, support the Umayyad claim to legitimacy, as could the neutral Murji'ites. The only theologians willing to take both a theoretical and a practical stance against the Umayyads were the Kharijites. Not only did they hold with the Qadarites that sin was possible; they wished to banish the sinner from Islam, and by force of arms if necessary. In the Kharijite view, the true believer, the Muslim whose sinless conduct served to validate his faith, should take up arms against the "sinners" within the *Dar al-Islam* with as much vigor as he did in the *jihad* against the infidels across the frontier. That the sin in question was usually political led to explosive consequences.

The Umayyads, and later the 'Abbasids, neither of whom had a legitimate claim to the Caliphate in Kharijite eyes, frequently resorted to arms against attempts to put this excommunication into effect. The Kharijites raised for all Muslims the serious question of political and religious conscience while they presented to the theologians a challenge on the very nature of Islam. Was the Muslim someone who recited and accepted the *shahadah* or someone who lived according to the Law of Islam? Did sin jeopardize one's membership in the *ummah?* The question was a political one, because the *ummah* was political and the Caliphate a political office. The Kharijite answer was a resounding yes; sin was apostasy.

On purely pragmatic grounds that answer was intolerable, and even those Kharijites who managed to win a measure of political control in one area or another frequently backed off from the earlier enthusiasms of the sect. Most Muslims would probably have assented to the opposite view, that Islam was essentially a profession of faith (*iman*) that committed one to live, as far as possible, in accordance with the Law of Islam. The two elements, faith and good works, were not completely unconnected, nor were they, as the Kharijites would have it, absolutely identical.

This was very much the view taken by Hasan al-Basri in his public teaching. The grave sinner was still a Muslim, but by his sin he put himself in the position of being what the *Qur'an* called a "hypocrite," a judgment of moral censure without the Kharijite implication of apostasy. Others were unwilling to go even that far. The Murji'ites knew that the Prophet was in Paradise and that the Christians, Jews and others who denied Allah were destined for Hell; but on the fate of other Muslims they could do no more than suspend judgment. Faith was not like a shirt that was taken off at the commission of a sin and put on again with repentance: *iman* was rather an indelible trait that could be obliterated only by an explicit denial.

The debate was apparently a lively one at Basrah in the early eighth century. Kharijism was still very much alive in Iraq, and it may have been Hasan's intent to steer a course between Kharijite and Murji'ite when he took his stand on "hypocrisy." It would have been impossible, in any event, for such a well-known figure to avoid being drawn into the controversy. In the end, however, it cost Hasan some of his followers, chief among them Wasil ibn 'Ata' (d. 748), a student of Hasan's who was credited with being the founder of a movement called Mu'tazilitism.

Wasil was probably as little a formal theologian as most of his contemporaries. Men were attempting to understand the *Qur'an* in the light of what was occurring around them. And what was happening in the eighth century was that the Umayyads, a dynasty whose legitimacy had been questioned by some from the start, was under increasing *religious* attack from the politically active Kharijites and the ideologues of the party of 'Ali. The Umayyads, who attempted to defend their ground on the basis of *Realpolitik*, were vulnerable to charges from pietists who did not like their style, from lawyers who had become dissatisfied with customary law as a ground for Muslim life, from theological idealists like the Kharijites who saw Islam as a "community of saints" and, finally, from the disappointed supporters of the House of 'Ali.

The latter were politically quiescent since the disaster visited upon Husayn ibn 'Ali at Karbala' in 680 and the abortive revolt of al-Mukhtar and the *mawali* in 687. No direct descendant of 'Ali came forward to assert a claim to the Caliphate in the face of the apparently unshakable Umayyad grip on that office. In lieu of political activism, the 'Alid theoreticians contented themselves with arguing about the past—whether Abu Bakr, 'Umar and 'Uthman had any real title to the Caliphate. The *Shi'at 'Ali* could agree, of course, on the vilification of 'Uthman; but the degree of their passion can be better measured by their attitudes toward Abu Bakr and 'Umar, both of whom had been accepted by the *ummah*, though neither had been designated by the Prophet.

Wasil was much involved in the question, and his stance here may be more indicative of his place in Islam than his alleged position at the head of the file of Mu'tazilites. Wasil broke with Hasan on the Kharijite question of sin. Hasan held that the sinner should be judged, but he was unwilling to brand him an apostate, while the Murji'ites argued for the latitudinarian view of suspending judgment on sinners. Wasil attempted to thread the needle once again: the grave sinner, he held, was neither an infidel à la Kharijism nor a believer in one of the roles put forward by Hasan and the Murji'ites; he was, rather, in an "intermediary state."

Wasil too, it appears, was suspending judgment on the internecine disputes surrounding the Battle of the Camel, but he did take a position on the status of the *Rashidun*, a stand which allows us to locate him rather precisely on the political spectrum: Abu Bakr and 'Umar were both legitimate Caliphs, but 'Ali had a better claim to that office than 'Uthman. Wasil stood, then, over against the Umayyads and close to what was developing as moderate Shi'ism, the set of attitudes even then, in the thirties and forties of the eighth century, associated with Husayn's grandson Zayd ibn 'Ali.

After the murder of Husayn the leadership of the 'Alids—and, as it was later maintained, the spiritual direction, or Imamate, of the Shi'ites—passed, in unremarkable circumstances, to his son 'Ali (d. 710). It was a sublimely uneventful period for the 'Alids, most of whom lived peacefully in Mecca and Medina. 'Ali ibn Husayn had two sons, and at the death of the elder, Muhammad al-Baqir, in 731, there occurred what appears to have been the first major difference among the followers of the 'Alids. Who was to succeed al-Baqir as *Imam*, his younger brother Zayd or his own son Ja'far? The greater number of the Hejaz Shi'ites declared for Ja'far, but Zayd too found supporters for his claim to the Imamate.

The exact circumstances are not clear, but in 740 Zayd allowed himself to be tempted into actions which were construed by the Umayyad authorities as rebellion. That it should have occurred at Kufah is not surprising, nor is the fact that Hisham's governor suppressed the disturbance with ease and rapidity. Zayd's uprising was of little or no political consequence in the troubled playing-out of the Umayyads' reign. Where Zayd left his mark was on the history of Shi'ism, particularly by his raising the issue of the succession in the Shi'ite Imamate, and in offering a moderate alternative to some of the extreme theories being propagated in the circle of al-Baqir and his son Ja'far al-Sadiq.[71]

Wasil may have been influenced by some of the Zaydi theses and so, too, may one of his contemporaries, 'Amr ibn 'Ubayd (d. 761), a *mawla* of Balkh and another former follower of Hasan whom the Mu'tazilites later claimed as one of their own. The two men, Wasil and 'Amr, differed on some points but they stood together on the essentially pro-'Alid line, sent representatives into the provinces, including Khurasan, to propagate their views, and 'Amr at least, who survived into 'Abbasid times, was a revered figure at the court of Mansur. But if either had anything to do with the furthering of 'Abbasid claims, we are uninformed on the subject. All that can be said is that they were part of the pro-'Alid sentiment arising in some pious and learned circles in the first half of the eighth century. Later in that same century, and more forcibly at the beginning of the next, the Mu'tazilites held somewhat similar views but located them in an entirely different intellectual context. Between Wasil and the Mu'tazilite eminence Abu al-Hudhayl intervened the massive and alien influence of a new metaphysic.

The Kharijites withdrew from the main body of the Muslim *ummah* in the name of a theocratic Islam. They called down a plague on all parties by appealing to a higher authority and, in so doing, they raised questions even more fundamental than their intent suggests. The Kharijites asked, in effect, who was a Muslim and provoked responses on what was Allah. The answer to that latter question was, of course, in the *Qur'an*. But the Qur'anic response was not a response: it implied no question but merely asserted and described, and in terms familiar to most of the Prophet's auditors, who had worshiped Allah before Muhammad had begun to preach his message. Allah was a personal and spiritual, albeit anthropomorphized, deity who created and ruled this world and, through his Prophet, called men to a fellowship

---

71. For the consequences among the party of 'Ali, see Chap. VIII, pp. 572–575. What Zayd himself held on some of these complex questions is uncertain, since the works preserved under his name are almost certainly the product of some of his later partisans.

dedicated to his worship, with a promise of reward for those who obeyed and a threat of punishment for those who did not.

Questions did eventually arise concerning that portrait, provoked by the evolution of the fellowship of believers and the death of the charismatic Prophet. Who would reply? Revelation was closed and the Successors of the Prophet laid no claim to a *magisterium.* Islam had perforce to respond to its own questions, with both questions and answers conditioned by their historical contexts. The context at Siffin had been political, but elsewhere the emphases were different. Politics was not absent from the Basrah of Hasan al-Basri, but other themes too can be heard, that of personal piety, for example, and questions of law. The climate would not have been very different at contemporary Mecca and Medina, save for one fact: the presence in Iraq of a growing number of converts drawn from the local Aramaean population and from the Iranians farther east.

The spread of Islam appears on maps as the extension of its military conquests, but behind the expanding frontiers of the *Dar al-Islam* were large bodies of people who either entered the *ummah* long after the armies had passed them by or else remained attached to their original beliefs. Officially Islam was concerned only with the juridical regulation of the non-Muslims within its borders; it neither proselytized nor persecuted the "Peoples of the Book." The actual situation was far more complex. The Islamic tax structure theoretically encouraged conversion, and the Arabs' early disinclination and inability in the face of the burgeoning administrative complexities of empire opened doors to the skilled and ambitious who could profess Islam.

The closure of the Muslim with the non-Arab, whether converted or not, provided, then, a new dimension to the context in which questions on the nature and powers of Allah were being posed at Basrah in the mid-eighth century. As far as we can reconstruct those conversations, the questions and answers unfolded dialectically, in the manner of Islamic jurisprudence. The substance of the discourse was Islamic, as were all the participants. But there were unseen witnesses—Wasil, for one, was aware of them—and some at least of the proposed solutions bear the marks of neither the *Qur'an* nor the findings of the lawyers. The version of Allah put forward by a certain Jahm ibn Safwan, for example, appears to owe far more to Plotinus and Parmenides than to anything uttered by the Prophet of Islam.

A great deal is known about translations done into Arabic from the Greek, and we can trace in some detail versions of the works of Greek philosophers made from about 800 onward. Before Ma'mun, however, the ground is far less firm. There are consistent reports that early Mu'tazilites of the reign of Harun were reading in the Greek philosophers, but we are at a loss to say whose books they were reading or how those works came into their hands. And yet the mystery runs deeper. The heresiographers identified many of those Mu'tazilite positions with those held half a century earlier by a group called the Jahmiyah. Their founder was Jahm ibn Safwan who professed what was, for that time and that milieu, an extraordinarily provocative theology and who was executed for political subversion in the waning days of the Umayyads. Jahm too gives the impression of having read Greek philosophers, though not, perhaps, of the variety that later became standard in Islam.

Whatever the source of his inspiration, Jahm appears to regard the universe from some Neoplatonic point of view. His version of Allah, for example, is not unlike Plotinus' One. God is not being; he is undefined and unlimited; he is neither his attributes nor his names, both of which are outside him and so created. Thus, both the power and the knowledge of Allah are created things, as is his utterance, the *Qur'an*. The utter transcendence and the ontological nakedness are pure Plotinus, and the projection of the divine attributes into created realities outside the First Principle recalls, though not in quite so explicit fashion, the Plotinian hypostases of Intelligence and the dynamic World Soul, the latter modified in Jahm to divine "power."

All of this had a most peculiar ring to the orthodox. They might applaud Jahm's desire to exalt the transcendence of Allah, but not at the price of separating him from those qualities which the *Qur'an* itself used to describe the Godhead: Allah is knowing and willing and powerful. Jahm had converted "power" into the most effective form provided by Greek theology, a unique and simple cause of everything; but in so doing he had relegated the traditional Qur'anic "power" to the status of a created being. Philo had done the same thing to Yahweh, and in somewhat the same fashion, but only after the Jews had become accustomed to speaking of God's wisdom and his speech as if they were something outside of him. There was as yet no such manner of speaking in Islam, and so Jahm's excursion into the metaphysics of cause and effect clashed abruptly with the anthropomorphic language of the *Qur'an.*

Though the traditionalists did not as yet perceive it, they were being presented with a dilemma. Jahm's single cause rendered all else an effect, a position that was, in the light of the *Qur'an,* an attractive one as far as its denial of human causality was concerned; according to Jahm, neither men nor bodies can possess true creative power, or even will or choice. The traditionalists could, and later did, assent to this, even at the price of placing a fearsome metaphysical "void" between the effects and their unique Cause. Perhaps the *Qur'an* already understood and intended that. Allah received no increase from man's acceptance of him nor suffered any loss from man's rejection. He cares and cares not, an attitude that makes tolerable the commonly held Islamic thesis that man's salvation or damnation is foreordained.

The traditionalist could console himself with the contemplation of the various "signs" (*ayat*) present in the natural order to illustrate God's way with the world. But this is cosmology and not sacramentalism; there is no supernatural dimension *within* the Islamic cosmos, none save the *Qur'an.* The revelation of the *Qur'an* was the Muslim's Incarnation, the sacramental intrusion of the eternity of Allah into the mortal cosmos that has its being in time. Jahm could not have it so. The cord was cut and the *Qur'an* became just another of the *ayat,* a natural sign pointing from effect to cause. Later traditionalists like Ahmad ibn Hanbal were revolted by this view and attacked both the Jahmiyah, who had originated the thesis, and the Mu'tazilites, who made it their own.

By his severe rationalism Jahm moved the question of the nature of God, his unity (*tawhid*) and his attributes into the forefront of conversations that up to that point had been struggling to disengage sin from treason on the one hand and from apostasy on the other. Hasan al-Basri knew nothing of the *tawhid* debate, but the evidence for his disillusioned follower and Jahm's contemporary Wasil is somewhat more circumstantial. We are told that at least some of Wasil's activity was turned toward missionary polemic, to the refutation of both Islamic heretics and nonbelievers all over the *Dar al-Islam.* It is precisely these latter, and particularly the dualist Manichaeans and Zoroastrians, with whom there was a quarrel over the unity and justice of God. Under the title of *zindiq,* dualists like Ibn al-Muqaffa' posed a new threat to Islam, and Wasil and his missionaries went out to confront them, armed, it would appear, with the strange new dialectic of Jahm ibn Safwan.

Both Wasil and Jahm had their differences with the Umayyads. Wasil's political stance can be inferred from his position vis-à-vis 'Ali, whom he considered preferable to 'Uthman as Caliph. Jahm's opposition to the regime has more direct testimony. Jahm, whose politics resembled the Murji'ite suspension of judgment, was the resident ideologue of a revolt that plagued the Umayyad administrators of Khurasan for more than ten years. Its leader was an Arab, Harith ibn Surayj, but his supporters included many *mawali,* who consistently reacted to such calls in the light of their own goals of social and economic equality in Islam. The Umayyad governor Nasr ibn Sayyar finally caught up with Harith in 746. Jahm was executed and the movement ran its course.

The last quarter century of Umayyad control in Khurasan was filled with many such political brush fires. Unwittingly the Umayyads or their agents provoked their own crises. When Hisham's governor Ashras ibn 'Abdallah made the first real effort to Islamicize Transoxania his very success created, as has been seen, fiscal chaos. Muslims were taxed at lower rates than non-Muslims and so conversions among the Iranians and Turks of Transoxania diminished Arab privilege accordingly. The Iranian landlords were equally unhappy with conversion because the egalitarian quality of Islam, no matter how stoutly resisted by the Arabs, was already undermining the old feudal order in the East.

While the *mawali* struggled to win a more spacious place for themselves in the new order, the Arabs, who had colonized Khurasan in considerable numbers, continued to waste themselves fighting over obscure points of honor imported into Khurasan from their now distant past on the Syrian and Arabian steppe. And beyond the Sogdian frontier were the Turks. Harith is a good example of both the climate and the tactics of Khurasan. His movement fed on social and economic unrest, but it was preached in the name of an expected *Mahdi*–Khurasan was almost as fertile in Messiahs as Palestine–who did not impress the Umayyads, but relied on the military support of the Turks, who *were* impressive to the lords of the province.

Khurasan, a rich province far from the Umayyad centers of power, was a tempting base for rebellion. The intellectual atmosphere in Basrah and Kufah was doubtless headier, and the streets of the Iraqi cities were filled with propagandists for every conceivable point of view. But the Umayyad armies could reach easily into Iraq, as had been demonstrated on a convincing number of occasions. They did not, however, reach quite so readily into Khurasan. The most important sectaries of the mid-eighth century, the Kharijites and the 'Alids, both understood this, but it was left to one branch of the latter to convert the possibilities into brilliant execution.

The 'Abbasids were not, of course, 'Alids except by self-designation. 'Abbas was an uncle of the Prophet, half-brother to Muhammad's father 'Abdallah and to Abu Talib, the father of 'Ali. He came to Islam relatively late, probably in 630, but so too had the Umayyads of Abu Sufyan. 'Abbas was a prosperous man–he had the pilgrims' water concession at Mecca both before Islam and after–and, like 'Uthman, he put at least part of that wealth at the disposal of the new Muslim community from his conversion until his death in 653. His service to the *ummah* was faithful but in no way distinguished, despite the later retouching of his role by 'Abbasid propagandists.

The family had, it is clear, no claim to the Caliphate either by political election, direct descent or charismatic power. Indeed, the first 'Abbasid to appear as a genuine political figure was 'Abbas' great-grandson Muhammad, who began laying claim to the Caliphate from about 718. That claim was apparently based on the alleged bequeathing of the title to Muhammad the 'Abbasid by one of the house of 'Ali, Abu Hashim, son of the Muhammad who was the offspring of 'Ali and a Hanafite woman. Hasan and Husayn were both sons of 'Ali and the Prophet's daughter Fatimah, but it was this collateral branch of the 'Alids represented by the son of Muhammad ibn al-Hanafiyah that delivered the tokens of legitimacy into the hands of the 'Abbasids.

After the disaster of Karbala' the Hasanid and Husaynid branches of the house of 'Ali had lapsed into political quietism. They did not vacate their claims to rule the *ummah*, to be sure, but they took no steps to press those claims against the early Umayyads. It was not until the accession of the 'Abbasids and the disappointment of whatever hopes they might have had on that occasion that the descendants of Hasan and Husayn allowed themselves to be prompted into overt political action. Muhammad ibn al-Hanafiyah was more forward, however, and permitted himself to be used by al-Mukhtar and the extremists among the *Shi'at 'Ali* at Kufah in 685. The bloody suppression of Mukhtar did nothing to dissipate the Shi'ite partisans of Muhammad ibn al-Hanafiyah, and at his death in 700 many of his partisans transferred their allegiance to his son Abu Hashim.

There at Kufah in the sedition of al-Mukhtar and the hapless Muhammad ibn al-Hanafiyah appear the unmistakable traces of the kind of esoteric Shi'ism that the mainstream of the later Shi'ah was so carefully to disavow. The Kufah group was known as the Kaysaniyah, a subdivision of the phenomenon unlovingly lumped together by the heresiographers as "extremists" (*ghulat*) in that they transgressed, in the name of the preeminence of 'Ali and his descendants, the essential humanity of Islamic prophethood: for the *ghulat* the *Imam* was more than a man; he was, by either divine infusion or metempsychosis, a divine being.

The Kaysaniyah held some such views about Muhammad ibn al-Hanafiyah and later about his son Abu Hashim. At the death of the latter without offspring in 716, a schism occurred among his followers. Not all of the Kaysaniyah accepted the story of the transference of the Imamate to Muhammad the 'Abbasid and so they maintained that Abu Hashim had not died at all but was merely "hidden," a notion that later found its way into more moderate Shi'ite ideology. Others among the Kaysaniyah apparently accepted the transference and went over to the 'Abbasid party.

Muhammad the 'Abbasid's claim to the Caliphate rested, then, upon an "extremist" premise: the transference of Abu Hashim's charismatic powers to himself, thence, after his death in 743, to his son Ibrahim, and finally, after Ibrahim's execution by Marwan II in 748, to the latter's brother Abu al-'Abbas, who reaped the reward of thirty years of propaganda and assumed the Caliphate. The later 'Abbasids disavowed their *ghulat* origins and rested their claims to legitimacy elsewhere—on the dubious merits of al-'Abbas himself, for example—but the evidence is overwhelming that they accepted, used, and then discarded the support of the extreme Shi'ites. And the chief centers of such support were in Khurasan.

The burden of holding Khurasan for the last Umayyads fell to the old campaigner Nasr ibn Sayyar, who governed there from 738 to 748. He reserved most of his severity for the Turks, who were pushed further back onto the steppe, while the Iranian Sogdians were treated with leniency, even those who had earlier converted to Islam and apostatized. No such leniency was shown to the 'Alid pretenders, and when one of them, Yahya, the son of the Husaynid Zayd who perished in Kufah in 740, came to Khurasan in 743, Nasr took prompt action: Yahya was arrested and crucified. The governor's quick repression of the 'Alid Yahya is in marked contrast with the amnesty he granted to Harith, who was nominally under the same banner but was in fact a local dissident protesting against local conditions.

Nasr also extended the Arabization and Islamicization of the empire to its eastern provinces. It was he who, under orders from Syria, reversed 'Umar II's policy and removed all non-Muslims from the Khurasanian *diwans*. He likewise ordered that henceforth its registers were to be kept in Arabic instead of the local Pahlevi. Some form of Persian was doubtless the common speech of Khurasan, and farther east, across the Oxus, the Iranian dialects of Sogdian and Khwarazmian still reigned unchallenged. Eventually these latter would be overwhelmed by either Arabic or Turkish, but the Iranian speech of Khurasan, by replacing its defective Pahlevi script with the more supple Arabic one, survived to find its own voice a century and a half after Nasr replaced it in the *diwans*.[72]

---

72. See Chap. IX, pp. 644–645.

For all his energy and intentions, Nasr did not solve the problems of Khurasan. He was himself a northern Arab, the successor of a Yemenite as governor in this province, and so a figure of contention among the Arab tribes there. Tribal tensions lay close to the surface in Khurasan, ready to be exploited by the next, and last, attempts at wresting the land from the Umayyads, that engineered by Abu Muslim. Abu Muslim was neither an Arab nor a Sogdian but an Iranian *mawla* attached to the Arabs of Kufah. There he was drawn into the same faction of the *Shi'at 'Ali* that stood behind Zayd ibn 'Ali a few years later. His mentor appears to have been a radical Shi'ite, but later, after a season in a Meccan prison in 741, Abu Muslim came under the instruction of the 'Abbasid *Imam* himself, Ibrahim ibn Muhammad, who sent him into Khurasan in 747 to direct the planned revolt there.

Abu Muslim's operations in Khurasan were skillfully handled. He rallied to himself not only the out-of-power Yemenite Arabs, but the non-Muslims upon whom the chief tax burden now rested, and finally, by some sophisticated manipulation, elements of the population that were only partially Islamicized. The heresiographers later turned Abu Muslim into a full-fledged religious innovator,[73] probably as a reflection of his earlier association with *ghulat* circles. This may be later Sunni propaganda, but the 'Abbasids were, at this time at least, still numbered among the ideological extremists and there is evidence of at least a political association between Abu Muslim and just such another contemporary innovator, the Iranian Bih'afrid.

Bih'afrid must have proclaimed his own prophethood in the same year that Abu Muslim came to Khurasan. That prophethood was a Zoroastrian one announcing the reform of the Iranian religion. The reform was unmistakably in the direction of Islam,

---

73. And the inspiration, if not the founder, of the curious sect of the Khurramiyah, who believed that the Imamate descended through Abu Muslim and then after his death through his daughter Fatimah. They held, in addition, a belief in the transmigration of souls, in the equality of all prophets and religions, and a hedonistic ethic. The Khurramiyah held a tenuous grip on one strong point or another, chiefly in Azarbayjan, down to the mid-ninth century.

some of whose practices, like daily prayer, almsgiving and the prohibition of wine, Bih'afrid incorporated into his revelation. The two men, the prophet and the revolutionary, appear to have worked together for a time, but in 749, when Abu Muslim was already crowned with success, he slaughtered his erstwhile ally at the request of a group that he judged more useful than Bih'afrid, the still powerful Zoroastrian clergy of Khurasan.

By 748 Abu Muslim and his supporters had taken Nishapur and driven Nasr from the province. His lieutenants meanwhile pressed the campaign further afield, Qahtabah in the west to the eventual destruction of the Umayyads on the Greater Zab and Abu Da'ud in the east. Their commander turned to internal affairs: Abu Muslim mercilessly rid himself of his Yemenite Arab allies and then provided a dark omen for the future by cruelly repressing a Shi'ite demonstration in Bukhara in 750. Again, this latter was an Arab affair prompted by religious rather than purely political motives and directed against the three years of continuous bloodletting by the 'Abbasids' premier agent. It availed nothing. Abu Muslim marshaled his now extensive army; Bukhara was taken and burned, and the Shi'ite rebels there suffered an exemplary death.

Marwan II, meanwhile, was fully engaged with enemies nearer to home, the Kharijites and still another wing of the Shi'ah, the partisans of 'Abdallah ibn Mu'awiyah, the great-grandson of 'Ali's brother Ja'far, who seized power in Kufah in 744 after attracting to his cause some of the followers of the dead Zayd ibn 'Ali. It was a few months after 'Abdallah's revolt that Marwan succeeded to the Caliphate. At first the Umayyad governor of Iraq appeared able to cope with the Shi'ite rebels, but once driven from Kufah they spread out into the provinces of Jibal, Ahwaz, Fars and Kirman, until almost all of western Iran was under their control.

Marwan had first to deal with the Kharijites, the implacable foes of the Umayyads since 661, but quiescent in Mesopotamia and Iraq since the successful campaigns waged against them by al-Hajjaj in the years between 692 and 698. Now, however, they took advantage of the disorders that marked the early years of Marwan's reign and summoned their strength for a final attack on the regime. By 745 the energetic Marwan had broken the Kharijites once again in their strongholds around Mosul[74] and could turn the main body of his troops against 'Abdallah ibn Mu'awiyah. Despite their apparent strength the Shi'ites too collapsed, and 'Abdallah unwisely withdrew into Khurasan, where Abu Muslim, the faithful servant of the 'Abbasid Imamate, had him executed in 747.

After 748 the 'Abbasids had no rivals in their assault on the Umayyads. But their adversary was still powerful; for three years Marwan had faced and defeated every challenge to his rule. In establishing himself he had, however, exposed the weaknesses of the regime. The contest between northern and southern Arabs passed from rivalry to open war at Marwan's accession. He threw in his lot with the northern Arab Qays in Mesopotamia and moved the entire apparatus of government from Damascus to the somewhat less hostile Harran. The outraged Syrians burst into open revolt and, during most of the time he was dealing with the Kharijite and Shi'ah uprisings in Iraq, Marwan was fighting a second war at his rear in Syria and attempting desperately to hold Egypt against invasion from the south.[75]

Until 748 the Caliph had held his ground everywhere but in Khurasan, which by then the Umayyads had irretrievably lost. Marwan celebrated his last triumph in the capture of the 'Abbasid *Imam* Ibrahim ibn Muhammad in 748, but the leadership passed easily to the latter's brother Abu al-'Abbas as the Khurasanian armies under Qahtabah approached Iraq from the east. They were already in possession of Rayy and Nihawand, and in 749 Qahtabah crossed into Iraq. Kufah was taken, and in October of 749 Abu al-'Abbas was publicly proclaimed Caliph.

---

74. The Kharijites of the Hadramawt were put down somewhat later, in 748.

75. The invaders were the armies of a great new empire arising in Nubia. From Aswan southward along both sides of the Nile lay great tribal federations like the Nobatae and the Blemmeyes who were well known to the Byzantines. They were reduced to tributory status in 453 and a century later they became Christians, and Monophysites. Muslim armies reached Nubia about 650, but apart from exacting treaties and tribute, they had little effect on the political life of the area. Indeed, they may have unwittingly welded the various kingdoms there into a new unity that led, in 745, to a large-scale invasion of Egypt and an assault on Fustat itself.

Marwan was at Harran, and at the beginning of 750 he finally bestirred himself in the face of a second 'Abbasid army approaching across northern Mesopotamia under the command of 'Abdallah, the uncle of Abu al-'Abbas. The two forces engaged on the banks of the Greater Zab, a northern tributary of the Tigris. The Umayyad tide was now running to full ebb: their squadrons were scattered, and there was little to stand in the way of the triumphant 'Abbasid march to Harran and finally Damascus. Marwan fled to Egypt, but he was captured and beheaded. The Umayyad line had come to an end.[76]

---

76. But only in the Near East. One member of the house, 'Abd al-Rahman, a grandson of the Caliph Hisham, barely escaped the blood bath that followed the battle on the Greater Zab. He escaped through Palestine and Egypt to North Africa. He crossed over into Spain in 755, claimed the Amirate for himself, and ruled there until his death in 788. Umayyad followed Umayyad at Cordova, until the last member of the family, Hisham III, was abandoned by his own subjects in 1031.

THE 'ABBASID CALIPHS

I. The Founding Fathers

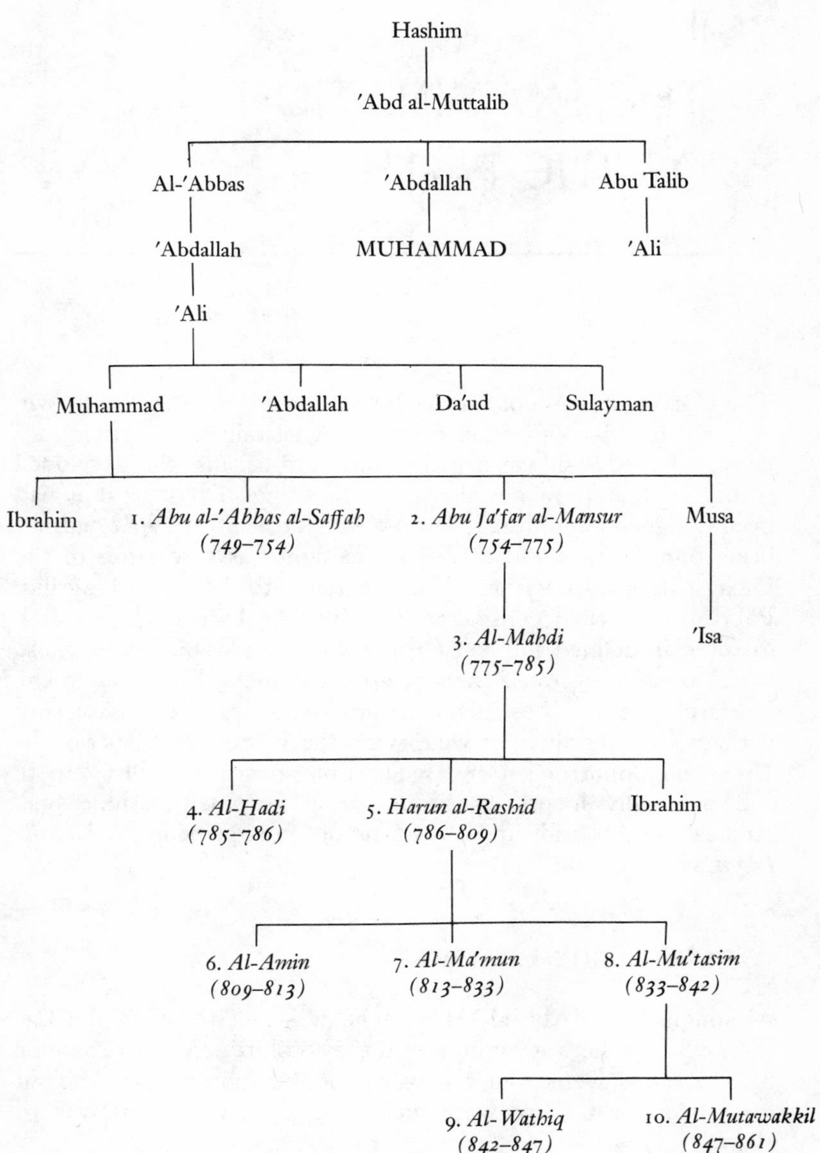

II

THE EXAMINATION OF THE FAITH

The Umayyads had not survived long enough to wrap themselves in the protective orthodox folds of an Islamic Law. Their successors the 'Abbasids managed it, but only because the developed theory of that Law was there for the using, almost as if it had been designed as an instrument of 'Abbasid legitimacy. It had not been, but the Law did come into existence as a reaction to the Umayyads' subordination of Islamic values to their own kingship. Political and tribal considerations aside, the Umayyads violated, in some ill-defined but very real way, the sensibilities of those Muslims who possessed the strongest and most direct ties to the Patriarchal Age. Those who designed and urged the Law, and perhaps the Kharijites as well, were the voices of opposition to Umayyad opportunism and secularism, an academically remote and politically inept opposition, but a genuinely Islamic one. And, as the 'Abbasids understood, no one could rule in the *Dar al-Islam* without them.

An Orthodox Caliphate

Although it was Abu al-'Abbas who was invested with the Caliphate in 749, he was by no means the absolute ruler that some of his successors were. Marwan was gone, but within the 'Abbasid movement itself there were men who possessed the power to

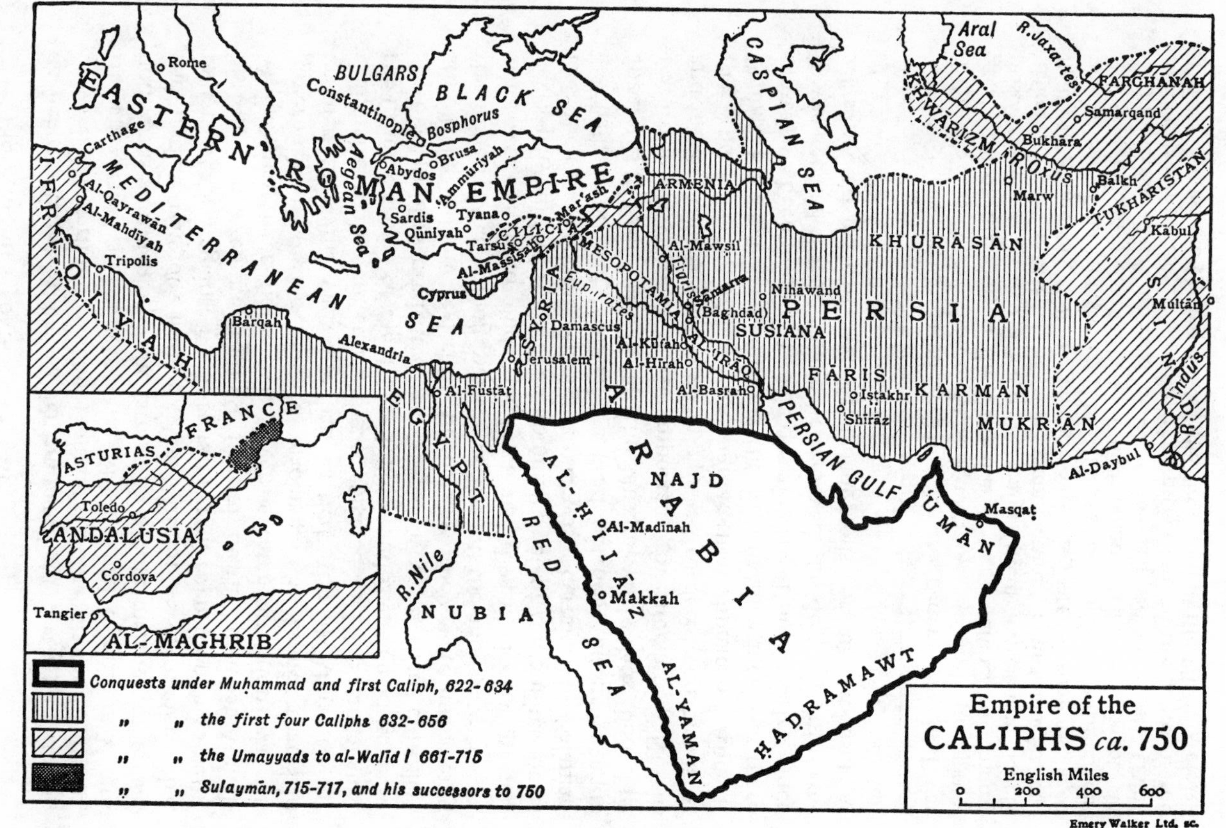
Empire of the
CALIPHS ca. 750
English Miles
0 200 400 600
Conquests under Muḥammad and first Caliph, 622-634
" " the first four Caliphs 632-656
" " the Umayyads to al-Walīd I 661-715
" " Sulaymān, 715-717, and his successors to 750
EASTERN ROMAN EMPIRE
MEDITERRANEAN SEA
BLACK SEA
CASPIAN SEA
Aral Sea
Aegean Sea
PERSIAN GULF
RED SEA
BULGARS
Rome
Constantinople
Bosphorus
Carthage
IFRIQIYAH
Al-Qayrawān
Al-Mahdīyah
Tripolis
Barqah
Alexandria
Abydos
Brusa
Ammūriyah
Sardis
Qūniyah
Tyana
Tarsus
CILICIA
Mar'ash
Al-Maṣṣīṣah
Cyprus
ARMENIA
MESOPOTAMIA
Al-Mawṣil
Tigris
Sāmarra
(Baghdād)
Euphrates
SYRIA
Damascus
Jerusalem
Al-Kūfah
Al-Ḥīrah
AL-'IRĀQ
Al-Baṣrah
Al-Fusṭāṭ
EGYPT
R. Nile
NUBIA
ARABIA
NAJD
AL-ḤIJĀZ
Al-Madīnah
Makkah
AL-YAMAN
ḤAḌRAMAWT
'UMĀN
Masqaṭ
PERSIA
SUSIANA
Nihāwand
KHURĀSĀN
FĀRIS
Iṣṭakhr
Shīrāz
KARMĀN
MUKRĀN
Al-Daybul
Marw
R. Oxus
KHWĀRIZM
Bukhāra
Samarqand
FARGHĀNAH
R. Jaxartes
Balkh
ṬUKHĀRISTĀN
Kābul
SIND
Multān
R. Indus
FRANCE
ASTURIAS
Toledo
ANDALUSIA
Cordova
Tangier
AL-MAGHRIB
Emery Walker Ltd. sc.

challenge Abu al-'Abbas. Chief among them was Abu Muslim, now seated without rival in Khurasan as the master of Arabs, Iranian *mawali* and Turks. Abu Muslim had campaigned with both arms and ideology, the latter an obscure mélange of *ghulat* and Iranian religious notions. Abu Muslim never invoked that potent weapon against his masters in Iraq, even though some of his followers attempted to do so after his death; but what Abu al-'Abbas may have noted with even greater attention was his governor's impressive military machine. The armies that had crushed the Umayyads and had carried Abu al-'Abbas to the Caliphal throne were still actively engaged in Khurasan against the Chinese armies of the T'ang dynasty and their Turkish allies.[1]

Abu Muslim's credentials for suspicion were, then, considerable. If he had any real rivals in the East, they were not among the military but among what was left of the moderate Shi'ah, who were coming to understand that an 'Abbasid victory was not necessarily an 'Alid one. The nominal chief of the Shi'ites, or at least their most visible representative, was a certain Abu Salamah al-Khallal who had been at the head of the 'Alid propaganda apparatus in Khurasan during Abu Muslim's early days there. His reward in the victory was the important governorship of Kufah, and it was Abu Salamah who in 749 had to decide on behalf of the 'Alids whether or not to recognize the Caliphate of Abu al-'Abbas. He acquiesced and took the oath of allegiance, but there must have been doubts in some quarters about his sincerity, since it was decided that he should be removed. To destroy him themselves would perhaps have been dangerous for the 'Abbasids at

---

1. The Chinese were mauled by Abu Muslim's generals on the River Talas in 751, and according to Muslim accounts, which did not pay a great deal of attention to the encounter, a large number of Chinese prisoners were taken to Samarqand, among them, apparently, paper-makers. Their knowledge of paper manufacture was introduced into Baghdad about 800, and the cheaper writing material soon replaced parchment in the chanceries. The Chinese took no such profit from the engagement. Talas marked the high point of Chinese influence in Central Asia. Over the next century they slipped back into China proper, leaving their rich commercial possessions in the hands of the Turkish tribes, the Qarluq east of the Jaxartes and the Uighurs closer to home.

this time, and so Abu al-'Abbas used his brother Abu Ja'far, the later Caliph al-Mansur, to sound out Abu Muslim on his willingness to dispatch the Shi'ite. Abu Muslim consulted the gods of politics and agreed. The deed was done by Abu Muslim's agents and the blame was put on the conveniently fanatical Kharijites.

Another of the Khurasanian Shi'ah, and a potential rival to both Abu al-'Abbas and Abu Muslim, was Sulayman ibn Kathir. He too was murdered about this time, and once again suspicion points to a collusion between the new Caliph and his governor in Khurasan. It was an odd failure on the part of Abu Muslim not to read his own death warrant in the murder of these two 'Alid propagandists. He may have connived at the deeds because he saw the victims as rivals rather than as paradigms of his own end. He was, at any rate, far too powerful to be toppled in the same way, and at Abu al-'Abbas' death in 754 Abu Muslim still governed in Khurasan, outwardly a loyal supporter of the new house but dangerously powerful in his own right.

It was Abu Muslim, too, who mustered the forces that carried Abu al-'Abbas' brother Abu Ja'far to the throne in despite of armed resistance to his succession. The new Caliph, now styled al-Mansur ("the Victorious"), however, had mistrusted Abu Muslim from the beginning and had counseled his brother to do away with his powerful viceroy in Khurasan. Al-Saffah had never felt secure enough to take that step, but al-Mansur, once he had dealt with his own rivals to the Caliphate, felt that he must. Abu Muslim was invited to present himself at court before returning to Khurasan. He was told by many that it would be unwise to do so, but Abu Muslim, oddly faithful to the end, did as he was bade and was peremptorily murdered.

Abu Muslim was the last of the major Shi'ite propagandists whose careful and dangerous work brought the 'Abbasids to the Caliphate. The first two Caliphs of that line coldly destroyed their Shi'ite agents, including Abu Muslim; there survived only the 'Alids themselves, the tokens of another, legitimist claim to the office. But whatever hopes the descendants of 'Ali may have harbored that an 'Abbasid victory against the Umayyads would lead to an 'Alid Caliphate must have quickly yielded to despair. The head of the Hasanid branch of the house, Hasan's grandson 'Abdallah, was apparently ready to accept the inevitable; he paid his dues to al-Saffah, who treated him with careful respect, and retired to Mecca. But 'Abdallah's sons Muhammad and Ibrahim were less willing to surrender the aspirations of the 'Alids into the hands of the Banu 'Abbas. Plans for a rebellion were hatched, plans which came to the ears of Mansur, who dispatched one of his own agents to serve as a provocateur in Mecca. The hapless 'Abdallah was easily entrapped into complicity and Mansur remanded him and the other 'Alids he could put his hands upon to prison, where 'Abdallah died sometime after 758.

The Hasanids had felt their expectations cheated when Abu al-'Abbas al-Saffah assumed the Caliphate in 749, and now his successor's treatment of the head of the family showed that they had little to expect from Mansur but further repression. Muhammad ibn 'Abdallah had been constructing an apparatus of sedition, but now that Mansur had passed over to the offensive, overt action was forced. Muhammad and his supporters freed the 'Alid captives at Medina in 762, but Mansur reacted quickly and in force, and the 'Alid revolt in the Hejaz was drowned in its own blood by Mansur's nephew 'Isa ibn Musa. Muhammad's brother Ibrahim was meanwhile trying to round up support in Basrah. There in lower Iraq the *Shi'at 'Ali* had more forceful partisans than the scholars and pietists of the Holy Cities, and some of the countryside round about actually passed into Ibrahim's control. Not for long, however. Mansur's Khurasanian troops, once again under the command of 'Isa, crushed Ibrahim and his supporters in 763.[2]

The 'Abbasids never intended to rule from Damascus as their Umayyad predecessors had done. Al-Saffah was proclaimed Caliph in Kufah, but he soon moved his court farther north, to al-Anbar on the Euphrates. Mansur was at first back in the south, at al-Hashimiyah, an encampment between Kufah and Hirah. For an 'Alid the site might have been ideal, but by now the 'Abbasids

---

2. Among the other aftereffects of this act was Mansur's decision to nominate 'Isa as his successor. At a later date the Caliph changed his mind in favor of his own son, and 'Isa had to be persuaded to waive his claims in favor of al-Mahdi. Blood ran thicker than nominations and al-Mahdi too had to ask 'Isa to step aside, this time in favor of the two princes Musa and Harun.

made no pretense of wearing 'Alid raiment and, moreover, the site of al-Hashimiyah was scarcely defensible, a decisive consideration for a new and shaky regime. Mansur chose again, this time more wisely, and in 762, under the supervision of the court astrologers, the foundations were put down for his new capital, *Madinat al-Salam*, the "City of Peace," more generally known, from the village it replaced, as Baghdad.

Baghdad was located on the west bank of the Tigris in the network of canals that connected that river with the Euphrates—al-Anbar was about thirty miles due west—and was set in the midst of a fertile and healthy plain not far north of al-Mada'in, the old Seleucid, Parthian and Sasanian capital of Seleucia-Ctesiphon. The city was carefully planned in the shape of a quartered circle, heavily protected by walls, canals and ditches, with a separate circular enclave at the heart of the larger city where the imperial quarters and *diwans* were located. The four quarters of the city, which could be closed and sealed at night, were settled by different ethnic or professional groups. Outside the city were the market and army camps.

Mansur moved into his still unfinished city in 763, and over the next few years the various quarters filled up. Directly opposite, on the east bank of the Tigris, the Caliph began the construction in 768 of a palace, mosque and camp for his son and heir al-Mahdi, and in due time, particularly after the Barmacids constructed their palaces there, the eastern city sprawled as widely as the original one on the west bank.

Intellectually, commercially and circumstantially, Baghdad inherited within the *Dar al-Islam* the role played by Alexandria in the old Hellenic *oikoumene*. Turbulent, cosmopolitan, invincibly successful, given more to scholarship and trade than to piety, the unrivaled center of arts and letters and the seat of the secular and religious power in Islam, Baghdad had, like its Egyptian counterpart, no past. Its present was frequently unruly, since rich and poor, Arab, Iranian and Turk, Shi'ite and traditionalist, Christian and Jew, scholar, merchant and soldier rubbed shoulders within its walls. Its only considerable drawback was a strategic one. The site was on the main route to Khurasan and provided, as Mansur noted, easy access to that important province. But it was remote from Islam's other frontier in Anatolia and from the western provinces. As Alexandria turned its back to Egypt and looked out on the Mediterranean, Baghdad faced the East. In founding it Mansur was, unwittingly, to be sure, surrendering his control of the West.

Mansur constructed Baghdad for internal rather than external reasons. The new city, the "City of Peace," was intended to begin a *novus ordo saeclorum* or, as the 'Abbasids called it, a "turning" (*dawlah*), in Islam. No longer would the Arabs rule as masters over defeated peoples. By reconciliation, by force if necessary, the dissidents would be brought together, a place made for the *mawali*, and Islam would pursue its course as a universalist religion with Baghdad as its symbolic Constantinople, Ibn Ishaq's *Life of the Prophet*, explicitly commissioned by Mansur, as its Gospel, and orthodoxy as its cachet.[3]

After the foundation of Baghdad the new mode of Muslim rule in the Near East becomes more evident. The Umayyads understood their role as Caliphs primarily as commanders in chief of the armies of Islam. They pushed forward the borders of the *Dar al-Islam*, while at home they attempted to preserve the rule of their house against insurrection. The Umayyads exhibited a discernible personal style during the century of their sovereignty,[4] but for the rest they left the administration of their empire in the hands of their *amirs* and the local municipalities. The 'Abbasids did not neglect the imperial style, but they encouraged as well the growth of an administrative bureaucracy which they themselves controlled and through which they could oversee, as their interests dictated, the *Dar al-Islam*.

In its earliest usage *diwan* meant the register in which were

---

3. All the previous Caliphs had ruled in their own name. Mansur, actually Abu Ja'far, was the first to assume an honorific and to characterize himself and his reign with *al-Mansur billah* ("Victorious by the hand of Allah").

4. The impression may not be a quite accurate gauge of the reality. The Umayyads can be read off only in their buildings, their court poets, and in the historiography of their opponents, who, like the Imperial Roman historians, concentrated their fire on the personalities of the rulers whose regimes they disavowed.

inscribed the pensioners of merit in Islam and, above all, the warriors (*muqatilah*) who stood at the heart of Muslim society under the Umayyads. These documents were kept in Damascus and the provincial garrisons, and were administered by the *amir*. It seems likely, too, that there arose a modest administrative apparatus around the registers and that the word *diwan* was already being used to describe both the register and the machinery by which it was administered.

In the latter half of the eighth century the demographic face of Islam was changing, however. Conversions were accelerating, and the *mawali* were forcing themselves into the counsels of state. The conquests too had slowed to a halt, and Islam's soldiery could no longer be paid out of booty. In the face of these changes the pension roll evolved into a military bureau that undertook to recruit, arm, and pay out salaries to the new professional army of the Khurasanian *mawali*.

'Abbasid Baghdad had two other major bureaus, a chancery and a department of finances, to regulate the now complex problems of records, taxes and archives. The Caliph could extend long clerical fingers into every corner of his holdings, and the method he used, where we can trace its antecedents, was that of the Shahs before him. The Umayyads had needed military commanders, *amirs*, but their 'Abbasid successors surrounded themselves with secretaries (*katib;* pl. *kuttab*) whose fields of ambition and power were the new Caliphal *diwans*.

The 'Abbasid *dawlah* was no longer the preserve of an Arab warrior aristocracy but was administered, in the style of other Near Eastern clerical regimes, by an aristocracy of service in which the Iranian *mawali*, by their skills and not by design, eventually took a prominent place. But it was a place shared with others, Muslim Arab lawyers, Aramaean Christian physicians and scholars, and Turkish soldiery. All these groups had their talents as well as their problems, and the Iranians in particular had a long tradition of Sasanian service behind them.

The Caliph had, then, new helpers in the business of administration. Chief among them was the vizier (*wazir*), who played an extraordinarily important role in the early history of the 'Abbasids. The word *wazir* is an Arabic one and means, in its nontechnical sense, "a helper." Its earliest use in a political context was in connection with al-Mukhtar who was called "the helper (*wazir*) of the family of Muhammad," a reference to his revolutionary services on behalf of the 'Alid cause in Kufah.[5] There was another such "helper" of the 'Alids, the same Abu Salamah who directed the Shi'ite propaganda in Khurasan, accepted the oath of allegiance on behalf of the still-undesignated al-Saffah and so became, in the later histories of the office, the first 'Abbasid "vizier."

Abu Salamah may have borne the title, but he hardly performed the functions associated with the vizierate under the 'Abbasids. For Mansur, and even more clearly under his son al-Mahdi, the vizier was a personal assistant, primarily a scribe, who conducted the Caliph's correspondence, supervised his personal wealth and, perhaps most importantly, was given charge of the education of the crown prince. It was doubtless this latter charge that shortly promoted the vizier into the chief counselor and confidant for each new generation of Caliphs.

The Umayyads had often delegated extensive powers to others —to Ziyad, to his son 'Ubaydallah, and to Hajjaj in Iraq, for example. Their office was, however, that of an *amir*, the military governor of an enlarged territory. The vizier's powers, on the other hand, were undefined and personal rather than geographical and military. That such a personal office was highly flexible in its application is immediately apparent, and before long the vizier was given, or expropriated, control over the Caliphal *diwans* and, in the cases of Harun al-Rashid and the sons of Khalid ibn Barmak, the military powers of the Amirate as well.

Khalid was originally associated with the 'Alids Muhammad and Ibrahim but was nonetheless taken on by al-Saffah and given an important financial post. Under Mansur he continued to exercise a considerable, if discreet, authority, and his grandson al-Fadl was raised as a foster brother to the Caliph's own grandson and the future Caliph, Harun, a relationship that was to have a profound influence on both men. The young heir to the throne, al-

---

5. See Chap. I, pp. 99–100.

Mahdi, was likewise placed under the tutelage of an experienced secretary-*mawla* to train him in the arts of government.[6]

When al-Mahdi assumed the Caliphate at the death of his father in 775 he already had some experience as Mansur's delegate in that office. He possessed as well the experienced tutor Abu 'Ubaydallah, who now passed, on al-Mahdi's accession, into the role of the chief secretary (*katib*) of the imperial government. Whether Abu 'Ubaydallah was or was not officially called by the name, he clearly exercised the powers later connected with the office of vizier. His expertise as secretary, financial overseer and appointments counselor made it natural for the Caliph to lean heavily upon his *katib* in the increasingly complex business of government, and it was probably under Abu 'Ubaydallah's influence that a major revision was made in the tax structure at this time—in place of a fixed taxation on produce, al-Mahdi instituted a method of proportional taxation that would take into account the size of the annual crop and fluctuations in prices.

Like most of his successors in office, Abu 'Ubaydallah eventually fell from grace. According to some, he was a crypto-Manichaean, but more likely he was dislodged by a rival, a certain Ya'qub ibn Da'ud, who earlier had been part of the circle of Nasr ibn Sayyar, the Umayyad governor of Khurasan, and then was implicated in the rebellions of 762. This last connection merited him imprisonment for most of Mansur's reign, but once he became the beneficiary of an amnesty, Ya'qub caught the ear of al-Mahdi and soon succeeded in dislodging Abu 'Ubaydallah.

The key to Ya'qub's success may have been a promise of solving the 'Alid problem. Since the bloody events of 762 in Medina and Kufah the Hasanids had held their peace. There was, however, activity among the Husaynid branch of the 'Alids, propagandistic rather than overtly political in nature. As later events

---

6. Al-Mahdi's literary education was not neglected. To act as his instructor in the traditional Arab arts of grammar and poetry Mansur reached among his political prisoners for al-Mufaddal al-Dabbi, a grammarian implicated in the revolt of the 'Alids in 762. The royal tutor put together the *Mufaddaliyat*, an anthology of 128 early Arabic odes, for the benefit of his pupil.

were to show, there was growing up among the followers of Zayd ibn 'Ali (d. 740) and of his nephew Ja'far al-Sadiq (d. 765) a serious body of theory on the Imamate. The full consequences were not felt until the reigns of Harun (786–809) and Ma'mun (813–833), but already al-Mahdi may have sensed the spirit of what was going on. It was during his Caliphate, at any rate, in 780, that the official 'Abbasid claim was changed from the earlier version of having been bequeathed the Caliphate by the 'Alid Abu Hashim to an emphasis on the virtues of al-'Abbas himself. The new account freed the 'Abbasids from their earlier 'Alid connections, but al-Mahdi nonetheless made some attempts at reconciling the Husaynids. And Ya'qub, who had connections with the followers of Zayd, was his instrument. Ya'qub, it was reported, zealously filled high government posts with known Zaydites.

The Zaydis were moderates in the Shi'ite spectrum, but the "extremists" and their Khurasanian congeners were not so tractable. The 'Abbasids' loose grip on the East, now, as under the Umayyads, a redoubt of rebels and reformers, created continuous problems for al-Mahdi's governors there. Not long after his accession the Caliph had to face a serious uprising of Kharijites in Khurasan. The Umayyads had dealt long and, in the end, unsuccessfully with the Kharijites, and Marwan's defeat of their loose but dangerous confederacy in 747 had signaled the end of the movement in Mesopotamia and Iraq. There were still Khawarij there under the 'Abbasids, but they were of a moderate stripe, disinclined to political action and the harsh measures and judgments of their Azraqi brethren.[7] Most of the extremists fled to eastern Iran, to Khurasan and Sijistan, and it was there that a certain Yusuf al-Barm, a *mawla*, led a fiercely contested uprising among the Kharijite faithful that had no real end until the time of Ma'mun.

---

7. One such group of moderates, founded at Basrah sometime about 685 by an 'Abdallah ibn Ibad and called after him the Ibadiyah, continued their scholarly and religious activity down into 'Abbasid times. Their "converts" spread across the *Dar al-Islam*, from Basrah to Oman, Zanzibar, and to Ifriqiyah and the Maghreb, where the Ibadis have had a long continuous history.

Social dissent may have reinforced the Kharijite call to action, but their primary appeal was religious, for a purified Islam as a "communion of saints"—with all others, whatever their view of Islam, banished as infidels and so subject, together with their wives and children, to the sudden penalty of political murder; since the time of Nafi' ibn al-Azraq the extreme Khawarij did not hesitate before assassination. They had condemned themselves, in fact, to outlawry by their extreme views, and it was only among those Kharijites who, like the Najdites and the Ibadis, had actually gained political control that extremism yielded to more pragmatic considerations. The Azraqis pursued their fanatic vision into oblivion.

The wraith of Abu Muslim continued to haunt Khurasan. After their leader's murder in 754, a number of groups came forward either to avenge his death or to claim his prophetic mantle. The shapes and motives of their concern remain obscure, but there is an unmistakable connection with Zoroastrianism and with Iranian theories of prophecy. One of the most striking of the disturbances connected with the legacy of Abu Muslim was that led by Hashim ibn Hakim, a native of Khurasan and an associate of Abu Muslim, who claimed that the prophetic emanation previously manifested in the Jewish prophets, in Jesus, and in Abu Muslim himself was now operative within him. Hashim was, in effect, a divine being, and to save his followers from the overpowering vision of his face—or because he was extremely ugly, as others said—he habitually wore a green veil across his features. The "Veiled One," al-Muqanna', made his first public claims in 776, and over the next few years he attracted numbers of peasants to his standard. His greatest triumph was the conquest of Bukhara, but the "men in white," as his followers were called, could not sustain themselves in the face of the Caliph's armies. Before the end, in 783, al-Muqanna' and a number of the faithful immolated themselves as the first step on their journey to Paradise.

Movements like that of Ibn al-Muqanna' appear to the modern historian as a highly complex and syncretized phenomenon compounded of both social and religious ingredients. The authorities at Baghdad were universally inclined to dismiss the first and reduce the religious elements to something considerably simpler than our own recipes demand. On the testimony of what followed, al-Mahdi read the chief danger to Islam as arising from the residual Manichaeism to be found among his subjects. In 763, the same year that al-Muqanna' was brought down, the Caliph established a special inquisitorial tribunal in Baghdad to root out and punish *zandaqah*, a usefully vague term generally understood at that time as crypto-Manichaeism and the same one used against Abu 'Ubaydallah and even earlier against Ibn al-Muqaffa'.

The *zindiq* (in Pahlevi *zandik*) was originally a Manichaean, so called by the orthodox Zoroastrians of the Sasanian Empire because he practiced *zand*, or interpretation, on the Avestan Scriptures. Within Islam the understanding of the term was considerably looser. In Iraq charges of *zandaqah* arose out of the transformation of the *diwans* of state by the influx of Iranian scribes and secretaries only recently converted to Islam. Their challenge to the literary ways of the Arabs gave rise to the controversy around cultural nationalism known as *shu'ubiyah*,[8] and the merits of Arab and Iranian were debated in literary circles until well into the tenth century. And if the 'Abbasids had some stake in Arab literary classicism, it was chiefly by reason of the connection of that classicism with traditionalist sentiment in religion.

The traditionalists (*ahl al-hadith*) had played their part in unseating the Umayyads and generally welcomed the 'Abbasids as defenders of the "customary way" (*sunnah*) in matters of religion. But *sunnah*, in religion as well as in literature, was associated in the traditionalists' minds with the Arab, the original beneficiary of Islam. The *mawali* had come to both Arabic and Islam by conversion, an acceptable route but one that did not always engender confidence in the results. Conversion to Islam was simple, a mere profession of faith, and it opened up ways to wealth, power and preferment. In many of the Iranian *mawali* families the practice of Zoroastrianism or Manichaeism lay but a generation distant and so for the pious, the envious or the merely suspicious, the accusation of *zandaqah* easily suggested itself.

The 'Abbasids had of necessity to live with both factions. The

---

8. See Chap. VI, pp. 401–407.

mawali dominated the government bureaus and were challenging Arab literary pretensions; the traditionalists, on the other hand, reigned supreme in the religious courts and in the study of the Islamic Law and the Qur'anic sciences. The former group enabled the 'Abbasids to rule; the latter legitimized that rule and, at base, represented popular opinion everywhere west of Iran. The brief 'Abbasid experiment of repudiating religious traditionalism conducted by Ma'mun and his two successors was obviously unsuccessful.

The precepts of Islam, associated as they were with an alien Arabism, must indeed have sat lightly upon many of the *mawali*. No secretary, al-Jahiz claimed, was even known to have taken the *Qur'an* as his bedside reading. Baghdad, its court and its *diwans* did not exude an odor of piety, and it was this secular and hedonist style apparent in both the lives and the poetry of the 'Abbasid courtiers that aroused the traditionalists and doubtless lay behind many of the charges of *zandaqah* raised in Iraq in the eighth century. Atheism, which was associated in the Muslim mind not with a complete denial of the existence of God but with a belief in an impersonal fate or some form of polytheism, was not always connected with a theological position but was often a rhetorical accusation of libertinage.

Farther east *zandaqah* meant something quite different. There at the edge of the Caliph's reach many men wore their refusal of Islam in a more provocatively open manner. The religious movements from Bih'afrid to al-Muqanna' did not conceal themselves under the cover of conversion. They rejected both the revelation of Islam and its Caliphal authority. They took up arms against the latter, but their ideological weapons, while not overtly Manichaean, owed something to that form of Gnosticism in their dualism and their insistence on a severe asceticism. If *zandaqah* implied libertinage in Iraq, it just as often suggested a suspicious asceticism in Khurasan.[9]

The *zindiq* was a hunted figure from the time Islam first came in contact with Iran in the mid-eighth century. By al-Mahdi's reign, however, *zandaqah* was somewhat more public than it had

---

9. An association that later led to serious difficulties for the Sufis; see Chap. VI, p. 426.

been earlier, not merely in its Khurasanian activist versions, but in learned circles in the capital, where, on the testimony of the historian Mas'udi, the works of Mani, Bar Daysan and Marcion, accredited dualists all, were circulating in Arabic translation[10] and treatises were being composed on the religious systems of these three men.

Mani and Bar Daysan, both of whom died in the third Christian century, still had their followers in the eighth,[11] and even though learned Muslims like Ibn al-Nadim, who was fairly well instructed on both men, could distinguish between the "Mananiyah" and the "Daysaniyah," the doctrines of the two had run together on many substantial points. In Muslim eyes both groups professed dualism, because they posited two eternal principles, light and darkness, as the causes of good and evil, associated in secret societies and practiced a strange asceticism.[12]

The fate of the Manichaeans, who left a trail of their own Scriptures behind them—the Daysaniyah were not scriptuaries in any but the Christian sense; they accepted the Gospels—is the better documented. They suffered grievously under the Sasanians in proportion as the Shahs advanced the notion of an Orthodox Zoroastrian Church, and as a result their energies were directed beyond the boundaries of the Sasanian Empire, as a competitor to Christianity in the West and as an aggressively proselytizing faith among the merchants and nomads of eastern Iran and Transoxania. A large number of fragments from the Manichaean Scriptures written in Syriac and the mercantile lingua franca of Central Asia—Sogdian—have been found scattered through the caravan cities between Balkh and the borders of China. There were Manichaean emissaries in Peking in 694, and shortly there-

---

10. Probably done from Syriac into Arabic by the son of Ibn al-Muqaffa'.

11. Marcion, however, did not, and his inclusion with the other two is likely a historical reflex. The Christian heresiographers frequently linked all three together and the Muslims continued to vilify them en masse.

12. The same "men in white" who followed the charismatic al-Muqanna' were, according to a Christian heresiographer, a feature of the Manichaean movement.

after the religion won its only national status when Manichaeism became the established religion of the Turkish Uighurs.

Down to 751 the great trade routes that wound across Central Asia between the steppe to the north and the Tibetan plateau to the south were in the hands of the Chinese. Their defeat by the armies of Abu Muslim at the river Talas was merely the beginning of the Chinese woes. T'ang China was racked with civil wars between 755 and 763, and to solve his problems the Emperor resorted to an expedient on which the Arabs would also one day rely: he summoned in from the Mongolian steppe his northern Turkish neighbors, the Uighurs.

The conversion of the Uighurs was doubtless accomplished by the Sogdians, Iranian commercial middlemen who ranged across Central Asia from their home in Transoxania to the Chinese capital at Lo-yang. The Uighur *khan* became the official protector of Manichaeism in China,[13] and the political master of the commercial oasis principalities, many of them Sogdian in culture, that ringed the Tarim basin in Sinkiang. In the eighth century these were merely Uighur colonies, but in the second half of the tenth century, when the Uighurs were driven from Mongolia by fresh bands of Turks, these caravan cities became the center of the Uighur domains.

Thrust by military pressures from their environment on the Orkhon into this highly cultured milieu, the Uighurs were the first of the Turkish peoples to move into the orbit of the higher cultures and to begin, by their adoption of the Sogdian alphabet, the long process of converting the Turkish oral tradition into a literary one. Their Manichaeism appears to have suffered in the

---

13. China under the T'ang dynasty was subject to a variety of religious influences from Western sources. In addition to Buddhists and Manichaeans, Nestorian Christians were established there from the seventh century. A bilingual pillar erected at Sian-fu explains, in Syriac and Arabic, that the Nestorian Church first came to China in 635 and was favorably received. It apparently flourished until about 840, when the disappearance of Uighur influence from China caused the Chinese to react against not only the Uighur-sponsored Manichaeism but all foreign cults, and particularly Christianity. Chinese Buddhism survived the pogrom, but Christianity and Manichaeism did not.

process. There were Manichaeans in Sinkiang, but there were Buddhists and Christians there as well, and the later Uighurs who lorded it in their caravan cities in the tenth century were mostly either Buddhists or Nestorians.

Until the Uighurs arrived in force in Central Asia the cities there had been, for long centuries, Indo-European at base. There was a mixture of Chinese influences, to be sure, but the predominant culture in Sinkiang was, on the evidence of the literature and art, either Iranian or Indian. The caravan cities reflected, in the end, changes on the steppe itself, which for three or four centuries had been dominated not, as of old, by Iranian tribes but by Altaic peoples, chiefly Turks. First the Tü-kueh, then the Uighurs, the Qarluq, and the Qarakhanids controlled the eastern approaches to Iran; and Sinkiang too, where Iranian culture had put down firm roots, had necessarily to reflect that fact. The Turkification of Sinkiang, and eventually of Bactria and Transoxania, began with the Uighurs.

Manichaeism had, then, a powerful redoubt in Central Asia where it peacefully shared oases and steppe with Nestorian Christianity and Buddhism, until Islam finally crossed the Oxus and won the Turks to itself. Most of its propagandists must have come to Iraq from eastern Iran once Islam had overthrown the hostile Sasanians. Their career there, at the heart of the Caliphate, was anything but happy, since both the Manichaeans and the Daysanites were far more than curious religious survivals from the third century; they were the bearers of an elaborate metaphysic and a considerable scientific heritage. This was only beginning to be understood in al-Mahdi's day, but later, during the reign of Ma'mun (813–833), when more of the dualists' intellectual foundations were laid bare, the Muslims were constrained to engage *zandaqah* as a theology rather than as an invitation to immorality or political dissent. For the time, however, al-Mahdi could still content himself with the blunt instrument of an inquisition.

Al-Mahdi died in August of 785 and almost immediately the oft-repeated mischief of a disputed succession began to appear. His two sons Musa and Harun, the former the governor of Jurjan, the latter of the border provinces of Azarbayjan and Armenia, each had his own advisers and administration. Both establishments had the seal of legitimacy upon them, and it was impossible to think that either would evaporate at the command of the other. Al-Mahdi must have known this and, at the moment of his death, was en route to Musa to persuade him to vacate his admittedly prior claim in favor of Harun. His chances of success, one suspects, were exceedingly slim.

In any event, it was Harun who displayed the magnanimity and acknowledged his brother as Caliph. Musa al-Hadi's reign was brief (785–786), confused and violent. The violence was directed chiefly at the remaining 'Alids and then, in the end, against the Caliph himself. Stories circulated at a later date that al-Hadi intended doing away with Harun on the very day he was himself murdered. There were equally plausible tales that the ruin of al-Hadi was encompassed by the formidable Queen Mother Khayzuran who, like her husband, favored their younger son Harun and bought him the throne with the blood of his brother.

Like his father before him, Harun came to the Caliphate with a full complement of *mawali* secretary-tutors who were skilled and ready to assume the running of the machinery of the empire. Chief among them was Yahya, son of the Khalid ibn Barmak who had been associated with the 'Abbasids from the early days of their struggle for power. Khalid had served, in one capacity or another, al-Saffah, Mansur, al-Mahdi and the Crown Prince Harun before his death in 781. During the reign of al-Mahdi he was assisted by his son Yahya, who in 775 was appointed governor of Azarbayjan. Yahya's own son al-Fadl was raised as the foster brother of the younger of the two 'Abbasid heirs, Harun. Now, with the accession of Harun, the family of Barmak reached the top of the Caliphal bureaucracy: Yahya was appointed vizier, the chief of the government *diwans* and the adviser of the Caliph, a post he held during seventeen years of unparalleled influence and power.

Yahya was only a second-generation Muslim. His grandfather Barmak—this was not actually a name but a title—was the hereditary superior, or *parmak*, of the famous Buddhist *stupa* located near Balkh. The monastery may have been destroyed during or immediately after the conquest of eastern Khurasan, but Barmak's sons emigrated, at any rate, to the new city of Basrah, embraced Islam and became the *mawali* of an Arab tribe there.

Yahya was a man of considerable government experience and close personal ties with both the Caliph and his mother, and he took a firm grip on the administration from the outset. He associated his two sons Ja'far and al-Fadl in his governance, so that Harun had in effect delegated vast powers to a triumvirate. Harun's predecessors had had assistants in the administration of the empire, and even in Mansur's time the *diwans* were professionally organized and staffed by lettered *mawali*. One *katib* or another had been the Caliph's chief administrator before, whether officially designated as vizier or not. No one of them possessed, however, the power of Yahya and his sons: they ran the *diwans*, had possession of the Caliph's personal seal, presided over the court of complaints and had a powerful voice in all appointments up to and including those of governors of the provinces.

The functions discharged by the two sons of Ja'far varied over the years. They were appointed tutors to the crown princes, al-Fadl for al-Amin and Ja'far for Ma'mun. In addition, al-Fadl was the governor of the frontier provinces of western Iran, where he put down an 'Alid revolt, and from 793 to 796 he presided over the administration of Khurasan. His governorship of that turbulent province was firm and successful; civil order was kept, a building program was begun, and Muslim rule was extended deep into Transoxania. Ja'far was a different sort. He too held governorships—Egypt, Syria and later Khurasan—but he was more frequently to be found in Baghdad. Harun enjoyed the company—and perhaps the sexual favors—of the witty, learned and elegant Ja'far, who, like his Caliph sovereign, threads his way through the narrative of the *Thousand and One Nights*.

Earlier, while he was still the heir, Harun had been given important responsibilities in his father's war against the Byzantines, a venture in which he had the assistance of both Khalid and Yahya. Now, during his own reign, he enlisted his own son al-Qasim in the fighting, which went on with only temporary interruptions during the twenty-three years of Harun's Caliphate. At first Harun contented himself with defensive measures, in rebuilding the ruined fortresses of the frontier and in establishing defense zones along the forward front in Anatolia and in the rear between Antioch and the Euphrates.

The Queen Mother died in 790, and thereafter Harun took a somewhat greater initiative in the governance of his vast holdings. The two sons of Yahya were securely in charge of the most troublesome of the provinces, and in 796 Harun, who once led a Muslim army to within sight of Constantinople, set up quarters at Raqqah on the Euphrates, where he assumed personal command of another Anatolian invasion. During the preceding ten years his lieutenants had been successful against the armies of Byzantium, and in 794 had even reached Amisus on the Black Sea. Now, with Harun in charge, there were further successes, but the fatal blow was never delivered, despite the fact that first the Emperor Constantine and then his mother Irene were deposed by their subjects between 797 and 802. The Byzantines still held the flanks of Anatolia by their possession of the Aegean naval stations like Cyprus, Rhodes and Crete,[14] and by reason of the dubious situation in Armenia, where Islam made little progress against the Christian nobility.

In the end, however, it was Harun's own troubles at home that harassed him as effectively as his Byzantine rivals. Shortly after the Byzantines ended the hostilities in Anatolia by agreeing to pay an annual tribute to the Caliph, al-Fadl lost his political footing at the head of Harun's government and was stripped of many, though not all, of his powers. The reasons, like those behind the total degradation of the Barmacid family four years later in 802, are not entirely clear, but al-Fadl's tolerant, if not favorable, policy toward the 'Alids clashed with Harun's own views on the subject, and that disagreement may have been the cause of his sudden fall from grace.

Harun, like Mansur and al-Mahdi before him, was deeply concerned about the various 'Alids in the empire and kept them under continuous scrutiny. In only one instance was there serious trouble, a revolt of one of Hasan's grandsons, Yahya ibn 'Abdallah in Daylam in 792. His presence there came about through the

---

14. The Arabs raided these islands and did considerable damage both before and during Harun's reign, but the strong points held and their naval installations were denied the Muslims until the next century.

connivance of the very man who was later sent to root him out, al-Fadl ibn Yahya, who had earlier provided the 'Alid with a safe conduct for himself and his men into the safety of remote Daylam. Al-Fadl, it is true, eventually negotiated Yahya's surrender,[15] but he displayed no more caution on his next 'Alid assignment. When Musa al-Kazim, the Husaynid, later acknowledged as the seventh Shi'ite *Imam*, was put under his guard, al-Fadl treated him somewhat more kindly than Harun thought proper, and the Barmacid was saved from the Caliph's wrath only by the intervention of his father, Yahya, who reassured the Caliph by proceeding directly to Baghdad and ordering the execution of the unfortunate Musa (799).

Musa's death must have had dangerous consequences for the chief 'Alid theologians. The best-known of them, Hisham ibn al-Hakam, who was an open adherent of Musa and his father, Ja'far al-Sadiq, had already died—probably in 795—before Musa met his end, but another of the Shi'ite divines of a far more activist bent was still in circulation. Sulayman ibn Jarir was reckoned a Zaydi Shi'ite—that is, one of the supporters of the Imamate of Zayd, son of 'Ali Zayn al-'Abidin. The Shi'ites were apparently in some disarray. Zayd had perished in an abortive revolt in 740, and since that time the *Shi'at 'Ali* were divided between the passivist leadership of Ja'far al-Sadiq (d. 765) and the uncertainties of Zayd's son 'Isa (d. 783). Harun was firmly in control, however, and the sons of both *Imams*, Musa ibn Ja'far and Ahmad ibn 'Isa, were kept under surveillance. Many of the Shi'ite activists seem to have gathered around Sulayman ibn Jarir, who in 792 recognized the Imamate of Yahya in Daylam. That too aborted, but Sulayman appears to have escaped retaliation.

In addition to the politicians and their religious supporters among the *Shi'at 'Ali*, Harun had also to reckon with the latest turnings in another stream of theological discourse that had been going on for nearly a century, first at Damascus, then in Basrah, and now in these latter days in Baghdad. The Umayyads had had

15. Harun treated his captive treacherously. Once Yahya was in his hands he repudiated the instrument of surrender drawn up by al-Fadl and had the 'Alid imprisoned and, in the end, executed.

their problems with the various advocates of free will known as the Qadariyah, chiefly because the ruling house found the opposing view, that Allah was responsible for all, more to their political taste. Under the 'Abbasids the issues had shifted somewhat. *Qadar* was still being debated, but the range of theological discussion had broadened to include the incendiary questions of whether or not the *Qur'an* was created, the ontological status of God's attributes and, inevitably, the nature of the Islamic Imamate.

Harun must have taken the position once espoused by the Umayyads and now paradoxically the property of Islamic traditionalists (*ahl al-hadith*). He pursued, it is reported, the leading Qadarite of the day, Bishr al-Marisi, for more than twenty years, while Bishr ibn al-Mu'tamir, one of the earliest of the new school of Mu'tazilites, whose theses were almost indistinguishable from those of Bishr al-Marisi, except for their more overt Shi'ism, was also imprisoned for a time. Ibn al-Mu'tamir was eventually released because of a popular outcry—he was a poet as well as a theologian—and lived well into the reign of Ma'mun to see his school established as the orthodoxy of Islam. There were other casualties; Ibn al-Mu'tamir's student Thumamah was also detained on charges of being a *zindiq*, and similar accusations were laid against the theologian Dirar ibn 'Amr.

Some of these theologians who had begun to gather at Baghdad, those known as Mu'tazilites and whose origins went back to some of the theses of Wasil ibn 'Ata' at Basrah, were making common cause with the Zaydite wing of the *Shi'at 'Ali*. Thus there came into being a mixed theological coalition of Mu'tazilites, Zaydis and Barmacid viziers set within the broadening cultural horizons of Baghdad. The Barmacids encouraged that broadening, and the new Mu'tazilites were nourished by it; under Barmacid patronage Arabic translations were made of Indian and Iranian works and, for the first time, of the writings of the Greeks.

This was not treason by any standard, and there is every sign that Harun encouraged his ministers' patronage of the translation activity. Without understanding the connection, Harun objected to the consequences of this intellectual cosmopolitanism. The opening toward Iran gave impetus to the swelling cultural nationalism of the Persians and fired the debate between Arab and Iranian; the admission of Hellas to Islam gave intellectual support to the new theology which Harun correctly judged was pro-'Alid in its orientations and, so, politically dangerous to the rule of his house. And in the middle of the web, somehow responsible, though not conspiratorially so, were the Barmacids.

Harun was engaged in the difficult dual role of Islamic traditionalist and cultural modernist. Both were the stated aims of 'Abbasid policy since Mansur, but now in Harun's day the tensions implicit between the two points of view were more evident and painful. A traditionalist consensus was emerging in the Islamic Law, and though at first the prestige of the lawyers of Mecca and Medina was placed at the disposal of the 'Alids—it was Malik ibn Anas who freed the 'Alids from their oath to Mansur in 762—there were signs that the authority of the *shari' ah* could be made to work for the 'Abbasids as well. The greatest of the lawyers, al-Shafi'i (d. 820), who left his mark on the entire Islamic legal tradition, was on familiar terms with Harun and his court at Raqqah and Baghdad, where he came into contact with the 'Abbasids' chief jurisprudents, Abu Yusuf (d. 798) and al-Shaybani (d. 805). Both men, followers of the legal tradition of Abu Hanifah and the Kufan school of law, served as *qadis* for Harun, the former as the first to hold the position of Chief Judge of the realm, and the latter as a judge at Raqqah and in Khurasan.

The 'Abbasids had yoked the Islamic Law and their own political authority in the office of the *qadi*. The fruits of that union may be seen not so much in the technical legal treatises of Shaybani as in the *Book of the Land Tax* composed by Abu Yusuf for Harun. In it the scholar and judge set out a blueprint for the Islamicization of the state to a degree never previously attempted since the days of the *Rashidun*. The Umayyads had possessed the power of the state but never had control of its ideology, which rested unhappily and impotently in the hands of the pietists of Mecca and Medina or with the various religious dissidents across their kingdom. From the beginning the 'Abbasids claimed both political power and ideology. At first it was to be the theories of the extremist dissidents to which they were drawn, but once firmly in control, the 'Abbasids repudiated the ideology of revolution and sought out an alliance with the conservative lawyers and traditionalists whom the Umayyads had neither controlled nor won.

And yet the Caliph must rule, not as a matter of personal privilege in a private kingdom but as the "Successor of the Prophet of God" over the *ummah*. For their model the 'Abbasids chose the administrative style of their Sasanian predecessors. The Caliph was transformed from *shaykh* to Shah and was enthroned at the center of the circular "City of Peace" on the Tigris. And at the same time the tribal registries of the early days of the conquest were converted into *diwans* in the Sasanian bureaucratic manner.

To staff this burgeoning organization the 'Abbasids took on as their collaborators the skilled and only recently converted Iranian *mawali* to serve as secretaries, diplomatists and tutors to the princes royal. Many began like the offspring of Barmak, in the lower bureaucratic echelons, and climbed to the summits of power trailing with them a string of clients, political, literary and financial. As a class the secretaries were literate in the Iranian manner rather than learned in the Arab style. The *kuttab* were unimpressed by Arab pretensions to the mother-wit of the desert, by the endless sagas of Bedouin raids and by genealogies that debouched, as one of them said, "in some camel driver of the Hejaz." For these they substituted their own pretensions, and Jahiz describes the secretaries' frequent sighs over "how efficiently the country was run under the Sasanians" and their obligatory conversational references to Ardashir, Khusraw Anushirvan and, for the more intellectually ambitious, Aristotle.

The Barmacids epitomized the type in all its suspect brilliance. They put their administrative talents at the disposal of the Caliphate and reaped an immense increase in wealth and prestige. At some point Harun must have calculated the debits and credits of that contract, weighed it against his own political goals and personal satisfactions, and judged that it should be abrogated. After his return from a pilgrimage to the Holy Cities at the end of 802, the Caliph suddenly ordered the execution of Ja'far, the imprisonment of al-Fadl and the surveillance of their father Yahya. It was in the eyes of many a stunning reversal of fortunes, and the Arab historians, who were deeply moved by the event, offered a great many explanations for the fall of the brilliant vizieral family.[16] No single explanation is adequate. Ministers had been turned out before, and very suddenly. Yahya and his sons had simply held on longer than most and so had stored up more wealth and more envy. Al-Fadl, it will be recalled, had already fallen from grace earlier in 799 for his pro-'Alid leanings, and on this occasion Yahya was merely interned. And so, perhaps it is only the sudden ferocity of the execution of Ja'far that wants explanation, and the repeated suggestions of a homosexual attachment between the two men suggest that the explanation may have to be sought on some deeply personal level rather than in politics or finance.

The empire went on without the Barmacids. Almost immediately after their disgrace Harun was once again at Raqqah readying an army to take up the war against the new Byzantine Emperor Nicephorus I (802–811), who had repudiated the treaty extorted by Harun from Irene in 798. Again there were local successes in Anatolia, but no real resolution. The war was turning to stalemate; the Arabs still held the initiative, but lacked the forces necessary to destroy the Byzantine defenses.

In 805 Harun was forced to break off his Anatolian campaign by events in Khurasan. Al-Fadl's governorship there had been highly successful, but he was replaced in 796 by a certain 'Ali ibn 'Isa ibn Mahan, the captain of the guard at Baghdad. Yahya had opposed the appointment–correctly, as it turned out–but the new *amir's* willingness to share with the Caliph the wealth he looted from the province counted more than the vizier's advice. 'Ali lay like an incubus upon Khurasan until Harun replaced him in 806.

Harun was in Khurasan in 805 to quiet the rising unrest generated by his rapacious governor, but it was only after his return to Anatolia that there broke out a full-scale revolt that cost 'Ali his post. The instigator was Rafi' ibn Layth, the grandson of the Umayyad governor Nasr ibn al-Sayyar, who in 808 seized Samarqand and gathered around him Turkish and Iranian allies from

---

16. One of the more romantic concerned a marriage between the Caliph's daughter 'Abbasah and Ja'far, which Harun had intended be purely nominal but which Ja'far unwisely consummated and so lost his life.

across Transoxania and as far away as Tibet. Harun responded by collecting a large army, but before the campaign was properly done the Caliph died at Tus in March of 809.[17]

On the fateful pilgrimage in 802 Harun had carefully—too carefully perhaps—set out the manner of his succession. Al-Amin, though slightly younger than al-Ma'mun, was of Arab stock on both sides and so was designated as Harun's first successor. He was bound, however, to accept Ma'mun, the son of Harun and an Iranian slave, as *his* successor. Ma'mun was confirmed in almost independent control of the eastern provinces, a provision that, in effect, divided the empire into two for as long as al-Amin ruled. The contract of succession was ratified by the Caliph and publicly exhibited at the Ka'bah in Mecca.

The Reign of Ma'mun

At Harun's death in 809 the evils inherent in his settlement of 802 burst into full flower. Al-Amin abided by the Meccan protocols for less than a year and then introduced the name of his own son into the Friday prayers, possibly at the instigation of his vizier Fadl ibn Rabi'. Ma'mun protested from Khurasan to no effect, and later in 810 Amin made formal announcement that his son and not Ma'mun would be his successor in the Caliphate. The declaration meant nothing less than civil war; Amin understood that Ma'mun would not yield and in the following year he sent an army against his half brother in Khurasan.

The contest was unequal from the start. Ma'mun had on his side both a legally unassailable position and the undivided support of Khurasan, where his Iranian ancestry doubtless strengthened his appeal. Amin, on the other hand, for all the purity of his blood, was the champion of neither the Arabs' interests nor those of Iran, nor was he totally credible as a ruler. He was ambitious but without possessing Ma'mun's ability or understanding.

17. The rebellion of Rafi' dragged on for another year, but his supporters saw the end before their leader, and when the Iranians and Turks drifted back to their homes Rafi' was forced to come to terms with Ma'mun.

Ma'mun's interests were equally divided among politics, religion and the quickening intellectual life of Islam; Amin consulted chiefly his own pleasures and the tutelage of the contemporary rhapsode of boys and wine, Abu Nuwas.

It took Ma'mun two years to deal with the forces of Amin. His generals Tahir and Harthama routed a succession of Caliphal armies in western Iran, and the only serious obstacle to their advance was Baghdad itself. It resisted the Khurasanian siege for a year, but in 813 the city finally fell. Shortly thereafter Amin was arrested in flight and murdered by Tahir's Iranian troopers. Ma'mun, meanwhile, made no move to enter the 'Abbasid capital. He placed Baghdad and Iraq under the supervision of Tahir, while he remained resolutely at Merv, the site of what was apparently to be the new Iranian capital of the *Dar al-Islam.*

Ma'mun's mentor during the difficult days after Harun's death was another Iranian *mawla* who played Ja'far to Ma'mun's Harun down to 818. Al-Fadl ibn Sahl and his brother Hasan were already high *diwan* officials under Harun, and it was al-Fadl who was appointed tutor to the Crown Prince Ma'mun after the fall of the Barmacids in 803. The occasion was also marked by al-Fadl's tardy public conversion from Zoroastrianism to Islam. As crown prince, Ma'mun was given, in a tradition that went back to Sasanian times, the governorship of Khurasan. Though he could have remained in Baghdad and allowed others to administer the province in his name, it was at al-Fadl's urging that Ma'mun accompanied his father east on the final expedition of 808 and thus at Harun's death was in a position to take firm and immediate control of the Khurasanian power levers.

After the fall of a severely damaged Baghdad Ma'mun was sole Caliph, a triumph that brought no peace. Amin still had scattered supporters farther west in Syria, and in Azarbayjan old religious forces were emerging anew. Ever since the days of Abu Muslim Iran had been agitated by a series of related religious movements based on a highly personal leadership like that of al-Muqanna' and constructed out of a syncretized body of belief and practice. One such faction was the Khurramiyah, which had its adherents as far back as 736, flared up again under Harun in 796 and 808, and broke out in full-bodied political revolt in 816, when an Iraqi jack-of-all-trades named Babak or Papak claimed that he was the reincarnation of an earlier Khurrami *Imam* and began to win converts in northern Azarbayjan.

Our information on the Khurramis' beliefs is neither entirely clear nor altogether consistent. Their system derived, like that of the Zoroastrians, Manichaeans and Daysaniyah, from a dual principle of light and darkness. Their ritual purity may also have owed something to Iran, but their belief in an *Imam* descended from the house of Abu Muslim is clearly Shi'ite in its orientation. Their enemies called the Khurramiyah hedonists and libertines, though this is perhaps a conscious or an unconscious misunderstanding of the practice of holding wives in common.[18] Finally, the Khurramiyah held a notorious belief in the transmigration of souls, a tenet they shared with the extremist Shi'ah and, of course, the Buddhists.

Whatever their theological origins, the Khurramiyah refused to the Caliph the allegiance they owed solely to their *Imam* or their charismatic prophets. Ma'mun was forced to take action, not so much in the defense of religious orthodoxy as in the name of 'Abbasid rule, which was being compromised both internally and externally by Babak, who was receiving encouragement and support from the Byzantines in nearby Anatolia. The local Muslim governors were incapable of containing the movement, nor were Ma'mun's generals any more successful. The Khurramiyah flourished, while Ma'mun changed his tactics to strike directly at the Byzantines rather than at their presumed agent Babak.

The Khurramiyah could perhaps be dealt with by military means, but Ma'mun's experiences with the Shi'ites prompted far more radical action. The male offspring of 'Ali's son Hasan—little was heard politically from the heirs of Husayn at this point—had not shown themselves politically adept, and the disturbances

---

18. The Mazdakites too (see Introduction, pp. 29–30) held wives in common, and the Christian writers across the frontier almost invariably interpreted the movement as libertinage. The Khurramiyah may have had a similar social program behind their community of wives, but it is more likely that their practice owed more to the Shi'ite practice of *mut'ah* or temporary marriage. Ma'mun, it is interesting to note, attempted to have *mut'ah* recognized by the traditionalist lawyers, though without success.

under Ma'mun appeared to follow the earlier motif in their fortunes: the coming-together of a political adventurer with the 'Alid heir, in this instance the former bandit general Abu al-Saraya, who was deeply involved in the civil war between Amin and Ma'mun, and the Hasanid Muhammad ibn Tabataba. They met toward the end of 814 and joined their forces in revolt against the regime at Kufah early the next year.

The rebels enjoyed some success at first. Abu al-Saraya held Kufah against a Caliphal army, and not even the death of Ibn Tabataba shortly after marked any decline in the revolt which in the course of 815 spread through southern Iraq and as far as Mecca. It was not ideology, however, but the soldiers of Abu al-Saraya who were its mainspring, and as soon as the vizier al-Hasan ibn Sahl could muster a large enough counterforce, Abu al-Saraya took to his heels and was run to ground before the year was out.

In the following year Ma'mun made an extraordinary political move: he summoned to Merv 'Ali al-Rida, the son of the murdered Musa al-Kazim and his father's successor as the not very active Husaynid *Imam.* Up to this point 'Ali had shown no more interest in politics than either his father or his grandfather and concentrated on scholarship in the Medina circles where he grew up. But Ma'mun was nonetheless determined to designate this 'Alid as his successor in the Caliphate, and 'Ali, though at the outset reluctant, finally accepted the oath of allegiance tendered him by the court at Merv.

It is possible to explain this remarkable choice on purely political grounds, as a long overdue act of reconciliation with the 'Alids, for example; but it is not at all certain that the act was a purely political one or, if it was, that Ma'mun correctly measured the consequences. Ma'mun's predecessors, who were as well aware as he of the growing polarization of the empire, ruled from Iraq but threw open the ways to both political preferment and intellectual prestige to the easterners who had first supported their house. 'Alid protests against the 'Abbasids were not provoked by that dynasty's favoring of Iraqis over easterners but by a totally different view of the Caliphate. Mansur and Harun both understood that, and so their encouragement of Iranian self-consciousness was accompanied by repressive measures against the 'Alids, even those who were quite clearly politically harmless.

Ma'mun was transparently sympathetic to the *Shi'at 'Ali*, and his sympathies drove him to a political gesture inconceivable to his tougher-minded father: he chose to rule from a provincial Merv rather than an ecumenical Baghdad, and he publicly announced that his successor as Caliph would be the 'Alid *Imam*. Only one note of caution was introduced; 'Ali al-Rida would succeed as Caliph not because he was the *Imam* but because he was best qualified for the task, a patently untrue proposition but a considered sop to traditionalist sentiment.

The Iraqis were not deceived, except perhaps in their assessment of the blame; they accused Fadl ibn Sahl of being behind the scheme. This appears most unlikely—the Banu Sahl could measure political consequences—but when the Caliph began to sense some of the Arab and traditionalist outrage against what he had wrought, he was quick to avail himself of the scapegoat created by public opinion. Finally convinced that unless he changed his policies he would lose Iraq—the 'Abbasid princes there had already proclaimed one of al-Mahdi's sons, the poet and musician Ibrahim, as Caliph—Ma'mun took the road to Baghdad in 818. It was, apparently, a punitive expedition, but en route a deeper strategy was revealed. Fadl ibn Sahl was murdered at Sarakhs, probably at Ma'mun's orders, and shortly after 'Ali al-Rida also met his end, though somewhat less certainly at the hands of Ma'mun. The Caliph ceremoniously buried his erstwhile heir near the grave of his own 'Alid-despising father Harun at Tus, and in 819 he continued on to Baghdad, where he reestablished himself as Caliph in the capital of the 'Abbasids. The question of the 'Alid succession was tacitly dropped.

Moving from Merv to Baghdad and disengaging himself from the conveniently dead 'Ali al-Rida brought no peace to Ma'mun or his realm. The 'Abbasid establishment in Iraq was not happy with Ma'mun's transparent Shi'ism, and the dead Amin still had his supporters in northern Syria, a particularly sensitive area by reason of its closeness to the Byzantine frontier. In 821 Ma'mun appointed as his governor of a vast region embracing both Syria and Egypt Tahir's son 'Abdallah, then a young man in his early twenties. Some difficult campaigns followed, and it was not until 826 that 'Abdallah finally brought the dissidents in Syria under control. He proceeded directly from Aleppo to Egypt, where for years a stream of Muslim emigrants from Spain had created havoc in the country. The action was swifter here: in 825 'Abdallah rid Egypt of the main body of the Cordovans, who then crossed over to Crete and wrested that island from the Byzantines.

Under Ma'mun it was already apparent that the empire could not be sustained as a whole. Spain was early lost to the Umayyads. Ifriqiyah had long suffered from Berber agitation, and when the Caliph's own Arab troopers revolted in 799, Harun had had to give over that province to the only man capable of pacifying it, Ibrahim ibn Aghlab. Ibrahim performed as promised, but he exacted his price from the Caliph: the province would contract to pay an annual assessment into the 'Abbasid treasury, but the governorship would henceforth be a hereditary office for Ibrahim's descendants. In Ma'mun's time a parallel situation developed in Khurasan. Once the Caliph had decided to leave Merv and take up residence in Baghdad, he entrusted the affairs of the province to his best military man, and a native Iranian, Tahir. Tahir's governorship in Khurasan was brief, but before he died in 822 he had made the essential declaration of independence: he omitted the Caliph's name from the Friday prayers. And yet Ma'mun could not do otherwise than acknowledge Tahir's son Talhah as the next governor there.

Disturbances continued to shake Iraq, Syria and Egypt, where the Caliph's brother and successor Mu'tasim showed himself incapable of dealing with the rebellious Copts, and Ma'mun had to take personal command. Al-Fadl had foreseen Ma'mun ruling over an empire where 'Abbasid and 'Alid, traditionalist and moderate, were reconciled in a politics of compromise. Already in 819 that vision lay in ruins. The antagonists were not reconciled; Ma'mun did not, however, surrender the cause. After 819 he moved back from his 'Alid politics but not from the Shi'ite and Mu'tazilite ideology that lay behind it. Khurasanians were no longer dominant in the army and the *diwans*, and nothing was being said about 'Ali al-Rida's son. Instead Ma'mun invested his efforts in a *bellum theologicum.* The opening shots were heard in 827, when the Caliph publicly promulgated the dogma of the creation of the *Qur'an* and the preeminence of 'Ali.

Both theses had Mu'tazilite support, and the first, that of the creation of the *Qur'an*, had been strongly pressed in Baghdad by Mu'tazilites and Jahmites alike. It had landed leaders of both factions, Thumamah ibn Ashras and Bishr al-Marisi, in prison during the reign of Harun, but now, under Ma'mun, Thumamah found more willing ears. Twice the Mu'tazilite theologian was offered the post of vizier by the Caliph. He declined the political office but continued to give theological advice. Ma'mun held back on the establishment of the Mu'tazilite version of orthodoxy, but only until 827 when Thumamah's student Ibn abi Du'ad became Chief *Qadi* and the Caliph was prevailed upon to make public declaration of his views.

The chronology is somewhat uncertain, but it may also have been about this time that Ma'mun founded his "House of Wisdom" in Baghdad. There is no evidence that it was intended as a Shi'ite propaganda center, but it surely rested upon the same intellectual ground already being cultivated by Mu'tazilite and Shi'ite alike, the translation and study of the Greek sciences. Ma'mun assembled a staff of scholars and translators to seek out Greek manuscripts and begin the work of translating them into Arabic. Works on philosophy, astronomy, mathematics and medicine were collected from as far afield as Constantinople.

The "foreign sciences" supported and encouraged so assiduously by Ma'mun may have suffered in the end by their association with the Caliph's Shi'ite and Mu'tazilite sympathies. The natural sciences like medicine and mathematics passed uncontested into Islam, but philosophy and theology, whether the latter be considered an independent discipline or as part of the fabric of the new Islamic dialectic (*kalam*), were linked in the minds of many with the dubious religious causes espoused by the Caliph.

Until Ma'mun's time orthodoxy was an ill-defined concept in Islam. Sectarianism was widespread and even violent at times; theses were proclaimed and anathemas exchanged. But Ma'mun was the first to use the Caliphate in an attempt to *define* orthodoxy. He published his theses on the *Qur'an* and the preeminence of 'Ali in 827. This claim to a *magisterium* was already an extraordinary step, though it was perhaps implicit in the earliest 'Abbasid view of the Caliphate as an Islamic rather than a purely secular office. Six years later the Caliph took steps to ensure conformity with his doctrinal statement. From his camp near

Tarsus Ma'mun addressed a rapid series of pastoral letters to his governor in Baghdad, with copies to the provinces, instructing him to institute a scrutiny (*mihnah*) of the lawyers and theologians of the capital on the subject of the *Qur'an*. Almost all of them yielded to the thinly veiled threat implicit in the charge and signaled their acceptance of the proposition that the *Qur'an* was created. A few held out, however, among them Ahmad ibn Hanbal (d. 855), whose repeated refusal to compromise his conscience eventually raised him to the position of martyr for the traditional orthodoxy and enormously enhanced the popular resistance to Ma'mun's elitist, intellectualistic approach to Islam.

The disruptive but provocative wrench given by Ma'mun to the fabric of Islam stirred responses far beyond the court at Baghdad. The Christian intellectual community of Mesopotamia and Iraq showed new signs of vitality, while farther east, in Fars and Kirman, the moribund body of Zoroastrianism stirred for the first time since the days of Khusraw I.

The Muslims were generous in accepting the followers of Zoroaster among the "Peoples of the Book" and, so, qualified to receive the special protective covenant (*dhimmah*) reserved for scriptuaries within Islam; the question of their own Scriptures must have been almost as confusing to the ninth-century Zoroastrians as it is to us. One book composed in Ma'mun's day, the *Denkart*, gives an elaborate history of the *Avesta* from Darius III to Khusraw I, but it is not at all clear what the author understood as the *Avesta*, whether the original Old Persian text, the Pahlevi translations, which were, as we can see, quite poor, or a larger, more comprehensive body of work called the *zand* and in which the original appears fleetingly as an occasional *lemma* in the midst of a great sea of gloss and commentary. Indeed, despite the interesting details in this account, it is uncertain whether the *Avesta* was even committed to writing at the coming of Islam.

It seems likely that the author of the *Denkart* was thinking of the third possibility, the *zand* that was manipulated in such a calculating manner by Shapur and Khusraw and whose unorthodox interpretation could lead to the charge of heresy. Thus came into existence the *zandik*, the "interpreter" who bedeviled the Sasanian clergy and who was still flourishing and bedeviling Muslim and Zoroastrian alike in Islamic times. The Manichaean was a species of *zandik* (in Arabic *zindiq*), or so at least he was judged by the Muslims; the Zoroastrians understood the *zandik* in a more specialized sense, however, as one who believed in a material cosmos produced and dominated by an equally material principle known as Time, the eternal and determining cause of the eternal universe.

This *zandik* position was almost certainly a version of the Zurvanism that had a periodic vogue in the Sasanian Empire, but the Muslim heresiographers tell a great deal more about it than the Pahlevi books. In Arabic the sect was called the Dahriyah (*dahr:* "eternity") and was said to include a belief in an impersonal and infinite Time, a denial of creation, providence and the prescriptions of positive religion and, the Zoroastrians would add, of the rewards and punishments of the afterlife.

Later students of the question find themselves in agreement with the orthodox Zoroastrians who condemned the *zandik:* whether called Zurvaism or Dahriyah, these beliefs are not Iranian in origin but derive from some other view of the world and its workings, Indian perhaps or Greek, or some combination of the two compounded of the Shahs' desire to open the Good Religion of Ahura Mazda to other, non-Iranian insights. Khusraw, we know, had both Greek and Indian works translated. Among the latter the *Upanishads* possess a similar notion of infinite time that serves, without the intervention of a personal creator, as the source of all the temporal modalities of this world, a view that combines easily enough with the Aristotelian notion of prime matter as an undefined cause of all being.[19]

Khusraw had thought that he could control the tension between those alien ideas and the original Zoroastrian belief in a personalized and spiritual God to the benefit of a Catholic Zoroastrian Church. His scheme had little chance to prove itself; his inept successors and the disastrous wars with Heraclius

19. The Muslim heresiographers did not, however, confuse the syncretisms of the Dahriyah with Aristotelianism. For al-Ghazali, for example, Aristotle belonged among the "theists" together with Socrates and Plato.

brought his empire to its knees, where the Arab conquerors of Iran found it in the mid-seventh century. Christianity and Judaism both survived the Muslim invasion, in straitened circumstances surely, but as still-functioning religious communities within the *Dar al-Islam.* For the Zoroastrians the Muslim conquest was a disaster. Despite its *dhimmi* status, Mazdaism went into a rapid and perceptible decline. Under the Sasanians it had been the established church of the empire, but once it was deprived of that state-supported cohesiveness, Zoroastrianism became the religion of individuals under the governance of a rapidly disappearing hierarchy. The Christians and Jews of Iraq had centuries before Islam to adjust to life in a City of God set down in an alien City of Man; for the Zoroastrians it was a totally new and fatal experience.

Deserted by its own intellectuals and the feudal landowners who were its support, and actively pursued by the Muslim authorities, particularly in Khurasan, Zoroastrianism did display one final, creative surge of energy before disappearing into the religious limbo once reserved for the old Roman *pagani.* In Kirman and Fars, the last redoubt of Islamic Zoroastrianism, there were signs of life in the ninth century; they are not always easy to read, but they are essential to an understanding of Mazdaism over the previous three centuries.

There have been preserved from the ninth century a number of Pahlevi treatises, whose contents and authors are as interesting as they are obscure. The chief among them, the *Deeds of Religion,* or *Denkart,* was mostly the work of Aturnfarnbag, a contemporary of Ma'mun who took part in a public debate before the Caliph sometime about 825. The first two books of the *Denkart* have disappeared, and the seven that remain are a very mixed encyclopedia of dogma, polemic, historical narrative, a life of Zoroaster and a veritable Avestan *zand.* Aturnfarnbag was not, however, a *zandik;* he was an orthodox dualist somewhat in the style of Khusraw I. So too was Mardan Farrukh, the somewhat later author of *The Decisive Solution of Doubts,* a work addressed to another Zoroastrian explaining the essentials of Mazdaism and refuting the claims of the Muslims—particularly the Mu'tazilites—Christians, Manichaeans and Jews. There is a third work, *The Original Creation,* or *Bundahishn,* of an unknown author but likely from the same period, which sets out a Zoroastrian account of creation whereby the Good Spirit Ohrmazd is the agent of creation who fashions the universe from the body of Infinite Time, an indication, perhaps, that a kind of mitigated Zurvanism is at work.

Zurvanism was not quite dead in the ninth century but it does not appear to have had many propagandists. There are fatalistic notes characteristic of Zurvanism in the *Spirit of Reason* (or *Wisdom*) and what appears to be a Zurvanite view of creation in the *Selected Works* of the Zoroastrian priest Zatspram. The brother of the latter, Manushchihr, was likewise a member of the Zoroastrian clergy, the chief priest of the provinces of Fars and Kirman and, like his brother, a religious writer. We have his *Religious Resolutions,* a mixed work of dogma and ritual—ritualistic questions were still highly important in the ninth century, particularly those dealing with purification—but of considerably greater historical interest are his *Letters,* written in 881, one of which reveals the rivalry that was then dividing the Zoroastrian hierarchy, a council of priests summoned to Shiraz to settle what was threatening to become a schism in the community and, finally, his differences with his brother Zatspram, whose opinions appeared in the eyes of Manushchihr more like Manichaeism than a genuine form of the Good Religion.

After this there is very little. The Pahlevi renaissance, kindled perhaps in equal measure by the intellectual liberality of Ma'mun and the subsequent rise of an Islamic orthodoxy under Mutawakkil, flickered briefly and then died. Even as the priests were writing it, Pahlevi was an expiring linguistic phenomenon, harnessed to an impossibly difficult alphabet and understood only by a small learned class, and probably imperfectly by them. The Iranian intellectuals turned instead to Arabic, and the merchants and peasants to a simpler form of the national language, what the Arabs called *dari.* The *Avesta* too lay buried beneath the confused layers of the *zand.*

In the tenth century the Iranian national spirit and Zoroastrianism parted ways, the former into the *shu'ubiyah* movements in Islam and eventually into a marvelous reflowering of Persian history, epic and lyric out of the lowly *dari* speech;[20] the latter into oblivion or exile. In the tenth century there began the Zoroastrian migrations to India, where a new community, the Parsees, cherished the belief and rituals in the old books.

If he had any opinion at all on the subject, Ma'mun probably stood with the Mu'tazilites against all forms of dualism, Manichaean or Zoroastrian, even though all three groups were drawing upon the growing body of "rational," though hardly secular, science available in Arabic in the ninth century. For the latter two, Manichaeism and Zoroastrianism, natural science, whether of the Greek or Indian variety, was by then a familiar quantity long since woven into the elaborate mythological tapestries of their beliefs; for Islam, which was still relatively innocent of myth, the encounter was more provocative and, in the end, more dangerous. In the light the orthodox Muslim, accustomed to the simplicities of Murji'ite, Kharijite and Shi'ite, came to see that the forest was filled with wolves.

Ma'mun devoted little time or attention to the swan song of the Zoroastrian clergy. His quarrel was with what appeared to him as criminally unenlightened conservatives within Islam, and without with the traditional Byzantine foe across the frontier. His preoccupations within the *Dar al-Islam* allowed him little opportunity to emulate his father's successes against the Byzantines, but Ma'mun did possess one weapon that proved useful—a Slavic soldier named Thomas, who had fled from Anatolia into Muslim territory in Harun's day. In 820 Ma'mun arranged, or connived at, Thomas' coronation as Basileus at the hands of the Patriarch of Antioch and, having equipped his revolutionary with money and soldiers beaten up from the border provinces, sent him back into Anatolia. Thomas raised the banner of revolt all through Byzantine Anatolia, where he put himself forth as the champion of image worshipers, the oppressed poor, and whatever ethnic groups had grievances against the regime.

The new emperor, Michael II (820–829), had few ideological resources with which to combat the immediately successful

---

20. See Chap. IX, pp. 644–646.

exhortations of Thomas. Most of Anatolia went over to the rebels, and by 821 Thomas had Constantinople locked in a state of siege. What Michael did have, however, was powerful allies, in this instance the Bulgars, whose *khan* agreed to come to the Emperor's assistance. In 823 the siege was broken. Thomas fled, was captured, tortured and executed.

It is not certain that Ma'mun would have greatly profited if Thomas, who was helped by the Caliph but was not his agent, had actually taken Constantinople. Ma'mun's own opportunity came from other quarters. 'Abdallah ibn Tahir had cleared the Syrian frontier of Amin's last supporters in 826 and then in the following year had flushed the Catalan immigrants from Egypt. The immediate effect was the Muslim conquest of Crete in the same year that the Caliph's nominal dependents, the Aghlabids of Ifriqiyah, gained their first firm foothold in Sicily.[21] Michael II had meantime been succeeded by his considerably less warlike son Theophilus (829–842), and the Caliph judged the time ripe for his own entry onto the scene.

Theophilus was, as Ma'mun knew, deeply preoccupied with Sicily, and the Caliph's plans were for nothing less than a decisive breakthrough into central Anatolia. The Muslims controlled the territories south of a line running from Erzerum to a point somewhat north of Tarsus in Cilicia, and for three years the Caliph and the Basileus, each engaged in serious ideological contests at home, struggled back and forth through the Cilician passes without a marked advantage to either side until Ma'mun's death at his camp near Tarsus in 833.

Ma'mun's second in command in Anatolia, his son 'Abbas, who had acquitted himself with distinction in the wars against the Byzantines, was not his father's first choice as successor. That was to be Ma'mun's brother Mu'tasim (833–842), whose chief ad-

21. The Aghlabids were brought onto the island by Euphemius, a former admiral of the Byzantine fleet, who had himself proclaimed emperor. When Constantinople gave signs of taking countermeasures against him Euphemius removed himself to Tunis and promised to hand over Crete to the Aghlabids. The offer was accepted with alacrity, and an army of ten thousand men was landed on the island.

ministrative post had been the governorship of Egypt. The Khurasanians of the Anatolian army preferred 'Abbas, but a major civil war was averted when 'Abbas persuaded his troops to accept his father's choice and take their oath to Mu'tasim.

The significance of the incident was not lost on the new Caliph. Ma'mun, like the 'Abbasids themselves, had come to power on Khurasanian arms, and if Ma'mun's policy veered off on an eccentric tangent after 819, the Khurasanians were still an important force in the *Dar al-Islam,* and there was, in addition, an almost autonomous dynasty settling itself into that province. 'Abdallah ibn Tahir who succeeded his brother as governor there in 829 showed himself a faithful, if nominal, servant of the Caliphate. 'Abdallah's power extended far beyond Khurasan; it was felt in Baghdad itself, where the Tahirids constructed a magnificent palace that served as the residence of the military governor of the city, a post they filled from the ranks of their own family.

To counteract the Khurasanians Mu'tasim turned where Ma'mun had turned before him, to the Turks. Turkish troopers had fought at the side of Rafi' in Transoxania in 808–810 and later took their place in Ma'mun's own army. Many of them came into the army as slaves captured in Transoxania and forwarded to Baghdad, ironically, as part of the annual Tahirid tribute to the Caliph. Slaves or free, the Turks provided Mu'tasim with a new praetorian guard, on whose loyalty he could rely and who proved their worth as soldiers in his later campaigns in Anatolia. The Turks did indeed make good soldiers, as Jahiz's essay *On the Exploits of the Turks* convincingly argued, but only indifferent citizens, and Baghdad with its Khurasanian and Tahirid attachments was the scene of frequent disorders, which the presence of a still-primitive Turkish soldiery only inflamed. It may be suspected that Mu'tasim found the Tahirid influence in Baghdad a more oppressive notion than civil disorder, but he resolved, at any rate, to move the court and his supporters to a more congenial location. Sixty miles north of Baghdad on the east bank of the Tigris he chose a new site for his quarters and proceeded to construct there the city and camp of Samarra, which from 836 to 892 served as the seat of the Caliphate and the capital of the empire. In the manner of Mansur, Mu'tasim collected materials, architects and artists from the breadth of the *Dar al-Islam* to grace his new city.[22] It rose on a lavish scale, as the considerable remains still testify, and Mu'tasim's successors, Mutawakkil in particular, continued to add to the city.[23]

If the use of Turkish soldiers, who eventually imprisoned the Caliphs within their splendid city, was implicitly suggested by Ma'mun's own later practice, Mu'tasim received other, quite explicit advice from his brother–to wit, to put his confidence in the Mu'tazilite *qadi* Ibn abi Du'ad rather than in his viziers. At his accession in 833, Mu'tasim followed that advice, at least in part. Ibn abi Du'ad was appointed Chief Judge and immediately took up the interrupted pursuit of the traditionalist Ahmad ibn Hanbal, whose case had remained unresolved at Ma'mun's death. Ibn Hanbal was interrogated by the *qadi* himself, and when he once again refused to submit on the prescribed theses, he was scourged and imprisoned. The confinement was not long, however; fear of popular demonstrations was stronger than the Mu'tazilite sentiments of the Caliph, and Ibn Hanbal was released.

Mu'tasim, it appears, did not entirely share the aggressive Mu'tazilite convictions of his dead brother. He accepted the advice of Ibn abi Du'ad, himself a relative moderate in both theology and politics, and Mu'tazilitism did indeed remain the officially defined orthodoxy of the realm, though perhaps for no better reason than that Mu'tasim feared to repudiate his predecessor's policy. Ahmad ibn Hanbal was, at any rate, left in peace as long as he made no pronouncements, an arrangement that apparently suited both sides in the conflict.

Mu'tasim did not, however, abstain from viziers, as his brother had counseled, and the years between 833 and 847 were charged with the interplay between Ibn abi Du'ad, the vizier Ibn al-Zayyat, and their respective supporters and clients. To the side, but only slightly so, were the new players in the drama, the Turkish commandants who controlled the guard at Mu'tasim's

---

22. Not entirely new, however. Marble was pillaged from earlier buildings, particularly in Egypt, and after he captured Amorium in Anatolia Mu'tasim carried back the gates of that city to grace his new capital.

23. The Great Mosque, with its extraordinary zigguratlike minaret, was part of Mutawakkil's contribution.

new capital at Samarra and were simultaneously governors of Mesopotamia, Egypt and Syria. The vizier still held the power of the purse, but the influence of the soldiery was becoming formidable.

The Turkish captains were not as yet interested, as they would be later, in the religious problems of the Caliphate; they contented themselves with the exchange of raw power in the form of troops attached to the person of the Caliph. These were predominantly Turkish, though there were some Iranian and Negro contingents, and all of them were under the command of a Turkish general officer who was, at the same time, chamberlain of the Caliphal palace and in charge of a "postal service" that did indeed deliver the mail but provided as well extensive intelligence reports from the provinces.

The first of those Turkish commanders, Afshin, came into prominence in the course of a fierce religious war that Mu'tasim had inherited from Ma'mun. Ma'mun had never come to grips with the anarchy being spread in Azarbayjan by the Khurramiyah and their leader Babak. That Caliph was preparing a direct assault on the rebels to be led by his most effective general, 'Abdallah ibn Tahir. 'Abdallah was in the course of collecting an army in Jibal in 829, when the death of his brother Talhah drew him to Khurasan, and Ma'mun had little choice but to permit 'Abdallah to take up the governorship of that province. Babak gained a few years' further respite when Ma'mun then chose to direct his main effort against the Byzantines rather than the Khurramiyah.

The few years of official neglect were used to advantage by the Khurramis, and by the accession of Mu'tasim the movement had spread southward from Azarbayjan into Jibal. In 835 Mu'tasim took up arms against Babak, and another of the empire's premier generals was sent out against him. Al-Afshin, as he was called,[24] was originally the ruler of a petty Transoxanian princedom who later served with distinction in the Caliphal armies in Egypt. Now installed in his new command, he tracked Babak and his

---

24. "Afshin" was actually a title borne by the rulers of Ushrusana, the territory of the lower Ferghana valley between Samarqand and Khojend.

peasant army for two years through difficult terrain. Even in the final closure Babak managed to escape into Armenia. Eventually he was betrayed into the hands of Afshin, and in 838 the Khurramiyah *Imam* was brought to Samarra, paraded before the crowds on the back of an elephant, and finally executed.

Once al-Afshin had delivered the rebels into his hands, Mu'tasim returned to the somewhat grandiose Anatolian plans of Ma'mun. In 838 two Muslim armies entered Anatolia, one of them under the command of Afshin, and later that year they were in possession of Ancyra and Amorium. Both Caliph and Emperor knew that a further advance to Constantinople was unlikely, and Mu'tasim withdrew to Tarsus under heavy pursuit. Only prestige was exchanged in Anatolia in 838—the Muslims gained a little; the Byzantines lost a little.

His successes in Anatolia did not distract Afshin from matters closer to home. His former princedom of Ushrusana was, like the rest of Khurasan, under the well-established control of 'Abdallah ibn Tahir, the governor of Khurasan whose province was coming to resemble an autonomous state within the *Dar al-Islam.* In the years following the Anatolian campaign Afshin became embroiled with 'Abdallah, whose influence in Baghdad he attempted to curtail by lending his support to the claims to independence of the rulers of Tabaristan. The remote province of Tabaristan on the southern shores of the Caspian belonged to the jurisdiction of Khurasan, and so it was the responsibility of 'Abdallah to deal with the revolt there. He put down the pretensions of the local ruler in some hard campaigning in 838–839. Afshin was implicated, but when he was brought captive to Samarra the charge was not treason but apostasy. Al-Afshin was, it is true, a relatively recent convert to Islam, probably from Buddhism, but the trial is more of a testament to the heated connection between religion and politics in ninth-century Iran than to al-Afshin's personal religious preferences.

The temperature increased perceptibly under Mu'tasim's son and successor al-Wathiq (842–847), who appears to have reinvigorated the *mihnah* against the traditionalists, while at Baghdad, Samarra and Basrah the Mu'tazilites reigned paramount as court theologians. Strong 'Abbasid dependencies ruled in Ifriqiyah and Khurasan, and it was the latter, the Tahirids, who by a curious irony became the refuge if not the champions of traditionalism in Islam. 'Abdallah ibn Tahir, who governed there until 845, and his son Tahir II after him were prompt to defend 'Abbasid legitimacy against 'Alids and opportunists alike; they did not, however, share the current acceptance of a Mu'tazilite version of orthodoxy, and the Tahirid court at Nishapur became a center for the "Sunnites," the conservative theologians who, like Ibn Hanbal in Baghdad, were waiting for a better day.

There was, to be sure, some opposition to the Mu'tazilites even in Baghdad. The ultraconservatives had for the most part gone to ground, but further to the theological left a kind of moderate conservatism was developing under the leadership of Ibn Kullab (d. 854). At about the same time the Zaydi Shi'ites, those who recognized the Imamate of Zayd ibn 'Ali, though at first allied to the Mu'tazilites, were undergoing internal dissensions. Zayd's grandson Ahmad ibn 'Isa, the last of the line to lay claim to the Imamate, had been imprisoned in Baghdad by Harun after receiving secret subsidies from the Barmacids. Ahmad escaped and made his way to the more congenial climate of Basrah, where he opened a literary attack on the Mu'tazilites. Ahmad died in 860, but even during his lifetime the leadership of the moderate Shi'ites was passing to another, al-Qasim, brother of the unfortunate Muhammad ibn Tabataba who had been used by the rebel Abu al-Saraya in 815. By descent al-Qasim belonged to the Hasanid branch of the 'Alids and not, like the late Zayd ibn 'Ali, to the Husaynids; he was, nonetheless, a Zaydi in his convictions,[25] and most of his theological positions were close to those held by the Mu'tazilites of Baghdad.

The Mu'tazilites

When Ma'mun assumed the Caliphate in 813 there occurred a turning in a signal theological battle being waged within the Muslim community. During his reign Islam was given its first authorized theological orthodoxy, which the Caliph undertook to

---

25. See Chap. VIII, pp. 572–573.

inspect and sanction. This was a new venture in Islam, and indeed theology itself was a novel and still-undefined calling for a Muslim scholar in the early ninth century. Islam began with a revelation that set out both a portrait of Allah and various guidelines to human conduct. The latter had been elaborated into a rationalized body of law under the later Umayyads, and legal orthodoxy was already well advanced by Ma'mun's day. Theology had lagged behind the law, however, and when the 'Abbasids replaced the Umayyads the theological dialecticians were only beginning to disengage problems about God, the universe and man from the almost suffocating growth of legal and political issues surrounding the 'Alid civil wars.

Theology had not entirely vindicated the autonomy of its object and method by the time of Ma'mun, but there were in Basrah and Baghdad men who might reasonably be described as theologians. Despite their not inconsiderable personal differences, they were known collectively as Mu'tazilites: Abu al-Hudhayl (d. 841), al-Nazzam (d. 855), Mu'ammar (d. 835), and Hisham al-Fuwati at Basrah; Bishr ibn al-Mu'tamir (d. 825), Thumamah ibn Ashras (d. 828), and Ibn abi Du'ad (d. 854) at Baghdad. After some difficult days under Harun, the Mu'tazilite theologians saw their point of view prevail during the Caliphates of Ma'mun, Mu'tasim and Wathiq. There was another turning with Mutawakkil in 847, and though there were Mu'tazilites after him, they had no official support and were exposed to the vengeance of the traditionalists and lawyers who had been the object of Mu'tazilite surveillance during the preceding decades.

The Mu'tazilites ended as heretics, execrated by the conservative wing of Islam and disavowed by the theologians of what came to be the orthodox persuasion. Their works disappeared and their opinions were memorialized chiefly in the unflattering remarks of the heresiographers. The situation is not greatly improved today—a few Mu'tazilite treatises have come to light[26]

---

26. Chiefly the *Book of Triumph* of al-Khayyat, a Mu'tazilite of Baghdad who died about 902, the *Satisfactory Work* and other treatises of 'Abd al-Jabbar (d. 1025), a judge at Rayy under the Buyids, and a number of Mu'tazilite heresiographies. The first work is a refutation of charges leveled against the Mu'tazilites by one of their own,

—but there can be surmised somewhat more than the Muslim sources chose to tell. We can trace somewhat more confidently, for example, the origins of the group, and we can assert what the heresiographers dissembled, that Mu'tazilitism was both a source and a major formative influence in what was, and is, orthodox Muslim speculative theology.

The beginnings of the Mu'tazilah are to be found in the questions raised and answered by a number of men whose activity has already been described: Ghaylan al-Dimashqi, Jahm ibn Safwan and Hasan al-Basri and his erstwhile disciple Wasil ibn 'Ata'. The followers of Ghaylan and Jahm eventually disappeared from the *Dar al-Islam* or were absorbed into other "schools"; Hasan and Wasil were, however, somewhat more fertile in successors. By their own accounts, the Mu'tazilites were constituted by the self-chosen "separation" (*i'tizal*) of Wasil and another disciple, 'Amr ibn 'Ubayd, from the circle of Hasan at Basrah. The immediate successors to Wasil and 'Amr's point of view are little more than obscure names, but the teaching of the two men, whatever its exact content, passed across that shadowy generation to the theologians who came into public view during the reign of Harun al-Rashid. Chief among these latter were Abu al-Hudhayl and the somewhat younger al-Nazzam. At the same time that Abu al-Hudhayl was active in Basrah, another branch of the Mu'tazilah was being founded in Baghdad by Bishr ibn al-Mu'tamir. Harun was uncertain about the politics of the new movement—it did not yet occur to Caliphs to worry about theology—and it must have been difficult in any event to reconcile the Baghdad Mu'tazilites' rather complacent attitudes toward the 'Alids with the 'Abbasids' own disengagement from the *Shi'at 'Ali*. Bishr was temporarily jailed for his views, but his students survived to enjoy the bounties of the pro-'Alid Ma'mun. Those were the golden years of Thumamah, Ibn abu Du'ad, Nazzam's disciple al-Jahiz, al-Shahham, al-Aswari and 'Abbad ibn Sulayman, the student of Hisham al-Fuwati.

The roll call of the Mu'tazilite teachers and their students gives

---

the archheretic al-Rewandi, while the recently discovered *Satisfactory Work* is an immense tract of systematic theology.

some idea of the historical shape of the movement, but nothing of what constituted the Mu'tazilites to begin with. On the evidence of their opponents, the loosely associated thinkers known as Mu'tazilites differed widely among themselves on important points. On some issues, however, there was agreement, and the Mu'tazilites themselves apparently acquiesced in the criterion of five basic theses. The Mu'tazilite was first a partisan of the unity (*tawhid*) of Allah, not merely as an affirmation of monotheism as understood by all Muslims, but in a special philosophical sense. Second, he affirmed the justice of God: Allah wished only good for the world and where sin did exist, it was the creation of man's free and responsible choice. Third, he discussed the nature of belief (*iman*) and its relation to sin and the commands of the *Qur'an*, the nature of the Law and tradition. Fourth, the Mu'tazilites took Wasil's "intermediate" position regarding the early Caliphs, that is, they recognized the legitimacy of the first three Caliphs as well as that of 'Ali, though there was disagreement on their relative merits. Finally, they promoted an active support of the observation of the Law.

On inspection, the five theses provide only indirect witness to the true origins of the Mu'tazilah or to their particular point of view. Many thinkers discussed these same points, and many if not all of the Mu'tazilites had far different questions on their agenda. The fourth point, that of the "intermediate state," is very primitive; it carried us back to the circle of Hasan al-Basri and may very well have been the original Mu'tazilite point of departure in politics. The first issue, that of the unity of God, is, on the other hand, of considerable metaphysical interest and seems to have been unknown to Hasan. Jahm appears to have been the first to have taken it up, though with what provocation or from what sources we can scarcely guess. Wasil's interest in *tawhid* is doubtful at best, but he at least points a direction: Wasil was a missionary and polemicist in the cause of Islam, and the two central Mu'tazilite theses of the unity and justice of God had a particular relevance to at least some of the nonbelievers within the *Dar al-Islam*.

The infidels against whom the Mu'tazilites labored to defend Islam will appear somewhat more clearly in the context of their physical and ethical theories, but the school may also be approached from its position in the debate surrounding the Islamic Law. At the time of the lawyer al-Shafi'i (d. 820) the Muslim legal spectrum was divided among three groups: the partisans of customary law (*ahl al-sunnah*) in the sense that that word was understood in the eighth century; the defenders of tradition (*ahl al-hadith*); and a final group variously described as proposing the method of "investigation" (*nazar*) or "personal opinion" and undoubtedly to be identified with the Mu'tazilites. The issue that divided the three groups was the interpretation of the *Qur'an*. The first maintained that as a legal instrument the *Qur'an* should be weighed somewhat pragmatically against the living local tradition of the law schools; the second that the *Qur'an* was the sole basis of the law and that the only permissible key to its exegesis was a tradition going back by unassailable witnesses to the Prophet or one of his Companions; the third group, the Mu'tazilites, placed an equally high value on the *Qur'an;* they differed from the traditionalists in that they wished to interpret it in the light of human reason.

On these legal grounds the Mu'tazilites appear to have been rationalists operating within the context of a revealed religion. Like their Christian contemporaries, they wished to understand that revelation in rational terms, unimpeded by either a local tradition or a body of traditioned exegesis that was, by the end of the eighth century, taking on the aura of a second revelation. By the time the Mu'tazilites came into favor at the beginning of the ninth century the first position, that of the *ahl al-sunnah*, had already been undermined; the fall of the Umayyads carried with it a discrediting of the pragmatic use of local tradition. The struggle was, then, between the traditionalists and the "partisans of speculation" on the issue of whether Allah could be grasped by natural cognition or only through God's unique and continuing voice speaking in the *Qur'an*, the *hadith*, and the consensus (*ijma'*) of the community. Already with al-Shafi'i the triumph of traditionalism was assured in the Law,[27] but in those speculative questions that had been raised in Islam almost from

27. See Chap. III, pp. 239–240.

the beginning, the issue was still being fought, as it would continue to be for the next three hundred years.

The Mu'tazilites were not the first speculative interpreters of the *Qur'an;* every Muslim divine since the death of the Prophet had been trying his hand at it. What the Mu'tazilites introduced into the practice was a speculative theory rooted in a set of rational principles, much in the same way that the Shi'ite reading of the *Qur'an* had certain political and religious premises. The Mu'tazilites never enunciated those principles, but preferred to conceal themselves behind the five traditional theses already described. The principles are evident nonetheless, and they are precisely those of the Greek rationalist tradition: that man's intelligence is an adequate instrument for acquiring the truth and that truth is most adequately expressed in intelligible terms.

Among the Greeks those premises had given rise to a physics, a metaphysics and an ethic describing the cosmos, God, and the good life for man. Christianity had had its effect in diminishing at least overt interest in the rationalistic ethic of late antiquity, and Islam too, as a revealed religion, paid only oblique attention to Hellenic-style ethics. But the Greek view of the cosmos and its workings and of the nature and activity of God was indissolubly linked with the rationalist premises that lay behind it; and so, too, in Islam the Mu'tazilites and their successors began their attempts at understanding the deposit of faith with a certain world view and a highly sophisticated theology that was far different from what operated in the mind of Muhammad or the speculations of either the traditionalist or Wasil ibn 'Ata'.

The intrusion of these new constructs and novel modes of understanding are first perceptible in the work of Jahm ibn Safwan, a far more likely sire to the Mu'tazilah than Wasil. Jahm had before him some vision of the world and God rationalized on a Neoplatonic model, and he proceeded to explain Allah in terms of that understanding. The Mu'tazilites followed in his path, not with one but with many world views, some of them crossed with non-Greek themes, but none of them even remotely resembling the *Weltanschauung* that lay behind the *Qur'an.* It is not by accident that the central Mu'tazilite thesis, that on the unity and transcendence of Allah, was precisely the one that lay at the heart of Jahm's speculations and was largely ignored by Hasan al-Basri and apparently by Wasil ibn 'Ata'. Religious politics and polemic were Wasil's style, not metaphysics; and if the Mu'tazilites were themselves not immune to the attractions of the *theologia civilis*, they did not make it their sole or most important concern.

No Muslim theologian of the eighth century could escape politics completely, but the Mu'tazilites took the problems raised by the history of the Islamic *ummah* and converted them into the stuff of philosophy. The process was complicated, to be sure, since most of these problems had already passed through the hands of the jurists and had been shaped by their concerns and their methods. One such was the central question of legal responsibility, a juridically framed discussion that arose from the political struggles of the years before and after Siffin, but which was for the Mu'tazilites an invitation toward epistemology rather than politics. Responsibility meant freedom or, more precisely, the freedom to act that appears in early theological debate as the "power" to act. The *Qur'an*'s unqualified insistence on both the omnipotence of God and the freedom of man challenged the theologians to present a rational explanation that would do justice to both.

For the Mu'tazilites the *Qur'an*-inspired dilemma raised two problems, not merely that of the operational extent of the human power to choose to act, but of the cognitional act that preceded the choice. Where the question narrowed to the performance of religious obligations, there the prior knowledge was the knowledge of God, and the Mu'tazilites were deeply involved in discussions on whether that knowledge of Allah was "given" to all men, so that they knew that they were acting morally in choosing to observe his law, or whether it was "acquired" by some and not by others, so that some men labored under what was, in effect, an inculpable ignorance.

"Given" was not the term current in theological discussions on the categories of knowledge. The Mu'tazilites divided cognition into "necessary" and "acquired" or "willed." Within the first category fell all the modes of knowing that are immediate and nondiscursive, and so infallible—sense perceptions and the intuitive grasp of axioms and first principles. Man has no real control over these ways of knowing and so is not responsible for them.

Where his responsibility does begin is in the second category, where discursive knowledge and the possibility of error have their place.

This distinction is very old among the theologians; even a proto-Mu'tazilite like Ghaylan recognized it. For him and for Abu al-Hudhayl the knowledge of the existence of God was of the a priori type qualified as "necessary" in that all men necessarily possessed it. But for these early thinkers the subsequent knowledge of the uniqueness of God and his revelation was "acquired" through a belief in the Prophet.

There is more than one difficulty here. There did not exist, it was clear, any immediate percept of God, and even Abu al-Hudhayl's equally immediate inference from the "sign" of creation to the Creator seemed somewhat less than immediate upon examination. One could, it appeared, come to a knowledge of God either through the process of discursive reasoning, which was, in the view of the next generation of Mu'tazilites, "acquired" knowledge, or immediately by a belief in revelation. Thumamah and his student Jahiz did not hesitate to draw the conclusion: the obligation to observe the Law rested solely and squarely upon the Muslim who had accepted the revelation; the nonbeliever could not be held culpably ignorant unless, of course, he denied the *possibility* of revelation or knew the truth and was prevented by his fanaticism from following it.

This somewhat abrupt exculpation of the infidels rested upon more than philosophical insight. In the atmosphere of Ma'mun's Baghdad, Thumamah's liberal stand justified and excused the Christian, Jewish and Zoroastrian beliefs of those other, non-Muslim residents of the *Dar al-Islam.* Intellectually it must not have been difficult to be indulgent. Contact with the sophisticated Christian version of speculation, which led in the end to beliefs quite different from Islam's, illustrated the complexity of the proofs for the existence of God; and to a degree that made it impossible to believe that it was an a priori knowledge of it. Abu al-Hudhayl may have been impressed by the fact that all men believed in God, but for Thumamah the crucial fact was the complexity of the paths that brought them there.

Nor was it any longer possible to be deceived that all men *did* believe in God. The developed literature of Islamic theology is studded with commonplace arguments derived directly from the skeptics of the later Platonic Academy. Most of these *topoi* are directed to showing the fallibility of sense knowledge and, in the end, were as little effective in undermining confidence in sense-based speculations among the Muslims as they had been among the Greeks. But, in addition to these literary arguments, which the Mu'tazilites knew,[28] the theologians had direct contact with quite another school of philosophers, who took sense knowledge quite seriously, to the exclusion, indeed, of all other forms of knowledge. They denied, as a consequence, the existence of both God and the human soul.

The members of this school, which had its origins in India, the Muslims called "Sumaniyah." Such radical sensualists of the Sumaniyah type are known in Indian intellectual history, and there is good evidence that they were represented in Baghdad at the time of the Barmacids (786–803)—who were themselves from a Buddhist family from eastern Khurasan—and that they were engaged in dialogue with Wasil ibn 'Ata' and Jahm ibn Safwan among others. The Sumaniyah may have made no converts, but they survived in the Muslim heresiographies as proof that it was possible to deny the existence of God and so render improbable the conviction that such knowledge was a priori.

Thumamah had good philosophical grounds for maintaining that the knowledge of God was totally within the realm of "acquired" speculation. If God is the object of speculation, then it must follow, according to Thumamah, that there will be those who do not, or cannot, arrive at such knowledge and that their ignorance is inculpable. Other, less theoretical, motives may have been urging him to the same conclusion. The struggle for social parity between Arab and non-Arab was still being fought, and Ma'mun's own cultural interests were catholic in their embrace.

---

28. The Muslims generalized most of these skeptics under the name of "Sophists," and indeed many of their arguments were similar to those brought forward earlier by Gorgias and Protagoras. But "Sophists" may be a false scent. In late antiquity the chief aficionados of such skeptical arguments were members of the so-called "empirical" school of physicians, and the path from them to Baghdad may well have led through the lecture halls of the Syrian hospital at Jundishapur.

More, the Hellenic learning now on display in the capital was creating a new generation of Muslim intellectuals, and the chief and almost sole guides to that learning were the Syrian Christians, who passed easily between Baghdad and Jundishapur. Thumamah's thesis both caught and sustained the liberal temper of the times.

The Mu'tazilites were one in their agreement that man is capable of knowing, whether it be immediately (and so "necessarily") through the senses or his grasp of the self-evident first principles,[29] or else mediately through discursive speculation. Knowledge presented the human will with a choice, and it is precisely in that choice, according to al-Nazzam, that man's freedom consists. And when choice flows into action, here too the Mu'tazilites, the partisans of divine justice, were unanimous in asserting that willed acts were caused by the volitional agent and, so, were his legal responsibility.

The Mu'tazilite vindication of human freedom drove divine causality from one corner of the universe, a consequence entirely unacceptable to the traditionalists, who feared that Allah's omnipotence was being undermined by such views. But there was more, and worse. Bishr ibn al-Mu'tamir, who learned his Mu'tazilitism from members of Wasil's circle at Basrah and later founded a branch of the movement in Baghdad, was willing to extend human causality even beyond the single, immediately willed action. Choice initiated a chain of serial causes. The first act was willed, but the subsequent ones in the series were likewise "generated" by the original agent, and he was responsible for them no less than the first. The series, Bishr conceded, unfolded according to strict physical laws governing bodies, but "according to" was not the same as "because of" and so the original agent retained responsibility. Not all of the Mu'tazilites agreed with this extension of human causality—Thumamah, Bishr's student, demurred[30]—nor were they all willing to follow down another

29. These were understood much in the same way that they were in the Greek tradition, by Aristotle, for example.

30. The standard *casus* for this principle was that of a man who shot an arrow but died before it struck and killed its target. Thumamah was unwilling to declare, as Bishr did, that the dead archer was an

parallel avenue of causality where their Hellenic-style epistemology was beckoning them.

Mu'tazilitism forced a second breach in divine omnipotence: man "created" not merely his voluntary acts but at least some of his cognitive ones as well. The distinction between "necessary" and "acquired" knowledge is found, as has been noted, among the earliest theologians and it represents, doubtless, the somewhat restrained recognition that the Muslims were willing to pay to the sovereign and autonomous Greek *episteme:* speculation "created" knowledge which was then "acquired" by the speculator. "Acquisition"—the term was first used by Wasil's student Dirar ibn 'Amr—is a modest-enough expression to get around the somewhat blasphemous "created." Bishr's "generation" (*tawlid*) was considerably more pointed, however, and the implications were not, at any rate, missed. Much of post-Mu'tazilite theology was devoted to finding other semantic paths around the embarrassments of "generation" in the name of preserving the omnipotence of Allah. Only he could create, and most Muslims were unwilling to grant that power to the premises of a syllogism.

The earliest Mu'tazilites knew little of syllogistic reasoning, though they were associated in the minds of their opponents with the introduction of a new type of discourse into Islam. Already in Shafi'i's time the Mu'tazilites were known as the *ahl al-kalam*, partisans of discourse or, better, of the dialectical speculation expressed in Greek by *dialexis*. The Hellenic *dialektikos* became in Arabic the *mutakallim* (pl. *mutakallimun*), and his science, *kalam*. Other etymologies have been proposed, and by the Arabs themselves: *kalam* as logic (*logike*) or as a scientific body of knowledge about God (*theologia*). But an inspection of the methods of the earliest *mutakallimun* shows that both formal logic and systematic theology were far from their thoughts.

From the beginning *kalam* was looked upon as an Islamic science and so had its place among the "traditioned" sciences; the Greek *theologia*, Aristotle's "first philosophy," held a completely independent position as the "divine science" (*'ilm ilahi*) among

---

ex post morte murderer, nor was he about to place the responsibility upon God. Rather, he embraced the paradox and declared it a deed without a doer.

the "rational" sciences. *Kalam* might be superfluous in the minds of many, but it was Islamic, nonetheless. Its adherents justified it on the grounds of its usefulness for the confirmation and defense of a faith already received from the Prophet. The *mutakallimun* never denied revelation, and their designation as rationalists must be understood within the rather restrictive confines of whether the Qur'anic revelation is better understood by the application of reasoning (*nazar*) or by reliance upon tradition.

The defense of the Muslim faith was not waged solely in Muslim terms, however. Both the method and the substance of the early *mutakallimun*, of whom the Mu'tazilites were simply the best-known example, owed something to outside sources. Those outside sources were not merely Greek, nor entirely philosophical. It is unlikely that they should have been, since the *mutakallimun*, at least since the time of Wasil, were making their defense of Islam not against conservative traditionalists, as sometimes appears from the Islamic sources where the traditionalists regarded groups like the Mu'tazilites as *their* adversaries, but against infidels and heretics of many stripes, very few of whom were either pure Hellenists or simply philosophers.

Among their other titles the Mu'tazilites were described as "partisans of dialectic," a designation that already sets them apart, in a quite significant way, from the philosophical tradition. For the Hellenic philosopher the dialectical argument, drawn from well-known *topoi* and proceeding across positions determined by polemic, was not the stuff of philosophical discourse. The scientific method in philosophy was the way of the syllogism: conclusions deduced rigorously from premises. The early Mu'tazilites were innocent of the possibility of syllogistic proof; they argued from "sign," not demonstration, and their preferred method was not very different from the analogical reasoning current among the Islamic lawyers.

A prolonged and studied encounter with Greek philosophy would eventually revolutionize the methods of the *mutakallimun*, but for these early theologians the more important influence was the constant and subtle interplay between what was emerging as a speculative theology and the older and more precocious science of jurisprudence. Earlier, Greek philosophers in the generation of Plato and Aristotle had turned to the already developed methodology of rhetoric, mathematics and medicine for the derivation of precise and coherent ways of philosophizing. Similarly in Islam, the previous coming of age of philology had its effects on the development of literary criticism. The early *mutakallim*, then, was confronted with the mature range of *sunnah*-based sciences, and they provided for him, whether he willed it or not, a methodological model for his own efforts.

To point the Mu'tazilites toward jurisprudence (*fiqh*) is not, however, to solve the problems of origins. *Fiqh* and *kalam* were not the only disciplines to use what the Greeks knew generally as the method of dialectic. Greek theology, particularly the Stoic version, had moved from demonstration to dialectic long before the coming of Islam, and the progressive infiltration of Christian theology by the dialectical methods cultivated in the Hellenistic schools of rhetoric is well documented. There are not many *kalam* works preserved from the earliest days, but the evidence suggests that they were cast in the form of disputations rather than of systematic treatises. Truly systematic works followed in time, and from Ghazali onward the *mutakallimun's* analogical and topical "proofs" yielded to the kinds of syllogistic demonstration long known to the Muslim philosophers.

The Mu'tazilites were not, then, the first philosophers of Islam, the forerunners of Kindi, Farabi and Ibn Sina, but the fashioners of a new dimension in the understanding of Islam, thinkers who chose to defend the Islamic revelation against rivals who accepted neither the *Qur'an* nor tradition. Cast in such a role, they might have been acceptable to the most conservative of believers. But the Mu'tazilites claimed more. They suggested, in varying degrees, that speculative reasoning not only was useful for the defense of Islam, but was necessary for its true understanding. How else, they argued, could the believer protect himself from doubt? There was no lack of alternative answers to that question, most of which the Mu'tazilites denounced as either inadequate or untrue. If conviction was the goal of the believer, it could be achieved only by understanding, and that, in turn, came only from rational investigation.

The conclusion drawn by the Mu'tazilites was a quasi-juridical one: the obligation to rational investigation was a religious obligation incumbent upon all Muslims. The more moderate *mutakalli-*

mun were unwilling to go quite that far and taught that the obligation did not bind all. The issue was, in any event, drawn, and the traditionalists reacted energetically. To the Mu'tazilites' *nazar* they opposed the jurists' *taqlid*, the acceptance of a proposition on authority. In law the principle rested upon the developing notion that the *sunnah* of the Prophet represented the only practical norm for the interpretation of the *Qur'an*, and that the *sunnah* was transmitted infallibly, it was coming to be believed, by the generation of the Prophet's Companions, in the form of "traditions."

The Mu'tazilites resisted the notion of *taqlid* in *kalam* as energetically as they did in the law. In their eyes *taqlid* was pointless since it provided no criterion for its own truth. Whether under Mu'tazilite pressure or not, the traditionalists did not attempt to propose a criterion. It was rooted in consensus: some traditions were exceedingly prevalent, and the fact of their general acceptance was the guarantee of the truth of their content. Among the Mu'tazilites, al-Nazzam in particular attacked the notion of "prevalence" and in a manner used by his own opponents against *kalam:* either the substance of the tradition is rationally coherent, in which case the "prevalence" adds nothing, or else it is false, and its widespread dissemination is merely misleading. Indeed, Nazzam doubted the very possibility of a consensus on points of doctrine, since each transmission was, in effect, a personal opinion, and the earliest generation of Muslims went to war among themselves over just such personal differences. Al-Shafi'i held that the Muslim community could not agree in error; Nazzam was convinced that it could.

There were those among the Muslims who knew that the *ummah* had, in fact, come to just such a consensus in error, specifically in its acceptance of Abu Bakr and 'Umar over 'Ali as its Caliph. This was the point of view of some of the *Shi'at Ali;* and if they were generally unimpressed by the argument from traditions that rested upon the authority of the Companions of the Prophet, they were in the end even less favorably disposed toward the Mu'tazilite theory of speculation. In later years the Shi'ites rejected the Mu'tazilite rationalism in favor of their own version of *taqlid*. By then the two groups had grown far apart in their ideology and politics, but earlier, in the waning years of the eighth century, when the Shi'ites still entertained political hopes and the Mu'tazilites were first emerging as a recognizable complex of scholars at Basrah and Baghdad, the fortunes of the two were more closely linked.

The Mu'tazilites claimed both Hasan al-Basri and Wasil ibn 'Ata' as their parents, and some of the theses later characterized as Mu'tazilite were in fact being discussed in Hasan's circle. As they are later described in the *kalam* works, those theses appear to rest solely upon theological issues, but Wasil was, as has been seen, a political theoretician as well as a theologian. His theology may well have flowed directly from his politics, and the eighth-century talk among Hasan's followers about the status of sinners and God's justice clearly depended on some prior assumptions regarding the Imamate of 'Ali, its legitimacy and the legitimacy of his three predecessors in that office.

The very *etymon* of the Mu'tazilite school, *i'itizal*, which means "separation" and which the Mu'tazilites themselves interpreted as Wasil's withdrawal from the following of Hasan, probably had its true origins in an earlier and far more political act, the "separation" of some of 'Ali's own supporters, who chose to assume a neutral position sometime between the battle of Siffin and 'Ali's submission to arbitration. They did not reject 'Ali's claims; they merely refused to fight on his behalf. It was in this political sense of the word that Wasil was a Mu'tazilite, a "separatist" who supported neither the Umayyads nor those Shi'ite extremists who wished to condemn out of hand all pretenders to the Caliphate save 'Ali.

The Shi'ite theologians of the first half century after the 'Abbasid succession to the Caliphate present a confused picture. There were, according to al-Jahiz, two main bodies of them, the Rafidites and the Zaydites. The first group was so called because they "deserted" (*rafada*) the claims of Abu Bakr, 'Umar and, of course, 'Uthman to the Caliphate, which is precisely the question that was being debated at Basrah during the declining years of the Umayyads. The Rafidites took a stronger view than that held by Wasil and later by the Zaydites; for them, Muhammad had designated 'Ali as his successor and so the Caliphates of the first three *Rashidun* were illegal. From the original 'Abbasid point of view, namely that the Caliphate had descended to al-Saffah through

'Ali's son Muhammad ibn al-Hanafiyah, the Rafidite contention would have been of no practical consequence. But sometime during the reign of al-Mahdi (775–785) the 'Abbasids had begun to advance a new claim to the effect that the Prophet had designated al-Saffah's ancestor, and Muhammad's own uncle, al-'Abbas, to be his successor. This proposal found little support in the *ummah*, but as long as they stood by it the 'Abbasids forced the Rafidites, and indeed all of the 'Alids, into opposition.

The Rafidite knife cut somewhat deeper than Abu Bakr and 'Umar; they rejected as well the testimony of all the Companions of the Prophet who had recognized those two men. Here was indeed a radical legal stand, since the great body of *hadith* upon which the edifice of the Islamic Law was being constructed rested upon the witness of those same Companions. Where, then, did the Rafidites propose to found the authority of the Law? Here the Rafidites had recourse to their own theory of the Caliphate and turned to the designated *Imams* who descended through the line of 'Ali's son Husayn down to Ja'far al-Sadiq (d. 765) and who were the guarantors of the genuine *sunnah* of Islam.

There is no evidence that the Rafidites were taking any overt political action to subvert the regimes of the 'Abbasids al-Mahdi and Harun al-Rashid. They were at this point still theologians and not revolutionaries, as can be seen from the activity of the best-known of them during the eighth century. Hisham ibn al-Hakam (d. c. 795) was originally a member of the circle of the Imam Ja'far and then later appears as a disputant with the Mu'tazilite Abu al-Hudhayl during the latter's passage through Mecca on the pilgrimage. On the basis of some very sparse accounts, Hisham held not only the Rafidite political theses but an embryonic metaphysic that identified existence with body and so led necessarily to a literal, anthropomorphizing reading of the *Qur'an*.[31]

---

31. Another trail back to Hisham leads from one of the earliest preserved heresiographies, the *Sects of the Shi'ah* of Hasan ibn Musa al-Nawbakhti (see Chap. VIII, p. 579), who used Hisham's earlier *Popular Differences on the Imamate*. Hasan ibn Musa's own work was largely incorporated into another heresiography, the *Views and Sects* of the Imamite Shi'ite Sa'd ibn 'Abdallah of Qumm.

The Mu'tazilites resisted Hisham and his views, but toward the other main body of the Shi'ah, the Zaydis, their relationships were far more complex. The Zaydis were somewhat less venturesome in their theology, but they took a far more active political posture than the Rafidites. None of the Rafidites was dabbling in politics during the difficult days under the early 'Abbasids, nor did the first generation of descendants from Hasan and Husayn show much zeal for rebellion. The Hasanids took regularly to emigration to the far west of the *Dar al-Islam*, where a number of dynasties later claimed descent from them, while Husaynids like Muhammad al-Baqir (d. 731) and the latter's son Ja'far al-Sadiq chose to spend their Imamates in circumspect piety.

But despite the appearances of calm, the Husaynid Muhammad al-Baqir's death provoked a major crisis among the *Shi-at 'Ali*. The principle of dynastic succession to the Imamate was by no means so firmly established as later Shi'ite writers would have us believe, and so at al-Baqir's death not all of his supporters transferred their allegiance to his son Ja'far. An important minority went over to al-Baqir's brother Zayd. Zayd met his end during an abortive uprising in Kufah in 740, and in the confused political situation surrounding the accession of the 'Abbasids, the focus of attention shifted to the Hasanids Muhammad and Ibrahim. Before his death in 748 Wasil had openly promoted recognition of the Imamate of Muhammad, surnamed "the pure spirit" (*al-nafs al-zakiyah*), and fourteen years later, when Muhammad was in open revolt at Medina, there were "partisans of free will" among his supporters. His brother Ibrahim at Basrah also had allies in the Mu'tazilah, Wasil's students among them.[32]

Zaydite and Mu'tazilite had similar political views. There were differences, surely—the Mu'tazilite followers of 'Amr ibn 'Ubayd made their peace with the 'Abbasids, while certain hard-line Zaydites stood close to the Rafidite refusal to recognize Abu Bakr and 'Umar—but on questions of who could be the *Imam* and who in Islam had in fact been *Imams* they were in reasonable agreement. Theologically, however, the distance that separated Zaydite from Mu'tazilite and both of those groups from a

---

32. But not 'Amr ibn 'Ubayd, who refused to recognize Muhammad when Wasil did and eventually took his oath of allegiance to Mansur.

Rafidite like Hisham ibn al-Hakam was at first considerably greater. Sulayman ibn Jarir, for example, a Zaydi *mutakallim* of the time of Harun, who had entered into debate with Hisham, strenuously defended Allah's determining power over the entire cosmos, man included. But while differing from the Mu'tazilites on the question of human freedom, Sulayman was as unrelenting as they in his rejection of anthropomorphism and his defense of Allah's unity.

Their agreement on Shi'ite political theses had created trouble for all three groups, Zaydites, Rafidites and Mu'tazilites, during the reign of Harun (786–809), but with the accession of Ma'mun in 813 there was a sudden reversal of fortune. The 'Alid *Imam*, Ja'far's grandson 'Ali al-Rida, was publicly declared Ma'mun's designated successor in the Caliphate, and even after Ma'mun's 'Alid intentions grew somewhat less fervid, he never relaxed his support of the Shi'ite-leaning theologians of the realm. Among the Mu'tazilites these were chiefly found in Baghdad where a branch of the Mu'tazilah had been founded by Bishr ibn al-Mu'tamir under the difficult circumstances of Harun's reign.

Baghdad Mu'tazilites appear close to the throne from the beginnings of Ma'mun's reign to his death twenty years later. Chief among them were Thumamah ibn Ashras and the *qadi* who played a central role in the *mihnah*, Ibn abi Du'ad. By then the group had a highly developed physics and metaphysics, but the Caliph was likely interested in neither. Ma'mun's problem was the political one of the 'Alids and the "partisans of the *sunnah* and the community." He had chosen to reconcile the 'Alids at the expense of the traditionalists, and so what Ma'mun needed was a practical test case and not a manifesto on the ontological status of substance and accidents.

Just such a political test was constructed out of the theological question of whether the *Qur'an* was created or uncreated. The choice was a shrewd one. To maintain, as the Mu'tazilites did, that the *Qur'an* was created had important political implications for the Shi'ah. It provided theological justification for the Shi'ite argument that the *Qur'an* and the reported traditions of the Prophet had been falsified at the expense of 'Ali, and by subtly downgrading the Muhammad-transmitted Book, the Shi'ites had before them the open possibility of a claim for an alternate or complementary source of revelation, the guidance of the Shi'ite *Imam*.

Neither of these motifs figures, of course, in the Mu'tazilite argumentation that was conducted in strictly dialectical terms. In their reduction of the *Qur'an* to a created object the Mu'tazilites were in fact being true to their metaphysics. The divine simplicity (*tawhid*) was defended by drawing a distinction between Allah and all of his attributes, including, in this case, his utterance (*kalam*). Allah is in his essence eternal, but all else is his creation, either directly, like his own utterance and knowledge, or through secondary causality, like the speech of men.

The traditionalists found this position quite unacceptable. They read the *Qur'an* literally and adhered to the belief that Allah, his *kalam* and all of his attributes were identical and eternal. Some of the traditionalists of the school of Ahmad ibn Hanbal went even further: the *Qur'an* is uncreated, both the Heavenly Book that is the speech of Allah and its earthly recitation by the lips of men. The distinction between the transcendental and human utterance was likely borrowed by the Hanbalites from the Mu'tazilites, but they did not avail themselves of the *distinguo* to compromise their position. There were others, however, for whom the distinction was useful.

Later, in the early tenth century, the theologian al-Ash'ari (d. 935) would attempt to mediate the rationalist theses of the Mu'tazilites and the fundamentalism of the Hanbalites, but he had predecessors in the Baghdad of Ma'mun. The *mutakallim* Ibn Kullab was unalterably opposed to Ma'mun and his court theologians. But his opposition was expressed as dialectically as the Mu'tazilites' own theses. Ibn Kullab took the distinction between Allah's utterance and that of men and argued that while the first was eternal, as an attribute subsisting in God's essence, its expression on the lips of men comes into existence in time.[33]

The *Qur'an* was, then, both created and uncreated. Ibn Kullab was in an exposed position. Somewhat like the Christian theo-

---

33. Ibn Kullab apparently could not bring himself to say that men "created" even the physical recitation of the *Qur'an*. One of his intellectual followers, the theologian and mystic al-Muhasibi (d. 857), had no such scruples. On Muhasibi, see Chap. VI, pp. 421–426.

logians at Chalcedon, he was trying to thread his way between a dialectically indefensible literal interpretation of the *Qur'an* and the Mu'tazilite wish to explain away the mystery. For Jahm and the Mu'tazilah the *Qur'an* presented no problem in ontology, any more than Jesus did for the Nestorians. But for Ibn Kullab and the *ahl al-hadith* the stripping away of Allah's characteristics and actions in the name of metaphysics seemed like an act of exegetical violence that led to an even wider separation of Allah from his creation.

Nor was the "speech of Allah" an isolated problem. Its political repercussions may have been of concern to the generation of theologians under Ma'mun, but it implicated, both before and after the first decades of the ninth century, the larger question of the attributes of Allah. These attributes (*sifat*) were in origin nothing more than the energetic predicates used to describe Allah in the *Qur'an,* where he is spoken of as performing various actions, like knowing, or characterized by certain qualities, like mercy and compassion.[34]

For the ordinary believer the Qur'anic predicates raised no serious problems, but they drew the theologian to speculation on two further points: is Allah to be conceived of as anthropomorphically as these predicates suggest—is he really "speaking" as we speak?—and what is their ontological relationship to his being? Is God the same as his speech?

Both questions had been posed earlier within Christianity and Judaism, and the first, at least, among the Greeks. All three had solved the problem of anthropomorphism relatively early on by choosing to interpret the passages in their revelation or myth in

---

34. In the theological discussions it is these latter, already hypostatized by linguistic usage into abstract nouns, that constitute the divine attributes, while the descriptive adjectives and participles, many of them of pre-Islamic origin, are Allah's "names" and the subject of pious and mystical contemplation rather than theological dispute. There are, according to one tradition, ninety-nine names of Allah, and he who recites them will enter Paradise. The cult of the divine names was widespread in Islam, as well as inquiries into their presumed esoteric meaning. The search for the "supreme name" which, if discovered, would lay bare the true identity of Allah was merely one exciting part of the quest.

nonliteral terms; on the eve of Islam there was no serious theologian willing to stand behind a strictly construed anthropomorphism. On the second point, however, both Judaism and Christianity had encountered serious difficulties. The God of the Greek philosophers, constructed backward from effects to cause, was defined in terms of an absolute Oneness that defied, in its triumphant Neoplatonic version, all attempts at introducing qualities into his being. Of secondary hypostases there was no end, but they were effects. It was the Greeks' final version of God, and he is as visible in Jahm ibn Safwan as he was in Plotinus.

Common sense suggested to the Muslim that Allah's Qur'anic predicates were somehow "consubstantial" with Allah himself, but only in the sense that a man's actions were his own. Whatever prompted him—certainly not Christian theology, which affirmed just the opposite—Jahm ibn Safwan attempted to play Arius to the Muslim community by subordinating Allah's attributes to Allah's essence. There was no Jesus to confound the problem, but there was the *Qur'an*, an Islamic "Word that was made flesh," which was, like Jesus, both consubstantial with Allah and at the same time "outside" him. The Jahmiyah found no support among the orthodox, but they succeeded in raising both an issue, the oneness (*tawhid*) of God, and a manner of solution that in the end reduced the traditionalists to a frustrating fundamentalism.

Jahm did, however, find support, or imitators, among the still-negligible ranks of the Hellenizers within Islam. One of them, Dirar ibn 'Amr, who lived at Basrah sometime about the end of the eighth century,[35] made explicit that the *Qur'an*'s descriptions of Allah are to be understood as nothing more than the denials of their opposites and so introduced in a formal way the *theologia negativa* that lies close to the surface in Jahm. Both men, Jahm

35. Dirar was likely a student of Wasil's at Basrah, but with a considerably greater flair for metaphysics. Where Dirar and the Mu'tazilites parted company, however, was on the question of free will. Dirar is the first theologian to have experimented with that later Ash'arite staple, the "acquisition" (*kasb*) of moral responsibility by men, while most of the Mu'tazilites preferred to grant man a real rather than an "acquired" dominion over his own acts.

and Dirar, represent what later Islamic orthodoxy called the "stripping off" of Allah's attributes, a charge that was also leveled at the Mu'tazilites.

In the Mu'tazilites' case the accusation was not entirely fair. The main body of the Mu'tazilah, with al-Nazzam at its head, did indeed deny any reality to the attributes, but at an early stage in the discussion one of them, al-Nazzam's teacher Abu al-Hudhayl, attempted a somewhat more nuanced position: God does possess attributes; he is knowing by reason of his knowledge, and so the attribute of "knowledge" may fairly be predicated of him. Allah's knowledge is, however, identical with his essence, though not identical with the other attributes.

With Abu al-Hudhayl's statement we have unmistakably returned to the thinking of Ibn Kullab, who held a similar compromise position on the *Qur'an*, and here, too, had attempted to work his way between the radical "stripping" of someone like Dirar and the literalism of the ultraconservatives whose embrace of anthropomorphism drove them to assert an absolute similarity between human and divine attributes. Ibn Kullab affirmed the existence of the attributes as qualities subsisting in the divine essence, not identical with that essence, as in Abu al-Hudhayl, but simultaneously like it and unlike it.

Ibn Kullab's compromise formula was not original with him. A generation before, in the time of Harun, the Rafidite Hisham ibn al-Hakam had proposed a similar solution, though with somewhat wider metaphysical implications. Hisham's two categories of being were bodies and their attributes, and these latter were, somewhat as Ibn Kullab later expressed it, neither bodies nor entirely separable from bodies. For the Mu'tazilites, who saw reality in far different terms, neither category was appropriate. The identification of existence and body reduced God to body—a conclusion that Hisham appears not to have recoiled from—and the peculiar ambivalence of the *sifat* denied them the kind of quasi substantiality that was demanded by the Mu'tazilites' physics.

The trail that leads back from Ibn Kullab to Hisham can be traced somewhat further. The witnesses are hostile, but a number of later theologians thought they knew where Hisham derived his philosophical insights. Mu'tazilites and anti-Mu'tazilites alike accuse Hisham of borrowing from the dualists, and particularly from the followers of the Edessan Theologian Bar Daysan (d. 222). Hisham is alleged to have gotten his "like and not like" formula from them, as well as his characteristic corporeality. The Daysaniyah, it appears, held that all existents, even qualities and universals, were bodies, a view that one pre-Islamic student of philosophy, Sergius of Reshayna (d. 536), claimed came to them from the Stoics.

From Stoicism to the Daysaniyah to Hisham is a difficult path to follow. The Daysaniyah were well known in early 'Abbasid times, and their works were circulating, along with Mani's, in Arabic translation. The details of their contents are not known, except that they dealt with cosmology, astrology and ethics; there are, however, hints enough on the substance of the Daysanite system in its Islamic version. Unlike the Manichaeans and somewhat in the manner of the Hellenic tradition, the Daysaniyah held that matter was a privative rather than an active principle. It arises rather than is, and its source is the mixture of the four pure elements. Once a metaphysics of light and darkness was superimposed upon this cosmology—darkness appears in the elements once they are mixed—a confusion seems to have arisen. Some of the Muslims accused the Daysaniyah of dualism, in believing in a good and evil God. The charge appears not to be accurate but to have derived from a supposed analogy with the Manichees, who did indeed believe in two Gods, the good identified with the light and the evil with darkness. The Muslims were not always careful in classifying their *zindiqs*.

Hisham was accused of taking his inspiration from a Daysanite named Abu Shakir, and the same name appears in an interesting context in the *Catalogue* of Ibn al-Nadim, where Abu Shakir is one of a number of men described as "crypto-Manichaeans." Though Ibn al-Nadim was writing two centuries after the event, he is an excellent witness on such matters and his list includes another, considerably more familiar name, that of Abu 'Isa al-Warraq, a well-known, if not popular, figure in Mu'tazilite circles and probably a contemporary of al-Jahiz. Abu 'Isa had, in fact, begun his theological career as a Mu'tazilite but then denounced the school—and possibly Islam as well—in favor of dualism.

Among the Mu'tazilites al-Nazzam was often accused of having dualist tendencies,[36] but the truth of the matter is more likely that the school began as Wasil's organized attempt at refuting the dualists. The Mu'tazilite thesis on the justice of God, normally understood by the heresiographers to refer to an intramural Islamic disputes, strikes at the heart of Manichaean ethical dualism, and their position on *tawhid*, an issue which appears abruptly among the theologians, seems calculatedly aimed against philosophical and theological proponents of corporeality like the Daysaniyah rather than at the naïve Islamic anthropomorphists.

The Mu'tazilites continued to use the term "attributes" to describe the characteristics of Allah, but for the most part they severed Hisham's tenuously expressed connection with being: the "attributes" were merely descriptive terms. To express really distinct attributes the Mu'tazilites from Abu al-Hudhayl onward turned to another term, "accident." It appears to be a simple turning, but by it Islamic theology was abruptly thrust into a metaphysics quite different from the Neoplatonic musings of Jahm or the quasi-Stoic attitudes of Hisham and the Daysaniyah.

The theory of atoms and accidents had a long history in Islam, and one form or another of it continued to be closely associated with *kalam*. Abu al-Hudhayl is generally reckoned the founder, but in his presentation, the earliest known to us, it is true, the system appears well thought-out and essentially complete, and so, perhaps, Abu al-Hudhayl was drawing upon earlier sources, either within Islam or without.

On Abu al-Hudhayl's view, reality is constituted by bodies: everything that exists, at least within our perceptions, is body. Bodies have their own constitutive elements, however, since an analysis of change suggests that they are conglomerates. The elements of their composition are what the Mu'tazilites described as "atoms" and "accidents." The first is substrate, an inert and absolutely unqualified ground in which all else inheres. The "all else" are the accidents, all the properties and qualities of a thing,

---

36. Many of these charges stem from Ibn al-Rewandi, a student of Abu 'Isa, who like his master defected from the Mu'tazilah; see Chap. VI, p. 469. The charges are refuted in detail by al-Khayyat in his *Book of Triumph.*

its quantification, and even such things as its composition, conjunction and contiguity of parts.

It is this latter, more formal type of accident that, by its adherence in atoms—perhaps six at a minimum—operates to bring together a body, that perceptible unit of experience that is a thing by reason of its self-coherence and its separation from other things. The formal, compositional accidents do not yet serve to explain the existential reality of the thing. For that, something more is needed, its "createdness," the creative act which initiates, continues, or terminates the actualization of this body in this time and place.

There is an obviously static quality to this view of being, a "freezing" of an existent at a given moment of time and the application of an analysis that yields discrete bits of states, activities and properties hypostatized into "accidents." The earlier Platonic tradition had shown inclinations in the same direction in isolating its "forms"; but Plato was led there by the conditions of an epistemology that was incapable of reconciling knowledge and process. Abu al-Hudhayl, on the other hand, appears to be in the grip of a special physics. That physics recoiled from admitting the infinite divisibility of bodies and so posited the atom, not in the sense of either Democritus or Epicurus, but as a restless alien in what otherwise appears like an Aristotelian division into matter and form.

The Mu'tazilite atom, like the Aristotelian prime matter, is pure substratum, the locus for the adherence of the accidents, with no quantities or qualities of its own. But there is no Aristotelian "form," with its concomitant notions of "structure" (*eidos*) and "act" (*energeia*), inhering in the atom but, rather, what appears to be a kind of hypostatized version of every predicate that may be said of a given object. The Mu'tazilite "accident" is a discrete, not a continuous, informing of the atom, and the cinematographic effect of Aristotelian being is exchanged for a series of still portraits. Abu al-Hudhayl attempted to get his stalled mechanism back into motion by insisting that the body perdures through a finite period of time; but the "body" in this case is neither the atom, which perdures but has no subsistent reality, nor the real existent itself, which is only *these* atoms with *these* accidents. The body that perdures is, then, *these* atoms with *some* of the more important accidents composed in more or less the same way.

The explanation must not have been very convincing, since even during Abu al-Hudhayl's lifetime al-Nazzam was forced to make resort to external sources of dynamism to "move" the relatively inert being. For Abu al-Hudhayl each existent is locked within itself; it is neither self-determining nor self-moving. There are, however, two beings in the system that are something more than actualized potentiality: God and man. Each is a mover and an actualizer that can affect reality outside itself. Man has, of course, soul and life and knowledge, but these are apparently little different from the "accidents" of all other bodies. But unlike those other bodies, the conglomerate that is man possesses a power that operates through a free act of his will. To the scandal of the orthodox, Abu al-Hudhayl made free to maintain that man creates, differently from God, but only in degree, not in kind. Thus, according to Abu al-Hudhayl, man can effect only motion and rest; other acts flow from these, but it was not clear to the various Mu'tazilites how far human responsibility should be extended along this line of generated effects.

To sustain and activate these discrete "moments" of being in Abu al-Hudhayl's system, al-Nazzam allegedly had resort not to the restricted power of man but to the infinite power of Allah: each body is continuously recreated in each moment of time. This thesis became a standard one in the atomism of the later *mutakallimun*, but it is not at all certain that Nazzam held it in exactly that form. In his view reality consisted solely in bodies, as it did for Hisham ibn al-Hakam, and "movements." This distinction is almost a moral one: "movements" are those acts, like praying, willing, knowing, et cetera, that are initiated by man; all else is body, either of the simple sort (hot, cold, red, etc.) or compound (fire is a composite of heat and light).

As far as we can make out, Nazzam held that God created all these "bodies" at one time and implanted in them a nature which governs their operation. But the bodies impenetrate each other or, to use another term favored by both Hisham and Nazzam, they lie "concealed" in each other. Thus perceptible beings, that is, composite bodies, are constantly changing, not because of the momentary quality of hot and cold but because of their passage in and out of each other.

The strange and convoluted metaphysics of atoms and accidents argued by the Mu'tazilites became the standard theory of the *mutakallimun*. The traditionalists regarded it with suspicion, and the philosophers with the disdain that Platonists reserved for the crudities of materialism. The Arab consensus was that the Mu'tazilites had borrowed it from the Greeks. This may be so, though the "atom" of Abu al-Hudhayl seems to fit somewhat uncomfortably between the atom of Democritus and Epicurus and the substance of Aristotle. His is an atom in the sense that it is, for all except Nazzam, an indivisible particle. But unlike the elementary particle of the Greek atomists it is completely devoid of characteristics of its own. And in its totally unqualified state the "atom" appears to resemble not so much the Aristotelian notion of substance, with its formal and structural connotations, as a discrete version of "first matter," potentiality rather than act. The Mu'tazilite "accidents," on the other hand, seem to have almost nothing to do with the Aristotelian *symbebekos* and to cover a range far broader than anything Epicurus intended by that term.

While not precluding the possibility of some far less visible connection, with Indian atomism, for example, the Mu'tazilite physics appears to be a hybrid constructed out of Greek materials. We recognize each of the elements, but we have never seen them in this particular configuration before. The Muslims themselves, who suspected Greek influence whenever they sniffed heresy, are of little help here. The Arabs had a direct and systematic knowledge of only Plato and Aristotle out of the thousand-year history of Greek philosophy that preceded them. What they knew of the pre-Socratics they derived, as we do, largely from the doxographies that were composed to serve as handbooks for the school disputes of late antiquity.[37] The Arabs' knowledge of post-Aristotelian philosophy came from similar sources, except

37. Their other major source, and our chief one on the subject, was the doxographies incorporated by Aristotle into his own works and those drawn upon by his commentators.

that here they suffered from a surprising and obvious ignorance of the history of philosophy and so had little or no context to which they could relate what they found in the school compendia in disembodied form.

The chief casualty of this ignorance was doubtless the Stoics. Since the Arabs' knowledge of Stoicism came from sources anonymous both to us and to themselves, we cannot begin to understand the extent or the forms of Arab Stoicism. It has already been suggested that some version of Stoic materialism had already entered Islam through the Daysaniyah and their alleged connection with the Rafidite Hisham ibn al-Hakam. Later, when direct access had been established with Plato, Aristotle, and their commentators, the Arab philosophers became Platonizing Aristotelians on a familiar model; but before that occurred, during the reigns of Mansur and Harun, the theologians, the Mu'tazilites among them, were drinking from other, more contaminated, springs, at least some of which appear to have been Stoic.

We will never know, perhaps, the sources of the Mu'tazilite theses in physics and metaphysics, because they arose not from translation of known Greek works but were mediated through the obscure non-Muslim groups like the ones embalmed in the pages of al-Ash'ari's *Views of the Muslims* and in the later heresiographies of Shahrastani, Baghdadi and Ibn Hazm. None of these writers was sympathetic to the Mu'tazilah, and they too knew little of what happened in Greek philosophy after Aristotle. On religious sects they did, however, possess valuable descriptive information, and some of this latter had come to maturity in Iraq and western Iran, where Syrian Christianity, both orthodox and heterodox, and various versions of Hellenic philosophy were creating mutants from which thinkers like Jahm ibn Safwan, Hisham and Abu al-Hudhayl could have, and probably did draw their inspiration.

Mutawakkil did not destroy the Mu'tazilites. Their theses continued to be debated all through the tenth century, and in the first half of the eleventh the movement was still producing important and sophisticated theologians. But the circumstances of their work had changed. In Ma'mun's time the Mu'tazilites were pioneers of an attitude that shook the traditional and popular view of Islam. Ibn Hanbal had arisen to defend that view, but his shrewd and spirited lawyer's brief did not meet the theological issues head on. That was being done by others, however, and with Ibn Kullab the possibility of an alternate *kalam* somewhat more attuned to the traditional values presented itself. The Mu'tazilites, whose prehistory was tied to positions first enunciated outside Islam, were unwilling or unable to move into that middle ground between themselves and the Hanbalites. The theological future belonged to the Kullabites, though it was possessed not in his name but in that of a former Mu'tazilite, al-Ash'ari.

III
THE ISLAMIC SCIENCES

Islam began with the *Qur'an*, a call that rang out like a trumpet in western Arabia in the early seventh century. In a great swirl of command and image that all but engulfed the mere mortal who served as his mouthpiece, Allah warned of the End and summoned his creatures to walk in the way of God. The summons was not simply to action, however. Allah and his Prophet charged the Muslim with both a knowledge (*'ilm*) and a penetrating understanding (*fiqh*) of God's revelation.

Muhammad was well aware that there were abundant examples of natural revelation: the world of nature is filled with "signs" (*ayah;* pl. *ayat*) manifesting God's power and dominion (45:3; 50:20). The most striking of the *ayat* were doubtless the miraculous powers given to other Prophets in confirmation of their message (43:46). Muhammad had no such powers; his *ayat* were the verses of Allah's *Qur'an,* and there are frequent occasions when he adduced them when challenged to produce wonders and miracles.

The shift of emphasis from the natural "signs" of creation to the extraordinary and privileged *ayat* of the *Qur'an* makes sense in the context of a Prophet attempting to verify his mission without benefit of miracle. Muhammad staked all upon the *Qur'an.* It was not simply a historically conditioned message from on high; this was an eternal Book sent down from heaven and faithful in every detail to its immutable prototype by the throne of Allah. Between its covers was the sum of divine wisdom: "We have sent a messenger among you, one of yourselves, to recite to you our *ayat*, to cleanse you, and to teach you the Book and wisdom" (2:151).

To cleanse the Muslim from paganism not merely as individuals but as an entire social and political community was the avowed intent of the Islamic Law. Wisdom appeared to follow from that, from acting in accordance with the positive precepts elicited from the *Qur'an*, and there is no evidence that the early Muslims were prepared to construe wisdom as a higher state of *theoria* to which they might mount from Islamic *praxis*. Knowledge (*'ilm*) was knowledge *of* the *Qur'an* and not knowledge *from* it. Understanding was harnessed directly to the needs of orthopraxy.

Ibn Khaldun (d. 1406), Islam's most sophisticated student of the philosophy of science, saw the point directly. "The basis of all the traditioned sciences is the legal material of the *Qur'an* and the *sunnah* of the Prophet . . . as well as the sciences connected with that material by means of which we can put it to use . . . There are many kinds of traditioned sciences because it is the duty of the Muslim to know the legal obligations God has placed upon him and others." It is a lawyer's vision of science as a propaedeutic to the formulation of precepts.

Ibn Khaldun's discussion of the "traditioned sciences" which are the Muslims' own is set down in a comparative context in his *Introduction to History*. They are contrasted in method and content to another view of science very different from what passed for science in Islam. By the time of Ibn Khaldun's writing, Islam had come in contact with another culture with its own concept of knowledge as science, and that other vision of wisdom had profoundly affected the Muslims' own.

This alien vision of wisdom, alien to Allah's explicit instructions that his revelation was the beginning and end of all knowledge, was that of the Hellenes. From Aristotle onward the Greeks regarded science (*episteme*) not simply as knowledge but a special kind of knowledge which by reason of its method had a unique claim to truth. Islamic *'ilm* was true in its source, which was Allah; the Hellenes' science, at least in its Aristotelian version,[1] was from man and had no need of the deity as either the creator or the guarantor of its truth.

Through the medium of translation the literature of one or another of the Greek sciences—*episteme* served indifferently to describe either the type of knowledge or organized bodies of such knowledge—began to be studied in Muslim circles in the second half of the eighth century. When they came to the complex notions that lay behind *episteme* the Arabs resorted to what they understood to be its vernacular equivalent, *'ilm.* Theologically it was perhaps an unhappy choice, since it rendered to the secular and rationalistic *episteme* a lexicographical share in what Allah had reserved exclusively to the *Qur'an.* The two were yoked together under the name of *'ilm:* the *episteme* that the *Qur'an* would judge a pretentious and dangerous vanity and the science of revelation that had no place in a canon reserved by the Greeks for knowledge by demonstration.

By the time this occurred the Muslims had already begun to extend the base of Qur'anic "science" well beyond the text itself of the Book. To penetrate the meaning of the *Qur'an* required more than a pure heart; it demanded, it now appeared, the specialized skills of the grammarian and the lawyer. From the perimeters of the *Qur'an* was emerging an articulated body of Islamic disciplines (*'ilm;* pl. *'ulum*), whose motives were appropriately religious but whose methods owed at least something to the same type of analytical and rational processes favored by the Greeks.

Following Aristotle, the Greeks drew up elaborate organizational schemes to illustrate the relationship of one science to another. Making was subordinated to acting, and the practical sciences, the favored domain of the Muslim scientist, in turn yielded precedence to the theoretical. The master science of philosophy, which provided the other sciences with their principles and direction, was the crown of the elaborate structure; it was not merely *episteme*, it was also *sophia*, wisdom.

---

1. There were, of course, competing views on wisdom, even in the generally rationalist Greek tradition. On the presence of this other Gnostic and occultist tradition in Islam, see Chap. V, pp. 270–286.

Eventually the Muslim too organized his new fields of intellectual endeavor in the manner that can be observed in Ibn Khaldun and many of his predecessors. The Hellenic schemes may have shown the way, but they can hardly have served as models. The Greek sciences mounted triumphantly to philosophy; the Islamic sciences depended, like a series of somewhat impoverished servants, from the revealed *Qur'an*.

Philosophy could presumably deal with the *Qur'an* in the same way in which the philosophers among the Greeks had dealt with their own home-grown theologians, the poets and mythographers. Hellenic epistemology and allegorical exegesis could snap up the *Qur'an* as easily as they had done with the *Iliad*, the *Theogony* and, more recently, the Bible. But for its part the *Qur'an* could never be adjusted to the self-proclaimed autonomy of philosophy. There were, in fact, from the time the Arabs began to read the Greeks, two contesting wisdoms in Islam, the "science of the *Qur'an*" and the "science of philosophy." The traditionalists would hear of no other than the first, while the Hellenizers among the Muslims did not hesitate to call the second by the name of wisdom (*hikmah*).[2]

The two bodies of "science" were never assimilated. They generally lay side by side in the various Arab attempts at classification, occasionally embarrassed by duplications and anomalies, but kept nonetheless in aloof separation as the "Muslim," "Arab," or "traditioned" (*naqli*) sciences on the one side, and the "Greek," "foreign," or "rational" (*'aqli*) sciences on the other. The Islamic categories were frequently crude and unsophisticated, while the Greek side of the ledger bore, like a talisman, a lucid Aristotelian and scholastic stamp.

What precisely constituted an Islamic science varied from authority to authority. Al-Khwarizmi (fl. 975–987), one of the

---

2. The terminology fluctuated, but "scholar" or "knower" (*'alim;* pl. *'ulama'*) was generally the designation applied to the student of the Islamic sciences, while "sage" (*hakim;* pl. *hukama'*) was reserved for the specialist in the Greek sciences. The "man of understanding" (*faqih;* pl. *fuqaha'*), which at first was a near synonym for *'alim*, was progressively limited to a specialized corner of the Islamic sciences, jurisprudence (*fiqh*).

earliest of the encyclopedists, simply lists jurisprudence, theology (*kalam*), grammar, writing, poetry and prose, and history,[3] while Ibn Khaldun, writing some four centuries later, included, after the propaedeutic language disciplines, the traditional sciences of Qur'anic reading and exegesis, the study of traditions concerning the Prophet, jurisprudence and its various divisions, theology, Sufism and the interpretation of dreams, the latter the sole surviving "science" from a day when the Arabs knew neither Hellenism nor Islam.

Ethnic origins apart, the differences between the two sets of sciences, Greek and Islamic, are precisely summed up in their designation as "rational" and "traditioned." Greek *episteme* on the Aristotelian model, whether philosophy, politics or zoology, had an internal-growth principle. Though nourished by a constantly growing body of empirical information, Greek scientific knowledge evolved from within in a self-consistent fashion. Muslim science was, on the other hand, "traditioned" in the strictest sense. The pre-Islamic Arabs had operated socially, politically and artistically on the principle of customary behavior or precedent (*sunnah*). The coming of Islam had done nothing to change that principle except to identify the *Qur'an* as the ultimate precedent, to be complemented, it soon appeared, by the *sunnah* of the Prophet.

Once the Book and the practice of the Prophet were accepted as the exclusive authoritative *sunnah* in the community, the major premise of the Islamic sciences was laid down. Salvation consisted in holding firm to the *sunnah*, and so the Islamic scientist was effectively the man dedicated to preserving and explicating the tradition, to retrieving it from the memories of men and to resisting its perversion by the ignorant or the unscrupulous. The scientist (*'alim;* pl. *'ulama'*) was, in the strict Muslim view, the collector and validator of an already deposited body of science (*'ilm*).

The *Qur'an* was a finished book, but the great body of traditions reported of the Prophet of God by his contemporaries knew no such limitation, and the *'alim's* energy as a collector was

---

3. This last was not so much the study of the discipline as a résumé knowledge of Near Eastern history.

well known in Islam. He coursed from one end of the *Dar al-Islam* to the other in pursuit of previously unreported *logia* of the Prophet. His zeal had nothing to do with induction; new principles could not and did not emerge from new material.

The Muslim scholar was not unaware of the problem of authenticity: *logia* were being forged as fast as the traditionalist could uncover them. To combat the practice the scientists developed their own elaborate methods of criticism. Their task was rendered somewhat simpler by the fact that, after a somewhat uncertain beginning, the material upon which they were working was made to conform to the underlying notion of tradition and so carried with it its own validation in the form of a list of transmitters and earlier collectors, its *isnad* (literally, "genealogy"), as the Arabs called it, which could be scrutinized and judged by the critic. Prophetic utterances, nuggets of grammatical and lexicographical information, and historical narratives all bore their own *isnad* that vouched for a blameless descent from an authoritative source.

The reality was not so engaging as the theory. The past could not be retrieved in its integrity. Nor were the *isnads* always intact, since the earliest generations of Muslims were frequently unaware of their later important role as the guarantors of a scientific process.[4] Finally, and most seriously, few among the *'ulama'*, no matter how devoted they might be to the principle of traditioned knowledge, could hold their ground unshaken by the incessant dialectical thrust of the "rational" sciences. Questions were asked. They had to be answered, reasons given, cases explained. The mimetic proximity of the Greek sciences eventually had its effect.

When questioned on any or all of these points, the Muslim had perforce to resort to some degree of intellectualization to extend or defend the ground of his own knowledge. Intellectualization introduced the subjective note, what the Arabs called "independent thought" (*ijtihad*), into the realm of the traditioned sciences. Convinced traditionalists fought it on the grounds that this

---

4. Whence modern criticism of the Islamic tradition takes it almost as axiomatic that the more perfect the *isnad*, the later the tradition to which it is attached.

constituted "innovation," but without much success. In the end at least some of them were willing to permit intellectualization if it was restricted to the modest extension of traditioned knowledge by means of analogy (*qiyas*).

To compare analogy to the speculative processes of Greek science struck Ibn Khaldun as disingenuous. Analogy did not develop the traditioned base of the Islamic sciences by inducing new particulars; it merely enabled the Muslim to assimilate the particulars because of a demonstrated resemblance between them and the first principles. The first principles themselves remained eternally intact.

Ibn Khaldun's judgment needs refinement. In some cases, like the study of traditions and law, the traditionalist position was strongly held. The victory was indeed a hollow one. Traditions had to be forged to satisfy the relentless need for change and at the same time to preserve the fiction of an unchanging deposit of faith. Outside the traditional Islamic Law there came into being, cloaked in subterfuge and indirection, another "rational" law based on inductively observed conditions or the pragmatic needs of the commonwealth. But in theology neither forgery nor subterfuge would do. The emetically acceptable analogy yielded to the more vigorous demonstration, and Islam had eventually to admit into the number of its own proper sciences a discipline that drew ever closer to a Greek-style *episteme.*

Philology as a Sacred Science

A Muslim's education arose from the simple injunction to read and understand the *Qur'an,* and the developed literary sciences, whether philological or aesthetic, had their common roots in the Arabic *Qur'an,* which was at once the sacred word of Allah and a miracle of perfection. From the first consideration developed the duty of a correct reading of the text, and from the second the scientific establishment of its claim to "inimitability."

The problem of reading was precisely that and not, as in Hellenic circles, the establishment of an authentic text. As has been seen, the textual problem was solved early in Islam, and so the Qur'anic scholar could confine his attention to the correct reading—or, more pertinently, the correct vocalization—of the text as it was recited or chanted. There was, quickly, one authoritative text of the *Qur'an*, but there was no unanimously accepted way of reading that text. Indeed, there must have been a great number of such, depending upon the various authorities of the first Islamic century. Later scholars like Ibn al-Mujahid (d. 976) attempted to restrict and canonize those readings—seven were finally admitted to the canon—but before standardization was made to prevail, aided, to be sure, by the introduction of an immense diacritical apparatus of signs and points that left no doubt as to the correct reading, the earliest devotees of the subject were confronted with an imperfectly written text and their own understanding of the workings of the Arabic language.

The "readers," specialists in the exact transmission of the *Qur'an*, may have been centered in the Hejaz, since it was there that one of the earliest identifiable students of the subject was to be found late in the seventh century. The "reading" of Abu 'Amr ibn al-'Ala' (d. 770) eventually became one of the seven canonical systems of dealing with the text, but what is significant is that his scholarly career, spent chiefly at Basrah, embraced the still undifferentiated roles of Qur'anic "reader," grammarian, exegete, and collector and transmitter of pre-Islamic poetry.

Later in Islam few men could claim mastery of all of those fields, each of which became in time an elaborately sophisticated science. But in the early days those Muslims—Caliphs and Companions of the Prophet among them—who seriously pondered the meaning of Allah's revelation gathered their philological, legal and historical meditations within the capacious confines of a commentary upon the *Qur'an*. There are a number of these works preserved from the first century after the *hijrah*, and others can be retrieved in part from the final resting place of many of them, the huge *Commentary* of the historian and exegete al-Tabari (d. 923).

Chief among Tabari's sources was the commentary written by Ibn al-'Abbas, the son of that 'Abbas who came late to Islam but whose descendants later ruled the community under the collective name of 'Abbasids. Ibn-al 'Abbas' lifetime overlapped the Prophet's own; he played a minor role in the Arab conquests and served for a year under 'Ali as governor of Basrah. From then until his death in 687 he lived in seclusion in Ta'if and devoted himself solely to a study of the *Qur'an*, the results of which he eventually published. It is a wide-ranging work—Ibn al-'Abbas and his students did not hesitate to consult Christians and Jews in their investigation of the Muslim Book[5]—but his method relied heavily upon philology. Ibn al-'Abbas sought out the opinions of others among the Companions on difficult words in the *Qur'an*, but he went as well to another rich but considerably more secular source, the works of the pre-Islamic poets of Arabia.

He did so by necessity. The recollections of the Companions might provide contextual enlightenment on verses of the *Qur'an*, but the only linguistic control material that the early Islamic scholar possessed was that body of profane poetry. Like the poetry, the *Qur'an* came out of a Bedouin *koine* that transcended local vernacular dialects. But that *koine* was, after all, a species of art-speech that was neither spoken (in the sense that it was colloquial) nor written. Though fixed forever in the *Qur'an*, it had no living support, and so, as Arabic moved out into the newly enlarged quarters of the *Dar al-Islam*, local and tribal dialects reasserted themselves, enriched and confused in turn by the "learned" Arabic of the *mawali*. In the second and third Islamic centuries, then, the only link with the Arabic *koine* was what was left of the Bedouin tradition, the tribal encampments where the old poems were still being recited by professional rhapsodes. The last resort of the "pure" *'arabiyah* was the desert and the steppe.

Arab poetry of the time before the coming of Islam—the "age of barbarism" (*al-jahiliyah*), as it was called—bursts forth with the same apparent suddenness as the Homeric epic among the Greeks. The very earliest of the preserved poems display a sophistication of form and diction that suggests that they were, like their Homeric counterparts, the products of a long, and unfortunately invisible, period of gestation among the Arab tribes. Imr' al-Qays, the first of the poets known by name—he

---

5. A practice which may explain why one of Ibn al-'Abbas' students, al-Mujahid (d. 722), could turn so easily in a direction forbidden to later, more traditional scholars and give the same kind of metaphorical reading to the *Qur'an*'s anthropomorphisms as the Jews and Christians gave to parts of the Bible.

died about 540—was already composing odes in the complex style that has characterized the genre from that day to this.

For the Arabs, poetry played as complex a role as it has for similar societies. The poet was still the *vates,* the inspired seer with powers somewhere between the magical and the religious. Like some Pythian priestess of the desert he couched his obscure oracles in utterances without a strong internal rhythm but with a repetitive and insistent end rhyme.

The rhymed prose (*saj'*) of the seer-poet was the stuff out of which the later art-poets of the sixth century fashioned their considerably more ornate odes. The *vates* remained on the Bedouin landscape until the coming of Islam—when the *Qur'an* usurped his functions—but even before that time he had been joined by a considerably secularized and naturalized counterpart. We cannot trace the steps whereby the loose *saj'* of the *vates* became the finely wrought poetry of the ode maker, but the transformation must have been complete sometime about 500, when the series of preserved masters begins.

The pre-Islamic ode, or *qasidah,* was a thematically stereotyped poem from twenty to a hundred verses,[6] characterized, like the *saj'* works, by an identical end rhyme but possessing as well an internal rhythm of high metrical subtlety. In his choice and use of these meters the poet was permitted considerable freedom, but the subject matter of the *qasidah* was governed by an almost inconceivably severe convention. The ideal *qasidah* began with a reminiscence provoked by a return to a place once known to the poet. He is struck by the changes time had wrought: the glories are gone, friends departed. The poet is then moved by a love recalled and the virtues of the absent lover are described. The body of the *qasidah* is chiefly descriptive, with exquisitely turned passages on drinking and hunting scenes and voyaging across the desert. Finally, there is an address to the poet's patron, an encomium of his virtues if the singer has been well rewarded; if not, the poet's disappointed expectations launch a highly satirical lampoon.

The *qasidah* was clearly a composite with the advantage of giving the poet a fine opportunity to display a variety of moods

---

6. Each verse or "house" (*bayt*) was composed of two hemistiches.

and techniques. Sadness and joy are there, as are nostalgia, pride, panegyric and parody. The whole was quite frankly an almost operatic showpiece in which the poet accepted the limitation of stereotyped themes and set about showing his virtuosity by his skillful manipulation of matter, language and figure.

The language of the *qasidah* poets was later judged to be the purest expression, after the *Qur'an*, of the genuine Arabic tongue. It was doubtless that. Conventional usage over a number of generations had produced an unimaginably fine, if artificial, dialect remote from the colloquialisms of vernacular speech and rich in expressions on a severely limited number of themes. All of this was faithfully reflected in the later Arabic dictionaries that based themselves almost exclusively on the artistic dialect spoken by none, but understood by poetry-loving Arab tribesmen from the Euphrates to Damascus and Mecca.

The sedentary tribes along the Byzantine and Sasanian frontiers, their town kinsmen in western Arabia and the nomadic Bedouin of the interior steppes all shared this common linguistic *koine*. Each tribe spoke its own vernacular dialect, but they were united in their use of a common *'arabiyah*, the language of Arabic poetry, which in Hirah and the Ghassanid encampments along the Syrian *limites*, in the commercial towns and agricultural villages of the Hejaz as well as in the Bedouin tents of the Najd provided a single ecumenical vehicle of artistic communication.

'Arabiyah, the language of Muhammad's *Qur'an* and the linguistic ground on which the philologists of the eighth and ninth centuries would later rear the structure of "classical Arabic," may have been the creation, in the first instance, of the Bedouin of the Najd, but it was carried throughout the still-modest Arab *oikoumene* of the sixth century by the professional rhapsodes, the *rawis*, who transmitted the stately *qasidahs* of the Arab poets.

The impressive body of pre-Islamic poetry was probably not written down until the end of the Umayyad era, but Arabic was not entirely an oral phenomenon in the days before Islam. Inscriptions written in a script that is recognizably the ancestor of the later Arabic one have been found from as early as 300. The great bulk of these inscriptions occur in Christian contexts, a fact that suggests that here in western Arabia as elsewhere in the Byzantine world it was Christian missionaries who took the lead in converting the oral tradition of their proselytes into a written language. Writing, it appears likely, must have flourished in the Arab towns of the Byzantine and Sasanian frontiers.

The evidence for the growth in the use of writing is particularly strong for Hirah, the capital of the Christian Lakhmid Arabs who served the Sasanians as mercenaries, and here too was the meeting place between what can only falteringly be described as "literary Arabic" and the still-oral tradition of the Arab poets. The details of the encounter are not known, but it must have been there at Hirah that the possibility of a *Qur'an* enunciated in the *'arabiyah* of the poets but quickly transcribed in a flexible written medium was prepared.

Hirah and other centers like it were also the chief ports of entry for the fairly extensive vocabulary of loanwords that can be perceived only marginally in the poets but is considerably more marked in the *Qur'an.* The Greek and Latin military jargon of the frontier and the abstract terms of the Christian culture of the Near East penetrated the local Arabic dialects and eventually came to rest in the *koine.* Most, if not all, of these terms had passed into some form of Aramaic before becoming domesticated in Arabic and particularly in the Christian Aramaic dialect of Syriac,[7] which had its own considerable contribution to make not only in the shaping of the *'arabiyah* but in providing both higher cultural concepts and the terms to express them.

The Bedouin world was a narrow one, and if the poet excelled at description, he had only a meager store of abstract ideas upon which to draw. He had perhaps little need for the latter in his poetry, but Arabic had the resources to develop such terms as its cultural horizons expanded. Homer too had written just such concrete poetry, and the Greeks had no great difficulty in transforming the Homeric language of things into the currency of philosophy and science. In due course Arabic was set to perform a similar feat, but in the sixth century its needs could more easily be served by borrowing than by invention. Many of the Christian Arabs already spoke a language with a full store of abstract terms and a highly technical vocabulary of religion and cult.

---

7. At base the Aramaic dialect used at Edessa whence it later passed into the *koine* of the non-Hellenized Christians of the Near East.

Some of the Syriac loanwords had Greek ancestry, but that was of little concern to the Arabs who neither knew nor cared for Greek. They incorporated into their own speech a fairly extensive glossary of Aramaic terms, either from Christian or from Jewish sources, which provided a kind of spiritual landscape for whatever religious discourse existed before Islam and indeed for the *Qur'an* itself.

Religion plays little or no part in the descriptive and lyrical *qasidah*, which may in part account for its survival into Islamic times. But religion was an important part of tribal life, and when Islam replaced those earlier religious preoccupations with its own *Qur'an*, it obliterated as well most of the literary traces of *jahili* literary discourse. We know from later testimony and from the mouth of the Prophet himself that the Arab tribes venerated their own specialized religious figures, among them the pre-*qasidah* seer-poet. Muhammad opposed these latter in strong terms and with his triumph they disappeared.[8] The Prophet took some pains to distinguish himself from the "seer" (*kahin*),[9] a kind of shamanistic medicine man who served the tribes in an oracular capacity. Muhammad presented himself as neither a seer nor a diviner, but the distinction may have been lost on at least some of his audience since he adopted a style that was not unlike that of the *kahins* and the poets: brief and enigmatic utterances couched in rhymed prose (*saj'*).

Very little of this was preserved into a later day. The grammarians and lexicographers of the eighth and ninth centuries ignored all of the pre-Islamic literary tradition save that of the *qasidah* poets. The lexicons are filled with the concrete descriptive terms favored by such poets, while they ignore the kind of borrowed religious terminology that had been making headway among the Syrian tribes and appears so suddenly and inexplicably

---

8. Their chief weapon of defense may have been abusive satire. That quality of Arabic verse did survive into Islam in the continuing competition of the tribes.

9. The word has obvious associations with the Hebrew *kohen*, but it was probably a native, rather than a borrowed concept, since the early Arab *kahin* was in no sense a priest like the fully developed Jewish *kohen*.

in the *Qur'an.* We are left with a curiously distorted picture of Arab literary history: a sophisticated prose *Qur'an* suddenly thrusting in upon a Bedouin society whose only literary concern appears to be with lovingly detailed descriptions of abandoned camp sites.

The earliest preserved poets of the Arabs are only partially realized historical persons; they are characters in their own fiction. Some of them were purely men of the desert, driven by some ideal or some slight to honor. Al-Shanfara', Ta'abbatah sharran and 'Antarah were all passionate men caught up in love and tribal warfare, as savage in their sentiments as they were refined in their expression. Softer, more temperate and reflective were the odes of Hatim, the Bedouin paragon of tribal generosity, of Zuhayr ibn abi Salma' and Labid ibn Rabi'ah.

All of these men lived their lives among the nomads; others were caught up in the richer climate of the Ghassanid and particularly the Lakhmid courts; Imr' al-Qays, the Kindite prince, was known as far afield as Constantinople. The wars of the Iraqi tribes Bakr and Taghlib spawned the odes of Tarafah ibn al-'Abd, 'Amr ibn Kulthum and Harith ibn Hillizah, all of whom moved in and out of Hirah. Al-Nabighah likewise served a patron at Hirah and then later at the Ghassanid court. Other lesser known poets were Jewish and Christian Arabs. All of them, Christian, Jew and pagan, Bedouin or court poet, impassioned or reflective, mined the rich, if confining, vein of the *qasidah*, and their language was the purest *koine 'arabiyah.*

The coming of Islam did not destroy the *qasidah.* It did change the environment of the Arab poet, but it provided as well a new incentive for the collection and study of the odes of the desert, an incentive that owed far more to theology than it did to literary considerations. The serious gathering of the *qasidah* poets appears to have begun toward the end of the Umayyad period and so we are in possession of nicely rounded poetical collections (*diwans*) attributed to a long series of poets beginning with Imr' al-Qays (d. c. 540) and reaching down to the time of Dhu al-Rummah (d. 735).

This impressive corpus of odes constituted the Arabic poetic legacy par excellence and has been endlessly studied and imitated down into modern times. Doubts have been cast upon its authenticity, at least in the form in which it now exists. Suspicion has arisen from two sources. There are, in the first place, the Arabs' own doubts about the reliability of some of the earliest collectors like Hammad al-Rawiyah (d. 771) and particularly Khalaf al-Ahmar (d. 796) who suffered the unfortunate distinction of being a poet in his own right and not averse to inserting some of his own fine imitations into the older *diwans*. Nor had the conversion of an oral tradition into a written one inspired a great deal of confidence, especially at a time when, for not dissimilar motives, there was apparently a large-scale falsifying of religious traditions.

In the end there is probably little reason to doubt that in the *diwans* of the pre-Islamic and Umayyad poets one is dealing with generally authentic material, though not perhaps in the precise form in which it was originally composed. Arab poetry was a notoriously conservative art form, and if certain modifications of tone and style are observable among the poets under the Umayyads, it is no more than one might expect in the changed circumstances of the life of the Arabs.

From the beginning the *qasidah* was a calculated literary act rather than a spontaneous outpouring of personal sentiment. Among the poets of the new Muslim centers of Basrah and Kufah the *qasidah* began its inevitable progress toward preciosity as it deserted the specialized Bedouin ethos for which it had once been the prime literary medium. City life was replacing the memory of the desert and the social change was reflected in the appearance of a major new theme, poems celebrating the virtues of wine and the pleasures of drinking. The earlier *qasidah* gave a considerable place to both boasting and satire. Both motifs remain, transformed, however, among the Iraqi poets into panegyrics of the new political and religious dynasts or slanging matches commemorating the tribal strife that plagued the Umayyad kingdom.

The triad of poets who made their reputations praising the Umayyads and attacking one another—al-Akhtal (d. 710), al-Farazdaq (d. 732) and Jarir (d. 732), were all Arab and Iraqi in origin, Akhtal a Christian from the Taghlib tribe in upper Mesopotamia and the other two from near Basrah. Patronage drew them into the Umayyad orbit in Syria, where their archaistic style suited the ruling house's nostalgia for Bedouin ways. The form and many of the traditional *qasidah* themes are present in their work, but something in the tone has unmistakably changed. Power now lay close to the poet's hand, a new political power unknown to the *jahili* singer who served only his tribe. The Umayyad poet was a praised and pampered panegyricist of royalty and its defender against the enemies of the regime. Tribalism had not, however, disappeared; the Arabs carried it with them into Syria and the Umayyad laureates attacked one another's tribal pretensions with a savage scurrility much appreciated by their Arab audiences.

The Hejaz too had changed. Mecca and Medina, briefly at the center of the Islamic *oikoumene*, lost their capital role after the accession of the Umayyads in 661 and became an odd combination of places for pious resort for scholars, pilgrims and religious dissenters and repositories for the new wealth of Islam. There was nothing of Geneva about the Holy Cities of the Hejaz. Despite occasional outbursts of political trouble, life was good there and the new *jeunesse dorée* of Mecca and Medina produced, during that century of the Umayyads, a distinct new development in Arab poetry. The lengthy *qasidah* was modified into the briefer *ghazal* and suffused with a highly charged and subjective lyricism.

The Hejazi lyricists like 'Umar ibn abi Rabi'ah (d. 710), Jamil (d. c. 700-710) and his contemporary, the famous "obsessed" poet "Majnun," extended the horizons of the restrictive *qasidah*. The personality of the poet, his pleasures and pains of unrequited love, replaced the stereotyped descriptions and predictable boasts of the ode. The effect was not, however, a lasting one. The passion of philologists like Abu 'Amr for the genuine Bedouin *qasidah* and the later influence of rhetoric upon all forms of poetical composition in Arabic stifled the Hejazi mood. It was in Persian rather than Arabic that Ibn abi Rabi'ah and his fellows had their eventual success, in the *ghazals* of Rudaki and his Iranian descendants.[10]

It was the *Qur'an* that drove Ibn al-'Abbas, Abu 'Amr and the other philologists back to the Bedouin poetry. There in Abu 'Amr's impressive collection of archaic literary material was the

---

10. See Chap. IX, pp. 646–647.

lexicographical documentation for his manner of reading the Sacred Book. From it came as well the first tentative steps toward a systematic Arab grammar.

Abu 'Amr's work was all of a piece, but with his immediate disciples there was a certain dissolution of the unity. In Khalil ibn Ahmad the focus was on lexicography and metrics, while in al-Asma'i one can detect a perceptible drift away from the connection of Qur'anic "reading" with the collection of the old poetry and the pursuit of the latter for its own sake, or better, for social and ethnic motives rather than purely religious ones.

The Arab tradition did not credit the noted Basran scholar al-Khalil (d. 786) with the absolute parentage of lexicography; like much else in Islam the origins of the "science of language" (*'ilm al-lughah*) were pushed back into the Patriarchal Age, in this instance to 'Ali. Such stories are highly dubious, but the insistent point that the compiling of lexicons was somehow connected with the influx of nonnative Arabic speakers into Islam is not unlikely.

Al-Khalil's *Book of 'Ayn* could have been of little consolation to the puzzled *mawla*. It took its name from its first letter entry, *'ayn*, whose place at the head of the file was dictated by phonetic rather than alphabetic principles. Al-Khalil knew the traditional alphabetic order of Arabic well enough, but he chose to arrange his dictionary according to the progression of sounds from the back to the front of the mouth, from *'ayn* to *mim*, with the four "weak" consonants, *waw*, *ya*, *alif* and *hamzah*, grouped together at the end.

A reasonable defense might be presented for this novel order but, within the letter divisions, further and somewhat less defensible complications appeared. Words were first separated according to the number of consonantal "roots" they possessed and then, within each of these categories—biradicals, triradicals, etcetera—further distinctions were drawn between words possessing one or more "weak" consonants among their roots. Having once settled into a root structure, al-Khalil proceeded to reproduce *all* the existing permutations of those roots.[11]

---

11. Thus under the triradical '-L-M there was found not only *'alima* but also *'amala* and *lama'a*.

As complex as it was, from al-Khalil's *Book of 'Ayn* descended the entire line of Arabic lexicons. The chief later innovation in arrangement was that introduced by al-Jawhari (d. 1007), whose *The Sound* used something closer to an alphabetic principle, but arranged the words according to their final consonants and so produced, in effect, a rhyming dictionary. Its rhyming successors, the prodigious *The Arabic Language* of Ibn Manzur (d. 1311) and the *All-Embracing Ocean* of Al-Firuzabadi (d. 1414) continued to dominate the field, even though some of the philologists of Kufah were early experimenting with lexicons based on the more practical alphabetical principle.

The alphabetical arrangement appears to have had its greatest success in what may be termed specialized lexicons. Two of the most striking examples, are from al-Zamakhshari (d. 1144), the Mu'tazilite, Qur'anic commentator, grammarian and rhetorician. His *Surpassingly Strange Expressions in the Hadith* is an alphabetically arranged lexicon of peculiar expressions in the *hadith* literature, a subject of venerable interest among the philologists, while *The Foundation of Eloquence* used a similar approach to words which had a metaphorical usage markedly different from their literal meaning. Zamakhshari's *Foundation* supplied both for the student of rhetoric.

If al-Khalil had some dubious predecessors as a lexicographer, he had none, dubious or otherwise, as prosodist; the discovery and classification of the meters of Arabic poetry was his achievement alone. The persistent end rhyme of the *qasidah* was evident to everyone, but al-Khalil perceived, or heard, that the ode also possessed an internal rhythm flowing from a regular succession of long and short measures. Al-Khalil distinguished sixteen such metrical patterns in his *Book of Prosody*,[12] and both his analyses and his names for the patterns became the standard for all later prosodists.[13]

Al-Khalil was an Arab of Oman in western Arabia; his student

---

12. The book itself is lost, but its contents can be reconstructed from later authors dependent on al-Khalil.

13. Including Western Orientalists. The complex and detailed explanation of Arabic prosody by al-Khalil and his successors inhibited all but the very daring from starting anew on the metrical analysis.

and successor as the chief Basran philologist was a *mawla* of pure Iranian ancestry, Sibawayh of Shiraz (d. c. 800), who paradoxically became the founder of Arabic grammar. His grammar, known simply as *The Book*, analyzed, in the scholastic manner of Basrah, the morphology and syntax of Arabic by recourse to the *Qur'an*, the *jahili* poets and the growing tradition of grammarians, chief among them his teacher al-Khalil.

Sibawayh's *Book* had no pretensions to being a descriptive grammar of how Arabic was spoken or written; rather it pursued a relentlessly normative path: this is the manner in which *'arabiyah*, the genuine language of the Arabs, *should* be used. As with al-Khalil and parallel to what was occurring in the contemporary law schools, the appeal of Sibawayh's grammar was to a tradition buttressed with a wealth of illustrative or, better, confirmatory examples; the linguistic *sunnah* of the Bedouin in both idiom and vocabulary was the absolute norm.

For the Arabs Sibawayh represented the philological method associated with the scholars of Basrah: the enunciation of patterns based on normal (normal, that is, in the canonical poets, not on the streets of Basrah) linguistic usage and capable of extension through analogical reasoning. The rival school of Kufah proceeded somewhat more phenomenologically. Usage was validation; if a linguistic form was attested in the ancient poetry or among the Bedouin, it was normative. At first sight more permissive, but at base more pedantic, the Kufan scholar sought out, revered and preserved the rare and the obscure in the diction of the past.

In a theoretical sense the revelation of the Arabic *Qur'an* marked the final perfection, and so the end of the evolution, of the Arabic language. But just as the *Qur'an* could be understood, in the traditionalists' view, only by recourse to the *sunnah* of the Prophet, so the Arabic of the *Qur'an* was effectively glossed only in terms of the poets of the *jahiliyah* and, curiously, of the Umayyad era. But there the canon was closed; beyond the *Diwan* of Dhu al-Rummah there was no acceptable standard of usage. If a later Basran scholar wished to decide on a grammatical point for which there was no precedent in the *Qur'an* or the poetical literature, he turned not to contemporary usage but, like the canon lawyer, to the argument from analogy.

There was nothing distinctly pious in this. Philology, launched on the wings of Abu 'Amr's piety, learned to navigate under its own power. Even under Abu 'Amr's own disciples new impulses are discernible, mixed with the old, perhaps because they are thrown into relief by the rapidly shifting social background. The unassumingly religious al-Asma'i (d. 828) was gathered from Basrah into the capacious folds of Harun's patronage at Baghdad, where the scholar could witness first hand the changing times and the new imperial affluence that sounded the doom of even Bedouin memories.

For al-Asma'i the Bedouin poetry represented more than the key to the *Qur'an;* it was the literary vehicle of the original Arab life style, still cultivated by the Bedouin of his own day but appreciated only by the connoisseurs among the new literati of Baghdad. Whether from motives of pious scholarship or, as seems more likely, of scholarly nostalgia, al-Asma'i continued to collect the ancient poetry as Abu 'Amr had done and to compile, on the basis of that poetry, his lexicographical evidence.

Another motive may have begun to come into prominence at this point. For al-Asma'i the Bedouin poetical speech was more than a reflection of the past; it was also its guarantee, and the scholar's distillation of the *koine* into normative rules insured the survival of pure Arabic. On the other side the *mawali*, newcomers to Islam and strangers to its language, had an obvious need of learning Arabic, the sacred tongue of their new religion and an increasingly important lingua franca all over the Near East. Just such a pressure from outside aspirants into its own linguistic community had produced the first grammars during the Hellenistic age, and it is probable that the *mawali* of the eighth century, like the *barbaroi* of third-century Egypt, hastened the codification of grammatical systems in the normative style of Sibawayh.

Al-Asma'i was a Sunni of Arab stock; Abu 'Amr's other major disciple, Abu 'Ubaydah (d. 825), was just such a *mawla* from Iraq and a Kharijite by conviction. No desert nostalgia gripped him. His scholarly interest was in the history and culture of the Arabs, now only tenuously connected with the *Qur'an*, and Abu 'Ubaydah's collection of poetry and traditions bearing on Arabism was not prompted by a desire to defend the Arabs or, likely, to attack them, even though some of the later partisans of Iranian self-advertisement seized upon his unflattering findings with undisguised delight.

By the time of the death of Abu 'Ubaydah in the first quarter of the ninth century Arabic philology had already come to maturity and there were in existence highly rationalized systems of grammar, lexicography and metrics. The work of enlargement and refinement continued—philology was from its origins a pious as well as a scholarly discipline—generally untroubled by any but methodological quarrels between the savants of Basrah and Kufah.

The philologists were, however, fishing in troubled waters. They were more than cultural anthropologists attempting to limn the rapidly disappearing traces of their own linguistic past; they were prescribing the usages of the past as a norm for the present at the same moment that they were announcing the demise of that past. The closing of the philologists' canon at Dhu al-Rummah did not, of course, end the writing of poetry. There were 'Abbasid as well as Umayyad poets, and not all of them heeded the philologists' advice. New styles evolved and from them was born the kind of "modernism" that held serious implications for 'Abbasid Islam.

The task of replying to the innovations of the poets fell not to the philologists but to the adepts of a new science, that of eloquence or rhetoric (*balaghah*). To translate *balaghah* as "rhetoric" may have its etymological justifications; it is, nonetheless, highly misleading. The original Greek notion of an art of persuasive speaking directed toward action was alien to classical Arabic *balaghah*, which was in essence an analysis of style, and indeed of poetical style. Forensic and political oratory, which presided over the birth of Greek rhetoric, had nothing to do with *balaghah*.[14]

There was no lack of an oratorical tradition among the early Arabs whose fascination with the "word" was the equal of the Greeks'. Oratory was even built into Islamic ritual in the form of the *khutbah*, or sermon, preached during the Friday mosque services. *Balaghah* may have had some connection with the pre-

14. When the Arabs wished to speak of rhetoric in the Greek sense they used not *balaghah*, but *khitabah*, "oratory."

Islamic oratorical style, though less likely with the *khutbah*, which, in imitation of the restrained expression of the *Qur'an*, must have been considerably less flamboyant than *jahili* oratory. Little is, in fact, known of the oral prose of the period of *Rashidun* and the Umayyads, and when a literary prose began to appear toward the end of the reign of the Umayyads, it owed as much to Iranian influences as it did to the native Arab tradition.

The somewhat overwrought prose of the 'Abbasid chanceries might well have provided adequate ground for stylistic analysis, but what actually occurred was that 'Abbasid prose became a center of controversy by reason of its cultural content, while the first students of *balaghah* addressed themselves rather to the continuous but evolving tradition of Arabic poetry.

Poetry too, it is true, had been caught up on the periphery of the debate regarding cultural norms, and among the traditionalists it was strongly felt that poetry, which rested, as they saw it, at the center of the Arabic literary tradition, was an essential ingredient in the formation of the cultured man. What was meant by poetry, of course, was the canon assembled by the philologists, untroubled as yet by the storm over "modernism." Some idea of this rather severe approach to Arabic poetry as seen from a literary rather than a technical philological point of view may be gotten from Ibn Qutaybah's (d. 889) *Poetry and Poets.*

Ibn Qutaybah's treatise was written to introduce the chancery secretary to what was needful for him to know about poetry. It is largely an anthology, but there are some modest efforts at criticism as well. Form and content are distinguished, and Ibn Qutaybah could discern well enough the difference between *disciplina* and *ingenium* in the work of the poet. But when he came to speak of poetical faults, these were chiefly violations of the canons of rhyme and prosody that had already been formulated by the philologist; the issues of the "new style," innovative use of metaphors, similes, and the like, were not discussed. To ignore them, as Ibn Qutaybah did, was to ignore the most important development in contemporary poetry.

The new 'Abbasid society, for whom the Bedouin days were a rapidly fading memory, was having its effect on the contemporary poet. The stately but frigid *qasidah*, which had been captured by the philologists for their own purposes, was safe only in the hands of the conservative archaizers, who attempted to duplicate the traditional form with all its growing obscurity. The "moderns" had little respect for the architectural integrity of the *qasidah*. They dissolved it into shorter, more lyrical segments. Poetry moved closer to song, away from Bedouin concision and formalism, toward a more personal and internalized utterance.

Criticism was rendered doubly difficult by the moral issue. *Jahili* poetry knew nothing of Islam but it did express a morality. The Bedouin ethos could be read there, some of it stern and ennobling, some of it less so, but all well cloaked with a literary and ethnic nostalgia. The "moderns" abused the form and mocked the content of the *qasidah*. Restraint, whether in imitation of Bedouin severity or prompted by the simple prudential concern to survive under an Islamic dispensation, was not the moderns' style. Their iconoclasm was all of a piece, and even though the Islamic courts were not always models of Islamic piety, some of the sensitive were outraged.

The philologists ignored their contemporaries and confined their critical attention to the older and more traditional *qasidah* poets. They felt no need for a defense of their choice, and so there was far more verbal, syntactical and metrical analysis than aesthetic criticism in their work. Aesthetic considerations were left to the theologian and the Qur'anic commentator.

The incentive for the conversion of these dimly realized standards into a systematic approach to the art of poetical eloquence arose not from newfangled poets like Bashshar ibn Burd (d. 784) or Abu Nuwas (d. 810), but from the traditionalist poets who borrowed the rhetorical tricks of their more revolutionary contemporaries. Abu Tammam (d. 846) and his student al-Buhturi (d. 897), Syrians both, were old-fashioned *qasidah* poets with some decidedly modern turns of diction and trope that disturbed the sensibilities of an audience used to the good old lays.

The novelty to be found in their work was called *badi'*, a term at first used in something close to its original meaning of "creativeness"—and suggestively close to the anathematized "innovation" (*bid'ah*)—but in the end more specifically as "the new style," characterized by certain unfamiliar metaphors and similes that had begun to turn up in contemporary poetry. This manner of writing found its defender among one of its own practitioners, the son of a Caliph, Ibn al-Mu'tazz (d. 908), who was later himself to sit upon the Caliphal throne for one day in December, 908. Ibn al-Mu'tazz was a considerable poet, but his place in theory rests upon *The New Style*, a book in which he attempted to defend the various forms of poetical ornamentation by classifying them and then proceeding to show that they were present in all of Arabic literature from the *Qur'an* and the *jahili* poets onward.

The issue was so important that by his work Ibn al-Mu'tazz almost singlehandedly created a new science of diction (*'ilm al-badi'*), and his successors took up the refinement of what he had begun. Abu Hilal al-'Askari's (d. 1004) *The Two Arts* expanded Ibn al-Mu'tazz's schema. Psychological and philosophical underpinning was provided by 'Abd al-Qahir al-Jurjani's (d. 1078) *Secrets of Rhetoric*, and in the age of Arabic encyclopedism, a final schematization was set out in al-Sakkaki's (d. 1228) *Key to the Sciences* and its commentaries.

In its final, classical version the science of eloquence was made up of three divisions dealing with concepts (*ma'ani*), exposition (*bayan*), and embellishment (*badi'*). The first had to do with the various types of sentences and their use, whether, in Ibn Khaldun's example, one ought to say "Zayd came to me" or "There came to me Zayd." The distinction between *bayan* and *badi'* was, however, somewhat tenuous. Both had to do with figures of speech, but the category of *bayan*, which by definition explored the ways in which a given idea might be expressed, confined its attention to the three figures of comparison, metaphor and metonymy. All the others, whose number had grown considerably from Ibn al-Mu'tazz's original list, were grouped under *badi'*.

Al-Sakkaki can hardly be called a literary critic; literary taxonomy was somewhat closer to what he accomplished in his final dissection of poetical eloquence. Nor was there any help from the Greeks. Hellenic influence remained tangential at best—a few technical terms here and there appear to have had Greek antecedents—and the rich ideological background that shaped both rhetoric and poetics for the Greeks was replaced in Islam by a struggle that was about tradition and history, rather than philosophy.

At least some of the Arabs knew about what the Greeks had done. The *Topics*, *Poetics* and *Rhetoric* of Aristotle were all translated into Arabic in the tenth century and passed through various hands among the philosophers. But as one of its Arab editors said of the *Rhetoric*, "This work is not very useful"—particularly since neither the translators nor the commentators could make much sense of the wealth of inductive examples cited by Aristotle. The *Poetics* in particular appears to have been translated more from a sense of Aristotelian piety than from any conviction that the text contained something of real value.

Al-Farabi, the most considerable Platonist in Islam, knew something of the Platonic view of poetry as well, but it played little or no role in his political theory and, like Aristotle's *Poetics*, had no discernible impact outside the ranks of the philosophers. Nor is it difficult to see why. The Greek poetic labored under Plato's indictment of the poet on epistemological and moral grounds; the Arab poet trailed no epistemology after him. He did, however, raise moral issues, and not merely by the way he lived. Poetry was, as has been noted, intimately connected with the explication of the *Qur'an*, and by that connection poetry fell into place as part of the *sunnah* structure imposed upon, and accepted by, 'Abbasid Islam. Innovation, whether in law, in custom or in poetry, was offensive to the traditionalists, and it is significant that the poetical licenses indulged in by "modernists" like Abu Tammam often attracted more attention than the personal license of their lives.

Rhetoric too was tied by the fourth-century Greeks to dialectic and so to philosophy. *Balaghah* knew no such resonances. It consisted chiefly in straightforward analysis, innocent of both the philosophical implication and political function it had once possessed in Hellas. The Greeks, and particularly those in the Aristotelian tradition, were also skilled in formalistic analysis and could distinguish tropes with as much dexterity as the Arab masters of *badi'*. But the larger context of rhetoric was never quite forgotten in Hellenism, even by the ornamentmongers of the Second Sophistic.

Balaghah began as a defensive reflex against charges of "modernism" and ended, except for the somewhat extraordinary figure of al-Jurjani, as either a propaedeutic for the study of the stylistic marvels of the *Qur'an* or as a recondite subcategory of the encyclopedists.

The Qur'anic route to a theory of aesthetics probably antedated even the crisis of the Ancients versus the Moderns that provoked the treatises of Ibn al-Mu'tazz and his successors. Muhammad himself had drawn attention in that direction by inviting his competitors and detractors to compose an equal to his Arabic *Qur'an,* and his claim for the inimitablility (*i'jaz*) of the *Qur'an* became a cornerstone of Muslim apologetics. Both al-Jahiz and Ibn Qutaybah addressed themselves to the stylistic, as opposed to the purely linguistic, qualities of the Sacred Book.

By the time of the Mu'tazilite rhetorician al-Rummani (d. 996) *balaghah* was firmly connected with Qur'anic exegesis as one of the ways in which a Muslim might explain the *i'jaz* of the Prophet's work. The Ash'arite theologian al-Baqillani (d. 1013)[15] composed the classic treatment of the theme in his *Inimitability of the Qur'an,* and the application of literary criticism to the *Qur'an* was obligatory for the later standard commentaries: the *Discoverer of the Truths of Revelation* of al-Zamakhshari (d. 1144), and the derivative *Keys to the Mystery* of Fakhr al-Din al-Razi (d. 1209) and the *Heights of Revelation* of al-Baydawi (d. 1286).

Finally, eloquence might be enlisted in the cause of Islamic sectarianism. Al-Sharif al-Radi (d. 1015), the aristocratic poet who served as the head (*naqib*) of the 'Alids of Baghdad under the Buyids, collected the discourses and letters of 'Ali in his *Path of Eloquence.*[16] Though the Shi'ite tradition has few doubts on the subject, modern Western scholarship has not always judged kindly the authenticity of the documents in the *Path of Eloquence.* Whatever the case, the work has had an immense and enduring effect on Arab letters, Sunni and Shi'ite alike. The *Path* is, in fact, remarkably free of polemic and special pleading.

---

15. See Chap. VIII, pp. 586–588.
16. The work is sometimes attributed to his brother and successor as *naqib,* al-Sharif al-Murtada (d. 1044); see Chap. VIII, pp. 582–583.

Whether or not they accepted the claims of his descendants to the Caliphate, Muslims were agreed in their reverence for 'Ali, and they assented to the traditional judgment on his skill and learning. Al-Radi appears not to have been propagandizing for himself,[17] but glorifying, on an ecumenical scale, his illustrious ancestor.

The Islamic Law

Equipped with a knowledge of the sciences of grammar, lexicography and eloquence, the Islamic scholar could then proceed to what was, by the mid-ninth century, the next step in his ideal progress toward an understanding of the *Qur'an:* a critical knowledge of the traditions (*hadith*) that told of the customary behavior (*sunnah*) of the Prophet and so were the sole basis for a valid interpretation of his revelation and the understanding of Allah's law for men.

This view of the law was a new one in Islam. The Umayyads, who as Muslims accepted the revelation of the *Qur'an,* had little interest in extracting from it a body of ideally formulated law to govern God's commonwealth. The Umayyads ruled as they could; they relied on local assistance, Muslim and non-Muslim alike, and they delegated powers once held personally by earlier Caliphs who governed the Islamic *ummah* from within the provincial confines of Mecca and Medina. A justice unencumbered by ideology was administered in the Umayyad provinces by local judges or *qadis* who were appointed by the governor and beholden for their offices to the political administration.

Under the Umayyads the law was still pragmatic, local and open to the influence of established custom. It was during this time, before the erection of a theoretical and closed structure of a specifically Islamic Law, that the jurisprudential norms of the community took on most of the foreign coloring that they were

---

17. Though he was a direct descendant of the Shi'ite *Imams,* al-Radi lived during a period of "occultation" when the main body of the Shi'ah, the Imamites, had surrendered their immediate political ambitions for the hope of an eschatological Messiah; see Chap. VIII, pp. 576–578.

eventually to possess. If there was such borrowing, it was modest indeed. The obvious possibility of taking over either concepts or methods from the sophisticated structure of Roman law has been investigated, but with extremely meager results. By the time of the Arab conquest Roman law in both its theory and its practice had been receding from the eastern provinces for over a century. Justinian had centralized most of the teaching of law in Constantinople, and the famous law school at Beirut was merely a memory when the Arabs took that city. War and heresy had had their effect, and the administration of justice in the eastern Roman provinces was largely in the hands of local bishops at the beginning of the seventh century. We are not well informed on what basis they rendered their judgments, except that they had frequent recourse to arbitration.

From the wreckage of the Roman legal system the Umayyad administrators took what they could. They borrowed the office of the Byzantine market supervisor almost intact. At first he continued in his secular role of watching over fair practice in the markets, but later he was more obviously Islamicized as the *muhtasib* and invested with some of the rudimentary police functions described in the *Qur'an*. The ubiquitous Islamic institution of the *waqf*, property whose usufruct was inalienably applied to some charitable purpose, was later understood by the community as a product of Islam, but it too appears to have originated in the grants made for pious Christian purposes and sanctioned by Byzantine law.

These are not overly impressive examples of borrowing by one legal culture from another, and this in an area where one had a right to expect a great deal more. For Sasanian law, about whose theory we know very little, there is a parallel lack of evidence, though here too there may have been some influence on institutions. Sasanian practice may have been at work in the evolution of the Islamic *qadi*, for example. There was more of this kind of institutional mimesis, particularly in the *diwan* structure of the 'Abbasid state, but by then the Islamic Law, which generally ignored the organs of government, had taken on its essential features.

When disenchantment with the Umayyads began to take firm root in pious circles, the focus of its complaint came to bear on the Caliphs' method of administering justice out of a pragmatic blend of Qur'anic injunction, local custom and the discretion of the *qadi*. Toward the end of Umayyad rule, in the generation at the beginning of the eighth century, just such an opposition began to take shape in the cities of the Hejaz, Iraq and Syria itself. Scholars remote from the practical considerations of the *qadi* urged the movement of the Law onto somewhat more theoretical bases than Umayyad practice. The law of the community should indeed be founded upon custom—for such was the Arab way—not, however, as exemplified in the rulings of local jurists and administrators, but rather as understood by professional jurists, the scholars at Kufah, for example, or Medina, who had reached a consensus on disputed points of the law.

There was no great disagreement among the scholars at these various centers on either principles or methodology. Their aim was simply to Islamicize the law by substituting Qur'anic prescriptions and ideals for local administrative practice. How this was to be accomplished in detail was at this point still left to the local scholars, the nucleus of the later "schools of law" (*madhhab;* pl. *madhahib*). These jurists at Kufah and Medina, who had no responsibility for the actual administration of justice, professed to scorn the personal discretion practiced by the Umayyad judges. They held instead for a more bookish and theoretical approach which relied heavily on the method of analogical reasoning (*qiyas*).

Analogy was nothing new in the Near East; it was in wide use in both Byzantine and Talmudic legal circles well before the coming of Islam, and it was an equally familiar procedure for the development of arguments in Christian theology. The ultimate sources for this kind of "rhetorical" argument may well have reached back into Hellenistic school practices; but, for the Muslim jurisprudent of the first decades of the eighth century, analogy represented a way of proceeding systematically[18] to the

---

18. Though not philosophically. For the difference between analogy (*qiyas*) and its related forms of rhetorical argument on the one hand and the technical "demonstration" (*burhan*) favored by philosophy on the other, see Chap. IX, p. 704.

extension of Qur'anic precepts into areas that were either unforeseen or nonexistent under the terms of the original revelation. It was a method that obviously permitted and even encouraged an evolutionary quality in the law, but by forcing the jurist to articulate the connective tissue between his ruling and the original precept from which it depended analogy served as an effective check on purely arbitrary opinions.

To justify their position the lawyers of Mecca, Medina, Basrah and Kufah had recourse to a principle of considerable importance that was then emerging in pious circles. The lawyers had long been familiar with the notion of "custom," but what they had meant by that term was something that has been described as "the living tradition of the place," a compound of idealized norms and actual practice. Now, at the beginning of the eighth century, a new understanding began to replace that view. The lawyers sought to justify their own consensus on the law by referring backward to the wisdom and authority of an earlier generation whose faithful followers they presumably were.

To cast tradition backward to an older and higher authority was not an uncommon practice as the Umayyads approached their end-time. The golden days of the first, pre-Umayyad Caliphs were recalled—it was at this point that the first four Caliphs began to be called "the right-directed ones" (*rashidun*)—and pointed contrasts were drawn between the earliest believers, those revered "Companions of the Prophet," and the degeneracy of the Umayyads. 'Abbasid and 'Alid political aspirations fed eagerly on such talk, but there was a genuine piety involved as well. Here and there men designated in the sources as "traditionalists" (*ashab al-hadith*) called for a return to primitive Islamic values; in their view the answers to all questions of behavior were to be found in the *Qur'an* and in the customary practice (*sunnah*) of the Prophet himself.

The traditionalists were not lawyers, but by their invocation of Prophetic authority they moved a question that led into the vitals of the law. Systematically applied, their reliance on the *Qur'an* and the *sunnah* of the Prophet would undercut both Umayyad customary practice and the current scholarly reliance upon local consensus. The legal scholars of the mid-eighth century apparently found it difficult to resist the call to One Islam and One

Islamic Law, and the works of the most eminent jurists of the period, Malik ibn Anas (d. 795) at Medina and Abu Hanifah (d. 767) at Basrah, reflect the ambivalence of their position. They had been strengthening their systems by appealing further and further back into the Islamic past and eventually to the witness of the generation immediately after the Prophet's own. But their pursuit of the principle of Islamic precedent was neither as wholehearted nor as systematic as that of the traditionalists, who would accept no authority other than the Prophet of Islam.

At stake was the evolutionary quality of Muslim Law. The traditionalists stood for an Islam that was theoretically complete when revelation ended at the Prophet's death. Nothing could be added and nothing subtracted. The lawyers at Kufah and Medina, on the other hand, saw the law as an organism whose progressive growth was slowly urged forward by the personal investigation (*ijtihad*) of the learned jurists. For the traditionalists, all forms of *ijtihad* were anathema, whether in the naked putting-forth of an arbitrary personal opinion or, what was becoming common among the jurists, the more systematic and circumspect reasoning by analogy.

Salvation came, as frequently in Islam, through compromise in the guise of reform. A former member of the Medina school, Muhammad ibn Idris al-Shafi'i, argued decisively for the traditionalist posture in law. According to Shafi'i, not only was the *Qur'an* the basic source of the Islamic Law; the Book had its sanction and unique method of interpretation in the *sunnah* of the Prophet. This latter, the extra-Qur'anic sayings and deeds of the Prophet as reported in the body of traditions (*hadith*) descending from him, enjoyed in Shafi'i's view the same degree of inspiration as the *Qur'an* itself, and these same *hadith*, or rather the generation of the Companions who transmitted them, came to share the infallibility of the Book.

Shafi'i did permit other "sources" to the legal theoretician; he allowed, for example, the legal prescriptions established by consensus, but not as that notion was formerly understood in the schools, as the agreement of scholars in a certain area, but as the common assent of the entire Muslim community. Further, one could invoke consensus as a legal justification only in the event that the *Qur'an* and the *hadith* were silent on a subject, on the establishment of the Caliphate, for example. The very same conditions applied to the fourth and last of the "sources" permitted by Shafi'i, the personal extension of legal prescriptions on the basis of analogical reasoning.

Shafi'i's position on the sources of the Islamic Law prevailed, and in a remarkably short time. The law schools, those of Malik and Abu Hanifah chief among them,[19] became traditionalist in the sense argued by al-Shafi'i: they accepted the principle of the legal priority of the *Qur'an* and the *sunnah* of the Prophet over established practice and local tradition. And almost at a stroke Shafi'i and the traditionalist point of view converted a generation of theoreticians into antiquarians. Which "traditions" among those in circulation genuinely reflected the words and deed of the Prophet? There was no critical help to be had from the substance of the tradition, since, as presumably inspired material, it was not subject to purely personal opinion. Scholars were forced to inspect the chains of transmitters, the "genealogy" (*isnad*) attached to each tradition, to determine whether or not such an utterance or such an act could indeed be attributed to the Prophet.

Islam did, doubtless, possess an authentic oral and written tradition on the Prophet which went back to the testimony of various of his first followers. According to the traditional Muslim account, those who had an immediate experience of the Prophet began to write down their recollection of his sayings shortly after his death. These written scraps of recollection remained in their original disconnected state until the time of the Caliph 'Umar II (717–720), who commissioned a certain Abu Bakr ibn Hazm to bring together in one collection the traditions recorded by or from the first generation of Muslims. The project was interrupted by Ibn Hazm's death, but it was accomplished by one of his contemporaries, al-Zuhri (d. 742). Zuhri's collection must have been simply that, since the Muslim version of the evolution of *hadith* places their grouping into separate and coherent units somewhat later, in the last quarter of the eighth century.

Most of the traditions collected in this fashion were made up of

---

19. On the Hanafite "resistance" under the cover of theology, see Chap. VI, pp. 462–463.

two easily distinguishable parts, the text or body of the tradition prefaced by a formulaic expression of the chains of men who passed on this particular tradition. The first part, the genealogy of the tradition, employed a terminology which most often suggested that its transmission was oral: "So and so related to me . . ." or "So and so recounted to us . . ." or strung out into "So and so related to me that So and so had related to them that So and so had recounted to them . . ." wherein the first name in the chain is the author's immediate source and the last name is that of the "Companion of the Prophet" who was the original reporter.[20] But despite the oral implications of the expressions in the *isnad*, it appears that the transmission had most often to do with written traditions and that it was books that were being verified orally in the presence of their editor or collector.

This may indeed have been the way in which traditions were noted down, collected and arranged in the first century and a half after the *hijrah*. Their status in the Islamic Law is, however, quite another question. Traditions from the Prophet are liberally cited in the chief pre-Shafi'ite work of Muslim jurisprudence, the *Paved Way* of Malik ibn Anas, and some of them are almost certainly genuine. But since they were in no sense juridically binding and did not have to justify their own authenticity by an impeccable *isnad*, many such traditions are only doubtfully attested, and then not always followed as a norm of behavior.

Once, however, the traditionalists and then their legal propagandist al-Shafi'i had established the *sunnah* of the Prophet as the unique legal norm, traditions began to appear with increased frequency, and each possessed an *isnad* of ostentatious correctness. Supply went out to meet demand, and though the results did not much alter the substance of what a Muslim might or might not do, the new crop of traditions did limit both the premises and the practice of personal interpretation. The law ceased to be

---

20. At first the term "Companions" was restricted to the actual associates of the Prophet, but as a technical term in the study of traditions it came to be extended to all who could have been, on the most generous chronological and geographical grounds, an eyewitness of the Prophet. The last of the "Companions" died about the turn of the first Islamic century.

evolutionary in an effective sense, and the jurist could lean no further than he could bend the exegesis of a *hadith*.

Spurred on by the theological and juridical identification of *hadith* and revelation, the collection of traditions accelerated. By the time of al-Shafi'i the traditions concerning the Prophet had passed through five or six sets of hands, and with each passing generation these now legally precious *hadith* had become progressively more scattered across the breadth of the *Dar al-Islam*. The pious collector was condemned to a life of almost constant journeying—encouraged, however, by the sure knowledge that he was traveling the "road of God."

The enormous amount of material collected in this fashion was obviously quite inconstant in quality. There were mutually contradictory traditions, those with incomplete chains of transmitters, and others with multiple weaknesses. The texts themselves contained material that ranged on occasion from the trivial to the superstitious, or was transparently Jewish or Christian in origin. A great many were overtly and outrageously political in their inspiration. There were many in the ninth century who criticized the rising tide of *hadith*. Some resorted to mockery, while others, like the new rationalists in Islam who accepted the *Qur'an* but were averse to the notion of an authoritatively traditioned explanation of revelation, lodged even more trenchant criticisms against the *hadith*. To resolve the obvious difficulties of the tradition system, scholars devised a critical method for the study of the *hadith* that would enable them to sort out the "sound" from the "weak" traditions.

Modern scholarship has attempted the same task—with far different results—and has worked over both the text (*matn*) of the *hadith* and its chain of transmitters (*isnad*); the ninth-century Islamic scholar preferred to concentrate on the *isnad*. He tried to determine first, whether it was *possible* for the men listed in the *isnad* to have transmitted the tradition in question and, second, whether they were reliable by reason of their moral probity.

The linchpin of the system was clearly the Companion from whom the *hadith* reputedly originated, whence it spread like ripples across the generations of later transmitters. The student of tradition thus had need of a great deal of biographical material on the early Islamic personages, and some scholars devoted themselves to the task of providing it.[21] With this information in hand, chronological connections could be made and some reasonable defense given of the probity of the Companions.

In the end little was accomplished on this latter point; a consensus developed that affirmed the probity of the Companions of the Prophet en masse, not excluding Abu Hurayrah (d. 678), who is credited with a penchant for joking as well as the transmission of some 3,500 *hadith*, and against whom a great deal of *hadith* criticism, medieval and modern, has been directed. The scholars contented themselves with probing the consistency of the *isnads*, weeding out some of the weakest, and trying to reconcile the sometimes conflicting texts of those that remained.

By the mid-ninth century *hadith* criticism—or, more accurately, *isnad* criticism—had proceeded to the point where the newly authenticated *hadith* could be brought together for the use of the lawyers. The practical point of such collections is clearly displayed in the first preserved specimen of the genre, that put together by al-Bukhari (d. 870). All the traditions contained in it are "sound" (*sahih*)—the work itself is called *The Sound Collection*—with respect to their *isnads*, but they are arranged according to their applicability to the categories of jurisprudence, and the work includes Bukhari's own remarks as to their legal application.

The collection of Bukhari was quickly accorded canonical status in Islam and was followed by other, similar and equally authoritative collections by Muslim (d. 875), Ibn Maja (d. 886), Abu Dawud (d. 888), al-Tirmidhi (d. 892), and al-Nasa'i (d. 915). Taken as a whole, the six collections represent the body of traditions accepted as valid, and therefore juridically binding, by the *'ulama'* of the second half of the ninth century. The description of the *sunnah* of the Prophet was essentially complete; beyond these canonical *hadith* the Muslim had to be guided by his piety, or his sectarian leanings.[22]

---

21. See pp. 261–263.

22. The Shi'ah did not accept the authority of the Companions as a whole but only that of 'Ali and his partisans, and thus their traditions differed from those of the Sunni canon. The Shi'ite *hadith* were not assembled as a whole until the time of al-Kulini (d. 939); see Chap. VIII, p. 582.

Earlier, al-Shafi'i had set forth his theory of the four sources of the Islamic Law: the *Qur'an;* the *sunnah* of the Prophet as reflected in the traditions; the consensus of the entire Muslim community; and, failing all else, the application of analogical reasoning. Shafi'i may have invoked the principle of consensus to eradicate the claims of local custom and practice in the eighth century, but here in the ninth the Muslim jurists had come to a number of significant ecumenical consensuses: the acceptance of Shafi'i's basic principle of the priority of the *sunnah,* the formulation of a body of authenticated *hadith* that enunciated the *sunnah,* and, by the beginning of the next century, an acceptance of each other's claim to orthodoxy.

The former local traditions of Medina and Kufah became, under this dispensation, the Malikite and Hanafite "schools of law." The disciples of Shafi'i formed another such "school," and later in the ninth century the fourth and strictest *madhhab* grew up around the teachings of Ahmad ibn Hanbal.[23] The differences among the four on points of law were not great, and in a sense they were all Shafi'ites in their attitude toward the *Qur'an* and the *sunnah,* differing from him only in the degree to which they permitted recourse to the secondary source of personal extension of the law by analogical reasoning. The Hanbalites, for example, and the minor and parallel school of the Zahirites[24] refused to accept any form of personal interpretation. Between them the four schools divided the *Dar al-Islam,* sharing orthodoxy, popular respect, and an essentially common view of the Islamic Law, a view that was al-Shafi'i's.

In the end consensus turned out to be a far more potent force than al-Shafi'i could have foreseen. Consensus, with its attendant notion of infallibility—there was, naturally enough, a prophetic *hadith* to the effect that "my community will never agree in

---

23. See Chap. VI, pp. 465–468.
24. Founded by Dawud ibn Khalaf (d. 883) and so called because of his insistence upon the literal (*zahir*) interpretation of the *Qur'an.* The Zahirites had a certain vogue in Spain, where they claimed the allegiance of the famous scholar-poet Ibn Hazm (d. 1064), but they never attained the same ecumenical status of the other four schools.

error"—was not only the guarantor of the other three sources of the Law; it served as the base and justification of important elements in Islam that were either unsanctioned in the *Qur'an* and the *sunnah*, like the institution of the Caliphate, or were expressly opposed there, like the cult of saints. In both instances the practice of the Islamic community won out and then found its theoretical justification in the principle of consensus.

It was the final consensus of the mutual acceptance of the schools that closed the formative period of Islamic Law. Once the four schools assented to their mutual claim to authority and, in effect, agreed to disagree on the rest of the details, no other basic approach to the law could be permitted except there be another consensus, a possibility that was, by consensus, ruled out. It was, as later affirmed, "the closing of the gate of independent thought."[25]

The prescribed disappearance of new, evolutionary, or independent thought and the beginning of the era of acceptance-on-authority (*taqlid*) left within the bounds of orthodoxy the legal systems of Malik ibn Anas, Abu Hanifah, al-Shafi'i and, latterly, Ahmad ibn Hanbal and, on the outside, a scattering of Sunnite legal dissenters and the entire body of Shi'ite law.

The four orthodox schools were devoted to the enunciation of the "way" of Islam, its *shari'ah* or, to be somewhat more accurate, to the understanding (*fiqh*), of the *shari'ah*. The Islamic jurisprudent (*faqih;* pl. *fuqaha'*) did not understand his task as unfolding the sacred law—it was complete at the death of the Prophet, the term of both the *Qur'an* and the *sunnah*—but rather in penetrating it. The position found, perhaps, little support in practice, since both consensus and particularly analogical reason-

---

25. The gate of independent thought was closed more firmly for some than for others. The Hanbalite school particularly, whose positions among the mutually acceptable schools was at first the least secure—it did not in principle admit analogical reasoning—saw the difficulty of a self-defining consensus, and at least the later Hanbalite lawyer Ibn Taymiyah (d. 1328) claimed the right to a personal legal opinion, not merely for himself, but for all jurisprudents since the generation of the Companions.

ing[26] could be applied for purposes of unfolding the *shari'ah* into areas where it did not, or could not, originally apply.

The *shari'ah* had claim to govern the entire range of actions that constituted a man's life: his relations with Allah through acts of cult and ritual; his relations with others, either hereditary or contractual; and his relations with the state in the sense of penal law, taxation and constitutional arrangements. Not all categories were equally developed, and the Muslim *faqih,* once he had mastered the theory of the sources of the law, concentrated chiefly on the area of ritual obligations, personal status, inheritance and contracts. He studied the Qur'anic passages and *hadith* pertinent to the subject and paid attention to the differences among the four orthodox schools. The *faqih* was a scholar; he had no hand in administering or applying the law, which was the work of the *qadi,* though he might, on occasion, be asked to render an opinion (*fatwa*) on a particular point of the law.

The classical statement of the *shari'ah* came to term as an ideal treatment of concrete duties. At root it attempted to extend the principles of Islam to the entire spectrum of man's actual behavior. It provided, much as Stoic ethical theory did, a moral yardstick, calibrated from *obligatory* through *indifferent* to *forbidden,* for human acts. The *shari'ah* is filled with what appear to be hard, pragmatic considerations, but the appearance is deceptive. In its exaltation of *sunnah,* its recognition of consensus as its only evolutionary element, its closing of the "gate of independent thought," and its continued refusal to allow a meaningful place to local or customary practice, the Islamic Law restricted itself to a splendid and detailed description of a society that *should* be.

By its immense authority, the *shari'ah* made a great deal of human activity conform to the norm. The pious struggled to achieve the concrete ideal, but the society as a whole moved inexorably onward and left its political masters little choice but to legislate around the *shari'ah* and finally, in modern times, to abrogate it.

---

26. One means of extending analogy, for example, was to affirm a statute without Qur'anic or *sunnah* support on the grounds that the welfare of the community demanded it. The principle of the common good, or *istislah,* was most frequently invoked by the Maliki school.

One of the early advisers to the 'Abbasid Caliphs, the Iranian savant Ibn al-Muqaffa' (d. 757), writing at a time before al-Shafi'i had imposed a traditionalist *sunnah* on the law, urged al-Mansur to take the local diversities, then supported only by the consensus of scholars in one center or another, into his own hands, to unify and codify the law in his own name and make this Caliph-promulgated *shari'ah* binding on the *qadis* of the empire. Mansur declined to play the role of an Islamic Justinian, and the tide of *Qur'an* and *sunnah* was running so swiftly that soon it was impossible for anyone to do so. The 'Abbasid *qadis* were indeed bound by the *shari'ah*, but a *shari'ah* elicited from the *hadith* and propounded by legal scholars independent of Caliphal authority. And the Caliph was bound to that same *shari'ah* as securely as the *qadis* were.

How complete was the reversal of Ibn al-Muqaffa's position may be seen from the attitude of Harun al-Rashid. This Caliph had as his Chief *Qadi* the eminent jurist Abu Yusuf (d. 798), a remarkable and tradition-oriented student of Abu Hanifah who composed, at the request of the Caliph, his *Book of the Land Tax*. In it he set forth for his ruler—the Successor of the Prophet—the accepted *shari'ah* position on public finance and taxation.

Abu Yusuf was one of the few such scholars tempted from the schools onto the perilous political terrain of a judgeship. The 'Abbasid *qadi* was in theory bound only to the *shari'ah*, but he was in fact a political appointee dependent on the benevolence of his sovereign. Generally the scholars held themselves aloof from the administration of justice, even *shari'ah* justice, and contented themselves with serving as *muftis*, men who by their learning could deliver an authoritative opinion (*fatwa*) on a disputed point of law.

In theory, the *shari'ah* covered the entire *forum externum* of human life, individual and social; in practice, it was invoked almost exclusively on such matters as marriage, divorce, inheritance and pious trusts. It rapidly showed itself too cumbersome to handle criminal justice and too idealized to provide a workable base for constitutional law. In its broad outline the Islamicization of the law—which was begun by the traditionalists, was continued by the lawyers of the mid-eighth century and was crowned by the work of al-Shafi'i—corresponded to the stated ideals of the new dynasty of the 'Abbasids. The Banu 'Abbas, unlike the Banu Umayyah, proclaimed their intent of establishing God's commonwealth on earth.

Wide avenues of recourse developed, meanwhile, around the jurisdiction of the more earthbound *qadi:* criminal justice was given over to the secular arm of the police; public order was the responsibility of an officer borrowed in the earliest Umayyad times from the Byzantines and Islamicized by the 'Abbasids, the market inspector, or *muhtasib,* who operated under the broad Qur'anic mandate to "encourage good and discourage evil"; and finally, the 'Abbasid Caliph, for all his stated good will toward the *shari'ah* and all his benevolence toward an Islamic commonwealth, went his own legislative way under the concealing rubric of enacting not law (*shari'ah*) but merely "policy" (*siyasah*).

Fiqh was the culmination of a purely Islamic education that began with the rudiments of reading and writing, progressed to a recitation and memorization of the *Qur'an,* and then to its exegesis, linguistic and legal, with the aid of the sciences of philology, eloquence, tradition and jurisprudence. In practice the latter fields were highly technical disciplines with a claim to be sciences in their own right, but they all reflected the condition of Islam in their unmistakable orientation to the *Qur'an* and their still-remarkable connection with the oral tradition of the Bedouin.

From Epic to History

The Muslim's link back to his past was more than mere nostalgia or the reflex of tribal pride; it was a theological necessity, as it was for the Jew and the Christian before him. For all three "Peoples of the Book," revelation was the dominant event in human history in that it must not be forgotten; to forget was to perish utterly. Nor could the links that connected the present generation with the original deposit of faith be allowed to grow blurred. Thus, the latter-day Muslim, who received that revelation by both Book and tradition, had perforce to be historian and theologian, hurrying toward a future Judgment and at the same time peering over his shoulder to assure himself that the indispensable links with the orthodox past were intact.

The Christian was in much the same predicament, but his historical obligations were considerably simpler. The Christian had the living tradition before him in the person of the bishop and, if he wished, like Eusebius, to view the tradition in a more social way, in the form of an *ekklesia*. The Muslim had no bishop and no Church; he had only a single Caliph, who claimed neither inspiration nor *magisterium*, but was the head of a social and political community, the *ummah*. Islam, submission to the will of Allah, was in its essence a personal act, but in a larger understanding it was the *Qur'an*, the tradition, and the state. The Muslim was condemned to history.

As far as we can see, he began to write it down in one form or another shortly after the death of the Prophet, and within a hundred years after the *hijrah* Islam had a substantial and developed body of historical writing. That is our perspective, but we cannot be sure of its accuracy. Literature under the Umayyads is largely a reconstruction painfully pieced together from what can be sifted out of works written after 750. And by 750 there had already come into being that mélange of what had once been the history of the Jews, Arabs, Byzantines and Persians, which was joined with the Prophet's own legacy to form Islamic history.

The pre-Islamic Arabs' sense of history was conditioned by their political development. Only in the south of Arabia had a society reached the level of institutional sophistication where a continuous and articulated record of the past was preserved. Elsewhere the Arabs lived chiefly as nomads, and their needful memory of the past was satisfied by genealogies, the only archive the Bedouin must possess. Tribal genealogies were kept with some care, and the Muslims' continuing interest in that element of their past is attested to by the fact that the Caliph 'Umar (634–644) commissioned three genealogical specialists to compile a register of the data.

'Umar's action may have been prompted by more pragmatic concerns than a mere curiosity about his own and his followers' Arab past. The genealogical lists were compiled in connection with the army muster rolls that were intended to serve as a criterion for the distribution of their new wealth among the Muslims.[27] The deed had far-reaching consequences; by connecting a Muslim's merit with his tribe 'Umar wittingly or unwittingly linked Arabism and Islam. In the address he gave on his "pilgrimage of farewell" the Prophet prided himself on his doing away with the pagan Quraysh's "veneration of ancestors," that endless boasting about the proud deeds of past members of the tribe that was the chief staple of Arab poetry. 'Umar gave the lie to that boast in the most effective manner possible, by consulting tribal genealogies in the distribution of spoils.

'Umar did not create the mischief of tribalism in Islam; he merely gave it official encouragement. Its effects could be seen everywhere. Different tribes settled into separate quarters in the new Arab cantonments in Iraq and Khurasan, and in Kufah it may have been just such tribal differences, with the social and financial implications imposed upon them by 'Umar's decree, that led to the first Shi'ite uprisings there. The period of the Umayyads is filled with the sounds of political and literary warfare between tribes living everywhere from Syria to Khurasan but tracing their descent to ancestors originating in northern or southern Arabia.

The chief weapon in this tribal warfare was precisely what it had been in the pre-Islamic days, the considerable powers of the Arab poets to praise or insult. But genealogists too did their work, and there were even attempts at denying that this or that tribe was Arab at all. Traditions were put in the mouth of the Prophet to the same end.

The usefulness of the Arab genealogist did not end with tribal strivings. There were other wars on another terrain where the skills of the genealogist could be used with telling effect. Those other contests were called by the Arabs *shu'ubiyah*, cultural nationalism, and its protagonists were the Iranians, whom tribalism demeaned to the status of "clients" upon their conversion to Islam. The struggle of the "foreign" Iranians to gain equality in Islam went forward on many fronts in the ninth century,[28] but in the present context it summoned forth the genealogist once

---

27. See Chap. I, pp. 83–84.
28. See Chap. VI, pp. 401–408.

again to examine pedigrees and to unleash his considerable knowledge of scandalous stories and skeletons in tribal closets.

The Arab genealogist was far more than a memory bank for fathers and grandfathers. The oldest and best of those specialists in Islam, Daghfal (d. 685), provided the Caliph Mu'awiyah with information on language and the stars as well as on family trees. The genealogist was in fact the repository of much of what passed as history in the pre-Islamic Arabia of the Bedouin, the "narratives" (*khabar;* pl. *akhbar*) and the "battle days of the Arabs" (*ayyam al-'arab*), the latter a mixed account in prose and verse. In these tales the virtues of the tribe were rehearsed; breeding and heroic deeds were closely entwined threads in the Arabs' self-image.

The poet and the genealogist, the latter in his dual role of "narrator" and expert on family trees, combined to entertain and instruct the pre-Islamic Arab. The ode and the *akhbar* were, for all that, disembodied fragments of a historical record, and not continuous records of the past. Then, quite suddenly with the coming of Islam, the feats that once had provided grounds for boasting and satire became, when they reoccurred, the subject of sacred history. The raids (*maghazi*) and the prideful contests of the pre-Islamic Arabs were transformed into episodes in a Holy War fought, as part of a providential plan, for the greater glory of Allah and the establishment of the *Dar al-Islam.* As members of the Islamic *ummah* instead of a blood clan, the Arabs began to make social and political history. Its remembrance was a foregone conclusion.

Muhammad was the watershed in the life of the Arabs. By his message he rendered their past as nothing, a "period of ignorance" (*al-jahiliyah*). He tried to turn their attention away from that Arab past and the tribal present to the future Judgment, where their actions would be weighed on new scales. The Prophet took away the future prospect of history and substituted for it an eschatology.

If their future offered a Judgment but not history, Muhammad did provide his followers with a new kind of historical past. He had no interest in the "battle days of the Arabs"; he was the "Seal of the Prophets," the scion of another line of aristocrats that stretched back across the millennia. As a revelational religion,

Islam had a past founded upon its position as the reformation and perfection of those other revelations to the Jews and Christians. In place of their tribal genealogies the Arabs were given a prophetic pedigree, Muhammad's own, that went back through both Jesus and the Jewish prophets to Moses, Abraham, and even Adam.[29]

These were not unfamiliar names to many of Muhammad's listeners, and those among them who were Christians or Jews were already part of that tradition. Now all were: every Arab—and eventually every Muslim of whatever origin—took his place in a world history begun at Creation and sealed at the revelation of the *Qur'an* to Muhammad. And in the end they would all stand before the Judgment.

The eschatology preached by Muhammad was an individual one, and it is unlikely that he saw beyond the moral activity of the individual to the collective moral activity of his community—in short, to its history. He died before he knew what he had wrought, and it was his successors as head of the community who had to descend to the dimension of political history. In 632 Islam was barely institutionalized. It had at hand the instruments of expansion in its armies, but none of the apparatus to convert individual action into a social action that was at the same time Islamic. Nor did it inherit from the founder the means to guarantee its own connection with the receding but now crucial past. No Apostles were chosen; no Paraclete would descend.

It did not take the Muslims long to realize what had occurred and to take hold of the past. The Caliph 'Umar signaled their embarkation into history by sealing the *hijrah* of the Prophet as the beginning of a new, Muslim era (*ta'rikh*) in world history. The dead Prophet's associates, many of them gathered at Medina even as the arms of Islam were moving out across the *oikoumene*, laid up the memories of his life and deeds together with the *Qur'an*. There was no coherence in these scattered memories,

29. The notion may have had its earliest effects among the genealogists. Daghfal traced some of his genealogies back to Biblical figures. Hence too the tracing of the ancestry of all the Arabs back to Abraham's son Isma'il.

even though some of them may have been written down even at this early stage; they were passed on in the cities of the Hejaz piecemeal and at random.

The men upon whom later Muslims depended for their collective memory of the Prophet were soon enshrined as a special class of "Companions," and the next generation consulted them on matters that pertained to "Muhammad's custom," his *sunnah*. In doing so they were acting little differently from their pre-Islamic ancestors; tribal life in Arabia was severely governed by custom and precedent. There was a difference, however: when the Prophet spoke, he appealed to no other authority than that of Allah. Islam was a break with the tribal *sunnah* in the name of an immediate revelation of God's will.

Muhammad's own intent may have been to replace precedent with a Book revelation on the model of what he understood of the Jews and Christians, but his own followers, who did not, for the most part, come from among the "Peoples of the Book," converted their experiences of him back into *sunnah*. They accepted the Scriptural premise of the revelation of the *Qur'an*, but Muhammad's own sayings and deeds became for them a new and peculiarly Muslim *sunnah*.

We know of no Arab customary law being committed to writing in the pre-Islamic period, but the ambiguity between the Scriptural *Qur'an* and the new "*sunnah* of the Prophet" may have led some of the Companions to commit their recollections of the latter to writing shortly after Muhammad's death. Writing, it appears, was far more common in the earliest years of Islam than once thought. The *Qur'an* was written down in Muhammad's own lifetime, and written traditions about the Prophet and commentaries upon the *Qur'an* give evidence of having followed soon after.

Some of those recollections of the Prophet pertained to legal matters—to wit, his various extra-Qur'anic rulings on a great variety of problems confronting the *ummah*. But others stood closer to the stuff of the pre-Islamic epics on the "battle days of the Arabs." In content the raids of the Prophet in the years after 622 were little different from the *maghazi* of his tribal ancestors, and it appears likely that the Companions transmitted what may be called the epic of the Prophet in much the same way they had transmitted the epics of the Arabs, in the form of disconnected narratives, or *akhbar*.

The material began to be organized in a somewhat more coherent form in the century of the Umayyads. The *maghazi* narratives probably had biographical material attached to them from the beginning, but the first man to have brought them together into something resembling a continuous biography of the Prophet may have been 'Urwah ibn al-Zubayr (d. 713). With his successor in the work, al-Zuhri, the very word "biography" (*sirah*) began to be employed, and still another Umayyad editor of the Prophet's *maghazi*, Musa ibn 'Uqbah (d. 758), whose interests in the genre extended to the "raids" of the Caliphs as well as the Prophet, used the annalistic method to organize his work.

The term of this development is the *Life of the Prophet* by Ibn Ishaq (d. 767). That, at least, is what it is called in the version we now possess, the one edited by Ibn Hisham (d. 834). This latter recension is indeed a biography of Muhammad in which the various *maghazi* narratives and other traditions concerning the Prophet have been set out in chronological order. Ibn Ishaq's original appears to have been somewhat more ambitious, however; it began with an account of Creation and a sketch of Biblical history.

This was, as has been seen, Muhammad's own perspective on history, and the *Qur'an* contains frequent reflections on Creation and on the Jewish and Christian traditions that preceded Islam. Muhammad's followers had access to considerably more elaborate information on those subjects, and the evidence points to the probability that it came from Yemenese sources. We do not know a great deal about the historical tradition in southern Arabia, but two of the earliest historians of Islam wrote on the Himyarites. The first of them, 'Abid ibn Shariya, whose life was contemporary with Muhammad's and who survived into the middle of the seventh century, was a collector of moral *exempla* from the past, an interest that may have led him to compose his *Narratives of the Yemen*, an early example of the "battle days of the Arabs" genre as it applied to the Yemenite tradition. More historical and more universal was the *Kings of the Himyarites* by Wahb ibn Munabbih (d. 732). Wahb belonged to the generation of the Companions and like many of them wrote about the "raids" of early Islam. But he knew of other things as well; Wahb's view of history came from the Judaeo-Christian tradition and his vision extended, as theirs did, back to Creation.

Wahb and others like him opened Islamic channels not merely into the notion of world history but into the rich legendary narratives of the Christians and the Jews. Two early converts from Judaism were also helpful in supplying literary material to fill out and supplement the Biblical narratives in the *Qur'an.* 'Abdallah ibn Salam (d. 663) was a Jew of Medina who accepted Islam after the *hijrah* and was later closely associated with both 'Umar and 'Uthman. Most of his information may have gone into Islamic circles in oral form, but only a few years later another Jewish convert from the Yemen, Ka'b al-Ahbar (d. 662), wrote works on a great variety of subjects including Adam and Eve, Moses and Alexander the Great.

All of this new material was put to use by Ibn Ishaq and other Muslim historians to enlarge the Prophet's understanding of the world from Adam's day to his own. Muhammad introduced the Muslim to world history, but the details of the *praeparatio Quranica* came from Jewish and Christian *haggadoth* and *apocrypha,* which were in some undefined way connected with southern Arabia, where we know that both faiths had made strong inroads in the sixth century.[30]

The traditions in Ibn Ishaq's *Life* concerning the Prophet himself probably came from Medina where the author spent most of his years before coming to the new capital of Baghdad in 763. It was at Baghdad that the *Life* was written down, reportedly at the behest of the Caliph al-Mansur (754–775). Since it did have Caliphal patronage it must have been intended, at least in part, as a bit of political propaganda for the ruling house.[31] There may have been another motive at work, however. It is possible to think of the *Life of the Prophet* as an attempt to supply the missing part of the Gospel of Islam. The *Qur'an* was merely the *logia* of Muhammad, without narrative or biographical context. That context had been passed down among the Arabs of the

---

30. See Introduction, pp. 21–22.
31. See Chap. I, p. 70.

Holy Cities, had been gradually shaped by Ibn Ishaq's predecessors, and was now being presented to the *Dar al-Islam* as a formal biographical document with the Caliph's seal upon it.

Between Muhammad's own lifetime and the time that Ibn Ishaq put together his *Life* there had grown up about the Prophet and his teaching a new awareness that is faithfully reflected in the traditions incorporated in Ibn Ishaq's work. In the *Qur'an* Muhammad is insistently described as a mere man whose only claim to miraculous power was the fact that he was the recipient of a miraculous revelation. Some, at least, of his followers did not see him in the same way: the *Life* draws upon *hadith* in which extraordinary deeds are attributed to the Prophet. Here too contact with Christianity may have left its mark; the Muhammad of the *Life* stands much closer to the typology of the Hellenic-Christian holy man than does the more unassuming mortal who glimmers through the pages of the *Qur'an.*

Much more has been added to the *Life*. There are no genealogies or descriptions of raids in the *Qur'an*, but the *Life* is filled with both. Biblical events merely touched upon in the *Qur'an* are fully fleshed out in the later work. Frequently we do not know where this new material has come from, whether from versions of Biblical legends already circulating among the pre-Islamic Arabs and preserved by scholars like Ka'b al-Ahbar and Wahb ibn Munabbih or from the interior of vivid and pious imaginations.

The Biblical and *maghazi* material apart, Ibn Ishaq's *Life* is constructed upon *hadith*. Modern criticism has no great regard for the historicity of these traditions related of the Prophet on legal and dogmatic matters, and the same charges can be leveled against the hagiographical and historical "traditions" assembled by Ibn Ishaq for his biography. Some of them are, indeed, tendentious, particularly those that deal with issues alive in the mid-eighth century. The role of Mansur's ancestor 'Abbas has been magnified, and likely that of 'Ali too, while Abu Sufyan of the Banu Umayyah is shown in a less favorable light.

For the rest, the general lines of Ibn Ishaq's account are probably to be trusted. The *Qur'an* does contain the most authentic material on Muhammad's career in that it is transmitted without alteration from the subject himself. But its purpose is so little biographical and its historical references so opaque that, without the *hadith* material collected by Ibn Ishaq and others, our knowledge of the life of Muhammad would be negligible.

Another Medinese collector of traditions, al-Waqidi (d. 823), came to Baghdad in 796 and composed a similar historical work for Harun and his vizier Yahya. Waqidi's series covered roughly the same ground as Ibn Ishaq's original, and in the same way, except that it began with the birth of Muhammad. Just as later attention focused selectively on the *Life* of Ibn Ishaq, so for the "raids" of the Medina period it was al-Waqidi who was read. Ibn Ishaq had himself extended the *maghazi* of the Prophet into the era of the Caliphs, where they were gradually converted from "raids" into "conquests." His conquest book is lost, but al-Waqidi drew heavily upon it for his own work entitled *The Conquests: Syria, Egypt, Iraq and Ifriqiyah*. Traditions on the same subject were still being collected by al-Baladhuri (d. 892), whose *Conquests of the Lands* is the complete account of the Arab invasions we now possess.[32]

While the revelation to Muhammad marked a turning point in the affairs of men, his death held no such implications. Historians like Ibn Ishaq and al-Waqidi continued their narratives of the raids uninterruptedly across the events of 632, accounts which only gradually left off being narratives of the conquests and became the "era [*ta'rikh*] of the Caliphs." The line of evolution was natural enough, but the organization of the events, now highly complex, and as political as they were military, must have posed a considerable problem for the prospective author of an "era work" (*ta'rikh*).

A solution to the problem of organization may have been developing over the years, but the most eminent proponent of setting down events according to the year of their occurrence was the historian-traditionalist and Qur'anic commentator al-Tabari (d. 923), whose *History of the Prophet and the Kings* is,

---

32. Baladhuri was, in addition, a considerable genealogist—his *Genealogy of the Nobles* is preserved—as any historian of the period had necessarily to be.

in its general form, not unlike the composite work of Ibn Ishaq. Once past the *hijrah*, however, Tabari employed the annalistic form and grouped his narratives by year down to 914. The arrangement is orderly, if not always enlightening in its connections, but the narratives within each year are presented as they always had been: mixtures of prose and poetry, with the introductory chains of transmitters, lying side by side. Whatever critical insight went into the work was lavished chiefly on a scrutiny of the *isnads*. Patterns of causality were foreign to the *khabar* form and so foreign to al-Tabari who was, in the end, an Islamic traditionalist and not an Arab Thucydides.

Was the annalistic form a borrowing? Among the Arabs' neighbors and predecessors, the Byzantines—Theophanes, a century before Tabari, for example—wrote history in the annalistic arrangement, while the Iranians favored a grouping of events according to dynasties and reigns. The Arabs were not much given to translating Greek histories, whether pagan or Christian,[33] though it is absurd to think that a translation was necessary to cause the Arabs to seize upon this simple annalistic device which was first used by Musa ibn 'Uqbah.

There is, however, abundant evidence that al-Tabari was well acquainted with Iranian historiography. In its earliest examples the pre-Islamic part of the Arabs' ventures into world history were compounded of a rather disorganized blend of Jewish and Christian narratives about the patriarchs, prophets and Jesus. They may have known something of the more secular history of Iran as well, probably from oral sources, but from the middle of the eighth century the Arab historians had at hand translations, done from Pahlevi into Arabic, of the Sasanians' history books. The Arab chronicler could read in such diverse material as the epic romance of the *Res Gestae of Ardashir*, the *Book of the Crown* on the organization of the Sasanian Court, or the more historical *Book of Kings*, the latter two in the translation of Ibn al-Muqaffa' (d. 757).

---

33. The only direct evidence for such a translation is that for the version of the Christian Orosius' *Against the Pagans*, a copy of which was sent to Spain by the Byzantine Emperor Romanus in 948 and translated there, though with some difficulty.

A knowledge of the Iranian historical epic and a somewhat organized sense of the dynasties of Iran is already evident in Tabari, and even earlier Iranians writing in Arabic, like Ibn Qutaybah (d. 889) in his *Sources of History*, and al-Dinawari (d. 895), in his *Long Histories*, had drawn from the same sources. Al-Mas'udi (d. 956), whose historical encyclopedias are filled with Iranian historical information, records seeing in Istakhr in 915 a lavishly illustrated copy of an Iranian king book that had first turned up in 731. Nor was that the only kind of information at hand. King lists that were only loosely related to the epic tradition but had their origins in the calculations of Sasanian astronomers and astrologers were also known to Islam. Two easterners, Persians by birth, Hamzah al-Isfahani (d. c. 970)[34] and al-Biruni (d. c. 1050) were much interested in chronology, and some at least of what they knew came from Sasanian scholars, perhaps through the earlier Islamic astronomers Abu Sahl al-Fadl ibn Nawbakht, the court astronomer of Harun al-Rashid and a translator from Pahlevi into Arabic, and Abu Ma'shar al-Balkhi (d. 886) whose *Book of the Thousands* included a primitive and highly impressionistic history of science.[35]

Tabari's perspectives were, then, somewhat wider than those of Ibn Ishaq a century and a half earlier. But he was, nonetheless, a historian of the old style, engaged in what was essentially a pious work rather than a disinterested intellectual pursuit of historical truth. For Tabari, as for Muhammad himself, Islam was connected to the earlier "period of ignorance" only through the thread of the Judaeo-Christian prophets, now reinforced by at least some sense of Iranian history. But there were others in Islam who saw the past as more than either a *jahiliyah* or a *praeparatio Quranica*.

At about the same time that it was discovering the Sasanian past of Iran with the help of its Persian converts, Islam was being introduced to another kind of history, to the past as culture. With his reception of the "Greek sciences" the Muslim came to

34. Who describes his requesting a Byzantine captured in the wars to translate a Greek history for him. The captive's son helped with the Arabic.

35. See Chap. IV, pp. 271–272.

recognize himself as the legitimate heir to an intellectual tradition stretching down from the mythic past to ninth- and tenth-century Baghdad. History could also be written in *its* terms as well as in the traditional patriarchs-prophets-Muhammad-*ummah* strain. An early attempt at such a project can be seen in the *History* of al-Ya'qubi (d. c. 897), the Shi'ite savant who served his patrons the Tahirids in Khurasan until their fall in 873 and then moved on to Egypt. His *History* is, in its later, Islamic sections, much like that of Tabari, except that it is much less carefully done, without Tabari's attention to *isnads*, for example, and has a distinct Shi'ite bias. But the pre-Islamic section is, in part, a genuine cultural history of various peoples from the Indians to the Greeks and the Romans. For the latter Ya'qubi was clearly working from a philosophical rather than a strictly historical source, so what he knew, and what his reader was told, about Hellenic achievements was couched in terms of Plato and Aristotle rather than Pericles and Augustus.

Al-Mas'udi read his pre-Islamic history in the same fashion, as a blend of cosmogony, Judaeo-Christian sacred history, a dash of king lists, and a large serving of cultural history, particularly that of people like the Indians and the Chinese, about whose political past he knew nothing. Tabari, who lived in Baghdad during the height of the translation activity there, either did not know or did not care about this view of history. He was at heart a *hadith*-monger (*muhaddith*) to whom Hellenic cultural history was an available but unopened book.

Tabari's way of writing history—*ta'rikh* was, after all, an "Arab science"—called forth a long line of imitators. After him it could be taken for granted, however, that the groundwork had been permanently put down: Ibn Ishaq on the life of the Prophet, al-Waqidi on the *maghazi*, Baladhuri on the conquests, and Tabari on the "era of the Caliphs." Later historians generally contented themselves with picking up the *History* where their predecessor had put it down. Only occasionally would the horizons broaden, as when one or other of the Sabians of Harran, heirs of another, more comprehensive tradition like Thabit ibn Sinan (d. 975), took up the task of continuing al-Tabari's work.

World history also had its attractions. In the hands of a

Miskawayh (d. 1030) or a Tha'alibi (fl. c. 1021)[36] the genre began to mature into something more philosophical and interesting; but there was, unfortunately, little or no sequel. With the exception of Ibn al-Athir's (d. 1233) *Perfection of History*, world histories continued to be written much as Tabari had written his. The only notable innovation was not a happy one, the invasion of history by biography.

Neither the Greeks nor the Muslims regarded biography as a subdivision of history. For the former it was an ethical genre, and for the latter it was chiefly an instrument for the criticism of traditions. Biography was implicit, to be sure, in the original Islamic approach to history as a link to revelation as construed by the Arab genealogist. The history of the Prophet, his raids, and the subsequent conquests all carried the workings of Allah's providence into areas of social and political activity. But that activity was, from the first, transmitted in narrative pieces (*akhbar*), each of which was guaranteed by its own chain of transmitters. For Tabari these *isnads* were still of crucial importance, because he looked upon the narratives as "traditions" (*hadith*) that were, from the jurist's point of view, the substance of Islam.

If *akhbar* was the stuff of Islamic history, then the study of *isnads* was, in a sense, its historiography. On that supposition there were surely more historiographers than historians in Islam. The same men who transmitted the *maghazi* were also, as has been seen, specialists in the manner of their transmission–in short, genealogists. Al-Waqidi was such, and it was one of his students at Baghdad, Ibn Sa'd (d. 845), a scholar contemporary with important developments in Islamic jurisprudence, who brought together the biographical information attached to the *akhbar* and arranged it in the form most useful to the lawyers and students of tradition. Ibn Sa'd set out his biographies in "layers," or "classes" (*tabaqat*), beginning with the Prophet's own and then proceeding first to the "class" of the Companions, who were

---

36. On the littérateur Tha'alibi, a contemporary but different man, see Chap. VI, p. 410.

the original informants on traditions related to the Prophet, and then to each succeeding generation of transmitters.

The *Classes* of Ibn Sa'd is the beginning of the rich vein of collective biography in Islam. Its intent was neither politicoethical, as was most Greco-Roman biography, nor edifying in the manner of Christian hagiography, but to collect certain kinds of information on those men who were with the Prophet from the beginning—the battle of Badr is Ibn Sa'd's first checkpoint—and who transmitted to later generations of Muslims details about his life and sayings. From that intent flowed Ibn Sa'd's choice of material on his subjects: the times of their birth and death, the circumstances of their lives as Muslims, and evidence of their intelligence, memory and probity.

Ibn Sa'd's perspective was a narrow functional one, but it proved eminently useful to the jurisprudents for whom it was obviously designed. It followed the exact form of the chain *isnad* and so gave the student of tradition a valuable tool for the evaluation of *hadith*. The method proved popular in all branches of the traditioned sciences and soon there were *tabaqat* collections on every class of Muslim scholar from grammarians and lawyers to Sufis and poets. What is more remarkable, perhaps, was its extension to scholars in the so-called "rational sciences," which had no connection with the original premise of the *tabaqat* work. Thus, the Spaniard Ibn Juljul (fl. c. 987) wrote a *Classes of Physicians and Learned Men*, and the later Damascene physician Ibn abi Usaybi'ah (d. 1270) produced his *Sources of Information on the Classes of Physicians*.

As generation was added to generation down through the course of Islamic history, the "class" principle became increasingly unwieldy, not in the writing but in its use. The reader simply could not retrieve the material he was looking for. The solution lay, as it did for the lexicographers, in an alphabetical arrangement. This was the order followed by al-Qifti (d. 1248) in his *History of Learned Men*, which is devoted to the same body of Hellenic-style intellectuals as in Ibn abi Usaybi'ah's work, and thereafter it became commonplace. Islam's two massive "dictionaries of national biography," Ibn Khallikan's (d. 1282) *Obituaries of Eminent Men* and al-Safadi's (d. 1363) *Supplement to the "Obituaries"* are alphabetically arranged.

The theological and legal concerns of the traditionalist biographer came in the end to dominate the writing of history in Islam. Biographies made their appearance among the yearly entries of "ecumenical" histories with the publication of *The Rightly Ordered Things,* a world history by the conservative Hanbalite theologian Ibn al-Jawzi (d. 1200), and long before that time they were a staple in the flourishing tradition of local history.

In pre-Islamic Arabia there was little interest in local history; the Bedouin had little sense of place and so no local pride. Elsewhere in the Near East it was the imperial tradition that dominated the work of historians. Sasanian history writing appears to have been quite simply the *res gestae* of the Shahs, and the Byzantine historians too thought in terms of empire and not of provinces and towns. We know there was local pride among the citizens of the Eastern Roman Empire, but it more often inspired the rhetorician or the poet than the historian. If the local spirit did manifest itself anywhere in men's historical consciousness it was in ecclesiastical history. Church history too was ecumenical, but it rested more often than not upon a local episcopal tradition of the type that still lies close to the surface in the *Church History* of Eusebius. Individual Sees kept track of their bishops, their martyrs and the acts of their local synods, and among the Syrian Christians there was even a strong tradition of local chronicles.

With the exception of the Syriac chronicles, which continued to be written under Islam and may have influenced local Arabic historiography in Syria and Mesopotamia, the Islamic historian of his native place owed nothing to his Byzantine or Sasanian predecessors or to Church historians. Local Muslim histories had motives but not models. One motive may have been the conquest itself, the desire of those in Medina to receive reports of the newly conquered territories. There are stories of such requests for information going out to local authorities in the first century of Islam, but it is uncertain how seriously they should be regarded.

If such requests were made, they were fulfilled on at least one occasion, in the *Conquest of Egypt and the West* by Ibn 'Abdalhakam (d. 871). This is more than a mere conquest book in the style of Waqidi or Baladhuri; it is a genuine local history of

Egypt and includes, as the conquest books do not, historical material from the pre-Islamic life of the land. An even more remarkable—if less historical—example of the use of pre-Islamic material in a local work is *The Crown* of al-Hamadhani (d. 945), a work that is preserved only in fragments, but apparently reviewed the history of the Yemen from the beginnings of the house of Himyar down to the Muslim conquest.

In other instances it was theology rather than either pride or curiosity that prompted local history. One of the earliest examples of the genre, the *Narratives of Mecca* of al-Azraqi (d. 837), focused not on the history of the city as a political or social unit but upon the Ka'bah and the rites connected with it. Sites are described, inscriptions reported, and legends are told, but Azraqi's aim is to give a theological and liturgical topography and not to write the history of Mecca.

The most common form of Islamic local history is the type that began to appear at the end of the ninth century. Both Ahmad ibn abi Tahir's (d. 893) *History of Baghdad* and Bahshal's (d. 905) *History of Wasit* are essentially the collected biographies of local *hadith* transmitters with an introductory essay on the topography and history of the city itself. Their purpose was no different from Ibn Sa'd's own, except that they restricted their attention to the scholars of one locality. And as in the more general "class" works, the arrangement in the local versions yielded in the tenth and eleventh centuries to an alphabetical order. It was then that the most finished and influential example of the genre appeared, the *History of Baghdad* of al-Khatib al-Baghdadi (d. 1071). Its biographies are arranged in alphabetical order, but otherwise it is identical in form to the ninth-century examples: an elaborate topographical introduction to Baghdad followed by the collected biographies of the city's most famous scholars.

In these dictionaries of biography, national or local, the entire intellectual achievement of medieval Islam is displayed in the lives of thousands of Muslims, Christians and Jews, almost all learned in the manner of their times, tending and adding to the West's most profoundly bookish culture before the introduction of printing. Islam's ultimate ideal was neither the ascetic, the soldier, nor the statesman, all of whom might claim their inspiration from the Prophet himself, but the *'alim,* the man who possessed knowledge. Muhammad had imposed only five obligations upon the believer: the *shahadah,* fasting, tithing, prayer and the pilgrimage—to which the Muslim added, like a sixth sacrament, *'ilm,* knowledge.

And yet knowledge was never an end in itself. In his attempts at reconstructing the past the Muslim historian was engaged in a practical and pious act that was related to and descended from the collection of *hadith,* the study of classical poetry, and the recitation of the *Qur'an.* If he had any other purpose it was—and here his pre-Islamic antecedents are clear—to entertain in the manner of the Arab storyteller or to edify on the model of the Iranian epic moralist.

For the Arabs, history fell among the "traditioned" sciences, a category of knowledge that had its paradigm in the transmission of *hadith.* Like its model it was long on exactitude, which it sought to achieve by recounting two or more narratives of the same event, but short on analysis. The traditionalist historian, like the theologian, believed that Allah was the universal cause and that the ground of history was the theater of providence, where instruction was given on the ways of God and not on the folly or wisdom of men.

IV
THE RECEPTION OF HELLENISM

The Muslim cultivated his home-grown sciences of *Qur'an*, *hadith*, and *fiqh* within the Arab enclaves of Medina, Basrah and Kufah. His intellectual experiences during the first Islamic century in Alexandria, Antioch and Seleucia-Ctesiphon, those other centers of a non-Arab and non-Muslim culture, are impenetrably veiled from sight. It is only at the court of the 'Abbasids at Baghdad that one can finally perceive the intellectual confrontation of Islam, Hellas and Iran.

The changes that came about from that meeting were immense, despite the fact of their concealment beneath a vigorously maintained Arabism. The pre-Islamic Arab had a poetical tradition of considerable vitality, but little else that might serve to give him an enduring cultural identification. The revelation of Islam supplied something of that latter, and during the first century after the *hijrah* the interplay of tribal and literary Arabism with the book revelation of the *Qur'an* created a Semitic cultural complex not unlike that of Judaism during its postexilic phase.

The Hasmonaean Pharisees and their descendants, the rabbis, may have learned something from Hellenism in their treatment of the Law, just as the jurists and grammarians of Basrah may have experienced the ill-defined influences of Roman law and Greek grammar. But a closer Jewish contact with Hellenism eventually produced something more, the Alexandrian Philo, and it would not have been difficult to predict that once Islam came under the direct influence of that same Hellenism the effects of syncretism would be equally remarkable. The only wonder is that it took more than a century for a Philo to come forth from Islam, and why it occurred in the new city of Baghdad and not in Hellenism's venerable center of Alexandria.

The early Caliphs understood that if Islam were to survive it needed both protection and reinforcement. Instead of pouring their Arab troopers into the old urban centers of the Near East, where they would have been swallowed up by the Hellenic or Iranian majority, they cantoned them in new Arab towns where they were, in effect, the majority. Fustat, Kufah and Basrah were totally Arab and totally Islamic, and if others came there, they came as petitioners at the seats of power and patronage. In such a deliberately protected environment the Arab sciences thrived under the care of Muslim savants.

Baghdad was a different kind of settlement. Associated with neither the Arab camps nor the old Iranian capitals, it was a new city of the Islamic *oikoumene*, where Muslims, Christians and Jews, Arabs, Syrians, Greeks and Iranians all came together on what was close to neutral ground. Baghdad was Islam's Alexandria, a commercial emporium and the seat of political power, built in expectation and unencumbered by either nostalgia or jealousy. And once the ground had been prepared, Islam's Philos came forward by the score into the discernible light of history.

In 987 or 988 the Baghdad bookseller Abu al-Faraj Muhammad ibn al-Nadim completed his *Fihrist*, or *Catalogue*. The work may have been begun as a bookseller's hand list, but the author's own learning and curiosity and the bracing intellectual climate of Buyid Baghdad eventually produced something far different; the *Catalogue* is nothing less than a tenth-century encyclopedia of the literary arts and sciences of Islam. From calligraphy to alchemy, Ibn al-Nadim noted down, with biographical and historical comments, the sum of the books of Islam.

Ibn al-Nadim's tastes were happily catholic. Though a Shi'ite by conviction, and likely a Mu'tazilite as well, he interested himself in the entire range of the Islamic and foreign sciences. What we know of the early history of the Muslim theological sects and of such non-Muslim groups as the Sabians, Manichaeans and

Daysanites comes immediately and indispensably from the *Catalogue*. And it is to the same source that we owe most of our knowledge of the progress of Hellenism in Islam. Across the dense pages of the *Catalogue* it is possible to trace, with a convincing amount of detail, the enormous translation activity from Greek, Syriac and Pahlevi into Arabic.

The translations described by Ibn al-Nadim could not have begun much before 750, and they were all but complete by the time of the author's death sometime toward the end of the tenth century. For the sustained transmission of the fruits of one culture into the native idiom of another, the activity of those two and a half centuries permits little comparison in history, even in the omnivorous history of Hellenism. Hellenism had met and transformed other cultures before, but normally through a native intelligentsia that had already learned Greek. The encounter of Hellenism with an Arab Islam was, however, remarkable: the Muslim accepted neither the language nor the humanistic values nor, he thought, the religion of the Greeks; his borrowings came exclusively through translation and were severely limited to a technical and scientific Hellenism.

The acceptance of Hellenism through translation was a deliberate choice on the part of Islam. In the eighth and ninth centuries Islam was still an established religion with an established language, Arabic, which was, on the Muslim view of revelation, the speech of Allah himself. It was many centuries before either Persian or Turkish, whatever their prevalence on the streets of Islamic cities, could gain a grudging place in official Islam. Greek never found a place there after 'Abd al-Malik dislodged it from the chanceries of Damascus; and few, if any, of the Muslim scholars associated with the Hellenic sciences knew a single word of the original language of the works they so thoughtfully pondered.

Islam's second choice of a technical over a humanistic Hellenism was, in fact, no choice at all. In the centuries before the Arabs came into contact with that culture, the humane values of the Hellenic legacy were either absorbed or transformed or discarded by Christianity. As a result, the rich hoard of scientific learning transmitted almost intact to the Arab was accompanied by little understanding of Greek *paideia,* the cultural and humane ideals of Hellenism. This easy separation of the head from the trunk reflects ominously on the educational practices of late antiquity, when higher education must have been so severely professional in tone and content that it was possible to pass to others the curricula of the natural sciences, medicine and philosophy without any intimation that they were once part of an *enkyklios paideia*, a general education that included grammar and rhetoric.

Rhetoric was the chief vehicle for the study of humane letters in late antiquity. It was a popular subject, and there were endowed municipal chairs in that discipline scattered over the provinces of the Eastern Roman Empire. There was one province, however, that was, despite its high standards in medicine, philosophy and the mathematical sciences, notoriously disinterested in rhetoric: Egypt. Alexandria conforms very precisely—far more closely than Antioch, for example—to a hypothesized source for the Arabs' Hellenism, an intellectual center strong in philosophy and the sciences (particularly medicine and mathematics) and weak in rhetoric and law. Alexandria was, of course, somewhat more than that; it was the chief nurse of Greco-Oriental occultism.

We are not particularly well informed on the higher schools in the early Byzantine Empire. Something is known of the teaching of philosophy at Athens and Alexandria in the fifth and early sixth centuries, and at Athens at least we observe the presence in the curriculum of some curious items like the *Chaldaean Oracles* and the numerological musings of Nicomachus of Gerasa. Matters were somewhat more traditional at Alexandria, or appeared to be, and yet the scientific tradition there is illuminated by a series of men who were somewhat more obviously alchemists and astrologers than physicists and astronomers.

The declining school learning of late antiquity was merely a part, albeit for us the most familiar and sympathetic part, of the intellectual interests of the contemporary intelligentsia. Many of the best men were drawn away to other pursuits, to the new Christian theology or into the extensive penumbra of the occult sciences. In the form of theurgy, occultism had long since penetrated the preserves of the Platonic schoolmen and under the rubric of Gnosticism was firmly, if somewhat heterodoxically, entrenched among the Christian theologians. And beyond these formal bases of operation occult learning in alchemy, astrology and "Bolean" physics extended deep into the intellectual life of the later Empire and early Byzantine times. Its talisman was the name of Hermes Trismegistos.

The Arrival of Hermes

Hermeticism was an exceedingly complex phenomenon. It was, in the first instance, a body of myth and legend surrounding Hermes and others in his circle: Hermes was an apostle, a divinely inspired sage who brought to men a knowledge of the arts and sciences and the myths told of Hermes'—or the various Hermes'—experiences with the Babylonians, Egyptians and Greeks. The second ingredient of Hermeticism was the substance of Hermetic knowledge. It was at the same time practical and theoretical; the works in the Greek *Corpus Hermeticum*, which is mostly theoretical and speculative—a kind of "scholarly Hermeticism" as it has been called—were accompanied by an immense variety of tracts on practical hermeticism, that is, instruction on the operation and manipulation of natural substances. The Hermeticist knew the occult powers of things and how to make them work. He represented the most advanced technology of antiquity.

It was the scholarly Hermeticism that owed the most obvious debt to Greek philosophy and science, and it obliquely acknowledged that debt by linking one or another of the Hermes' to the Greek philosophical tradition—by making him the teacher of Pythagoras, for example. The connection redounded to the credit of both sides: it gave Hermeticism the cachet of intellectual enlightenment and the prestige of the Greek thinkers, while it made philosophers like Plato and Aristotle part of a continuing tradition that was divine in its origins and ecumenical in its scale.

Together with the mass of Hermetic lore the Arabs received a number of stories on the person of Hermes himself. They were taught by their Iranian informants that the original Hermes dated from antediluvian times, that he was in fact a grandson of Adam, and that one or another of the Hermes' known to them was a migrant bearing the wisdom of Babylon into Egypt. In the end Islam synthesized Hermes into the already-composite portrait of the Qur'anic Idris and the Jewish Enoch. It is not certain when this transmigration of Hermes into an Islamic setting took place, but as early as 845 Jahiz knew of the identification of Hermes-Idris, and Abu Ma'shar writing about the same time confidently stated that the Harranian sage Hermes was the grandson of the Hebrews' Adam and the Persians' Gayomart, and so, identical with the Biblical Khanukh (Enoch) and the Qur'anic Idris. Mas'udi likewise says that Enoch-Idris is the same as Hermes and adds that this identification was made by the Sabians. If the Sabians were responsible for inserting Hermes into the Idris-Enoch complex, then it is likely that the identification began to be diffused at the time when, as shall be seen, the *Dar al-Islam* took official notice of the Sabians of Harran, during the final days of Ma'mun. Abu Sahl al-Fadl ibn Nawbakht, Harun's Iranian librarian, knew nothing of it.

It was not, then, his association with Idris that originally recommended Hermes to the Muslim. Rather it was his position in the history of science that was being propagated in the Baghdad of Harun by scholars like al-Fadl and was accepted in the next century by Abu Ma'shar al-Balkhi and in the tenth by the considerably more sober and better informed Ibn al-Nadim.

In Ibn al-Nadim's *Catalogue* the sketchy description of the passage of the Platonic and Aristotelian school corpus into Islam is preceded by a series of somewhat disjointed narratives that provided the Muslim reader of the tenth century with an account of the origins of science and of Greek philosophy. The first and second of Ibn al-Nadim's narratives, those derived from Abu Sahl al-Fadl ibn Nawbakht and from Abu Ma'shar, purport to return to the very origins of scientific knowledge. And though they were reporting on different parts of the story, both men drew upon some common or complementary source.

According to their composite account, science began in Babylon and passed thence into Egypt and India. The substance of this "science" was primarily cosmogonic, but its understanding was unaccountably blurred by some "original sin," and it was not until some later time that the true understanding of the origins of the universe was recalled or restored. Centuries afterward, during the reign of the king Tahmurath according to Abu Ma'shar, there came to Babylon reports of a flood "in the west." Alarmed, Tahmurath ordered the construction of a repository on the citadel of Jayy near Isfahan and concealed there the books of human wisdom.

Greece plays little or no role in this version of the origins of science, nor is there any reason it should. Ibn al-Nadim was using two sources who were committed to a Babylonian and Iranian origin of learning. That the learning in question was chiefly astrological is no less obvious. Al-Fadl ibn Nawbakht (d. 815), the older of the two authorities, was an Iranian who specialized in translations from the Pahlevi in Harun's "Treasure House of Wisdom," while his father had been the court astrologer of al-Mansur and had assisted in that capacity at the laying-out of the city of Baghdad. Abu Ma'shar may have been somewhat more the Hellenophile, but he too was an astrologer and relied far more earnestly on Iranian than on Greek sources in his work.[1]

Howsoever much these men inclined toward Iran, they both knew of at least one Greek sage, Hermes. Indeed, Abu Ma'shar knew three by that name, encouraged, doubtless, by the stereotyped epithet *trismegistos* applied to Hermes in the sources. The earliest of the three lived before the Flood. He was the first to study the sciences and constructed the pyramids in Egypt. The second was identical with the Hermes of al-Fadl's account of postdiluvian Iraq. A king, Dahhaq ibn Qay, founded a city, likely Babylon, and constructed in it seven (or twelve) astronomical shrines for seven scholars, among them Hermes. The coming of an unnamed prophet shattered this golden age of learning in Iraq, and Hermes eventually left for Egypt, where he became king. Later authors obviously copying from Abu Ma'shar connected this Hermes with Pythagoras, either as the teacher or as the student of Hermes. The latest of the Hermes' was the Egyptian sage associated with the body of Greek (and Latin) texts that bear his name, the so-called *Corpus Hermeticum*, the Egyptian

1. Earlier in his life Abu Ma'shar had been a rather conservative student of *hadith* and a critic of al-Kindi's penchant for philosophy. He underwent a "conversion" to philosophy at the latter's instigation, but in the end Abu Ma'shar gave himself over to astrology.

summa of Gnosticism and alchemical science. This same Hermes was the sire of Asclepius, who passed his father's scientific and philosophical learning to the Greeks.

This view of intellectual history was put together in scholarly circles at the court of Harun (786–809), well before the days of Hunayn ibn Ishaq and of al-Kindi, and so, earlier than the full impact of scholastic Hellenism upon Islam. Even earlier, Mansur had shown an interest in the "foreign sciences"—Jurjis ibn Jibril ibn Bukhtishu' came from Jundishapur to Baghdad as Caliphal physician in 765—but that interest was neither entirely philosophical nor entirely Greek in its object. Jurjis and his successors from the Buhktishu' family were Hellenically trained, but another family that came into prominence in Mansur's reign, the Nawbakhti, looked, as we have seen, in quite different directions. The founder of that line, Nawbakht (d. c. 777), was an Iranian convert from Zoroastrianism to Islam and an astrologer of considerable influence at court. And it was from his son Abu Sahl al-Fadl, likewise an astrologer and bilingual in Pahlevi and Arabic, that Ibn al-Nadim drew his account of the early history of science.

Harun too was interested in Greek science and philosophy. The Bukhtishu' retained their position at court but were joined by another Jundishapur alumnus, Yuhanna ibn Masawayh, the Christian to whom Harun entrusted the task of translating the Greek medical works taken during the various Muslim forays into Anatolia. Abu Nuh, the secretary of the Nestorian Catholicus Timotheus, edged forward the still relatively unsophisticated translation work on the Aristotelian logic and another obscure scholar, Sallam al-Abrash, is alleged to have translated the *Physics*.

Sallam probably had the patronage of the Barmacid family, but those recent converts from Buddhism to Islam had interests far more catholic than Greek science. Yahya ibn Khalid, who commissioned the translation of Ptolemy's *Almagest*, was personally responsible for having Indian medical works translated into Arabic. Other scholars connected with either the Barmacids or Harun's library labored at turning both Sanskrit and Pahlevi works into Arabic. Abu Sahl al-Fadl was among these latter; in the words of the *Catalogue*, "he was relied upon because of his knowledge of the books of Fars," which included works of "Hermes the Babylonian" translated into Pahlevi during the reign of Shapur.

The Muslim savants of the late eighth century were well versed in Persian, Indian and Greek astronomy, astrology, medicine and alchemy, and this at a time when they knew Aristotle only in an epitome and apparently possessed no knowledge of Plato at all. Within a few years Ibn al-Bitriq, Ibn Bahriz, Ibn Na'imah, all Christians, began the work of translating Aristotle, Plato and the Neoplatonists. This scholastic tradition, patronized by Ma'mun, came into Arabic directly from Syriac or even Greek prototypes and without the notable Iranian contamination to which the stories told by Al-Fadl and Abu Ma'shar bear eloquent, if symbolic, witness. They describe the state of historical knowledge under Harun and Mansur: with the assistance, it would seem, of Iranian astrologers, Hermes Trismegistos was domesticated in Islam a generation before either Plato or Aristotle found a firm base there.

Scholastic philosophy did nothing to impede the growth and diffusion of Hermeticism in Islam. Indeed, their coming together was like the mutual rediscovery of an old ally. The Greeks and Romans at the end of antiquity were persuaded of the identification of Hermes with the Egyptian god Thoth—the Theuth of Plato's *Phaedrus*—and were equally convinced that the works circulating in Greek under the name of Hermes Trismegistos were a genuine reflection of remote Egyptian antiquity. The philosophers of the Renaissance embraced the imposture with equal enthusiasm, and it was only in relatively recent times that Western scholarship judged the *Corpus Hermeticum* as essentially the creation of late Greek piety and learning.

The Arabs possessed, on the testimony of the *Catalogue*, a wide range of *Hermetica* including versions of the Hermes myth as well as works of theology, cosmology and physics that were the substance of the Hermetic "revelation." The extent of the latter may be measured in the alchemical Book Ten of the *Catalogue*, with its bewildering profusion of names and titles. The major figures are Hermes—the Babylonian Hermes of al-Fadl—Ostanes, Zosimus, Khalid ibn Yazid, Jabir ibn Hayyan, the Sufi master Dhu al-Nun al-Misri (d. 860), Muhammad ibn Zakariya al-

Razi (d. 925), Ibn Wahshiyah (d. 904), his contemporary al-Ikhmini, a Christian monk named Stephen, the 'Alid Sufi Abu Bakr al-Sa'ih al-'Alawi, Kindi's student Dubays, and the extremist Shi'ite Al-Shalmaghani (d. 934).[2]

The list points to some of the directions penetrated by Hermeticism in the late tenth century. The *Shi'at 'Ali* consistently claimed Jabir as one of their own and linked him with the *Imam* Ja'far al-Sadiq (d. 765), who was himself credited with alchemical works. Ja'far's other companions are not, in fact, very well known except from what can be read in the Sunni heresiographers. Abu al-Khattab (d. c. 762) came to rest in those collections as an early example of the Shi'ite *ghulat* by reason of his divinization of both Ja'far al-Sadiq and himself. The *Catalogue* connects two other famous members of Ja'far's circle with Abu al-Khattab, Maymun al-Qaddah and his son 'Abdallah, the reputed founders of the Isma'ili wing of the Shi'ah. Another man who belonged to the same group around Ja'far was the early Shi'ite *mutakallim* Hisham ibn al-Hakam (d. 795).

Ibn al-Nadim offered another characterization of Maymun al-Qaddah: in addition to being a follower of Abu al-Khattab he was also a Daysanite, a latter-day adherent of the early Christian theologian of Edessa, Bar Daysan (d. 222). We know little of what to make of this. Though they could distinguish the two on a number of points of doctrine, the Muslim heresiographers often linked the Daysaniyah with the Manichaeans, generally on the grounds that both schools argued for the eternity of the elements and held for two ultimate principles, light and darkness. What the Muslims knew was that Mani, who was described by Ibn Hazm as a "monk in Harran," had a serious disagreement with Bar Daysan on the nature of the metaphysical principle of darkness. For Mani it was alive, but for Bar Daysan matter was dead and so created evil only by "nature and necessity," a function not unlike that of the substrate in Plato's *Timaeus* and a far cry from the matter-with-reason of Mani.

---

2. Shalmaghani belonged to an intellectual circle that included, not always on friendly terms, Thabit ibn Qurrah and two later members of the Nawbakhti family, Abu Sahl Isma'il and his nephew Hasan ibn Musa.

Bar Daysan is not to our eyes a clearly defined figure. Some of that obscurity may have arisen from the shifting positions of those who claimed his name over the following eight centuries. Though interested in astrology, he was not, it appears, part of the occult Hermetic tradition associated with Harran. Bar Daysan was a Christian, and so his myth was a Christian, not a Hermetic, one, even though it was invaded by the sensibilities of his highly syncretized milieu. The knowledge of the doctrines of Bar Daysan must have arrived within Islam through Syrian Christian channels, even though the Muslim heresiographers preferred to associate him with Mani because of their preoccupations with the problems of dualism. Ibn al-Nadim appears not even to have been aware that he was a Christian.

In Ibn al-Nadim's day there were Daysaniyah in Khurasan and China, but earlier the sect had reportedly thrived in the marshlands of southern Iraq, in the same area that spawned the "Sabians of the marshes" or the "Nabataeans," another archaic survival in Islam. These strange people were almost certainly the Mandaeans, a Gnostic sect that had its origins within later (but possibly pre-Christian) Judaism as an ascetic, baptist society with its centers in eastern Jordan, the former haunts of the Nabataeans. Some of these so-called Nasoraean Jews may have been absorbed within Judaeo-Christianity, but another branch of the "baptizers" migrated eastward sometime before the destruction of the Temple in 70 and, after passing through Harran, found their refuge in the marsh areas of lower Iraq.

The Mandaeans may well have been Gnostics before they departed from their camps in the Transjordan, but their literature, at any rate, dates from after their arrival in Iraq and testifies to the incorporation into a very early form of Jewish Gnosticism of ideas derived from both Babylonian and Iranian sources, the importance given to the seven planets, for example, and the Mandaean form of the Gnostic savior myth.

None of this painfully reconstructed history of the Mandaeans was evident to Ibn al-Nadim, who contented himself with brief comments on their practices and who seems to say that they were originally Manichaeans. The reality was, in fact, quite the reverse; there was a Mandaean sacred literature before 300, or at any rate early enough for Mani to borrow from it. And it must surely have been the existence of these Scriptures that prompted Muhammad to include the "Sabians" in the *Qur'an* (2:62; 5:69; 22:17) as "People of the Book."

It would appear unlikely that Muhammad had direct access to the Sabian-Mandaean Scriptures. Ibn al-Nadim credited them with no titles, but he did know of other, somewhat more secular "Nabataean" works, chief among them the *Nabataean Agriculture,* a work purportedly done by Ibn Wahshiyah but more likely the creation of the Shi'ite Abu Talib Ahmad ibn al-Zayyat (d. c. 951). The purpose of the *Nabataean Agriculture* remains obscure, but it is obviously Hermetic, and like the *Hermetica* in Greek its pretended antiquity—it claims merely to be a translation from the original Nabataean (Aramaic) of the older Semitic learning of Mesopotamia—is largely fable.

Most of the material in the *Nabataean Agriculture* is, in fact, pre-Islamic, though it does not return to the remote patriarchal times of the Arabs' imaginings. Much of it is Greek, but there are also considerable traces of Mesopotamian lore, a combination which points once again to the besetting problems of Near Eastern syncretism. In the five-odd centuries spanning the birth of Christ, the Near East presents a series of religious and quasi-religious phenomena compounded out of motifs drawn from all over Western Asia. Gnosticism is one such, Mandaeism another, and the typology can be multiplied through various Jewish and Christian sects and the occult sciences like astrology and alchemy. Scholars' attempts at disengaging and assigning to their appropriate sources the various themes within these complexes have been only partly successful at best, least of all their efforts at speaking with historical preciseness on the when and where of these obvious syncretisms.

The problem and its attempted solutions reflect upon the search for the origins of parallel phenomena in Islam. The routes whereby Hellenic *scholastic* material passed into Islam are well marked in the pages of the *Catalogue,* and their exploration leads directly to Farabi engaged in the study of the *Metaphysics.* But the occult knowledge possessed by Farabi's contemporaries did not necessarily travel over parallel, albeit underground, paths. Much of what has been described as Hermeticism may have been on the site long before Islam, in the hands of people like the

Mandaeans, Syrian Christian groups like the Daysaniyah, the theologians of the well-established Babylonian rabbinate, the Hellenized priesthoods which were still active in Babylon and elsewhere in the first Christian century, or in later times the Hellenic and Hellenized philosophers at the court of Khusraw Anushirvan.

The territory in lower Iraq occupied by the Mandaeans-Sabians in the second or third Christian century was the breeding ground in the ninth of the Qarmatian wing of the Isma'ili Shi'ah.[3] None of the earliest Isma'ilis, those associated with Ja'far al-Sadiq in the eighth century, were explicitly connected with the Mesopotamian Sabians, though Maymun al-Qaddah was accused, as has been seen, of being an adherent of the Daysaniyah, who were once strong in those regions. The charge appears somewhat unlikely. There was nothing in Bar Daysan of the *batin-gnosis* approach to knowledge, no spiritual emanations, no continuing revelation through an *Imam.*

Whatever its claims to political and dynastic legitimacy, theoretical Isma'ilism was the creation of those obscure men connected in one way or another with the *Imam* Ja'far. None of their work has been preserved intact, but the degree to which some form of Neoplatonism invaded the preserves of Isma'ili Shi'ism by the mid-tenth century can be observed in the highly systematized theories of the Brethren of Purity at Basrah.[4] The Brethren acknowledged the prophethood of Hermes, an admission rendered easier by the Sabians' prior identification of Hermes with the Qur'anic Idris, but the most overt expression of Hermeticism in the *Epistles* of the Brethren is reserved for the fifty-second and final *Epistle* in our collection. It is here, in this collection of magic and theurgy, that the debt to the Sabians is explicitly confessed, the Sabians' connection with the Greeks is maintained, and the ultimate origins of science are traced, as they were in the various Hermes legends, to Egypt and Babylon.

The entire passage is an important source of information on the sect of the Harranians, who flourished, if only for a brief time,

---

3. See Chap. VIII, p. 596.
4. See Chap. VIII, pp. 613–616.

under Islam and left their profound mark on Isma'ili Shi'ite and Sunni alike. In the first part of the ninth chapter of the *Catalogue,* Ibn al-Nadim has another lengthy description of the same sect. He names as his first source al-Sarakhsi (d. 899), who derived his account in turn from his teacher al-Kindi. This initial part of the narrative describes some of the rituals and taboos of the Sabians, but the hand of al-Kindi is most evident in the final equation of Sabian physics and theology with the contents of the Aristotelian curriculum.

After the Kindi-Sarakhsi account, Ibn al-Nadim proceeds to his other sources on the Harranian Sabians including a Christian's narrative of how Ma'mun first became aware of their existence. The Caliph insisted upon the conversion of these obvious pagans, but the "Harranians" devised a way out of the impasse: they identified themselves with the Mandaean "Sabians" mentioned in the *Qur'an* and so sought to move into the shelter reserved in Islam for "Peoples of the Book." It was the same motive, doubtless, that brought Hermes into the orbit of the Qur'anic Idris.

There was a justice in this. The original invocation of both Hermes and Thoth in connection with the occultism of the *Corpus Hermeticum* was itself a subterfuge to convince the Hellenic reader of the impeccable Eastern antiquity of what was really the creation of the religious sensibilities of late Greco-Roman antiquity. Just as Hermes-Thoth was used to conceal the true nature of the original philosophical-theosophical mélange, so now Idris was summoned to give Hermes and Hermeticism an Islamic coloration by serving as a pseudepigraph for a pseudepigraph.

Enoch and Idris were late Islamic arrivals at Harran. During the Greco-Roman period the spiritual founding fathers there were Hermes and Agathodaimon, to whose patronage the local ritual and, somewhat more successfully, the considerable Harranian skill in the theory and practice of alchemy and astrology was bestowed. The alchemy may have been a local growth; its constant and almost exclusive concern with minerals suggests some kind of association with a metalworking guild. The planet cult, of which Muslim authors like Ibn al-Nadim, Mas'udi, the Brethren of Purity, Shahrastani and Dimashqi produced such detailed descriptions, was likewise very old at Harran, and its assimilation of the sophisticated scientific techniques of Babylonian astrology could have occurred on either of the two occasions when northern Syria and Babylonia were part of the same political organization, during the rule of the Achaemenians or that of the Seleucids.

Ibn al-Nadim's description of the various rituals practiced at Harran has unmistakably to do with something exceedingly primitive, survivals from another age that escaped at Harran the oblivion in which Christianity wrapped similar rites all across northern Syria and Mesopotamia. Hermeticism, on the contrary, was not, despite appearances and constant professions of antiquity, a primitive survival from a vanished world, and its mock antiquity stands in absurd contrast to the patently old cult practices of Harran.

Sabianism was far more than mere star worship: the Harranians possessed a physics and a theology. Kindi's account in the *Catalogue* reduced the Sabian philosophy to a somewhat too perfect image of Aristotelianism, but the Brethren's explanation of the philosophical premises of the Sabians' astrology, taken together with Shahrastani's report, with which it essentially agrees, reveals something far different. The Sabians believed in a creator God, remote in his transcendence. He is the One in his essence, but is present by infusion in the other spiritual beings who are his creatures, whether the angels or the souls of men.

Seven of the divine spiritual beings who are not mixed with matter were assigned the direction of the planets. Although the Sabians called the planets the "temples" of the spiritual beings, these divine beings did not inhabit them in the manner of souls or inherent forms but ruled them from without, while the planets in turn directed the rest of the material universe. The universe is the meeting place of the goodness of light—the One God was identified with Light by the Sabians—and the darkness of evil. The human soul is consubstantial with the divine beings but does not always realize its powers, because of its mixture, as form with matter, with the material elements.

God has mercy on some men, and those were the prophets. But for the rest a return to their homeland among the spiritual beings is attained only by a veritable Platonic *askesis*, the putting-off of the influences of the lower parts of the tripartite soul. How a man conducts himself in life determines his role in the next cycle of creation. In the Sabian view the species cease their reproduction at the end of a Great Year of 36,425 solar years. At that point begins a new cycle of material beings. The purified souls have since rejoined the spiritual beings on high, but those whose purification is not complete must suffer another reincarnation, either as men or, for the substantially impure, as beasts.

Although it is not stated explicitly, this body of cosmology, theology, physics and psychology probably constituted the esoteric teaching of the Sabians of Harran, what the Isma'ili Brethren called the "realities" (*haqa'iq*), while their elaborate rituals were designed for esoteric purposes. That the two were born at the same time or arose from the same religious sensibilities defies belief, however. We can only surmise that at some point which cannot at present be determined, but likely during Hellenistic times, the pagans at Harran fashioned for themselves a theology—that is, they attempted to explain their beliefs in terms of Hellenic rational discourse, albeit in a late, syncretized and occult form of that discourse. The experiment was not a complete success. The old cult and the new theology sat uneasily together, uncomfortably enough for Shahrastani to deduce the existence of two Sabian sects, the "spirituals" and the "idolaters," the latter likely the original "Sabians" of Harran, and the former equally likely the product of a contact with Hellenistic piety and science.

Kindi was correct when he thought he could perceive Aristotle through the outlines of Harranian theology, but only half so. What he did not understand was the highly syncretized nature of the Harranians'—and his own—philosophical inheritance. He says, "Their saying that God is unity, to whom no attribute applies and about whom no affirmative statement can be made, or any syllogism related, is similar to what is said in the *Metaphysics*." Kindi knew the *Metaphysics*—it had been translated for him by a certain "Astat" (Eustathius)—and so too did his Sabian contemporary Thabit ibn Qurrah; but Kindi also had before him another text masquerading as Aristotle which expressed sentiments far closer to the Sabian insights than the *Metaphysics*, the abridgment of parts of the *Enneads* known as the *Theology of Aristotle*.

There existed another Arab tradition on the origins of the Harranian version of the *theologia negativa*. Sa'id al-Andalusi's account of the history of Greek philosophy in his cultural history, *The Classes of Nations*, opens with the remark, already seen in the Brethren, that the Greeks' religion is like the Sabians'. How this came about historically is revealed shortly after: the oldest Greek philosopher was Empedocles, who learned his wisdom in Syria from King David's vizier Luqman. Among Empedocles' successors, Sa'id includes only Pythagoras, who was initiated into philosophy in Egypt by certain companions of Solomon who fled there; Socrates and Plato, who were both students of Pythagoras; and finally Aristotle, who was, of course, the student of Plato but also, in a sense, of Pythagoras, since his father, Nicomachus, was a student of Pythagoras.

The Greeks' own view of that history reads quite differently. Sa'id or his source has reversed the true chronology of Empedocles and Pythagoras to confer priority on the former. Later Greek lives of Pythagoras, like that in Porphyry's *Philosophical History*, do make him into an indefatigable traveler over the Near East; according to Porphyry, Pythagoras derived his wisdom from the Egyptians, Phoenicians and Chaldaeans, as well as from Arabs and Jews, who instructed him in the interpretation of dreams. There are, however, no similar traditions in the case of Empedocles, and the tiny fragment preserved from Porphyry on Empedocles does nothing more than state that he was the student and lover of Parmenides, a name which means nothing to Sa'id.[5]

Sa'id's characterization of Socrates is another departure from the later Greek tradition. Despite the fact that the later Platonists paid little or no attention to the ethical philosophy or political concerns of Socrates, he did, however, hold a central position in their understanding of the *history* of philosophy. Socrates was, again according to Porphyry, the "coryphaeus of the philosophers," an attitude that went back to the philosophers of the generation before Cicero, when the ethically oriented Stoics and Platonists came to regard Socrates as the founder of "modern philosophy" and claimed him as their own. The interest in ethics

5. And very little to Ibn al-Nadim. The name of Parmenides appears in the *Catalogue* only on a list that comes from John Philoponus and names the most famous physicians before Galen.

did not survive among the later Platonists, but the historical position granted to Socrates did.

Sa'id was not, however, writing history, but was obscurely enunciating a philosophical attitude that had its origins in the East and located its Greek ancestry chiefly in a long-dead Empedocles and Pythagoras. According to Sa'id, in Empedocles' own lifetime popular opposition forced his philosophy to go underground, where it was cultivated by "Batinites." In Islam its reappearance was connected with the Spaniard Ibn Masarrah and the early Mu'tazilites, who were, in Sa'id's view, the chief beneficiaries of Empedocles' insistence on the unity of God and his denial of the reality of the divine attributes.

The titles attributed to Hermes in the *Catalogue* are chiefly alchemical and astrological. Similar works were earlier circulating under his name in Greek, as well, but the preserved Greek *Corpus Hermeticum* is far more philosophical than occult, and its theology bears a marked resemblance to both Stoicism and Platonism. None of the *Catalogue*'s titles point in that direction, but at the end of the Kindi-Sarakhsi account of the Sabians, Ibn al-Nadim adds: "Al-Kindi said that he saw a book which these people [the Sabians] authorized. It was the 'Discourses of Hermes on Unity [*tawhid*],' which Hermes wrote for his son. . . . No serious philosopher can dispense with them and agreement with them."

The "Discourses on Unity" have been identified, without evidence, as the *Poimandres* of our *Corpus Hermeticum*. Given the content of the *Poimandres*, the identification appears highly unlikely. If we recall, on the other hand, that the information—and the editorial comment—came from al-Kindi, a philosopher of known Mu'tazilite leanings, and that the "unity of Allah" was *the* paramount Mu'tazilite issue, we are no closer to locating the "Discourses" in the *Corpus Hermeticum*, but we have uncovered al-Kindi's motive in praising whatever he read in the "Discourses" and can perhaps conjecture what he did read there. In al-Kindi's bibliography we find there among his controversial works various refutations of the Manichaeans and other dualists, a work on *tawhid* together with commentaries and, finally, a treatment of the differences that exist among the various sects on the subject of *tawhid*, and this despite the fact that they are all supporters of the divine unity.

Al-Kindi, we have seen, had already attempted to locate Sabian theology in the context of the *tawhid* question by what must have been a highly Neoplatonic reading of the *Metaphysics*, just as Sa'id al-Andalusi was to do with a similar reading of Empedocles. Sa'id was, however, far more explicit in drawing the historical conclusions: the Empedoclean (read "Neoplatonic") version of Hermeticism had a direct influence on the theology of the Mu'tazilite Abu al-Hudhayl. We do not know enough about the intellectual formation of Abu al-Hudhayl properly to comment on Sa'id's judgment, except to note that the theological positions formulated by Abu al-Hudhayl, who, despite the date of his death (841), belonged to the generation before al-Kindi, had not yet been fully exposed to the scholastic tradition in philosophy.

And yet the signs of exposure to some type of speculative theology on the Greek model are unmistakable not, as might be expected in the Mu'tazilite pioneer Wasil ibn 'Ata', but in one of his contemporaries, Jahm ibn Safwan (d. c. 745). Jahm must be read through the mercies of his opponents, but it is difficult to believe that he was not meditating (Pseudo) Empedocles or some other Neoplatonic source, the Hermetic "Discourses on *Tawhid*," for example, when he presented his own radical portrait of Allah as absolutely transcendent, beyond accidents, properties, or qualifications, and beyond being itself.

Further back in Islam it is impossible to go. Jahm antedates all the known translations of Greek *philosophica* into Arabic. He may have been relying on Syriac material, either Neoplatonizing Christian theologians—Pseudo-Dionysius had been available in Syriac since the sixth century in the translation of Sergius of Reshayna—or those of Harran, whose God Kindi described as "*tawhid*, to whom no attribute applies or about whom no affirmative statement can be made or any syllogism related."

It would be a mistake to characterize the entire Harranian tradition as Hermetic. In philosophy the line between Middle Platonism's flirtation with Neopythagoreanism and a full-blown occult Hermeticism was, in any event, a thin one. Pythagoras was extravagantly admired by his Neoplatonic biographers, and as much for his wondrous powers as for his philosophical perspicacity.[6] Indeed, Pythagoreanism had been closely linked with thaumaturgy since its revival by Nigidius Figulus in the late Republic. By the first century of the Empire, however, Pythagoras represented a metaphysics as well as a *bios,* as the later Platonists were well aware.

What was the impact of the Sabians upon Islam? As is the case in the parallel instances of the Manichaeans and the Daysaniyah, we do not possess the books of the sect nor even their history, but must rely on what can be read in the oblique *testimonia* of Mas'udi, Ibn al-Nadim, the Brethren of Purity, Shahrastani, Maimonides and Dimashqi, all of whom, with the exception of the sympathetic Brethren, regarded the Sabians of Harran as a somewhat exotic paganism given to the worship of planets and idols. Individual Sabians, by way of contrast, operated within the intellectual circles of tenth-century Islam with what appears to be considerably greater freedom than the *zindiq.*

Ibn Hazm ranked the Sabians among the *thanawiyah* (read "pluralists"). The point may have been technically correct as argued by Ibn Hazm in the pages of a heresiography, but by all appearances Sabianism was a myth, a *roman,* as it has been called, founded upon the historical survival in northern Mesopotamia of a pagan sect whose antiquity was obvious but not historically identifiable by the Muslims. Trading on this ignorance the Harranians managed to associate themselves with the Mandaeans of Iraq, who had no greater claim to antiquity but had the inestimable advantage of being accepted as "People of the Book." Thus, both groups were drawn into the Biblical complex of Enoch and Abraham, and by linking Enoch, Idris and Hermes the Harranians could assume the role of possessors of a wisdom that was both patriarchal and attractively Hellenic.

One philosopher who accepted the historical claims but not the conclusions to be drawn therefrom was Maimonides. He had seen the Sabians' books and found them interesting in that they provided the precise pagan context against which the precepts of the

6. The Arabs, on the other hand, knew Pythagoras chiefly as a moralist, as the author of the *Golden Verses*, which found their way into a number of Arabic gnomonological collections like Miskawayh's *Eternal Wisdom;* see Chap. VII, pp. 539–540.

Torah were revealed. Maimonides' *Guide for the Perplexed* dwells upon a number of those books: a defense of the community of the Sabians and a book on their rituals by a certain Ishaq the Sabian, a number of Hermetic Aristotelian pseudepigraphs, and particularly the *Nabataean Agriculture* of Ibn Wahshiyah.

Maimonides was little interested in the speculative side of Sabian Hermeticism; his obvious intent was to connect Sabian cult and ritual with the theurgic practices that rendered the Sabians reprobate to the Jews. Earlier Muslim authors like Ibn al-Nadim and Mas'udi were less concerned with drawing a moral than in describing what was a received element in ancient history, an element that had curiously survived in living form into the tenth century: the Hermes of whom the Greek and Iranian sources spoke was represented in contemporary history by the Sabians of Harran.

Even before the fall of the Umayyads these Harranian and other channels back into the hybrid Hellenism of late antiquity were open, and through them Greek learning was being made available to the Muslim. Much of it was obscurely Hermetic, but other strains reflect somewhat more clearly the philosophical school tradition of the fifth and sixth centuries. And despite the obvious later predominance of Aristotle in Islam, that school tradition was Platonic.

Plato: From Athens to Islam

There were many varieties of Platonism in Islam. One of the earliest of the Muslim theologians, Jahm ibn Safwan was promulgating, as we have seen, a view of God totally different from that of his contemporaries and yet remarkably like the negative theology current in later Greek Neoplatonism. Two centuries later an avowed Platonist, Muhammad ibn Zakariya al-Razi (d. 925), was drawing upon even more complex sources, including the philosophical and scientific tradition of the Sabians of Harran. The Sabians, in turn, appear to represent the survival of an occult Platonism long defunct within the Christian Byzantine Empire. Later the Isma'ilis, the Sufis, and the eastern partisans of the "philosophy of illumination" all bear witness, in varying degrees, to a persistent and vital Platonic legacy in Islam.

Platonism survived on its merits, but the high literary and scholastic quality of much of that tradition enables us to chart the paths of its survival. Methods, texts and curricula all passed into Islam through the hands of Syrian intermediaries who were themselves both schoolmen and sophisticated translators. The Arabs observed the passage of philosophy from Hellas into Islam and carefully recorded its progress. But not always with the same degree of understanding.

The history of the translations of Aristotle into Arabic is plain for the reading in the Arab bibliographers and historians and in the preserved manuscripts. Our chief source, Ibn al-Nadim, was exceptionally well informed on the Aristotelian corpus, its Greek commentators, and its Syrian and Arabic translations, both Islamic and pre-Islamic. But to turn from his convincing paragraphs on Aristotle to his entry on Plato is to desert understanding for mere information, some of it scarcely digested. And even after all of that information is collated and evaluated, it still remains difficult to say just how much Plato, whether in integral translations or in epitomes, the medieval Muslim actually possessed.

No Arabic version of a Platonic dialogue has been preserved. And yet Ibn al-Nadim, writing in the late tenth century at the height of Islam's reception of Hellenism, knew, principally on the basis of a written memoire by the Christian scholar Yahya ibn 'Adi (d. 974), of translations of the *Republic*, the *Laws*, the *Sophist*, the *Timaeus*, and finally the *Letters*. But as soon as we approach more closely to the works themselves, we find ourselves in the presence of epitomes rather than translations. We do have a translation of the *Timaeus*, but it was not done from the text of the entire dialogue. Instead, it is an Arabic version of Galen's *Synopsis of the Platonic Dialogues*. The Arabic is extant and it includes not merely a résumé of the *Timaeus*, but considerably smaller fragments of paraphrases of the *Republic* and the *Laws*. That the complete work also embraced the *Parmenides* we know from a reference in the preserved section, as well as Ibn al-Nadim's explicit statement in the *Catalogue*.

We cannot progress much beyond this. There is a summary of the *Laws* transmitted by Farabi which significantly omits the important Book X. Nothing comparable is extant on the *Republic*, but the references and citations of that work scattered through Arabic literature suggest that here too the Muslim philosophers had available a résumé, probably the one based on Galen's epitome of the dialogues as translated by Hunayn ibn Ishaq.

Since so many of the Arabs were working from paraphrases of Plato rather than integral texts of the dialogues, it is unlikely that they felt the same need for the elaborate apparatus of textual commentary that so impressively supported their work on Aristotle. The likelihood is confirmed by Ibn al-Nadim, who mentions only the commentary of Olympiodorus on the *Sophist* and possibly the *Theaetetus*. There was, in addition, Proclus' work on the myth in the *Gorgias* and his commentary on the *Phaedo*, a small part of which was translated.

From other sources we can add further details. At least some Arabs were reading Proclus' commentary on the *Timaeus* and on the *Republic*. Further, a work of Plutarch on the *Timaeus* is mentioned by Ibn al-Nadim in his section on Plato. It does not reappear in his later entry devoted to Plutarch, though he does list there a treatise *On the Soul*. Both citations probably refer to the one essay, Plutarch's *On the Production of the Soul in the Timaeus*, a work also known to Muhammad ibn Zakariya al-Razi. Finally, as Ibn al-Nadim also attests, the Arabs knew and used Theon of Smyrna's propaedeutic *The Order of Plato's Books and the Titles of His Works*.

Following directly upon his almost tabular treatment of Plato is Ibn al-Nadim's presentation of the biography of Aristotle and the elaborate and informed history of the Aristotelian translations. This emphasis was not a peculiarity of the *Catalogue;* whatever the actual content of their philosophical heritage, the Arabs regarded Aristotle as the chief of the file of Hellenic sages. He was better known and more highly esteemed than any other Greek thinker in Islam, and Farabi, the most considerable Muslim Platonist, was being measured not against Plato but against Aristotle when he was flatteringly called "the Second Master."

The *Catalogue*'s review of the post-Aristotelian philosophers reveals the same perspective. The list includes Theophrastus, Proclus "the Platonist," Alexander of Aphrodisias, Porphyry, Ammonius (Hermieu), Themistius, Nicolaus, Plutarch (of Chaeronea), Olympiodorus, Hippocrates, Epaphroditus, "another Plutarch," John Philoponus, and a final jumble of names drawn from another source and including Gregory of Nyssa and Theon of Smyrna, "whose periods and order of sequence are not known." In the entire group only Proclus and Theon are identified as Platonists; the rest are seen almost exclusively through the focus of an Aristotelian exegetical tradition.

Even in the rudimentary sequence of Hellenic philosophers presented by Ibn al-Nadim there is one striking near-omission: the founder of the very type of Platonism that consistently shows itself in the systems of the Islamic philosopher, Plotinus. Al-Qifti, who does devote a few lines to Plotinus, identifies him as an Aristotelian commentator. He knows that some of Plotinus' works were translated into Syriac, but he is forced to admit ignorance on whether or not they subsequently appeared in Arabic versions. We are somewhat better informed; the Arabs did study Plotinus, but inevitably as a *pseudepigraphon* of Aristotle, or anonymously, or under what appears to be a pseudonym, "the Greek Elder (*al-shaykh al-yunani*).

An abridgment of *Enneads* IV–VI circulated in Arabic under the title of *The Theology of Aristotle*, and additional Arabic texts not included in *Theology*, but paraphrasing the same Plotinian passages as that work, have come to light over the last thirty years. Neither the new material nor a careful study of the old has brought the question of the identity of the "editor" or of his motives any closer to a solution. If it can be conceded that someone abridged and rearranged the latter half of the *Enneads* without, at the same time, holding him responsible for the attribution of the results to Aristotle or to anyone else, then Plotinus' student and confessed editor Porphyry is a not unlikely candidate. The substitution of Aristotle for Porphyry could have been an honest mistake. Porphyry's introduction to the Aristotelian logic, which was widely diffused in Syriac, was already an integral part of the *Organon*, and so a similar Porphyrian reworking of an Aristotelian theology would not have appeared unlikely to the sixth- or seventh-century reader.

Why the philosophers under Islam were so transparently Neoplatonists and at the same time were so oblivious of the true nature of their Platonism that they could not identify its author is one of the abiding mysteries of *falsafah*. To say that they simply did not care defies both the evidence of the *Catalogue*, which was obviously attempting to trace out some kind of philosophical lineage for the Arab thinkers, and our own knowledge of the historical attitudes of the later philosophical schools. The lecturers at Athens and Alexandria knew whence they had come. The Academy had adopted Aristotle into its curriculum, but it never lost sight of the fact that it was a Platonic school. Truth lies in Platonic orthodoxy, Plotinus had taught. His Greek successors did not forget the lesson, but the Arabs, who had just as much a claim to the Platonic tradition as Damascius or Olympiodorus, did not recognize their affiliations.

In talking about the late scholastic tradition we mean nothing more than the history of the Platonic schools. At the beginning of the third Christian century the schools of Epicurus, Zeno and Aristotle were moribund, if not dead; after 200 there existed among the Greeks of the Empire only the Platonic schools at Alexandria and Athens and their lesser reflections at Apamea and Pergamum. And in the end, on the eve of the Muslim invasion, there was only Alexandria. The final masters at Alexandria, and their solitary Platonic contemporary at Athens were, however, deeply invested in the study of Aristotle.

Somewhere within this paradox rests the explanation of the Arabs' confusion about their own philosophical identity. The Athenian Academy traced its mixed Platonism of the second and third centuries from the insights first of Plotinus (d. 270) and then of Porphyry (d. c. 306), Iamblichus (d. 325) and Proclus (d. 485), a combination that proved dangerous and finally deadly to Athenian Platonism. The pains of this transformation were lost on the Arabs, though they had perhaps inherited, without understanding it, the dissimulations that enabled the Alexandrian Platonists to outlive their Athenian colleagues.

Dissimulation is a charge that can likely be sustained against the Platonists of Alexandria; but, for the Muslims and Christians under Islam, the alleged subterfuges of an Ammonius or an Olympiodorus had yielded to mere ignorance, to the point that the Arabs could, though Platonists, somehow consider themselves Aristotelians, could believe that the *Enneads* really did constitute the "theology of Aristotle," and that Porphyry's greatest achievement was his explication of the *Categories*. And beyond Porphyry the mystification was almost total.

The Arabs knew almost nothing of Iamblichus. He turns up twice in Ibn al-Nadim's history of the Aristotelian corpus, as a commentator on the *Categories* and *On Interpretation*. But in the first case, and likely in the second as well, the citation is derived secondhand through Simplicius. Ibn al-Nadim knew something more about Iamblichus, but just as in the case of Plotinus, it was under a different name: Iamblichus the commentator of Aristotle is the identifiable "Amlichus," while Iamblichus the author of *On the Mysteries of the Egyptians* is transformed into the mysterious Anebo ("Anabun") the priest to whom Porphyry directed the original letter that in turn had provoked Iamblichus' response.

The reference to "Anabun" occurs within Ibn al-Nadim's bibliographical survey of the works of Muhammad ibn Zakariya al-Razi under the title, "A Criticism of the Book of Anebo Against Porphyry Concerning a Commentary on the Teachings of Aristotle on Theology." We do not, of course, possess the Greek of Porphyry's *Letter to Anebo*, though the Arabs certainly did, at least in part; but neither its Greek reconstruction, nor the analysis of Iamblichus' response guides us even remotely in the direction of the *Metaphysics*. It is equally unlikely that they point in the direction of the *Theology of Aristotle*, which some of the Arabs connected with the name of Porphyry, since the *Letter to Anebo* was written long before Porphyry arranged the essays of Plotinus into what was to be the *Enneads* and so prior to any possibility of commenting upon them.

Among other things, Porphyry's *Letter* dealt with the delicate relationship between speculative theology and practical theurgy. Porphyry was in doubt on the question, but Iamblichus' response was unequivocal: theurgy is superior to theology. Nor was that all. The theology of the Easterners—the Egyptians, Chaldaeans, Magi, et cetera—was superior to that of the Greeks. Greek theology was first the writings of Plato, summed up in the *Timaeus* and the *Parmenides*, to which he would add the works of the poets from Homer onward. The net of Eastern theology was thrown equally wide, but for Iamblichus and most of his successors it was constituted, in effect, by the *Chaldaean Oracles*.[7]

Neither of these themes, the extension of Greek theology beyond the purely philosophical tradition and the extension beyond the Hellenic *paideia* itself, was the innovation of Iamblichus. The emphasis and conviction were, however, new, and from Iamblichus onward non-Greek *theologia* and a marked interest in *theourgia* were characteristics of Athenian Platonism until Justinian closed the Academy in 529. There were theurgists too within Islam, but no one of them, with the possible exception of Muhammad ibn Zakariya al-Razi, belonged to the school tradition that was the Muslim's principal inheritance from later Platonism. The Arab scholastics were immune to the Iamblichan virus.

The Arabs knew little of the fortunes of later Platonism. Of Proclus and Simplicius they possessed considerable textual evidence, but it was unaccompanied by any sense of the position of these philosophers in the evolution of later Platonism. Indeed, Athens appears to have disappeared completely from their historical perspectives. In the two earliest treatments devoted by Arab authors to the history of later Greek philosophy, those of Farabi and Mas'udi, the fortunes of philosophy are tied not to Athens but to Alexandria and Rome. The Greek source upon which they were relying was clearly Peripatetic—Andronicus of Rhodes figures prominently in the account—and late as well, since it alleges that the Christian Emperor Theodosius closed down the Roman branch and so confined the study of philosophy to Alexandria alone. There is no mention of Athens or, indeed, of Platonism.

The Arabs, it appears, were far more interested in Proclus than they realized. Ibn al-Nadim's entry under his name identified him as a Platonist, as the "successor" of Plato, and the author of an imposing list of works, including the *Elements of Physics* and the *Elements of Theology*, a commentary on the *Golden Sayings* of Pythagoras, and in a more precisely Platonic context, a book on the myth (*mathal*) in Plato's *Gorgias*.

---

7. A collection of oracular utterances put together from miscellaneous sources by a certain Julian, who lived during the reign of Marcus Aurelius.

The list is interesting but hardly complete. Our Greek versions of Proclus' *Commentary on the Timaeus* cover only half of the dialogue, but the evidence appears unmistakable that Proclus' exegesis covered the entire *Timaeus* and that the Islamic philosophers possessed it in an Arabic version. Ibn al-Nadim also mentions, somewhat obliquely, that Proclus was the author of a treatise refuted by John Philoponus. This alludes to the eighteen questions or proofs *On the Eternity of the World* which are known in Greek only from their citation in Philoponus' imperfectly preserved refutation. Two versions of the original have turned up in Arabic, neither complete, but both extremely valuable. The older version, translator unknown, is preserved in two Istanbul manuscripts, while the latter is the work of Ishaq ibn Hunayn.

There are other small texts that may or may not be Arabic versions of Proclus, but by far the most considerable piece of Proclus known to the Arabs was the treatise "On the Pure Good" and called, in its Latin version, the *Liber de causis*. The material in the *De causis* is surely Proclan, as Aquinas had already observed, and derived from the *Elements of Theology*. But for the Arabs, or at least for most of those who addressed themselves to the question, the work was attributed to Aristotle. The question of who extracted the *De causis* from the *Elements of Theology* and circulated it under the name of Aristotle is as unsettled as that surrounding the *Theology*, whether it was a Greek or a Syrian Christian before the coming of Islam, or whether it was done in Islamic times by al-Farabi in the east or the Jew Dawud in the west.

In sum, the Arabs knew Proclus as a late Platonist and absorbed his metaphysics, as they had Plotinus', as an undistinguishable part of the Neoplatonist synthesis of Plato and Aristotle. His work on Pythagoras probably appeared to be a rather harmless gnomonology, while the Proclus who admired Pythagoras the *Wundermann*, who commented on the "theology" of the *Chaldaean Oracles*, the mystery adept and theurgist, was ignored by the Islamic tradition. Of theurgy the Arabs had perhaps some sense, but not through the ordinary scholastic channels described by Ibn al-Nadim.

One of Proclus' fellow students at Athens under the brief

tenure of Syrianus as scholarch (432–437?) was Hermias, and from him descended the final series of Platonic philosophers at Alexandria down to the time in 616 when Stephen deserted that city for the university in Constantinople. At Athens itself Proclus' immediate successors, Isidore and Zenodotus, were not distinguished. We are aware of them solely from Damascius' *Life of Isidore*, an important historical source denied to the Arabs; no trace of their own work is left. There were, in addition, difficulties with the Christian authorities. Even Proclus, who could be prudent when need be on the subject of his paganism, was forced to go into exile for a year, and his successors were less careful until Justinian finally closed the Academy in 529 and confiscated its property.

There followed the curious and interesting sojourn of the seven Athenian philosophers, including the current Platonic "successor" Damascius and his student Simplicius, at the court of Khusraw I at Ctesiphon. Their stay there was exceedingly brief, less than a year, perhaps, before their return to Byzantine territory under the terms of the peace treaty of 532, and so it is probably dangerous to draw many conclusions from it. But Khusraw's intellectual credentials are well attested from other sources. Both Procopius and Agathias, two contemporary Byzantine historians, testify to his interest in Greek philosophy, particularly Plato and Aristotle, whose works he had translated for himself, so that, according to the incredulous Agathias, "not even the *Timaeus* would escape him." So it was claimed, but Agathias for one was not persuaded.

Khusraw, it would seem, was served by philosophers whose chief preoccupations were Aristotelian, either of the Christian variety, like those of Paul, who as a Christian was interested chiefly, if not exclusively, in the Aristotelian logic,[8] or of a chastened Platonic paganism, like those of Simplicius who upon his return to Athens after 533 devoted himself exclusively to

8. There is considerable confusion here about three men, all named Paul. Two of them were bishops of Nisibis, but the third was Khusraw's court philosopher, who is reputed to have written in Pahlevi. Two of his reworkings of the Aristotelian logic are preserved in their Syriac translations.

commenting upon Aristotle. Despite the remark of Agathias there is no trace of a Pahlevi *Timaeus,* unless it existed, as it frequently did for the latter-day Greek Platonists, under the cover of a discussion of the proofs for the eternity of the *kosmos* in the *Physics* and *On the Heavens.*

On his return from Persia, Damascius was well into his seventies, but Simplicius still had an active career before him, likely at Athens. But not as a teacher. Lecturing had ceased forever in the Academy, and Simplicius became a library scholar, whose chief monument is in his commentaries on Aristotle. Of these the Arabs appear to have known only those on the *Categories* and *On the Soul,* the latter of which was in Syriac and may have constituted, on the basis of the *Catalogue*'s description, a transcript of his teacher Ammonius' lectures on the subject. They did not possess the extensive commentaries on the *Physics* and *On the Heavens,* though the Arabs were well instructed on the controversies that unfolded there.

At different points in these latter two commentaries Simplicius took up the task of refuting an Alexandrian contemporary, the Christian John Philoponus, who had earlier written two works on the subject of the eternity of the world: *On the Eternity of the World against Proclus,* written in 529, and *Against Aristotle,* a treatment in six books of Aristotle's views expressed in the *Physics* and *On the Heavens.* We do not possess the Greek text of the latter work of Philoponus and must reconstruct it from Simplicius; the Arabs, who did not have the pertinent commentaries of Simplicius, could still read the work of Philoponus, and it had, in fact, an enormous influence in Islam.

How Philoponus and Simplicius, both students at Alexandria of Ammonius who had, in turn, matriculated with Proclus at Athens, came to be debating Aristotle and not Plato in the first half of the sixth century carries us back to Ammonius himself. Like his father, Hermias, Ammonius had gone to Athens for his philosophical education. Both men, father and son, eventually returned to Alexandria to teach and write, Hermias on Plato,[9]

9. The preserved commentary on the *Phaedrus* is really his transcription of Syrianus' lectures on the subject. The Arabs do not seem to have been aware of this scholastic phenomenon, except unconsciously

and Ammonius chiefly on Aristotle. The work was published in his own name and those of his students, Asclepius and John Philoponus. The interest in Aristotle is not strange in someone trained in a Platonic tradition that had been studying Peripatetic works at least since the days of Plotinus and Porphyry, but the *publication* of almost exclusively Aristotelian material is curious and abrupt. And among its results was the fact that the Arabs, who had a limited literary access to late antiquity, regarded Ammonius and his successors almost entirely as Aristotelian commentators.

Ibn al-Nadim's brief notice on Ammonius (d. c. 520) is drawn from Ishaq ibn Hunayn's *History of Physicians*. It identifies him as an Aristotelian exegete who lived some time after Galen. In addition to the commentaries on the *Categories* and *Topics*, whose Greek originals are no longer extant, the *Catalogue* cites the titles of three other works: *An Exposition of Aristotle's Doctrines about the Creator*, *Aristotle's Intentions in His Books*, and *Aristotle's Proof of Oneness*.

It would be interesting indeed to be able to read the first of these. Did the student of Proclus trim his theological sails, perhaps, as it has been conjectured, for monetary considerations, and so turn aside the mounting Christian pressure that led to the closure at Athens? There is even some evidence that Ammonius may have undergone a forced conversion. Whatever occurred, it did not prevent Ammonius from continuing to lecture on Plato; though he, or his students, published his courses on Aristotle, Ammonius kept up his Platonic interests in the classroom. Some of his immediate students like Damascius and Olympiodorus could still report on Ammonius' views on Plato; but for the Arabs, who had only his books, or reports about his books, Ammonius was an Aristotelian commentator.

Ammonius' students dominated both Athens and Alexandria during the next generation; the Athenian "successor" Damascius, who was unknown to the Arabs, and his student Simplicius; Olympiodorus, Asclepius, and John Philoponus at Alexandria.

---

in the case of Simplicius' commentary on *On the Soul*. Thus they possessed far more Ammonius and far less Philoponus than they imagined.

Olympiodorus produced a number of Platonic commentaries, but only one of them, that on the *Sophist,* was extant or known in Arabic, together with his commentaries on the Aristotelian *Meteorology* and *On the Soul.*

Olympiodorus, who was almost certainly not a Christian, appears to have moved nonetheless to a more accommodating position with Christianity, but there is no mention of a Christian in the *Catalogue* until the next of Ibn al-Nadim's entries, that on John Philoponus, "a bishop over some of the churches of Egypt, upholding the Christian sect of the Jacobites." The same passage closes with what became a standard Arab confusion on the dates of John: "he lived during the days of 'Amr ibn al-As," that is, until the Muslim conquest of Egypt.

John "the grammarian" (*al-nahwi*), as the Arabs called him and as he styled himself (*grammatikos*) in his own works,[10] was a well-known figure in Islam as an Aristotelian commentator, a medical writer and historian,[11] and, considerably more obscurely, as a Christian theologian.[12] Over the years John's career turned away from his earlier scholastic work under Ammonius. His redaction of his professor's notes on the *Physics* dates from 517, but by 529, the same year that Justinian closed the Academy for its flagrant paganism, Philoponus was working in a far more Christian vein. In that year appeared his *On the Eternity of the World against Proclus*, followed shortly by the complementary *Against Aristotle*, a twofold attack on the current Neoplatonic position on the eternity of the *kosmos.*

The attack on Aristotle was frontal, but in refuting Proclus'

---

10. His other title, *philoponus,* which refers to his pious militancy on behalf of Christian causes, was also known to the Arabs; on the guild of the *philoponoi* at Alexandria, see Chap. V, p. 376.

11. Ishaq ibn Hunayn's *History of Physicians,* a major source of the *Catalogue*'s treatment of the history of ancient medicine, drew heavily on John. It is by no means certain, however, that John Philoponus is the same person who wrote the medical works circulating under that name in Islam; see Chap. V, p. 377.

12. Ibn al-Nadim describes him as a student of "Sawari," perhaps Severus, the Monophysite Patriarch of Antioch in 512–538, who much earlier, before 488 at any rate, had studied rhetoric at Alexandria; see Introduction, p. 20.

reading of the *Timaeus* Philoponus had some support from earlier Platonism. Proclus himself names two men who read the *Timaeus* as advocating creation in time, Plutarch of Chaeronea and Atticus, and Philoponus can adduce Atticus' predecessor as *diadochus,* Calvisius Taurus, who headed the Academy under Hadrian and Antoninus Pius. All of these citations may, however, go back only as far as Porphyry's own commentary on the *Timaeus.* The Muslims, who shared Philoponus' view of creation in time, were highly interested in the controversy and could follow it closely through Arabic versions of the *Timaeus* (albeit in an *epitome*), the *On the Heavens* and *Physics,* Proclus' *Arguments* and his commentary on the *Timaeus,* and Philoponus' refutation. But they knew and cared nothing for the rest of Philoponus' career after 530, his progressive involvement in theology, and his final bout with tritheism.

In the Arabs' version of the history of philosophy Olympiodorus' Christian students Elias and David have no place.[13] The last-known scholarch at Alexandria, Stephen, was summoned to Constantinople sometime about 616 to assume a teaching post there. His portrait among the Arabs is thin but congruent with the Greek sources. Stephen's commentaries on the *Categories* and *On Interpretation* were extant in Arabic, as well as some medical writings. There is a further odd tradition of "Stephen the ancient" who translated certain works on "The Art" (of alchemy) for the Umayyad prince Khalid ibn Yazid (d. c. 705). Another part of the tradition derives Khalid's instruction in alchemy from savants summoned from Alexandria, one of whom was the Syrian Marinus, who had studied with Stephen. Whether this is the same

---

13. Nor do the Christian Platonists of Gaza: Aeneas, Zacharias, the bishop of Mytilene, and his brother Procopius. The Gaza intellectuals of the early sixth century generally appear to have been interested more in rhetoric than in philosophy, but they were, nonetheless, heirs to a genuine philosophical tradition. Its origins were at Alexandria, where Aeneas studied with Hierocles. Zacharias was a fellow student there of the Monophysite theoretician Severus of Antioch, and his Syriac *Life of Severus* provides us with most of what we know about university life in Alexandria in the late fifth century.

Stephen is uncertain, though the attribution of alchemical works to him is widespread in Greek.

This is the end of the philosophical tradition of late antiquity. Stephen, who served Heraclius, touches the chronological limits of Islam. The Arabs who followed pieced together their knowledge of that tradition from the philosophical texts available to them and from a far less easily identified set of historical perspectives. Both, however, betray their origins in a clear way: clustered around the works of Aristotle are the names of the great commentators from the Platonic school tradition at Alexandria from Ammonius in the fifth century to Stephen in the seventh. From there it is possible to trace the connection back to Porphyry in the fourth century, the man who introduced the textual exegesis of Aristotle into the curriculum of the Platonic schools.

Considerable nuances can be added to this on the basis of the texts that have actually been preserved. There is, of course, Aristotle and Plato, the former in integral Arabic versions and the latter in résumé, a situation that once again points to Alexandria, where from Ammonius onward the publishing emphasis was on the Aristotelian lecture courses and where the scholars lectured on *texts*. Oddly, there are at present no textual remains of the great Alexandrian commentators discussed so knowingly by Ibn al-Nadim. It is difficult to believe that the exegetical works of Simplicius, Olympiodorus, Ammonius *et al.* were *not* once preserved in Arabic; but if they were translated, transcribed and studied, the texts themselves have since disappeared without a trace.

What has been preserved over and above the texts of Plato and Aristotle is of a somewhat different orientation: the work of two Peripatetic paraphrasts, Nicolaus of Damascus and Themistius, and a number of treatises by the Aristotelian Alexander of Aphrodisias. Were these three men important in the curriculum at Alexandria in the fifth and sixth centuries? We do not know. The second group of Greek philosophical texts derives not from the Aristotelizing Alexandrian school tradition but from the Neoplatonists. As has been seen, the Arabs did in fact possess texts of Plotinus and Proclus, though they were transmitted, from some unknown point in time, under false attributions to

Aristotle. Finally, there was available in Islam a body of philosophical material from the pre-Plotinian period of Platonism, chiefly from Galen and Plutarch of Chaeronea.

Some of these anomalies are easily understood. Alexandrian Platonism made its peace with Christianity, ignominiously, perhaps, with Ammonius, subtly with Olympiodorus, and overtly with John Philoponus. Thus it survived into the seventh century, long enough to transmit its scholastic attitudes to the Arab philosophers and to commit its ostensibly Aristotelian curriculum to the pages of the *Catalogue*. It has been suggested that one of the fruits of Alexandrian prudence was precisely the sliding of Plotinus and Proclus into the safety of an Aristotelian curriculum under assumed names. The abbreviation of the *Enneads* may well have been the work of Porphyry, done for the best—or worst—of academic motives, but its circulation as the "theology of Aristotle" is not necessarily the doing of the same person. That this person or persons were cautious or frightened Platonists of the sixth century is an attractive possibility, particularly since that century produced just another such pseudepigraph, the body of Proclan theology masquerading as the literary output of a Christian contemporary of Saint Paul, Dionysius the Areopagite.

An Aristotelian curriculum superficially purged of the Platonic theology that was its normal complement in the philosophical schools of later antiquity may have had another point of origin. The Arabs' knowledge of the history of philosophy ran thin, as has been seen, at a point sometime before the lifetime of Plotinus. Their views of the later Alexandrians were founded on the connection of those scholars with the Aristotelian texts of the standard curriculum. They were less well informed on the Alexandrian school itself, except to acknowledge that there were teachers in Baghdad about 900 who somehow traced their intellectual lineage back to Alexandria.

The men who did most of the translating into Arabic did not, however, belong to that same line of philosophers. They were physicians trained at the medical school of Jundishapur and, so, as much interested in Galen as they were in Aristotle. And when we look once again to late antiquity we note that the details of the Arabs' version of the history of medicine began to grow dim at somewhat the same point where their philosophical perspectives did—that is, the lifetime of Galen (d. 199). There are important figures later than Galen—Oribasios and Paul of Aegina, for example—who are mentioned in the *Catalogue*, but the author does not know precisely where to locate them in the history of medicine. Their names, like those of the Alexandrian Platonists, came, it would appear, from the title pages of their translated works and not from history books.

It seems highly likely, then, that the Arabs derived at least some of their notions of the history of philosophy and a great deal of their interest in the texts themselves from an Alexandrian medical tradition grounded in Galen and with little or no interest in the theology of later Platonism. Galen's works stood at the heart of Alexandrian medicine. It was Galen too who insisted on the importance of a philosophical education for the physician. And it was Galen, we may suspect, who gave to that physician his picture of the history of philosophy, a portrait whose final resting place was, by way of John Philoponus, Ishaq ibn Hunayn's *History of Physicians*. In the *Catalogue* the chronology for both Porphyry and Ammonius, the latter explicitly derived from Ishaq, is measured against Galen's lifetime. And when Ibn al-Nadim does refer to his chief post-Galenic historical source, the *Philosophical History* of Porphyry, it is by way of his philosophical friends at Baghdad and not from the Jundishapur medical tradition.

When we put aside the bibliographical notices and turn to Islam's philosophers the same anomalies reappear. All of the philosophers, from al-Kindi to Suhrawardi and his successors, were to some extent operating within the Platonic tradition, at least in the sense of the syncretizing of Plato and Aristotle that had been current in philosophical circles since the early days of the Roman Empire. Among those philosophers, Muslim and Christian, al-Farabi stands somewhat apart. He was the most self-consciously Platonizing of the philosophers, both in his understanding of Plato and his familiarity with the texts. But neither Farabi's interest in Plato nor his approach to the dialogues conforms to our understanding of the patterns of the final, Neoplatonic stages in the Platonic tradition.

Al-Kindi, the earliest of the philosophers, and one whose work seems to antedate, since it antedates the translations of Hunayn, the full impact of Alexandrian medical scholasticism upon Islamic philosophy, is a historically predictable Muslim Neoplatonist of the Proclan variety. Farabi, however, was drawing from other sources. There is, for example, his elaborate reworking of the Platonic politics of the *Republic* and the *Laws*. There were, to be sure, peculiarities in Farabi's reading of this latter dialogue, due perhaps to the historical circumstances of his own theological position within Islam; but the mere fact that he could read both dialogues as political treatises and not merely as a discussion of the immortality of the soul and a primer in theology unmistakably separates Farabi from almost all of his immediate pre-Islamic Platonic predecessors.

Plato may have had his own difficulties with the practical value of political activity for the philosopher, but in his own day the *polis* was still the unique focus of moral activity for men, and the concern with morality that he shared with his master Socrates combined to produce an elaborate and earnest political theory. Later Platonism had little recollection of either Socrates or the *polis*,[14] and it read the dialogues with quite different emphases. Its eyes were directed not toward the political associations of the City of Man, but upward toward the "intelligible universe" whither man's divine and immortal soul strove to return.

Farabi's political theorizing is unmistakably Platonic, however; it rested firmly on his reading of the *Republic* and the *Laws*, two works of considerably varying importance in later Platonism. We can now reconstruct with some accuracy the Platonic curriculum favored by the Neoplatonists. It proceeded from I *Alcibiades* through the series *Gorgias* (politics), *Phaedo* (catharsis of the philosopher), *Cratylus* (names), *Theaetetus* (concepts), *Sophist* and *Statesman* (physics), *Phaedrus* and *Symposium* (theology),

---

14. Another peculiarity of the Islamic tradition was its veneration of Socrates the moralist. The *Catalogue* lists among Kindi's works a number devoted to Socrates. They are included in a group devoted to "politics"; but on the basis of their titles they appear to have been extracted from the *Phaedo*. The later Platonists read that dialogue not as a testimonial to Socratic ethics but as a treatise on psychology.

to end with the treatment of the Good as the Final Cause in the *Philebus*. The characterizations are not, of course, Plato's but probably go back to Iamblichus, who bore the chief responsibility of arranging the dialogues in a curricular order and assigning a specific interpretation to each.

The *Timaeus* was by no means neglected. The series described above constituted what might be described as the "long course"; it was resumed in its essence by the two dialogues which the later Academics embraced as the *summa* of Platonism, the *Timaeus* and the *Parmenides*. Each dialogue had its own proper exegesis, and even within the longer curriculum of ten dialogues—out of the thirty-five in the Thrasyllan canon—a further selection was imposed; not all the parts of each dialogue were studied. The exegesis of the *Sophist*, *Statesman*, and perhaps the *Phaedrus* was restricted to their myths, the *Theaetetus* to its central digression, and the *Symposium* to the speech of Diotima. The *Republic* and the *Laws*, which were not even in the curriculum, suffered a similar compression; interest in the *Republic* fastened on the myth of Er, and that in the *Laws* on Book X.

The contrast with Farabi is striking. He worked over the whole of the *Republic*, and Book X is precisely the one he ignored in his own treatment of the *Laws*. The epitome of Plato's philosophy reproduced by Farabi tells a similar story; it is a survey of a Platonic curriculum that is considerably different from the one in fashion among the Neoplatonists. It is closer to the first of two Platonic bibliographies reproduced by Ibn al-Nadim and explicitly credited, for both its titles and its order, to the second-century Platonist Theon of Smyrna. In its order this latter differs from the Thrasyllan tetrarchies, an arrangement the Arabs knew about but which they or Theon attributed to Plato himself. The manuscript is garbled in places, but the list in the *Catalogue* appears to begin with two translated titles, *Al-Siyasah* (*Republic?*) and *Al-Nawamis* (*Laws*), and then proceeds through a series of transliterated Greek titles from the *Theages* down to what seems to be the *Statesman*. Unlike the case of the Aristotelian corpus, Ibn al-Nadim knows little of the translation history of each dialogue. He notes Arabic translations for the *Siyasah*, the *Nawamis*, and the *Sophist*, and at another point Galen is said to have made an abridgment of the *Parmenides*.

There is no mention in the list of the *Apology*, *Philebus*, *Symposium*, *Lysis*, *Epinomis* and *Letters*, all of which appeared in the Thrasyllan canon, while the *Philebus* and the *Symposium* were central in the Neoplatonic curriculum.

This series is followed immediately by another that is based on Ibn al-Nadim's own knowledge and may represent the identifiable Plato circulating in Islam: the *Timaeus*, "Relationships," "a book of Plato to the Cretan on the laws," "Oneness," "his dialogue on the soul, the intelligence, substance, and properties," "sense perception and pleasure," the *Timaeus* again, the *Theaetetus;* "the Education of Young Men," and the *Letters*. The difference between Theon's list, reproduced almost literally by Ibn al-Nadim, and what was actually available to the philosophers is striking. Equally striking is the fact that neither list corresponds to the curriculum of the Neoplatonic Academy.

Nor is there much in common between Farabi and the fifth-century Academy. His First Cause was not the utterly transcendent Neoplatonic One but an intelligent Creator. There is no trace of theurgy in Farabi; his prophecy is naturalistic rather than mystical, derived, to a great extent, from the Peripatetic Alexander of Aphrodisias.[15] And there is, finally, Farabi's extraordinary interest in politics.

In a sense none of this requires explanation. Farabi was a Muslim and his God is the activist Creator of the *Qur'an* whose message was, no less than that of Jesus, an ethical one. Islam was a political as well as a religious community, but it was almost completely innocent of any sacramental basis for a theurgy in the style of Pseudo-Dionysius. And yet Farabi's theories, for all their originality, are explicitly and consistently derived from Greek archetypes. Some of his reading was obviously Plato; but no scholastic philosopher came to Plato in private. He approached the dialogues with the exegetical attitudes and apparatus that comprised Platonism, the Platonic tradition.

By the time it reached Farabi that tradition had been evolving for over a millennium, from Aristotle's original revisions of his master's teachings to Christianity's own expropriation of the

---

15. See Chap. VII, pp. 507–509.

version of those teachings current in the sixth century. From what point in that tradition were Islamic philosophers like Farabi drawing their perspectives? There is some evidence that the Arabs in general and Farabi in particular had access to a form of pre-Plotinian Platonism, and most likely that in vogue among the so-called "Middle" Platonists of the early Roman Empire.

It is difficult now to assess that possibility, since the eventual triumph of Plotinian Neoplatonism in the Academy reduced those earlier representatives of the tradition to a mere shadow. Much of what can be retrieved goes back to a source well known to the Arabs, Porphyry of Tyre. Porphyry was regarded by the Arabs chiefly as the author of the *Eisagoge* and as an Aristotelian commentator, while his connection with the exegesis of Plato was ignored, even though there were grounds for suspecting it. The Islamic philosophers had in their hands Porphyry's *Philosophical History* in four books, the entirety in Syriac and half, perhaps the first half, in Arabic. Ibn al-Nadim himself had seen Book IV in Syriac. If so, he saw the life of Plato, since, according to a well-known Middle Platonic perception of history, Porphyry's work ended with Plato.

The *Philosophical History* provided Arab authors with biographical details on the early Greek philosophers, but from a doctrinal point of view Porphyry's *Concordance of the Philosophy of Plato and Aristotle* had a far more profound effect in Islam, or so it appears. It was not, however, the first such work; Plotinus' teacher Ammonius Saccas was preaching just such a concordance a century before Porphyry. The Arab bibliographers do not mention by name a *Concordance* by either man; indeed they did not know the name Ammonius Saccas at all. So, while the probabilities remain that Porphyry's work was the direct source of such syncretizing among the philosophers—of Farabi's *On the Agreement of the Opinions of the Two Sages*, for example—it is not to be excluded that the influence of Ammonius was at work, if only indirectly.

Porphyry's positions were not, of course, identical with those of the long-dead scholars of Middle Platonism; he was, after all, a student of Plotinus, even though the Arabs were unaware of that affiliation, and it was precisely his somewhat dimly perceived

Neoplatonism that bothered the Islamic philosophers. His *Points of Departure for the Intelligibles*, known in the Arabic tradition as *On the Intellect and the Intelligible*, was a kind of Neoplatonic handbook based, like the *Theology*, on the *Enneads*. It included among its other arguments a defense against Middle Platonists like his former teacher Longinus, of the absolute transcendence of the One and a discussion of the mode of union between the intellect and the objects of its intellection.

The notion that the mind somehow becomes its object in the act of intellection was a commonplace in Peripatetic circles, but the manner of its "becoming" was a matter of some dispute. In his *Points of Departure* Porphyry argued for an ontological unity between intellect and intelligible. Among the Arabs, who drew a great deal of their psychological theory from Alexander of Aphrodisias, Ibn Sina resolutely rejected that interpretation, which he explicitly attributed to Porphyry's *Points of Departure*. Ibn Rushd, who seems to have had trouble with that same work, though on different grounds, spoke unfavorably of Porphyry. He did, however, regard him as a Peripatetic, albeit a strange one.

Some of the material on pre-Plotinian Platonism may have come to the Arabs, as it has to us, through the hands of Porphyry. But they had more direct access. Plutarch was available in Arabic, and the Islamic philosophers had a detailed and sophisticated knowledge of Galen, the student of Gaius and Albinus. Further, Galen's connection with Platonism was somewhat better understood than Porphyry's. His epitome of Plato's dialogues was in circulation in Arabic, for example, and bore his name upon it. But, for the Arabs, Galen was also part of the Aristotelian tradition; his commentary on the *On Interpretation* was preserved, his association with Alexander of Aphrodisias was stressed, and one major account of his life emphasizes his Peripatetic teachers. The reason is not far to seek: at least some of the biographical information on Galen in Arabic came from John Philoponus.

There is no mention in the Arab bibliographers of the fourth- or fifth-century work often ascribed to Galen in the manuscripts, the *Philosophical History*. What they did possess, however, is one of the sources of that work that bore, in Greek and Arabic, and equally incorrectly, the name of Plutarch, the *Placita Philos-*

ophorum. The Arabic version was by Qusta ibn Luqa and was widely read in Islam. The Pseudo-Plutarch, like the Pseudo-Galen after it, was a doxography rather than a history; it collected opinions of philosophers and arranged them under topic headings, chiefly in the physical branches of philosophy.

The Arabs had in their hands another such Neoplatonic doxography, this one unknown from the Greek sources, Pseudo Ammonius' *The Opinions of the Philosophers*. This was first known from citations in Biruni and Shahrastani, but now the text itself has been discovered in an Istanbul manuscript. It appears to stand closer to the *Placita* than to that other form of handbook wisdom transmitted from antiquity into Islam, the gnomonology. There was an abundant sampling of the wit and wisdom of the Greeks available in Arabic, and it was incorporated into works like Hunayn's *Anecdotes*, Mubashshir's *Epitome of Wisdom*, and Abu Sulayman's *Garden of Wisdom*.

The diffusion of these scholastic handbooks in Islam has made it difficult in the extreme to trace to their sources opinions held by the philosophers on Plato or anyone else. The historical knowledge of a Kindi or a Farabi could derive from an integral text of the author in question, an epitome, or a doxography. Simplicius, writing in the sixth century in Athens, still had pre-Socratic texts in his hands but not as many of his contemporaries elsewhere possessed the same kind of library resources. And it is even less likely that the Arabs did.

What the Arabs did know, even within the anonymous confines of the school tradition, were two different strains of Platonism: the Neoplatonic version of Plotinus and Proclus, and an older Platonism taught in the Roman schools during the second and third centuries. The first was rendered all but faceless by the body of pseudepigraphy with which someone, pagan Greek, Christian Syrian or Muslim Arab, felt it necessary to conceal the traces of Neoplatonic metaphysics. The second points insistently to Galen and may have come to the Arabs directly from Middle Platonic sources. Or there may have survived within the all-pervasive Neoplatonism of the fifth and sixth centuries, perhaps at Alexandria, a minor and subdued strain of Middle Platonic conservatism to which the Arabs were the principal heirs.

The Syriac and Arabic Aristotle

The seventh book of Ibn al-Nadim's *Catalogue* is devoted to philosophy and science. In it the author gives a long and highly detailed account of how Aristotle was translated into Arabic. Beginning with the *Categories*[16] and proceeding, treatise by treatise, through the entire Aristotelian corpus down to the *Metaphysics,* Ibn al-Nadim tells us what he knew of the translation history, Syriac and Arabic, of each work and the Greek commentaries on it. The order and arrangement of his treatment of the *Aristotelica,* as well as the long biographical treatment that precedes it, derived from some ancient curriculum of a type well known to Ibn al-Nadim and his contemporaries, a curriculum that did not harbor within its structure the various Aristotelian pseudepigraphs. The Arabs, including Ibn al-Nadim, had few hesitations about the spurious Aristotle, but they made no effort to incorporate him into their inherited and better-informed curricula.

Ibn al-Nadim may have had some expert instruction in philosophy from Abu Sulayman al-Sijistani (d. 990), the Christian Yahya ibn 'Adi (d. 974), and others, but his limitations were nonetheless severe; like most of his contemporaries the author of the *Catalogue* had little or no idea of the evolution of the Greek philosophical tradition before it came into Arab hands, and especially of the curricular relationship between Plato and Aristotle. We are not a great deal better instructed on those subjects, but we do have some sense of why Aristotle so obviously, if superficially, dominated the Muslim perception of philosophy. As has already been pointed out, thinkers like Porphyry, Ammonius and

---

16. The medieval Muslims possessed some disguised passages from the early Aristotelian dialogues, but since their formal knowledge of Aristotle was based upon a curriculum that did not include the dialogues—these works passed out of philosophical vogue about 200, shortly before Aristotle was incorporated into the Neoplatonic curriculum—they were generally unaware of this phase of Aristotle's development.

Simplicius, who appear in our own histories of philosophy as members of the Platonic school tradition, were known to Ibn al-Nadim and the Islamic Hellenists as Aristotelian commentators. All these men did work on Aristotle, of course, but we can identify them, as the Arab bibliographer could not, in a larger historical context.

On the witness of Porphyry's biography of his teacher, Aristotle was carefully and critically studied by Plotinus. Porphyry himself did the same, and in a somewhat more systematic manner than Plotinus, whose approach to philosophy was formed by his own teacher's informal seminars. There may have been some sense of curriculum in the Platonic school tradition before Plotinus, a notion that was ignored by Plotinus but reasserted by Porphyry. And it is clear from Porphyry's own work that Aristotle was part of that curriculum. Porphyry was the first Platonist to produce formal commentaries on the treatises of Aristotle, a fact that guaranteed, in the sequel, that Aristotle would be studied in the Platonic schools.

According to the view that emerged in the post-Porphyrian school tradition, there were two major branches of philosophy, that which had to do with the various manifestations of sensible reality, the study known generally as physics, and that which devoted itself to the contemplation of suprasensible reality, that is, theology—or, to use the word favored by later Platonic pietists, "mystical viewing" (*epopteia*).[17] Whatever role ethics may have played in the scheme, it was severed, as has been seen, from its original connection with politics and reduced to the status of a cathartic preliminary to the study of philosophy.

The position of logic was paradoxical. In the original Aristotelian view logic was a method, or an instrument (*organon*), and not a part of philosophy. This was a departure from Plato's teaching, which united dialectic and metaphysics, philosophy and philosophizing, in an intimate and inviolable union. The later

17. The word was borrowed from the description of the final revelation to the mystery initiate at Eleusis, a "viewing" of the sacred drama. The assimilation of philosophical terminology to the jargon of the mystery religions was pronounced among the later Platonists.

Platonists continued to pay lip service to the Platonic ideal, but in reality they were dogmatists and not dialecticians. Whatever they may have said about dialectic, they used logic as a tool, and in the manner set down by Aristotle. Porphyry installed the logical *Organon* at the starting point of the curriculum and it remained there during the rest of the history of the school.

From the *Organon* the Platonist proceeded to the study of the Aristotelian philosophy proper, particularly the physical and psychological treatises. When Proclus was doing his studies at Athens in the fifth century, the Aristotelian part of the curriculum took two years. At its completion the student was ready for natural theology, a theology that was, of course, Platonic and centered upon the exegesis of the *Timaeus* and the *Parmenides*. Beyond that lay the sacred theology of the *Chaldaean Oracles*.

This was, we are certain, the standard curriculum in the only surviving philosophical school in late antiquity, the Platonic. It was not, however, what was passed on to the Arabs. What they knew of a curriculum came from translated examples of a standard "introduction to Aristotle" and not from what was actually being taught in the schools of Athens or Alexandria. The laying-out of the Aristotelian treatises from the *Categories* to the *Metaphysics*, the arrangement found in the *Catalogue*, and the one that determined the structure of most Arab encyclopedias of the "foreign sciences," was not a curriculum at all. Rather, it was an academic "division of the sciences." The simple fact is that neither we nor the Arabs have much information on the actual curriculum of any Aristotelian school.

The use of the *Rhetoric* and the *Poetics* is a case in point. Alexander of Aphrodisias, a Peripatetic writing about 200, refused both treatises a place in the *Organon*, while among the later Platonists, at least since the time of Ammonius at Alexandria, they were reckoned a part of the logic. The *Organon* was thought to deal with both terms (*Categories*, *On Interpretation*, *Prior Analytics*) and modes of reasoning. Strict demonstration (*apodeixis*) was taken up in the *Posterior Analytics* and its illegitimate versions in the *Sophistical Refutations*. The *Topics* and *Rhetoric* studied the methods of dialectical reasoning, the type appropriate to the orator, the jurisprudent and, as it turned out, the Muslim theologian. The *Poetics*, finally, had to do with a third form of discourse, one whose premises were neither true nor likely but, rather, in Farabi's expression, imaginative.

The Platonists discussed these matters as theoretical problems connected with the parts of philosophy; very few of them indeed devoted their efforts to actually lecturing upon either the *Rhetoric* or the *Poetics.* The Arabs dutifully followed along and included both works in their scheme of the *Organon,* even though they were generally baffled by the contents of the treatises. Paradoxically there are more recorded treatments of the *Rhetoric* and the *Poetics* at the hands of Arab authors than there are from the later Greeks. Scholastic piety could go no further.

The history of the *Politics* provides a parallel example. Though it finds its place in all the curricular schemata, the *Politics* appears not to have been translated into Arabic at all. It has sometimes been suggested that the reason for this is that the political treatises of Plato replaced the *Politics* in the later schools. In one sense this is true; the later Neoplatonists did pay close attention to certain aspects of both the *Republic* and the *Laws.* But that interest was in no way political; and while it is perfectly clear that the Aristotelian *Politics* was largely neglected by both Greeks and Arabs, it is equally clear that there were circulating in Islam treatises that purported to be Aristotle's thinking on political subjects.

Modern scholars have not been overly impressed by the claims to authenticity of the body of letters bearing the name of Aristotle in Greek, Arabic, Latin and Hebrew during the Middle Ages. But the Arabs, like the others, accepted their share of the windfall as authentic. And while many of the letters are unabashedly Hermetic,[18] some, at least, are political in content. The letters, many of them addressed to Alexander, are not, at any rate, either philosophical or analytical, but belong somewhere in the middle ground between politics and ethics inhabited by the "Mirror for Princes" type of work. That territory, we know,

---

18. Including the so-called "Treasure of Alexander," a treatise on talismans directed to Alexander by Aristotle, who had in turn received the information from Apollonius of Tyana, in Arabic "Balinus." The historical Apollonius lived about three and a half centuries after Aristotle.

was cultivated by later Peripatetic scholars, nor is there anything intrinsically improbable in Aristotle's communicating with a former student on the subject of politics.[19]

Whether authentic or not, the Aristotelian correspondence in Arabic had no visible effect on the theories of Farabi or any other political theoretician in Islam. They ended, instead, frequently ground exceedingly fine, in the somewhat shapeless pages of the Arabic gnomonologies, where they provided nothing more substantial than striking proverbs. Politically they were of little interest in Islam.

At base the Arabs learned about Aristotle from school books, particularly the introductory-type work known as the *eisagoge*,[20] not from the living tradition of any school, which would have been, in any event, Platonic. Their school books were written by Platonists, Porphyry among them, but of that the Arabs had no way of knowing, since the Platonic theology which would have revealed the true identity of a Porphyry, an Iamblichus or a Proclus had disappeared or, rather, had been concealed, as has been seen, under a pseudepigraphical mask, that of Aristotle.

The Arab celebration of Aristotle, to which Ibn al-Nadim bears such detailed witness, was a novel event in the Near East. During the preceding five centuries all who studied the philosopher did so from a far more limited pragmatism than that which the Arabs brought to the task. The Neoplatonists did grant him a place in their curriculum, but it was a subordinate one. And the Christians too, when they discovered their own need of Aristotle, were even more severe in their restrictions on his use.

The Christian use of Aristotle was, in the end, more important than the restrictions placed upon it. The works of the great eastern Neoplatonists appeared in no other language but their original Greek until the coming of Islam; Christianity and its theologians leaped cultural frontiers, including that which separated the Hellenes from the Semites of the Aramaic-speaking

---

19. A case has recently been made for the authenticity of one such letter preserved in Arabic and called *On Governance*. If this is indeed the *Alexander or On Colonies* mentioned by Aristotle's ancient bibliographers, it reflects some radical departures in Aristotle's thought.
20. See Chap. V, pp. 332–333.

East. Before there was an Arabic Aristotle there was a Syriac Aristotle, who served, in this limited capacity, the cause of Christian theology.

Though Syriac literature was properly a creation of Christian times, the Aramaic-speaking peoples of the Near East had been living within a Hellenized milieu since the time of Alexander's conquests. And if at Edessa the contact between Aramaean and Hellene produced a literature that was overwhelmingly Christian in its sentiments, the same contact at nearby Harran brought forth a far different kind of cultural mix: pagan, scientific and occult, rather than meditative, ascetic, musical and primarily Christian. Harran produced no literature until the days of the Muslim conquest, but what was otherwise revealed there shows that Greek learning had been at work in the Semitic centers of the Near East for a considerable length of time and that not all of its offspring were impeccably Hellenic.

As was later the case with the Arabs, attention has been most easily drawn to the scholastic Hellenic tradition among the Syrians, their explicit borrowings from Plato and Aristotle, for example. But they too had their hybrids. There was an extensive and early alchemical literature in Syriac, as well as other works treating of the occult properties of things and their manipulation. Much of this was, as usual, anonymous or concealed under a false name. One of the earliest historical figures drawing on the Greek legacy, and an essentially nonscholastic part of that legacy, was Bar Daysan (d. 222), the founding father of what had become by Islamic times the sect of the Daysaniyah.

The Edessa of Bar Daysan, who was born in 154, was still an insecurely Christian island in a surrounding sea of pagan Semitic cults, Gnosticism, and thriving Jewish communities in northern Syria and Mesopotamia. It was a commercial and intellectual crossroads, and Bar Daysan's teachings reflect all the multiple interests of that time and place: Persian ideas competing with Greek, and Babylonian with Jewish, all incorporated into the thinking of a well-educated Christian unconfined by later, more severe notions of what constituted orthodoxy and what did not. Some of those interests were unmistakably Greek, Stoic it has been surmised, though not necessarily derived from Syriac translations of Greek philosophical works. Bar Daysan wrote in

Syriac—his *Book of the Laws of the Countries* was composed in that tongue—but second- and third-century Syria was necessarily and effectively bilingual, and there would be nothing unusual or unlikely in Bar Daysan's reading the Stoics in Greek.

Bar Daysan's precise sources cannot be tracked: they were probably unprotected by the rigors of a school tradition and, so, already hybridized before they came into his hands. The phenomenon is common enough among the early Greek fathers—Origen, Bar Daysan's slightly younger contemporary, is a typical example—and the Greeks for their part had not yet begun the work of putting together their final version of a philosophical curriculum, the one incorporating Plato and Aristotle. Porphyry was two generations after Bar Daysan.

The Christian embrace of scholastic Platonism of the type prevalent in the schools from Porphyry to Proclus was hesitant and, in the end, indirect. The Neoplatonists were among the severest intellectual critics of Christianity, and neither the polemics of Porphyry, the attempts at a Neoplatonic restoration by Julian,[21] nor the theurgic pieties of Proclus reassured the Christian intellectual that there was some common ground between Jerusalem and Athens. The revival of the doctrines of Origen on the preexistence of the soul and the controversies they provoked in the sixth century made the Christian theologians even more cautious on the subject of Plato—and that, paradoxically, at the very moment when a major piece of Neoplatonic metaphysics was beginning to circulate in the East under the name of Dionysius the Areopagite.

Origenism was, however, a theological diversion in the sixth century. The central issue continued to be the Christological debate begun in the previous decades and inflamed, not settled, by the decisions of the two councils at Ephesus in 431 and 449, and that at Chalcedon in 451. The fathers assembled at Chalcedon had condemned Monophysitism, but by the mid-sixth century both Egypt and Syria were largely Monophysitic in their sympathies and conviction. The great ideologue of the sect was

---

21. Ibn al-Nadim has a number of pieces of information about Julian. It was he, according to the *Catalogue*, who revoked the Christian ban on the study of philosophy.

Severus of Antioch (d. 538), but their strength lay in the labors of missionaries, not theologians, men like Jacob Baradai (d. 578), who, through the friendly influence of the Empress Theodora, was consecrated bishop of Edessa and, in the years that followed, almost singlehandedly reconstituted the sore-pressed Monophysite hierarchy in the East.[22]

Severus was a theologian of some subtlety, and the Christological controversy itself was intricately interwoven with semantic considerations. The Chalcedonians, Monophysites and Nestorians were engaged, as none other of their predecessors, in a *bellum lexicographicum* fought over the meanings of *substance*, *nature*, *person* and *hypostasis*. The terms had arisen gradually into view since Nicaea, but by 500 none could follow the turnings of the polemic without considerable instruction in what had unexpectedly come to be a guide to the theological warfare, the *Organon* of Aristotle.

The theologians of Antioch may have been the first to lay their hands on the new weapons, and because they were exegetes rather than metaphysicians in the Alexandrian style, they found the logical Aristotle of greater use than the theologian Plato. The primary exegete in the Antiochene school, "The Interpreter," as he was called, was Theodore of Mopsuestia (d. 428). His approach to Scripture was carefully literal and historical, and his exegetical instruments were dialectical in the manner of Aristotle rather than allegorical in the style of Plato and the later Platonists.

Whatever judgments may be made about Theodore's own orthodoxy,[23] he held for the East Syrians the same position that he held at Antioch, that of the authoritative exegete of the Christian Scriptures. We do not know a great deal about theological

---

22. And who gave his name to the "Jacobite" churches of the Monophysite persuasion; see Introduction, p. 26 above.

23. Though he reputedly influenced Nestorius, Theodore was condemned at neither Ephesus nor Chalcedon; see Introduction, pp. 18–19. During Justinian's reign, however, he was anathematized at the Second Council of Constantinople in 553. Condemned along with Theodore on that occasion were his students Theodoret of Cyrrhus and Hiba of Edessa, the latter of whom had the works of his master translated into Syriac.

instruction at Antioch, but it seems highly likely that during Theodore's lifetime, or in the century following, the training in exegesis was preceded by some kind of instruction in the Aristotelian logic, since the introduction of Theodore's works and methods into the Syriac-speaking school at Edessa was marked by the simultaneous appearance of the *Organon* in the curriculum there.

The school at Edessa, founded during the lifetime of the famous Ephraem the Syrian (d. 373), was the center for higher theological studies among the Aramaic Christians of the East, both those within the borders of the Roman Empire and those farther east under the rule of the Sasanian Shahs. During the first half of the fifth century instruction at Edessa was closely tied to the theology of Antioch, and it was during that period that the works of Theodore were translated into Syriac and made the basis of the program of studies. The translations were done under the direction of Hiba, a teacher at the school and later bishop of Edessa. He had as collaborators Kumi, Proba, who was probably not on the teaching staff, and a certain Ma'na who, at this stage of his life, was engaged in Greco-Syriac translations, but later prepared Pahlevi versions of various Syriac liturgical works. Proba, in addition to working on the Theodore project, turned his hand to the Aristotelian logic. Parts of his translations of Porphyry's *Eisagoge* and Aristotle's *On Interpretation* and *Prior Analytics* have been preserved, and the *Categories* too must have come into Syriac at this time.

In 431 the Council of Ephesus condemned Theodore's student Nestorius. The connection of the Edessan teachers both with Nestorius and with Antioch created troubles in Syria at this time and, particularly, when Hiba, the great champion of Theodore of Mopsuestia, was promoted to the bishopric of Edessa in 435. Hiba protected the school until his death in 457, but thereafter the faculty at Edessa, still faithful to the Antiochene tradition, was discomforted by the rising tide of Monophysitism, until 489, when the Emperor Zeno ordered the school closed for good.

Even before that final closure the faculty had begun to migrate from Edessa to the friendlier atmosphere of the Shah's territories to the east. They included Narsai, who had been the director at Edessa for twenty years and who, sometime after 471, crossed the frontier to Nisibis and opened there a new school or, rather, a continuation of the old school in a new location. In the genuine Antiochene and Edessan tradition the scholarch was also "The Interpreter." But if exegesis was the principal concern of the school, it was undergirded by instruction in the elements of writing, including the copying of manuscripts, and in reading the Scriptures of Syriac-speaking Christianity.[24]

It is difficult to draw many conclusions about the substance of the curriculum at Nisibis except that it was, on the face of it, resolutely theological. There are, however, some interesting occasional illuminations. Sometime between 488 and 496 the Shah Kavad requested his religious minorities to submit a statement of their beliefs. The head of the East Syrians, the Catholicus, responded by having translated from Syriac into Pahlevi a work by one of the teachers at Nisibis. Its contents are described as "the divine essence, the Trinity, the works of the six days of Creation, the fashioning of man, the creation of the angels, the fall of Satan, the end of things."

Somewhat more revealing is the work of another Syrian called "Paul the Persian" in the Byzantine sources. This Paul, a different man from the Paul who was connected with Khusraw's court, debated a Manichaean in Constantinople in 527 and later wrote for Junilius, the Quaestor of the Sacred Palace, a Greek version of the hermeneutical textbok used at Nisibis. This *Parts of the Divine Law*, which in its Latin version found its way into the hands of Cassiodorus in Italy, shows the now close relationship between the Antioch-Edessa-Nisibis exegetical tradition on the one hand, and the Aristotelian logic on the other. The first part is quite simply the adaptation of a Porphyrian-Aristotelian "how to approach the study of a book" to the reading of the Bible; the pedagogical terminology is lifted directly from the early Syriac translation of *On Interpretation*.

The second section of the *Parts of the Divine Law* lays down in a didactic manner the theological principles in the study of

---

24. It was one of the "readers" at Edessa, Narsai's student Joseph Huzaya, who composed the first Syriac grammar. Among the Syrian Christians no less than the later Muslims, philology was a sacred science.

Scripture: God, his essence and power, the divine names, creation and providence; the present world, its creation and governance, accidents and an analysis of free will and its works; finally, the world to come. Again, the method is scholastic and Aristotelian, and the resemblance to what Muslim theologians were discussing in the eighth century is no less striking.

Not long afterward the school of Nisibis fell upon hard days. In 540 one of its teaching staff, Mar Aba (d. 557), was named Nestorian Catholicus at Seleucia-Ctesiphon, but the promise of the event came to nothing when Khusraw Anushirvan closed down the school and shortly afterward sent the new Catholicus into exile. Before that occurred, however, Mar Aba had begun to give theological instruction at the Sasanian capital. It did not compensate for the loss of Nisibis, where the closing of the school, albeit temporarily, dispersed the faculty, but did spawn new, if minor, centers of Christian learning in Iraq and western Iran. None of them attained the reputation of Nisibis, but there was, after 540 and during the last century of the Sasanians' rule, some form of higher Christian education at their capital. Somewhat later, Syrian Christian physicians began appearing in Sasanian court circles, and at the reopened school of Nisibis a medical faculty suddenly appeared.

The last great director at Nisibis was Henana, who, after a stormy career of thirty years as "The Interpreter," led the bulk of his students and faculty out of Nisibis into a form of self-imposed exile. This occurred about 600 and the school never recovered. The immediate cause of the dispute was Henana's attempts at replacing Theodore of Mopsuestia and the Antiochene exegetical tradition with something palpably more Alexandrian and Platonic. For many of his contemporaries Henana's "reform" was tantamount to a betrayal of their position to the Monophysites, an extremely uncomfortable suggestion in the last decade of the sixth century.

By Henana's day the Aristotelian logic was thoroughly domesticated in Syriac. Medicine too was obviously flourishing. The Alexandrian medical curriculum was translated into Syriac at the beginning of the sixth century by West Syrians and must already have been in use at what was emerging as the Nestorians' chief medical center, Jundishapur in Khuzistan. The material was

Hellenic, but its study did not necessarily imply a knowledge of Greek. The only East Syrian churchman of the sixth century who is credited with a knowledge of Greek is Mar Aba, who was educated at Nisibis but had to return to Edessa to learn Greek.

The West Syrian interest in Aristotle manifested itself somewhat later than that of the Nestorians. The connection of Theodore and, by implication, of Nestorius with Aristotle may have inhibited an early move in that direction, even though the East Syrians used the Aristotelian dialectic for purposes of exegesis rather than for the construction of a Christology. The preserved curricula of the East Syrian schools emphasize hermeneutics to the exclusion of almost all else, and the exegete's need of Aristotle was a limited one, to provide the formal schema upon which to lay out the explication of a text.

In Monophysite circles, Hellenized or Syrian, the needs were somewhat different, and the polemic that grew up in the wake of Chalcedon shows that both sides, the Monophysites and the Chalcedonian Dyophysites, had come to understand that the Christological argument was not merely a Scriptural one but had to do with new concepts unknown to the Gospels. The Chalcedonian John of Damascus (d. 750) underlined in the introduction to his *Source of Knowledge* the need for a careful definition of terms in the Christological disputes. The remark was essentially apologetic, a defense of the use of a science which was still considered "pagan": it was necessary to understand dialectic to refute the heretics.

The first part of the *Source of Knowledge*, the so-called "philosophical chapters," provided the eighth-century Christian theologian with an introduction to a dialectic transparently adapted from the Neoplatonic "introductions" to Porphyry and Aristotle current at Alexandria in the sixth century. Adaptations they must have been, since no one of the preserved *eisagogai*, neither those of the pagan Ammonius nor those of the Christians David and Elias, conform exactly to John's presentation. John, it appears, was not reading directly in the Alexandrian Neoplatonists.

There was little need to do so. For two centuries before John, theologians on both sides of the Chalcedonian divide were pursuing the same line proposed by the Damascene: Severus among the Monophysites, Leontius of Byzantium and Theodore of Raithu among the Chalcedonians. Whether they, in turn, were drawing their dialectical material from Alexandria is a more difficult question. The presentation is so thin and so anonymously scholastic that identification is rendered almost impossible. Some of the Alexandrians were, of course, Christians as well as professional philosophers, John Philoponus and Stephen among them, and one such may have prepared the kind of summary treatment of the Aristotelian logic that served the technical needs of theologians like John of Damascus.

Severus, since 512 the Monophysite Patriarch of Antioch, was also an alumnus of Alexandria, though not of the philosophical school. Sergius of Reshayna, on the other hand, studied both philosophy and medicine at Alexandria. This was during his Monophysite days; later he went over to the Chalcedonian position. Before his death in Constantinople in 536 Sergius, whose intellectual formation was wider and deeper than any of the sixth-century writers in Syriac known to us, was personally responsible for the translation of a great mass of Hellenic material into Syriac. Much of it may have been done under Monophysite auspices. It shows, at any rate, the same interest in the Aristotelian dialectic manifested by the other parties to the Chalcedonian dispute: a translation of Porphyry's *Eisagoge*, an elaborate commentary on the *Categories*, and smaller works on *On Interpretation* and *Prior Analytics*.

Thus far Sergius' labors were little different, though they came a century later, from the East Syrians' work on Aristotle or from what his own successors among the West Syrians were to do. But, unlike both groups, he was not merely a churchman[25] but a broadly educated physician, whose translations into Syriac included most of the basic works, chiefly Galen, in the medical curriculum at Alexandria, a number of popular moral treatises by Isocrates, Plutarch, Lucian, and Themistius, selections from some of the Greek gnomonologies, the entire body of the recently

25. Indeed, he was not a theologian at all, though he was deeply involved in the sixth-century version of the politics of theology, notably by his services as a legate between Ephraem, Justin's energetically Chalcedonian Patriarch of Antioch, and Agapetus, the bishop of Rome.

appeared writings attributed, falsely, to Dionysius the Areopagite,[26] and, less certainly, some occult treatises.

This combination of translation subjects appears to us a highly unlikely one, but only because it in no way coincides with our meager information on what was being studied in the West Syrian schools. Sergius' Syriac Galen was almost certainly in use in the newly important East Syrian medical centers, since it later formed the basis of the Arabic version of the same works by the Nestorian Hunayn ibn Ishaq, an alumnus of one of those centers. The Plutarch and the Isocrates remain puzzling, but another side of Sergius' work makes somewhat more sense. Among his translations was one of the tract entitled *On the Universe*, a work of Stoic origins falsely attributed to Aristotle, and Sergius himself wrote something called "On the Universe according to Aristotle." Sergius, it would appear, was involved in a contemporary controversy best known in Greek from the work of another Alexandrian philosopher, John Philoponus.

In 529 Philoponus had taken up weapons, as has been seen, against both Proclus and Aristotle on the subject of the eternity of the universe. The Arabs, we know, were well instructed on that aspect of the controversy. What they did not know was that somewhat later, between 546 and 549, John had offered a partial recantation in a work entitled *On the Creation of the Universe*, which was dedicated to the Monophysite Patriarch of Antioch. In it Philoponus made his own modest attempt at baptizing Aristotelian science by bringing it under the aegis of Mosaic wisdom. Even though he may have preferred Moses to Aristotle on some disputed points, Philoponus did attempt to bring the two wisdoms into alignment.

Philoponus' efforts at constructing a Christian scientific Aristotelianism were not greeted with universal acclaim, and there is reason to think that Sergius was engaged in a similar project and met with the same kind of opposition. Not unnaturally, the opposition came from Nestorian circles. The later Nestorian Catholicus Mar Aba came west from Nisibis sometime about 525 to see the Holy Places, as he explained, and to debate with the

---

26. It has even been suggested that Sergius is himself an excellent candidate for the authorship of those pseudepigraphs.

notoriously paganized Sergius. The Sergius in question is almost certainly Sergius of Reshayna, who was well known among the East Syrians. We do not know whether Mar Aba fulfilled his wish to confront Sergius, but he had his way, albeit through an intermediary, against the Alexandrian Monophysite Philoponus on the subject of cosmology.

Mar Aba's travels took him to Alexandria and then to Constantinople, where he came into contact with a Nestorian named Cosmas, the author of a curious work entitled *Christian Topography*. The *Christian Topography* was another trial at enunciating a Christian science, derived, as the author himself tells us, from the teachings of Mar Aba. It was directed against those false Christians who had hastened to embrace the science of the pagans at the expense of the wisdom of Scripture. Chief among these latter was John Philoponus, whose *On the Creation of the Universe* was alleged to have had as its target the teachings of Theodore of Mopsuestia. The *Christian Topography* was to be the common answer of Cosmas and Mar Aba against the detractors of Theodore.

When Mar Aba began his travels the theological atmosphere of the Empire was firmly Chalcedonian. Monophysites were zealously pursued by the agents of the stanchly orthodox Emperor Justin (517–527). One of their victims was John of Beth Aphtonia (d. 537), a Monophysite theologian and abbot of the monastery of Mar Thomas in the Syrian port city of Seleucia. Justin's unremitting support of the Council of Chalcedon and the subsequent abdication in 521 of Severus from the See of Antioch forced John into the same kind of exodus imposed upon the Nestorian scholars of Edessa half a century before. Together with the teachers at Mar Thomas, he migrated to a place near Callinicum on the Euphrates, where he founded the monastery of Qenneshre.[27]

From the results in the next century the move from Seleucia to

27. Callinicum had become, at about the time of John's arrival there, a center of feverish Monophysite proselytizing under the direction of one of Severus' agents, John of Tella; see Introduction, p. 23. There was another monastery with a similar name, Qenneshrin, located near Chalcis in Syria.

Qenneshre signaled a major transfusion of Hellenism into the West Syrian Monophysite community. The work of Sergius was carried forward along the same broad lines represented by the translations of the earlier scholar. Greek must have been taught and studied at Qenneshre, even though the effects are not visible until a century after its founding. Severus Sebokht (d. 667) worked on the Aristotelian logic in Syriac, particularly the *On Interpretation,* which Severus apparently used in a Syriac version done from the Pahlevi by Khusraw's court scholar Paul, the *Prior Analytics* and the *Rhetoric.* He was also an astronomer of note—he was likely the author of the Syriac translation of Ptolemy's *Tetrabiblos*—a mathematician and a cosmographer.

Severus produced an entire generation of Hellenically trained scholars: Jacob of Edessa (d. 708), Athanasius II of Balad, Monophysite Patriarch from 683 until his death in 686, and Jacob's student George (d. 724), bishop of the Arab tribes of Mesopotamia. Jacob was trained at Qenneshre and then at Alexandria before he was appointed bishop of Edessa, probably about 684. There were difficulties in his diocese, and he retired from the See and taught at various monasteries until his death.

The Monophysite Jacob was the chief intellectual among the Syrians of the seventh century, a man whose interests stood close to those of Sergius in the preceding century, the result doubtless of a similar training at Alexandria. He was a poet, historian, Biblical exegete, grammarian[28] and tireless letter writer. A great many translations from the Greek circulated under his name, including a new version of the *Categories.* Another work gave some brief definitions of the key philosophical terms in the Christological dispute: *hypostasis, substance, nature, form* and *person.* Finally, Jacob also turned his hand to another genre well known among the Greek theologians but not previously attempted in Syriac, a *hexaemeron,* the six days of Creation explicated in terms of the most sophisticated secular learning of the day.

The range of neither Athanasius nor George was as wide as Jacob's. Both were concerned with Aristotle, however. Atha-

---

28. It was Jacob who introduced into Syriac orthography the vocalization signs derived from Greek vowels.

nasius translated Porphyry's *Eisagoge*, which had already been done by Sergius, and glossed other parts of the *Organon.* George provided new translations, with commentary, on the *Categories, On Interpretation, Prior Analytics* and *Topics*. The lifetime of all three men was intersected by the Muslim invasion of their homeland. Their work and that of their predecessors in the Syrian schools was, however, ignored for the present by the Arab rulers of the Near East, who as yet had no need of Aristotelian dialecticians. When they did, the versions of these three seventh-century Syrians formed the basis of their own translators' work.

The Umayyads gave their support to Christian bureaucrats and poets, but made no move to patronize the Hellenic-style learning, whether in Greek or in Syriac. Nor is it likely that the Syrians expected it. A generation after George, the Maronite Theophilus of Edessa (d. 785) was still cultivating the same ground of the Aristotelian logic, presumably for the same theological motives that moved his Christian predecessors. If he did eventually come to the notice of the Caliph al-Mahdi (775–785), it was as an astrologer and not as a translator of Aristotle. Theophilus' versions of the *Prior Analytics* and the *Sophistical Refutations* were both done from Greek into Syriac, a language of no conceivable interest to al-Mahdi.[29]

Already, with Theophilus, there were connections with Islam but the purely Christian adaptation of Hellenic learning in Syriac that had begun in pre-Islamic days went on uninterrupted by the new order of things. Moses bar Kepha, who died in 903 and whose life spanned almost all of the ninth century, was for forty years the Jacobite bishop of Mosul. He wrote entirely in Syriac, and his works included scriptural exegesis,[30] liturgical and homiletic writings, what appears to have been a commentary on the *Celestial Hierarchy* of Pseudo-Dionysius, various original treatises on theology including one on the freedom of the will

29. Theophilus also translated Galen into Syriac, and, according to one source, was responsible for an otherwise unknown Syriac version of Homer.

30. The only part of it that is preserved is his exegesis of *Genesis* in the *hexaemeron* style of his Jacobite predecessor Jacob of Edessa. It is a major source on the teachings of Bar Daysan.

and another on the soul and, finally, a commentary in the well-worn Syrian style on the logic of Aristotle.

The new Arabic versions of Greek works did not have the same impulse as that which had earlier moved the Syriac translators and which continued to inform the interests of Moses bar Kepha, a careful cultivation of the opening treatises of the *Organon* as a modest propaedeutic to Christian theology. This Syrian school tradition eventually found rich soil for growth in Islam, but not until about 900, long after the Arabic translation movement had found its own sustenance. The desire to read Greek works in their own tongue arose within the Muslim Arabs from scientific rather than theological or philosophical preoccupations.

Mansur's (754–775) interests were in medicine and astrology, and at least one of his contemporaries, al-Bitriq, "the Patrician," was translating from Greek or Syriac into Arabic. Al-Mahdi cherished the Aristotelian Theophilus as an astrologer. His successor Harun (786–809) likewise showed himself far more inclined to science than to philosophy. Sallam al-Abrash reportedly translated the *Physics* for him, and there were other men in his "Treasure House of Wisdom" working on mathematics and astronomy.

Harun did show some interest in the Aristotelian logic; at one point he commissioned the Nestorian Catholicus Timotheus and his secretary Abu Nuh to prepare for him a translation of the *Topics*. The Caliph's request may not have been totally disinterested; both Christians had publicly taken up dialectical weapons against Islam, probably during the days of al-Mahdi, and Harun may have been curious to inspect the ammunition somewhat more closely.

If this was his motive, the Caliph was somewhat behind the times. An Islamic dialectic had been developing for nearly half a century, if not in the well-illumined halls of Damascus and Baghdad, then within the confines of Basrah and Kufah. That early form of Islamic "dialectical theology" (*kalam*) may have had some Greek assistance. No immediate Greek links have been detected, but Harun had an extremely suspicious regard for those Islamic theologians, and his curiosity about the *Topics*, a prime source, together with the *Sophistical Refutations* and the *Rhet-*

oric, for dialectical disputation, may be saying something indirect but important about the evolution of Islamic theology.

Out of those obscure discussions in Iraq evolved the group of Mu'tazilites who had settled somewhat uneasily into Baghdad by Harun's day. The early Mu'tazilites have no demonstrable connection with the translation movement, but their elevation to orthodoxy by Ma'mun (813–833) coincided with a new burst of energy on the part of the translators as well as a turning toward more purely philosophical material. Ma'mun's "House of Wisdom," though doubtless the continuation of Harun's earlier library, became a more formal center for research, and many of the contemporary translators were connected with it and, so, with Caliphal patronage. An arrangement was made with the Byzantine Emperor, probably Michael II, for the sending of teams of scholars into Byzantine territory in search of manuscripts. Among the newly discovered treasures were Euclid's *Elements* and Ptolemy's *Almagest*.

The continuing interest in science included Aristotelian science, and Yahya, the son of the earlier al-Bitriq, translated or paraphrased for Ma'mun Aristotle's *On the Soul*, *Meteorology*, *On the Heavens*, and *On Animals*. The pseudepigraphical *Secret of Secrets*[31] also bears Ibn al-Bitriq's name as translator, and that other major piece of falsification, the excerpts of Plotinus known as the *Theology of Aristotle*, may likewise have dated from Ma'mun's period or shortly after. Its translator is named as Ibn Na'imah, a Christian of Emesa who also shows up as the translator of the *Sophistical Refutations* and the *Physics*.

Ibn Na'imah's versions, like those of an otherwise unknown contemporary, Eustathius, who worked on the *Metaphysics*, served as the basis of al-Kindi's studies. Kindi (d. c. 870), the first philosopher in Islam, was nourished, then, on a philosophical tradition that had no obvious connection with the Syrian theologians, whose concerns with Aristotle did not much transcend the logical *Organon*. His introduction into philosophy was liter-

31. This Aristotelian pseudepigraph, which was widely read in its Arabic, Hebrew, Latin and European vernacular versions, is actually a composite work combining information and instruction on political science, medicine, astronomy and astrology, talismans and magic.

ary and unmistakably scholastic. It was a remarkable act of resuscitation to revive, through books alone, a type of philosophical concern not seen in the Hellenic tradition since the early sixth century. The long list of Kindi's works included by Ibn al-Nadim in his *Catalogue* ranges across the entire Aristotelian canon—logic, physics, psychology and metaphysics—and far beyond into preserves of Euclid, Ptolemy and Hippocrates.

On the testimony of his preserved works Kindi was an essayist and synthesizer; but during his lifetime the ground was being prepared in Baghdad for the appearance of the true textual scholar. The translations available to al-Kindi were still relatively crude. One of his contemporaries, Hunayn ibn Ishaq (d. 873) was, however, sharpening the philological tools of the translator. Hunayn, a Nestorian Christian of Hirah trained in Syro-Hellenic medicine by Yuhanna ibn Masawayh[32] was a product of the Jundishapur tradition. He was taken into the famous translation organization of the Banu Musa and, under their auspices, he accompanied manuscript-hunting expeditions into Anatolia, where he became skilled in Greek. Hunayn was eventually appointed the personal physician of the Caliph al-Mutawakkil (847–861).

The great bulk of Hunayn's translations were of Hippocrates and Galen, where he used Sergius' exemplars, but he worked on Plato and Aristotle as well; according to Ibn al-Nadim he translated the *Categories*, *On Interpretation*, the *Analytics*, *On Generation and Corruption*, *On the Soul*, and the *Physics* together with Alexander's commentary. All of these were done from Greek into Syriac, sometimes with the help of older Syriac translations, and then passed on to one of his associates, his son Ishaq, his nephew Hubaysh, or Stephen the son of Basil, Musa ibn Khalid, or Yahya ibn Harun, to prepare an Arabic version. Great care was taken to consult the best available manuscripts, and there were painstaking collations of the Greek original with whatever Syriac versions were extant. The translations themselves were finely done, faithful to the Greek and yet with an obvious concern to exploit the supple Arabic idiom to its fullest extent.

---

32. See Chap. V, p. 383.

By 900 the Arab scholars had in their hands excellent versions of a great many of the Aristotelian writings, genuine and spurious. At about the same time they unexpectedly fell heir to another part of the Hellenic tradition. According to the accounts of Farabi and Mas'udi, the philosophical school at Alexandria continued to operate right through the Arab invasion of Egypt, a fact unsuspected from the Greek sources. The faculty did not remain long in Alexandria, however. Sometime about the middle of the eighth century they migrated to Antioch and then, during the reign of Mutawakkil, to Harran. Finally, two and a half centuries after the Arabs took Alexandria, the progeny of the philosophical faculty arrived in Baghdad and began to give instruction there. The date was sometime about 900, and the instruction was almost certainly in the Aristotelian logic.

The three Harranians who were reported to have begun teaching in Baghdad were all Christians: Quwayri, Yuhanna ibn Haylan, and Abu Yahya al-Marwazi. Of the first little is known except that he wrote commentaries on the Aristotelian logic in some kind of tabular form. Yuhanna ibn Haylan probably had similar interests, and though no specific works are attributed to him, we do know that al-Farabi read the *Categories*, *On Interpretation*, and the *Prior Analytics* with Yuhanna, not improbably in Arabic. Of al-Marwazi, on the other hand, Ibn al-Nadim reports that all he wrote was in Syriac.

Among al-Marwazi's students there was a Muslim, Ibn Karnib, and a Nestorian Christian, Abu Bishr Matta (d. 940). Ibn Karnib appears to have succeeded al-Marwazi as the "head" of the new Baghdad teachers. We cannot be sure what that meant in circumstances where there were teachers but no evidence for a school. But if he did so, it must have meant a considerable broadening of the "curriculum." Farabi somewhat patronizingly remarked that the Syrian Christians contented themselves with studying the Aristotelian logic up to but not including the apodictic, or scientific, mode of proof described in the *Posterior Analytics*,[33]

33. The assertion is in the main true, but not accurately put. The Syrians did ignore the *Posterior Analytics*, but they concerned themselves with the various rhetorical proofs treated in the *Topics*, *Rhetoric*, and *Poetics*.

while he himself had read, under a Syrian Christian teacher, straight through the *Posterior Analytics*. Farabi may have been referring primarily to the curriculum in logic, but Ibn Karnib came to philosophy not through the *Organon*, as most of the Syrians did, but from the Hellenic scientific tradition. Both his father and his brother were eminent mathematicians, and the *Catalogue* describes Ibn Karnib himself as both a theologian (*mutakallim*) and a physical scientist.[34]

Abu Bishr Matta's earliest training was in ecclesiastical circles, at the monastery school of Dayr Qunna southwest of Baghdad. Later at Baghdad itself he studied first with the Christian Abu Yahya al-Marwazi and then with the Muslim Ibn Karnib. Unlike his fellow student Farabi, who was only a commentator, Abu Bishr produced both commentaries and translations of Aristotle from Syriac into Arabic: a commentary, possibly based on Themistius, on the *Prior Analytics* and the earliest known Arabic version of the *Posterior Analytics*;[35] translations of the *Sophistical Refutations*, *On Generation and Corruption* (with the commentary of Alexander of Aphrodisias and perhaps that of Themistius), the *Poetics* and *On the Heavens*.

Abu Bishr's scholarly labors, when taken with those of his contemporary al-Farabi,[36] show the influence of the scholastic tradition among the early philosophers of the *Dar al-Islam*. Both men were instructed directly upon the texts, something denied to al-Kindi, and they could handle those texts as knowingly as any fifth-century Neoplatonist of the schools. They possessed as well a familiarity with the same range of scholastic instruments as their predecessors: introductions, résumés, and commentaries on differing scales. Farabi's works include such scholastic staples as an introduction to the sciences, a reconciliation of Plato and Aristotle, a study of the intentions of Aristotle in his *Meta-*

---

34. We know he wrote a commentary on part of Aristotle's *Physics*.
35. As Farabi already noted, the earlier Syrians generally neglected the *Posterior Analytics*. Its first Syriac translation, and the basis of Abu Bishr's Arabic version, was prepared by Hunayn and his son Ishaq.
36. Among the Aristotelian works directly commented upon by Farabi were the *Categories*, *On Interpretation*, the *Analytics*, *Sophistical Refutations*, *Poetics*, *Physics* and *Ethics*.

physics, an *eisagoge* to the study of the Aristotelian corpus, and a setting-out of the preliminaries to the study of Aristotle.

After his education at Baghdad, Farabi left the 'Abbasid capital for the court of the Shi'ite Hamdanids at Aleppo. In doing so he may have cut himself off from the expanding circles of philosophers in Islam. Whatever influence he had—and it was considerable—Farabi exercised it through written works, upon readers without the same kind of access to, or interest in, the texts upon which his own studies were founded. Abu Bishr, on the other hand, who continued to work in Baghdad, had his own students as his successors, and it was they who incorporated his textual commentaries in the ongoing work of explicating Aristotle. Chief among them was the Monophysite Yahya ibn 'Adi, the principal Baghdad philosopher and theologian of his day, an accomplished editor and commentator of Aristotle, and Ibn al-Nadim's chief informant on things philosophical.

The studies of Yahya and his students and successors of the next generation, Ibn Suwar, Ibn Zur'ah and Ibn al-Tayyib, continued to be directed toward texts and commentaries. By this time the Greek, Syrian and Arab strands had run together to form a continuous tradition of learned textual exegesis. The earlier translations of Hunayn and his predecessors were corrected and embellished with commentaries to provide excellent textbooks for formal instruction.

As often happens, more is known about the textbooks than about the instruction. Baghdad's only institution of higher studies in the ninth century was Ma'mun's "House of Wisdom," which probably did not survive the transference of the capital from Baghdad to Samarra. There were still libraries in various cities, however, and one in particular in Basrah founded by Ibn al-Nadim's contemporary Abu 'Ali ibn Suwar—not the same man as Yahya's student al-Hasan ibn Suwar—possessed books on the secular sciences. We are further informed that instruction was given there and that the teacher was a Mu'tazilite *mutakallim*.

The other branch of the Mu'tazilites, those in Baghdad, are probably connected with another foundation, the "House of Science" organized by the Buyid vizier Shapur ibn Ardashir in 993. His motives are not far to seek: the rival Isma'ilis had opened their own academy, the Azhar, in Cairo only a few years before.[37] Ibn Ardashir was himself a Zaydi Shi'ite, and he lived during a period of increased rapport between the Zaydis and the Mu'tazilites of Baghdad. The fruit of their collaboration may have been the library-school at Basrah and the new academy at Baghdad.

If it is possible to connect the Mu'tazilites with both Ma'mun's "House of Wisdom" and Ibn Ardashir's "House of Science," no one of the known philosophers was affiliated with the latter institution. Most of them were Christians, and Ibn Ardashir's academy had a marked Muslim orientation. Philosophical discourse, if not the careful, technical training revealed by the Baghdad textbooks, must have taken place elsewhere, in the private salons (*majalis*) that flourished in Buyid Baghdad or in the "market place of the booksellers," the gathering place of Christians, Muslims and Zoroastrians.

The Baghdad philosophers were editors as well as essayists and polemicists, and their editorial work was directed, as all such since the fifth century, toward the Aristotelian corpus. They were, however, no more Peripatetics than their Greek or Syrian predecessors had been. The Baghdadis' philosophical premises were those of Neoplatonism: an Aristotelian logic and physics undergirding a Plotinian view of the great cosmos and its God. Farabi, the "second master" after Aristotle, stood at one end of that tradition, and Ibn Sina, the author of medieval Islam's definitive Aristotelian encyclopedia, stood at the other. Both were Platonic theologians.

---

37. See Chap. IX, p. 636.

V

THE FOREIGN SCIENCES

Following Aristotle's own programmatic remarks about the classification of the sciences, Peripatetic scholars, and particularly those associated with the school in Alexandria in the fifth and sixth centuries, generally introduced their students to a study of the Aristotelian corpus through an elaborate discussion of the division of the sciences. Once the divisions and distinctions were articulated, they served in turn as a classification device for the Aristotelian treatises themselves. Thus, the Alexandrian course of studies, which would eventually reach Plato's theology, began with a highly stylized introduction (*eisagoge*), which set out for the student the various definitions of philosophy, its classification into distinct disciplines, the major philosophical schools, the biography of Aristotle and a bibliography of his works. Only then was the student ready to take up the reading and study of the *Organon*.

The *eisagoge* complex, which was early circulating in an Arabic version, was particularly fruitful in Islam. It introduced the Arabs to the scholastic methodology of late antiquity, taught them what they knew of the history of philosophy and, most pertinently in the present context, provided a theoretical overview of what came to be called the "foreign" or "Hellenic" sciences. We cannot say precisely how the *eisagoge* complex got from authors like John Philoponus and Ammonius into Arabic, but the transit was surely made; even the earliest of the Arabs' own "division of the sciences" works, al-Farabi's *Enumeration of the Sciences*, for example, bear the unmistakable imprint of a Greek *eisagoge*.

The Arabs followed, with some minor variations,[1] the Aristotelian division of scientific knowledge into logic, the physical sciences, first philosophy or metaphysics, and the practical sciences of ethics, economics and politics. These were the "rational," or "foreign," sciences, enhanced from time to time by additions of uncertain origin. Farabi tacked on "linguistic science" before logic, and then added both jurisprudence (*fiqh*) and another "theology" (*kalam*) after politics in an attempt to do justice to Islam's contribution to science. But he likewise had a "science of weights" and "mechanics," which he inserted among the mathematical disciplines, additions that were almost certainly made by the Greeks themselves.[2] Some few years later, in 976, al-Khwarizmi, whose classificatory *Keys of the Sciences* already dealt with the "Arab" and "foreign" sciences in separate categories, included among the latter both the art of medicine and the more ominous *al-kimiya'*, alchemy.

The Mathematical Sciences and Geography

By "mathematical sciences" the Arabs understood what the Greeks had understood before them, the "quadrivium" of arithmetic, geometry, astronomy and music, with a few secondary additions, some of them, like optics, of Greek origin and others, like the "science of dividing inheritances," of purely Islamic concern. The latter three, geometry, astronomy and music, are all

---

1. Which had to do chiefly with the position of logic. Was it, as the Stoics held, a genuine branch of philosophy, or merely, as the Aristotelians maintained, a propaedeutic "instrument" (*organon*)?
2. Some of these additions correspond to treatises circulating among the Greeks, and later among the Arabs, under the name of Aristotle. Most of the pseudepigraphs dealing with problems in the physical sciences probably date from the Lyceum shortly after Aristotle's death and arise out of the work of Theophrastus and particularly of Strato of Lampsacus, surnamed "the physicist," when the school took a decided turn toward material naturalism.

unmistakably part of the Greek heritage in Islam, nourished and enriched, it is true, by Indian mathematics; it is only in the first, arithmetic, that the line of historical descent reveals something more complex.

The earliest of the Muslim mathematicians, Muhammad ibn Musa al-Khwarizmi—not the same man as the author of the *Keys* cited above—was active in Ma'mun's research center and library, where he did important studies on both Indian astronomy and Greek mathematical geography. But his reputation rests on his mathematics and, particularly, on his famous treatise *The Concise Calculation of Restoration and Confrontation*, part of whose Arabic title, *al-jabr*, provided the European languages with a term to describe the new mathematical method introduced by al-Khwarizmi.[3]

Al-Khwarizmi's "algebra" was, in effect, a new way of solving equations, first by "restoring" normalcy to an equation by bringing its negative terms up to a positive value through addition, a process which was repeated on the other side of the equation; and second by "confronting" similar and congruent terms on either side of the equation and eliminating them. When the work was translated into Latin by Gerard of Cremona and Robert of Chester, two twelfth-century contemporaries working in Spain, it appeared novel indeed, since they knew nothing of the even earlier Greek excursion into algebra by the third-century Alexandrian Diophantus. But even if they had had Diophantus available in translation, it is not likely that the Latins would have found the *Restoration and Confrontation* familiar, since it was apparently independent of even the Greek experiment in algebra.

Khwarizmi may not even have known of Diophantus—the earliest translation of the latter's work from Greek into Arabic is credited to Qusta ibn Luqa (d. c. 912)—but he made it clear at the outset that he was not working along Greek theoretical lines, which he did, to some extent, know. His was to be a practical arithmetic, useful, for example, in the ever-important calculation of inheritance shares. He then proceeded to construct his "alge-

3. Whose own name, transformed into the Latin *Algorismus* or *Alcorithmus*, added still another term to European mathematical nomenclature.

bra," which is at once more primitive than Diophantus', in that it is still completely in the form of prose recipes instead of the symbols with which Diophantus had begun to experiment, and at the same time more sophisticated in its increasingly obvious separation of number from geometry.

A second work of al-Khwarizmi had an equally profound influence on the West. The Arabic original of his *Addition and Subtraction* is lost, but a Latin translation entitled *On the Indian Numbers* survives to bear witness to at least one stage of the passage of the "Arabic numerals," which the Arabs themselves called "Indian" (*Hindi*), from India to Europe. The Hellenes had employed a cumbersome system of computation in which they used a different letter for each numeral up to nine, and additional letters for the decades, hundreds and thousands. The system had two major disabilities: the lack of a place-value notation made complicated calculations extremely difficult; and, more seriously, the entire number system was so closely tied to geometry that its inability to handle fractions, the so-called "irrational numbers," and negative values created in time almost insurmountable obstacles to mathematical progress.

In the period after Alexander's conquests the Greeks were introduced to another system, the Babylonian, which was sexagesimal rather than decimal and had the enormous advantage of the notion of place value. Not only did ease of calculation flow from the system; value by position effectively severed number from quantity and thus, by removing the inhibition against fractions, set Babylonian mathematics on its own road to algebra. Greek astronomers knew and admired the Babylonian number system, and Claudius Ptolemy introduced it into his *Mathematical Collection* where fractions are treated sexagesimally; and there appears, moreover, a special symbol to indicate "no units in this position." This is, of course, the function of zero, and to denote it Ptolemy used the abbreviation "o" for *ouden* ("nothing").

Sometime between 200 and 600, Greek and Babylonian mathematics passed into India, where there already was a decimal number system with place values. The Indians used separate symbols for the numbers 1 to 9 and then, by arranging these same nine digits in different columns, could express any higher number desired. And at some point they added the zero, the same "little circle" known to Ptolemy and later borrowed from the Indians by the Arabs and called "the empty" (*al-sifr;* "cipher").[4] Whether or not the Indians borrowed the zero from the Greeks, they integrated it into their decimal system as no Greek had done and produced, on the eve of Islam, an elegant and economical system of calculation.

The Arabs knew about "Hindi reckoning" from about 770, when there were Indian astronomers at the court of al-Mansur, but its use in pure mathematics, as opposed to astronomy, apparently had to await the work of al-Khwarizmi under Ma'mun. In his *Addition*, the Indian digit symbols were used and thereafter became standard in Islam.[5] They were written somewhat differently in the far-western provinces of the *Dar al-Islam*, and it was in that Maghribi form that the "Arabic numerals" passed into Europe, accompanied and explained by the Latin version of al-Khwarizmi.[6]

Al-Khwarizmi's effect on mathematics, Islamic and European, was incalculable, but his own originality cannot properly be judged. Even if his mathematical antecedents were patently not Greek, was he, as has been maintained, merely drawing upon the persistent tradition of Babylonian algebra, now joined to the liberating calculation methods of India? The Babylonian hypothesis is attractive, but since it rests upon a mathematics

---

4. "Zero" comes from the same Arabic word, via the medieval Latin *zephirum*.

5. Earlier the Arabs had used, like the Greeks, letters to represent numbers. The letter-numbers did not completely disappear from Islam, but their use was largely confined to magical and occult purposes.

6. The study of the Arabic numerals in Spain may have been confined to learned circles at first, but in 1202 the merchant-scholar Leonardo Fibonacci of Pisa, who lived for a time at an Italian trading station in North Africa, published his *Book of the Abacus*. Though its intent was theoretical, the book convinced many Italian merchant bankers that the new "Arabic" system of calculation was far superior to the old Roman one. Leonardo is also known to have traveled to Constantinople, and it may have been through him that the Byzantines too learned to use the Indian numerals. They appeared, at any rate, in Byzantine mathematical calculations during Leonardo's lifetime and were still a novelty in the Empire in the thirteenth century.

invisible for almost a millennium between the Seleucids and al-Ma'mun, it remains no more than a hypothesis.

Elsewhere in Islamic mathematics the Babylonian hypothesis has little need of being invoked; the Hellenic and Indian antecedents are clear. From Euclid in the third pre-Christian century to Pappus exactly six centuries later, all the major Greek mathematicians were translated into Arabic: Euclid's *Elements* with the additions of the Byzantine Hypsicles in Books XIV and XV by Hajjaj ibn Matar (c. 800) and Ishaq ibn Hunayn (d. 910); a number of Archimedes' treatises by Thabit ibn Qurrah (d. 901) and others; the *Conics* of Apollonius of Perge directly or under the supervision of a family of mathematicians known collectively as "the sons of Musa ibn Shakir" and by Thabit ibn Qurrah; the treatises of the Hellenistic trigonometer Menelaus by Ishaq ibn Hunayn, Thabit ibn Qurrah, and others; Autolycus by an unknown hand; Diophantus by Qusta ibn Luqa; and Pappus' commentaries on Euclid by Abu 'Uthman al-Dimashqi (c. 917).

Nor was this all. Many of these works were accompanied by translations of their Greek commentaries and then further illuminated by a long line of Arab exegetes. Euclid, for example, after the original translation by Ibn Matar about 800, immediately began to attract Arab commentators, first al-Jawhari (fl. 829), then al-Mahani (fl. 860), Thabit ibn Qurrah, al-Nayrizi (d. 922) and a whole series of savants stretching down to the Persian poet and mathematician 'Umar al-Khayyam (d. 1123) who wrote, in Arabic, on both Euclid and al-Khwarizmi.[7] The line of Euclidean commentators could be continued down to the end of the Islamic Middle Ages and included most of the major philosophers: Kindi, Farabi, Ibn Sina and Ibn Rushd all concerned themselves in one way or another with Euclid, and Ibn Sina used the *Elements* to flesh out the mathematical sections of his encyclopedic *The Healing*.

This impressive list of Greek translations reflects most exactly

---

7. But who was, nonetheless, far more deeply within the tradition of Diophantus than that of his Arab predecessors. 'Umar could, however, handle cubic equations with ease, while Diophantus had confined himself to the quadratic variety.

the Greeks' own concentration on plane and spherical geometry, and mathematics' progressive absorption into the preserves of astronomy. Where real progress in mathematics was made, it was frequently the work of astronomers, a principle as evident in Islam as it was among the later Greeks. Two tenth-century examples are al-Battani (d. 929) and Abu al-Wafa' (d. c. 997), whose mathematics, derived from Greek sources like Euclid, Ptolemy and Diophantus, were placed at the service of their astronomical interests and produced rapid advances in trigonometry, a branch of mathematics in which the Greeks had taken only the first halting steps.[8]

For the Greeks the line of mathematicians that ran from Euclid to Pappus was a secular one. They knew, however, another mathematical tradition with roots in Pythagoras and its finest fruits in later Neoplatonists like Nicomachus of Gerasa, Iamblichus and Proclus. The Arabs were well aware of this second, more metaphysical view of number. It did not come to them, of course, from Pythagoras, about whose mathematics they knew as little as the later Greeks, which was very little indeed. Nor did they possess the mathematical works of Iamblichus or Proclus. But Nicomachus of Gerasa, the Pythagorean revivalist of the first Christian century, whom they often confused with Aristotle's father, the Arabs did know and study.

Nicomachus' *Arithmetical Theology* apparently was unknown to the scholars of the tenth century, but his other major work, the *Introduction to Arithmetic*, which became a standard textbook in the later Platonic schools,[9] was translated into Arabic by Thabit ibn Qurrah. It may have been more than a simple scholarly labor. Pythagoras, the Arabs thought, was from Harran, a remote member of that same community of Sabians in which Thabit himself played an important part.[10]

By all accounts Thabit was the first of those Harranians to reach Baghdad and leave his mark there. Muhammad ibn Musa of

---

8. It was not until the time of Nasir al-Din al-Tusi (d. 1274) that trigonometry began to emerge from the shadow of astronomy.

9. It was commented upon by Iamblichus, Philoponus and Proclus, the last of whom fancied himself a reincarnation of Nicomachus.

10. See Chap. IV, pp. 278–281.

the famous family of savants and patrons of learning found Thabit employed in Harran as a moneychanger, admired his style, and took him into his translation organization, which at that time included Hunayn ibn Ishaq. Thabit trained with Muhammad, was eventually introduced to the Caliph Mu'tadid (892–902), and became the effective head of the Sabian community in Iraq.

Thabit was comfortable in Greek, Syriac and Arabic, and had an active scholarly life as a translator, epitomizer and commentator of Hellenic scientific material, chiefly in mathematics, astronomy and medicine. His interest in Aristotle centered on the *Organon*, but at least one Platonic study was found among his works, "An Explanation of the Allegories in Plato's *Republic.*" It was not Thabit's only work on politics, nor was it the last time that a member of the family wrote on the *Republic*. His son, the physician Sinan, wrote a world history, which began, on the testimony of Mas'udi's somewhat critical notice, with a preface in the manner of Plato's *Republic*—that is, it proceeded from an analysis of the faculties of the soul to an understanding of the governance of the state.

Thabit's scientific interests are well attested; assessing his work as a philosopher is considerably more difficult. His bibliography shows that he devoted a great deal of attention to Galen, one of the chief routes whereby scholastic philosophy passed into Islam. Galen's *On Demonstration*, which had been translated into Syriac by a certain Ayyub and then into Arabic by Hunayn and his assistants, was given close study by Thabit. Only a few years later an otherwise unknown philosopher of Mosul, Abu Bakr ibn abi Thawr, was exercised by that same Galenic tract. There are strong Platonic reminiscences in Abu Bakr, and yet the only Islamic philosopher he cites is Thabit ibn Qurrah. On the face of it both Thabit and his son Sinan had an abiding interest in ethical and political questions, an interest that went back, as seems likely, to a study of Platonic psychology.

Thabit's son Sinan (d. 942) enjoyed an equally prestigious position in Baghdad, where he was in charge of the licensing of physicians for the practice of medicine in the capital. But despite his closeness to both Muqtadir (908–932) and Qahir (932–934), Sinan's Sabianism provoked difficulties. He resisted the importunities of Qahir, even to the point of fleeing to Khurasan, but in the end he embraced Islam. Others of his Harranian coreligionists were feeling the same pressure. The *Catalogue* of Ibn al-Nadim has preserved a list of "headmen" at Harran reaching from the time of 'Abd al-Malik down to the beginning of Ibn al-Nadim's own lifetime, when the succession appears to grow somewhat uncertain. From another source we learn that the last head of the Sabian community died in 944. There was some relief in 965 when a prominent Sabian, Abu Ishaq Ibrahim ibn Hilal (d. 995), became the chief secretary in the Buyid chancery and used his influence on behalf of his confreres.

By Ibrahim's day the Sabian intellectuals appear to have deserted the earlier scientific interests for the perhaps safer domain of belles-lettres and history. Both Ibrahim and Thabit ibn Qurrah's grandson, Thabit ibn Sinan (d. 975), were literary men rather than scientists, the latter a historian of some distinction but with a marked Hellenic cast. This marks the end of Sabian occultism, the obscure realm presided over by "Hermes Thrice Great." Science and occultism had come together at Harran as at no other place in Islam, and the scholars who issued from the ill-understood community of pagans were the most eminent practitioners of the "Hellenic science" since the bright days of Alexandria.

The Sabians specialized in mathematics and astronomy, and in the latter science it was once again the catholic patronage of the 'Abbasid Caliphs that led the strains of Indian, Greek and Iranian learning into Baghdad in the late eighth century and so prepared the ground for the Sabian savants in the ninth. The first signs of genuine astronomical activity are indirect, however. Two astronomers, almost certainly functioning more as astrologers, presided over the laying-out of Baghdad in 762: Nawbakht (d. c. 777), and Masha'allah (d. 815), the first an Iranian by origin and a known translator from Pahlevi, the second a Jew from Balkh. Both must have been using Sasanian astronomical data in their calculations. We know that there were tables of planetary motions compiled by Sasanian court astronomers, and more specifically that a major revision of those tables, called in Pahlevi *zik*, was undertaken by Khusraw in 556. The revision was likely based on an increased knowledge of both Indian and Greek astronomical calculations, and so in consulting the Pahlevi *zik*, whether in the original or in an Arabic version,[11] Mansur's astronomers were already being introduced into a complex tradition. Perhaps they had access to other astronomical sources as well. Nawbakht's son al-Fadl (d. 815) for one apparently knew a great many details of the Sabian version of the transmission of astronomical science from remote antiquity through Hermes Trismegistos down to its rediscovery by the Arabs.

The "rediscovery" was nowhere as romantic as Ibn al-Nawbakht and others would have it—there were many stories of buried books turning up in the ruins of forgotten cities—but came about through the more pedestrian route of translation. Later in the reign of Mansur, perhaps about 770, an Indian named Kankah who was resident at the Caliphal court translated the Indian astronomical tables, the *Siddhantas* (in Arabic *Sindhind*), from Sanskrit into Arabic. Kankah may have had some assistance, technical, if not linguistic, from the astronomer al-Fazari. Al-Fazari was encouraged in his collaboration by al-Mansur, and shortly after the translation of the *Sindhind* was completed, the Indian material was integrated, again by al-Fazari, into Islam's first proper astronomical tables (*zij*).

Under Harun there appears to have been an attempt to turn some of the Greek astronomers, notably Ptolemy, into Arabic. The results must not have been happy, however, and it was not until the reign of Ma'mun that there were scholars skilled enough to handle both the Greek and the mathematics of Ptolemy's *Mathematical Collection*—which was also known as *The Great Collection* (*Megale Syntaxis*), whence the Arabic corruption *al-Majisti*—the final Greek statement in astronomy. Involved in the work was the interesting Salm "the Harranian," an Aristotelian translator who also knew Pahlevi, was the director of Ma'mun's "House of Wisdom" in Baghdad and paid an official visit to Constantinople in search of manuscripts.[12]

---

11. The Arabic translation of the so-called *Shah's Tables* may have been the work of 'Umar ibn al-Farrukhan, but their earliest preserved form is in the reworking by al-Khwarizmi.

12. That was not the only reason for going to Constantinople. Ma'mun made persistent requests, through Salm and others, that the Emperor

The *Almagest* and Ptolemy's other major work, the *Tetrabiblos*, continued to be revised down to the time of Ishaq ibn Hunayn and Thabit ibn Qurrah, and the results were not judged satisfactory until near the end of the ninth century. Ma'mun encouraged the pursuit of astronomy in both theory and practice—the first observatory was set up in Baghdad at this time—and set Islamic astronomy off on its own path. The *zij* were revised by Yahya ibn Mansur and Habash al-Hasib. The more occult traditions of the East, already known to al-Fadl ibn al-Nawbakht, were combined with solid learning by Abu Ma'shar, a scholar whose interest in chronology was notably conditioned by the casting of horoscopes. Both he and his contemporary al-Farghani were well known to Europe in later Latin translation.

What the Arabs brought to developed Greek astronomy was little or no change in theory—the Ptolemaic geocentric system was accepted without demur—but a certain refinement in observation and a more skillful use of mathematics. The two Harranian astronomers Thabit ibn Qurrah and al-Battani (d. 929) were both accomplished mathematicians, and the latter, a convert to Islam from Sabianism, brought to Ptolemy's still primitive trigonometry based on chords a new and more productive approach through the calculation of sines, tangents and cotangents. At the same time the accumulating observational data collected from observatories spread across Iran were incorporated into a series of new astronomical tables from those of al-Khwarizmi to the *zij* prepared in 1437 for Ulegh Beg.

The final subject in the ancient mathematical quadrivium was music. The Arabs treated it both as an art (Gr. *techne;* Ar. *sina'ah*) and as a theoretical science (Gr. *episteme;* Ar. *'ilm*), and the philosophers among them devoted more than passing attention to the *'ilm al-musiqi*. The ancient authorities on harmonics, Aristoxenus, Euclid, Nicomachus of Gerasa and Ptolemy, were all well known in translation. Their angle of approach was, of course, mathematical, but the Muslim philosophers who followed

---

Theophilus send to him in Baghdad Byzantium's most famous mathematician, Leo. Theophilus refused the requests, but Leo's reputation suffered no harm from the offer and he was later made head of the Imperial University.

in their steps, and who also treated music as a branch of mathematics presided over by Pythagoras, had some thought of music as an art and in the style of Plato explored its ethical implications.

Dependent from the basic quadrivium sciences of arithmetic, geometry, astronomy and music were the derived sciences of optics and geography. The first was a descendant of geometry, and among the Greeks optics was almost the private preserve of the geometers. The towering figure of Islamic optical science, Ibn al-Haytham (d. 1039), knew the geometers' work—he wrote commentaries on the optical works of Euclid and Ptolemy and for years supported himself simply by making and selling copies of their works—but the Muslim scholar was also a theoretical and experimental physicist,[13] an astronomer of some note and a physician. He never practiced this latter speciality, but he brought from it to his study of optics a knowledge of the anatomy of the eye that no geometer could hope to possess. There was a pragmatism about Ibn al-Haytham's work, and his studies on the nature, refraction and reflection of light that are summed up in his *Optics* were accompanied by a sophisticated and quite extraordinary experimentation. He ascertained, for example, that the Hellenic theory of vision, that visual contact took place between the sun's rays, those given forth by the eye and the perceived object at some point outside the eye, was simply not true. According to Ibn al-Haytham, light passed only *into* the eye, through its proper lens.

There is much that is typical and much too that is superlative in Ibn al-Haytham the scientist. He was educated in a classical tradition, Aristotle, Euclid, Apollonius of Perge and Ptolemy, but he was not so overawed by it that he followed slavishly where the masters had led. Privately pious, he was a thoroughgoing rationalist in science. He was patronized by the state and harassed by it. He was a polymath on the common Islamic model,

---

13. While still living in Basrah he proposed a method for regulating the annual flooding of the Nile. This exciting piece of information was brought to the attention of the Fatimid Caliph al-Hakim, who summoned Ibn al-Haytham to Egypt, where the scholar quickly realized the impossibility of his proposal. He had to pretend madness until the Caliph's death to escape Hakim's disappointed wrath.

and yet he did rigorous and sustained work in all the disciplines he put his hand to.

The Greeks possessed two geographies: one, related to astronomy and concerned with determining through mathematical means the exact location of places, is represented by Ptolemy's *Geographical Description;* the other, the bastard offspring of ethnography, travel literature, philosophy and history, can be observed in the pages of Herodotus, Strabo and Arrian. The first descended in direct line to Islam via the normal translation route. Ptolemy's mathematical geography was translated or, perhaps better, adapted, not once but many times. The first to have done so may have been Ibn Kurdadhbih in the middle of the ninth century. If this is so, and Ibn Kurdadhbih says it is, his own geographical work went off in a very different direction. Almost contemporary was the translation of Ptolemy done for the philosopher al-Kindi, who had a lively interest in geography, which he passed on to his students, and who wrote a number of works on the subject himself.

A third, almost simultaneous reworking of Ptolemy was done by the astronomer and mathematician al-Khwarizmi, and from it emerged his own similar work, *The Image of the Earth,* which, like Ptolemy's original, was accompanied by a map. The same scholar was involved in one of al-Ma'mun's own geodetic projects, the measurement of a degree of latitude in the open spaces near Mosul. The results are complicated, first by later reports about the uncertainty of the figure and, second, by modern disagreement on how to convert that figure into miles or kilometers. By any reckoning the degree was calculated larger than it is.

After al-Khwarizmi the Ptolemaic legacy of mathematical geography passed through the hands of successive generations of astronomers: al-Farghani; Thabit ibn Qurrah; al-Battani; al-Hakim's court astronomer in Cairo, Ibn Yunus (d. 1009); and al-Biruni. At the same time the Arabs, who gave no evidence of knowing anything about either Herodotus or Strabo, were creating their own tradition of descriptive geography. The same Ibn Kurdadhbih who had busied himself with Ptolemy wrote a *Book of Routes and Kingdoms* in 846, and it was only shortly after that that a student of al-Kindi, Ahmad al-Sarakhsi, wrote a similar work with an identical title. Both works were essentially itineraries, like the earlier Roman *Parthian Stations* of Isidore of Charax, a description of routes and distances between towns.

The "stations"-type work, and its maritime sister, the *periplous*, was a practical handbook for travel, in the first instance for official travelers of the army and the *diwans*—Ibn Kurdadhbih was himself an official of the Postal Service—but, in a society so seized by wanderlust as the Islamic, eventually for private travelers as well. For much of the medieval period the *Dar al-Islam* lay open from Spain to India for the curious adventurer, the pious pilgrim and the wealthy merchant, to travel its routes and observe its sights. Many of them recorded their travels for no other motive than pleasure. Two of the earliest examples, the description of Ibn Fadlan's diplomatic mission on behalf of the Caliph to the Volga Bulgars in 921–922 and of Abu Dulaf's similarly motivated journey into China for the Samanids in 942, must be reconstructed from later authorities, but thereafter we are in full possession of a number of remarkable accounts: the *Journey* of Ibn Jubayr, who in 1182–1185 traveled from his Spanish homeland through Syria, Iraq and Egypt to Mecca and then returned by way of Sicily; the Persian *Book of Travel* of the poet and philosopher Nasir-i Khusraw who traveled the Near East in 1045–1052 and was converted to Isma'ilism during his stay in Cairo;[14] the Hebrew *Itinerary* of the Spanish Jew Benjamin of Tudela, who visited Jewish communities at Constantinople, Jerusalem, Baghdad and Alexandria on his travels through the Near East in 1160–1173; and the *Gift of Observers* of Ibn Battutah (d. 1377), who roamed the *Dar al-Islam* and the lands that lay outside, from Timbuktu to China, for nearly thirty years.

All these books are essentially entertainments with an immensely rich vein of eyewitness observations collected by intelligent men. Their information, and that collected by others like them, did not come to rest there; it was collected and arranged in patterns different from the simple chronological line of the traveler. Early in Islam, from the ninth century onward, there appeared in Arabic both descriptive geographies in the manner of

---

14. See Chap. IX, pp. 641–642.

Strabo and a body of works that rest somewhat awkwardly between cultural history and natural philosophy.

Descriptive geography, as far as we can trace its beginnings, appears to have originated close to Hellenic circles. The earliest extant example, the *Book of Lands*, was written by al-Ya'qubi (d. 897), a scholar whose ecumenical *History* shows a close knowledge of Greek cultural and philosophical sources. Ya'qubi operated in much the Herodotean fashion in his geography, drawing upon literary sources where available, but supplementing his account out of his own travel experiences and the inquiries he made of the natives in the lands he visited. The researches of the Hellenic-style scholar and the observations of the traveler were combined into a broad, geographical panorama that embraced economic, social and political history, as well as the topography of Egypt, Syria and western Islam.

Scholarship is more in evidence than observation in the geographical works produced in the "school" of al-Kindi. The philosopher's own interest, as concerned Ptolemy and others, was toward mathematical geography, and his student al-Sarakhsi has already been noted as the author of a "stations." It was another student of al-Kindi, Abu Zayd al-Balkhi (d. 934), a native of Khurasan and a protégé of the Samanid princes there, who moved unmistakably into a more fully descriptive method in geography. The genesis of Balkhi's *Images of the Climes* is obscure—it may have consisted in descriptive passages connected with an earlier map—but it set Arabic geography on its descriptive way, and al-Balkhi's successors, al-Istakhri (fl. 930) and Ibn Hawkal (fl. 977), contented themselves with revising al-Balkhi's original work. In 985 al-Muqaddasi wrote his *Best Division*, which was still based on the Balkhi tradition but profited from the author's own extensive travels around the *Dar al-Islam*.

Each of these geographies was accompanied by a map or, rather, by a series of maps ranging from a general outline of the entire *Dar al-Islam*, the Mediterranean, Persian Gulf and Caspian, followed by the various provincial divisions, Syria, Egypt, et cetera, with considerably greater detail lavished on the eastern provinces. The detail is a relative thing, since the maps were all highly schematized and paid little attention to either the actual shape of the physical features or the mathematical precisions based on latitude and longitude that the Greeks had already begun projecting on their maps. The south, as was customary on all the Arab maps, was at the top of the page.

Greek precision returned to Arab map making with al-Idrisi (d. 1166), the Moroccan Muslim who served at Palermo in the Norman-Arab court of Roger II of Sicily (d. 1154) and for whom he prepared his world map and accompanying description, popularly called *The Book of Roger*. Idrisi's training was solidly within the Hellenic tradition—he had studied the botanical works attributed to Aristotle and Theophrastus, for example—and his map was done in the classical tradition of a quadrangle representing the known world, not merely the *Dar al-Islam*, and divided vertically by ten meridians of longitude and horizontally by seven parallels of latitude.[15]

Arabic scientific geography did not proceed much beyond this point, even though detailed knowledge of topography within the *Dar al-Islam* continued to accumulate, locally often on a prodigious scale, and was incorporated into local histories rather than geographical works proper,[16] or came to rest in medieval Islam's *summa* of descriptive geography, the *Dictionary of the Lands*. This alphabetically arranged dictionary of geography was the work of Yaqut (d. 1228), a Greek by birth, who was brought to Baghdad, reared as a Muslim, and worked in the still-lavish princely libraries all over the Near East. Like Yaqut's dictionary of national biography, the *Dictionary of the Lands* is a vast encyclopedia in which is collected, from literary sources and Yaqut's own travel experiences, information not only on places but on the men associated with them in Islamic history.

The final form of Islamic geography arose from a direct but

---

15. The division into horizontal "climates" (Gk. *klimata*—Ar. *iqlim;* pl. *aqalim*) was common among the Greeks from the time of Eratosthenes and Hipparchus, and under Islam these "climates" were invariably seven in number. Both the Arabs and the Greeks may have been working from older Babylonian prototypes, but the invasion of astronomy by astrology gave to the inhabitants of those zones certain characteristics determined by the planets that ruled them. This kind of astrological ethnography was already being practiced by Ptolemy in his *Tetrabiblos*.

16. On the local histories, see Chap. III, pp. 263–264.

indefinable contact with Hellenism, and perhaps even with the related Christian tradition. The cultural and dynastic histories of ancient peoples, still kept separate in the geographical and historical works of Ya'qubi, ran together in al-Mas'udi (d. 956), who produced in his *Golden Meadows* and *Notice* a type of encyclopedia rather than either a history or a geography. Both works open with an introduction that begins as a cosmology and evolves, under the influence of Greek astronomical consideration, in the direction of a Ptolemaic geography. Mas'udi's intent was not, however, mathematical, and he soon veers off into a cultural history of the "seven nations of antiquity" before returning, in a later historical section on the kings of Greece, to a survey of natural history from an Aristotelian point of view. Natural, cultural and political history were all within Mas'udi's purview and, if Ya'qubi is Islam's Herodotus, one must return at least as far as Posidonius to find a parallel to Mas'udi.

In Islam the cosmological and geographical introduction became, after Mas'udi's example, a common way of beginning a world history; no more than ten years after Mas'udi's death al-Mutahhar ibn Tahir al-Maqdisi composed his *Book of Creation and History*, a similar, if somewhat more pious and considerably less learned, version of the Mas'udian encyclopedias. At least parts of the work of both men bear some resemblance to a genre already well known in the East. Christian authors often displayed their own learning in cosmology, geography and natural history in the form of a commentary on the opening chapters of *Genesis* entitled *Hexaemeron* or *On the Six Days of Creation*. The type was well known in Syriac both before and after the *hijrah*, and one of the earliest *summas* of Syrian learning under Islam, the *Book of Treasures* of Job of Edessa (d. 814), though not cast in the form of a *hexaemeron*, stands close to that genre in its organization and content.[17]

The *hexaemeron* continued to enjoy a vogue among the Syriac-

---

17. Job—or Ayyub, as he was known to the Arabs—was a well-known translator of Galen from Greek into Syriac and it has been proposed that he was the real author of the Hermetic *Secret of Creation* attributed to "Balinus." That latter work was probably put together in pre-Islamic times, however.

speaking Christians, particularly the thirteenth-century Jacobite encyclopedists Severus bar Shakko (d. 1241) and Barhebraeus (d. 1286). The Muslim polymath had no such literary form, of course, but could exercise his encyclopedic talents in other ways, in Qur'anic exegesis, for example, in the prologues of world histories, or in the broad surveys of natural history that owed as much to Aristotle as they did to Ptolemy and the geographers. These latter were purely secular works, much like al-Jahiz's *Book of Animals*, and yet they possessed no connection, as Mas'udi's work did, with political history. Later Islam was fertile in such encyclopedias of natural history, beginning with Zakariya ibn Muhammad al-Qazwini's (d. 1283) *Marvels of Creation*, the first and probably the best of the genre.

Between al-Khwarizmi and al-Qazwini, Islam produced scores of men who are respectable if not towering figures in the history of science. What is far more impressive than their absolute stature, however, is the breadth of their learning. Greek science appears to have come into Islam as a coherent and integrated program that produced polymaths more regularly than isolated and specialized geniuses. We are at a loss to explain how, in lives choked with action, men could accomplish so much across a wide span of intellectually demanding scientific disciplines. Ibn Sina (d. 1037) has not been much mentioned here in connection with the Hellenic sciences. He was primarily a philosopher and a physician, and created a large body of work in both fields. And yet his range across the natural sciences from mathematics to music and astronomy is staggering, as is that of the later Nasir al-Din al-Tusi (d. 1274).

Though surpassed by Ibn Sina as a philosopher and Tusi as a theologian, the greatest of Muslim scientists and the archetype of the Islamic polymath, at least as far as the Hellenic sciences are concerned, was al-Biruni (d. c. 1050), a scholar whose work was untranslated and so unknown in Europe until modern times. A native of Khwarazm, where he was born sometime around 970, al-Biruni knew the life of the political exile and opportunist, almost as thoroughly as did Ibn Sina. In his trekking from patron to patron across northern Iran, Ibn Sina never allowed himself to fall or be enticed into the hands of the increasingly important Turkish *amirs*. If al-Biruni had any such qualms—he was raised a

Shi'ite—he suppressed them and learned to accept the Sunni orthodoxy of the Turks: after serving the Samanids, Ziyarids and Khwarazmshahs in turn, Biruni was carried away from his homeland in 1017 by the victorious troops of the Turk Mahmud of Ghazna and passed the rest of his life as the official astronomer of Mahmud, his son Mas'ud, and his grandson Mawdud.

Earlier in his career, before the years at Ghazna, Biruni had received his training in the "foreign" sciences: mathematics, astronomy, physics, medicine and *materia medica.* A product of this early period was his elaborate study of calendars and eras, his *Traces of the Past*, compiled about 1000 and based on a corrected version of what he had studied in people like Abu Ma'shar and on his own computations. His "capture" by Mahmud opened more earthly perspectives, however. Biruni went to India in the van of Mahmud's armies and stayed on in the new Ghaznavid province to teach the sciences, to learn Sanskrit, and to observe Indian society at first hand. The result of this quarter century of study and reflection was the *History of India*, completed in 1030, an extraordinary Muslim assessment of an alien civilization by an observer who had entered, as no other Greek, Arab or Iranian, before him, into another culture. India is there complete: its geography and topography, its manners, customs, and beliefs, its literature and its laws, all described by a detached but sympathetic scholar with the intellectual equipment to do the job. Biruni's *History of India* is Islamic science's finest monument.

There was more after this, his *Canon of Mas'ud*, an Islamic astronomical *summa* comparable in scope and learning to Ibn Sina's *Medical Canon*, a further work on mineralogy and, when he was over eighty, a considerable work on drugs. There were some 180 of Biruni's works in all, most of them scientific treatises composed in Arabic, but with a scattering of Persian works as well, and all written in the spirit of enlightened scholarship that typified the coming-together of Iranian, Arab and Hellene at its best.

The Occult Sciences

Among Biruni's other works is one entitled *Instruction on the Elements of Astrology*, which became a standard introduction to that popular subject. Once again, even in Biruni, one can see the two faces of Islamic science; the secular tradition of trigonometric functions, astronomical tables and schemes of world chronology was accompanied and contaminated by a parallel tradition of horoscopes, astral influences and elaborate theories of the descent of occult wisdom from the hoary past into the bosom of Islam. At the side of al-Battani, the student of Ptolemy and exegete of his works, stood Abu Ma'shar, a devotee of Hermes and the Harranians.

Biruni was by no means extraordinary in his commitment to two disciplines that we would judge totally incompatible. Ptolemy himself had almost identical interests and suffered as little embarrassment as Biruni did in cultivating both astronomy and astrology. Each discipline had authentic credentials that established it as a science; and if astrology was somewhat less exact in its predictions, as Ptolemy willingly conceded, it was no more so than ethics, for example, with respect to geometry.

The latter comparison is borrowed from Aristotle, who knew nothing, however, of astrology as a science and so was mute on its merits. The promotion to scientific status of astrology, alchemy and the other occult arts of Oriental antiquity occurred after the lifetime of Aristotle, and yet the processes that led to this signal extension of the scientific curriculum were already in motion in his day. The records indicate that there was a Babylonian among Aristotle's classmates in the Platonic Academy. It is an interesting and significant fact, since toward the end of Plato's life, near the mid-point of the fourth pre-Christian century, there are signs that Greek intellectuals were deserting their traditional disdain for what other peoples were pleased to consider *their* wisdom.

The Greeks were always curious about the eastern *barbaroi* and were eager, as no other people in the world were eager, to learn about others; the notion of being instructed by such was, on the other hand, simply laughable. That attitude was changing, however, in the fourth century, and the young Aristotle was willing to entertain the possibility of a history of wisdom that began before the Greeks and included such an unlikely—unlikely a mere generation earlier—figure as Zoroaster. By Aristotle's death the world itself had changed. In the wake of Alexander, the

Greeks found themselves masters of a political empire that included, for the first time in their history, non-Greeks, the *barbaroi* of the clergy lands of Iran, Mesopotamia, Palestine and Egypt. It should have been a moment of Hellenic triumph; it signaled instead the beginning of a period of profound and shattering self-doubt.

The Greeks' closure, as suitors rather than investigators, with those other, eastern traders in wisdom was not everywhere uniform. The Jews did not much attract them; a revealed law as the repository of wisdom said nothing to the psephophile Greeks. As time passed the Hellenes did come to appreciate somewhat more deeply Jewish monotheism and piety, but the narrow notion of tribal survival was as profoundly uninteresting to the newly ecumenical Greeks of the third century as it was later to the Romans. The other high cultures of the East, those of Iran, Babylon and Egypt, did possess, on the other hand, more intriguing keys to the mysteries of the universe and of the natures in it.

The Babylonian and Egyptian priesthoods were at low ebb when the Greeks arrived to rule those lands. On the evidence, they told all to their new masters, who were, after all, neither bandits nor warlords but the prestigious Hellenes. And out of the exchange came a new hybrid wisdom in which the religious occultism of the eastern priesthoods was grafted onto the Greeks' intellectualistic and public *philosophia*, while for their part, the easterners became Hellenized.

The progress of Hellenism into the vitals of the indigenous religions of Iraq, Iran, Egypt and Palestine is not very well known, except in the case of the Jews, since their history has survived. The mutations that were wrought within Hellenism can be traced in some detail, however. There were early changes within the Greek philosophical schools—in the growth of an astral theology, for example—but they did not at the outset destroy the public and acquired nature of philosophy itself. There were signs, however, of other stirrings, notoriously the resurrection of a long-dead Pythagoras in the new guise of miracle worker and proponent of the occult. The historical Pythagoras may have been just that—we cannot tell with certainty—but the scholastic masters of the fourth century, Plato and Aristotle, preferred to think of him as a philosopher and a scientist.

In the end the chief survivors among the Greek philosophical schools, the Platonists, embraced the occult with a passion. Plotinus in the third Christian century stood almost alone in his resistance to what most of his philosophical contemporaries and successors judged to be an alternative, and superior, way to truth, a conning of the great oracular collections like the *Chaldaean Oracles* in an attempt to extort from them a mastery of the secrets of nature. The stars and planets, divinities all, were scanned and implored to work their will benignly upon men. Proclus, the head of the Platonic Academy in the fifth century, thought he might be the reincarnation of the Pythagorean numerologist Nicomachus of Gerasa.

The philosophers' acceptance of the occult was in some sense fitting, since it was they who had provided the theoretical grounds for the conversion of the varied star and nature lore of the East into the very model of Hellenic sciences. There was nothing exotic about the theories themselves; they were drawn from the purest Peripatetic and Stoic sources. Later devotees chose to dissemble and to invoke the names of more ancient and less Hellenic sages, but the true, if unwitting, fathers of the occult sciences were Aristotle and Posidonius, the former by his analysis of physical change and the latter by his classic statement of the Stoic notion of cosmic sympathy.

For the mathematicizing physics of the Academy Aristotle had substituted his own emphasis on the qualities of material beings, an emphasis that yielded a new analysis of change in the physical world. States of being were identified as the passage in and out of the matter of different "forms" on either the accidental or the substantial level. "Form" was a reassuringly Platonic term, but Aristotle's alternate expression was a somewhat more accurate description of the phenomenon: the operational and dynamic components of being were "energies" (*energeiai*) or, as the later tradition preferred to call them, "powers" (*aretai, dynameis*).

The exchange of quantitative for qualitative analysis removed physics from the preserve of the mathematician and placed it, quite unintentionally, in the hands of the occultist. Aristotle's dynamic view of being harked back to something much older in Greek philosophical thinking, when it was first freeing itself from primitive animism. Aristotle's philosophical version of this animism was rational and secular, but when transplanted to Egypt and elsewhere in Hellenistic times, it raised echoes of other animist traditions which still had religious associations clinging about them. Hellenized eastern scientists, chief among them Bolus of Mendes in Egypt, understood Aristotle's "powers" as the occult properties buried deep within being, and they interested themselves not so much in the empirically observed operation of such powers as in their infallible manipulation.

Aristotle's analysis of change was closely and uniquely tied to physical processes. For his occult successors matters were not so simple. The effects of a magnet upon iron or the moon upon tides, for example, could not be so explained, nor could all those practical techniques for altering material things and their appearances that had been developed over the centuries by the eastern priesthoods and had been concealed from the understanding of the laity by an elaborate cover of symbol and code.

There were other explanations at hand, however, and the occultists of late antiquity took eagerly to them. Chief among them, and the cornerstone of occult science, was the Stoic theory of cosmic sympathy. From the beginning the Greeks had regarded the universe as some kind of organic whole, and by the time of Posidonius, a Hellenized Syrian who lived in the second pre-Christian century, the view had found its refined statement: the universe as a whole and the various powers deployed within it are bound together in a network of mutual interreaction (*sympatheia*).

To understand the natural sympathies and antipathies of one power with respect to another was to possess the key to their manipulation. There were still immense difficulties, of course; the real "powers" of things were obscurely concealed deep within the entrails of being and so were inaccessible not so much to Aristotle's discursive reasoning as to a great deal of practical experience, the kind of experience, one might add, that had long been the private and secret property of the eastern priestly guilds.

The emphasis on experience over against speculative knowledge is more than simply a bow in the direction of those proto-alchemists and protoastrologers who had been germinating within the Egyptian and Babylonian priesthoods. It shows that what was beginning to emerge was not merely a science (*episteme*) directed toward understanding but an art (*techne*) that aimed at practical results. Aristotle was content with the analysis of natural change; his alchemist successors wanted to alter and divert natural processes for their own ends. More, they shared the skepticism of their philosophical counterparts on the usefulness of unaided human reason.

In principle the occult sciences might have been as thoroughgoingly secular and rationalistic as the sciences cultivated by Aristotle. Ptolemy, for one, was a secular astrologer in that he considered the powers of the planets as purely natural phenomena subject to the laws of physics. Nor did he feel any need to call upon the help of the gods in taking the measure of those powers. Ptolemy was, however, a rarity. For most of the occultists the powers of natural substances were as psychic as they were physical, and their pursuit was an unmistakably religious one.

The later Hellenic scientific establishment was overrun with partisans of the latter view, but they regarded themselves as successors of Plato and Aristotle and spoke with equal reverence of the sages of an older wisdom, Moses, Solomon, Zoroaster, Cleopatra and particularly the Greek god Hermes and his Egyptian counterpart, Thoth. They circulated their own work under the names of those same sages—the first historical person whose name appears on a preserved alchemical treatise is Zosimus in the fourth Christian century—not only to claim the authority of antiquity but to conceal themselves from the malevolent and increasingly powerful attentions of Christianity.

There was no shape to Hermeticism, just as there was none originally to Hermes. Some of it was thinly disguised Greek theological speculation placed at the service of a supposed Hermetic revelation; some of it was science, Greek and Babylonian in the main; the rest was magical recipes. And the whole was cast over with an elaborate and false veneer of Egyptian antiquity. The cachet of Oriental antiquity helped to sell Hermeticism in a world that now revered rather than despised the eastern *barbaroi:* "From the East, Light," to which one could now add "and Wisdom and Salvation."

One group among the eastern *barbaroi* still languished in their barbarism, even under this extended franchise. The sixth-century Arabs neither drew upon nor contributed to this exchange of wisdom. Some of the frontier tribes were Christians and served, as has been seen, as mercenaries for the Byzantines and Persians; but the great number of Arabs lived isolated from the high cultures of Alexandria, Antioch and Seleucia-Ctesiphon as nomads within the Syrian steppe or dwellers in the towns of the Hejaz. Their wisdom was parochial, their sciences had to do with survival, and their magic and demonology was that of a folk culture.

The magical legacy of the Arabs runs throughout the *Qur'an.* The objects of the Muhammad's "warnings" at Mecca were the pagan and superstitious Quraysh, but his rivals were the nameless *kahins*, seers, diviners and poets who like him claimed access to the all-too-present supernatural world of the Arabs. That world was populated, as has been seen, by the *jinn*, those half-personified forces of nature who were a little less than gods and somewhat more than men. The *jinn* were often malevolent toward men, but some among the Arabs had made pacts with those preternatural powers and so were privy to the secrets which the *jinn* had extorted or stolen from the gods.

Muhammad believed in the *jinn* as firmly as any of his contemporaries. He scorned, however, those *kahins* and others whose *jinn*-inspired knowledge gave them power over their fellowmen, and he deeply resented any comparison between his own message and what a *kahin* or poet may have received from a *jinn.* He believed too that the *jinn* could be tamed. The *Qur'an* (2:102) reflects pointedly on the mastery of the art of binding the *jinn* to good ends. Some Jews, it appeared, had claimed that Solomon was a magician. Muhammad disagreed: the *jinn* were controlled by Solomon, and some of them, here called "Satans," plotted to revenge themselves on the king by teaching men magic (*sihr*). This was evil medicine indeed, and the believer should have nothing to do with it.

Solomon's power over the *jinn* was God-given, and so the marvelous things he accomplished with their help–Rabbinical and Islamic legend is filled with such stories–constituted what the later jurists and theologians judged "permissible," or "white," magic; what unscrupulous men like Muhammad's contemporaries the *kahins* might effect by cooperating with the *jinn* was, on the other hand, strictly forbidden by Islamic Law.

Muhammad's point of view reflects his own belief in the real existence of *jinn* and the possibility of magic that flows from it. Similar beliefs were shared by his followers throughout the history of Islam, and there was an ongoing interest in the various means of binding those supernatural forces to achieve a desired effect. Amulets, talismans, magic recipes and formulas abounded at all times among the Muslims, and the perhaps oversubtle distinction between "white" and "black" magic was not very carefully observed in many quarters.

Ibn Khaldun (d. 1406) instructed the readers of his *Introduction to History* that the difference between miracle and sorcery was that the saintly worker of miracles is supported by the power of God, while the sorcerer achieves his effects either through his own psychic powers or with the help of the *jinn*. The introduction of psychic powers into the discussion reflects Ibn Khaldun's own point of view as a philosopher, but for Muhammad, and even for most of Ibn Khaldun's own contemporaries, the psyche had very little to do with it. For them magic was formulaic and mechanistic, and the powers which such instruments harnessed were not merely those of the philosophically conceived soul but the occult powers deep in the being of all things.

On a popular level this view of magic is probably another residue of animism, but in their passage from Mecca and Medina to the centers of other, older cultures the Muslims came to appreciate other perspectives that converted magic from folklore to the status of science. We have already seen how they discovered, even before their meeting with Plato and Aristotle, the glamorous figure of Hermes Thrice Great and with him the varied buried treasures of Greek and Oriental occultism.

The Hermetic literature in Arabic is as historically complicated as it is in Greek, since it circulated in both languages under false names: Hermes ("Hirmis"), Apollonius of Tyana ("Balinus"), Empedocles, Pythagoras and even Aristotle. Again, like its Greek prototype, Arab Hermeticism served as a cover for everything from the most standard kind of Neoplatonic philosophy and theology to works on alchemy, astrology, talismans and outright magic. And yet, despite the very obvious signs that Arab

Hermeticism issued from Greek antecedents, few if any of those antecedents have been found. The immediate sources remain unknown.

One of the most popular of the Arabic works attributed to Hermes was the so-called *Treasure of Alexander*, to which the Caliph Mu'tasim was directed in a dream in 838. He was instructed to dig in the foundation of the recently conquered city of Amorium in Anatolia and there discovered a book written in golden letters and identified as *The Treasure of Alexander*. Mu'tasim had it translated from its original Greek into Arabic and so gave to the Muslim world a genuine Hermetic encyclopedia, author and origins unknown. After an introductory chapter on the occult properties of things, the *Treasure* ranges easily over their manipulation in the animal, vegetable and mineral kingdoms and concludes with a tract on the preparation and use of talismans.

There is much more of this lying unpublished and unread in "Hirmis" manuscripts scattered through Near Eastern libraries and much too under the closely associated name of Balinus. We know something of the historical Apollonius of Tyana, enough to realize that the biography of that wonder worker of the first Christian century written by Philostratos in the third is a highly idealized portrait. The Arabs knew neither in any detail. What they did possess was a number of works on alchemy and talismans bearing the name "Balinus." The chief among them is another Hermetic encyclopedia entitled *The Secret of Creation*, a book not unlike the *Book of Treasures* written in Syriac by the Christian Job of Edessa sometime about 817. In at least one manuscript the Balinus work professes to be a translation from Syriac, but we are so ill informed on its history that there is no agreement on whether there was a Greek original at all.

These are merely two examples of a great mass of occult material, most of it Greek in origin, that somehow found its way into Islam. We are almost helpless in tracing its descent from Greek through Syriac into Arabic, save perhaps in the case of astrology, where there was a well-defined Greek school tradition that did not fear to reveal names.

For the Muslim, as for the later Greek, scientific astrology received its classic statement in the *Tetrabiblos* of Ptolemy, a work available in Syriac in the translation of Severus Sebokht (d. 667) and in Arabic in an often-revised and commented-on version by Ibrahim ibn al-Salt. According to Ptolemy, the catalyst of the entire structure of cosmic sympathy is the fifth element, the *aither*, out of which the heavenly bodies are composed and whose "effluences" effect changes in the four sublunary elements—earth, air, fire and water. Thus a precise knowledge of the positions and movements of the heavenly bodies will give the investigator some understanding of their terrestrial counterparts.

For Ptolemy there was no question of the heavenly bodies' exercising their *will* on earthly affairs. His language is frequently anthropomorphic, but the operation of the powers is pure physics and, on the postulate of cosmic sympathy, perfectly natural. Nor was he unaware of the difficulties and deficiencies of the investigation. The causes operating on sublunary beings are highly complex and not always comprehensible; environment, genetics and individual differences all make the task of the scientist a forbidding one and his findings subject to considerable error.

In the second book of the *Tetrabiblos* Ptolemy applied the scientific method of astrology to questions of national characteristics. The first and more universal form of astrological prognostication is "that which relates to whole races, countries and cities," while the second is that which deals with individual men. What follows in Book II is more ethnographical than political, though the Arabs were to convert the method to more practical political ends. Nor did it pass without objection. There was a long tradition of philosophical opposition to astrology and, with the coming of Christianity, a theological opposition as well. The Syrian Christian Bar Daysan, who was once an astrologer himself, wrote his Syriac *Book of the Laws of the Countries* in part to refute the Ptolemaic theory by recourse to the realities of ethnography: people who should on astrological grounds exhibit similar national characteristics have in fact very different laws and customs.

The Ptolemaic astrological premises, though they can hardly be described as naturalistic, owed little to the highly religious synthesis of astrology, magic and metaphysics that later captivated Platonic theologians and Hermetic scientists alike. Plotinus, for example, had little regard for astrology, but within the very next generation of Platonists Iamblichus not only affirmed the value of astrology but began to assert its connection with the metaphysics of his school.

The general effect of Neoplatonism on the earlier theories of astrology was to replace the view of the universe as an organic network with one that posited vertical lines of force descending from the supreme One to the lowest levels of being. The chain effect characteristic of all phases of Neoplatonism gave to the heavenly bodies a new role as intermediaries. They became links in a descending chain of spiritual substances emanating from the One. More, they were material living beings, divine in their intelligence and incorruptible in their matter. In the astrological scheme it was the planets that passed on in differentiated forms the generic "effluence" and power they received from the higher beings above themselves. And while an astronomer like Ptolemy might contemplate their movements as paradigms of regularity, these celestial intermediaries were endowed by his successors with a kind of wild vitality.

The philosopher Ibn Sina (d. 1037) illustrates how this late Hellenic theorizing on the heavenly bodies came together in a nonoccult form in Islam.[18] For Ibn Sina, as for the Greeks, the human body-soul relationship provided abundant evidence for the power of the soul to work its effects immediately upon its own body, in the excitation and repression of sexual desires, for example. The Intellects and Souls that govern the celestial bodies have even greater powers; they not only bestow the original immanent forms on natural existents, they are likewise capable of affecting those forms and so also the bodies in which they dwell. Finally, certain spiritually gifted human souls are able, by reason of their connection with the transcendental Intellects of the spheres, to serve as channels of communication for those celestial

---

18. Ibn Sina's own bouts with occultism were relatively mild. Though he granted the heavenly bodies a will of their own (see Chap. VIII, p. 632), he denied the possibility of astrology and expressed the gravest doubts that metals could in fact be transmuted. There are, however, a few minor treatises on occult subjects attributed to him, including one on the mysterious letters prefixed to certain *surahs* of the *Qur'an*.

powers. The miracles of the saints and the prophets are formally nothing more than the effects that heavenly bodies can work on other bodies by reason of cosmic sympathy. They only appear miraculous when they are transmitted through the intellects and wills of mortal men.

Late antiquity was overrun with the activities of a great swarm of minor gods, the prolific tribes of *daimones* who compensated by their hyperactivity for the increasing remoteness of the High God of the philosophers. There was a strong element of folk religion in the later Greek fascination with these lesser spirits, but not even the remote precincts of the Academy were immune to their influx, and the folk *daimones* eventually shuttled with agility up and down the Neoplatonic chain of being.

The planets had, then, both a physical and a spiritual effect on material beings here below, the first through the various occult "powers" flowing into things and the latter through the sometimes highly personalized workings of the gods and *daimones*. Or so a Greek would call them. The Jew Philo of Alexandria had introduced another consideration: the *daimones* of the Greeks were no other than the angels of Judaism. The Neoplatonists welcomed the identification, and angels became an important part of the celestial landscape well before the coming of Islam. Muhammad knew of the Biblical angels, and their religious role in Islam grew, rather than diminished, over the years. Muslim Hermeticists and philosophers had little difficulty in assimilating them to their own purposes.

The astrologers of Islam followed the lead of their ancient sources and cast "nativities" with a fine abandon. The official support they received from Caliph and Sultan alike must have calmed whatever religious scruples they originally possessed: almost every Islamic ruler from the insouciant early 'Abbasids to the ultraorthodox Turks had court astrologers like Nawbakht and Masha'allah, men who could be counted upon to give advice on everything from the founding of a city to the fighting of a battle.[19]

---

19. At least one of them got too close to the front. Ma'mun's astrologer, Yahya ibn Mansur, was killed in one of the Caliph's campaigns against the Byzantines in 830.

There was orthodox opposition, to be sure, and polemical literature against astrology had as distinguished a history in Islam as it did in Christianity. Philosophers and theologians alike took up the cudgels. Al-Kindi and his students were devotees, but on the other side Farabi, Ibn Sina and Ibn Rushd among the philosophers, and among the theologians Ash'ari, Ghazali and the Mu'tazilite 'Abd al-Jabbar were all opposed. In the fourteenth century the conservative Hanbalite theologian Ibn Qayyim al-Jawziyah (d. 1349) and the liberally educated Ibn Khaldun both denounced "the science of the laws of the stars" (*'ilm ahkam al-nujum*), as it was called, as fraudulent and irreligious.

The translation history of the earliest star tables available to the Muslim astronomers and astrologers shows that it was far more than Greek notions that were being introduced into Islam. The Iranian tradition in astronomy was strongly represented among the savants who served Mansur, al-Mahdi and Harun. And given the history of that discipline under the Sasanians, it is not entirely surprising that those same men should turn out to be somewhat more astrologers than astronomers. It was the Sasanians, for example, who pioneered the attempt at writing history in astrological terms, an example that found many imitators in Islamic times.

Before the coming of Islam the Arabs had practiced some modest charismatic divination, but the Sasanians' peering into the future was done methodically and scientifically. The science in question was astrology, and the reasoning behind astrological prognostication was simple and straightforward: events have horoscopes just as men and nations do. The rise of a house or a kingdom could thus be charted, and since the movement of the heavens was a cyclical one, some judgment could be rendered on the future of the political institution in question.[20]

---

20. As a matter of actual practice the Muslim astrologers, and probably the Sasanians before them, used the conjunction of the two "superior" planets Jupiter and Saturn. In its rarest form their conjunction signaled the transfer of political authority, while the more common conjunctions of those same planets marked the rise of rebels and revolutionaries. Another meaningful conjunction was that of the two "unlucky" planets, Saturn and Mars, in the sign of Cancer. This was the signal for upheavals, political, social and natural. Among al-Kindi's

According to an obviously later story, Khusraw Anushirvan consulted his vizier on how much longer the Iranians could expect to rule before the domination of the Arabs began. He was told that the founder of Arab rule would be born in the forty-fifth year of his reign and, since the planet of the Arab domination was Venus, that domination would last for the period of Venus, one thousand and sixty years. The prediction was obviously a highly optimistic one, but there were those among the Arabs whose calculations were different or whose expectations were less hopeful.

The earliest preserved response to that same question within the *Dar al-Islam* is that of Theophilus of Edessa, the Christian translator of Aristotle and al-Mahdi's court astrologer. The question must have become a standard one for astrologers and obviously found great favor among promoters of self-fulfilling prophecies. Masha'allah (d. 815), the philosopher al-Kindi,[21] his student al-Sarakhsi (d. 899) and Abu Ma'shar (d. 886) all gave their predictions, which were based, in every instance, upon astronomical calculations going back to Sasanian times.

On the testimony of Ibn Khaldun, who devoted an entire section of his *Introduction to History* to predictions and divination, al-Kindi's work on the subject predicted the fall of Baghdad and of the 'Abbasid dynasty in the thirteenth century and the coming of the Messiah in 1298–1299. Ibn Khaldun had never met anyone who had personally seen the treatise in question, but he knew it was popularly called *The Book of Jafr* in imitation of an earlier work by the Shi'ite Imam Ja'far al-Sadiq (d. 765).[22] Kindi's book was probably a harmless enough exercise in astrology, but the earlier *Book of Jafr* was notorious in Islam for containing within its closely guarded pages the sum of the Shi'ite *gnosis*.

---

works was one entitled "The Two Maleficent Planets in the Sign of Cancer," which may be the original name of the preserved essay predicting the duration of Islam.

21. See Chap. VI, p. 439.

22. *Jafr* is a word of somewhat obscure etymology. It possibly refers to the parchment upon which Ja'far's book was written, but it soon came to be used as a general term for divination.

The Shi'ite *Book of Jafr* made no claims to being science on the Hellenic model; its authority rested, as Ibn Khaldun pointed out, on the special powers of "unveiling" granted by Allah to the descendants of 'Ali. It was, in effect, a wisdom born of a secret revelation. Islam's astrologers from Kindi to Biruni calculated, on the other hand, from observed data. And if a great deal of that data was Sasanian, the postulates behind their work were pure Hellenic. Kindi in particular was a close student of Ptolemy, and even earlier, during the reign of Harun, scholars at the Caliph's court were pondering the hexameters of Dorotheus the Syrian, an obscure astrologer whose *Pentateuch*, originally written in Greek, was translated from Pahlevi into Arabic by 'Umar ibn al-Farrukhan, the same man who translated the Sasanian astronomical tables and wrote a commentary on the *Tetrabiblos*.

The early astrologers of Islam were not prodigal with theory, and it appears that they may have concentrated on the more practical applications of the art favored by the Sasanians. But not always along the somewhat austere lines of Ptolemy. Their connection with Harran had made them Hermeticists, and Hermetic astrology had drunk deeply of the theosophy favored by both magicians and astrologers in late antiquity.

A philosophical version of late Hellenic astrology, sketched against an unmistakably Neoplatonic metaphysics, is presented in a document which made no attempt to conceal its Harranian and Hermetic origins, the *Epistles* of the Brethren of Purity.[23] There is another such, this time considerably overgrown with formulas and recipes, in a work entitled *The Sage's Intentions*, an elaborate occult encyclopedia falsely attributed to the Spaniard al-Majriti.[24]

The Sage's Intentions is lavish not merely in its detailed descriptions of the workings of the individual planets on human affairs in general, but in the precise correspondences between the

---

23. See Chap. VIII, pp. 613–616.

24. The genuine Majriti, who was a mathematician and astronomer of some repute, died in 1105, while our occult author wrote sometime between 1045 and 1055. The *Sage's Intentions* was translated, in a somewhat altered form, into Latin under the title of *Picatrix*—a corruption of "Hippocrates"—and provided Europe with its most influential introduction to both the Hellenistic and Islamic versions of the Hermetic sciences.

heavenly bodies and plants, minerals, animals, and even parts of the human body. It was not, of course, a novel undertaking, even within Islam itself. As early as Masha'allah, the Arabs had worked themselves into the rich mix of Hellenic astrological occultism. We have a Latin version of one of his works on the fixed stars, wherein he describes "according to Hermes" the "sympathies" between various of those stars and the appropriate minerals, plants and talismans.[25]

The occult and obviously non-Islamic quality of this learning bothered not a few Muslims, and the Neoplatonic theories that lay behind it raised other problems as well. The notion of the star souls as spiritual emanations that served as intermediaries of the divine power contradicted the conservative orthodox position that Allah's unique creative power rendered all secondary causality otiose. "It has been proven," as Ibn Khaldun put it in his attack on astrology, "that there is no agent but Allah," a sentiment that ran nicely counter to what was once the prevailing Hellenic view that God was so remote that he *needed* intermediaries. Some of the Hellenizing Muslims who had a care for orthodoxy, and most of them did, went to considerable lengths to integrate—or conceal—the astrological premise by casting around the star souls a calculated Islamic nomenclature, just as Philo had done by identifying the Greeks' *daimones* with the angels of later Judaism. The philosophers frequently operated in this fashion, and the Agent Intellect, the intelligence that is the tenth and lowest emanation from the First Cause and has an important function in both human intellection and the theory of prophecy,[26] was sometimes called "the Holy Spirit" and sometimes "Gabriel."

---

25. The talisman (Gr. *telesma;* Ar. *tilmsan*) was a gem-inscribed image of one of the decans, the thirty-six godlike figures who ruled the various divisions of the circle of the zodiac. The decans were originally Egyptian gods of time, who were associated in threes with each sign of the zodiac in Greek times. The Arabs' notions about the decans were rather vague, but Masha'allah's figures clearly derive from them. The chief Arab authority on talismans was Apollonius-Balinus, who was linked backward to Hermes and forward to Aristotle and Alexander. Part of his *Treasure of Alexander* concerned talismans.

26. See Chap. VIII, p. 629.

The effect of the heavenly bodies on the sublunary world was only part of the far-ranging consequences of the theory of cosmic sympathy. The tightly forged, but concealed, links that ran through all of nature transformed physics, botany, mineralogy and medicine, whether among the Greeks or their Arab successors. The notion of occult and divine powers promised the scientists of late antiquity far more spectacular results than their more secular predecessors. Between them, astrology and alchemy divided the heavenly and earthly sciences. They shared the same world-view, the same physical and metaphysical principles, and differed chiefly in that astrology, which reflected on the eternal and determined causes of nature, had to content itself with a mere predicative knowledge of the future, while alchemy could attempt to change nature in the realm of the shifting causes characteristic of the sublunary world. Alchemy was the technology of astrology.

Each science had at its disposal a vast and sophisticated body of learning accumulated from different cultures over the millenniums. Greek alchemy had earlier assimilated the guild knowledge of the Egyptians, and its Muslim version could draw upon additional information from Iran and India. Lapidaries and botanical works falsely attributed to Aristotle found their way into Arabic, with many accretions en route.[27] By the time they reached the Arabs through their Syrian versions both the origins and the viewpoints of such works were hopelessly confused, and under Islam they were supplemented by knowledge coming from India, generally through a Pahlevi or Syriac intermediary, and transmitted in most cases by members of the faculty at the medical school at Jundishapur. Thanks to one of their Indian members, scholars there were reading *The Book of Poisons*, a work on poisonous plants recently translated from Sanskrit into Arabic and at the same time were consulting the "secular" works

---

27. Two such works, *On Metals* and *On Plants*, which certainly issued from the Aristotelian school in the generation of Theophrastus, were written in the naturalistic tradition of the later Lyceum. It was only somewhat later that they became entangled in the Hermetic version of science with its emphasis on the occult "powers" of things.

on simple and compound drugs by Galen and Dioscurides and quasi-Hermetic tracts like the *Physiologus* or the *Geoponica,* which were mixed encyclopedias on the characteristics of animals, plants and minerals and were well known in Syriac.[28]

From this fertile soil of learning, lore and pure imagination grew the potent tradition of Arab alchemy, "The Art" (*al-sina'ah*), as the oldest authorities called it.[29] And if the earliest Islamic astrology carries the Arabs' connection with Greek works of science back to the reigns of Mansur and Harun, their connection with Greek alchemy is earlier still; according to the Arabs' own version of the story, the first Muslim adept of "The Art" was Khalid, son of the Caliph Yazid I. In the *Catalogue* of Ibn al-Nadim, Khalid, who was still alive in 720, is credited with a number of alchemical treatises, one of them in verse, and early authorities like Jahiz and Mas'udi were unanimously agreed that he was an alchemist. The *Catalogue* supplies further details: Khalid summoned a number of scholars from Egypt to translate from Greek and Coptic into Arabic various alchemical tracts for his use. Among the translators was a certain "Stephen the Elder,"[30] and Khalid himself supplies the name of one of his teachers,

---

28. The Syrians and the Arabs both had translations of the *Georgics,* which was widely attributed to Democritus but was probably put together by Bolus of Mendes in Egypt during the second century B.C. The Arabs possessed, moreover, a reworking of Aristotle's *On Plants* by Nicolaus of Damascus in the translation of Ishaq ibn Hunayn and the revision of Thabit ibn Qurrah, possibly Theophrastus' *History of Plants,* the *Georgics* of Anatolius of Beirut (fourth–fifth century), of "Balinus" (fifth century), and of Cassianus Bassus (sixth century), the latter work translated first from Greek and then from a Pahlevi version. On the most notorious of the Arabs' "Georgics," the *Nabataean Agriculture* attributed to Ibn Wahshiyah, see Chap. IV, p. 277.

29. The Arabs also knew the Greek derived term *al-kimiya',* and though this term eventually came to be used for the entire science, it was at first applied to actual and somewhat disreputable attempts at transmuting base metals into precious ones.

30. Often confused in some of the later accounts with the Neoplatonic philosopher of the same name who was summoned by Heraclius from Alexandria to teach in Constantinople, and with another "Stephen the Monk," a tenth-century alchemist.

Marinus, a Roman who had migrated to Alexandria and studied alchemy there before being taken on by Khalid.

The various testimonies by and concerning Khalid have been called into serious doubt, because there was almost no evidence for translations from the Greek before the time of Harun, let alone in the era of the Umayyads. That judgment stands in need of serious revision. The witness of Ibn al-Nadim and the bulk of the preserved translations speak directly to the scholastic tradition in Greek philosophy and science, and it is true that in that tradition most of the translation activity began with Harun and Ma'mun. But in the so-called occult sciences, where pseudepigraphy was the prevailing practice, translations were being done far earlier than was once thought probable, and the likelihood that Khalid did sponsor such and was, in effect, an alchemist with access to Greek learning in some form must be seriously entertained.

What precisely was translated is not easy to say. Both Crates of Mallos and the influential Apollonius of Tyana were almost certainly represented at this stage and, if the period is extended down to the reign of Ma'mun, one can add the name of the Byzantine alchemist Zosimus (c. 400), various pseudepigraphs of Socrates, Plato and Aristotle, and possibly the works known as *The Emerald Table* (*Tabula Smaragdina*) and *The Convention.*[31] These are the unmistakable sources of Arab alchemy and if, as now seems likely, they represent the work of anonymous Greek scholars of the period between 400 and 600, then the course of Greek physical science after Zosimus, an exceedingly ill-known period, has at last revealed itself.

The full reworking of these Greek treatises first becomes visible in the work of the sixth Shi'ite Imam Ja'far al-Sadiq and his disciple and associate Jabir ibn Hayyan (d. c. 815). Just as in

---

31. Also known from its Latin translation as the *Turba Philosophorum.* It was literally a convention of his "disciples" summoned by Pythagoras to correct some mistaken ideas, chief among them the belief that alchemy may only be learned by a secret oral tradition. The assembled sages included Parmenides, Socrates and Plato, as well as Moses and Ostanes.

the case of Khalid, doubts have surrounded the scientific work of both these men, particularly Jabir's, whose immense preserved bibliography and sophisticated theories have suggested later, perhaps tenth century, hands at work. Ja'far, on the other hand, had a reputation but very little extant alchemical work to support it. In neither case, however, is it intrinsically unlikely that things were as the ancient authorities said they were: that the doyen of theological Shi'ism interested himself in alchemy,[32] and that Jabir had available the intellectual resources to become the eighth century's most eminent scientist.

According to the traditional accounts, Jabir was the son of a druggist who was executed by the governor of Khurasan in 725 for Shi'ite activities. Jabir himself may have been an agent for the Shi'ite underground in Kufah. He studied alchemy with both Ja'far and a Christian monk whom he met in Syria. He had a good connection with the Barmacids—Yahya ibn Khalid was reputedly his student—but after their fall Jabir was forced to live in concealment in Kufah until his death at the age of ninety, probably in 815. He also bore, somewhat inexplicably, the title "Sufi."

Jabir wrote, on his own telling, some five thousand-odd books. Ibn al-Nadim has recorded a substantial number of titles under his name, and an equally imposing array of works are attributed to him in preserved manuscripts. They cover a broad range of topics: alchemy, philosophy, medicine, physics, mathematics, astronomy, magic and, interestingly, a series of "emendations" of Homer, Pythagoras, Archigenes, Democritus, Socrates, Plato and Aristotle.[33]

By Jabir's own characterization, the alchemist is a manipulator of nature, not by a kind of trial-and-error process, but through a scientific understanding of how natural objects, animal, vegetable

---

32. A Gnostic-type esotericism set in early among supporters of the 'Alids. Al-Mughirah ibn Sa'id (d. 737), for example, was already indulging in speculation on the secret properties of letters in a way not very different from Ja'far's *Book of Jafr*, and another in that same circle, Abu al-Khattab, had a well-deserved reputation as a theological "extremist"; see Chap. VIII, p. 578.

33. Only the *Emendations of Plato* are preserved.

and mineral, are constituted and how they function. The alchemist must study the four basic elements of earth, air, fire and water, and the four basic properties of warm, cold, dry and wet.[34]

The alchemist's particular attention is directed toward gold, since this metal is the perfect natural substance, a perfectly balanced combination of the hot and dry (sulphur) and the cold and wet (mercury). All other metals are formed on exactly the same principles, but they differ from gold in that their constituent proportions are in one way or another faulty. The alchemist's intensive study of properties ends, then, in the production of an agent, and elixir (*al-iksir*), which is potent enough to resolve and so redress the imperfect balance of other metals and thus convert them into perfect gold.

Jabir's cosmology and physics have, for all their professed "emendations," obvious Aristotelian antecedents. Where he departed sharply from those antecedents, however, was in his rare desire to convert the Greeks' qualitative physics of powers and energies into a quantitative science. In the Jabiran system composition is essentially a mixture according to fixed proportions. This is the central theme of Jabir's *Book of Balances* and the heart of his theory. For its implementation he invoked another theory, the occultists' conviction that there is a necessary connection between letters, numbers and natures.[35]

On this unhappy premise Jabir could reduce any substance to number simply by converting the letters of its name into numbers and assigning the numbers thus represented to the various substantial qualities like hot, cold, dry and moist. The number of qualities, their degrees and the proportions that existed between them were derived by another device that was also mathematical but owed nothing to quantitative analysis, the magic square.[36]

---

34. For Jabir these latter are not merely properties of things. They are rather substantial hypostases somewhat in the manner of the Platonic "forms" and dwell in a sphere beyond that of the physical world.
35. And so also music and speech. For Jabir, speech is both the product of convention and a substantial and natural quality of the soul.
36. A magic square is the arrangement of numbers in such a way that each column and each row, as well as the two diagonals, all yield an

Jabir claims to have learned his magic square from "Balinus," and indeed the works of that obscure figure appear to have been a major source for the Muslim alchemist. Jabir also knew and used a number of alchemical pseudepigraphs attributed to Socrates and Plato,[37] but there is an even greater reliance on what he thought to be Aristotle. Jabir did know a great many of the genuine treatises and gives verbal quotations from them:[38] but he was equally interested in the spurious Aristotle of the *Istamakhis*, the *Istamatis* and the Hermetic *Treasure of Alexander*.

Among the earliest of the preserved Islamic alchemists to cite Jabir's work in their own were the notorious occult "agriculturist" Ibn Wahshiyah in the ninth century and Muhammad ibn Umayl al-Tamimi at the very end of the tenth. Like Jabir, Ibn Umayl still had direct access to the pseudepigraphs of late antiquity, and the pages of his *Silver Water* are filled with citations from the various alchemical works of Hermes. His slightly older contemporary, Muhammad ibn Zakariya al-Razi (d. 925), on the other hand, accepted neither Hermes nor Muhammad as a repository of a revealed wisdom and so was immune to the historical presuppositions that informed the Hermetic tradition, that of an esoteric knowledge transmitted from the dawn of ages and embracing the knowledge of both matter and spirit. Razi's training was in the secular version of Greek medicine and philosophy,[39] and his major "alchemical" work, the *Secret of Secrets*,

---

identical sum. Jabir's magic square, and the determinant of his mathematical ratios, was a relatively simple one:

4	9	2
3	5	7
8	1	6

37. One such ascribed to Plato in Arabic is the so-called *Book of the Laws* bearing the same title as the genuine Platonic dialogue but with a very different content.

38. Arabic citations which do not agree with our extant ninth-century versions. Either Jabir had access to early but unknown Arabic versions of the *Aristotelica*—which seems very unlikely—or he was drawing upon Arabic translations of epitomes.

39. See Chap. VI, pp. 440–445.

is more thoroughly chemical than anything produced before or long after in Islam. Instead of esoterica it traded in the analyses of substances and the processes and techniques whereby they might be combined. The elaborate alchemical symbolism is all there—there was no other way to speak of such things except in the inherited language—but beneath it is a sophisticated knowledge of medieval chemistry.

Razi's alchemical successor, "Al-Majriti," already noted as the author of a major work on astrology, the *Picatrix*,[40] and the two "Jabirans" al-'Iraqi (13th century) and al-Jildaki (d. 1342) have little to add to the theories already outlined by Jabir and Razi. There were refinements of technique and apparatus, but the scientific theories behind the work were those already put forward by the Neoplatonists and alchemists of the fifth and sixth centuries.

There were few who denied the alchemists' physical and philosophical theory, but there was more than one voice raised against the reality of the transmutation of metals or anything else. Kindi, Farabi and Ibn Sina, all of whom were drawing upon the same philosophical sources as the alchemists,[41] wrote treatises against the practical claims of alchemy. Ibn Sina was explicit in his acceptance of the theory of the composition of metals, but he was equally certain that they could not be transmuted and that the writings of Jabir and Razi were thus filled with palpable nonsense.

Neither these nor other voices—there is an elaborate round-table debate on alchemy in Tawhidi's (d. 1023) *Pleasure and Conviviality*—drove occultism from the bosom of Islam. It long survived philosophy itself; and even when serious new work ceased to be done in the secular sciences, the occultists were still busy collecting, cataloguing and explaining the techniques of mastering nature. Increasingly those techniques were magical rather than scientific in any sense understood by a Kindi, a Razi

---

40. His alchemical tract, the *Sage's Step*, recommends a careful study of Aristotle, Jabir and Razi.

41. It is noteworthy, however, that neither of the two chief alchemical theoreticians, Jabir and Razi, subscribed to the Neoplatonic theory of emanation embraced, in varying degrees, by the philosophers.

or even a Zosimus. The most popular of the later Islamic treatments of the occult, the *Golden Sun of the Sciences* of al-Buni (d. 1225), is nothing more than an enormously credulous encyclopedia of magic. Buni's "sun" is the alchemists' gold, but its light is fixed almost exclusively on magical recipes, numbers and amulets.

Medical Learning in Islam

Despite the historical pretensions of alchemy, the Muslims' first contact with the methods, techniques and literature of a fully constituted science was likely in the field of medicine, which was already well established in theory and practice across the Semitic East before the expansion of Islam. Here, at any rate, the Muslim scholar could join a living tradition; in almost every other instance he was engaged in the resurrection of a well-preserved but moribund body of knowledge.

Medical science in Islam was, quite simply, Greek medical science. The physical and physiological theories on which most of the medical literature in Arabic was constructed were Hellenic, as were the methods of diagnosis and cure of human illnesses. Nor is the reason complex. Islam learned its medical theory and practice from Syrian physicians who were educated by the books and teachers of Alexandria and taught their Muslim colleagues to appreciate and to use the standard Alexandrian medical curriculum. Islam's proper contribution to the intellectual process was to encourage, by official patronage and private interest, the translation of that curriculum, and much more besides, into Arabic.

The foundation of that curriculum was the theoretical and practical work of Galen, the Hellenized Roman physician of Pergamum, who died about 200. Galen was an enormously gifted synthesizer who summed up the medical achievements of the previous seven centuries in a large number of Greek treatises which, together with the Hippocratic corpus, served succeeding generations of physicians in the East—Roman, Byzantine, Syrian and Arab—as their education and their ideal.

Galenic medicine and, so, Islamic medicine after it, were

founded upon a view of man's physical constitution dominated by the four basic humors—blood, phlegm, yellow bile and black bile—whose mixture in varying degrees within the body determined the organism's health or illness. Ethics, aesthetics and mathematics all converged upon this view of illness as an imbalance of the humors, a disproportion or violation of the natural "mean." The task of the physician was, then, the redress of the imbalance. The change of the humors took place within the organs of the body—in the "cooking" of the digestive process, for example—but the Greek physician concentrated in the first instance on external factors like environment and diet. Failing this, he might proceed to the use of drugs. Earlier Greek physicians did not much favor their use, but in late antiquity therapy by simple or compound drugs became increasingly common. Finally, the physician could resort to surgery.

This view of disease and its cure owed as much to philosophy as to clinical experience. Galen was a distinguished clinician and anatomist, but he was equally convinced of the importance of philosophy for medicine—one of his works, later translated into Arabic, bore the title *That the Best Physician Is a Philosopher*—not merely because it provided the physician with a fundamental physical theory of the macrocosm to which the human microcosm was obviously related, but also because it was the final authority on scientific proof.[42]

With the exception of the Hippocratic corpus and the *Materia Medica* of Dioscurides, for which they had integral translations, the Arabs knew most of Galen's predecessors through the latter's elaborate criticisms and comments. From Galen's own day they knew and used Rufus of Ephesus' therapeutic works and Soranus on gynecology. Among the later Hellenic physicians the Arabs had direct access to the ambitious medical encyclopedia of Oribasius (d. 403), the *Therapeutics* of Alexander of Tralles (d.

---

42. The Arabic Galen provided the Muslim philosopher with a synopsis of the Platonic dialogues (see Chap. IV, p. 287) and a number of commentaries on the Aristotelian *Organon.* Galen also engaged in philosophical controversy with his Peripatetic contemporary Alexander of Aphrodisias, and on this too the Arabs were well instructed through translations.

605) and in the seventh century, the derivative *Memoranda* of Paul of Aegina and the *Pandects* of the priest Ahron. Both of these latter men studied and taught at Alexandria which had become, under the Christian Roman Empire, the almost unique center for the study of medicine.

The Christianizing of the empire had no effect on either the theory of medicine or its teaching at Alexandria, but it did leave its mark on one important area of medical practice. The Roman Empire had both clinics, where doctors could ply their trade on a modest scale, and some kind of medical facilities for the use of the military. But with Constantine a new institution appeared under Christian auspices. The Emperor founded various hostels (*xenodocheia*) for the use of Christian pilgrims. Some of them had medical facilities attached, and out of this complex of travelers' inn and clinic came the first genuine hospitals (*nosokomeia*), institutions whose primary function was the boarding and the treatment of the sick.

From Constantine down to the Muslim invasion, both the Church and the Christian emperors founded hospitals throughout the eastern provinces of the Empire. Often they were connected with church buildings and monasteries, and in some cases the earlier association with a pilgrims' hostel continued. Justinian constructed the famous Samson hospital in Constantinople and built another with two hundred beds in Jerusalem. Every large city must have had some form of a *nosokomeion*, and Alexandria, where the medical tradition was strong, had several. We are told of the Melchite Patriarch John the Almoner founding several lying-in hospitals there, each with forty beds, and then throwing them open to the ill and wounded fleeing from the Persian advance into Syria in 610.[43]

It was also in Alexandria that the cult of the Empire's two most famous physician-saints, John and Cyrus, had its center. The church honoring them was located at Canopus just outside the city, and there and elsewhere the saints presided over a great variety of miraculous cures. Earlier the various temples of Asclepius had been the sites of similar cures, but with the coming of

43. When the Sasanian armies reached Egypt shortly after, John himself became a refugee; see Introduction, pp. 36–37.

Christianity both the methods and the results of temple incubation were transferred to churches and their presiding saints. The long-dead saints would appear to the ill in their sleep and prescribe invariably successful cures. "Where now are those braggarts Hippocrates and Galen and the other tens of thousands who think they are physicians?" triumphantly cried the anonymous author of a collection of such medical miracles.

The followers of Hippocrates and Galen continued to have their share of the business. Some of the sick were driven to the churches to seek their cure for less than spiritual reasons—physicians' fees and the painful horrors of surgery were commonplace complaints in antiquity—but many needed more secular forms of assistance, and here too the Church intervened. There were throughout the Near East guilds of Christian volunteers organized on a semimonastic basis to render help and care to the sick and the poor. The best-known of them was that of the *philoponoi*, "God's laborers," they were called,[44] who had their own hospital for the poor in Alexandria.

Most of this network of secular and religiously inspired medical facilities was still operating when the Muslims burst into the eastern provinces of the Byzantine Empire. The medical school at Alexandria continued to function, and two of its faculty who had a profound influence on Arab medicine, Paul and Ahron, were teaching there when the Arab armies arrived. Thereafter the record is obscure. We are told that the school was transferred to Antioch under 'Umar II (717–720), thence with its library to the scientific center of northern Syria, Harran. This was about 850, but when the final act was played out in Baghdad about 900, it was not medicine but philosophy that the Harranians began teaching in the capital.[45]

Between Paul of Aegina and whenever it was that medical instruction ceased being given in Greek may belong the few otherwise unknown names associated with medical works whose original language was reportedly Greek but which are known

---

44. For one of their number, John, who left his mark on Islam, see Chap. IV, pp. 297–298.
45. See Chap. IV, pp. 328–330.

only in Arabic citation: John the Alexandrian,[46] Stephen, Gessius, Marinus, and someone whom the Arabs called "Anqilawus." All these men were engaged in what appears to have been the final major undertaking of Alexandrian medicine, the preparation of the "Alexandrian Summaries," a synopsis of sixteen major treatises of Galen.

The Syrians of the East were, after the Romans, the chief heirs of Hellenic medical science. One such Syrian Christian, Sergius (d. 536), a priest and physician of Reshayna in northern Mesopotamia, was trained, as has been seen, at the still-flourishing medical school at Alexandria late in the fifth century, and he eventually translated its basic medical curriculum into Syriac. Though Sergius was himself a Monophysite and later a Chalcedonian, at least some of these medical translations were dedicated to a Nestorian bishop, an indication that they may have been intended for use not within Roman territory—the Syrian school at Edessa had been closed down in 489—but in one of the Nestorian centers in the Sasanian Empire.

The chief Nestorian theological school was at Nisibis, and in the end it had a medical as well as a theological faculty; but a far more likely destination for Sergius' medical translations was the curious settlement at Jundishapur, the city founded in Khuzistan by Shapur I for his Roman captives in the war against Valerian. Between its founding in the third century and its later emergence under the early 'Abbasids as the chief Syrian medical center in the Near East not much is known about Jundishapur, but physicians trained there in the ninth century knew of Sergius' translations and based their own Arabic versions on his.

There is not much left of the Syrian medical literature of pre-Islamic times. Its best-preserved example is probably the anonymous medical compendium that was written sometime after Sergius' lifetime and was still being used as a medical source by writers of the ninth century before they had more direct access

---

46. Unless he is indeed identical with John Philoponus. The Arabs thought the two men were the same, but there is no independent evidence that John Philoponus was a physician or that he wrote, as the Arab bibliographers claimed, commentaries on Galen or a *History of Physicians*.

to the Hellenic tradition. More informative are the writings of Syrian physicians and scholars writing in the ninth century. Job of Edessa (d. after 823), the author of the encyclopedic *Book of Treasures*, was still engaged in the translation of Galen for his Syriac-speaking colleagues, while Yuhanna bar Sarabiyun put together, sometime about 873, a Syriac medical compendium (*kunnash*) that shows an easy familiarity with the traditional Greek sources.

From all the evidence the Syrian medical tradition from Sergius in the sixth century to Job and Bar Sarabiyun in the ninth was an offshoot of Greco-Roman learning on the subject, and was nourished by its literary and personal connections with Alexandria. Syrian physicians like Sergius were trained at Alexandria, and the medical synopses which later served as textbooks in Islam, and which the Arabs understood were in use in Jundishapur, were as a matter of fact Alexandrian handbooks.

How soon Sergius' Syriac version of the Alexandrian medical canon began to be read at Jundishapur and how the curriculum there was shaped around it cannot now be said. All that is known is that under the Sasanians the physicians of Jundishapur were highly regarded, and that at the time of Khusraw I (531–579) Zoroastrian and Christian physicians in Iran appeared to know each other's work and were both drawing on the common source of Greek medical learning. At one point during his reign Khusraw was treated by a Christian physician, Joseph, who had trained in the Byzantine Empire, possibly with Sergius, and who later became the Nestorian Catholicus in succession to Mar Aba, another scholar well versed in both Greek science and the work of Sergius.[47]

Just as pious Muslims would later turn to the *Qur'an* for instruction in medical matters, so in Sasanian Iran the *Avesta* was regarded as a repository of medical learning. At least it was treated as such by the Zoroastrian commentators who extracted from those sacred texts a series of rules governing not only the cure of ailments, but the behavior and recompense of physicians. They recognized, as the Greeks did, the standard cures through medication, surgery and fumigation—there was less of a concern

47. See Chap. IV, pp. 321–322.

for "environmental medicine"—to which they added a kind of sacred medicine which relied heavily upon incantation.

It was not an unnatural connection. Not all Greek physicians were naturalists in the style of a Hippocrates or a Galen; Alexander of Tralles, for one, who was well known in Islam, did not hesitate to resort to cures through amulets and other forms of sympathetic magic. As in alchemy, the bonds between spirit and flesh were taken seriously on both sides of the Roman frontier. Thus even the physician of the body had to be skilled in those ailments of the soul that often were the cause of physical ills. The "cure for the ailments of souls," a common motif in the later works of Muslim mysticism, were of equally great concern to the physicians of Sasanian Iran.

Khusraw's court physician Burzoe reveals other dimensions to Sasanian medicine.[48] The Pahlevi translation of the Indian fable book *Kalilah and Dimnah,* known in Sanskrit as *Panchatantra,* was his work, and he prefaced the collection with an autobiographical narrative filled with reflections about himself, his training and his attitude toward medicine.[49] His father was of the Sasanian military aristocracy and his mother from a priestly family. Burzoe's first love was medicine. It brought him success but no peace of mind, and what should have been the high point of his career, a journey of medical research to India under the patronage of the Shah, ended with his bringing back samples of Indian wisdom and not, as Khusraw hoped, an antidote for mortality.

With the accession of a sympathetic Khusraw II in 590 a Christian was promoted to the position of *drustbad,* or chief physician of the realm. This was Gabriel of Shiggar, who reputedly gained his eminence by curing the Shah's Christian wife Shirin of sterility.[50] It may have been his unique medical act;

---

48. On Burzoe, see Introduction, p. 32.

49. The *Kalilah and Dimnah* was translated into Arabic by Ibn al-Muqaffa' (d. 757), but not everyone has been convinced that Ibn al-Muqaffa' did not write the preface himself and attribute it to Burzoe to conceal its somewhat dangerous sentiments.

50. With the assistance of Saint Sergius, the Christian holy man whose memory was venerated at a basilica at Rusafah on the Euphrates. In 590 Khusraw made a dedication there of a gold cross suitably engraved in Greek.

thereafter the *drustbad* appears to have spent most of his time meddling in the complex and explosive ecclesiastical politics of the time.

Gabriel does not cast much light on the history of medical learning in the Near East before Islam. The Nestorian medical tradition is undoubtedly present, but only in the darkened background during the last century of Sasanian rule in the East. Physicians, including Christian ones, stood closer to the throne in Iran than they did at Byzantium, where practical medicine was the concern of both the Church and the state and where theoretical instruction in the science was given at a few great centers like Alexandria.

The Arabs themselves were remote from any form of scientific medicine before Islam. That they suffered from a great deal of sickness is certain, and their vocabulary was expanded to describe the ills the Bedouin flesh was heir to. For their remedies they possessed, however, only an unsophisticated folk medicine, and the term "physician" (*tabib*) was granted to anyone who knew how to apply them. Magic was one remedy, and it appears to have been often prescribed. This was the medical context into which Muhammad was born, and though the *Qur'an* itself shows little interest in physical ills and their cure, Muhammad himself had a number of opinions on the subject, or so it is reported in the traditions.

It is not unlikely that the Prophet was consulted on the bodily ailments suffered by his followers, and some at least of the many *hadith* on that theme must be genuine; they are congruent, at any rate, with contemporary medical thinking among the Arabs. Falling as they did from the mouth of the Prophet, the medical *hadith* were considerably more than folk recipes. Caught up in the general sanctification of Prophetic "traditions," the medical *hadith* constituted in time the matter of a special science, "Prophetic Medicine," which acted like a magnet for forged traditions on everything from the proper clothing to how to administer the evil eye.[51]

Prophetic Medicine was a favorite library pursuit of lawyers

---

51. And was inexorably followed, among the ranks of the Shi'ites, by a "Medicine of the *Imams*."

and tradition collectors, but anyone who could afford it and knew better resorted to a physician trained elsewhere than in the *hadith*. The "foreign" physician appeared early in Islam. The Caliph Mu'awiyah (661–680) had two in his entourage, both Christians. Their names, Ibn Athal and Abu al-Hakam, are pure Arab, and so we do not know how or where they were trained, except that they were both skilled in drugs and, as Christians, probably had nothing to do with Prophetic Medicine. Another physician, this time bearing the Greek name of Theodocus, was the personal physician of the Umayyad governor of Iraq, al-Hajjaj, and he appears to have composed medical works on the preparation of drugs, though in what language is unknown.

The first clear link with Hellenic medicine occurs at the time of Marwan I (684–685), when a Syriac-speaking Jew of Basrah, Masarjawayh, translated from Syriac into Arabic the *Pandects* of the Alexandrian priest and physician Ahron. The Syriac version was the work of an otherwise unknown "Gosios" and must have been accomplished sometime between 640 and 680. Details on Masarjawayh are lacking, but if the attribution is authentic,[52] this medical compendium was the first Hellenic work to find its way into Arabic.

A silence then falls over the sources, but there is evidence from the first major medical works preserved from 'Abbasid times, those by Ibn Masawayh and 'Ali al-Tabari, both of whom were working during the reign of Mutawakkil, that between 750 and 850 Arabic translations were being done from either Greek or Syriac medical works, probably at Baghdad under the auspices of Mansur or Harun.[53] In 765 Mansur summoned to his new capital Jurjis ibn Jibril ibn Bukhtishu' (d. c. 771), the Christian who was the head of the medical school at Jundishapur, to serve as his personal physician; and though neither he nor his son nor his grandson who followed him in the post was personally much

52. There is another (or the same?) Masarjawayh, likely a Christian, who lived at the end of the eighth century.

53. Another important but uncertain piece of evidence is the authenticity of the works attributed to Jabir ibn Hayyan, many of them on medical subjects with explicit references to Hippocrates, Galen and others.

interested in medical theory, their presence at the 'Abbasid court was the signal of the new Muslim interest in Greek learning, including the art of the physician.

And not Greek learning alone. Under the auspices first of Mansur and then of Harun and his Barmacid viziers, Indian science too began to be studied in Baghdad. The learning of India was already known to the Sasanians, as has been seen, and the symbiosis between the Syro-Hellenic tradition of Jundishapur and Indian medicine was already well under way at the court of Khusraw I. Mansur's scholars concerned themselves with Indian astronomy and astrology, but it was the Sanskrit tradition in medicine that excited the interests of Yahya the Barmacid, who invited various Indian physicians to Harun's court and so initiated the work of translating the Indian medical books into Arabic.

With one notable exception, the *Book of Poisons* by "Shanaq," the results of Yahya's interests must be read out of the works of two Muslim authors who wrote in the ninth century and whose works show a fairly detailed knowledge of what they identified as Indian medicine, 'Ali al-Tabari's *Paradise of Wisdom,* written about 850, and the somewhat later *Comprehensive Book* of Razi.[54] Their testimony, when put beside the explicit remarks in Ibn al-Nadim's *Catalogue,* leaves little doubt that Indian medical texts were indeed being translated from Sanskrit into Arabic, with or without a Syriac intermediary, late in the eighth century.

The *Catalogue* supplies some names, and the most substantial among them is that of Mankah, one of the group of Indians brought to Baghdad by Yahya. Mankah worked at Harun's hospital in the capital and according to one report eventually embraced Islam. He is credited with a number of translations, but only one of them survives, the *Book of Poisons* written by "Shanaq." This latter is actually the Indian Canakya, and a comparison of the Sanskrit work preserved under his name with the

---

54. These are only the earliest and clearest examples of the Muslims' knowledge of Indian medicine; the same kind of material is present in the work of later authors like Abu Mansur al-Muwaffaq of Herat, the tenth-century author of a Persian book on drugs (see p. 392), and al-Biruni, Islam's most sophisticated connoisseur of things Indian.

Arabic *Book of Poisons* shows that the two treatises, though differing on many points, are indeed related. According to Muslim accounts, Mankah translated "from Indian into Persian,"[55] whence it came into Arabic under the hand of al-'Abbas ibn Sa'id during the Caliphate of Ma'mun.

Muslim authors like Tabari and Razi knew other Indian medical works by Susruta and Caraka, and these too must have found their way into Arabic before the *Paradise of Wisdom* was written in the middle of the ninth century. But what the Arabs learned from their classical Indian mentors in medicine was a great deal of information, particularly in pharmacology, and very little theory. Arab medicine as a science was neither created nor sustained by these interesting early contacts with India but by an intensive study of Hellenic theory. Both Tabari and Razi, who appreciated Indian medicine, recognized it as a secondary growth.

The activity of Harun's Indian savants appears to have centered around the hospital (*bimaristan*) founded in Baghdad by the Caliph and the first of many in Islam. It too had its connections with Jundishapur. One of the Bukhtishu' family, Jibril, supervised its organization. Masawayh worked there after a distinguished career at Jundishapur, and later his son Yuhanna (d. 857) became the director of the Baghdad *bimaristan*. Yuhanna ibn Masawayh wrote his own medical work in Arabic, the first important Christian physician to have done so, and somewhat later in his career he led the earliest organized attempt at turning the body of Hellenic medical literature into Arabic. Ibn Masawayh was himself responsible for some of the translations, which were done on Greek manuscripts gotten at Ancyra and Amorium during Harun's campaigns against the Byzantines in Anatolia. What they were like we cannot say, since they are lost, as are those of his contemporary Abu Yahya al-Bitriq (d. c. 800), who undertook the translation of some of Galen's works.

There would be many translations to follow, but the best evidence for the progress of Islamic medicine in the mid-ninth

---

55. What "Persian" means in this context is probably *Syriac*, a notice that ties Mankah somewhat more closely to Christian Jundishapur than to a purely Muslim context.

century is the encyclopedic *Paradise of Wisdom* of 'Ali ibn Sahl, the son of a Christian scholar (*rabban*) of Merv. 'Ali began his own career as the secretary of a local ruler in Tabaristan, but during the reigns of Mu'tasim, Wathiq and Mutawakkil (833–861) he was connected with the Caliphal court at Samarra. He converted to Islam and, like Jahiz, won favor in Mutawakkil's eyes by publicly attacking Christianity in a *Refutation of the Christians* and by an equally spirited defense of Islam in his *Book of Religion and Empire*.

The *Paradise of Wisdom* is a convincing sign of how little we know of how the Muslim of the early ninth century came by his medical learning. An interesting appendix to the work is given over to Indian medicine and this accords with the Barmacids' encouragement of translations from Sanskrit into Arabic in the previous century; but 'Ali al-Tabari was also well instructed on the Hellenic medical classics, Hippocrates, Galen, and others. And however he came to this knowledge, it was apparently not through the translations of those authors by Hunayn ibn Ishaq. Like Ibn Masawayh before him, 'Ali al-Tabari may have been drawing immediately upon Syriac works.

The *Paradise of Wisdom* is professedly a compendium designed to lead the student of medicine from the foundations to an understanding of therapeutics. Those foundations were profoundly philosophical and profoundly Greek. 'Ali described his father as a man learned in both philosophy and medicine, and it is apparent that his son shared this interdisciplinary view. The name of Aristotle, for 'Ali simply "the Philosopher," appears as often in the opening chapters as that of Hippocrates, and it was Aristotle's physical and psychological treatises that provided the material for 'Ali's summary exposition of the organization of the cosmos and the physical and psychic constitution of man. The *Paradise* was intended, after all, for "the physician of the body and the soul."

'Ali al-Tabari's introduction to the *Paradise of Wisdom* is standard Greek medical theory as synthesized by Galen and compacted into handbooks by his successors. 'Ali's knowledge of them may have been synthetic as well, drawn from Syriac handbooks not unlike his own. But there also appeared in his book the new name of Hunayn ibn Ishaq, the gifted physician and translator who finally promoted Islamic medicine to the point where the best Greek and Roman practitioners and theoreticians had left off. Tabari knew of Hunayn but not of his new translations from the Greek; for the Hellenic tradition he was still relying on the older Syriac versions and what he could learn from Job of Edessa's *Book of Treasures*.

Hunayn (809–873), the son of a Nestorian Christian druggist of Hirah, studied medicine at Jundishapur and Baghdad under both Jibril ibn Bukhtishu' and Ibn Masawayh, and then spent two years in Byzantine Anatolia, where he learned Greek and hunted down manuscripts, perhaps under a commission for the family of mathematicians known as the Banu Musa. By birth a Syriac speaker and now a student of Greek, Hunayn went on his return to Basrah, where he studied Arabic with the lexicographer al-Khalil ibn Ahmad. The connection with Jibril led to favors from Ma'mun and then, when Ibn Masawayh died in 857, Hunayn was appointed to succeed him as the personal physician to al-Mutawakkil. Al-Mutawakkil himself died in 861, but Caliphal patronage continued under his successors for another ten years. In the end, however, Hunayn was involved in a court intrigue and died, out of favor with the Caliph and his own Catholicus, in 873.

In 856 Hunayn wrote a letter summing up his translations to date of the corpus of Galen: he had at that point translated from Greek into Syriac or from Syriac into Arabic over 125 treatises of the Roman Empire's most eminent medical man. For each treatise Hunayn remarked on the translation history and gave some brief indication of the techniques that he and his associates, notably his son Ishaq and his nephew Hubaysh, used in doing the translations. One man normally did the Syriac version and handed it over to a second for the Arabic; or else they used one of the earlier Syriac translations, by Sergius, for example. In any case they were careful to work from the best manuscripts available and to collate both manuscripts and previous translations before beginning their own work. Hunayn reviewed and revised the work of the others, as in the case of Stephen's translation of the *Materia Medica* of Dioscurides, where Stephen had considerable difficulty in finding the right Arabic expressions for the technical terms and so frequently resorted, as earlier the Syrians had done, to transcribing Greek names into Arabic letters instead of translating them. Hunayn, with his considerable knowledge of Arabic lexicography, supplied the correct Arabic terms.

The results were remarkably good translations, congruent with our own best Greek texts and done on Greek manuscripts that are far older than those on which the modern editor of Galen works.[56] Later Arab editors were to work over, though not substantially revise, his translations of Aristotle, but the work of Hunayn and his "school" of translators on Galen, Hippocrates, Rufus of Ephesus, Oribasius, Dioscurides, and Paul of Aegina remained the unrivaled standard.

Hunayn's connection with Hippocrates and Galen ran back through the medical schools at Alexandria. The work of both physicians was transmitted to the Arabs enclosed within the protective folds of a "canon" that referred not so much to questions of authenticity as to which texts were basic to a medical curriculum.[57] In the case of Hippocrates there were ten such works, and, for Galen, sixteen. There were also bio-bibliographical treatments of both authors, not unlike that given to Aristotle in the philosophy courses at Alexandria.

The clearest indication that the Arabs inherited a curriculum rather than individual manuscripts of an author who happened to interest them is the so-called "Alexandrian Summaries," a digest of sixteen treatises of the Galenic canon. Its form is unmistakably that of a schoolbook, but Hunayn has provided more explicit confirmation. In his letter on his translations of Galen he set down his own list of twenty basic texts and then added that these were the books and this was the order of their reading followed in the medical school at Alexandria, the same books and the same order that are followed "even to this day by our Christian compatriots in their schools." The Christians' school was, of course, Jundishapur, and other of Hunayn's own works show something of the academic style there, his propaedeutic *Introduction to*

---

56. Most of the extant Greek manuscripts of Galen date from the fifteenth century. There is, moveover, a substantial amount of Galen preserved *only* in Arabic translation.

57. The Arabs did understand that the Hippocratic corpus was a composite work done by a number of different hands.

Medicine, the catechetical *Questions on Medicine*, and a diagrammatic treatment of the same subject.

Hunayn was far more than a translator; he was one of Islam's better-known ophthalmologists. His *Ten Questions on the Eye* was actually little more than a compendium of Greek theory on that organ, and though it was criticized on that score even by Muslims, it and Hunayn's other works on the subject set the standard of ophthalmology for Islamic physicians.

With Hunayn's son Ishaq (d. 910) the Muslim received his first instruction on the history of medicine. That history was Greek, and Ishaq probably translated and reworked a *History of Physicians* attributed to "John the Grammarian," perhaps John Philoponus or an Alexandrian physician of the same name living a century after Philoponus. Ishaq or his source did attempt to sort out the chronology of the ancient physicians,[58] and so was perhaps justified in calling his book an "era-work" (*ta'rikh*), but much of what was found there belonged to the same kind of "ethical biography" favored by the Greeks and now becoming popular in Islam. Ishaq ibn 'Ali of Edessa's *Culture of the Physician*[59] contained a number of such biographies of both ancient and Islamic physicians, and Ishaq's contemporary Ibn al-Daya (d. 910) wrote a *Narratives of Physicians* in much the same vein.

A great deal of this material came to rest in the great biographical dictionaries of physicians by al-Qifti (d. 1248) and Ibn abi Usaybi'ah (d. 1270), but Ishaq's *History of Physicians* found a more proximate use. He supplied Ibn al-Nadim with most of what the latter knew about Greek medical history up to the time of Galen—the *Catalogue*'s chronology of physicians living after Galen is exceedingly sparse. Ibn al-Nadim's interests lay in bibliography rather than in anecdotes, but there were those who found employment for the anecdotes as well, Abu Sulayman al-Sijistani in his *Garden of Wisdom*[60] and al-Mubashshir in his *Epitome of Wisdom* written in 1049.

---

58. And even to relate them, though not very successfully, with Iranian dynastic chronology.
59. On this genre, see Chap. VI, p. 410.
60. Abu Sulayman's *Garden* deals only with Greek savants, but it was brought forward into Islamic times by 'Ali ibn al-Qasim al-Bayhaqi (d. 1169) in his *Continuation*.

Two of Ishaq's contemporaries who had far wider scientific interests devoted at least part of their energies to medicine. The Sabian Thabit ibn Qurrah is far better known as a mathematician and philosopher, but the important medical collection *The Treasure* is probably from his pen; the author knew, at any rate, a good deal about both Greek and Indian medicine. The former provided him with his theory, but *The Treasure* had its own interesting comments to make on the detection and cure of diseases. Another wide-ranging scholar was Qusta ibn Luqa (d. 912) of Baalbek, one of the rare men of his time who could, like Hunayn, work in Greek, Syriac and Arabic. Like Hunayn, too, Qusta improved his Greek across the Byzantine frontier in Anatolia and then, beginning about 860, worked as a translator for various Caliphal patrons in Baghdad. Qusta's translation work through half a century ranged across the entire scientific and philosophical spectrum from Galen, Hero and Euclid to Aristotle, where he translated Alexander of Aphrodisias' and John Philoponus' important commentaries on the *Physics*.

Qusta, too, was far more than a translator. His own work centered largely on astronomy, mathematics and medicine—more than fifty of his medical works are preserved in manuscript—and it shows, almost a century before Ibn al-Nadim wrote his *Catalogue*, the degree to which Greek scientific learning had succeeded in creating not merely new Arab scientists but a genuine polymath. Qusta's intellectual formation owed nothing to Islam except its patronage; he was an Alexandrian suddenly restored to life in Baghdad in the ninth century.

To that same generation of the Sabian Thabit ibn Qurrah and the Christians Ishaq ibn Hunayn and Qusta ibn Luqa belonged the *Dar al-Islam's* most famous physician, who recognized neither Christianity nor Islam, Muhammad ibn Zakariya al-Razi.[61] He studied medicine at Baghdad—with whom is not certain—then at his native Rayy. After another stay in Baghdad, probably as the director of a *bimaristan*, he returned to Rayy for good and was in charge of the hospital there until his death.

---

61. See Chap. VI, pp. 440–445.

Razi's bibliography, compiled and annotated by al-Biruni, comprises 184 works on a great variety of Hellenic sciences, including 56 devoted solely to medicine. Of these, two have gained a particular celebrity. The *Comprehensive Book,* is an immense posthumous medical encyclopedia based on Greek, Syriac and Indian literary sources, and on Razi's own considerable clinical experience. Earlier he had written for the Samanid prince of Khurasan a shorter type of *kunnash* entitled *The Medicine of Mansur,* in which he provided an annotated epitome of Greek medical theory in anatomy, physiology and *materia medica,* and its application in surgery, toxicology and the cure of fevers.

Razi's reputation in Islam rested principally upon his control of the immense Hellenic medical learning displayed in the *Comprehensive Book,* but modern students of his work have been more impressed by another quality of Razi, his obvious interest in and aptitude for clinical observation. The elaborate theorizing of the *Comprehensive Book* is sprinkled with Razi's own observations on symptoms and cures, and in another of his works, *On Smallpox and Measles,* those two infectious diseases, not well understood by Razi's Greek predecessors, were given a classical descriptive analysis.

Razi was both a physician in the Hellenic naturalist tradition and an authentic, if mitigated, alchemist. Though the combination appears contradictory to our eyes, it was not entirely unnatural in ninth-century Islam. Astrology and alchemy rested upon the same scientific premises as medicine. Kindi, who wrote frequently on medical subjects, was a convinced astrologer,[62] and one of his treatises is addressed precisely to their combination, *On the Application of Astronomical Signs to Medicine.* In the next generation the Christian Ibn al-Salt al-Katib wrote a handbook on astral medicine (*al-tibb al-najumi*). For them as for Razi, the external and occult properties of things were part of a single complex, and their study, the preserve of physics, medicine and alchemy, was purely scientific. *Occult* was not a synonym for *supernatural* as we understand that latter word, nor was

62. See p. 363 and Chap. VI, pp. 438–439.

medicine restricted to the cure of physical diseases. Another of Razi's works, *On Spiritual Medicine*, belongs to a tradition that goes back to the Sasanian and Greek theoreticians of the art.

An argument has been made, by one who was both an Islamicist and a physician, that Razi was the greatest medical man produced under Islam. What is more important than the superlative is the fact that Razi, whatever his relative position, had many rivals. The science of medicine (*'ilm al-tibb*), already at full maturity between 850 and 900, attracted generation after generation of skilled and learned men who had at their disposal not merely a rich literary tradition but excellent clinical facilities. In the first half of the ninth century Baghdad was dotted with *bimaristans*, each supported by its own inalienable endowment (*waqf*), staffed with physicians trained in specialties, and provided with teaching facilities. There were even traveling dispensaries in Baghdad, and the entire hospital system in the capital had a medical superintendent.[63]

The Buyids continued the earlier practice of patronizing medicine, and one of the finest and most elaborate of the medieval *bimaristans* was founded in Baghdad by 'Adud al-Dawlah in 982.[64] An old, but patently incorrect, tradition connects al-Razi with the foundation of this hospital. The first director is uncertain, but a more likely candidate than the long-dead Razi is 'Adud al-Dawlah's own physician, 'Ali ibn 'Abbas al-Majusi (d. 994), the "Haly Abbas" of the medieval West, and the author of a medical encyclopedia known by a variety of titles—one of them, *Al-Kunnash al-maliki* became *Liber Regius* in Latin translation—which opens with an interesting critique of the author's Hellenic and Islamic predecessors, including al-Razi, whom 'Ali found either too long in the *Comprehensive Book* or too brief in the *Mansur*.

To remedy this, 'Ali ibn 'Abbas wrote his own *kunnash* dedi-

---

63. The first to hold the post was the Christian physician and translator Abu 'Uthman al-Dimashqi, who was appointed in 914 by the vizier 'Ali ibn 'Isa. He was succeeded by the Sabian Sinan ibn Thabit, the personal physician of the Caliphs al-Muqtadir and al-Qahir.

64. On Buyid Baghdad, see Chap. VII, pp. 529–535.

cated to 'Adud al-Dawlah. The *Royal Collection* is indeed an improvement on the *Comprehensive Book* in that it organized in a clear and practically useful way the knowledge essential for a physician in the diagnosis and cure of diseases. At about the same time Abu al-Hasan al-Tabari, the personal physician of Rukn al-Dawlah (932–977) who studied with the same teacher as 'Ali ibn 'Abbas, was reducing Hippocratic medicine to an equally useful form. His *Hippocratic Treatments* was intended to introduce the medical student who had no philosophical background to diagnosis and therapeutics. After a preliminary treatise on the various technical terms Abu al-Hasan classified the diseases according to the affected part of the body, from the head to the internal organs.

Medical and philosophical circles in Baghdad were closely connected from the beginning, and their association became even closer in the tenth century. The Christians Ibn Zur'ah (d. 1008), Ibn Suwar (d. 1017), and Ibn al-Tayyib (d. 1043) were all both physicians and translators or editors of Aristotle. The last-named lectured at 'Adud al-Dawlah's hospital in the capital and had another philosopher-physician, Ibn Butlan (d. 1063), as his student and also trained one of Islam's most famous ophthalmologists, 'Ali ibn 'Isa, surnamed "the oculist" (*al-kahhal*),[65] who died in the middle of the eleventh century and was the author of the influential *Memorandum of the Oculists*, where for the first time in the literature a surgical anesthetic is prescribed.

The Buyids did not neglect the provinces, and from Rayy to Khwarazm there were physicians of some clinical skill and a solid theoretical foundation. In Khwarazm, al-Biruni had met two of them, the Christian 'Isa ibn Yahya al-Masihi, a native of Khwarazm like Biruni, and his gifted Muslim student Ibn Sina. Biruni went off to Ghazna in 1017, but the other two, master and disciple, must have left in the opposite direction some years earlier. Ibn Sina, who was only eighteen years old when he was with al-Masihi, on his own testimony had been practicing medicine for

65. The "professional" derivative of the word *kuhl* ("kohl") the preparation of antinomy used as both an eye treatment and a cosmetic in Egypt from the earliest times.

two years before that. "Medicine," he noted in his autobiography, "is not a difficult science and naturally I excelled in it in a short time."

The rest of the passage suggests that Ibn Sina was largely self-educated in medical theory—al-Masihi is gracelessly omitted from the autobiography—and chiefly in the library of his Samanid patron Nuh ibn Mansur (d. 997). The young Ibn Sina was a voracious reader and the library was apparently an excellent one, and so the clinical results were generally happy.[66] Given a brief period of leisure, Ibn Sina composed his *Medical Canon,* which quickly became one of the standard medical textbooks in Islam, chiefly, one supposes, for its arrangement and Ibn Sina's prestige rather than for its impressive learning; its advance on similar earlier works by Razi and 'Ali ibn 'Abbas was negligible.

Though Ibn Sina and Biruni wrote the bulk of their work in Arabic, they did not completely scorn Persian as a vehicle for scientific prose. The vernacular tradition was growing stronger in Iran in the eleventh century, and in medicine it had a longstanding native tradition to draw on. Even in the earliest medical writings under Islam many of the drugs bore Persian names as a barely audible testimony to a Sasanian pharmacology. The first scientific work in Persian prose was a drug book, *The Fundamentals of the True Properties of Remedies,* written by Abu Mansur al-Muwaffaq of Herat under the patronage of the Samanid al-Mansur (961–976), the father of Ibn Sina's own patron.

The Iranian sequel was constant, if not distinguished. The philosopher-physician was as familiar a figure in Iran as he was in Baghdad and Cairo, though he normally chose to write in Arabic. Fakhr al-Din al-Razi (d. 1209), for example, Ibn Sina's theological opponent, also commented upon his *Canon,* but in Arabic. About a century after Ibn Sina, Iran received its own *Canon* in

---

66. Ibn Sina failed, however, to cure himself of the "colic" that followed upon his frequent indulgence in sexual activities. Though final, the test was not, perhaps, entirely fair, since his enemies were tampering with the dose.

Persian, *The Treasure of the Khwarazmshah,* dedicated to Qutb al-Din Muhammad (1097–1127) by Zayn al-Din Sayyid Isma'il al-Jurjani (d. 1136). Like its Arabic ancestors, the *Treasure* is an immense work, but we can only speculate about its use, since almost nothing is known about medical education in eastern Iran. We do know that there were in those parts physicians, princely patronage and an informed understanding of what was going on in the *bimaristans* farther west. So much can be deduced from an intriguing glimpse of the intellectual life in Iran provided by the *Four Treatises* written in Persian by Nizami 'Arudi in about 1155 for his Ghurid patrons in Afghanistan.

The medieval medical historian allowed no such obscurity to fall upon affairs in Iraq, Syria and Egypt. At Baghdad in the generation after Ibn al-Tayyib the medical scene continued to be dominated by Christians: the restless Ibn Butlan, who ended his life in a monastery in Antioch after some unfortunate experiences with colleagues in Egypt; his friend from the Baghdad days and the last prominent member of the famous Bukhtishu' family, Abu Sa'id 'Ubaydallah (d. 1058); and Ibn Jazlah (d. 1100), who converted to Islam in 1074 and who, like Ibn Butlan, pioneered a new pedagogical technique in medicine by reducing diseases and their cures to a tabular format reminiscent of the astronomical tables. The final great name in Baghdad was likewise a Christian, Ibn al-Tilmidh (d. 1165), the director general of the Baghdad hospitals and the teacher of a great number of students who in the subsequent years spread out through the new hospitals in Syria and Egypt.

Under the Greeks and Romans, Alexandria in Egypt was, with Pergamum, the foremost center of medical studies in the ancient world. It is certain that it was still functioning when the Arabs arrived there, but for the new conquerors of Egypt Alexandria was a Byzantine enclave which they neglected in favor of Fustat. The Greek sciences were not much cultivated in that military and commercial city, and medicine too appears to have languished in the Umayyad and 'Abbasid province. Fustat did not even possess a hospital until Ibn Tulun had one constructed there in 872–874. But in 969 a new power came to Egypt, the Fatimids, and with them an interest in the Greek sciences in general—

Isma'ili theory rested heavily upon them—and medicine in particular.[67] Their vizier in Cairo, Ibn Killis (d. 990), the real founder of al-Azhar, had as his personal physicians the Palestinian pharmacologist al-Tamimi and the gynecologist al-Baladi, two respectable, if not distinguished, theoreticians.

Distinction came to Egypt under al-Hakim (996–1021), the erratic Caliph who drew tighter the links between Hellenic learning and Isma'ili propaganda. He founded his "House of Science" in Cairo in 1005 to serve the Isma'ili cause along the lines already explored by the Brethren of Purity.[68] Al-Hakim's court was graced by a number of physicians including the famous Ibn al-Haytham and 'Ali ibn Ridwan (d. 1068), a sometime astrologer—he wrote a commentary on Ptolemy's *Tetrabiblos*—and the medical man with whom Ibn Butlan became engaged in controversy during his stay in Cairo in 1050.

The debate, of which we have an elaborate report, ranged widely from medical minutiae to profound questions of medical education and philosophy. Ibn Ridwan was at a distinct disadvantage; he was self-taught in medicine, while Ibn Butlan had studied with the learned Ibn al-Tayyib in Baghdad and had traveled widely. The final word probably belonged to the Christian, but Ibn Ridwan had no reason to be ashamed of his work. His *Prevention of Bodily Ills in Egypt* is a masterly study of environment and health in Cairo and one of the best Islamic works on infectious diseases.

In the next century the powerful rulers of both Syria and Egypt endowed their capitals with magnificent new hospitals, Nur al-Din's in Damascus sometime after 1154 and Salah al-Din's in Cairo in 1171. The two *bimaristans* drew medical talent from all over the *Dar al-Islam* and especially from among Ibn al-Tilmidh's students at the 'Adudi Hospital in Baghdad. From the West came the Spanish Jew Musa ibn Maymun (Maimonides), who had arrived in Egypt as an *émigré* about 1165. It was the last

---

67. See Chap. IX, p. 639. The Fatimid *Mahdi* 'Ubaydallah took into his personal service at Qayrawan the Jewish physician Ishaq al-Isra'ili (d. 932), a native Egyptian, who was attached to the court of the Aghlabids in Ifriqiyah.

68. See Chap. VIII, pp. 613–616.

troubled days of Fatimid rule in Egypt, and with the change of dynasty Maimonides passed into the service of the new Ayyubid house as the personal physician of Salah al-Din's son, al-Malik al-'Aziz.[69] Salah died in 1193, and between 1200 and 1218 the Syrian and Egyptian holdings of his family were united under his brother al-Malik al-'Adil who in 1210 appointed his own physician, the Damascene al-Dakhwar, a medical superintendent of both provinces.

Despite his administrative duties, al-Dakhwar (d. 1230) continued to write, chiefly commentaries on Galen and Hippocrates, and to lecture at the Nuri *bimaristan* in Damascus. It was one of his students there, the medical historian Ibn abi Usaybi'ah, to whom we owe much of what we know about Islamic physicians and their work. Another student of al-Dakhwar was Ibn al-Nafis (d. 1288), the extraordinary theoretician who deduced the minor circulation of the blood centuries before it was suspected in the West.

Islam knew, then, the entire range of the Hellenic quadrivium and its related sciences. But it knew them as disciplines rather than as a curriculum. Under the Romans and their Byzantine successors all of these same sciences were reduced to the handbook form best known from the preserved Latin examples and in that manner became part of a state-supported school system spread from Gaul to Anatolia and Egypt. The Muslim inherited the handbooks and, unlike the Romans, eventually searched out the authors behind them; what they did not inherit was the schools. Thus the *eisagoge* complex became a purely literary device instead of the pedagogical instrument it was originally intended to be. The Hellenic sciences became the preserve of the scholar while remaining outside the mosque schools and *madrasahs*, which taught only the "Arab sciences." Not even the extraordinary "academies" like the "House of Wisdom" founded by Ma'mun in Baghdad or the similar institution organized by al-

69. Maimonides' medical works were all written in Arabic, but were soon translated into Hebrew. The best-known is his *Aphorisms*, mostly taken from Galen but including a few of his own reflections. He also composed an epitome of Galen, a commentary of the *Aphorisms* of Hippocrates, and some original treatises on various medical problems.

Hakim in Cairo were schools in the Greek or Roman sense; they were more properly research centers for advanced work in the sciences. Only in medicine, where the *bimaristan* undertook to give some formal instruction, could the interested student indulge his attraction to the Hellenic sciences by going to school. In all other cases he had to seek out private instruction, just as he did in philosophy.

Across the border, within the Byzantine Empire, education meant, even in that most Christian of states, education on the venerable Hellenic model. In Islam there were some who possessed such an education, and the figure of the Hellenic *hakim* stood near the center of the intellectual life in Islam. But at the same time it was possible to be adequately educated on a completely different and in no way inferior model, as a lawyer or a *littérateur* without the slightest knowledge of or interest in Hellenic learning. There were highly educated Muslims who had never heard of Euclid, Ptolemy or "Aristutalis."

VI
THE SEARCH FOR THE CENTER

The Arab, once the inhabitant of oasis and steppe, dismounted from his conquests and settled into new quarters in the Near East. Some of these were of his own making, like the garrison cities of Fustat, Basrah and Kufah, and they reflected in their somewhat disorderly way the tribal values and structure of his earlier life. Others were the former show places of Hellenism, Antioch and Alexandria, for example, or even older cities like Jerusalem, Damascus and Gaza, which were hybridized versions of Greek and Semitic styles.

What was left of the Greek style was little more than marble and limestone in the eighth century. The proud Near Eastern *poleis* with their tradition of civil autonomy had long been in decline, and from the time of Justinian onward the urban communities of the Eastern Roman Empire were governed either by a local bishop or by a military commander who dispensed a version of martial law over an entire province. By the time the Arabs came to those cities the local government aristocracy, the *curiales,* were ruined and the institutions of self-government, the magistracies and councils descended from the classical Hellenic *polis,* were little more than a memory. Of a thousand-year tradition of municipal self-government in the Near East the Muslim Arabs inherited only the keepers of records, scribes and bureaucrats who could work in the Caliph's chancery.

Of Greco-Roman magistracies they probably felt they had little need. The new Arab conquerors ruled in the name of an Islamic Law and not the Theodosian Code, and that Law of Islam, which descended in the main from tribal practices regulating the conduct of individuals, knew and cared nothing for municipal autonomy. City, town and village were all equal and undistinguished parts of the Islamic *ummah*. They were ruled, according to their size, by a delegate of the Caliph, a member of his family or, more frequently in the mid-ninth century, by a military commander from a rising new caste, the Turkish captains who were assuming the military mastery of the Caliphate.

The Arabs changed the shape of the older Hellenic cities into which they settled. Many of the *poleis* had been planned settlements, laid out, as the landscape permitted, according to a rational and regular scheme that reflected the political and economic structure of the *polis:* broad avenues and an open market place, gymnasia, temples and government buildings. The Arabs crowded in and over the ground plan and in time changed the face of the Greco-Roman city into a far more irregular organism. Avenues became streets, and streets lanes. Only a mosque was needed; the Muslim governor lived where and how he could.

The chief garrison towns of Fustat, Basrah and Kufah were purely Arab creations, raw and unfinished in appearance. Their original purpose was military, to canton the Arab troopers, but they shared directly and proportionately in the booty won by those troopers, and their prosperity attracted other, nonmilitary interests. These were commercial in the first instance, but soon the garrison towns of Iraq became centers of the new intellectual life of an Arab Islam, where piety and nostalgia came together to create the early Islamic sciences around the study of the *Qur'an*.

The Umayyads ruled from Damascus, a Syrian city not of their own making. The 'Abbasids won their victory in the East and ruled from there, not, however, in the unwalled and unprotected garrisons of Basrah and Kufah, but in a new Islamic "City of Peace," which was, paradoxically, a palace fortress. Mansur likely had the garrison towns in mind when he put down the plans of Baghdad; but, unlike the *amsar*, his city came about from design and possessed not a governor's house but an imperial palace. The new city was strongly protected by its circular walls. Within them, troops were quartered, and outside, in the rapidly growing environs of the Round City, lived the 'Abbasids' clients and auxiliaries, now no longer exclusively Arab, but polyglot in the manner of the new empire.

The City of Peace was an international capital adorned with the rich rewards of success and thronged by the victors, their captives and their clients. The Caliphs lived like grandees in their courts. They brought new life to a moribund Iraq and illuminated even remote corners of Iran only fitfully visible under the Sasanians. In the sometimes odd and sometimes skillfully authentic accent of acquired Arabic, the Iranian *mawali* came to serve where their fathers had served before them, in the *diwans* of the Caliphal court. Christians too, unconvinced by Islam, attended the Caliphs as physicians and interpreters of another culture, the Hellenic, which they had preserved as carefully as their religion.

The mix was rich and teeming with new life. Hellenism and the Iranian tradition were thrust in upon the rapidly maturing "Arab sciences" with profoundly shocking effects. Had their collision been simply an intellectual one, the terms of a peaceful syncretism would doubtless have been painless. As it was, not merely were value systems concealed behind the classificatory schemata, but national aspirations too were at hand. The Arabs were still haltingly but not unsuccessfully attempting to reconcile the Bedouin ethos that continued to give them their Arab identity with the supratribal claims of Islam. When they were confronted with a scientific Hellenism that was in some way connected with Christianity, and with an Iranian wisdom with its own Zoroastrian and Sasanian resonances, the clash of religion, politics and culture had necessarily to be painful.

In one form or another these shocks of encounter occasionally became the Caliph's concern, when his *qadis* had to deal with charges of heresy, for example; but more generally, during the first century of the 'Abbasids, the three-cornered battle between Arabia, Hellas and Iran was fought on paper by secretaries and scribes, by propagandists, philosophers and poets, and on the twin issue of *adab* and *shu'ubiyah*.

A Muslim Paideia

The notion of an Arabic literary tradition is only imperfectly revealed within the capacious connotations of the word *adab*. In its earliest use among the Arabs *adab* meant something close to *sunnah*, the customary norms of behavior, the Bedouin style displaced by Islam and for which it eventually substituted its own concept of "the *sunnah* of the Prophet." The substitution was far from complete: *adab*, though refined by Islam, continued to carry the meaning of a certain time-honored and, so, praiseworthy manner of behavior. What constituted such behavior changed, of course, with the shifting of the Islamic political and cultural focus from Mecca and Medina to the urban centers of Syria and Iraq. Bedouin refinement yielded to urban refinement, and in this latter sense the man who possessed *adab* was characterized by his wit, his civility and his elegance.

Urbanization was accompanied by intellectualization. The practice of Islam took up company with the study of Islam and generated the science of jurisprudence. *Adab* too progressed from behavior to understanding. Toward the end of the Umayyad period the man of *adab*, the *adib*, was identified by his learning not in the religious sciences but in the secular learning inherited from the pre-Islamic tradition, an interest in and an understanding of the "battle days of the Arabs," the *jahili* poetry and the antiquities of Arabia.

This is where matters stood past the turn of the second Islamic century. Under the rubric of *adab* the pre-Islamic culture of the Arabs survived the coming of Islam because it had found a legitimate place as an *ancilla revelationis*, as when Ibn Ishaq, the biographer of the Prophet, drew on his pre-Islamic sources to erect a kind of "Evangelical Preparation" for the coming of Islam. It was not, however, the term of its evolution.

Under the first 'Abbasid Caliphs the Muslim community took cognizance of the traditions of the conquered peoples—not, to be sure, overtly in their religious manifestations, but in the more secular form of Greek learning and the complex literary and ethical tradition of Iran. The effect of this new learning on the structure of the intellectual life in Islam has already been discussed; here it is a question of its repercussions on what had been evolving as *adab*, the culture of the Muslim gentleman. The Greek translations brought a new vision of the universe and some of the marvels therein; historical and geographical perspectives were opened. Their passage into Islam aroused apprehensions among some of the pious traditionalists who understood the dangers of the new learning. But in circles connected with the cultivation of *adab* the novelties of Hellenism, which came to the Arabs chiefly in a technical, methodological and informational sense—they learned little of true Greek *paideia* or of Ciceronian *humanitas*—caused little controversy.

The Arabs' introduction to Iranian culture was, however, of a different sort. Even as reported by the Greeks of an earlier day, the Iranian tradition was bound to the ethical and moral sensibilities of an aristocratic chivalry. Some of the literature embodying that ideal may have been available in its Pahlevi version, but with its translation into the new Islamic *koine*, Arabic, particularly from the time of Ibn al-Muqaffa', the popular and courtly ethic of the Sasanians made its appearance among the *mawali* newly come from Khurasan into the 'Abbasid *diwans* of state and caused to flourish the somewhat formless Iranian "nationalism" (*shu'ubiyah*) that is plain to read in authors—writing in Arabic—from the ninth to the twelfth century.

Shu'ubiyah is a far from simple notion; it is highly uncertain, for example, how far it should be extended from its cultural base into the area of political action. It is by no means apparent that the 'Abbasid Caliphs or their viziers, who directly or indirectly encouraged the literary work of the *mawali*, intended thereby to promote a sense of Iranian separatism. The debate between the champions of "Arabism" and "Iranianism" had its social and religious implications, certainly; the *mawali* were striving to gain an equal footing in an Islamic community that up to the middle of the eighth century had given pride of place to the native Arabs and whose intellectual life was dominated by the "Arab sciences" flowing from the twin sources of Arab poetry and an Arabic *Qur'an*.

Much of the controversy swirled about the office of the vizier and the lesser secretaries (*katib;* pl. *kuttab*) in the chancery. The vizier was by origin, and remained in practice, a secretary whose professional cachet was not policy but the written word. His developed duties were extensive: a master, on the one hand, of the nuances of protocol and, on the other, of the Islamic sciences upon which the 'Abbasid Caliphate had chosen to base itself. As *mawali,* which most of them were, from a variety of non-Arab backgrounds, their own Islamic formation sat lightly upon most of the viziers and secretaries. They were perforce *arabisants,* but they apparently fed more avidly on other cultural nourishment, the norms of Sasanian protocol and the Iranian literary tradition, both of which were in vogue in Caliphal circles since Hisham and Marwan II.

In the *Golden Meadows* written by Mas'udi in 947 one such borrowing from Iran is touched upon almost casually in a discussion of legendary stories. There was in Pahlevi, we are told, a collection of stories known as *The Thousand Tales* but now called in Arabic *The Thousand Nights.* They were constructed around a frame story having to do with a king, his vizier, and the latter's daughter, Shirazad. Ibn al-Nadim writing in 987 knew somewhat more. According to his *Catalogue,* the historian al-Jahshiyari was editing a collection of similar materials from Iranian, Arab and Greek sources before he died in 942.

What both authors were referring to is clearly the earliest history of *The Thousand and One Nights.* We, who possess the entire collection scattered in a number of different arrangements across a varied manuscript tradition, are scarcely able to add more to that history. It seems probable that the original frame story of the vizier's daughter who saves her own and her father's life by telling a different story on each of many nights is Indian in origin and had been grafted onto the *Thousand Tales* before these latter came into Arabic. We also know that the original tales, whatever their number, were constantly growing by accretion both before their passage into Islam, when the Indian Sinbad stories were added to the collection, and constantly afterward. The Islamic additions are themselves rich and interesting, some of them romances, folk tales or simply gossip from Baghdad, others joined to the *Nights* in Mamluk Egypt down to about 1500, when the recensions as we have them were essentially complete.

Each layer that modern scholarship has stripped off *The Thousand and One Nights,* the Indian, Iranian, Baghdad, Cairene and others, has its own interest, but the collection as a whole points to both the catholicity of taste in Islam and the very mixed nature of its inheritance. Baghdad in the tenth century stood upon a broad highway leading eastward to Iran and India and westward to the Christian and Hellenic culture of the Byzantines. Intellectual and literary goods flowed in both directions, and Islam, despite its devotion to its Arab origins, openly exacted its duties from them all.

In the *Catalogue* of Ibn al-Nadim there is an imposing list of titles of other works translated from Pahlevi into Arabic, and at least a few of them can be attributed to Ibn al-Muqaffa', an Iranian convert from Zoroastrianism to Islam, who served as secretary to the last Umayyad governor of Kirman and who later received the patronage of Mansur. The Caliphal favor was not of long duration. Mansur wearied of his young client's impiety—or his rationalism—and had him executed, aged thirty-six, in 757.

Ibn al-Muqaffa' 's translations from the Pahlevi, some of which like the *Thousand Tales* derived ultimately from Indian sources, found a wide readership in Islam. The *Kalilah and Dimnah* circulated in his Arabic translation, then in a poetical version by the Iranian Rudaki (d. 940) and finally in a prose reworking, again in Persian, by Abu al-Ma'ali (c. 1145). The Arabic of his *Book of Kings* is now lost, but that too was extensively used by later historians. There were other translations and adaptations of Pahlevi ethical literature, most of them known today only from their citations and use in writers like Tabari, Ibn Qutaybah and Biruni.

Ibn al-Muqaffa' did more than render available a body of Iranian literary material to the Arabic readership in Islam; by his own *adab* compositions he introduced norms of Sasanian protocol and style into secretarial circles and fashioned one of the earliest experiments in a literary prose style in Arabic. He, his modest predecessors and their numerous successors in mining the Sasanian books were almost all men of the *diwans*. Their humbler talents at copying letters and protocol documents were bought and paid for by the state, which found that it had acquired their wider literary interests as well.

The 'Abbasid viziers were not dismayed by these decidedly non-Arab preoccupations. They subsidized the literary arts, and many of them were authors in their own right. We do not know how deeply and personally the viziers were involved in the dispute over the Arabic versus the Iranian literary tradition; there is no evidence to show that any one of them was committed to a political *shu'ubiyah*. Even the purely literary struggle may have been confined to the ranks of the secretaries, where reasons of state were of minor importance and where social conflict could take place without serious political repercussions.

The Kharijites had already raised the theological and political issue of the equality of all believers—in a considerably different context, it is true, but with unmistakably pertinent conclusions for the contemporary generation of *mawali*. The Kharijite dispute ended on the field of battle, but the issue of *shu'ubiyah* raged across the written page.[1] *Shu'ubi* writers delighted in denigrating the predominant Arabism and its pretensions. Of what avail was it to have a long and pure genealogy if it ended in nothing more impressive than a Hejazi camel driver!

The proudest boast of the Arab after the Arabic *Qur'an* was the impressive body of Bedouin poetry being assembled and studied by the philologists. This stood close to the heart of the *adab* question, since the *qasidah* illustrated in both form and content the traditional modes. The *jahili* poetry, of course, had nothing to do with Islam, and even in its extension down into the Umayyad period it showed little serious concern with properly Islamic values. The *qasidah* had a life independent of both Muhammad and the *Qur'an*.

Attacks against the *qasidah* came not from without, from some spectacularly revived representative of the Iranian bardic tradition, but from the poets working within the genre itself. Umayyad poetry, and particularly the style practiced by the erotic poets of the Hejaz, was carried forward into 'Abbasid times by Bashshar ibn Burd (d. 784). Though the family had Iranian antecedents, Bashshar grew up in the lively intellectual milieu of Arab Basrah, where he knew the philologists of the circle of Abu

---

1. Though not without its politicoreligious dangers. The term *zindiq*, for example, was broad enough to cover anyone from a public Manichaean to someone whose Islamic convictions were, even on purely literary grounds, suspect.

'Amr ibn al-'Ala' and had some connection with Wasil ibn 'Ata'. All of these threads ran together in his own life: Bashshar was a convinced *shu'ubi*, an occasional Mu'tazilite, possibly a Shi'ite, and was accused, probably with good reason, of *zandaqah*. He served as panegyricist for the eastern Umayyad governors and possibly for the Caliph Marwan II. After the founding of Baghdad in 762 he took up residence there. He was a favorite of Mansur, but ran afoul of the *zindiq*-hunting al-Mahdi, who engineered his murder.

While adhering to the general conventions of the *qasidah*, Bashshar stretched the form from within, particularly in his erotic elegies, by his strong personal tone and his adventuresome innovations in poetical diction. The latter had, as has been seen, a specific effect on the development of an Arabic aesthetic, but it is Bashshar's special tone that is unmistakably present in the poets of the next generation—in Abu Nuwas for example. The sober structure of the Arab *qasidah* was in the process of being dissolved by another, alien sensibility which was sensual and innovative, rather than piously Islamic, and owed as great a debt to the new urbanism that flourished under 'Abbasid auspices as to the Iranian pride to which Bashshar for one had frequent resort.

His successor in the new style was Abu Nuwas (d. 810), the son of a *mawla* father and a Persian mother. He studied at Basrah and Kufah, where he received instruction in both the traditional poetry and the philological sciences. Abu Nuwas' own poetical career unfolded at Baghdad and then, after the sudden fall of the Barmacid viziers, with whom he was closely associated, in Egypt. The poetry of this period may have been chiefly of the traditional panegyric sort, but after his return to Baghdad, and particularly under the pleasure-loving Caliph al-Amin (807–813), Abu Nuwas found a milieu congenial to his own inclinations. His poems threw over the old forms and themes, and concentrated on the staples of his own hedonistic ethic: drinking and eroticism.

The poetry of Abu Nuwas illustrates the subtle difference between *shu'ubiyah*, the Iranian reaction to Arab pretensions of cultural superiority, and the spirit of literary modernism that considered the traditional Bedouin poetry outmoded. There is Iranian material, historical and linguistic, in the *Diwan* of Abu Nuwas, but it was part of his natural cultural formation and not an acquired weapon against Arabism as such. The poet was well versed in the traditional Arab disciplines, and he wrote by choice in Arabic; his objection was to the confinement of the classical *qasidah*. Some of this was, doubtless, literary pose; most flowed directly from his own poetical temperament; almost none was inspired by ideological or political conviction.

In the contest between *ars* and *ingenium* it was often the first that won out in the soul of the Arabic literary artist. But not always. In the *Diwan* of Ibn al-Rumi (d. 896), a poet of Byzantine descent who sought, but never gained, official recognition at Baghdad, there are signs of something deeper than skill at figures and finely wrought diction: an almost unparalleled understanding of his own experience. Something similar, though accompanied by a more remarkable grace, can also be seen in the poetry of al-Mutanabbi (d. 965), the temperamental court poet of Sayf al-Dawlah at Aleppo. Just as he had read Ibn al-Rumi, Mutanabbi was read in turn, and was attended to, by al-Ma'arri (d. 1057), a native Aleppan, blind from his youth, cranky, eccentric, and an altogether singular poet in an age of artistic conformity.

Despite the occasional figure of a Mutanabbi or a Ma'arri, Arabic poetry remained firmly caught up in the grasp of the conservative philologist and the precious rhetorician; the *qasidah* and the *ghazal* were the limits of its efforts. At least some of the philologists' interest in the traditional form of Bedouin poetry was promoted by something more than piety. The living language was evolving as rapidly as the mores of Islam; and if that fact is concealed beneath the conservative form of the *qasidah*, it must have been clear enough to the grammarians and lexicographers of Basrah, Kufah and Baghdad, where non-Arabs were joining the Islamic *ummah* in increasing numbers. The philologists held their ground, perhaps at the price of fossilizing both poetry and their own sciences, but the new styles and the new social consciousness of a heterogeneous Islam found other outlets.

The *shu'ubiyah* movement served that end. It caused Islam to reexamine the assumption that its culture was necessarily Arabic. To put it in strictly literary terms, the partisans of *shu'ubiyah* were demanding the admission of foreign elements, here specifically Iranian elements, into the notion of *adab*. Put thus, the demand was eventually met: both Iranian and Hellenic learning were included in the formation of the *adib*. On a larger scale, however, and still speaking in literary and cultural terms, the *shu'ubiyah* movement was a failure. Incorporation was not equality, and from the end of the ninth century, when the issue was effectively settled, down to the end of the Islamic Middle Age, the Muslim gentleman was characterized by a culture that was unmistakably, if no longer exclusively, Arabic.

The resolution of the *adab* controversy came about largely through the efforts and prestige of one man, al-Jahiz (d. 869). He was born at Basrah and came to Baghdad sometime between 818 and 825, when al-Ma'mun was in the course of establishing Mu'tazilitism as the orthodoxy of Islam. Jahiz was highly connected at the capital. He was the intimate of Ibn al-Zayyat, the vizier of both Mu'tasim and Wathiq, and the *éminence grise* of the Mu'tazilah, the Chief Qadi Ibn abi Du'ad. It was the latter who saved Jahiz's skin when the Mu'tazilite interlude came to an abrupt end with the death of al-Wathiq in 847. Jahiz survived under the new orthodoxy of al-Mutawakkil (847–861), again by the power of his friends and by promptly lending his pen to Mutawakkil's anti-Christian policy; his *Refutation of the Christians* may have saved Jahiz's life in an increasingly hostile milieu.

Jahiz was one of the first in Islam to explore what it was to be "modern" and at the same time a Muslim. In his day, modernism consisted in asserting the use of reason in the newly emerging theology as well as in science, art and history. Reason meant for Jahiz the Hellenic tradition even then coming into learned circles in Iraq. Jahiz was given to brandishing his considerable command of the Greek sciences, particularly in natural history,[2] to lay the residual superstitions of the Bedouin cosmos. He knew and understood the ways of men, their differences and what made them different. In a staggering number of works Jahiz dispensed instruction on geography, anthropology, ethnography, zoology and botany in a tone that was both enlightened and amused.

Despite Jahiz's immense stylistic influence, not everyone was enchanted. Some doubted his seriousness, as Lucian's contempo-

2. His *Book of Animals* was a storehouse of such information, much of it derived from Aristotle.

raries had doubted his, but it was his theology that was most disquieting. The use of reason in constructing a theology and indeed the very possibility of a theology were theories associated with the Mu'tazilites and fiercely resisted by the traditionalists. Jahiz was certainly one of the former—he studied with al-Nazzam at Basrah—and he unhesitatingly took up the pen in their behalf.

It was not on his theology, naturally, that al-Jahiz's reputation rested, but on his undisputed superiority as a prose stylist and essayist, his elegance, his wit and his learning. Culturally he was a traditionalist; he gave no hearing to the partisans of *shu'ubiyah*. The *adab* of the Muslim was Arabic; its heart was in the *Qur'an* and in the sciences that derived from the Book, and its language was Arabic. Other people had their contributions to make,[3] but they were no substitute for a Muslim wisdom expressed in the language of Islam, Arabic.

Jahiz attacked the *shu'ubiyah* and its Iranian pretensions in a number of essays, but his chief statement on the subject of *adab* was the *Book of Argument*. It is a large and rambling book, a series of discourses rather than a *summa*, but one that portrayed by its style and encyclopedic range the physiognomy of the new Muslim *adib*, a somewhat new figure in Islam but one who was granted, largely through Jahiz's winning portrait, permanent rights of domicile in the Islamic *oikoumene*.

The work of al-Jahiz was the diffuse outpouring of an inventive *littérateur* who had yoked his points of view to the sensibility of the artist. Ibn Qutaybah (d. 889) was at once more pragmatic and programmatic. Almost all of his published work

---

3. There were writers enough to celebrate the virtues of the Iranians, but Jahiz was one of the first to pay serious attention to the later rulers of the Islamic Commonwealth, the Turks. In his *Exploits of the Turks* he gave them high marks for their military prowess, their innocence of the vices of civilization, and their orthodoxy. In another work, *The Superiority of the Black Race Over the White*, al-Jahiz, whose grandfather was a Negro, essayed to restore the reputation of the "black man," by which he understood everything from an Indian to an Egyptian and an Ethiopian. It was well worth the doing, however. Every Muslim was equal before Allah, but as a social class the black was clearly somewhat less equal than the others.

converges upon a single theme, the formation of the secretary, a project which he viewed against the current controversy between Arab and Iranian *adab*. Ibn Qutaybah, who was himself of Iranian origin, was an Arab traditionalist, equally opposed to Iranian claims of cultural superiority and to the rationalism spreading in theological circles in Baghdad and Basrah. In law and theology, Ibn Qutaybah belonged unmistakably with the traditionalists; in *adab* he stood on the side of the Arabs.

Ibn Qutaybah was not, however, a reactionary. Like Jahiz, he preferred eclecticism. While upholding the superiority of Arabism, he could admit to his pedagogical works the cultural inheritance from Iran. In his *Culture of the Secretary* and *Book of Knowledge* the history of Iran is set down next to the history of the Arabs; and the learning of the Greeks, no less than the traditional sciences, was offered for the education and edification of the would-be secretary. Significantly it is only in his *Book of Poetry and Poets* that the Arabs know no rivals.

The *adib* of the tenth and early eleventh centuries was a literary gentleman of considerable refinement and equal learning, both sacred and profane, with a marked preference for the profane. His two eminent predecessors, al-Jahiz and Ibn Qutaybah, had made knowledge of the "foreign sciences" respectable and even necessary for the formation of the cultured man, and the nonprofessional but accomplished scholars of the next generations ranged widely and unconcernedly across Islam's inheritance from the non-Islamic past.

It is, perhaps, misleading to draw the line too finely, but even among those cultured *prosateurs* whose literary preferences ran to world histories, anthologies and encyclopedias, the seams dividing the two cultures, the Arab on the one side and the Hellenic or the Iranian on the other, can be grossly observed. Some, like Mas'udi, Tawhidi and Miskawayh, clearly preferred their borrowed inheritance, while others, notably Isfahani, Tanukhi and Tha'alibi, cultivated an *adab* distinctly Arab in tone.

Abu al-Faraj of Isfahan (d. 967), though born in Iran, was of the purest Arab stock, a Quraysh descended from the line of the Umayyads. Oddly, he was a Shi'ite as well, and he found his patrons in the Shi'ite courts of the Hamdanids of Aleppo and the Buyids of Baghdad. Intellectually Isfahani descends from the early philologist-editors of Basrah and Kufah, crossed with the new *adab* consciousness of the 'Abbasid age. His *Book of Songs*, on which he worked for half a century, is an anthology of 'Abbasid and earlier poetry interspersed with biographical sketches and historical notes on the poets and their work. It became the indispensable handbook for the Arab-style *adib*.

Isfahani's student al-Tanukhi (d. 994) cast his net somewhat wider. His *Deliverance After Misfortune* is an anthology of cases, many of them drawn from history, to illustrate the always-popular theme of the reversal of human fortunes.[4] His *Table Talk* is a massive collection of anecdote and reflection, and it caught the flavor of judicial and *adab* circles in Baghdad in the same way that Tawhidi had caught that of the philosophical salons.

By the time Tha'alibi (d. 1038) put together his *Unique Epoch*, an anthology of contemporary poets, the love of ornamentation that characterized Arabic poetry from the beginning had begun to degenerate into unbridled lust. Rhetoric ran riot among the poets, as it did among almost all the literary men of the day, and with its triumph over sensibility the *adab* preached and practiced by Jahiz came to the term of its evolution. With his philologist's training Tha'alibi could be instructive and entertaining in turn, but never in the integrated sense in which Jahiz had balanced style and learning.

Al-Jahiz and Ibn Qutaybah had resolved one aspect of the *adab* question, but they by no means halted the evolution of the term. Jahiz and his successors and imitators understood the word as connoting a general, almost encyclopedic culture. But at almost the same time *adab* was beginning to acquire the more specialized meaning of the particular knowledge necessary to perform one or another professional function. Thus there came into existence an extensive literature on the *adab* of the vizier or the secretary or the *qadi*.[5] The specialization of the meanings of *adab* was perhaps

---

4. Tanukhi's was the third such work with the identical title in a deliberate series of imitations.

5. Thus, two genres of works converge on these offices: the *Res Gestae of the Viziers*, like those of al-Jahshiyari (d. 942), the same chamberlain of the vizier 'Ali ibn 'Isa who was working on the *Thou-*

a normal evolution, but it had the further effect of reducing the Jahizian legacy to a small corner of a previously wide domain. Nonspecialized *adab* ceased to mean general culture and came to signify a kind of baroque belletrism.

Arabic baroque was the result of the isolation of the writer from the broad spectrum of interests and activities that had characterized him in the period from Jahiz to al-Tawhidi, the arrival, in short, of the professional literary man condemned in academic isolation to a Hellenistic preciosity and extravagance. The *adib* of the ninth and early tenth centuries was a polymath who dipped his pen into everything from Greek philosophy to Arabic prosody. Islam continued to produce such polymaths through most of its history, but they were generally learned men and no more; the wit and sophistication of *adab* did not concern them. Sometime about the middle of the eleventh century the *adib* deserted the intellectual life, where Jahiz had firmly placed him, for the more refined climate of art.

He deserted as well the terrain prepared by the new culture of the 'Abbasid scribes with their supple and brilliant prose for the somewhat more treacherous ground of *saj'* or rhymed prose. Preciosity is not an intrinsic characteristic of the *saj'* style; it was used throughout the *Qur'an*, for example, in a restrained yet forceful and effective manner. The preciosity may well have developed within the same chanceries that were the seedbeds of the classical prose style.

As far back as 'Abd al-Hamid, the secretary of Marwan II, the chancery style had shown itself capable of overblown and rhetorical effects, and by the middle of the eleventh century these qualities had carried all before them. One of the chief architects of the new rhetorical style was Ibrahim ibn Hilal (d. 995), the Buyid vizier and historian, whose protocol instructions set the mode. The contemporary Hamdanids had their own resident rhetorician in Abu Bakr al-Khwarizmi (d. 1002), and the Ayyubids could later boast of the services of al-Qadi al-Fadil (d. 1200),

---

sand Nights, and those of Hilal (d. 1056), the nephew of the Sabian historian Thabit ibn Sinan; and the works *On the Culture of the Vizier* of the sort attributed to the mystic al-Hallaj (d. 922) and the jurist al-Mawardi (d. 1058).

who set the proper literary and rhetorical tone at the court of Salah al-Din.

The work of these three exemplars still belongs to the rhetorical extension of the specialized "*adab* of the secretary." Preciosity was proceeding apace in poetry as well. It was already present in the contrived abuse hurled at one another's tribe by the Iraqi poets under the Umayyads, and when it was taken up for analysis by the literary critics its success was assured among a select if not always very wide audience.

Academic poetry and the increasingly complex chancery style, singly or in concert, all but overwhelmed Arabic letters in the eleventh century. Set pieces of narrative or description, frequently cast in the form of an "epistle" (*risalah*) and inevitably expressed in the *saj'* style, were broadcast with the unmistakable and single-minded purpose of glorifying the stylistic refinement and sophisticated learning of the writer rather than enlightening the reader.

Within the narrowing confines of a purely literary *adab* the omnipresent *saj'* style formed, if it did not produce, at least one formal innovation in Arabic letters. A number of experiments were attempted by the *littérateurs* of the late tenth century, but the richest in consequence was the "encounters" (*maqamat*) of al-Hamadhani (d. 1007) who strung together the highly appreciated set pieces within the structure of a series of meetings between a narrator and a scoundrel hero whose changing circumstances and clever elusiveness gave the author a remarkable opportunity to display his wit, his learning in a variety of areas, and his readiness at narrative *saj'*.

The notion of a picaresque Euphues, for all its unlikely combination of art and artlessness, had an extravagant success in the version of the *maqamat* composed by al-Hariri (d. 1122), the *littérateur* of Basrah who composed his *Encounters* for the vizier of the Caliph al-Mustarshid. The fifty biographical episodes and the final repentance of the learned but rascally Abu Zayd, as told by a certain Harith ibn Hammam, caught the Arab imagination as few other literary deeds have done. It was the climax of *adab* as both finesse and learning.

Literary *adab*, once it was loosed from its earlier immediate connection with Hellenic learning and Iranian history and wisdom, never quite escaped the academic constrictions exploited but endured by al-Hariri. His successors in Arabic had little distinction in an age when Persian poetry was in brilliant flower.

The classical interlude marked by the equilibrium between form and content was of exceedingly brief duration in Arabic letters. Al-Jahiz was its beginning and very nearly its end. Thereafter the baroque *saj'* took captive the domain of the *littérateur;* for the others, they cultivated a kind of *adab* that was nothing more than vocational skill. Literature was not the only loser. The Hellenic sciences, after their brief but bracing encounter with a living literary tradition, declined once again into the forbidding scholasticism that had been their only style since late antiquity.

A Conscience for Islam: The Early Sufis

The annals of Islamic biography are filled with examples of men who pursued, then rejected, one or another of the ideals proposed to the Muslim by the traditionalist, the lawyer and the *littérateur.* Between them, aridity and worldliness drove Muslims down other paths, which had as their goal neither orthodoxy nor orthopraxy but a complete renunciation of the world and an immediate experience of God.

The *Qur'an* taught in clear terms the worthlessness of worldly goods in the eye of eternity, and it was no less urgent than the Gospels in holding before the minds of men the terrible vision of the Judgment. But where the early Judaeo-Christian, already schooled, perhaps, by an Essene environment, faced the end-time with a rigorous *askesis,* the first Muslims found themselves in the grip of an eschatology of the present, wherein, prior to that final summoning before the Throne, they had to meet and overcome the trial of political survival. The earliest Muslim *askesis* was a struggle to found Allah's community, not, as in Christianity, within their own hearts, but in the dimension of history and in the face of a determined political and social opposition.

There is an unmistakable tension in Islam between the claims of history and those of eternity. Muhammad preached more than conversion; he founded a community, and his life, like the *Qur'an* itself, was filled with the often-petty details of organizing, administering and judging the complex relationships of men dwelling on the hither side of the vale of tears. But the very same body of traditions that describe Muhammad engaged in the business of running the business of God leave no doubt that the Prophet of Allah led a life of austere self-discipline unmoved by either the wealth or the power that followed upon the initial successes of Islam.

We cannot be certain, but the more traditional renunciation of the world that appears within the ranks of the Prophet's earliest followers may have been motivated by the very success of the *ummah* in winning a place in the world. Its transition from a maligned and oppressed political minority—as a mere religious minority they would probably have provoked little attention—to the status of international power was terrifyingly rapid, and with it came both wealth beyond expectation and the equally new experience of Muslim contesting against Muslim in civil war.

We know something of the scandal provoked by the terrible events of the years, between 656 and 661, when perhaps only the bravest attempted to remain neutral in the strife of parties and the conflicting claims to power, status and the truth of Islam. The not very distant days of the Prophet must have appeared simple in comparison, when the first beleaguered Muslims led a fearful but cohesive existence supported by the presence of Muhammad and the conviction that they were doing the will of Allah.

What Allah willed was somewhat less clear in the second half of the seventh century. In the midst of dissolving certainties many lost their primitive Islamic innocence in a manner spared the earliest Christians. Among the immediate disciples of Jesus there were neither generals nor governors of a new City of God. Christianity spread slowly outward through the synagogues of the Diaspora, and the spirit of the new enterprise produced missionaries, preachers and ascetics, each, doubtless, with Jewish antecedents. Their deeds are chronicled in the *Acts of the Apostles*. Islam possesses no such document; the "Acts of the Companions" are rehearsed in the various "Conquests of the Lands" that chronicle not the workings of the Holy Spirit but the military successes of Islamic arms and their passage into civil war.

For many of the dimly perceived generation of the Companions the only response to civil war was to take sides, though not always out of self-interest, surely. There were many among them whose conversion to Islam had been religiously motivated and whom later history remembered as men of genuine piety who possessed, if not ambition, military prowess or administrative skill, then that newest and feeblest of moral instruments, an Islamic conscience. One such was Abu Dharr al-Ghifari (d. 652), a very early convert to Islam who had followed the conquests to Damascus, where he proceeded to lecture Mu'awiyah, then still governor of Syria, on Muslim morality and was forced by 'Uthman to return to Medina for his pains. Others of the Companions were somewhat more prudent, Hudhayfah (d. 657) for example, one of many whose consciences were revolted by the behavior of 'Uthman but who attempted, like many after him, to draw a distinction between reprehensible personal conduct and legitimate authority.

Neither Abu Dharr nor Hudhayfah were sectarians in the same sense as many of their contemporaries. They were simply experiencing in a painful way the growing tension between the ideals of Islam and the realities of empire, an experience most deeply felt perhaps by those who had no share in that empire. The original choice had been between Islam, which stood with Allah, or paganism, which stood against him. Now it appeared there were choices to be made *within* Islam, and after 656 the moral message of the *Qur'an* had to be reinterpreted in some new intra-Islamic sense.

The Muslim had little cause for surprise. The Pharisees and Christians among the Jews had attempted just such an internal moral reform of their parent body, and even then the Christians of the seventh century were exclusively concerned with the same question; theirs was not a choice of whether or not to be a Christian, but of what Christian vocation to follow within a Christian society, layman or cleric, married or celibate, the Prescriptions of the Law or the Counsels of Perfection?

Muhammad preached Islam to nonbelievers but gave no counsels of perfection to those who embraced it. He was aware, however, of the Christian's options, and there are numerous references in the *Qur'an* to the Christian priest and monk, some critical and some laudatory. The crucial text is one that occurs in *Surah* 57:27: "And we [Allah] put in the hearts of those who followed Jesus compassion and mercy and the monastic state. They instituted the same—we did not prescribe it to them—only out of a desire to please God. Yet they observed it not as it ought truly to have been observed. And we gave to such of them as believed their reward; but many others of them were evildoers."[6]

Later the Muslim community would read this text in a pejorative sense and then produce as its counterpart the Prophetic tradition to the effect that "there is no monasticism in Islam." But for the first two centuries or more the verse was understood as rendered here: monasticism was a characteristic Christian practice that had been encouraged, though not prescribed, by Allah, and there were good monks and bad.

There was, as a matter of fact, no monasticism in primitive Islam. Muhammad founded no monasteries, neither counseled nor imposed vows, and nowhere made the suggestion that there were different paths to salvation for different Muslims. On all the evidence, Muslims fashioned counsels of perfection for themselves out of their own sensibilities and their understanding of the example and preaching of the Prophet.

The implication, if not the prescription, of asceticism was of course present in the *Qur'an*'s own dark underlining of the contrast between this world and the next. That contrast may have been somewhat neglected in the fevers of the conquest, but the deeds of the civil war brought Muslims to introspection and, with it, a recollection of the judgment. The example of Christian ascetics of Syria may have played its part as well,[7] but imitation led the Muslim not to the establishment of monasticism with its

---

6. Translation after Massignon based on what was apparently the oldest understanding of the text. The later pejorative reading of the same passage is illustrated in Pickthall's version: ". . . and placed compassion and mercy in the hearts of those who followed him [Jesus]. But monasticism they invented—We ordained it not for them—only seeking Allah's pleasure . . ." where "monasticism" is separated from and opposed to the praiseworthy "compassion and mercy."

7. The supposition is somewhat weakened by the fact that the earliest centers of Islamic asceticism were not in Syria or Mesopotamia but in the Hejaz and Iraq, in the purely Arab cities of Basrah and Kufah.

celibacy and obedience to a superior but rather to a heightened sense of genuinely Islamic self-denial which manifested itself principally in a simplicity of life in the face of the rising luxury and worldliness of the Muslim elite.

Some of these early Islamic ascetics were notorious enough to have left their names embalmed in a spare list compiled by al-Jahiz. He called them ascetics, but certain among them bear another name, that of "Sufi." Later Arabic lexicographers allowed their fertile imaginations to range freely over the etymological possibilities of the word, but *suf* almost certainly refers to the woolen cloak worn by the Christian monks and later the common costume of Muslim ascetics. Thus Jahiz names among the Sufis, "those who wear the woolen cloak," a certain Abu Hashim of Kufah, who sometime about 760 migrated from his native Kufah to Ramlah in Palestine and founded there what tradition chose to call the first Islamic "convent" (*khanqah*).[8] To call it such may be mischievous as well as misleading. Abu Hashim was not the herald of monasticism in Islam, and those who lived in his *khanqah* in no way constituted a monastic community on the Christian model.

Out of Jahiz's list of ascetics, "weepers" and hell-fire preachers only one name emerges into firm historical substance, that of Hasan al-Basri (d. 728). Born at Medina in 643 and raised at Basrah, Hasan lived through the civil wars as an adolescent, fought on the Islamic frontier in Afghanistan, and then returned in his early forties to take up an active career of teaching and preaching at Basrah. He was often in trouble with the Umayyad governor al-Hajjaj for his outspoken comments on the regime, and though he probably never took part in an open insurrection, there were times when his only safety lay in hiding. With the accession of the pious 'Umar II in 717 Hasan received his due: he

---

8. The chief rival to this claim to priority was the community of ascetics at 'Abbadan at the head of the Persian Gulf. The community at 'Abbadan was lodged, however, in quite another type of building, a *ribat*, or fortified stronghold, which served as a defense and lookout point against invasion, particularly by sea, and where religious exercises were an ordinary part of the daily routine. It was only later, when the *ribat* began to lose its military usefulness, that it became principally a monastic compound.

was appointed *qadi* of Basrah. He may never have served in that office, but he continued his public instruction down to his death in 728, at age eighty-five.

Hasan's role in the theological controversies that swirled about the later Umayyads has already been described, but the Sufis too claimed him as one of their own. And with justice. Hasan was by no means a scholastic—most of his dogmatic teaching is in the form of "questions," and his moral teaching must be retrieved from his public sermons[9]—but in his teaching one can perceive the coming-together of the strands of Islam's nascent theology with the random and pragmatic asceticism of Iraq. According to Hasan, it was not enough for the Muslim merely to act; he must reflect upon his action, whether it be ritual or supererogatory, with the end of purifying his intention.

This is a totally new note in Islamic asceticism, the translation of personal holiness from the exterior act into the realm of the heart, and Hasan's chosen instrument is reflection, a scrupulous attention not merely to the act but to one's motives in performing it. By striking this particular emphasis, Hasan was opening a middle path between a purely juridical approach to religious duties, where the performance was all and the intention nothing, and the affective piety whose partisans, the fire-breathing preachers, wandered the towns of Iraq in increasing numbers during Hasan's lifetime.

Hasan's middle way between the lawyers and the popular preachers is the beginning of moral theology in Islam. His point of departure was, of course, the *Qur'an* and the *sunnah* of the Prophet, but there is theorizing too. Some of it derived from Hasan's connection with the current debates on free will which shaped his thinking on the quality of the moral act. In Hasan's view some men are "invested" by God with their actions and thus possess no great share in the responsibility, such acts are not the principal ground of morality. Morality rests elsewhere, in man's complaisant acceptance of God's will and God's reciprocal benevolence toward men. So the *Qur'an* spoke of those in Paradise: "Allah was pleased with them and they with Him."

---

9. Many of them reproduced by Jahiz as models of the genre.

The mutual acceptance of Allah and man soon yielded, in that same Basrah milieu, to the bolder thought of the love of God. Among the earliest of Hasan's disciples, 'Abd al-Wahid ibn Zayd (d. 793), for example, who was connected with the foundation of the ascetical community at Abbadan, there was still a reluctance to admit that man was capable of achieving a fully consummated love of the transcendent God. Most contemporary ascetics contented themselves with speaking of a "desire" for God, or even a "friendship" between men and Allah, but one of 'Abd al-Wahid's associates at Basrah, Rabi'ah (d. 801), the former flute girl turned mystic, openly declared not merely the possibility but the reality of divine love. She loved God, she wrote in some verses preserved under her name, in two ways: with a self-interested love that was motivated by her own gain and a purer type of love that loved Allah for his own sake.

Rabi'ah's scorn for a love motivated by the joys of Paradise—in one of her prayers she asked to be excluded from Paradise if her motives were directed toward that end—did not prevent her contemporaries from speculating on the vision of God that awaited them there. So Rabi'ah's friend Rabah ibn 'Amr (d. 796) explained that final vision in terms of a divine "illumination," a notion with a rich future, but one that at this stage may imply no more than an analogy with the role of light in natural vision. 'Abd al-Wahid had meditated the same reality, and the disciple who carried his teachings from Basrah to Syria, al-Darani (d. 830), while publicly proclaiming his reticence on the subject, shared those same illuminations with more private audiences. They were, in the style of the day, eschatological. Darani spoke vividly on the joys of Paradise and affirmed without hesitation that the holy man would indeed see Allah face to face at the Judgment.

From the cantonments of Basrah and Kufah the new asceticism and its attendant theory srpead with the Arab colonists into Khurasan. The earliest to have borne the title of Sufi there was Ibrahim ibn Adham (d. c. 776), a native of Balkh who was converted from an early career of dissipation by a divine call and thereafter devoted himself to a life of strenuous self-denial, a practice which evolved in the hands of his chief disciple, Shaqiq (d. 810), into the doctrine of complete trust in God.

One tradition has Ibrahim explaining to a disciple during his later pious wanderings in Syria, that he had acquired mystical knowledge through converse with a Christian monk. This is not impossible—Christian Syria knew both Gnostics and a particularly fierce type of asceticism—but the entire life of Ibrahim is so embroidered with legend, his family origins, for example,[10] that it is difficult to construct anything solid upon the information there. Another early holy man of the Gnostic type, the Egyptian known as Dhu al-Nun, "he of the fish," is surrounded by equal uncertainty. What we do know is that during Ma'mun's inquisition Dhu al-Nun was arrested for denying the creation of the *Qur'an*, that he was sent under escort to Baghdad, and that he was freed by Mutawakkil not long before his death in Egypt in 860.

According to later authorities, Dhu al-Nun was far more than a simple ascetic. His bibliography is a pastiche of alchemical treatises; he is frequently cited as the transmitter of traditions going back to the Shi'ite Imam Ja'far al-Sadiq; and he was the first, according to some reports, to have introduced into Islamic spirituality the notion of a mystical knowledge distinct from the normal modes of cognition. At first sight this appears to be an odd combination of interests, but as a matter of fact it can be duplicated by two further steps backward in time: to Ja'far himself, an alchemist of repute and the originator of a mystical and illuminationist exegesis of the *Qur'an*, and his student—and the reputed instructor of Dhu al-Nun in alchemy—Jabir ibn Hayyan, Islam's most notorious alchemist and himself the bearer of the title of "Sufi."

It is probably impossible to sort this out today. Occult and Gnostic ideas were circulating in Islam in the mid-eighth century, far earlier than once thought likely. Alchemy was a branch of the physical sciences, but it was also a spiritual discipline devoted to the "transformation" of souls, and there is nothing

---

10. His genealogy makes it clear that he was an Arab, and yet he is described in the tales as "the son of the ancient king of Khurasan." The portrait of the begging prince has suggested to some a borrowing from the stories surrounding the Buddha. Balkh was, at any rate, the center of Buddhism in Khurasan.

impossible in its being grafted onto Muslim religious sensibilities, even at this early date. Alchemy as a mystical discipline was concerned with an occult wisdom, the same type that Ja'far allegedly found concealed in numbers and names, and the alchemist cast simultaneously in the role of the mystic is not, on the face of it, an unlikely combination.

From the little we know of Dhu al-Nun, he had gone far beyond the asceticism of the first Islamic holy men. Exterior *praxis* was yielding, in the early ninth century, to a more affective spirituality, to the experience of the love of God and, in the case of Dhu al-Nun, to a visionary excitement at the prospect of confronting the object of his love on the Day of Judgment. That day could be summoned up by the lover through his own imaginative efforts, and thus the experience could be savored before the event. The vision promised by God to his friends at the end-time was near at hand in Dhu al-Nun; ecstasy was foreshortening the route to eschatology.

The summoning of these eschatological visions into the imagined present is probably the basis of the claims that Dhu al-Nun introduced mysticism into Islam and was the first to articulate its various stages. It is neither possible nor necessary to pass judgment on the question of absolute priority; what can be said is that a new path was being opened to the holy man and that Dhu al-Nun was one of its explorers.

Not everyone was prepared to hurry down the same path. One of Darani's Syrian associates, Ahmad ibn 'Asim al-Antaki, the date of whose death is still uncertain, was also turning asceticism into more interior channels of spirituality. His own work, *The Cure of the Ailment of Hearts*, and what others have said of him show Antaki more concerned with the purification of consciences than with the visionary recitals of the Judgment. He too admitted to an experimental knowledge of God, but the way to it leads not through ecstasy but through solitude and reflection.

Whether Antaki came to these conclusions on his own or was inspired by his better-known but younger contemporary al-Harith al-Muhasibi (d. 857) is concealed within the obscurity surrounding the relationship between the two men. Passages in Muhasibi's *Book of Solitude* are attributed by some to Antaki, and the latter, despite the fact that he was apparently older, may well have been one of Muhasibi's students. Whatever the case, both men, Antaki and Muhasibi, belong to the tradition of rationalized spirituality that in Muhasibi's case at least has clear lines of affiliation back to Hasan al-Basri. There is another quality that distinguishes the two men. Muhasibi had the benefit of exposure to the new *kalam*, and though he did not always agree with the conclusions of the theologians, he was obviously aware of and influenced by the methods of the Mu'tazilites of Basrah, where Muhasibi was born sometime about 781, and later of Baghdad, where he spent most of his active career.

Not a great deal is known about the details of Muhasibi's life. There is a stongly autobiographical passage in his *Book of Faithful Counsels*, but like the later example from the pen of al-Ghazali, who pointedly had Muhasibi in mind in writing his own spiritual biography, it is long on reflections but short on factual information.

According to the account in the *Faithful Counsels*, Muhasibi was deeply discouraged by the sectarianism into which Islam had fallen, the result, in his analysis, of men allowing themselves to be ruled by their own desires. He found salvation, he tells us, among men who valued the next world more than this, who based themselves on the *Qur'an* and the *sunnah* and observed the Law with scrupulous exactitude, who avoided disputatious wrangling and counseled instead a simple love of God. Muhasibi does not further describe his spiritual guides with their obviously conservative bent and their eschewing of all sectarianism, but it seems likely that they were not the ascetics of his time but some group of the traditionalists (*ahl al-hadith*).

Muhasibi was, of course, far from being a simple *muhaddith;* it is truer to characterize him as a sophisticated, if conciliatory, exponent of the *kalam*, a position that rendered him suspect to his natural allies, the Hanbalites. The consequences became apparent when Mutawakkil reversed the theological positions of his predecessors and restored Ibn Hanbal to prominence in Baghdad. Muhasibi had to desert that city for Kufah in 846, and though he did return to Baghdad shortly before his death in 857, it was a return without honor or even recognition.

Some of Muhasibi's preserved works are devoted to *kalam* questions, but his fame in Islam depends more certainly upon his moral writings, his *Mindfulness of the Rights of God*, the *Cultivation of Souls*, and the already-mentioned *Book of Solitude* and *Faithful Counsels*. In them Muhasibi set out, on lines already sketched by Hasan al-Basri, a blueprint for the spiritual life of the Muslim. The tone is unmistakably intellectualistic and the insights are more convincingly those of a moral theologian than those of a mystic. They spring, in the first instance, from Muhasibi's profound understanding of the sources of moral conflict within man, his narrow and superficial self-seeking, which Muhasibi localizes in the faculty of the "self," and which he contrasts with that other, more penetrating faculty of the "heart" whereby man is taken out of himself and turned toward his Creator.

Muhasibi meditated long and seriously upon this distinction of faculties, and his portrait of the "self" and its works is persuasively realistic. The "self," directed as it is toward self-gratification, gives rise to unbridled lust for the goods of this world, friendships, preferment, psychological and corporeal gratifications and, at root, the besetting sin of mankind, hypocrisy. Muhasibi showed no mercy in condemning the folly of this spiritual vanity both in obvious worldlings and in some of the popular religious types of his day, the various ascetics, preachers and *Qur'an* readers, whose well-advertised piety served merely to cloak their pride. Included in this dim estimate are the wool-clad Sufis; on balance, Muhasibi seems to have preferred the custom of an older generation of ascetics who had no distinctive garb, but he was far less disturbed by the Sufis' innovations in dress than by their obvious succumbing to vanity.

For Muhasibi the cure for self-esteem and its desires lies in the understanding that God has implanted in men and that enables them to distinguish between what is useful and what is harmful to them. All men possess this understanding with regard to worldly things, but only the Muslim has the true "understanding from Allah," which is directed toward salvation. Unlike the Mu'tazilites who pressed from the necessity of "understanding" into a full-blown *kalam*, Muhasibi reasserted at this point his traditionalist premises: understanding implicates knowledge, but this knowledge is, almost uniquely, a knowledge of the *Qur'an* and the *sunnah*.

Though the alternatives were not yet fully developed, Muhasibi's prescription for an Islamic spirituality described a path between the theoretical learning of the theologians and the jurists on the one hand and the immediately inspired "experiences" of the mystics on the other. Intellectualist to the extent of prizing the intention above the deed, Muhasibi constructed a program for the ordinary Muslim rather than for the scholar or the man of extraordinary spiritual gifts. His spirituality is designed, like Aristotle's ethics, for the *spoudaios*, the reasonably serious man capable of experiencing the fear of God and of reflecting upon his own deeds. It is a regime of means and balances, a personal "holy war" against the passions with the intent not of extirpating them but of bringing them under control.

Others in Islam, less conscious perhaps than Muhasibi that the *jihad* was directed against the "self" as the principal moral spokesman for the "world," had been drawn to a rigorous and even extreme asceticism. The Khurasanians in particular had stressed an almost absolute abandonment to God, to the point of taking no pains for one's own welfare, an attitude that had led some to embrace a radical poverty. Neither the principle nor the practice was congenial to Muhasibi. The self-renewing activities of the "self" could not be curbed by the quietism implicit in the Khurasanians' attitudes. Despite their protestations, man was, on the testimony of the *Qur'an*, responsible for his acts; in the realm of morals God did not do all.

The first step in the progress to spiritual perfection is, according to Muhasibi's own view, the development of a scrupulous conscience that scrutinizes not merely forbidden things but even, in the manner of the Pharisees' "fences of the Law," all actions of even doubtful rectitude. Cultivating a profound fear of God was helpful in this direction, and Muhasibi advocated the private use of the public techniques of the popular preachers: to represent to one's own imagination and to meditate upon the Last Things.

Self-examination (*muhasabah*) is the hallmark of the system and won for the author his sobriquet "al-Muhasibi." It is directed most appropriately toward *intended* action, and this focusing upon the morality of intention was the foundation stone upon which a true Islamic conscience could be built. Here too Hasan al-Basri had gone before, but for Muhasibi the examination of conscience was not a single and isolated arm in the personal *jihad;*

it is man's most salutary and potent weapon for purifying one's intention and so conquering the "self."

For Muhasibi, intention was all, and without it even canonically prescribed acts like the ritual prayers were worthless. The Muslim at prayer must reflect upon what he is doing and saying, that he is, in effect, conversing with God. Intention renders prayer more intimate, and as the most internalized of all the "Pillars of Islam," prayer encompasses within itself all the other obligations of the Muslim. But for all its attractions, the ritual prayer must yield, in Muhasibi's view, to a still more familiar form of address, the "private conversations" between creature and Creator in which the worshiper addresses God directly in his own words.[11]

One form of private prayer, probably the most common one, was that known as the "recollection of God" (*dhikr*), a constant repetition of the divine name, and though it has a place in Muhasibi's scheme of things, neither it nor the more public and more affective "spiritual concert" looms as large in his consideration as they do in that of later Islamic mystics. Introspection, not ecstasy and visions, was Muhasibi's style. He was enough of a traditionalist to hold, as many Mu'tazilites did not, that the just "saw" God "with the sight of the eyes" in the next world, but that beatific vision was never granted in this life. A man might have a vision of, or picture to himself, the pleasures of Paradise or the horrors of Hell as if they were really present. That was, however, a vision with "the eyes of the heart" and falls short, both in method and object, of the beatific vision after the Judgment.

In this latter context, Muhasibi quotes with approval the opinion of Dhu al-Nun—the two men were together in Baghdad after Dhu al-Nun's vindication and before his return to Egypt—even though they came to that vision from widely differing angles. Muhasibi was a *mutakallim* whose approach to the problems of the spiritual life was, if not dialectical, at least soberly rational; the Egyptian was a visionary and an occultist, and if we do not entirely understand his connection of the two, we can perceive

11. In Muhasibi's version the "conversation" is still one-sided. God does not answer directly, as he does to later mystics.

that he regarded spirituality as essentially a problem of the affections and their manipulation.

Muhasibi's counterpart in Khurasan was the *mutakallim* and ascetic Ibn Karram (d. 869) of Sijistan, who received his spiritual formation at the hands of various Sufis in Herat, Merv and Nishapur.[12] Muhasibi's "just balance" was not much in evidence in Khurasan, where Ibn Karram's embrace of poverty and the life of the mendicant was typical of the local tradition. In other ways, however, Ibn Karram differed from the main thrusts of Khurasanian spirituality. Abandonment to God did not mean to him man's abandonment of moral responsibility or, as some Khurasanians were beginning to suggest, the actual seeking of moral reproof as a sign of one's disengagement from worldly values and judgments. This school of thought, dubbed by later authors "the partisans of censure" (*malamatiyah*), had its beginnings at Nishapur during Ibn Karram's lifetime in the teaching of Abu Hafs al-Haddad (d. 873) and Hamdun al-Qassar (d. 884).[13] With them antinomianism made its formal entry into the Sufi tradition; and when Sufism bethought itself of its own orthodoxy in the next century, it was precisely that issue that provoked the most serious attacks and the most fervent defenses.

Ibn Karram's corrective to this new radical asceticism came, as Muhasibi's did, from an insistence on the reflective quality of the moral act, a quality that differentiated it from the simple act of faith on the one hand and from the belief that God "created" all of our acts on the other. Ibn Karram's interest in these questions and his resistance to both a simple fideism and the unthinking pursuit of self-denial betray him as a theologian. He argued, much in the fashion of Antaki and Muhasibi, from *hadith* rather than dialectic, but his problems were those of *kalam*. Although both Ibn Karram and Muhasibi took their stand closer to the center than did the Mu'tazilites, their moderation did not render

---

12. For Ibn Karram's work as a theologian, see pp. 462–463.

13. Most of the information on them comes from al-Sulami (d. 1021), whose fame rests primarily on his anecdotal biographies of Sufis (see Chap. VIII, p. 558) but who also wrote a preserved *Treatise on the Malamatiyah*.

them acceptable to either the traditionalist or to the Ash'arites who later occupied much of that same terrain.

Ibn Karram suffered imprisonment at the hands of the Tahirid governors of Khurasan for his views—the charge had to do with his claims to private revelation; severe asceticism had always been regarded with suspicion by the political authorities in Khurasan—but he was eventually released, and he ended his days in Jerusalem. There his disciples may have taken still another step in the social evolution of Sufism: they established a "resort of ascetics" that may actually have borne the title of "convent" (*khanqah*) and was further distinguished by the fact that it was also a *locus* of instruction. Whether that instruction was in Hanafite law—most of the Karramiyah belonged to the Hanafite *madhhab*—or, as seems far less likely, in Karramiyah *kalam*, the rationalist presumptions of Ibn Karram's views are clearly underlined.

The intellectualist Sufi, whether Muhasibi in the ninth century or al-Ghazali in the twelfth, dominates the portrait of Muslim spirituality for the simple reason that he was the maker of the portrait. As the literary spokesman for Sufism he explained in measured and reasonable terms what he and his fellows were about. The other Sufis, those whose piety was revealed, without benefit of theory, in their lives alone or in an occasional preserved cry of ecstasy or sorrow, are reduced to illustrative footnotes in the works of the theoreticians or to strings of anecdotes in the great biographical collections. Later the "intoxicated" Sufis, whom orthodoxy often wished to but could not quite forget, found their voice in Gnosticism or poetry, Arabic and Persian; but even in the ninth century Sufism was, despite its visible literary features, an experience rather than a set of propositions.

The experimental side of Sufism—and the fears of the traditionalists regarding it—becomes more pronounced as the ninth century turns into the tenth, when the "sober" Sufi of the pen must write more forcibly and more rapidly to render intelligible what his colleagues were feeling in their fevered hearts and seeing with the eyes of the soul. But for the present he was doing something else: he was fashioning, as no lawyer could, a conscience for Islam. By his life style the simple ascetic convicted

Islam of worldliness, while the more reflective Sufis of the literary tradition undertook to convert that almost instinctive reflex of "conversion" into something that was capable of reforming not just individuals but the entire Muslim community.

Hasan al-Basri and Muhasibi began the process of spiritualizing the Law by suffusing it with the ardor of nascent Sufism, and their work came to term in the elaborate urging of Ghazali's (d. 1111) *Revitalization of the Sciences of Religion.*[14] Neither Ghazali's monumental work nor its modest forebears would have been possible, however, without those pious souls who had experienced Islam in this new spiritual way and whose experiences were distilled into an authentic Muslim ethic.

The principal difference between Muhasibi and Ghazali was that the latter had more than experience to convert into ethical theory. Ghazali possessed a view of the origins, nature and workings of the soul far more sophisticated than Muhasibi's somewhat crude precisions about the "self" and the "heart." It did not come to him by simple reflection upon experience; it was quite obviously inherited from the riches of Aristotelian psychology and ethics, of which Muhasibi apparently knew little or nothing and Ghazali a great deal.

Others in Islam would turn to the Hellenic material in an effort to construct a humanistic ethic in which a Muslim too might share. Not so the "sober" theoreticians of Sufism, Ghazali himself included. Their goal, like the *Qur'an*'s, was a supernatural perfection, and however much they may have expropriated Greek concepts, they did not share in Hellenism's ideals; for the Sufi the perfection of man lay not in this world but in the next.

A New Revelation: Falsafah

In the ninth century Islam had its first experience of a new kind of intellectual, the *faylasuf*. His name was not Arabic, but merely a loose transcription of the Greek *philosophos* and his interests lay nowhere among the traditional Arab sciences. He was the

---

14. See Chap. IX, p. 713.

adept of a new science, philosophy (*falsafah*), known but never previously practiced in Islam. The scholar, *littérateur*, sage, prophet and saint all preceded the *faylasuf* in the *Dar al-Islam* and they long survived his disappearance. But by his brief presence he touched them all, and Islam itself.

The origins of *falsafah* in Islam are as transparent as the etymology of its name. Philosophy came from the Greeks, and the Islamic *faylasuf* had to seek his spiritual parentage in another culture and another time, in the Athens of the fourth century before Christ. Or so he thought. His true parents were much closer to home, among the Alexandrians and Christian Syrians of the fifth and sixth Christian centuries. The seven-century error was of no great consequence; Islam's problems with *falsafah* lay elsewhere.

Falsafah was substance and method, both inherited. The substance was what could be found in the great edifice of the sciences that the Greeks had been constructing as rigorously as they knew how over the millennium between Thales and Simplicius. Progress had been steady in all of them, and if the pace of their growth seemed to flag in some areas in the fourth and fifth Christian centuries, it was surely because the Hellenic sciences were simultaneously nourishing their own secondary growths, the precocious occult sciences and the new Christian theology. Further, they labored under the increasing strain of their own presence.

From the days of Plato and Aristotle, the Greek sciences were housed in schools. Though it was not apparent at the time, their new base of operations altered the evolution of those sciences. Searchers became masters, and students were transformed into disciples by their passage through the schools. The ironies of Socrates and Plato were converted into dogma and Aristotle, antiquity's most insistent spokesman for empirical research and cumulative progress along the path of truth, was assigned the status of Holy Writ. In the end there were no more philosophers; there were only Platonists and Aristotelians.

The Islamic *faylasuf* (pl. *falasifah*) received the Writ as piously as others before him. It had been worked over for centuries, modified in some areas and enlarged in others, argued, synthesized and compacted into textbooks. It was an organized and impressive body of learning. By the time of its arrival in Islam the great body of sciences that rested on the bases of logic and was crowned by the "first philosophy," or metaphysics, had come together in a single unified curriculum whose parts were the various "foreign sciences" and whose acknowledged masters were Plato and Aristotle, Galen, Hippocrates, Euclid and Ptolemy.

Some of this material had been studied by 'Abbasid scholars well before the first *faylasuf* appeared in Islam. Mansur, al-Mahdi and Harun had all promoted, in one way or another, the pursuit of Hellenic learning no less than the wisdom of India and Iran. None of it conformed, perhaps, to the *Qur'an*'s ideal of learning, but these alien bodies of knowledge must have appeared at the outset worldly rather than threatening to the concerned Muslim.

What *falsafah* added to the accumulating pieces of the Greek sciences was an epistemological claim. It brought before the Muslim an alternative theory of wisdom that simultaneously exalted itself and set down in an inferior position the channel of revelation opened by the Prophet of Islam. As clearly as the *Qur'an* itself, the *Posterior Analytics* proposed to tell wherein lay the truth. The *faylasuf* came to Islam bearing a new revelation, and he had necessarily to answer to the old.

The first of the new Islamic philosophers, an Arab as he was proudly known, was Abu Yusuf Ya'qub ibn Ishaq called al-Kindi by reason of his descent from the esteemed tribe of the Kindah. He was educated at Basrah and Baghdad, and as far as we can tell, it was in the Baghdad of Ma'mun and his immediate Mu'tazilite successors that al-Kindi spent most of his creative life as a philosopher. His works bear dedications to both Ma'mun and Mu'tasim, and the philosopher served as tutor to the latter's son Ahmad. The reversal of religious policy under Mutawakkil in 847 cost al-Kindi his position, prestige and his considerable library. He was still alive in 870, but must have died shortly thereafter.

Kindi is a transitional figure in Islam, a new growth out of the context of Mu'tazilite *kalam*. Though he shared some of the basic attitudes of the Mu'tazilites, Kindi understood, if he did not always put into practice, the great differences that separated the *kalam* of the contemporary theologians from the newly discovered discipline of *falsafah*. *Kalam* was a method, perhaps chiefly apologetic, of getting at the truth. Its problems were those raised by the *Qur'an* or elicited by the history of the Muslim community. *Kalam* drew freely from its environment both to describe and to solve its problems, from the Greeks, it seems, for their physical theory of atoms and accidents, and likely from the Manichaeans as the target of Mu'tazilite polemics on the unity and justice of God.

Al-Kindi must have been well aware of this since the impressive list of his works includes titles on some of the favorite Mu'tazilite topics; but his own position was quite different. He was a *faylasuf*, not a *mutakallim*, and philosophy was an autonomous discipline with its own problems, methods and tradition. By the most generous reckoning, Mu'tazilite *kalam* reached no further into the past than Hasan al-Basri, while Kindi consciously took his place in a file that stretched back past the Prophet to Aristotle, Plato and Socrates. The problems of *falsafah* had been enunciated as early as Parmenides and Pythagoras, and their accepted manner of solution was set out in the methodological treatises of Aristotle's *Organon*.

Al-Kindi was not always at ease with the Hellenic method of scientific demonstration, and later philosophers were often critical of his proofs. He accepted it in principle, however, and affirmed its two corollaries, that scientific knowledge was essentially deductive and that philosophy was the master science capping all of human wisdom. The Mu'tazilah were at best ambivalent on the first of those propositions and ignored the second. They possessed, as has been seen, an epistemology that permitted them, as it permitted Aristotle and al-Kindi, to derive a set of a priori and immediate first principles, but there was no consequent effort to construct a science from those principles in the manner of an Aristotle or a Euclid. Instead they were used dialectically to test the positions of Islamic lawyers and traditionalists.

Al-Kindi operated very differently. Among his preserved essays[15] is one *On the Definitions of Things*, wherein he set forth, in the assured and succinct manner of the practitioner of an old

---

15. According to one source, al-Kindi was the first to use the epistolary essay as a vehicle for philosophy.

trade, definitions of some of the basic terms of philosophy. Among them is "philosophy" itself, and al-Kindi had ready at hand a variety of definitions from an etymological one, in which it is explained by the Greekless but confident Kindi that *faylasuf* comes from two Greek words, *fala* meaning "lover" and *sufa* meaning "wisdom," to the Platonic "assimilation to God" and the Aristotelian "science of being." All these definitions came to Kindi from the *eisagoge* complex current in late antiquity; and yet he was not a Hellenic archaeologist but a member of a living tradition, and so he passed them on without further comment or explanation.

Kindi's borrowed definitions hardly did justice to the enormous range of *falsafah* as it became known to the Arabs. It was not a single science but a *body* of disciplines, the highly professional studies of the Hellenic higher schools that are reflected in both the arrangement of Aristotle's works by his academic editors and in the curricula pursued in those schools. The philosopher, whether Greek or Muslim, was an encyclopedist. His range was expected to cover everything from the propaedeutic logic, through the physical and mathematical sciences, to "first philosophy," theology or metaphysics. All these sciences neatly ordered in their ranks along the path to theology are reflected in Kindi's own immense bibliography. The Mu'tazilite interested himself within the narrow confines of what constituted "Islamic questions"; al-Kindi inherited an entire curriculum.

The upwards of two hundred titles, only a fraction of which are actually preserved, attributed to al-Kindi by his bibliographers cover the ancient curriculum. His treatments, where we can judge them, are derived in most cases from classical prototypes, some of them textual but more, doubtless, in the form of epitomes and summaries. There was a progressive closing with the original Hellenic texts by the *falasifah*, the effect, largely, of the coming of the Alexandrian remnant to Baghdad in 900, but al-Kindi stands at the beginning of the movement and, like the earliest Latin scholastics, preferred paraphrase and summary to textual commentary.

And, as in the Latin West, it may have been the quality of the texts themselves that determined Kindi's approach. He was not himself a translator, but he stood close to a number of translators whose work he supported and perhaps to some extent directed. The results of the labors of Ibn Na'imah, Eustathius and Ibn al-Bitriq were adequate, if somewhat crude; but they came nowhere near the standards of the versions available to the later *falasifah.* The differences in technical sophistication between Kindi and Farabi (d. 950) spring from more than personal achievement; Farabi had available, as Kindi did not, the translations of Greek works prepared by Hunayn ibn Ishaq and his atelier.

Kindi was, then, a *faylasuf* of the type that was to become familiar in Islam. The Mu'tazilites may have been drawing upon Greek Stoic material for their peculiar form of atomism, but as far as philosophy was concerned, there was only one well from which to drink in late antiquity; and if Islam were to connect itself with a living philosophical tradition, then that tradition was the version of Platonism formally propagated by Plotinus and Porphyry. When it reached Islam the current Neoplatonism was a fairly coherent, if highly syncretistic, system. It was academic in tone, scholastic in its methods and pedagogy, sober and generally secular, apart from the pietistic nuances given it by the pagan Proclus and the Christian John Philoponus. It believed in both God and human reason, in intellectual as well as moral virtue, and in an organic and providentially ordered universe.

In al-Kindi's case we are given a rare view of an immediate source of his own philosophical attitudes. Among the works of Aristotle Ibn al-Nadim lists something called "The Theology of Aristotle" which has since been revealed as an abridgment of Plotinus's *Enneads.*[16] Whether the original editorial work was done earlier by a Greek, a Christian or someone within the *Dar al-Islam,* the preserved Arabic text was known to have been translated by Ibn Na'imah, a Syrian Christian, and revised for al-Mu'tasim's son by al-Kindi. In what that revision consisted we have no present way of knowing, except that it was not textual; al-Kindi had no Greek.

---

16. Significantly, it is not listed within the general schema of Aristotle's works but in a kind of appendix. Nor did al-Kindi note it in his own version of that same schema, *On the Number of Books of Aristotle,* which is based, like the *Catalogue*'s outline, on a fifth- or sixth-century introductory lecture on Aristotle.

What is certain is that Kindi had before him, and worked on, a premier piece of evidence supporting the contention that had been heard at least as far back as Porphyry, namely, that the doctrines of Plato and Aristotle were one. The "Theology" appeared to bear this out in detail, though it was, in fact neither Plato nor Aristotle but Plotinus. Kindi accepted it as genuine, however, and the "Theology" represented for him and most of the later *falasifah* an authentic and traditional description of the universe and its workings.

Kindi's own theology is exposed in his *First Philosophy*. It is neither Aristotle nor Plotinus but a new and somewhat unexpected combination of the two. Philosophy, the study of the causes of things, is divided by Kindi into two parts: physics, the search for the causes of mutable material substances; and the science of "what is above physics" whose object is immutable and immaterial being and whose proper method is the Hellenic-style demonstration. The supreme object of this first philosophy was for al-Kindi, as it had been for Aristotle, the First Cause, the One, the Eternal.

The God of al-Kindi owes little to Aristotle, however, or even to the *Qur'an*. It is unmistakably another version of the God of the Philosophers drawn along lines suggested by Plotinus but modified in one important respect by Kindi's Muslim sensibilities. The unity of God is asserted against both partition and predication: the One has no parts, attributes or qualities. Like his fellow Mu'tazilites and like the entire Platonic tradition before him, Kindi was a partisan of the "unity" (*tawhid*) of Allah. God does act, however. He is the first and unique Agent in that he performs the elemental act: he brings things from nonbeing into being.

Some such view may have stood behind the earlier musings of Jahm ibn Safwan. If so, Jahm borrowed the conclusions without embracing the tradition; al-Kindi accepted the tradition, the Hellenic *paradosis*. But like Proclus and Philoponus before him, both of whom attempted to make their philosophy conform to a kind of revelation, Kindi was a believer. As a Muslim he accepted the revelation of the *Qur'an*, and so at the outset he was forced to confront the intellectual dilemma that plagued *falsafah* to the end of its days, the apparent conflict between the revealed deposit of faith and the conclusions of philosophy.

Later *falsafah* was fertile in solutions to the dilemma, most of them developed from the well-worn Stoic distinction of a tripartite theology for philosophers, poets and statesmen wherein the truths of revelation were relegated to the figurative and allegorical parables of the "poets" (read "prophets") as a kind of theology for laymen who were incapable of understanding the higher and purer truths of the philosopher. Many after him in Islam were willing to accept that solution, but Kindi was not. He understood well enough the difference between the philosopher and the prophet. The former trafficked in a "human wisdom," which was won only after much toil, research and striving and which was expressed in rather opaque terms. The prophet, on the other hand, received his "divine wisdom" effortlessly, as a reward for his personal moral probity, and his statement of it was clear and concise. Between the two the palm clearly belonged to the prophet, and al-Kindi may have been the first and last *faylasuf* to award it to him.

The philosopher was not denied his own claims; the divine truths of revelation and the human ones of philosophy were, in fact, identical. As Islam grew somewhat more sophisticated in the ways of the philosophers, not many Muslims could accept that proposition at face value. Ghazali's later *Incoherence of the Philosophers* was devoted to demonstrating to the *falasifah* that a number of their basic propositions flatly contradicted the *Qur'an* and so were at worst heretical and at best temerarious. Kindi was as aware of this fact as Ghazali was, and he made a strenuous effort to meet it head on, not by quoting the *Qur'an* to philosophy but by demonstrating, as Ghazali did, that the suspect propositions were not the necessary conclusions of a scientific proof.

In Kindi's day the crucial issue was that of creation. The Muslim, Christian and Jew could live in blissful concord on the subject of the creation of the universe from nothing at a given moment of time, but the standard Neoplatonism was almost unanimous in its affirmation of an eternal and necessary creation worked upon what appeared to be an eternal and absolute matter.

A Muslim philosopher intent upon following that tradition might very well have chosen to bring his talents at allegorical exegesis to bear on *Genesis* or the *Qur'an,* but Kindi preferred another course, though not of his own devising, to be sure.

Earlier in the career of philosophy the awkwardness of a willed and temporal creation from nothing had been raised by the Platonists Porphyry and Proclus in their attacks on the intellectual pretensions of Christianity. The case for the Judaeo-Christian version of creation was made by John Philoponus in both his treatise directed *Against Proclus* and in the later *Against Aristotle,* wherein he undertook to defend on philosophical grounds the finiteness of the universe in its origins and its end.[17] The latter treatise is lost in Greek except for Simplicius' remarks upon it in his Aristotelian commentaries, but the Arabs knew it well enough. Kindi drew upon it, as did the Jewish theologian Saadya Gaon (d. 942). Farabi, the faithful *faylasuf,* attacked it, while the Christians Yahya ibn 'Adi and Ibn Suwar not unnaturally affirmed it. Philoponus' work was still being used, directly or indirectly, as late as Maimonides and Ibn Rushd.

Kindi may not have read Philoponus' *Against Aristotle* in an integral translation; his arguments lacked, at any rate, something in finesse. The chief among them was based on the composition of the universe: what is composed, either in three dimensions or from matter and form, is finite and so necessarily created. Composition from matter and form was, of course, an Aristotelian legacy to later Platonism and was as comprehensible to Kindi as it had been to Philoponus. But the proof appealed as well to those other creationists, the *mutakallimun,* whose own atomic physics was remote from the Aristotelian variety. When the Philoponus proof passed through their hands, possibly by courtesy of al-Kindi, the necessary adjustments were made; composition from matter and form yielded to composition from atoms and acci-

---

17. With some help from the Platonic tradition itself. Plato's *Timaeus* appears to describe a temporal creation at the hands of a personal artificer. Most Platonists, including Aristotle, read the temporal and personal elements in that account figuratively, but that interpretation was by no means unanimous; see Chap. IV, p. 298.

dents, and thus both the physics of *kalam* and Muslim orthodoxy were served.

The philosopher and the prophet had both spoken, then, on the subject of creation and their teachings were identical. There was one truth, even though there were two roads that led to it. The way of the prophet was, on Kindi's view, superior in its ease, clarity and conciseness. How the prophet functioned Kindi was not, however, able to explain. From Farabi onward the capacious categories of Greek epistemology were opened to embrace prophetic as well as philosophical knowledge. In so doing the *falasifah* were likely following where the interests and sensibilities of their Hellenic predecessors had already led, but Kindi was either unaware of or disinterested in such speculations. For him prophecy was a "divine wisdom" in a sense that fell outside the categories of human intellection.

Kindi's own theory of intellection rested firmly on Greek bases, and particularly on the studies of Aristotle's psychology made by the commentator Alexander of Aphrodisias. Alexander had addressed himself to the terse and opaque remarks on the human intellect in the third book of Aristotle's tract *On the Soul.* In the course of his explanation Aristotle had described a passive or material intellect that operates within and is totally dependent on the body. But because it is passive this intellect cannot provide its own dynamism in the passage from potency to act, the actuality of knowing the intelligible form of things. For this it requires another intellect already in act, which is described by Aristotle in another place as coming "from outside" and comparable in its effect to illumination from a light source.

In his exegesis of this passage Alexander distinguished what appeared to him to be three intellects engaged in the process of human intellection: the purely passive material intellect; the habitual or "acquired" intellect, that is, the material intellect when it actually knows the intelligible form of an object; and finally the active intellect which is impassible, divine and located outside the body. The latter is, according to Alexander, the Divine Intelligence that serves as the First and Final Cause of the Aristotelian universe. This may indeed have been Aristotle's intention, but an early and Platonizing Aristotle and not likely the author of the otherwise naturalistic psychology put forward in the treatise *On the Soul.*

Kindi's own view of the functioning of human intelligence is put forward in his *On the Intellect* and it obviously owes a great deal to the articulated intellects of Alexander's presentation. Alexander is nowhere mentioned, however, and the Islamic reader is assured that he is receiving the genuine views of Aristotle. What follows that assurance is not purely Aristotle, and even though Kindi's intellects are the same as those of Alexander, he understood the entire operation to function naturalistically. Kindi's multiple intellects operate totally within the categories of act and potency and the conversion of sensible forms into intelligible forms. Alexander's equation of the active intellect with God is nowhere in sight, nor are the conclusions drawn by the later Platonists, Greek and Muslim, from that identification.

One such view does not make al-Kindi a naturalist on the model of Strato of Lampsacus. The physics of his universe was Aristotelian, but the sensibilities are those of a Stoic, a Platonist and, to no small degree, those of a ninth-century Muslim theologian. Kindi's view of the soul, for example, is deeply Platonic. The soul may possess the full range of Aristotelian faculties, but in its essence it is the single divine substance of the *Phaedo.* Divine in its origins and divine in its ultimate destiny, the soul at death must undergo a cathartic journey through the spheres before it can finally be restored to that "other place."

Kindi was not a contemporary of Plato and Aristotle, however; he was, as they were not, an astrologer of a type that came into prominence in Hellenic circles only after the death of Aristotle. Out of the later Greeks' contact with Babylon and its priesthoods had arisen a new Hellenistic astrology that wedded Greek scientific theory to both the piety and the elaborate observed data of the Babylonian priestly guilds. The theories were those already discussed, a universal "sympathy" that linked, by way of "effluences" of the *aither,* the supralunary and sublunary worlds in a network of interreaction.[18]

Al-Kindi subscribed fully to these premises, most notably in his

---

18. See Chap. V, p. 354.

work *The Proximate Efficient Cause of Generation and Corruption,* and found their Stoic resonances useful for his own Muslim purposes: the effects of the heavenly bodies on human history are manifestations of the will of Allah. The directive force of the universe was not now, as the Stoics had once taken it, an immanent Reason directing all to a common good, but a transcendent God who not only had created the universe but continued to rule it through his providential instruments, the planets.

Kindi had other pious uses for his astrological learning. Astrology was for him a serious science, and he was capable, as has been seen, of writing astrological history in the best Sasanian manner. On astronomical grounds he predicted that Islam would survive for 693 years: "In the conjunction that dominates Islam, Venus is in 28°42′ of Pisces. The remainder is thus 11°18′, and since there are sixty minutes to a degree, the duration of Islam will be 693 years." This in Kindi's view was what human reason was capable of telling about the future. Revelation was then allowed to speak. Kindi converted to their numerical values the isolated letters that stood at the head of various *surahs* of the *Qur'an* and they too added up to 693. Reason and revelation were once again shown to be two paths to the same truth.

Kindi's scientific naturalism was balanced, then, against his obvious conviction about the truth of the Muslim revelation. The affirmation of both modes of access to the truth, the "human wisdom" of philosophy and science and the "divine wisdom" of the *Qur'an,* had the further advantage of allowing him to combine the two in a single argument. Kindi read the *Qur'an* in the open, almost rationalistic manner of the contemporary Mu'tazilities, confident that science, grammatical, lexicographical and philosophical, could do no other but cast a complementary light on the truths of the Sacred Book.

Kindi's confidence in revelation may have extended beyond the *Qur'an.* As has already been remarked, one of Ibn al-Nadim's major sources on the Sabians of Harran came from Kindi by way of his student al-Sarakhsi. In his narrative Kindi performed a quite remarkable reduction of the Sabians' scientific methodology, physics and metaphysics to those of the Aristotelian system. The Sabians' doctrines were not, as a matter of fact, the findings of philosophy but the product, according to the Sabians themselves, of a revelation from Hermes. And for al-Kindi that revelation turned out to be identical, just as his own Muslim *Qur'an* was, with the conclusions of Peripatetic philosophy.

It would be interesting to know the context in which Sarakhsi was quoting al-Kindi on the Harranians. The master found no disagreement between the philosopher and the prophet, not even at Harran; the student denied prophecy outright. Was the Harranian passage intended by Sarakhsi to show that the Sabians had stolen the teachings of the Greek philosophers and disguised them as a Hermetic revelation, as indeed they had? We cannot say, nor can we answer the question that puzzled Biruni: since Sarakhsi considered the prophets as charlatans, how can he quote verses of the *Qur'an* to sustain his theses?

Kindi and Sarakhsi stood close in their over-all interests. Both had studied the Harranians, and both men were, perhaps not coincidentally, convinced astrologers; Sarakhsi too had calculated the duration of Islam. Both had done considerable work on the logic of Aristotle, and Sarakhsi had prepared, quite in the Kindi manner, epitomes of many of the treatises of the *Organon*. Sarakhsi too was reported to have had Mu'tazilite sympathies—they may have cost him his life[19]—and yet like his teacher he rejected the Mu'tazilite atomic physics for the new Aristotelianism.

Kindi admitted the philosopher into Islam, but he was not yet willing to allow him to supplant the Prophet. One who was, and in a radical way that not even the boldest of Muslim Hellenists was prepared to concede, was the physician, alchemist and *faylasuf* Muhammad ibn Zakariya al-Razi (d. 925). Apart from his alchemical and medical works, which had a just celebrity in Islam and in the West, not much is known of this thinker who was notorious in Muslim circles as an archheretic, a *zindiq* without peer who drank from every tainted spring emptying into Islam.

Not unexpectedly there is not a great deal of Razi the meta-

---

19. He was executed in 899, possibly at the command, and certainly with the connivance, of Mu'tadid (892–902), whom Sarakhsi had tutored before his accession to the Caliphate.

physician and theologian left to be read.[20] There are lists of titles preserved by Ibn al-Nadim and al-Biruni, but their content must be reconstructed out of what rebuttalists had to say of them. Razi's formal training was in medicine at hospitals in his native Rayy and Baghdad. He had no formal connections that we know of with the Peripatetic philosophers working on the texts of Aristotle in Baghdad during his lifetime; philosophically and technically Razi belonged rather to the generation of al-Kindi.

In philosophy Kindi was the kind of Platonizing Aristotelian familiar from late antiquity. We know what he was reading and, thanks to the scholastic apparatus surrounding Greek philosophical works, how. Razi too had access to translations of the philosophers—Plato's *Timaeus* for one, and Plutarch's reflections upon it—but what emerged from his meditations was not a transformed Aristotelianism but a system that, for all its oddity in our eyes, Razi himself identified as Platonic.[21]

The men upon whom our knowledge of Razi depends, principally the Isma'ilis Abu Hatim al-Razi (d. 934),[22] Nasir-i Khusraw (d. after 1070)[23] and the later encyclopedist al-Katibi (d. 1276), were not in agreement with that identification. Nasir-i Khusraw made a convincing case that Razi had plagiarized his physical theories and their theological implications from a certain Iranshahri, a shadowy figure of the eighth century who held some unorthodox views of his own—he found the traditional religions not much to his liking and went about promoting one of his own devising—and who is cited by Biruni as an expert on the Iranian calendar, the culture of India and Manichaeism.

According to Nasir-i Khusraw, Iranshahri had speculated that

---

20. His most general systematic work appears to have been his *Theology*, which is, however, known to us only through citations by later authors.

21. Among Razi's preserved titles there are, however, commentaries on Aristotle's logical works as well as on the *Physics*, and all the evidence suggests that he knew Aristotle fairly thoroughly.

22. The chief Isma'ili missionary in Tabaristan with whom Razi engaged in controversy on the subject of prophecy. Much of Razi's position on the subject can be reconstructed from Abu Hatim's preserved *Signs of Prophecy*; see Chap. VIII, pp. 612–613.

23. See Chap. IX, pp. 642–643.

certain of the attributes of God, his knowledge, capacity, action and power, were made manifest in this world as time, space, movement and body. What Razi was said to have done was to take these manifestations, separate them from God, and give them an eternal reality of their own. Thus was Iranshahri's exercise of allegorical exegesis in the philosophical mode taken over by Razi and converted to heresy pure and simple.

We cannot judge the truth of this charge, since we know nothing of Iranshahri's theology beyond what Nasir has chosen to tell us. But the five eternal principles—he also called them substances—posited by Razi, to wit, the Creator, Soul, Matter, Void and Eternity, are not, as a matter of fact, identical with Iranshahri's God and his "manifestations."[24] Each of Razi's principles has, on the other hand, distinct Platonic antecedents that run back through the history of exegesis to the *Timaeus*. The *Timaeus* was read in a variety of ways in the Platonic schools, but the only commentator explicitly connected with Razi's understanding of that dialogue is Plutarch of Chaeronea, a partisan, no less than Razi was, of the creation of the world in time.

Razi's position on the temporal creation of the universe, a position that ranged him with Plutarch and John Philoponus against the main body of later Platonists,[25] was not the result of Islamic piety or of a desire to do justice to the Qur'anic account of creation. Indeed, he could make no sense of a creation *ex nihilo*. In his account of "creation" one of the five eternal principles, Soul, which in its original state possessed life but not yet knowledge, conceived a passionate lust to be united with Matter. Its desire could not be gratified as long as that Matter remained in its primordial state of formlessness, and since Soul was incapable of inducing form into primitive Matter, the Creator in effect connived with this weakness of Soul and brought into being a universe within which Soul was dispersed as individual souls in dwellings of articulated matter, that is to say, bodies.

Thus, as a result of the "fall" of the Soul there came into

---

24. Motion, for example, which in Iranshahri's scheme of things is a separate "manifestation," is for Razi an essential attribute of bodies.
25. Among Razi's other lost works is a "Refutation of Proclus."

existence the world of bodies endowed with life without understanding. Matter was transformed into bodies composed of atomic particles and fragments of void, and all the qualities of body—save movement, which is a property of the atoms—arise from the number and density of the atomic composite. The absolute Void is filled with such bodies and becomes space; and Eternity is reduced by its contact with movement into mere time.

The most elaborate description of Razi's cosmology comes from al-Katibi, who says that it was identical with the teachings of the Sabians of Harran. The charge had been made before. Mas'udi (d. 956) cited Razi as the author of a work on the Sabians, and far more explicitly the Spaniards Sa'id al-Andalusi (d. 1067) and Ibn Hazm (d. 1064) derived Razi's belief in transmigration from the same source. Razi notoriously held such a doctrine, as did others in Islam from far different motives, but not everyone was convinced that the Sabians alone were to blame. Pythagoras was also brought into the lists, and we are told that the tenth-century Christian Aristotelian Yahya ibn 'Adi studied the theology of Razi as a prime exemplar of Pythagoreanism.

The Sabians, Manichaeans, Brahmans and Pythagoras were all charged with the responsibility of having shaped the irreligious and heterodox philosophy of Razi. Many of the attributions came from Razi himself and may have been intended to mislead; Islam knew other instances of putting difficult or unlikely doctrines into the mouth of an alien tradition. Razi's self-confessed Platonism was real enough, however, even though it is not exactly the Platonism of a Plotinus, a Porphyry, or a Proclus. Instead of a single transcendent and spiritual cause Razi posited five eternal coprinciples which are substantial hypostases but not emanations from a unique First Cause.

One could elicit such a scheme from a reading of the *Timaeus*, as has been said, and perhaps Platonists of the obscure period before Plotinus were reading it so. What is less certain is that the same dialogue could be read to construct Razi's peculiar brand of atomism. A Platonist like Plutarch was still concerned with the influence of Epicurus in the second Christian century, but Razi stood, for all his atomic physics, remote from the tradition of

Epicurus. Razi's God was both demiurgic and provident, and for him the human intellect was no mere conglomerate of atoms but part of the divine substance itself.

At the heart of Razi's philosophy is a paradoxical soteriology. The Creator was moved with pity for the fallen Soul and provided it with a means of salvation: there came forth from the Creator a part of his substance, reason, whereby the individualized soul might come to an understanding of its true origins and so eventually free itself from matter. At first glance this appears to be some form of Manichaean salvation myth, and indeed it has often been asserted, both in his own day and this, that Razi was influenced by the Manichaeans.[26] The charge does not appear well founded. The existence of an eternal Matter was posited on cosmological and not moral grounds. Morality enters the scene only with the "lust" of the Soul, and in the sequel the material world is the creation of a good demiurge and not, as in Manichaeism, of some evil creator.

Once the human soul realizes its origins, it does seek to free itself from material desires, and the human soul does precisely the same in Plato without the benefit of Manichaeism. Further, salvation comes through reason, an "emanation" from God's own substance.[27] Thus Razi's cure for mortality turns out to be not a secret Manichaean *gnosis* but something unmistakably Hellenic, the public wisdom of philosophy available to all according to their abilities: neither an elitist *gnosis* nor an Islamic prophet is necessary for mankind's salvation.

Razi's denial of the need of prophecy brought him into conflict with Sunni and Shi'ite alike, but it makes him equally remote from the oracle-ridden theology of Proclan Neoplatonism. And yet Razi stood athwart a very similar tradition that sought to relate philosophy not to oracles but to the occult powers of

---

26. By Biruni among others, and this despite the fact that Biruni's own list of Razi's works includes one against "Sisinnius the Manichaean."
27. Soul may be an eternal principle, but Razi's "reason" is very like the "intelligence" that is the first emanation in Neoplatonism. It comes forth from God, albeit *after* the formation of the universe, necessarily and not by reason of any divine choice. The emanation of reason is the most Neoplatonic feature of Razi's world view.

nature. He was unmistakably an alchemist, and he defended its study as a necessary propaedeutic to philosophy. In the end it is not, however, alchemy that brings a man to that "other world" but rather philosophy, the supreme science. Proclus came to the *Chaldaean Oracles* after theology; for Razi philosophy was the end of the quest.

Razi's resistance to prophecy, whether in its usual Judaeo-Christian-Islamic form of a public and social revelation or in its esoteric Shi'ite manifestation in the person of an infallible *Imam*, held him close to a naturalistic theory of knowledge. The Platonist Farabi would develop a theory of naturalistic prophecy out of late Peripatetic speculation on the imagination, but the Platonism of Razi did not much exceed the bounds of physics.

Razi acknowledged the sage but denied the prophet. His wise man was not, however, the divinely inspired bard or the oracles so highly praised by later Platonism but the intellectual "striver," a Plato or an Aristotle whose accomplishments were the results of investigation, not inspiration.

Razi's intellectual naturalism had no sequel in Islam. He survived as a scientist, while his denial of prophecy in favor of reasoned speculation was universally denounced as something alien to Islam. Razi refused to conceal himself within the artifices of allegorical exegesis, as his mentor Iranshahri was perhaps already doing, or by saying, as Kindi had, that there was no conflict between the truths of philosophy and those of the Muslim revelation. He was unique in announcing that revelation had no truths and that those who claimed to be prophets were in fact mere impostors. Plato was the only prophet and his revelation was *falsafah*.

Reaction and Reform

The fragile favors granted by Ma'mun and his immediate successors to the theologian and the philosopher were short-lived. A small coterie of intellectuals, themselves under grave suspicion of heresy, could not sustain the Caliphs; for that the Caliphs had to rely on their Turkish pretorians, first at Baghdad and then, after 836, in the palace fortresses at Samarra. And when al-Wathiq

THEOLOGICAL MOVEMENT

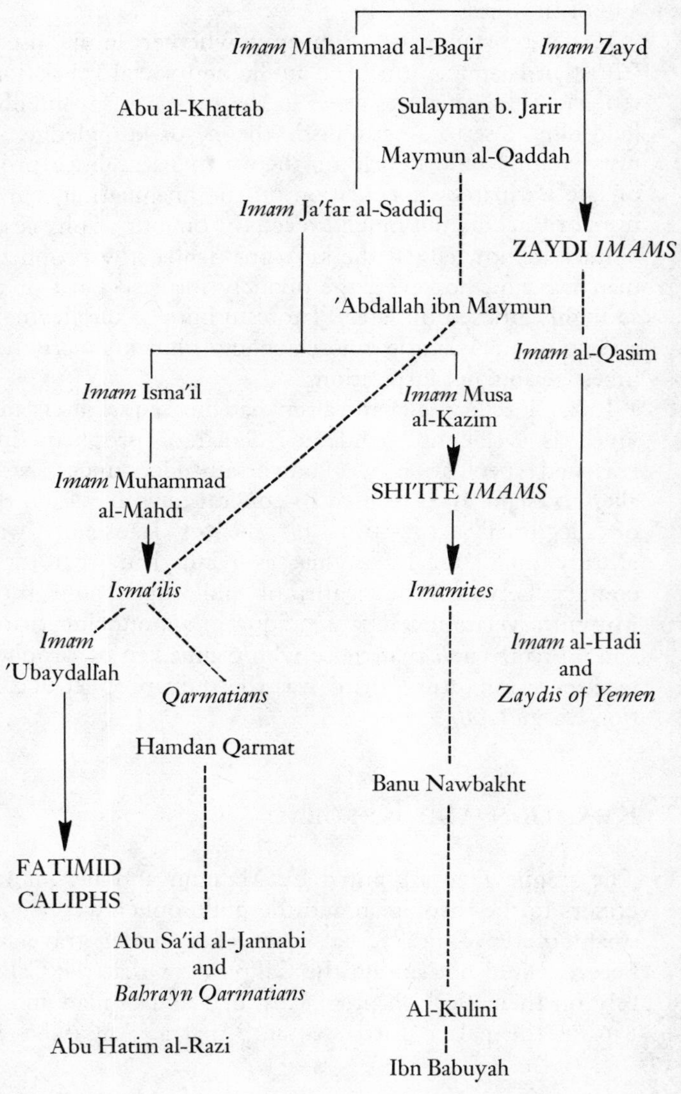

AND SECTS (c. 700–1000)

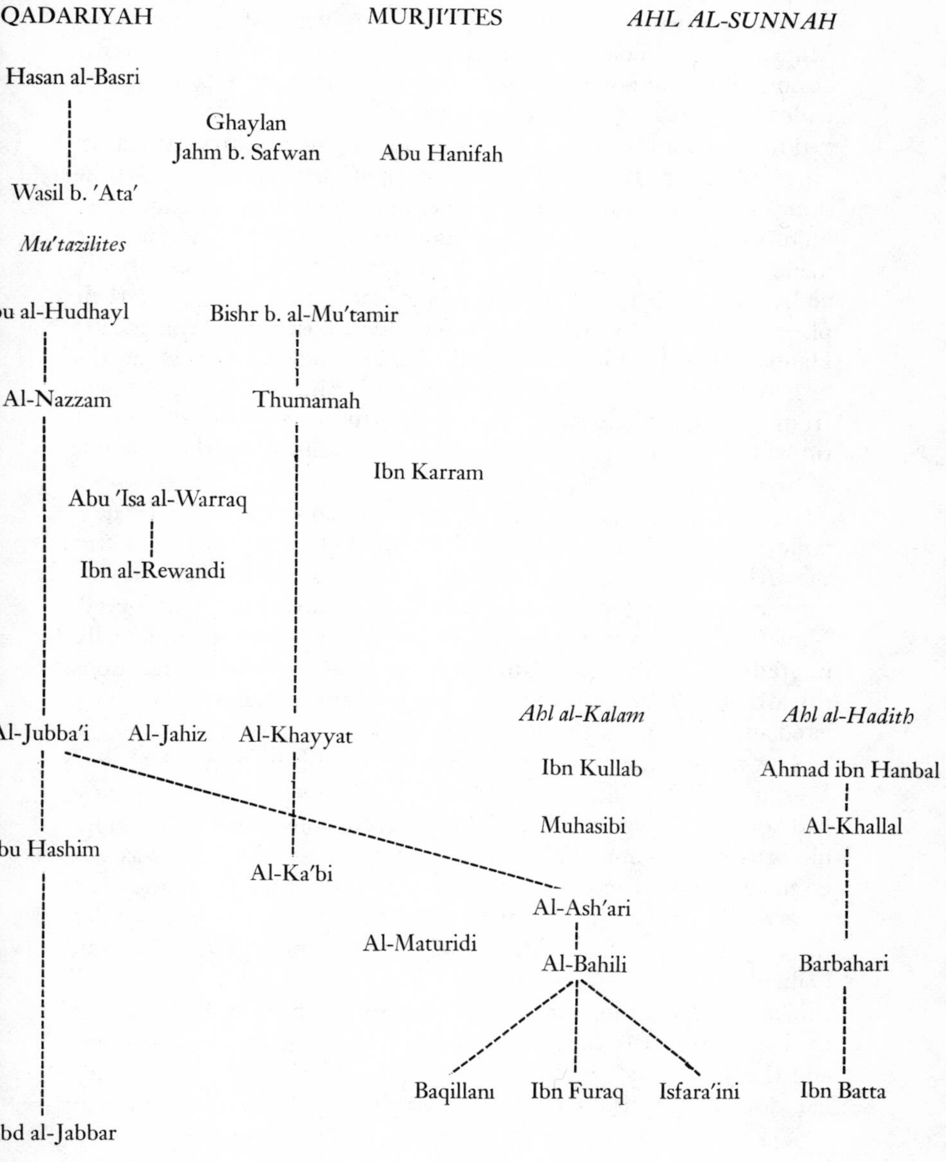

died in 847 without having appointed a successor, it was the candidate of the Turkish captains who prevailed, al-Wathiq's brother Mutawakkil (847–861). They had chosen, it soon appeared, a man with a policy; within a year of his accession Mutawakkil reversed the religious program of his three predecessors. He summoned a committee of conservative lawyers and bade them restore the traditionalist ideology.

The discontinuance of the *mihnah* did not at first affect its chief architect, Ibn abi Du'ad. The *qadi* had suffered a stroke soon after Mutawakkil took office, and though he continued to hold his post in name until 851, most of the actual decisions were made by his son. Imprisonment and confiscation did eventually come, and both father and son died in disgrace in 854. In their place was put Ibn Akhtam, reputedly chosen by Ahmad ibn Hanbal himself. The elderly theologian who had stood at the targeted center of the purge for fifteen years was brought forth from retirement and was offered by Mutawakkil the charge of tutoring the crown prince. Ibn Hanbal declined on the grounds of his age; he died in 855.

The 'Alids immediately felt the consequences of the new policy. Since Ma'mun's brief flirtation with 'Ali al-Rida in 817 the 'Alids could hardly be said to have enjoyed official favor; they were merely pressed rather than systematically persecuted. Now under Mutawakkil they were overtly and energetically hunted, and in 851 the Caliph left no doubt as to his intentions toward the *Shi'at 'Ali:* the tomb of Husayn at Karbala' was violated and all pilgrimages to the place banned.

The *mihnah* instituted by Ma'mun had been directed against Muslims and Muslims alone. Mutawakkil's reversal of that policy had, on the other hand, serious repercussions for the religious minorities of Islam. The triumph of the traditionalists was accompanied by severe persecutions of Christians, Jews and that mass of heretics and unbelievers that the orthodox lumped under the rubric of *zindiq:* Manichaeans, Daysaniyah, Zoroastrians, Dahriyah, et cetera.

Zandaqah with its taint of polytheism had been judged suspect by Islam from the beginning, but the position of the Christians and the Jews was very different. The recognition of their peculiar doctrinal position vis-à-vis Islam had led to a distinction in their juridical status and the creation of the category of *dhimmah* or protected minority with its discriminatory obligations and covenanted guarantees. Juridical status, which was invested with an eternal quality by Islamic jurisprudence, did not, however, reflect the subtly shifting relations between the contracting parties. The statute was set down by a minority group of conquerors but was administered by a ruling majority who sensed their own need of the *dhimmis* as well as both the challenge and the threat that such people posed to Islam.

In Iraq the status of Christians was bound up with the problem of the *mawali* who began to dominate in the chanceries from the beginning of 'Abbasid rule. Nestorian scribes took their place at the side of converted Iranian secretaries in the imperial bureaus, and the Barmacids and other viziers patronized *mawali* and Christians alike. The secretaries' intellectual pedigrees ran back into Iranian sources, however, while the Christians were heirs to quite another tradition, that of the Hellenic sciences. From Mansur's day, or perhaps even earlier, the Christian physician was a familiar figure at court, and when Ma'mun founded his "House of Wisdom" sometime around 830 the connections between Caliphal patronage and Christian learning became even more intimate.

The physicians of Jundishapur and the translators who began the conversion of Greek wisdom into Arabic functioned principally as scholars rather than as Christians. But their Christianity was known to their contemporaries, who noted the fact in their works. During the entire period, the more than half a century stretching across the reigns of Harun and Ma'mun, the Nestorian Church, the main body of Christians east of Syria and Egypt, was in a flourishing state, due in large measure to the aggressive leadership of the Catholicus Timotheus (780–823). The strength of the Church lay among the Aramaic peoples—whom the Arabs somewhat contemptuously called "Nabataeans"—of middle and upper Mesopotamia; and while Christianity lost the Arab tribes to Islam,[28] the rate of loss among the Aramaeans was steady but slower. There was no question of making new converts among

28. The last Christian Arab tribe, the Banu Tanukh, were forcibly converted to Islam by al-Mahdi in 780.

the Muslims, a dangerous and illegal maneuver in any event, and so Timotheus concentrated his efforts on missionary work outside the *Dar al-Islam* and particularly in Central Asia, where the Christian hierarchy was strengthened and expanded. From the eighth century until Mongol times Nestorianism was a powerful religious presence on the steppes and in the oases of Central Asia.

In Baghdad itself, where the Catholicus had his residence, Timotheus was as well known at court as the members of the Christian Bukhtishu' family who served the Caliphs as physicians,[29] and he had even done some translating at the Caliph's specific request. The Caliphs of the period much fancied public disputations and Timotheus engaged in one such on Christianity before al-Mahdi. The Catholicus' secretary and collaborator, Abu Nuh, was somewhat more direct; he is reported to have composed a refutation of the *Qur'an.*

The religious climate appears free and open, and perhaps it was in Baghdad before 847. There were, however, local quarrels, the obviously diminishing number of Christians in Syria and Palestine, and in Egypt the continuing legacy of Umayyad oppression; between 725 and 773 there were six Coptic uprisings in Egypt, each put down with severity. The juridical status of the Christians dictated an inferior social and economic position for the *dhimmis;* it remained to the local authorities to decide how literally the discriminatory regulations concerning taxation, dress and the general pattern of social behavior would be enforced. In Egypt, where the Copts were totally at the mercy of the local governor, the regulations were by and large enforced, while in Baghdad, where the Christian community had direct access to the Caliph, they were not.

With Mutawakkil's decision to embrace a conservative version of Islam, the statutes began to be enforced in Iraq as well. Nestorians were winnowed out of the *diwans,* and what had been a

---

29. Relations apparently were not always smooth between the Catholicus and the Royal Physician, the two Christians with the most immediate access to the Caliph. Timotheus excommunicated Jibril ibn Bukhtishu', and on later occasions the Bukhtishu' family asserted its right to have a say in the selection of the Catholicus.

sometimes friendly and illuminating dialogue between Christianity and Islam assumed the harsher tones of polemic. Two attacks on Christianity are preserved from Mutawakkil's time, the physician 'Ali al-Tabari's *Book of Religion and Empire* and al-Jahiz's *Refutation of the Christians.*

Both works relied heavily on Scriptural exegesis. The Muslim was committed to the proposition that the Christians and Jews had distorted the Scriptures and the polemicists set out to show how it was done. But the Muslim had also to accept the proposition that Muhammad was the term of the Judaeo-Christian revelation, and the Christians for their part were quick to point out that neither the Old nor the New Testament knew anything about the coming of this new Prophet. Exegesis ran off into theology, where the Muslim not only had an essentially different view of Jesus from that held by his opponents, but also had inherited a great deal of legend, myth and *midrash* about figures in Christian and Jewish history; the *Qur'an*'s apparent confusion, for example, of Mary the sister of Moses with Jesus' mother provided the Christians with a broad and inviting target.

Much of this quickly became standardized so that later anti-Christian polemicists like Ibn Hazm and al-Ghazali had a sophisticated knowledge of the weaknesses of the other side and could recite the Scriptural *cruces* as easily as a verse from the *Qur'an.* With Jahiz, on the other hand, an essayist rather than a professional theologian, the attack on Christianity took on an interesting social dimension. The contemporary Christians, Jahiz conceded, were more acceptable than the Jews: they were cleaner, better educated and wealthier; Christians rode to the hounds, played polo and wore fine clothes. In fact, they were pretentious to the point where the Muslim was beginning to feel inferior in their presence. No need, Jahiz asserted, and he proceeded to score his theological points.

As the passages in Jahiz suggest, the source of Mutawakkil's *furor theologicus* ran deeper than appearances. Islamic history was later written by traditionalists and Shi'ites to whom Mutawakkil appeared to be acting out of personal religious conviction. So he may, but the Caliph was in a desperate position. The grandiose buildings at Samarra, to which Mutawakkil added more than his share, were despoiling the treasury, while the Caliph, who was caught between vizier, *qadi* and Turkish captain, was rapidly losing what remained of his powers. In a last convulsive effort to restore the situation, Mutawakkil carried his case to the people by espousing the popular conservative theology against elitist Mu'tazilitism. The Christians and Jews were pawns in a game of political theology, offered up to the traditionalists in exchange for their support of the regime.

Mutawakkil's repressive measures against them had severe and far-reaching effects on those Christians of the *Dar al-Islam* who fell immediately under the Caliph's control and who did not possess, as the Nestorians to some extent did, firm enough connections with the Muslim establishment to weather the storm. The regulations on distinctive dress and other identifications, some of which went back to Harun al-Rashid, were strictly enforced. In Egypt, which had a tradition of severity toward Christians from the Umayyads' time, the situation was further complicated by wholesale Bedouin migrations into the country. Among their prime targets were the largely unprotected monastic communities that were the backbone of Coptic Christianity. The Bedouin savagely plundered the famous convents of the desert, and those monks who survived did so only by converting their monasteries into fortresses. The face of the Near East was changing into a Muslim one, while the Christians were reduced by the battering to the position of a beleaguered minority.

The Caliphs Mansur and Harun had thought they could maintain the equilibrium between Islamic orthodoxy on the one side and the cultural mélange represented by the intellectuals, the *mawali* and the Christians on the other. The brilliant and mercurial Ma'mun lost his nerve, however, and destroyed that perilous balance. Mutawakkil, instead of adjusting it, took a dangerous gamble that succeeded only if success is judged to mean the continued existence of the Caliphate and its possession by his house. Once given its head by Mutawakkil, a radical conservatism settled deep into the marrow of Islam until it eventually took over the life of the organism. An open, liberal and evolutionary Islam did not disappear at a stroke in 847. What did occur was that Islam officially vacated a large area of intellectual concern, which was summarily expropriated by others, in the first instance by an invigorated Shi'ah, and in the end Islam unleashed its reactionaries instead of taming them.

The Mu'tazilites were in the front line of this struggle, but not a great deal is heard of them after Mutawakkil's repudiation of their version of orthodoxy. That Caliph's successors were far more concerned with the politically dangerous 'Alids than with the increasingly subtle metaphysics of the Mu'tazilah. *Kalam* was, moreover, a private enterprise; it had no place in the curriculum of Muslim institutions of higher learning, where advanced instruction was given in the Qur'anic and *hadith* sciences and where jurisprudence was the primary concern.[30] The Mu'tazilites were a *school* only in the sense that they were a *sect;* they did not constitute, in any event, the only kind of school that Islam knew at that point, to wit, an orthodox legal *madhhab*.

Mu'tazilite teaching, whether private or semipublic,[31] must have continued at Basrah and Baghdad in the latter half of the tenth century. Something, though not a great deal, is known of the major figures of the sect. The Basran group was led by al-Jubba'i (d. 915) who was eventually succeeded in that role by his son Abu Hashim (d. 933), while the somewhat less influential Baghdad Mu'tazilah had as its head al-Khayyat's student Abu al-Qasim al-Ka'bi (d. 931). Despite their common opposition to the "partisans of tradition," the two groups had their own mutual differences, many of them springing from questions raised in the preceding generation by Thumamah and al-Jahiz.

As has already been seen, the two earlier Mu'tazilites had attempted to reduce the obligation to belief—and in this context, to Islamic belief—by attacking Abu al-Hudhayl's contention that the knowledge of God was given a priori and so was of a necessitating kind. With al-Jubba'i the Basrah Mu'tazilites returned to the question. Their conclusions were similar to Abu al-Hudhayl's, but they were reached by a different route. For Jubba'i it was not the direct knowledge of God that was given in

30. See Chap. IX, p. 681.
31. The latter in the form of the "discussion conference," or *majlis al-nazar*, which was open to all interested parties; such gatherings were a constant feature of the intellectual life of Muslim cities from the tenth century onward.

the first instance. That comes about through a somewhat complicated psychological process initiated by a spiritual uneasiness arising out of man's recognition of his created state. That recognition leads to further understanding that his peace can only be restored by knowledge. Man reflects, and the pondering creates an anxiety that drives the rational being to reason as a cure, and so also as a good. Reason then teaches him that God exists.

The issue at stake here was the primitive Mu'tazilite one of justifying the existence of a rational theology independent of revelation. Jubba'i's explanation was directed toward establishing the moral value, and so the absolute necessity, of speculative reason. His chain of effects descending from a primary psychological intuition was designed to lead around the obvious *crux* raised by Thumamah and Jahiz, that there was no primary concept of God. The reliance on that intuition merely raised a further residual difficulty, however. In the contemporary metaphysics there was no place for the kind of "uncaused" and primary intuition that started Jubba'i's chain of reactions.

His son and disciple Abu Hashim attempted to correct the intuition into something more comprehensible; he introduced the notion of Allah's grace. God is knowing, and so knowledge is a good. By an act of his grace Allah intimates the same to man by bringing about this primary but anxious insight about himself and the world. Once the initial "dangling" causality had been explained, the rest of Jubba'i's series could unfold on its necessary way toward speculation.

The traditionalists' opposition to the Mu'tazilite theses on the necessity of speculative knowledge was based on its apparent undercutting of the economy of revelation. If Allah could be, and indeed must be, apprehended by human reason, what was the point of the Prophet's revelation? When Abu Hashim spoke of Allah's communicating to man the primordial insight into his created state, he was referring not to Allah's message in the *Qur'an* but to a private speech directed to the individual. Was there a place for the Prophet in a scheme where Allah spoke directly to the intelligence of individual men?

The apostate Mu'tazilite Ibn al-Rewandi had posed exactly that question to his former associates, and there were others—al-

Kindi's student Sarakhsi and the physician Razi among them—who for one reason or another concluded that in a rationalist system prophets were otiose. The Mu'tazilites did not go so far. Some, like Abu Hashim, invoked a distinction in the Law: unaided reason could indeed deduce many of the prescriptions of the *shari'ah,* but other commandments—the fast of Ramadan, for example—were not grounded in reason and so could be known only through the benefit of a public revelation. Others preferred to avoid such a distinction and attempted to defend the need of a public revelation solely in terms of its being a humane shortcut through the difficult and protracted process of intellectual speculation.

What attracted later attention to Abu Hashim was not, however, his refinements on his father's notion of an obligatory speculation, but rather his own peculiar contribution to the continuing debate on the attributes of Allah. The earlier discussion had gone off into the metaphysics of atoms and accidents, but already in the generation of Abu al-Hudhayl some of the Mu'tazilites had begun to investigate other aspects of the question. For Abu al-Hudhayl an existent was a "something" and so possessed for him, as it had for Hisham ibn al-Hakam, certain corporeal associations. The identification of "thing" and "existent" posed some grave difficulties, however, when it was brought into the discussion of God's knowledge. At first sight the only alternative to "something" was "nothing," the nonexistent, and so it seemed to follow that God could not know a thing until it became an existent, a "something." The position was an awkward one in that it placed the eternal omniscient God in a position of ignorance until such time as the world was created, or, to put it another way, it made God's knowledge dependent on contingent beings.

An early attempt at avoiding this conclusion was proposed by Abu al-Hudhayl's student Hisham al-Fuwati, who suggested that before creation God knew only one thing, that beings would be created. Thus before creation being was a "known" and afterwards it was an existent "thing." This was not the only possible solution. One could, for example, maintain the eternity of "things" and so save God's knowledge at the expense of his creation,[32] or one could turn to the resources of atomism and suggest that God knew the atoms from all eternity, though not the qualifying accidents that converted those atoms into "things."

What was happening, clearly, was that the bond between being and "thing" was weakening as the Mu'tazilites came to understand the differences between absolute nonbeing and some intermediary stages of relative being. What the Greeks had come to from an analysis of change provoked by Parmenides' conundrums about nonbeing, the Muslim approached from the side of revelation that posited a creator God who had to know before he could create. Al-Fuwati had begun with his tentative steps toward a purely intelligible being, and his contemporary al-Shahham, likewise a student of Abu al-Hudhayl, proceeded further. He proposed the existence of a "possible nonbeing" that exists in the mind of God before it becomes an existent. Thus, where the early *mutakallimun* recognized only the disjunction nonexistent/existent (= thing), the next generation of Mu'tazilites proposed the more sophisticated disjunction of nonbeing/being, with the latter further subdivided into possible being and existent being.

The terminology continued to change as the latter disjunction took hold, but atomism did not easily lend itself to such distinctions. Possible being was, within the context of the discussion, some kind of noetic being, but the distinction between atoms and accidents, which arose out of what must have been a very different kind of discussion, allowed little room for such noncorporeal entities. What was needed was a different kind of distinction, that between matter and spirit, to enable the intelligibles to enjoy some degree of being, if not perfect existence, in the mind of God before creation. Both the Platonic "form" and the Aristotelian "essence" provided just such a possibility, and among the later Mu'tazilites the shading off of Abu al-Hudhayl's atom into an Aristotelian essence is clearly perceptible.

Abu Hashim's entry into the controversy marked a reversion to something older in *kalam*. His contribution to the debate on

---

32. This was the solution of another obscure but important sect running back to pre-Islamic times, the Dahriyah, who held for the eternity (*dahr*) of the world and time.

the nature of being came on the related subject of Allah's attributes. The divine attributes raised exactly the same ontological questions as God's knowledge of being, and the early affirmation and denial of the attributes hinged on their ontological status and its relation to the being of God. Ibn Kullab, it will be recalled,[33] had proposed a compromise formula: the divine attributes were not the same as Allah nor entirely separable from him. Abu Hashim's response was in the same vein. He proposed that the attributes were neither identical with God's being nor apart from it; they were "modes" of Allah's being.

Abu Hashim's "modes" may be no more than a reflex upon Ibn Kullab's earlier attempt at finding some ground between existence and absolute nonbeing, but the terminology of this later formula suggests other possibilities. For the Stoics too the supreme genus of being was the "something," and they had distinguished one existent from another precisely by its "mode of being." Earlier traces of Stoicism in Islam were mediated through the Christian sensibilities of the Daysaniyah, and here too Christian *kalam* cannot be excluded. In the eighth century John of Damascus revived an earlier explanation of the Trinity which understood the three divine Persons as the "modes of being" of a single substance. Abu Hashim, the Stoics, and John of Damascus were all facing the same problem and their solutions are remarkably similar: there is between a fully constituted existent and absolute nonbeing an intermediate degree which all three parties to the problem called the "mode of being."

Al-Jubba'i died in 915 and was succeeded as head of the Basrah Mu'tazilites by his son Abu Hashim. He may have made known his choice of successor even earlier, since in 912 the Mu'tazilah lost another theologian who was reputed to have been in line for the position of scholarch, Abu al-Hasan al-Ash'ari (d. 935). According to a source dating some two and a half centuries after the event,[34] al-Ash'ari, then a Mu'tazilite follower of al-Jubba'i, had a vision of the Prophet in which he was commanded to

---

33. See Chap. II, pp. 198–199.
34. The Damascene historian Ibn 'Asakir (d. 1176) whose *Refutation of the Calumniator's Lying* is the source of most of what we know of Ash'ari's life.

devote himself to the religious sciences. When Ash'ari interpreted this to mean that he must surrender the study of *kalam,* the Prophet appeared once again and admonished him that this science too was useful. In 912 Ash'ari mounted the pulpit of the mosque in Basrah and made public announcement of his repudiation of the Mu'tazilah.

The account of the vision may be tendentious, but its content sums up well enough Ash'ari's intention of aligning himself with the "partisans of custom and the community" and of giving the lie to his former Mu'tazilite colleagues. Whether piety, disenchantment or thwarted ambition brought about the "conversion" of Ash'ari is not the point here; the more important, and equally difficult, question is What did he actually accomplish? The later orthodox tradition in theology claimed that it was "Ash'arite" and so invested its alleged founder with the prestige of a "centenary reformer," one of the men who appear at the turn of each Islamic century to renew the vitality of Allah's religion.[35] It is not easy, then, to disentangle the man from his reputation.

There are extant a number of Ash'ari's own works, notably the *Exposition of the Principles of Religion,* the *Highlights of Polemic against Deviationists and Innovators* and the highly important heresiography, *Views of the Muslims.* Among his other works known only by title, Ash'ari devoted monographs to special questions raised by the Mu'tazilites on the divine attributes, free will, and the central issue of the creation of the *Qur'an;* he composed, in addition, an impressive number of polemical treatises against the "materialists," Rafidites, Ibn al-Rewandi, the logicians and philosophers. Finally, there is the preserved text of the *Vindication of the Science of Kalam,* a work whose authenticity has been questioned. It is only doubtfully attested by later authors, and it raises, in fact, the central question of what Ash'ari intended.

On the basis of the *Exposition* alone Ash'ari appears to be a genuine convert from the *kalam* of the Mu'tazilites back to the

---

35. Ash'ari's immediate predecessors in this gallery of religious heroes were thought to be the Caliph 'Umar II and al-Shafi'i and his successors al-Baqillani and al-Ghazali, a wholesome if not entirely representative lot.

traditionalism of Ahmad ibn Hanbal. If the *Vindication* is genuine, however, then the picture must be revised to make room for Ash'ari the chastened but still unreformed *mutakallim*. There is no doubt that the later Ash'arites undertook to defend and even to strengthen *kalam* as a legitimate methodology for the Shafi'ite lawyer. But it is not at all clear that Ash'ari himself saw it the same way. The traditionalist pieties of the *Exposition* create at least the suspicion that the moderately rationalist Ash'ari was the creation of classical Ash'arism and not, as the tradition held, vice versa.

The *Exposition* is filled with expressions like "We confess that God has two hands, without asking how." The statement is pure Ahmad ibn Hanbal in its literal acceptance of the *Qur'an's* anthropomorphic descriptions of Allah and its simultaneous refusal to impose an allegorical or rationalistic exegesis upon the text. Like the Hanbalites, Ash'ari also accepted the Caliphate of 'Uthman, the various eschatological details that the Mu'tazilites explained into allegorical oblivion and the uncreated nature of the *Qur'an*. But on free will the luminous Hanbalism begins to cloud over when Ash'ari affirms that while God is the sole agent of all acts, men somehow "acquire" them. "Acquisition" is hardly Hanbalism; it is rather the suggestion of an earlier *mutakallim*, Dirar ibn 'Amr, on how to preserve God's omnipotence and at the same time satisfy man's sense of freedom in moral acts. On the evidence, Ash'ari had by no means deserted *kalam*, nor did he pretend he had.

If Ash'ari's goal was to be an orthodox *mutakallim*, it was scarcely a novel enterprise. Ahmad ibn Hanbal's own contemporary Ibn Kullab had attempted something quite similar against the Mu'tazilites, and in Ash'ari's own day there were those among the eastern Hanafites who were exploring the same possibility. Ash'ari was well aware of Ibn Kullab and his school, and in the *Views of the Muslims* he connected their positions adroitly with his own. Like Ash'ari himself, Ibn Kullab ran into Hanbalite opposition to his use of *kalam*, and in a curious piece of historical archaizing the Hanbalite Ibn Taymiyah (d. 1328) was still treating Ibn Kullab as an adversary some five hundred years after the event.

The case of the Sufi al-Muhasibi is somewhat more complex.

Ibn Hanbal had a number of harsh things to say of Muhasibi, and some at least of them had to do with Muhasibi's theories on the love of God and the possibility of man's achieving it. But according to other accounts, Ibn Hanbal accused his contemporary of heresy (*bid'ah*) and of having to bear a heavy burden of responsibility for the *mihnah* by reason of his support of *kalam*, presumably of the Mu'tazilite variety.[36] Muhasibi did interest himself in the theological questions of the day, that of the divine attributes for example, but it is not at all certain that he argued them dialectically in the manner of the Mu'tazilites. His preserved works rely heavily on *hadith* arguments.

What Ibn Hanbal may have found far more objectionable, however, was Muhasibi's persevering trust in the power of reason as an instrument for attaining the truth. As we have seen, Muhasibi was speaking primarily in a moral context, where intelligence is a discriminating power between good and evil, but if Ibn Hanbal's somewhat violent reaction is to be taken seriously, the Sufi's intellectualism may have extended into speculative realms as well.

On dogma Ash'ari, like Muhasibi, made no compromise with the Mu'tazilah. His *Highlights* is a work of polemic directed precisely against the Mu'tazilites,[37] and in it he denied outright that the *Qur'an* was created, that Allah possessed no attributes distinct from his essence, and that man created his own acts, all fundamental and strongly held Mu'tazilite theses. But despite the lavish praise heaped on Ibn Hanbal in the *Exposition*, there is also the dubious witness of the *Vindication of the Science of Kalam* aimed against those among the Hanbalites who refused to accept Ash'ari's eager embrace. The argument in the *Vindication* rests largely upon Qur'anic passages and *hadith*, but the author is, nonetheless, unable to conceal the true bone of contention between himself and the traditionalists, the relationship between

36. Whatever their precise cause, Ahmad ibn Hanbal's reproaches apparently had their desired effect, the isolation of Muhasibi. It is reported that only four people appeared at his funeral.

37. Ibn al-Nadim reports that Muhasibi too wrote works against the Mu'tazilites.

truth transmitted by authority (*taqlid*) and that acquired through speculation (*nazar*).

The Mu'tazilites were almost unanimous in their denunciation of those who would accept the truth of a proposition on the authority of another. From Abu al-Hudhayl to Abu Hashim the same theme occurs: whatever its value in the Law, where the principle operates in the form of consensus, *taqlid* is unacceptable in theology, since it cannot lead to true knowledge. The only dissenter that we know of was al-Ka'bi who preferred to concentrate on the conclusion rather than the method of reaching it. If a man affirms a truth on someone else's authority, he is still asserting a truth and for him *taqlid* has led to knowledge. The sophisticated theologian might stand in need of speculation, but in Ka'bi's view the common man did not. His Basrah contemporary Abu Hashim would not have it so. Knowledge of God without some kind of proof was not knowledge at all, and so it followed for Abu Hashim that the man who rested upon *taqlid* was in no sense a true believer. Speculation was, then, absolutely necessary for salvation.

For Ash'ari the case was not so simple. The believer did stand in need of some speculatively derived knowledge, but Ash'ari was equally unwilling to condemn, as Abu Hashim did, the simple man who accepted the authority of others in matters of faith; he was not an infidel (*kafir*). Who was a believer and who an infidel was, of course, an early and important juridical issue, and Ash'ari betrays his Mu'tazilite antecedents in equating the believer's faith (*iman*) with the intellectual's understanding (*'ilm*): there cannot be belief without understanding, and there is no understanding without some kind of speculative knowledge.

In Ash'ari, or better, the Ash'arites, the analysis of the act of faith centers on an inner assent construed every bit as intellectually as the Mu'tazilites were accustomed to do. The interior quality of faith was not a Mu'tazilite contribution to Islam, to be sure. Earlier, when the Kharijites had raised the question in the juridical form of "Who is a Muslim?" their insistence on orthopraxy as the sole criterion was countered by another, more interiorized point of view. The Murji'ites held that an exterior profession of belief was enough to qualify one as a Muslim in the eyes of the community, while God alone could read and judge what was in the heart. The jurist Abu Hanifah (d. 767), who was a Murji'ite in his theology, took a similar position. This was before the rise of the Mu'tazilites as a distinct sect, and even though there were wide differences between the later Hanafites and the Mu'tazilah, at least part of the struggle that went on between Ash'arism and Mu'tazilitism during the tenth and eleventh centuries had to do with the control of the Hanafite school of law.

Measured against the traditionalism of al-Shafi'i and Ahmad ibn Hanbal, Abu Hanifah's attitude toward the roots of the Law was cautiously rationalistic. He claimed legitimacy for some element of personal discretion in jurisprudence against the rising claims for tradition as the exclusive operative base for the Islamic Law. Faith, too, required understanding as the ground for the interior assent that is far more critical than external acts in making a man a Muslim. This was the view among the Hanafites at Kufah, but in the east some of the school went even further. Ibn Karram (d. 869), a teacher in Khurasan who fell afoul of the Tahirid princes there on more than one occasion, was not a lawyer but an ascetic and a *mutakallim.* Thanks to their passage through more orthodox hands, Ibn Karram's teachings are not well known, but he did found what the later heresiographers regarded as a sect that included, down to the beginning of the eleventh century, a considerable number of eastern Hanafite lawyers.

What rendered Ibn Karram doctrinally suspect was a somewhat naïve attempt at reconciling a version of atomism with the *Qur'an*'s description of God. He took the Mu'tazilite position that Allah was a "substance," or, in the terminology of the times, a "body," still, in the ninth century, a working term for "being." Ibn Karram then awkwardly placed this philosophically and materially conceived "body" upon the "throne" described in the *Qur'an* and in so doing convinced the traditionalists that he was a flagrant anthropomorphist. There was more of this, but the heresiographers who tell the tale were all Ash'arites and ignored or obscured what was more likely the real point of Ibn Karram's efforts, to construct an orthodox *kalam* within the liberal confines of the Murji'ite-Hanafite tradition.

Ibn Karram stood close to the Murji'ites on the issue of faith.

The juridical problem was resolved for both by a mere verbal profession (*shahadah*), but there stands behind that verbal *shahadah* a complex of spiritual acts in which the mind's knowledge and the heart's assent are vital. And like Abu Hanifah and the Mu'tazilites—whom the Karramites strongly opposed on the question of the divine attributes—Ibn Karram held firmly for the freedom of human action and, in the spirit of the Hanafite school, for a flexible interpretation of the *shari'ah*.

The Baghdad Hanbalites regarded the Karramiyah among their adversaries throughout the tenth and early eleventh centuries, principally on the issues of freedom, anthropomorphism and the Murji'ite-inspired separation of faith from the observance of the Law. The contest with the followers of Ibn Karram, however, took place not in Baghdad but in the eastern provinces, where Karramites were near to being the official theologians of the Ghaznavids until 1017.[38] Thereafter the Karramites' influence diminished, but they survived long enough to pass on some of their ideas to another group of theologians who had a somewhat happier fate in the struggle for orthodoxy.

The history of theology in Islam was shaped by the later Ash'arite predominance within the ranks of the Shafi'ite lawyers, and their material and outlook is colored by a self-serving defense of *kalam*. But *kalam* had other defenders besides the Ash'arites and the suspect Mu'tazilites. Ibn Kullab was one, Ibn Karram was another, and later, again under the legal banner of Abu Hanifah, there was al-Maturidi (d. 944) of Samarqand.

Maturidite *kalam* merged in the end with Ash'arism or died with Mu'tazilitism, but by reason of the fact that it was Hanafite rather than Shafi'ite, in law other diflerences arose between it and the version of *kalam* being propagated by Ash'ari. The Maturidites followed the lead of Abu Hanifah in supporting human freedom and responsibility, a position bypassed by the Ash'arite doctrine of "acquisition." They avoided at the same time the radical Ash'arite stance on the absolute obligation to speculative knowledge. For the Maturidites, speculation was better than *taqlid*, but even that latter reliance on human authority can lead

38. See Chap. VIII, pp. 588–591.

to truth and so is not to be scorned. The Maturidites did not write off the simple believer, as the Ash'arites were inclined to do. They attempted instead to instruct him, and whatever is left of Maturidite literature is precisely in the form of creeds and catechisms and not treatises on *kalam*.[39]

The Hanbalites did not much attend to the followers of al-Maturidi, who were neither strong in Baghdad nor, indeed, very distinct from the Ash'arite school of *kalam*. Between the Hanbalites and the *mutakallimun*, whether of the Shafi'ite-Ash'arite or the Hanafite-Maturidite persuasion, there were, however, fundamental differences that ran in and out of the interwoven fabric of *fiqh* and *kalam*. The struggle between Hanbalite and Ash'arite was fought, after all, on the subject of orthodoxy, on who had claim to the allegiance of the "partisans of *sunnah* and the community."

In the tenth century, doctrinal orthodoxy meant only one thing, membership in one of the four or five recognized law schools. *Kalam*, which was the issue between them, was not, however, jurisprudence, and so the notion of an Ash'arite "school" would have seemed exceedingly strange to most of the contestants. For the traditionalists, *kalam* was a method and not yet a discipline; and so the question posed by them and responded to by the Ash'arites was quite simply, Does *kalam* have a legitimate place in any of the schools of law?

The tension between *kalam* as a method and as a discipline runs through all the debates of the tenth and eleventh centuries. The Hanbalites were lawyers attempting to defend the Law, and the Ash'arites had to meet them on those terms. In the end they were successful and Ash'arite *kalam* gained a permanent foothold in the Shafi'ite *madhhab*. The Mu'tazilites' early relationship to jurisprudence is not entirely clear, and even though there is some evidence that they too were attempting to infiltrate the Hanafite school, they never found any place there, a failure that proved to be fatal. The Hanbalites operated from the strongest position of

39. Notably the *Articles of Belief* of Abu Hafs al-Nasafi (d. 1142) of Samarqand and the little poetical catechism, *The Qasidah*, of al-Ushi (d. 1173) of Ferghana. Both were frequent objects of later commentaries.

all: they fought from within the acknowledged orthodoxy of their own school.

The fortunes of the Hanbalites are not always easy to discern after the accession of Mutawakkil in 847 and the death of Ibn Hanbal eight years later. Mutawakkil undertook to restore the "partisans of *sunnah*" to a position of prominence at court, and Ibn Hanbal was invited to play a leading role in the restoration. He declined on grounds of age and infirmity and the responsibility passed to others. Chief among the old man's disciples was his son 'Abdallah (d. 903) and Abu Bakr al-Khallal (d. 923). 'Abdallah was particularly engaged in the transmission and edition of Ibn Hanbal's collection of almost thirty thousand acceptable *hadiths* in a book called *The Well Attested*,[40] while al-Khallal was one of the many Hanbalites who collected the *responsa* given by the master during his lifetime.

This latter work, *Queries*, together with his *Refutation of Zindiqs and Jahmites*,[41] represents the kernel of Ibn Hanbal on dogmatic questions. He was not, as sometimes appears, a proponent of anthropomorphism, but he was equally opposed to the stripping down of the Qur'anic portrait of God in the name of some fancied allegory or for the purpose of making Allah conform to the apophatic necessities of the rationalists' deity. Ibn Hanbal took the *Qur'an* seriously, not to the point that every word had to be read literally—which would convert Allah into a somewhat overgrown man—but with an understanding that there is between God and man some mysterious gulf bridged by the revelation of an eternal *Qur'an* but not entirely accessible to man's intelligence or human formulas. He affirmed the givens of the Sacred Book and then went on to affirm the mystery as well: I accept, without knowing how.

---

40. Ahmad ibn Hanbal made the original selection of traditions and organized them according to the earliest name to appear in the chain of transmitters. 'Abdallah's editorial work was apparently not considerable.

41. The Muslims, who show an almost infinite inventiveness in categorizing heresies, could also be disconcertingly generic on occasion. *Zindiq* was one favorite catch-all, and in Hanbalite eyes "Jahmite" had the same somewhat cloudy but ominous associations.

Ahmad ibn Hanbal was certainly not anti-intellectualistic; at every step of the way he practiced "personal investigation" (*ijtihad*) in the formulation of the Islamic Law. What he opposed was the rationalism inherent in the Mu'tazilite positions, a rationalism that in his own day had led to a denial of the eternal and uncreated *Qur'an* and the stripping from Allah of his Qur'anically attested attributes. But Ibn Hanbal and his successors found themselves in the position peculiar to all opponents of *kalam:* the choice of weapons belonged to their adversaries.

In Ibn Hanbal's day the *mutakallimun* had mastered the dialectical method (*'ilm al-jadal*) but had not yet enlisted in their service the systematic literary presentation of those arguments that had long been in use among the Greeks and that would, from Ghazali onward, be the normal form of discourse among the theologians. Ash'ari's own works were in various forms, but like the Mu'tazilites whom he renounced and then attacked, he favored the dialectical—"they maintain; I respond"—form of the heresiography. But framed in both are the elements of an older, predialectical construct known as a "credo."

From its earliest preserved example,[42] the Muslim "creed" consisted in a number of loosely linked propositions which represented the statement of one scholar or one school on the disputed questions of the time. Ash'ari's credo is no more organized than its three or four predecessors from other schools; but it is far more complex, if for no other reason than that the horizon of polemic had broadened immensely since Abu Hanifah's first creed a century earlier. And though Ash'ari's creed now included profound metaphysical questions unknown to the earlier examples, it was not, however, dialectical; like all the others of its kind, it stated rather than argued its beliefs.

Six such creeds have been preserved from Ibn Hanbal, each transmitted by one or another of his disciples. The form remained popular among the Hanbalites despite the obvious inadequacy of the nonresponsive credo in the face of a skilled partisan

42. The so-called *Fikh Akbar I* dating from c. 767 and attributed to Abu Hanifah. The "profession of faith" (*shahadah*)—"There is no God but Allah and Muhammad is his prophet"—is older but belongs to another genre.

of dialectic. But some at least of Ibn Hanbal's followers did not shy away from more direct confrontations with the adversary. His son 'Abdallah, who had grown up under the *mihnah*, addressed both the Mu'tazilites and the Rafidite Shi'ah in his *Book of Sunnah*, and somewhat later Abu Bakr al-Khallal, the tireless editor of Ibn Hanbal and the student of his sons, began the process of converting the loosely associated followers of the founder into the Hanbalite *madhhab* by writing and organizing the biographies of those scholars in his *Classes of the Followers of Ibn Hanbal.*

Al-Khallal showed a deeper interest in politics than any of his Hanbalite predecessors. The members of the school were, after all, "partisans of the *sunnah* and the community," and if the Mu'tazilites were the chief sinners against the first, it was the *Shi'at 'Ali* that most seriously threatened the unity of the *ummah.* The Caliphs had to face increasingly overt challenges to that unity in the last half of the ninth century, but for the Hanbalite theoreticians the fundamental question, phrased, like most other contemporary issues, in juridical terms, hinged on the legitimacy of the first four Caliphs. The Rafidites rejected all the predecessors of 'Ali out of hand, while the Zaydi Shi'ah and the Mu'tazilah contented themselves with discussing the preferability of 'Ali. For the Hanbalites the consensus of the community had spoken out clearly: Abu Bakr, 'Umar, 'Uthman and 'Ali had all been recognized by the community and so were legitimate Caliphs. And so also, by implication, was Mu'awiyah, which was exactly the position held by the earliest "partisans of the community" under the later Umayyads.

Al-Khallal appears either not to have known or not to have cared about his somewhat older Baghdad contemporary al-Ash'ari. Another member of the school, al-Barbahari (d. 941), who like al-Khallal was a third generation Hanbalite, was, however, aware of the notorious former Mu'tazilite. His *Book of the Sunnah*, another polemical credo, is reported to have been the provocation of Ash'ari's *Exposition.* It is not impossible; Barbahari's work is a spirited defense of *taqlid* against the rationalist claims of *kalam.*

Barbahari had little difficulty in appraising the value of metaphysics, but politics gave him somewhat more trouble. During his lifetime the tide of Shi'ite dissent was mounting against the 'Abbasid Caliphate. Armed rebellion was commonplace, and Barbahari as a defender of the unity of the community argued for the absolute obedience to constituted political authority. He also believed, like every good Muslim, that the good should be supported and evil actively suppressed, but in this case the evil was the Shi'ite activity in Baghdad, a city which was at this time, and remained for many years afterward, forcefully Hanbalite in its sentiments.

Ahmad ibn Hanbal had borne the repressions of the *mihnah* with remarkable patience, but once Mutawakkil had declared in their favor, the later Hanbalites showed no reluctance to confront the enemies of Islam in a direct and even violent manner. For twenty years between 921 and 941 Barbahari was involved in a series of public incidents in Baghdad in which his followers assumed with gusto the obligation of seeing to it that the letter of the *shari'ah* was being observed in cult as well as dogma. Shi'ites, *zindiqs* and Mu'tazilites were all fair game, and the perfervid Hanbalites were not always patient with distinctions. The historian and exegete al-Tabari ran afoul of the Baghdad Hanbalites in a public dispute in 921. He was accused of harboring Shi'ite and Mu'tazilite sympathies, and when he died two years later the Hanbalite zealots opposed his being granted a Muslim funeral.

In the first decades of the tenth century the political and religious landscape had changed to a considerable extent from what it had been under Ma'mun a century earlier. The same principals were on the scene, but their fortunes had altered. The Mu'tazilites had lost their favored position at court but had gained in coherence; what had been a group of scholars and polemicists joined under the elastic rubric of Mu'tazilite had become over that century a school or, as their opponents called them, a sect. In Barbahari's day the Basrah branch was directed, as has been seen, by al-Jubba'i's son Abu Hashim (d. 933), while Abu al-Qasim al-Ka'bi of Balkh (d. 931), was the scholarch in Baghdad. Increasingly the two branches exercised their dialectical skills for each other's benefit and were drawn into ever finer subtleties by a growing awareness of the philosophical tradition.

The Mu'tazilah had other internal problems. Al-Ash'ari was by no means the first defector from their ranks. Abu 'Isa al-Warraq had departed some time toward the middle of the ninth century and had gone over, it was reported, to *zandaqah*. Later one of his students, Ibn al-Rewandi (d. 910), went the same route. This latter complex personality is known only by indirection. Al-Jahiz had earlier written a work entitled *The Excellence of the Mu'tazilah*, now lost, in which he proposed to defend his teachers and colleagues from Rafidite calumnies. A former Baghdad Mu'tazilite, the Iranian Ibn al-Rewandi, refuted it in his *Shame of the Mu'tazilah*, which is also lost. We know about the controversy and the arguments it provoked from both sides, because a response to the *Shame* is extant, al-Khayyat's *Book of Triumph*, which reproduces long passages from Ibn al-Rewandi.

Ibn al-Rewandi may still have been a Muslim when he wrote against the Mu'tazilah; at least part of the *Shame* is directed toward sustaining the Rafidite Shi'ah against their Mu'tazilite adversaries. Ibn al-Rewandi did not, at any rate, remain within Islam. Under the influence of Abu 'Isa he embraced *zandaqah*, and the debris of titles that represents his literary legacy shows among them a refutation of the *Qur'an*, a denial of prophecy and a defense of the eternity of the world.

Ibn al-Rewandi's book damaged the Mu'tazilah—his arguments show up in many later authors—but it must not have done much good for the Rafidites in whose camp he briefly alighted en route to *zandaqah*. His mentor Abu 'Isa had carried on a similar flirtation under almost identical circumstances, and the fact that two such well-known apostates had left the *ummah* through the passage clearly marked "Mu'tazilite" and "Shi'ite" could not have reassured the traditionalists about the orthodoxy of those two way stations to perdition. And those who, like the Hanbalites, had occasion to remember the unholy alliance of Mu'tazilite and Shi'ite in Ma'mun's day must have taken a grisly satisfaction at the impious scandal.

THE 'ABBASID CALIPHS

II. The Heirs of Mu'tasim (842–991)

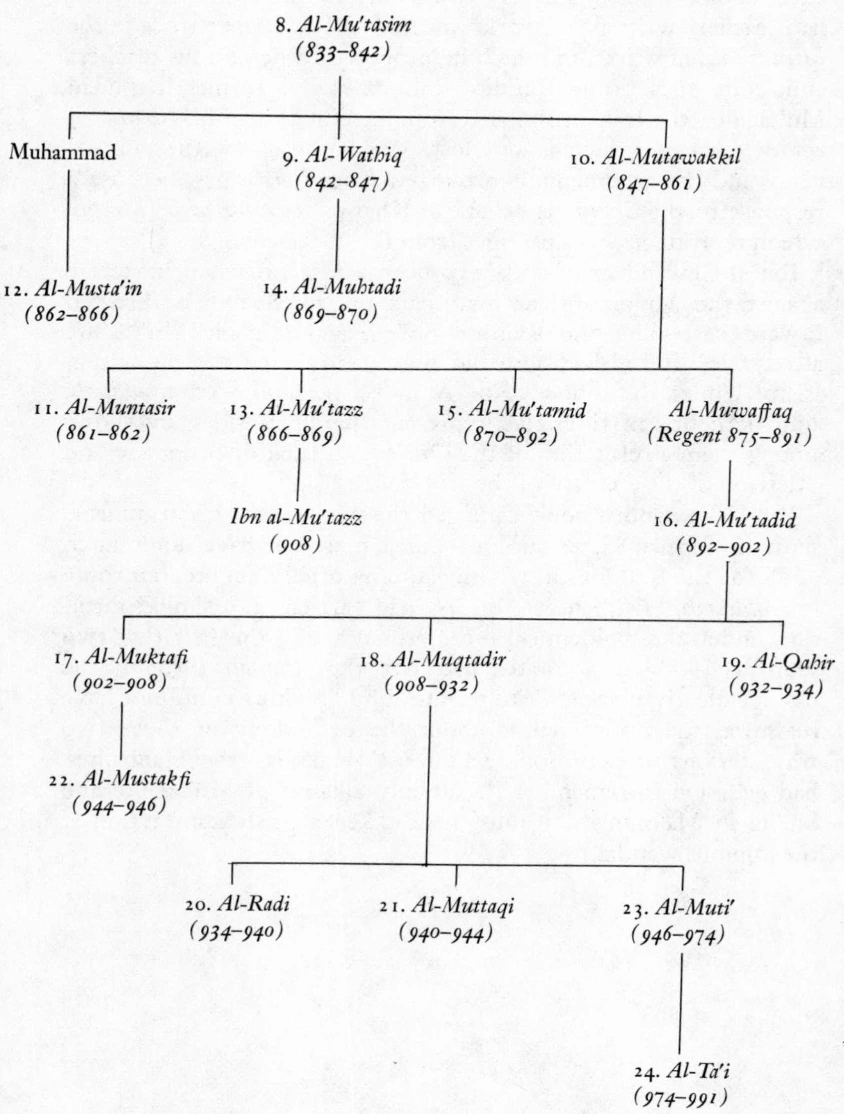

VII
THE IGNORANT CITY AND THE VIRTUOUS CITY

The emperor remained at the heart of Roman history from the time of Augustus to the fall of the last Autocrat of the Romans in the Turkish siege of Constantinople in 1453. There were weak emperors and strong ones, but the power of the office was never entirely lost. Basil in the eleventh Christian century was no whit diminished from what Diocletian had been in the third. The lands of the Empire had shrunk from what Augustus had once possessed, but Basil wielded even greater powers than Augustus; he directed a highly centralized government apparatus, was the sole source of law in the Empire, and claimed as well some degree of jurisdiction over something Augustus had never known, an Ecumenical Christian Church; *Isapostolos*, "Equal of the Apostles," was a title far richer in implication than that of *Pontifex Maximus.*

From the beginning the Caliphate was different. "Successor of the Prophet of Allah" had no justification in revelation, and the powers of its tenant were nowhere spelled out in the *hadith*. Traditionally the Arabs were governed by customary law, but it was the *sunnah* of a tribal society, which the Islamic polity was not. Even after "the *sunnah*" came to be understood as "the *sunnah* of the Prophet," there was little help for a Caliph who by then possessed neither the legislative powers nor the theological *magisterium* of the Founder. Upon his accession the Caliph was acknowledged by an oath of allegiance; his contemporary in Constantinople was consecrated at the high altar of Hagia Sophia.

The problem of the Christian emperor often arose from the tension between the two mature societies, the *imperium* and the *ekklesia*, over which he had to exercise his jurisdiction. At the outset the Caliph ruled, without benefit of charisma or consecration, an embryo indifferently developing into a military caste. 'Umar's military elite did not survive the 'Abbasid revolution, however; the new Muslims of non-Arab blood served, in increasing numbers, as Islam's soldiers, secretaries, intellectuals and finally its governors. There was power in all those positions, a power unregulated by constitutional control. Allah's commonwealth was richly endowed with contractual legislation, but it had no political constitution and the Caliph was powerless to provide one.

The Umayyads guarded their power as a matter of personal privilege, first in the manner of pre-Islamic *shaykhs*, then somewhat unaccountably as late-Roman emperors without benefit of a Roman constitution and, finally, as reflections of the Sasanian Shah. The latter was the 'Abbasid model as well, except that theirs was more markedly Islamic in its pretensions than the preliminary Umayyad version.

The notion of the Caliph as an Islamic Shah was at best a fragile conception that may have worked far too well in its political consequences. The Iranian society over which the Shah ruled was a feudal one, where baronial landowners and a powerful clergy contested for the Shah's attention or his power. The Shah exercised dominion over both groups; he was the largest landowner in the state and in some undefined fashion he was the head of the Mazdaean "Church."

Technically, Islam had neither feudal landowners nor a clerical caste on the Indo-Iranian model. But as the state evolved in early 'Abbasid times, the provincial *amirs*, through whose hands the taxes for Baghdad passed and who controlled the army musters in their provinces, behaved almost precisely like the Shah's satraps during the declining days of both the Achaemenian and Sasanian empires. And in place of a clergy there grew up in Islam a clerical elite of lawyers and secretaries who between them dominated the

Islamic Law and the administration of the state. By the mid-ninth century the Caliph's collaborators had become his rivals.

The Dissolution of the Commonwealth

In 861 Mutawakkil was assassinated by the same Turkish pretorians who had carried him to power over the corpse of his brother. In the years that followed the deed, three of his own sons and two of his nephews came to the tottering throne within the grandiose but dangerous palaces at Samarra. The immediate cause of Mutawakkil's death was the public announcement that the succession had not been settled upon his eldest son Muntasir, but upon a younger offspring from his favorite Greek concubine. The Turkish captains, who supported Muntasir and had his private encouragement, took matters into their own hands. With Mutawakkil slain, the younger son Mu'tazz was imprisoned and Muntasir ascended the throne in despite of his dead father's wishes. Six months later Muntasir too was dead, under circumstances of sinister obscurity.

This time the Turks chose at their pleasure, and their pleasure fell upon one of Mutawakkil's nephews and a grandson of Mu'tasim, al-Musta'in (862–866). Apparently it was not a unanimous choice, and the hapless Musta'in and his supporters were driven from Samarra by the dissidents. The exiles set up a rump court at Baghdad, while at Samarra the generals summoned Mu'tazz from prison and finally thrust the Caliphate upon him. Two Caliphs could hardly coexist in the strained circumstances, and the adherents of Mu'tazz marched upon Musta'in in Baghdad in 865. There was resistance there, but after a ferocious and protracted siege (865–866) the city fell. Musta'in agreed to abdicate—he was assassinated almost immediately after—and Mu'tazz (866–869) ruled briefly, without a rival. Within three years he too had fallen from favor at Samarra; he was beaten, forced to abdicate and assassinated.

Baghdad bore the visible marks of the struggles of those years, but the damage to the Caliphate ran far more deeply elsewhere. In 864 the Zaydi Shi'ites managed to accomplish what no other

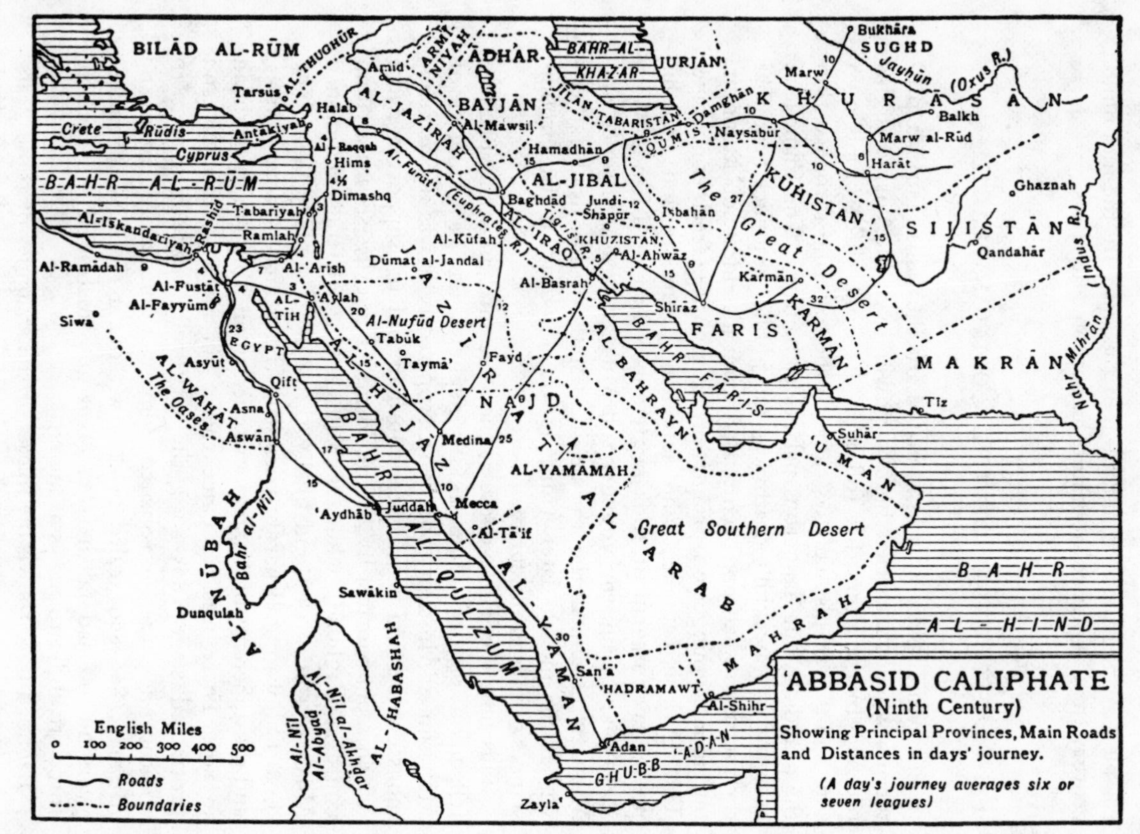
'ABBĀSID CALIPHATE
(Ninth Century)
Showing Principal Provinces, Main Roads and Distances in days' journey.
(A day's journey averages six or seven leagues)
English Miles
0 100 200 300 400 500
Roads
Boundaries
BILĀD AL-RŪM
AL-THUGHŪR
ARMINIYAH
ĀDHARBAYJĀN
BAHR AL-KHAZAR
JURJĀN
JILĀN
TABARISTĀN
QŪMIS
KHURĀSĀN
SUGHD
Bukhāra
Jayhūn (Oxus R.)
Marw
Balkh
Marw al-Rūd
Harāt
Naysābūr
Damghān
KŪHISTĀN
The Great Desert
SIJISTĀN
Ghaznah
Qandahār
Nahr Mihrān (Indus R.)
MAKRĀN
Tīz
KARMĀN
Karmān
FĀRIS
Shīrāz
BAHR FĀRIS
AL-BAHRAYN
'UMĀN
Suhār
BAHR AL-HIND
MAHRAH
HADRAMAWT
Al-Shihr
'ADAN
Adan
San'ā'
GHUBB
Zayla'
Tarsūs
Halab
Antākiyah
Crete
Rūdis
Cyprus
BAHR AL-RŪM
Al-Raqqah
Hims
Dimashq
Tabarīyah
Ramlah
Rashīd
Al-Iskandarīyah
Al-Ramādah
Al-Fustāt
Al-Fayyūm
Siwa
Al-'Arīsh
AL-TĪH
Aylah
EGYPT
Asyūt
Qift
Asna
Aswān
AL-WĀHĀT The Oases
AL-NŪBAH
Bahr al-Nīl
Dunqulah
Al-Nīl al-Abyad
Al-Nīl al-Akhdar
AL-HABASHAH
Sawākin
'Aydhāb
Juddah
Mecca
Al-Tā'if
BAHR AL-QULZUM
AL-YAMAN
Āmid
AL-JAZĪRAH
Al-Mawsil
Al-Furāt (Euphrates R.)
Tigris R.
Hamadhān
AL-JIBĀL
Baghdād
Jundi-Shāpūr
Isbahān
KHŪZISTĀN
Al-Ahwāz
AL-'IRĀQ
Al-Kūfah
Al-Basrah
Dūmat al-Jandal
JAZĪRAT AL-'ARAB
Al-Nufūd Desert
Tabūk
Taymā'
Fayd
NAJD
AL-HIJĀZ
Medina
AL-YAMĀMAH
Great Southern Desert

'Alids had accomplished since the days of 'Ali himself, the establishment of an independent Amirate in Tabaristan south of the Caspian Sea.[1] The Zaydi Amirs of Tabaristan did not, of course, acknowledge the legitimacy of the 'Abbasid Caliph at Samarra, but the Caliphate was little better served by those who did; the Aghlabids in Qayrawan[2] and the Tahirids in Nishapur all ruled, son after father, at their own discretion.

The Tahirids had first come to prominence in Islam because of the military services that the Iranian *mawla* Tahir performed for Ma'mun in the civil war against Amin. In the sequel Tahir was given a wide jurisdiction in Khurasan and Transoxania, while his son 'Abdallah was given similar powers in Baghdad, Syria and Egypt. Eventually 'Abdallah succeeded his father and elder brother at Nishapur (828–845), while other members of the family held high government posts elsewhere, in Baghdad, for example, where a Tahirid traditionally served as chief of police.[3]

In the 860's the Tahirid line in Khurasan was in jeopardy. In nearby Sijistan a new power was rising, that of "the coppersmith" (*al-saffar*) called Ya'qub. He and his brother 'Amr stood at the head of a movement in Sijistan which seems to have had as its chief preoccupation the defense of the local population from the anarchical Kharijites who roamed the country at will in the face of the Caliph's feeble agents.[4] There are frequent examples in the *Dar al-Islam* of the local proletariat taking their security into their own hands, sometimes under the guise of a religious war, when the local authorities proved impotent,[5] and Ya'qub may have been the leader of just such a hastily formed militia.

---

1. See Chap. I, p. 124, and on Zaydi ideology, Chap. VIII, pp. 574–575.
2. Who, as Baghdad was being besieged, were in the final stages of their conquest of Sicily.
3. It was a Tahirid in that post who directed the defense of the city against Mu'tazz's Turkish legionaries in 865–866.
4. The Kharijites had come to Sijistan in flight from the Umayyads; see Chap. I, pp. 134–135. By the mid-ninth century most of them had slid gracelessly from ideology to brigandage pure and simple.
5. So those irregular city militias at Baghdad and elsewhere that appear in the official historians as "worthless vagabonds" (*'ayyarun*); see Chap. IX, pp. 660–661.

But whereas the others never emerged from an obscure anonymity, he welded his irregulars into a political power.

The targets of that power were all of Ya'qub's immediate neighbors: the provinces of Kirman and Fars to the west, a still largely pagan Afghanistan to the east, and the Tahirid domains in Khurasan. Ya'qub was in full control of Sijistan by 867; two years later he raided Shiraz and soon afterward took Balkh. In 873 his motley but well-paid troops overran Khurasan and drove the last of the Tahirids, Muhammad (862–873), from Nishapur. The Caliph refused to recognize this doubtfully loyal commando, but it did not matter. Ya'qub plunged onward into Tabaristan, plundered Rayy, and then returned and expropriated the treasury at Shiraz.

It was enough for the Caliph Mu'tamid and his regent, his brother Muwaffaq. In 875 they recognized Ya'qub al-Saffar as Amir of Sijistan, Khurasan, Tabaristan, Kirman and Fars, and gave him in addition the military command of Baghdad once reserved for the Tahirids. Ya'qub was apparently unimpressed. He no longer had to request; he could take. His armies marched upon Baghdad and Muwaffaq came down from Samarra to oppose him. Somewhere south of Baghdad the two forces clashed. Ya'qub was defeated and withdrew, and even though it was not apparent at the time, the Saffarid threat had passed. At the death of Ya'qub in 879 his brother 'Amr (879–901) continued to exercise sovereignty over the vast Saffarid domains with the reluctant but inevitable acquiescence of the Caliph; but the explosive energy that nearly propelled Ya'qub into Baghdad was gone. The Caliph was not at present strong enough to dislodge 'Amr, nor he to control Iraq.

In 868, a year after Ya'qub al-Saffar seized control in Sijistan, a new 'Abbasid governor arrived in Egypt. The Turk Ahmad ibn Tulun came not in his own name but in that of his stepfather, a slave soldier to whom Mu'tazz had given the charge of Egypt. Whatever Mu'tazz may have intended, it was Ibn Tulun who took control and for nearly twenty years Egypt was a thoroughly independent princedom under the severe but enlightened rule of the Caliph's nominal *amir*. The Saffarids were opportunists whose only progress in the underdeveloped lands of Sijistan was from self-survival to self-aggrandizement; in Egypt autonomy was put to quite different ends: secure behind the new *amir's* professional slave army of Berbers, Sudanese and Turks, and enriched by taxes once sent to Baghdad, the commercial and agricultural fortunes of Egypt thrived. A new city was laid out immediately to the north of the old garrison of Fustat, and between 876 and 879 at its heart Ibn Tulun constructed his chief architectural monument, a cathedral mosque of spacious and imposing dimensions on the model of the one already raised by his nominal masters in Samarra.

At Samarra meantime the pretense of sovereignty was kept up. At his accession in 870 the new Caliph Mu'tamid, a brother of Mu'tazz and the successor of the ephemeral Muhtadi (869–870), made a division of his empire. To his son Ja'far al-Mufawwad he gave the western provinces of Ifriqiyah, Egypt and Syria, while the Caliph's brother Abu Ahmad al-Muwaffaq was appointed Amir of Iraq and Arabia, and then in 875 was designated the second successor to the Caliph—Ja'far was the first—with control over the entire East. The younger man was an ineffective figurehead, but al-Muwaffaq almost immediately took over the role of Caliphal regent.

On Muwaffaq fell the burden of protecting the Caliphate from the encroaching forces of disintegration. In 876 the Saffarids were beaten off the approaches of Baghdad, while at the same time the regent was engaged in a bloody thirteen-year struggle against a rebellion in southern Iraq. For a number of years before the reign of Mu'tamid (870–892), a certain 'Ali ibn Muhammad, a native of Rayy who claimed, probably falsely, to be an 'Alid, was preaching insurrection in Bahrayn and Basrah. He apparently had little success, at least until he found his true constituency, the pagan black slaves (*zanj*) from East Africa who for years had been pressed into labor gangs to work the salt flats east of Basrah. 'Ali publicly proclaimed himself the *Mahdi* in 869, and in the name of an egalitarian, Kharijite-style Islam, led the enflamed *zanj* into open revolt.

Slavery was a pre-Islamic institution in Arabia, and the bulk of the slaves in the Hejaz were, even then, blacks from across the Bab al-Mandab. Islam did not abolish slavery, but the *Qur'an* did attempt to mitigate the institution, by forbidding the forced prostitution of female slaves, for example. Further, the Islamic

Law, which had a great deal to say about slavery insofar as it concerned personal contracts, recognized only two legitimate means of continuing the practice: a man or woman came into slavery only by being born of slave parents or by falling a captive in war. Muslims could not enslave Muslims, but conversion did not necessarily lead to manumission.

The great majority of slaves within the *Dar al-Islam*—Greeks, Turks, Berbers, Slavs, Nubians and East Africans—were employed in either domestic duty or soldiering. Some did work on the farms of their owners, but there is little evidence of the type of collective forced labor on plantations earlier practiced by the Romans on Sicily. The *zanj* workers on the sugar cane plantations around Basrah were an exception and, as it turned out, a dangerous one. Conditions were intolerable, and 'Ali's call to rebellion fell upon receptive ears. Under their new leader the *zanj* burst out of their plantation bondage. In 870 they took the port of Basrah, and in the following year, with the enthusiastic help of the local Bedouin, who scented the prospect of loot, they fell upon Basrah itself and sacked the city.

The Arab historians' accounts of the rebellion of the *zanj* are highly detailed. They are tendentious as well, as when 'Ali's 'Alid genealogy is mockingly dismissed. What they do not provide is any very clear idea of the ideology behind the political disorders. The *zanj* did not generate a sect and so found no place in those repositories of unsuccessful projects, the heresiographies. Nor was 'Ali's Shi'ism of the eschatological sort favored earlier by al-Mukhtar and later by the Qarmatians in those same regions. Again, he did not join forces with the nearby Saffarids who were likely far less interested in ideology than he. The sources generally concur that what 'Ali was preaching to the *zanj* was some form of Kharijism, which in its extreme form mandated death to all, even other Muslims and children, who did not accept the Kharijite understanding of Islam.

Kharijite, like *zindiq*, was a convenient label in medievel Islam and served to describe and explain everything from social unrest to the purest forms of anarchy. The complaints of the illiterate *zanj*, many of whom did not even speak Arabic, were surely of a social and economic rather than a theological order. Their goal was not a utopian society free of the very institution that held them in bondage; 'Ali promised his followers that they too would possess slaves. Quite simply they were oppressed; and whatever 'Ali may have had in mind, his followers turned first against their immediate tormentors and, once free of the plantations, gave themselves over to pillaging the commercial centers of southern Iraq. Either because they could not or they would not, they did not occupy their prizes.

The Caliph's reaction may have been as little motivated by theology as the action of the rebels. The *zanj* had effectively cut off Baghdad from the Persian Gulf and so had disrupted the rich maritime trade with India and the East, to the advantage, one might add, of Ibn Tulun in Egypt. Ships that were diverted from the troubled areas at the head of the Persian Gulf put in instead at the Egyptian ports on the Red Sea.

The repression of the revolt took many years of hard fighting under novel circumstances. The *zanj* enjoyed the bravery of men with little to lose, were skillfully led and occupied difficult terrain. As has been said, the rebels did not attempt to hold their victimized cities, but they took refuge in the swamps and canals that crisscrossed the Iraqi marshland. Formal warfare in the ninth century was borne chiefly by the cavalry, but here the Caliph's armies had to take to long boats and flush the rebels out of the marshes, company by company, under a hail of arrows.

At first Mu'tamid attempted to handle the situation himself, but the various punitive expeditions sent against the rebels in the years after 871 were ineffective. There was, moreover, the pressing business of the Saffarids. It was Muwaffaq who defeated these latter and it was the regent who took command of the suppression of the *zanj* in 880. He dispatched his son at the head of an expedition in force against lower Iraq, but this too was unavailing. It was not until 883, with Muwaffaq himself at the head of his troops, that the camp capital of the "slave republic" fell.

The war against the *zanj* was a triumph for the regent, but it brought other problems in its wake. In 877 Muwaffaq requested or demanded increased payments from the Caliph's dependent in Egypt, Ibn Tulun. The demand was a legitimate one; Ibn Tulun had evicted the Caliph's finance officer from the province, and with the exception of a small sum forwarded to Baghdad, Egyptian tax revenues were remaining within the borders of Egypt.

Ibn Tulun, who had the support of the Caliph as a foil against his own powerfully waxing brother, did increase the allotment to Baghdad on this occasion. It did not satisfy Muwaffaq, however, who saw in the governor of Egypt a rival of his own power. And he knew what was happening to the maritime trade from India.

In 878 a legate was sent out to Egypt at the head of a Caliphal army with orders to remove the fractious *amir*. He failed and Ibn Tulun responded by sending his own army into the Caliph's domains in Palestine and Syria. There was little resistance there, and the new territories were added to the growing Egyptian estate. In 882 Ibn Tulun went so far as to invite the Caliph to join him in Egypt. Mu'tamid, who was by then totally at odds with Muwaffaq, was willing and had actually set out on his way before he was intercepted by his brother and returned to Samarra.

In 884, at the height of his glories, Ibn Tulun died, and in the manner that was becoming customary in those autonomous provinces of the Caliphate, he was succeeded by his twenty-year-old son Khumarwayh. The new *amir* ruled by no authority but his own and against the obvious wishes of the regent. Muwaffaq had by this time crushed the *zanj* and come to a settlement with the Saffarids, and so as soon as he heard of the death of Ibn Tulun he sent another army into Syria to wrest from the son what he could not save from the father. He was no more successful on this occasion than on the first, and in the end he consented to legitimize Khumarwayh's position by recognizing him and his descendants as superintendents of Egypt and Syria for a fixed period and in consideration of a fixed tribute. The Caliph's name would, of course, continue to be mentioned in the Friday prayers, an act that guaranteed little more than that Egypt had not fallen into the hands of an infidel or a Shi'ite. The arrangement was renewed by the next Caliph, Mu'tadid, who married Khumarwayh's daughter in the bargain.

Muwaffaq was not a popular ruler to his subjects, who had to bear the financial burden of his efforts to hold together the Caliphate. The Turks still possessed the military power within those lands, but there were other handles for leverage within the regime. On one side, generally on Mu'tamid's, stood the rich Shi'ite financiers and, on the other, with Muwaffaq, the increasingly important body of Christian secretaries who, like the

Shi'ites, sought to further their own sectarian ends by siding with the regent against his brother. There were frequent plots at Baghdad and the usual round of arrests, confiscations and murders.

Muwaffaq died in 891 and before the end he managed to have his son declared what he himself had been, the second heir to the Caliphate. With great alacrity the young man then did as opportunity so obviously bade him and had himself promoted to first heir, so that when the frustrated and enfeebled Mu'tamid died in 892 it was Muwaffaq's son Mu'tadid and not Mu'tamid's who succeeded him. And at Baghdad, not Samarra. Shortly before his death Mu'tamid transferred the Caliphal residence from Samarra back to Mansur's "City of Peace," where it remained until the Mongol sack of the capital in 1258.

Mu'tadid's (892–902) policy had of necessity to be different from his father's, since the treasury was now all but empty. There was money to be had in Iraq, however, chiefly from Shi'ite sources, and not unexpectedly the impoverished Mu'tadid took a markedly complacent attitude toward the *Shi'at 'Ali.* The Zaydi princes of Tabaristan were cultivated, and another 'Alid Amirate came to power in Yemen in 897. A Shi'ite family, the Banu Furat, were given control of the *diwan* of the treasury, and it was only with difficulty that Mu'tadid was persuaded not to promulgate a public defamation of Mu'awiyah, a move that would surely have provoked the Hanbalite extremists in Baghdad.[6]

Mu'tadid died in 902 and was succeeded by his twenty-eight-year-old son, al-Muktafi (902–908), who inherited both a strengthened Caliphate and the shattering problem of the Qarmatians.[7] These latter were revolutionary anarchists who had gained a foothold in Bahrayn and, despite Mu'tadid's efforts at rooting them out, had grown to such a pitch of strength that in 900 and 901 they were threatening Basrah and attacking cities the length and breadth of Syria. The Tulunid governor there had shown himself incapable of containing the Qarmatians' assaults, but a Caliphal army sent out in 903 was more successful, and the

---

6. On the Baghdad Hanbalites and the renewal of Shi'ite fortunes in the tenth century, see Chap. VIII, pp. 581–592.
7. See Chap. VIII, p. 596.

Qarmatians never quite regained their strength in Syria. Nor did the Tulunids. It was now possible to wrest not only Syria but Egypt itself from the degenerate grandsons of Ibn Tulun. It was done, and in 905 Muktafi's troops entered Fustat and reclaimed it for the Caliph. It balanced, perhaps, the loss of Khurasan to another Iranian dynasty, the Samanids, who nevertheless performed for the Caliphate the useful service of removing from that province the more dangerous Saffarids.[8]

In 908 Muktafi perished at the age of thirty-two, of a disease that had afflicted him from childhood, and the problem of the succession arose once again. The Caliph's own children were barely out of infancy and his brother Ja'far was only thirteen. There was, to be sure, another candidate with some popular support, 'Abdallah, the son of the former Caliph Mu'tazz and a grandson of Mutawakkil, who had passed most of his life up to this point in a kind of enforced seclusion rendered civilized by the pursuit of poetry and *adab*.[9] 'Abdallah ibn al-Mu'tazz was undoubtedly qualified to hold the office, too qualified, perhaps, in the eyes of the viziers and secretaries who saw in the teen-age Ja'far a useful and pliable instrument for their own eminence as well as the encouragement of Shi'ism.

By moving quickly the vizier al-'Abbas promoted Ja'far, now al-Muqtadir, to the throne. Just as quickly the partisans of Ibn al-Mu'tazz made their countermove. They assassinated al-'Abbas and just failed to murder al-Muqtadir with him. When Ibn al-Mu'tazz went to bed on December 17, 908, he was to all appearances Caliph; when he awoke the following morning his military support had vanished. The notorious "Caliph for a day" made a final futile effort to rally Hanbalite support to his side, went into hiding and was eventually betrayed, jailed and executed. Al-Muqtadir resumed his position, and at his side was the new and powerful vizier Ibn al-Furat.[10]

---

8. On the Samanids, see Chap. IX, pp. 645–649.
9. For Ibn al-Mu-tazz's accomplishments in these areas, see Chap. III, p. 232.
10. Who relentlessly pursued the opponents of al-Muqtadir. Among them was the mystic al-Hallaj, who was indicted in 909 but escaped and was not run to ground until three years later; see Chap. VIII, p. 556.

During the following years the vizierates of Ibn al-Furat and 'Ali ibn 'Isa show the prime minister at the height of his powers and exercising an almost total control over the Caliph's domains. These were shrinking, to be sure. The Samanids were firmly established in the East, the Qarmatians were lodged in Bahrayn and lower Iraq, and in Ifriqiyah another revolutionary branch of the Shi'ah had overthrown the Aghlabids and now gave no promise of refraining from Egypt. The vizier's powers were great, but at this point they were political rather than military; and so, little or nothing was done to arrest the palpable disintegration of the Caliphate.

The Caliph did retain some powers, the making and unmaking of viziers among them, and during the reign of Muqtadir (908–932) four major figures contested, with varying success, for that office: Ibn al-Furat, a Shi'ite of Iraq and a strong-handed, if greedy, minister; 'Ali ibn 'Isa, a moderate Sunni and an enlightened, pragmatic and efficient administrator; the Turk al-Khaqani, a religious conservative and only fitfully interested in the business of government; and finally Ibn Muqlah, uncertainly ambitious, anti-Shi'ite, but willing to temporize. Opposite them, as rival or co-conspirator, was the captain of the Turkish guard, Mu'nis.

The Caliph's viziers were all *mawali*, some of them of rather recent conversion, who were all but reared in the *diwans*. In the tenth century many of the secretaries in those same *diwans* were Christians whose intellectual formation was acquired in the Nestorian monastery schools of Iraq. Only a Muslim, Sunni or Shi'ite, depending on the current winds of religious politics, might become a vizier, and his chief administrative function, by way of delegation from the Caliph, was nothing less than the execution of the financial and legal prescriptions of the Islamic Law. But the Caliph had also possessed a large number of discretionary powers, and if at first they were merely channeled to subordinates through the vizier, the latter eventually came to initiate and control the measures of government and to submit them to the Caliph for little more than his signature. From the time of al-Muqtadir the vizier had in his hands the entire direction of the state.

The vizier's powers were by no means absolute. He had no real constitutional function of his own; all that he did was legally by way of delegation from the Caliph. Nor did he possess, on the other hand, the *de facto* powers vested in the captain of the guard. The military *amir* could act; the vizier had to persuade, cajole, threaten or bribe. Failure meant deposition or arrest.

In 924 the delicate balance that sustained the vizierate underwent a rude disequilibrium. The immediate cause was a savage attack by the Qarmatians upon a pilgrimage caravan en route from Baghdad to Mecca. The Shi'ite vizier was held responsible for this outrage against piety and public safety, and popular pressure drove Muqtadir from the embrace of his vizier into what he judged to be the stronger arms of the Turkish captain Mu'nis. Isma'ili propaganda, Fatimid successes in Egypt, a growing Byzantine confidence in Anatolia, public scandals and religious feuds had sapped the confidence of both Baghdad and the provinces. Salvation appeared to lie only with the military.

It did not, at least as far as Muqtadir was concerned. The Caliph was briefly deposed by a palace revolution in 929, and his brother was set in his place. Mu'nis' role in those events is ambiguous, but three years later the breech between the paramount military commander of Islam and his sovereign was complete. Muqtadir made the mistake of marching against Mu'nis, a piece of folly for which he paid with his life.

It was now Mu'nis who selected, perhaps on the advice of an eminent Shi'ite of the Nawbakhti family,[11] Muqtadir's brother to serve as Caliph. Al-Qahir (932–934) had been on the throne briefly during the earlier deposition of his brother. His present tenancy did not last much longer, and it was notable chiefly for an imposing, if inconsequential deed; by playing on the dissatisfaction of the Caliphal guard, al-Qahir encompassed the fall of Mu'nis.

If al-Qahir may be said to have had a policy, it was compounded of revenge against the former supporters of al-Muqtadir and of a violent anti-Shi'ism. A new Shi'ite power had arisen in the northwest corner of Iran, the Buyids of Daylam,[12] and they were even then occupying Jibal (932), Fars (934) and Kirman (936). Even closer to home the Caliph must have felt himself

---

11. On the Banu Nawbakht, see Chap. VIII, pp. 578–579.
12. See pp. 521–524.

surrounded by powerful men, whose attitudes ranged from sympathy toward the 'Alids, as in the case of Mu'nis, moderate Shi'ites like the Banu Nawbakht and the Arab dynast of Mosul, Nasr ibn Hamdan, to extremists like the ideologue al-Shalmaghani and the Banu Baridi of Ahwaz. Al-Qahir rid himself of Mu'nis and Ishaq al-Nawbakhti, and al-Shalmaghani was finally run to ground early in the reign of al-Qahir's successor. Only the Banu Baridi survived to plague the Caliphate yet a few years longer.

Al-Qahir was destroyed by the same troops that had enabled him to topple Mu'nis, and he was succeeded by Muqtadir's son al-Radi (934–940). The sources of the Baghdad regime's income were drying up. Powerful *amirs* like Ibn Ra'iq in Basrah and Hasan the Hamdanid in Mosul, or tax farmers like the Banu Baridi, the "sons of the postman,"[13] in Ahwaz were little inclined to send their taxes to Baghdad for the benefit of the various power seekers there. Al-Radi had little choice but to enlist one against the other. The first choice fell upon Ibn Ra'iq who in 936 was appointed Grand Amir, an office which effectively combined the functions of a military commander with those of a vizier.[14]

At the moment of Ibn Ra'iq's elevation there was little left of the Caliph's domains to defend. In the east the Samanids and the Buyids, in Tabaristan and the Yemen the Zaydi Shi'ite *Imams*, in Bahrayn and southern Iraq the Qarmatians, in Ahwaz the Banu Baridi, in northern Mesopotamia and Syria the Shi'ite Hamdanids, in Egypt a new *amir*, Muhammad ibn Tughj, and at his western frontier in Libya the Fatimids—all contested the Caliph's authority. Some denied his legitimacy altogether; others contented themselves with merely mentioning his name in the Friday prayers. In no case was the Caliph conceded a significant share of the revenues of the province.

Out of this mélange of anti-Caliphs and autonomous governors, only the *amirs* of Nishapur and Fustat could be accounted Sunnis, the Samanids aggressively so, while in Egypt it was prob-

---

13. The founder of the clan had had the charge of the lucrative postal service (*barid*).

14. The title may have been used earlier—by Mu'nis, for example—but the formal cession of the highest military *and* civil powers to one man begins with Ibn Ra'iq.

ably self-survival rather than any piety toward the Caliphate that prompted Ibn Tughj's spirited resistance to the Fatimid *Imams* of Ifriqiyah. Ever since the beginning of the tenth century the Fatimids' armies and propagandists were steadily advancing across North Africa toward Egypt. For thirty years after the 'Abbasids' restoration of their authority in that latter province, power was wielded in Egypt by a series of financiers who paid their dues to the Caliphs but were only dubiously capable of defending the country against either the Fatimid armies or the increasingly common Byzantine naval raids against the coast.

Egypt had need of a strong hand in the first half of the tenth century and found it in another Turkish adventurer, Muhammad ibn Tughj, who seized power in 935 and was recognized a few years later by al-Radi and the pragmatists at Baghdad as Amir of Egypt under the Central Asian title of *Ikhshid*. Ibn Tughj (935–946) was a military man—his father was the Tulunid general who defended Damascus against the Qarmatians earlier in the century—and he restored to Egypt the strength it had possessed under Ibn Tulun. The Fatimids were repulsed, and Egypt once again exercised control over Palestine and much of Syria. In Palestine there was little resistance to the *Ikhshid's* armies, but farther north in Mesopotamia they collided with the thwarted ambitions of Ibn Ra'iq.

Al-Radi's Grand Amir had not been able to sustain himself in Baghdad despite his enormous new powers. In 938 he was deposed by yet another Turkish captain, Bajkam, an event which won the vizierate for Abu 'Abdallah al-Baridi, the former tax collector of Ahwaz. Ibn Ra'iq was not totally desolated in the affair; he was granted a governorship in northern Mesopotamia, where in 939 he was contesting the *Ikhshid's* advance through Syria.

Ibn Ra'iq's ambitions continued to run more strongly toward Baghdad than to control of Damascus. He and the *Ikhshid* settled on a division of Syria and Palestine, and in 941 the Grand Amir was once again embroiled in the affairs of the Caliphate. Bajkam was murdered in the spring of that year by Kurdish brigands, and the new Caliph, Muqtadir's second son, al-Muttaqi (940–944), who owed his promotion to the throne to the Turk, had to cast elsewhere for new alliances, in this instance to the Banu

Baridi. Muttaqi's son and designated heir Abu Mansur was married to one of the Baridi daughters, and in the division of offices that followed, Abu Mansur was announced as Grand Amir and Abu 'Abdallah al-Baridi as vizier.

The first proposal came to nothing, since the Turkish troops had their own candidate, Tuzun. And the Banu Baridi could possess the vizierate only so long as they could hold Baghdad. By the end of 941 Abu 'Abdallah could no longer do that, because of his troubles with the military in Wasit, and in the interval Ibn Ra'iq was once again installed as Grand Amir. Early in 942 the "sons of the postman" returned in force. Muttaqi and his Amir had no practical alternative but flight, northward, to the protection of Hasan, the Hamdanid Amir of Mosul. Hasan's price for sanctuary and assistance was the deposition of Ibn Ra'iq and the marriage of Abu Mansur to his own daughter.

The Hamdanids' custody of the Caliph was of brief duration. Muttaqi was little more than a pawn between the Arab Hasan and the Turk Tuzun, both ambitious to possess the Grand Amirate, and it was Tuzun who prevailed. Muttaqi's only riposte was to attempt to interest the *Ikhshid* in his fate, but to no avail. When it suited the interests of Tuzun, he unceremoniously deposed Muttaqi and installed in his place not the expectant Abu Mansur but a son of Muktafi, 'Abdallah al-Mustakfi (944–946), who shortly ended by committing himself and the Caliphate to the protection of the Buyids of Daylam.

This dreary record of political impotence and progressive decline is in essence a simple one. As has already been remarked, the Muslim Caliph was neither a legislator in the style of the Byzantine emperor nor a teacher in the manner of the Christian bishop. From the beginning his chief duties were those of a military commander and administrator, powers that were intimately connected with the financial structure of Islam. The taxes and tribute prescribed by Islamic Law were collected by the Caliph's agents from the conquered and distributed to the Islamic elite as sustenance and reward for services rendered. Such an arrangement foresaw neither the growth of a military that was not part of that elite, but had nevertheless to be compensated, nor the development of a central government. And when the apparatus of scribes and bureaus came to full flower under the early

'Abbasids, the needs and claims of the "government," now centralized in the hands of the vizier, were no longer identical with those of Islam's salaried soldiers.

The Caliphs of the century between the reign of Mutawakkil and the coming of the Buyids had either given up or had wrested away from them both their administrative and military authority. The viziers had taken the first for themselves, and the Turkish pretorians the second. The two factions, the vizieral and the military, struggled for control around the Caliph, but it was a narrowing arena. In the provinces the separation of the civil (read "financial") and military powers had not yet progressed as far as it had in Baghdad. In that conjunction lay strength, and the provincial *amirs* could propose and dispose as they wished. The enfeeblement of the central government with its feuding Caliphs, viziers and captains was accompanied by the rise of powerful provincial dynasties.

The struggle at Baghdad was resolved in 936 with the appointment of Ibn Ra'iq as Grand Amir with full control of both the military and financial resources of the Caliphate.

It marked the effective end of the civil vizierate, and perhaps of the Caliphate as well. The Caliphs had taken profit from the envy of the vizier and the captain, but after 936 that tension was resolved and even the modest role of the *tertius gaudens* was denied the Caliph. Thereafter it was the Grand Amir, or the various candidates for that office, who was supreme in Baghdad.

Ibn Ra'iq's death in 942 was a signal to the *Ikhshid* that the route into northern Syria was once again open to him. It was, but only temporarily. Egyptian forces occupied the territories denied them by Ibn Ra'iq in 939, only to be dislodged two years later by a hand more powerful than their own, 'Ali, surnamed Sayf al-Dawlah, "Sword of the State," the brother of the Hamdanid *amir* of Mosul. Sayf al-Dawlah drove the *Ikhshid's* troops from Aleppo and Hims and established a new principality that ruled northern Syria for the next half century.

The Hamdanids who rose to prominence in Mesopotamia and northern Syria in the mid-tenth century were no upstarts in the round of Caliphal politics. They were a branch of the once Christian Arab tribe of the Taghlib, and the first of their number to distinguish himself, Hamdan ibn Hamdun, did so by fighting for the Caliph against the Kharijites in 868. Like many of his contemporaries, Hamdan rewarded himself by taking over a number of towns on the upper Tigris. In 892 Mu'tadid was strong enough to reduce some of those localities and Hamdan was captured and imprisoned. His son Husayn proved the loyalty of the family, however, by assisting in the reconquest of Egypt from the Tulunids in 905, and as a result Hamdan was freed.

Like his father, Husayn yielded to his own ambitions. He ran afoul of the vizier a few years later, was captured by Mu'nis and was executed in 918; his overt Shi'ite sympathies doubtless played a part. His brothers were more fortunate. One, 'Abdallah, was appointed Amir of Mosul in 905, and a second, Abu al-Hayja', helped resist the Qarmatian advance against Baghdad in 927 and so won for himself the same honor. In 929 Abu al-Hayja' was part of the abortive conspiracy to unseat Muqtadir for the benefit of al-Qahir, and he paid for his efforts with his life.

It was only a temporary setback to the fortunes of the family. The son of Abu al-Hayja', Hasan, was not to be deposed from Mosul by either the Caliph or his own relatives, and by 936 he was in possession of broad territories in upper Mesopotamia. It was Hasan who gave refuge to Muttaqi and his vizier Ibn Ra'iq, and after he arranged the assassination of Ibn Ra'iq, it was the same Hasan and his brother 'Ali who restored the Caliph to Baghdad in 942 and received in return the honorific titles of Nasir al-Dawlah, "Defender of the State," and Sayf al-Dawlah, "Sword of the State."[15] For somewhat less than a year Nasir al-Dawlah, né Hasan ibn Hamdan, filled the office of Grand Amir at Baghdad before pressure from Tuzun forced him to yield and return to Mosul.

The Shi'ite Arab Nasir resisted the Shi'ite Iranian Mu'izz al-Dawlah before Baghdad in 946, but he was nevertheless confirmed in the Amirate at Mosul by the triumphant Buyids. Mu'izz may have had little choice, and the confirmation did not, in any event, guarantee Nasir's financial support of the Buyids. Taxes arrived only rarely in Baghdad from Mosul, and Mu'izz al-Dawlah had frequent occasion to dispatch armies against the

---

15. On these titles, see p. 523, n. 47.

amir. Nasir's tenancy was uncertain during the sixties, and when he died in 969, it was in a not entirely glorious exile.

Hasan's son Abu Taghlib al-Ghandafar fared little better. It was now Mu'izz's son Bakhtiyar 'Izz al-Dawlah (967–978), who controlled Iraq in the Buyid name, and the two came often to grief. In the end they settled upon terms, and the concordat may have been al-Ghandafar's undoing. He supported Bakhtiyar against his newly ambitious brother 'Adud al-Dawlah (949–983), but in 978 'Adud met and defeated both of them. Ghandafar lost Mosul in the sequel and eked out the rest of his career scuttling between the Byzantines and various Islamic principalities in Mesopotamia and Syria.[16]

The seizure of northern Syria by the other son of Abu al-Hayja', 'Ali Sayf al-Dawlah, was formally recognized in 947 by the *Ikhshid's* son and successor as Amir of Egypt, Unujur (946–961). The new ruler of Egypt was not of the same stuff as his father, but it was of little consequence since the real power there lay in the hands of a Nubian slave-soldier, Kafur, who ruled first as regent and then, after the death of the *Ikhshid's* second son in 966, in his own name. Kafur could not afford to be much concerned with Sayf al-Dawlah and the distant Syria; from the west the Fatimids were drawing ever closer to his own Libyan frontier.[17]

In occupying Syria, Sayf al-Dawlah (944–967) performed for the Ikhshidids a service which they could not have sustained themselves, that of resisting the growing Byzantine strength in Anatolia. How well he acquitted himself in that task may be questioned, however. In the very year of his establishment in Aleppo (944), a Byzantine army invested the city of Edessa and carried off as their prize one of Christendom's most sacred relics, the cloth upon which Jesus was said to have wiped his wounded face and so left a portrait of his features. The miraculous portrait was then installed with pomp in Constantinople, an event that

---

16. The eventual Hamdanid loss of Mosul was not to the Buyids but to the seminomadic Arab tribe of the 'Uqaylids, who in the last decade of the tenth century controlled much of the area north of Baghdad.

17. See Chap. IX, p. 637.

enhanced the already enormous prestige of the architect of the campaign, the Armenian general John Curcuas.

The triumph of Christian arms over Muslim ones at Edessa was not an isolated event. As early as the reign of Leo VI (886–912) the Byzantines had begun to push their frontier eastward and southward across Anatolia. It was not yet the signal for a reversal, however; both the Turk Mu'nis and the Hamdanid Husayn led punishing raids into Byzantine territory between 915 and 917. Then the frontier grew quiet under a purchased peace and Byzantine energies were directed toward the Balkans for a spell. Within ten years all was changed: an energetic military man, Romanus I Lecapenus (919–944), was co-emperor at Constantinople and he had, from 923, a new commander on the Anatolian frontier, John Curcuas.

Curcuas' first victories were in Armenia, but Mu'nis was still a formidable foe and the Arab counterraids went on. Mu'nis fell, however, with the advent of al-Qahir and during the turmoil that followed at Baghdad Curcuas crossed the frontier and took Melitene from the Muslims (934). Curcuas did not press his immediate advantage—to his misfortune, as it proved, since the power vacuum in northern Mesopotamia was being filled by the Hamdanids. Even before he became Amir of Aleppo, Sayf al-Dawlah was chastising the Byzantines in Armenia and eastern Anatolia; Curcuas, meanwhile, was engaged in military projects elsewhere. In 942 he returned to the frontier and the great Byzantine offensive against Islam began. The Arab defenses in central Anatolia were shattered, and John and his troopers swept southward past the Tigris onto the plains of upper Mesopotamia. Amida fell, then Nisibis, and the capture of Edessa itself was averted only by the surrender of the prized icon of Jesus.

The climax of Curcuas' glory was also its end. He was removed from command toward the end of 944, and his fall was shortly followed by that of his patron Romanus I. South of the Taurus Sayf al-Dawlah was safely established in Aleppo, and for the next quarter century this skilled frontier fighter unsettled the Byzantine forces opposite him by the usual Arab technique of lightning summer raids from Tarsus up onto the Anatolian plateau. And after 950 these were more than mere raids: the Caliph Muti' (946–974) proclaimed, largely for Sayf al-Dawlah's benefit, a

Holy War against Byzantium. Not merely booty but paradise awaited the intrepid warrior for the faith, the *ghazi*, in Anatolia.[18]

The *jihad* went neither poorly nor well. For decades the Byzantines made no major move and Sayf undertook no decisive counterstroke. Indeed, during his most daring adventure, a foray deep into Anatolia in 960, Sayf was ambushed en route home and lost the better part of a force of thirty thousand men. And at the very moment that the Amir was taking his thrashing in the passes of the Taurus, the Byzantines' true strength was ominously revealed elsewhere: the general Nicephorus Phocas took and sacked Candia and drove the Arabs off Crete. It marked the effective collapse of Muslim naval control of the eastern Mediterranean.

In 961 Nicephorus was on the eastern front where he had first made a name for himself, and in February of the following year the Byzantine reconquest of Heraclius' lost eastern provinces began. Nicephorus thrust across the Taurus directly into Cilicia and Syria. The Muslim base at Tarsus was by-passed—Nicephorus returned and took it in 965—as he passed south and then east and stood at the end of the year at the foot of the citadel of Aleppo. Sayf al-Dawlah had ignominiously to flee his capital.

The figure of Sayf al-Dawlah withdrawing in discomfort from Aleppo is an unaccustomed one. The Hamdanid *amir* had a long and active reign, but his place in the annals of Islam may owe more to his publicists than to his actual accomplishments. Like most tenth-century princes, he patronized the arts, and the poets who shared his generosity reciprocated by leaving behind them a flattering portrait of the *amir* as a great *ghazi* warrior struggling chivalrously for the salvation of Islam. He was also, in the words of one of his admirers, "an accomplished scholar, a poet himself and a lover of fine poetry, and highly susceptible to words of praise."

If it was poetry and praise the *amir* craved, he must have been well satisfied. Hamdanid Aleppo housed the two most eminent Arab poets of the day, al-Mutanabbi (d. 965) and the *amir's*

18. One wonders how many of them were Sayf's own tribesmen. With the conversion of the Turks to Islam in 950 large drafts of Khurasanian *ghazis*, their work against the infidel Turks completed, passed westward into Armenia and Mesopotamia.

cousin Abu Firas (d. 968), as well as a clutch of lesser lights. The great anthologist of the Arabs' poetical past, Abu al-Faraj al-Isfahani (d. 967), who dedicated his *Book of Songs* to Sayf al-Dawlah, also found support there and, more pertinently, the poets and panegyricists of Sayf's own generation received *their* critical evaluation by a slightly later anthologist, al-Tha'alibi (d. 1038), who was still under the spell emanating from the Hamdanid court.[19]

Of the two archpoets, Mutanabbi enjoys the higher reputation, but Abu Firas may be more representative of the true Hamdanid style. He was Sayf's paternal cousin–his mother was a Greek–and was educated in Aleppo from the time the Hamdanids began their control of that city. When he came of age Abu Firas was appointed to the governorship of one or another of Sayf's vassal cities and accompanied the *amir* on his campaigns against the Byzantines. He was twice captured by the latter: first in 951, when he quickly escaped, and again in 962. On this latter occasion he was taken to Constantinople and remained in captivity until the exchange of prisoners arranged with Nicephorus Phocas in 966. After Sayf's death in the following year, Abu Firas' own political ambitions came into play. He was caught up in a conspiracy against the new *amir* Sa'd al-Dawlah (967–991), was captured and executed in 968.

Abu Firas was a traditional poet who worked in the classical *qasidah,* though in a relatively subdued style. The Shi'ite convictions of his family stood out strongly in his poems, and though he admired his cousin, his most famous work, *Odes from Byzantium,* is filled with reproaches against the *amir* for allowing him to languish in Constantinople far from his home and his friends. Arab literary criticism was never based on a pure poetic, however, and Abu Firas' reputation as a poet is suffused with the portrait of him as the perfect knight, poet and prince.

Abu al-Tayyib, called Mutanabbi or "the would-be prophet," is a far more complex figure, as a man, if not as a poet.[20] His early life is obscure, except that he was the son of a Kufan water carrier and spent some time in Syria. The next we hear of him he

---

19. On Tha'alibi's *Unique Epoch,* see Chap. VI, p. 410.
20. See Chap. VI, p. 406.

had been arrested by the Ikhshidid governor of Hims, possibly by reason of a connection with Qarmatian activity in Syria. Was it in this context that he received his nickname of "would-be-prophet"? It is as likely an explanation as any for the odd sobriquet. Upon his release he wandered about Syria and then in 948 came to Aleppo. For the following nine years Mutanabbi lived liberally on Sayf al-Dawlah's favors and gave in return a mighty torrent of panegyric. In the end they had a falling out, and after a few disappointing years in Fustat under the patronage of Kafur, Mutanabbi was murdered in 965 en route to the court of 'Adud al-Dawlah at Shiraz.

Here in the work of these two men is the foundation stone of Sayf al-Dawlah's reputation. Both Abu al-Firas and Mutanabbi were immensely popular poets, and they fixed the image of their patron in the minds of succeeding generations: a leader who not only typified the Bedouin virtues of bravery and generosity but added to them a characteristic Islamic note. "You are not only a king routing an equal," Mutanabbi said to him, "but monotheism itself routing polytheism."

The rout of polytheism was undertaken, be it noted, by a Shi'ite prince in the name of a Sunni Caliph. The Hamdanids made no effort to conceal their Shi'ism, which was not, in any event, overtly political in its ambitions. Mutanabbi may have been a Qarmatian early in his career, but his preserved poems are more given to panegyric than to preachments to revolution. Most of Sayf al-Dawlah's literary circle did, nonetheless, share the *amir's* religious preference: Abu Firas; Isfahani, who composed an 'Alid martyrology; and Abu Nasr Muhammad al Farabi were all Shi'ites.

In 942, the year in which the Hamdanids restored the Caliph Muttaqi to Baghdad, the elderly philosopher al-Farabi left the capital to take up residence in Damascus, a city which was soon to be part of Sayf al-Dawlah's own territory. Farabi's major political work, *The Views of the Inhabitants of the Ideal State*, was begun in Baghdad and completed in Damascus shortly after his arrival there and so antedates Farabi's immediate experience of the Hamdanid *amir*. But before he died in 950, the philosopher had another occasion to reflect on the science of politics, and in this work, the *Aphorisms of the Statesman*, Farabi may have provided his own somewhat oblique portrait of Sayf al-Dawlah.

The *Aphorisms* describes someone called, in Farabi's generalized way, "the second chief," a leader whom the polity is forced to accept in the absence of the almost unattainably ideal "first chief." It is not a portrait drawn from life—many of the traits are derived from philosophical rather than historical considerations—but something of Sayf is perhaps discernible there. "He should possess excellence of rhetoric and persuasion and in producing an imaginative impression. And at the same time he should be able to conduct the *jihad*." There had earlier been no mention of a Holy War in the political writings of Farabi. But there had been no Sayf al-Dawlah either, and no Byzantine counteroffensive in Syria. Farabi did not live to see his patron's flight from Aleppo and the collapse of the famous *jihad* in the face of Nicephorus Phocas.

After the capture of Aleppo, Nicephorus had to return to Constantinople to assert his own claim to the Byzantine throne, and when he returned to the Taurus in 964 he came as Autocrat of the Romans to face a considerably weakened Hamdanid Amirate. Tarsus fell, then Cyprus. Antioch capitulated after a painful siege, and Aleppo became a vassal of the Byzantine empire. The repercussions were soon felt in Baghdad. In 971 there were violent outbursts among the Sunni population of the capital, and in the same year the Buyid vizier levied a special tax on all the "protected minorities" of the city.[21]

Sayf al-Dawlah died in 967 and Nicephorus was murdered in Constantinople in 969. Again there was a lull on the frontier, and Nicephorus' successor, another eastern general, John Tzimisces (969–976), did not give his attention to the projected reconquest of Syria until 975, when it was not Aleppo, where Sayf's son Sa'd al-Dawlah ruled by the sufferance of the Byzantines, but Jerusalem itself that was the goal.

Tzimisces never reached the Holy City. His armies took Hims,

---

21. There were other, somewhat less expected consequences within the captured territory. For the first time in three centuries the Byzantine authorities had to face the problem of Monophysitism, and more than one Jacobite prelate fared far worse in Byzantine hands than he had in Muslim ones.

Damascus, Beirut, Acre, Tyre and Tripolis, Nazareth in Galilee and Caesarea on the coast west of Jerusalem. Why he did not take Jerusalem itself, which offered itself in surrender to him, is not easy to fathom. Events at home may have summoned him back to Constantinople, where he returned, in any event, at the end of his ramble through Syria in 975. In retrospect the campaign of 975 was little more than a patrol in force, rendered somewhat too important perhaps by its similarity to the Crusades. Despite the easy capitulation of its cities, neither Syria nor Palestine was occupied by the Byzantines. Antioch was a permanent Byzantine foothold in the province, but the hinterland, which was no longer firmly Hamdanid, fell under the control of the new Shi'ite dynasty that had overwhelmed the Caliph's *amir* in Egypt, the Fatimids.

The Hamdanid Sa'd al-Dawlah still ruled in Aleppo under Byzantine sovereignty, though under increasing Fatimid pressure from the south. The *amir* had on occasion to call for assistance from the Byzantine commandant at Antioch, who had in turn to summon the Emperor Basil II (976–1025). Basil was forced to leave the more urgent affairs in the Balkans to save the Muslim lord of Aleppo from the Muslim lord of Cairo. The latter was the Caliph-*Imam* al-Hakim, with whom Basil eventually compacted the disposition of Syria.

Al-Hakim's vagaries were well known in Egypt,[22] but not, apparently, to Basil, and the Emperor was likely taken by surprise when the Fatimid Caliph launched a violent persecution of Christians and Jews that reached its climax in 1009 with the destruction of the Church of the Holy Sepulcher in Jerusalem. Al-Hakim's savagery was unexpected in that it appeared to be motivated by purely religious considerations. Turkish tribesmen might appear on the Anatolian frontier in the full heat of their passion for the *jihad*, but their *amirs*, whatever image they chose to cultivate in the writings of their poets, behaved otherwise in their dealings with their Christian enemies abroad and their Christian minorities at home. These latter had, of course, a covenanted protection guaranteed by Islamic Law. Al-Hakim cared little enough for the *shari'ah*, but his ten-year persecution

22. See Chap. IX, pp. 638–641.

of the Christians, and particularly his destruction of the premier church in the *Dar al-Islam,* was as politically mindless as it was illegal.

There were no immediate military consequences, but what occurred under Basil's successors Michael IV (1034–1041) and Constantine IX (1042–1055) was more far-reaching in its effects than a mere punitive expedition. They negotiated with the Fatimids the reconstruction of the Holy Sepulcher at their own expense; and if this did not yet constitute a Byzantine protectorate over the Holy Places, it did insinuate a presumption of interest, a presumption that could be invoked not merely by the Emperor but by the other foreign lords of the thousands of Christian pilgrims who yearly arrived in Palestine from abroad.

In the immediate future it was neither Byzantines nor Europeans who threatened the Fatimid hold on Syria. Even before al-Hakim's mysterious disappearance in 1021, various Arab tribes of the Syrian steppe were moving into the political vacuum created by the enfeeblement of the Hamdanids. Their success was ephemeral, however. Fiercer warriors than they were beginning to make their appearance in Syria. The first Turkoman bands from the east arrived there in 1064, just as other of their fellow tribesmen were pressing into Anatolia to the eventual discomfort of the Byzantines. In 1078 the Turk Tutush took formal political possession of Syria, and thereafter the Fatimid claim to that province was reduced to the port cities of Acre and Tyre and, spasmodically, Jerusalem.

The arrival of the Turks in Syria put an end to an Arab political renaissance around the Fertile Crescent in the tenth and eleventh centuries. Its beginnings are obscure, but sometime after 900 the Bedouin of the Syrian steppe began to move into the settled areas of Iraq, Mesopotamia and Syria. The destructive raids of the Qarmatians in the opening decades of the tenth century may have set the tribes in motion; but whatever the cause, Arab dynasts came to share in the dismemberment of the Caliph's territories.

The Hamdanids of Mosul and Aleppo were merely the first and best-known of those Arab *amirs.* At their decay another Bedouin group, the 'Uqaylids, took hold of Mosul and soon had under their sway the entire breadth of northern Mesopotamia.

Aleppo fell to others, the Mirdasids, and it was they who struggled unsuccessfully for the possession of Syria against the Fatimids and their fellow Arabs the 'Uqaylids. A third Arab dynasty, the Mazyadids of the Asad tribe, ruled central Iraq from their fortified camp at Hilla near the site of Babylon.

All these Arab principalities were Shi'ite, and the Fatimids' inability to enlist them in their own Shi'ite cause was a crucial factor in the failure of Isma'ili arms and propaganda to overthrow the 'Abbasid Caliph. With the exception of the Hamdanids, the Arab *amirs* had largely predatory instincts and only provincial ambitions. Their Shi'ism was apparently more nostalgic than subversive, the last muted appeal for an Arab Islam. They fell, all of them, before the naked power of the Turks.

The Caliphs did not attend their salvation from such quarters. Indeed, it is doubtful whether they expected salvation at all. They had lost their power first to their viziers and then to their palace guards. Forces larger than themselves swirled about their palaces at Samarra and Baghdad. There was no need for a Caliphal Avignon; Baghdad itself would serve.

Farabi left the capital in 942 while the various power brokers struggled for the possession of the helpless Caliph. Not too many years later, shortly before his death in 950, he seemed to be reflecting on that event. "It is wrong for a virtuous man to remain in a corrupt polity. He has no choice but migration (*hijrah*) to a virtuous state, if one really exists in his own time. If not, then he is a stranger in this world and wretched in life; for such a man death is preferable to life."

The Ideal Polity: Farabi

The author of those reminiscently Platonic sentiments was neither an Arab nor a native of Baghdad. The family of Farabi originated, as his name indicates, in the district of Farab in Transoxania. Whether Farabi's father, who served as a military commander under the Samanids, was Iranian or Turkish is not known for certain, but his son, Abu Nasr Muhammad, wrote only in the ecumenical Arabic of his day. He was educated in

Damascus and Baghdad, and it was in the latter city about the year 900, when he was nearly thirty, that Farabi took up the study of Aristotle under the instruction of the Syrian Christians who had recently come to Baghdad from Harran as the surviving members of the Alexandrian philosophical tradition.[23] Farabi's name was particularly linked with one of them, Yuhanna ibn Haylan.

Farabi's career in Baghdad lasted over forty years, until 942, when he left that city and returned to Damascus, an event to which he later somewhat obliquely referred as his own *hijrah*. Farabi was a Shi'ite, and though we have no idea of his motives in leaving Baghdad in 942, it was at a Shi'ite court that he spent the final years of his life. The Hamdanid *amir* Sayf al-Dawlah, an Arab and a Shi'ite, occupied Aleppo in 944 and Damascus in the year following, and it was in his territories that Farabi spent the last six years of his life in honor and esteem. In 948 Farabi was in Egypt, not yet a Shi'ite domain. Two years later, on the road from Damascus to Ascalon, the eighty-year-old philosopher was murdered by thieves.

Farabi's major political works, *The Views of the Citizens of the Ideal State*, *Political Governance* and *Aphorisms of the Statesman*, all come from the final years of his life; the rest of his extensive bibliography cannot be dated with certainty. He spent half a century cultivating all branches of the Hellenic curriculum after his initiation into the Aristotelian logic in the years after 900, and much of his work from the logic onwards bears a strong stamp of Alexandrian scholasticism. The textual commentary was one of the preferred forms of Farabi's self-expression as a philosopher, as it had been for every Neoplatonist since the time of Porphyry.

As has been seen, the Alexandrians followed a more or less stereotyped format in their study of a philosophical work,[24] and bits and pieces of that same *eisagoge* complex are still visible in the form and style of Farabi's own writings. His knowledge of

---

23. The source of the information is Farabi himself; see Chap. IV, p. 328.
24. See Chap. V, pp. 332–333.

the history of philosophy, for example, must have come from just such an introductory lecture on philosophy,[25] as did the material in his *What Must Precede the Study of Philosophy*. The opening pages of his large commentary on Aristotle's *On Interpretation* read like an Alexandrian schoolbook: the intention of Aristotle in this work; its place in the corpus; its divisions; its point of departure, et cetera.

Apart from his commentaries, Farabi's most considerable scholastic undertaking was his *Enumeration of the Sciences*. The plan is academic, and the greater number of the sciences in question are those represented by an ideal Aristotelian curriculum with its major divisions into logic, mathematics, physics, metaphysics and politics. Preceding and following this Aristotelian core are set down three disciplines of somewhat more Islamic provenance. The linguistic sciences of grammar, writing, reading, prosody et cetera prepare for the study of logic,[26] while appended to politics are the two "Islamic sciences" of jurisprudence (*fiqh*) and dialectical theology (*kalam*).

There is only one theology in Farabi's scheme: it is the true "science about God" (*'ilm ilahi*), which stands in the place held by the *Metaphysics* in the Aristotelian curriculum.[27] *Kalam*, far from possessing any claim to be considered a true theological science, is reduced to a kind of defensive dialectic, and in Farabi's view held the same position vis-à-vis the genuine *'ilm ilahi* as the *Rhetoric* did to the *Posterior Analytics*. It was useful, but not scientific.

The place and necessarily brief remarks on metaphysics in the *Enumeration of the Sciences* contrast sharply with Farabi's other treatments of the same subject. He came explicitly to metaphysics

---

25. Best displayed in the preserved fragments of a tract entitled *On the Name of Philosophy and the Cause of Its Appearance*.

26. While many of Farabi's contemporaries were considerable philologists, his own interest in language was philosophical. His *Book of Letters* (see p. 501) is in part devoted to historical and analytical study of the connections between language, religion and philosophy.

27. Farabi, like Kindi, had no niche in his inherited schema for the other Aristotelian "theology" that he both knew and used, the epitome of Plotinus' *Enneads;* see Chap. IV, p. 289.

from three different directions. The first is the scholastic approach of the *Enumeration* and his *Intentions of the Metaphysics*, which owe their form and purpose to Greek academic sources. The other two methods of dealing with metaphysics are more peculiarly Farabi's own, and reveal far more instructively than the thin academic lines of the *Enumeration of the Sciences* his striking originality as a philosopher.

Many of Farabi's commentaries on the Aristotelian logic are cast in the form of a paraphrase or a continuous commentary on the text itself. What comes closest to being a Farabian commentary on the *Metaphysics*, his *Book of Letters*, is, however, a meditation suggested by the *Metaphysics* on a number of Farabi's favorite themes. The *Book of Letters* is essentially about language in a philosophical context and much of it is given over to the kind of lexicon that Aristotle or his editors inserted as Book Delta of the *Metaphysics*. But the investigation of language led Farabi into another fascinating topic, the historical relationship between language, philosophy and religion.

The connection between the latter two had already been investigated by one of Farabi's major sources. In the *Laws*, a work Farabi knew in epitome, Plato described the relationship between philosophy and religion in political terms. The *Book of Letters* came to the problem from a different direction. In it Farabi sketched a general typology of cultural evolution in which politics appears only during the final stages of the growth from the practical and popular arts, through the rhetorical arts, to philosophy. Both laws (*nawamis*)[28] and religion proceed from philosophical reasoning.

Farabi devoted an independent treatise to religion, *The Ideal Religion*, a work in which he described the duties of the ruler of the ideal polity with respect to religion. It is a short work and somewhat pragmatic in its intent. Religion for Farabi was an extension of the policy of the ruler. It grows out of the conversion of the truths of philosophy into the metaphors and symbols of a material social existence. Those truths constitute one immutable whole, but religion, like language, and law itself, is plural in

28. The Arabicized plural of the Greek *nomoi* and the same word used to translate the title of Plato's *Laws*.

its manifestations. Thus, *The Ideal Religion* is just one part of a larger complex seen in its total evolution in the *Book of Letters.*

Not surprisingly, then, Farabi's own metaphysics appear in a political setting. His *Views of the Inhabitants of the Ideal State* is a programmatic statement on the ideal commonwealth, which is the term of the evolution described in the *Book of Letters.*[29] The ideal ruler is one who looks upward in contemplation to the *philosophia perennis* and downward to his subjects, who are guided in their pursuit of happiness by the twofold instrumentality of law and religion. The ruler must understand before he can govern, and the citizens too must understand the same transcendental truths if they are to attain their goal of happiness.

The *Views* opens not with a description of the human forms of political association, but with a survey of the organization of the transcendental world beyond our own. That world, whose realities provide the substance of the "views" that must necessarily be affirmed by the citizens of the ideal polity, is, with one important modification, the intelligible cosmos of Plotinus and the Neoplatonists. At its apex is the First Cause, as remote in its transcendence as the Eternal of Kindi and the Allah of the Mu'tazilite successors of Jahm ibn Safwan. But for Farabi no less than Kindi, the First Cause was the Aristotelian Intelligence thinking Itself.[30] The austere mathematical attractions of the One as the ground and source of all being served the interests of neither the Christian nor the Muslim theologians.

In their description of the procession of the universe from the First Cause, Farabi and the other Arab Neoplatonists combined

---

29. In all his political writings Farabi paid close attention to the less than perfect alternatives to the "virtuous city." Some of these, like the varieties of the "ignorant city" (*madinah jahiliyah*), may owe something to Plato's analyses, but the correspondences are never exact, and Farabi was doubtless meditating the lessons of Islam's own political history. The very term *jahiliyah* carried strong Islamic nuances; it was for the Muslim the "time of ignorance" before the coming of the Prophet and the *Qur'an.* On Miskawayh's more direct use of Islamic history for ethical purposes, see p. 534.

30. As Farabi put it, he is intellect and the intelligizer and the intelligized. Immediately after this Aristotelian display Farabi proceeds to the justification of the various Qur'anic names for Allah.

Aristotle, Plato, Ptolemy and Plotinus in a most remarkable fashion. From the unique and simple Creator, who is capable, nonetheless, of noetic activity, comes forth, by reason of his unsurpassed goodness, the plurality of the universe. The first emanation from that First Cause was another Divine Intellect independent of matter. Its noetic activities differ from those of the First Cause in that they suffer distinctions. Thus, the first Caused Intellect is aware of (1) its principle, the First Cause whence it came, (2) itself and, in Ibn Sina's version of the descent, (3) the contingency of its own existence. These three "moments" in the intellectual activity of the first Caused Intellect generate three separate effects: (1) another Caused Intellect independent of matter, (2) a soul, and (3) a body, in this instance the body of the First Heaven. The emanation process continues down through the series of separated Intellects and heavenly bodies, each of the latter embedded in its own sphere, that of the fixed stars, Saturn, Jupiter, Mars, the Sun, Venus, Mercury and the Moon.

The Platonic tradition from Plotinus to Simplicius had been unanimous in its acceptance of a single First Cause from which all else proceeded in a serial descent, while for Aristotle God was the Final Cause, an object of love whose supreme goodness was not the cause of creation in being but of motion through love and desire. In the *Metaphysics* the heavenly spheres have their own proper movers as well, as many as were necessary to explain their complex celestial motions. These heavenly movers Aristotle described as Intelligences, and though he does not explicitly say so, it is likely through them that the First Mover communicates his desirable goodness to the world beneath.

In Farabi's version of the emanation scheme, the moving cause of Aristotle and the producing cause of the Platonists have been integrated into a single system, and Farabi himself supplies evidence on who was responsible for the synthesis. In his essay *On the Agreement of the Views of Plato and Aristotle* Farabi took up the critical question of the creation of the universe. Plato, on the testimony of the *Timaeus*, held for a creator; Aristotle apparently did not. The difference was not, however, a real one and Farabi can cite the "Theology of Aristotle" as part of his evidence to the contrary. Plotinus under the guise of Aristotle did, of course, help the case considerably, but there was more. Farabi referred as well to a work of Ammonius which dealt with both men's notions of the creator, "An Exposition of Aristotle's Doctrines About the Creator," and even before Farabi, Ammonius' student Simplicius had in his hands the same book that attempted to prove, and did, to the satisfaction of both Simplicius and Farabi, that for Aristotle the Unmoved Mover of the universe was also its Creator.

In late fifth-century Alexandria, then, the integration of Plato and Aristotle begun by Porphyry continued to exercise its influence on the philosophical faculty. The Aristotelian universe was provided with a Creator, and some alumni of the school, like the Christians John Philoponus and Zacharias of Mitylene, were even pressing the claims of a finite universe created in time. John Philoponus took up the case against Aristotle, while Zacharias addressed himself directly to Ammonius in his dialogue *Ammonius Or On the Creation of the Universe*.[31] The Arabs appear to have known nothing of Zacharias, but they did possess Philoponus' *Against Aristotle*, though Farabi for one was not convinced by it.

Farabi took up arms against Philoponus' finite universe on a number of occasions, but only the tract *Against John the Grammarian* has been preserved for us. In it the Muslim accused the Christian of misunderstanding Aristotle's arguments in *On the Heavens* and of attempting to refute what Aristotle did not attempt to prove, namely, the eternity of the world. Farabi was not sure why Philoponus did this, but he did have a suspicion. In making his case John was drawing on arguments supplied to him by his own religion (*millah*). John surely must have known the difference between religious arguments and philosophical proofs, but his treatise may have been designed for the consumption of his coreligionists, to persuade them that he did not share the opinions of the philosophers, "so as not to suffer," suggested Farabi, "the same fate as Socrates."

There are some indications among those same Alexandrian Greeks that other of Aristotle's views were making headway

31. On Zacharias, see Chap. IV, p. 298, n. 13.

among the Platonists. The first was his contention that there was noetic activity on the part of the First Cause. The earlier Neoplatonists had relegated Intelligence to the first emanation to flow forth from the supreme One, but Simplicius, for one, appeared willing to accept Aristotle's self-thinking Intellect as a First Cause, and by the Arabs' time the identification of First Cause and Uncaused Intelligence was complete: Kindi, Farabi and Ibn Sina all held for a self-thinking first principle of the universe. In the latter two philosophers the theory of separated Intellects operating upon animated celestial bodies had also been fully integrated into the Neoplatonic system of emanations and Ptolemy's nine concentric celestial spheres.[32]

Ptolemaic astronomy did not carry with it any necessary conviction about astrology, even of the mild Ptolemaic variety. Neither Farabi nor any of the philosophers or conservative theologians in Islam had the slightest doubts about the validity of astronomy; the "science of the stars" was a branch of mathematics whose purpose was the observation and measurement of the heavenly bodies. That is how Farabi understood it in his *Enumeration of the Sciences,* but when he came to write his *Notes on What Is Valid and Invalid in Astrology* the claims of astronomy had been extended by Farabi's own philosophical interests, and those of Aristotle before him, into the realm of physics.

On the basis of the theory of cosmic sympathy, which all the philosophers wholeheartedly accepted, the planets do affect the process of change in the sublunary world. The degree of their

---

32. The outermost sphere, that of the "first heaven," was another of Ptolemy's modifications of the Aristotelian physics and, by extension, of the Aristotelian theology as well. Ptolemy understood, as Aristotle did not, that the motion of the so-called "fixed stars" was not a single uniform motion; and once the motion of this sphere had been "decomposed" into two countermotions, it was necessary to posit still another sphere above it. This new "first heaven" was material and starless, and it was moved in its simple, uniform and spherical motion by a single Intellect. Farabi, the Brethren and Ibn Sina, all accepted the Ptolemaic correction; Ibn Rushd, on the other hand, remained faithful to Aristotle and his eight-sphere orthodoxy.

influences and effects are, in the physicists' view, computable from the observed phenomena. Astrology (literally "the study of the stars"), on the other hand, seeks to know what cannot be known, and so the astrologer has substituted his own guesses and pretenses for the prosaic but scientific calculations of the astronomer.

The wills of the separated Intellects that govern the celestial spheres play no part in the physically derived effects worked by the planets upon terrestrial matter. Those Intellects operated entirely within the confines of Farabi's epistemology, and their effects were experienced not so much in the domain of physics as in the souls of men. Divine intelligence was mediated downward through the separated Intellects until it reached the human intelligences that were, in Aristotle's phrase, illuminated "from outside." That outside source of illumination was the tenth and lowest of those separated Intellects, and in it Farabi found the keystone to both his theory of intellection and his explanation of prophecy.

Al-Kindi, who had inherited from some Peripatetic source like Alexander of Aphrodisias a naturalistic view of how men know, preferred the other, supernatural mode of cognition, the "divine science" of prophecy. The two methods of cognition were kept distinct by Kindi, for whom God was neither soul nor intellect; but few of his immediate Greek predecessors had done likewise, nor did Farabi and the rest of the Islamic philosophers. For the later Hellenic philosophers the illumination of men's minds from above was a persistently attractive question, and even though Kindi cared little for such concerns, Farabi appears to have been caught up in the center of their discussions.

The question of illumination and the possibility (or necessity) of a nonnaturalistic mode of knowledge arose out of a complex of problems. One of the issues at stake between Plato and Aristotle had been that of the "intelligibles" (*noeta*). For Plato they were transcendental substances; for Aristotle their only real existence was immanently within things. Thus, Platonic intellection (*noesis*) was a reaching out or a rising up somehow to touch the transcendental intelligible Forms, while for Aristotle intellection rested upon a process of abstraction whereby the intellect derived the intelligible forms from the material existents in which they were immanent and then realized, and so knew, those same intelligibles as universal essences. Aristotle did, however, recognize a type of intellection that had nothing to do with material beings: the intellectual activity of the First Cause in which thought and its immaterial object were identical.

At first it appeared that the Aristotelian view was going to prevail in the Academy. The scholars of the Platonic tradition in the centuries just before and after the birth of Christ converted the transcendental Forms of Plato into truly noetic entities, thoughts present in the mind of God. Their motive may well have been Plato's repeated suggestion that the Forms were paradigms for the Artist-Demiurge's fashioning of the universe. If the Demiurge was to be identified with a Divine Intelligence, then it was natural enough to conclude, even though the pertinent passage in the *Timaeus* suggested otherwise, that the forms were noetic, that they were the Demiurge's ideas, an identification that gave Platonism a God not unlike Aristotle's intelligent Mover.[33]

For their part the Peripatetics, at least as they are represented by Alexander of Aphrodisias, were having difficulties with the more modest immanent forms of Aristotle as universal essences individualized in matter. Though they could be abstracted and known by human intelligence, the Aristotelian essences apparently did not depend for their existence on that knowledge. Alexander was not so certain. It seemed to him that all the intelligibles had some kind of existential dependence upon an intelligence, either the intelligence of the First Cause or the human intellect of man. Alexander had an attentive reader in Plotinus, and the hypothesis mooted by Alexander appears in the *Enneads* in its most explicit form: the intelligibles do not exist outside an intellect.

---

33. But only in a position secondary to that of the immobile and changeless One. Not many Platonists were convinced by Aristotle's explanation that the First Mover had the "motion of immobility." To intelligize, even to intelligize oneself, was to be subject to process, a characteristic that made Aristotle's Mover an unlikely candidate for the First God but which rendered him perfectly suitable as a "Second God" who mediated between the unique and changeless One and the plurality of the universe.

There is more that Plotinus took from the Peripatetic Alexander and settled within a Platonic context. The intellect immanent in man does not stand to his soul as form to matter. The Platonic metaphor of the artist likewise made Alexander's suggestion of another, external intellect cooperating in the process of human intellection attractive. The immanent human intellect might be considered "like a form in a bronze statue," but there is another "which produces the form in the statue." Thus, for Plotinus the hypostatized Divine Intellect is the paradigm for all human thought, and the intellectual World Soul embraces within its intelligence all the forms and passes them on to matter where they are immanent as "reflections and copies."

The choice of a Divine Intellect as the model for its human counterpart lead Plotinus into considerable difficulty. If the human intellect is also divine and possesses all the intelligibles, then it must, in this view, constantly enjoy the kind of intuitive intellection that characterizes the Divine Intellect, and this despite its own decline into matter. Plotinus accepted the conclusion, but not many of the succeeding Platonists followed his lead. For them the fall of the human soul destroyed the possibility of the continuous intuition enjoyed by its divine counterpart.

For most of the Platonists man had to settle for a sporadic and occasional intellection, and here too they had available Alexander's suggestion of how this was to be accomplished, that is, the "divinization" of the purely passive human intellect by its contact with the First Cause in the act of knowing. We are not certain how far Alexander pushed that hypothesis, but his Arab translators, at any rate, thought they knew. Alexander's treatise *On the Intellect* has been recovered in Arabic in the translation of Ishaq ibn Hunayn, and in it what Alexander called "the intellect from outside" has become "the acquired intellect," a reading of Alexander's sense that left no doubt that in the act of intelligizing the human intellect became, albeit temporarily, the Divine Intellect.

The simplicities of that solution were unavailable to the later Greek Platonists. Between the Divine Intellect and its human copy were a number of other separated Intellects in the serial chain of being. Iamblichus set out one version of that series: there are Divine Intellects completely devoid of matter; beneath them are the intelligences of the heavenly bodies, the visible gods; then come in descending order the archangels, angels, demons (*daimones*), heroes and cosmic archons, each with its own functions and gifts.

Plotinus was likely the last Platonist capable of accepting Alexander's suggested identification of the human intellect and the Divine Intellect in the act of knowing. Thereafter the act of union, frequently expressed, as in Aristotle, in terms of an illumination, was mediated by one of the supernatural powers located above men, a planetary Mover in Aristotle's physical way of looking at things, or, more commonly among the later Platonists, a *daimon* or an angel. By the time of the Arabs that hierarchy of intermediate entities was stabilized, as has been seen, in the series of ten descending Intellects, the last of which, the tenth, was the direct link between man's mode of knowing and God's.

For Farabi, human intellection occurs where it did for both Alexander and Aristotle, in the passive faculty of the soul, the passive or hylic intellect. The Active Intellect, the tenth emanation from the First Cause, illumines the sensible forms stored up in human memory from sense perceptions and by that illumination activates them as intelligible forms in the passive intellect. The passive intellect thus becomes an intellect-in-act which possesses the former potentially intelligible forms as actually intelligized forms. The intellect has in this manner "acquired" actuality and has become, in effect, something new, an "acquired intellect."

In Farabi's epistemology the "acquired intellect" is the culmination of human cognition that is described in his essay *On the Intellect*. Through this new faculty the philosopher, the prophet and the mystic are all put in contact with the divine Active Intellect. Religious thinkers might designate that latter as the "Holy Spirit" or an angel, but for Farabi it was better described in Aristotelian terms. Very few people reach the state of intellectual perfection wherein they can establish such contact with the Active Intellect. They are, however, the true philosophers, and if they manage to combine the transcendental knowledge of the philosopher with the special qualities of the prophet, they are the ideal rulers of Farabi's ideal state.[34]

The faculty proper to the prophet as such is not the intellect but the imagination. In Greek theories of cognition the imagination was that faculty of the soul that presented to the passive intellect those potentially intelligible forms derived from the operation of the senses, the same forms that would be converted, under the operation of the Active Intellect, into actually intelligized forms. Though the Neoplatonic philosophers did not limit the functions of the imagination to this service it performed for the higher intellect, it was not until Farabi that the possibility of the imagination as a semi-autonomous creative faculty came to be explored.

Farabi regarded the imagination as likewise capable of taking the intelligible forms already present in the intellect by the act of knowledge and reproducing them mimetically under sensible, material aspects. The artist functions somewhat in this manner and, more to the point here, the philosopher-prophet. With the intellect of the philosopher he has established contact with the Active Intellect and the intelligible forms are present in all their splendor in his "acquired intellect." With the acutely developed imagination of a prophet he "re-creates" those intelligibles in sensible terms of the highest order.

Farabi's portrait of the philosopher-prophet was still well within the Greek philosophical tradition that recognized a non-discursive and intuitive grasp of intelligibility that occurs, usually of a sudden, near the end of the dialectical ascent to the truth, "the flight," as Plotinus described it, "of the alone to the Alone." The Platonists' enlarged analysis of the intellectual faculties of man and of a cosmic landscape dominated by emanations downward from the One provided Farabi with the intellectual grounds for his own understanding of prophecy. An upward-questing human intelligence and a downward-coursing Divine Intellect were central premises of Neoplatonism, and within them

34. Farabi nowhere suggests that by this contact with the Active Intellect man himself is divinized. It is a contact that is achieved, not an assimilation of the type described earlier by the Platonic mystics and later by their Islamic counterparts.

prophetism could be treated comfortably in cognitive terms rather than as an abnormal and arational activity.

The Greeks had no occasion, of course, to explain an actual historical revelation, and later Greek psychology, for all the sophistication that permitted it to analyze cognitive processes, was incapable of dealing with prophecy either as a historical event or as a social phenomenon. All intuition, the unitive grasp of intelligibility, was in a sense revelation, but in the Muslim theory this was merely a private business done for the sake of personal contemplation and one's own satisfaction, as it might have been for Plotinus; the Islamic Prophet, on the other hand, and those in the Judaeo-Christian tradition before him, had a social and historical function.

Farabi's use of the faculty of the imagination led easily into an explanation of the prophet as the revealer of truths to men. The true prophet, the man of transcendent intelligence, was also a man of surpassing imagination, and thus he was able to convert his intuition of intelligibility into the grosser forms of language and symbol and so communicate it to the masses and implement it in the form of law. There were Greek antecedents here too. The incapability of the ordinary man to grasp the substance of philosophy and the dangerous necessity of converting it into something more vulgar was a literary commonplace of Platonism.[35] When it was converted into political terms it led to Plato's notion of a philosopher-king ruling through his own person or that more earthbound extension of his understanding, the laws. Stoicism was operating under a similar prescription when it formulated its tripartite "theology" appropriate to the philosopher, the poet and the politician, each an operationally distinct way of communicating the same truth.

In Farabi's version of prophecy the prophet communicates his intuitions of intelligibility in the form of a figured revelation, the *Qur'an,* and a material law, the *shari'ah,* and it is precisely here that the philosopher's prophetic theory ran counter to Islamic orthodoxy. Not only did philosophy exalt itself over revelation;

---

35. This is the consideration that lies at the root of the Greek distinction between the "esoteric" and "exoteric" works of the philosophers, the former an explanation designed for adepts, the latter for the layman.

it failed to do justice to the historical mission of Muhammad. By casting prophecy into psychological categories Farabi and the rest of the *falasifah* could say nothing of the special quality of Islam nor of Muhammad's claim to be the seal and end of the prophets.

From his theory of how the prophet knows and speaks, Farabi, following in Plato's footsteps, gave himself over to a consideration of the political means whereby the special understanding of philosopher-prophet might be implemented in man's social associations. He acknowledged that absolute happiness is to be found only in the beatific vision after death, but once having paid his dues to the eschatology of Islam, he turned with enthusiasm to the investigation of how men can acquire the somewhat mitigated happiness that is their lot in this world.

The answer lies in the very structure of his works. Farabi's metaphysics occurs where it does in Plato, in the context of a work on politics, the *Views of the Inhabitants of the Ideal State*. And another work that sets the problem, *The Attainment of Happiness*, is the first part of a trilogy that culminates in the exposition of the philosophies of Plato and Aristotle.[36] Wisdom (*hikmah*) is clearly the highest value a human can strive for, and that wisdom is embodied in *falsafah*.

Farabi's interest in politics was unique in later Platonism. Plato's political writings were read selectively in the later Academy where the gaze of the professors was fixed steadily on the transcendentals. There are a number of titles in al-Kindi's bibliography that Ibn al-Nadim classified as "political," but they were, as far as we can see, ethical and gnomonological rather than political in either the Greek or the Farabian sense of the word.

In Farabi's view man's perfection consists in two sets of virtues, those connected with speculative wisdom (*'ilm, hikmah*) and those that flow from practical wisdom (Gr. *phronesis;* Ar. *ta'aqqul*). "Wisdom acquaints one with true happiness, and practical wisdom with what must be done to attain happiness." These two, then, are the operative considerations in the perfecting of man: *hikmah* is that which sets the ultimate end; *ta'aqqul* specifies the means whereby the end is attained.

---

36. See p. 520.

The most important area for the exercise of practical wisdom is the ideal polity where the ruler, "the first chief," combines within himself six qualities: speculative and practical wisdom, the power to persuade, a highly developed imagination, and the moral and physical strength to carry out his responsibilities. The polity ruled by such a man is bound together by love, which for Farabi is based on a community of thought and action. That thought is nothing less than a knowledge of the truths of philosophy, the metaphysical and physical system sketched by Farabi in his *Views of the Inhabitants of the Ideal State*.

Philosophy contemplates the first principles and demonstrates the truths that proceed from them. But the truths of philosophy are also promulgated in a concrete form by the lawgiver and expressed symbolically and imaginatively by the prophet. From those varied expressions of the unitive truth grow both the polity and religion (*millah*), from whose needs in turn arise the pragmatic disciplines of jurisprudence (*fiqh*) and dialectical theology (*kalam*).

Jurisprudence, like political philosophy, concerns itself with both thought and action. Dogma and morality alike are the preserve of the philosopher-prophet who rules the ideal state and they find their ultimate expression in the Law transmitted to men in the form of the Prophet's revelation. Jurisprudence is the study of that Law and of its extension by analogy into areas not explicitly covered by the original revelation. The dialectical theologian (*mutakallim*) is not concerned with extension as such. He rests upon the same principles as those enunciated by the jurisprudent; his task is to defend them.

Farabi regarded *kalam* as a purely defensive weapon operating on behalf of the givens of revelation. Indeed, in Farabi's view dialectical theology appears to have no method of its own but to rely on whatever is at hand to defend the dogmas and prescriptions of the Law: the evidence of the senses, the conclusions of reason, generally held opinions, allegorical exegesis and a wide variety of purely rhetorical arguments. In neither its purpose nor its methods should *kalam* be confused with genuine theology (*'ilm ilahi*).

Farabi was himself even less a political activist than Plato; his close scrutiny of political science was purely speculative. Contemporary political developments may well have provoked some of his elaborate analyses of imperfect polities, but there is no sign that he was preparing a program for a Shi'ite *Imam* or that he intended to play Plato to Sayf al-Dawlah's Dion. Farabi attempted to construct out of rational materials and the experience of history a humanistic ethic in which there was a place for both a revealed religion like Islam and the claims of the Hellenic philosophers.

The results doubtless exalted the philosopher at the expense of the prophet, but Farabi was more Hellenic than his immediate Platonic predecessors in that he took the social and political consequences of prophecy seriously; the happiness of human society in this world and the next depended immediately upon the lawgiver-prophet. Farabi was not engaged in speculation for the benefit of the rare philosopher who needed only metaphysics. His concerns were social, like Islam's own, and the revival of Platonic politics in the tenth century of the Christian era may have owed more to Farabi's Muslim sensibilities than to the mere continuance of the Hellenic tradition.

The Hellenic Enlightenment

The early Muslim's view of himself was troubled by a profound disorientation. Born in the desert and reared in the proud tradition of a tribal society, he grew to maturity in cities and sought out his identity in an ecumenical religion. Bedouin or city dweller, tribal Arab or catholic Muslim, the new citizen of the *Dar al-Islam* was torn between conflicting ideals and styles. The Greek had grown slowly from his feudal Bronze Age past into the fifth-century man of the *polis*. His ethical and social ideals had evolved with him, and over the course of five centuries the virtues of the Homeric warrior were transformed into those of the citizen, the *polites*. Odysseus' skill at speech became the rhetoric of the democratic assembly, and Achilles' beauty, speed and strength were gracefully metamorphosed into the athleticism of the gymnasia.

The Arab was cheated of the evolutionary process. The route from Bedouin to city dweller was traversed within one generation. The cities where he had first lived and ruled were not of his own making, nor did he share in their citizenship. His membership was in the Islamic *ummah*—God's community, whose very success thrust it into the fellowship of kingdoms and empires. His only guide was the Islamic Law, which regulated his worship of God and his contracts with his fellow Muslims; it gave him no instruction on how to rule, no model of a state, no ideal prince or ideal constitution.

The Muslim Arab had lost but still remembered the desert and the tribe. What the Greeks sublimated into *polis* institutions and athletic contests the urbanized Muslim fed upon in the form of literary nostalgia. He read about and celebrated his ancestors' speed, strength and daring, but no ideal of *kalokagathia*, excellence of body and spirit, beckoned him on; he built no gymnasia, no theaters, and no senate houses. He had need of only one building, the mosque;[37] his other monuments are the torrents of books, monographs and pamphlets that came forth from the intellectual and religious establishment of Islam. And there, where he recorded his deeds and his aspirations, the Muslim left his indelible self-portrait; what he was and what he wanted to be is plainly written out in Arabic literature.

Piety and learning were part of that portrait, and the eighth and ninth centuries are full of exemplars of a happy combination of the two, lawyers meditating upon the *shari'ah*, philologists visiting the camps of the Bedouin in the hopes of casting new linguistic lights on the *Qur'an*, pious scholars who spent a lifetime wandering in pursuit of sayings of the Prophet. At first glance the historian Mas'udi appears to conform to the familiar type with his journeying across the *Dar al-Islam* from Egypt to India and the China Sea. His apparently ceaseless traveling was not, however, in the pursuit of new *hadith* or to sit at the feet of eminent *shaykhs* in one or another corner of the Islamic world. His motive was more Hellenic than Islamic, a Herodotean search-

37. More specifically the cathedral mosque (*jami'*) from whose pulpit the Friday invocation was pronounced. The "pulpit" had at its inception nothing to do with sermonizing; it was the Prophet's, and then the Caliph's throne, an association that at first restricted the cathedral mosque to the chief city of the province.

ing out of the various peoples of the East, their history, manners and customs. The results appeared in a series of encyclopedic histories, of which only the *Golden Meadows* and the *Notice* are preserved. In them Mas'udi took as his province the entire history of the cosmos, natural, cultural and political, from Creation to his own day.

Mas'udi was one of the new scholars of Islam, a historian whose vision extended beyond Abraham, Moses and Jesus, and whose material was drawn not only from sacred traditions but from profane books, among them translations of Aristotle and Farabi's lost *Appearance of Philosophy*. The summoning of new actors upon the stage of history—Plato, Khusraw Anushirvan, the Sabians of Harran, Pythagoras and Hermes Trismegistos—had necessarily to add some new and alien nuances to the question, What did the Muslim intend to be?

The answer was patent; it was stated in the *Qur'an* and codified in the *shari'ah*, the Law of Islam, which in concrete and detailed terms set down the norms of acceptable conduct. As a historical phenomenon the *shari'ah* replaced another code, that of the pre-Islamic Arabs, or perhaps three other codes, if Christianity and Judaism are reckoned here. The resolution of one by the other was never complete, however. The old Arab chivalry which was embodied in the pre-Islamic poetry so assiduously if paradoxically cultivated by the pious conservatives never disappeared from Islam. As part of the issue of Arabism it stood over against the pretensions of an Iranian *shu'ubiyah*.

The Iranians had no quarrel with Islam as such, merely with the identification of Arabism and Islam. But just as the old Bedouin code of chivalry was part of the defense of Arabism, so the extensive ethical tradition of pre-Islamic Iranian literature became part of the disputed terrain between the two peoples. A considerable body of that ethical writing was translated into Arabic under circumstances no longer entirely clear to us and formed part of the subsequent ethical speculation in Islam.

The fourth and final element in the Islamic attempt to work out an ethic was what the Arabs and others learned from the Greeks. The Hellenic philosophical heritage in Islam is fairly well defined; what Plato and what Aristotle was being read, and whose commentaries thereon, is tolerably well known. In ethics, however, the Arabs drank deeply of a great variety of Greek works with no great cohesion. They knew the *Republic*, the *Laws* and the *Nicomachean Ethics*, but they read as well the *Oikonomikos* of Bryson,[38] the ethical treatises of Galen,[39] Plutarch, Themistius, the *Pinax* of Cebes, the *Golden Verses* attributed to Pythagoras, a number of Aristotelian pseudepigraphs connected with Alexander and a rich collection of anonymously transmitted ethical proverbs.

The Muslim had to seek his ethical identity somewhere in this mélange. Was he to be a Bedouin or a Sasanian knight? An imitator of the pious Abu Bakr in his simple-minded pursuit of an Islamic felicity or a devotee of the *bios theoretikos* exalted by the Greeks? The early Christian with his choice between Athens and Jerusalem, Cicero and Christ, must have appeared in an enviously uncomplicated position.

In practice the resolution of values was neither as syncretistic nor as complicated as might at first appear. The confrontation with Iranian ideals drew Muslim and "Arabist" into an alliance that was publicly and officially consummated by the *littérateurs* of the ninth and tenth centuries; the court might affect certain Iranian styles,[40] but Islam was officially Arabic. Where syncretism did not occur, despite serious and repeated attempts at making it work, was between this Arabo-Islamic morality and the Hellenic ideal of the supremacy of intellectual virtue.

Among the philosophers al-Kindi, al-Farabi and Ibn Sina, all

---

38. The Muslims generally followed the Hellenic division of practical philosophy into ethics (*akhlaq*), "household governance" (*oikonomia; tadbir al-manzil*), and political science (*'ilm al-madani*), and it was the treatise of this Neoplatonist of uncertain date who supplied most of what they needed to know about that second area.

39. Particularly his treatise *On Moral Dispositions*, which is known only indirectly in Greek but was translated completely into Arabic by Hunayn ibn Ishaq and is currently preserved in the form of an Arabic epitome.

40. But not ideology. Iranian wisdom was gnomic rather than philosophical and so, had more to do with style than with principle. Zoroastrian ethics represented neither an ideological threat nor a genuine alternative to the *shari'ah*.

attempted to shape an integrated ethics suitable to the intelligent Muslim. How much there was original in these efforts is now difficult to decide, since all three men had available, as we do not, a major interpretive commentary upon the *Nicomachean Ethics*, that of the Neoplatonist Porphyry, and were in addition drawing on the imperfectly known ethical systems that grew out of the synthesis of Plato and Aristotle current in the Hellenic schools from the second pre-Christian century onward.

The Arab philosophers were faithful followers of the late-Hellenic sentiment that Plato and Aristotle were in essential agreement in their philosophies. But they also understood some of the differences. Al-Kindi and Ibn Sina, for example, faithfully reproduce the Platonic version of the soul as taught by Galen, that it had three "parts" and that even the strictly irrational parts had moral dispositions appropriate to them. Farabi, on the other hand, followed the Aristotelian partition of the soul into vegetative, animal and rational faculties and adhered to the Aristotelian definition of virtue as a mean.

Against this inherited Hellenic background the Muslim philosophers conducted their exploration of the final good for man, whether it was happiness in the next world achieved by the observance of the *shari'ah* with the help of philosophical understanding, whether philosophy and religious wisdoms were equals and allies in the pursuit of happiness or, finally, whether true happiness consisted uniquely in philosophical wisdom, with religion serving as an inferior substitute for those incapable of leading the philosophical life.

Al-Kindi (d. c. 870) was an exponent of the first view. His orthodoxy is apparent in his understanding of philosophical wisdom as an auxiliary to theology, but in so doing he was equally apparently departing from the traditionalist position of his day by his willingness to construct a Muslim theology out of philosophy. For the traditionalists, a knowledge of the *Qur'an* and the *sunnah* was sufficient for man to achieve his end, and Revelation had no need of any "handmaidens" save those skilled in philology.

Much like his fellow Mu'tazilites,[41] al-Kindi saw the Muslim

---

41. See Chap. VI, p. 430.

committed to giving a rational defense of his faith through the means provided him by Hellenic philosophy. These were, in effect, the "rational sciences" that served as the support of the higher and revelation-based "traditioned sciences." Secure in the knowledge that he was leading the reader toward a true understanding of Muslim revelation, al-Kindi could proceed to erect his metaphysics and ethics out of the synthesis of Plato and Aristotle bequeathed to him by late antiquity.

Within the middle ground of opinion that attempted to do equal justice to both the revealed *shari'ah* and the speculative wisdom of the philosophers, a number of different postures were struck. Al-Farabi (d. 950) was an Aristotelian who had simply read more Plato than Kindi. He knew the Aristotelian psychology that underlay the moral theories of the *Nicomachean Ethics*, but he had also read, at least in an abridged version, the *Republic* and the *Laws* and so could locate the question of the happiness and the end of man in a fundamentally more political context than had been done by al-Kindi. Nor was the Islamic *ummah* the limit of Farabi's horizon; he was acquainted as well with the Platonic version of the parochial *polis* and the Stoic version of the world state.

Ibn Sina (d. 1037), while more actively engaged in politics than Farabi,[42] was less interested in its theory. He had, of course, ideas about the state. His theory of social origins, for example, was considerably more pessimistic than Farabi's Hellenizing view of man as a political animal who finds his happiness in mutual association. According to Ibn Sina, it is safety that man seeks in society and so he enters into a social contract to protect himself and his well-being. It is from the implementation of this contract that flows the need of law.

Ibn Sina was, for all that, more interested in the conditions of individual happiness than in the somewhat desperate circumstances of statecraft. He too had read Aristotle and his commentators on the soul, as well as his own Muslim predecessors, and from this emerged a detailed and imaginative Avicennan theory of the intellectual operations of the human psyche,

---

42. See Chap. VIII, pp. 619–620.

whether they had to do with the discursive understanding of the philosopher or the intuitive seizure of the prophet.

Prophecy is the coping stone in the theory of Islamic ethics. It bridges the distance between the will of Allah and the felicity of man. Through his Prophet the decree of Allah was converted into a moral imperative. For most Muslims the prophethood of Muhammad was simply a unique historical phenomenon that had occurred; for the Muslim who was also a philosopher it had necessarily to be more. To consider Muhammad as merely a historical figure would have made the *shari'ah* absolutely discontinuous with the naturalistic ethic inherited from the Greeks. Only by reducing "the Prophet" to "prophet" and locating him within the cadres of his own epistemology could the Muslim philosopher begin the difficult task of reconciling the *shari'ah* with the *Republic* and the *Nicomachean Ethics*.

In Farabi and Ibn Sina's view the prophet is superior to the philosopher in his mode of knowing, but philosophy is superior to the mere traditioning of revelation in that the latter descends through the lower faculty of the imagination and comes forth, for the benefit of the unphilosophical masses, in the form of a figured revelation, the *Qur'an*, and of a material law, the *shari'ah*. Precisely here, in the contest between philosophy and the figured revelation of a material law, did the philosophers' prophetic theory run counter to Islamic orthodoxy. Not only did philosophy exalt itself above historical revelation; it failed to do justice to the unique historical position of Muhammad and Islam.

Both *falsafah* and the *Qur'an* had to do with man's happiness, the first in its pursuit and the latter in its revelation. In the Greek rationalist tradition happiness consisted in wisdom, Greek wisdom, which was attained through the perfection of the human intellect. As we have seen, Farabi came to the question in precisely those terms in his *On the Philosophy of Plato and Aristotle* where epitomes of the teachings of the two philosophers are preceded by the professedly ethical treatise *On the Attainment of Happiness*.[43] Unmistakably, wisdom preceded happiness. Prophetic revelation, on the other hand, Islam's proper claim to

---

43. The three parts also circulated separately in Islam.

wisdom, was achieved by the perfection of a lower faculty, the imagination. The philosopher took his wisdom neat, in Plato and Aristotle—the pious believer, in sign and symbols.

Intellectual wisdom (*hikmah*) was, then, the highest form of human happiness, but consonant with the Greek sources that he was meditating, Farabi pursued the investigation of individual perfection into the larger context of the ethical master science, political philosophy. In three major works, *The Views of the Inhabitants of the Ideal State, Political Governance* and *Aphorisms of the Statesman,* he posed the question, What is the political association that, by its governance and institutions, can best insure happiness for its inhabitants? The ideal might well be the ecumenical world-state—the term, perhaps, of an expanding *Dar al-Islam*—but since that could not presently be achieved, Farabi expressed his preference for the "nation" (*ummah*) over the smaller Platonic *polis.*

Farabi's state was no other-worldly project on the model of Augustine's City of God; it was an ideal but attainable City of Man constructed on the triple foundations of *Falsafah, Qur'an* and *Shari'ah.* Farabi was enough of a Hellene to concede the center of the arch to the first, but he was also enough of a Muslim to bind philosophy and revelation into a practical political ideal for Islam.

Farabi's political sketches may have been, for all their transparently Platonic inspiration, a philosopher's meditation on the rising Shi'ite expectations of the second quarter of the tenth century. By the time of Farabi's death in 950 one revolutionary Shi'ite dynasty was entrenched in North Africa and was extending itself in the direction of Egypt. Syria and northern Mesopotamia were likewise in the hands of Arab princes of the Shi'ite persuasion, including Farabi's own patrons, the Hamdanids. And at the heart of the 'Abbasid Caliphate in Iraq and western Iran power was passing into the possession of a family of resolute Iranian and Shi'ite soldiers from Daylam.

The Iranian Daylamis, like the later Turks, were converted not by conquest but by missionary activity. But while the Turks received their initiation to Islam at the hands of simple but effective Sunni dervishes who ventured out onto the steppe, Islam came to the fastnesses of Daylam in the person of Shi'ite missionaries from the Zaydi principality in nearby Tabaristan.[44]

Among the Shi'ites abroad in the *Dar al-Islam* in the ninth century the Zaydis can be reckoned as moderates, political partisans of 'Ali and his family without either of the auxiliary programs of Gnosticism or social revolution, and in the sequel the Daylamis showed similar traits. Despite an early flirtation with the Isma'iliyah, the Daylami conquest of the heart of Sunni Islam was chiefly remarkable for an almost total absence of revolutionary political consequences.

The Daylamis had a long and well-deserved reputation as warriors for pay and profit, and among the Daylami *condottieri* of the first quarter of the tenth century, one, Mardawij ibn Ziyar, began to take and hold towns in the uplands south of Daylam. His troops were Daylamites, and if their chief motive was booty, their leader had at least the glimmerings of something more ambitious. Mardawij had once been solicited for the Isma'iliyah by the missionary Abu Hatim al-Razi, but his attacks against the thriving cities of Hamadhan and Dinawar had a discernible anti-Muslim cast, and some of his contemporaries were convinced that Mardawij had revanchist ambitions that featured himself as the new *Shahanshah* of Iran, a title in default since the death of Yazdigird III in 651.

Mardawij never lived to see his alleged ambitions fulfilled: after eight years of successes as far south as Isfahan, he was murdered by his newly recruited Turkish cavalry. The Turks, who were then as little politicized as the Daylamis had been earlier, took no profit from their act, and others stepped in to reap what Mardawij had sown. His brother Vushmagir held on to some few of his conquests along the Caspian, and a subsequent dynasty descended from Vushmagir, the Ziyarids, clung to their

---

44. The Zaydi Shi'ites of Tabaristan east of Daylam survived as an independent political entity from about 864 to 900, when a bloody and successful onslaught by the aggressive Samanids of Khurasan forced the Zaydi princes to acknowledge Samanid—and Sunni—sovereignty. The other major political wing of the Zaydis, those in the Yemen, were somewhat more successful at survival; see Chap. VIII, p. 574.

Tabaristan outposts by showing themselves somewhat more accommodating than Mardawij: they accepted first Samanid and then Ghaznavid sovereignty and, in the course of time, Sunni Islam as well.[45]

The chief beneficiaries of Mardawij's self-promotion from brigandage to politics were three brothers, 'Ali, Hasan and Ahmad, sons of an obscure Buya Panakhusraw.[46] In 945 the Daylami infantry and Turkish horsemen of the sons of Buya entered Baghdad to begin what has been called a "Daylamite intermezzo" in the history of the Caliphate. The Caliph al-Mustakfi (944–946) recognized the three brothers as "commanders" or *amirs*, and henceforth they bore, as a mark of honor, special titles to distinguish them.[47] Ahmad, now Mu'izz al-Dawlah, was *amir* of Baghdad and the Shi'ite custodian of the Sunni Caliph. Surprisingly, nothing happened: the Buyids remained Shi'ites and the Caliph, who was undoubtedly relieved to be able to deal with the pragmatic Buyids rather than with an Iranian archaeologist like Mardawij, remained a Sunni and continued to enjoy the immense prestige of his office.

---

45. The Ziyarids were not without a certain literary distinction. One of their *amirs*, Qabus (978–1012), was a poet of some repute in Arabic and Persian, and both Firdawsi and Ibn Sina graced his court for a time. A later Ziyarid, Kay Ka'us (1049–1090), wrote, sometime about 1083, a Persian "Mirror for Princes" entitled *The Book of Qabus* for the benefit of his son and successor. It was of little use to the young man; within ten years the Isma'ilis overran Tabaristan and brought the line of the Ziyarids to an end.

46. Buya's obscurity vanished in direct proportion to the growth in eminence of his sons, and later Iranian nationalists managed to trace his lineage back to the heroic Sasanian Shah Bahram Gor.

47. These honorary titles, or *laqabs*, began in Caliphal circles sometime about 900 and went into a relentlessly inflationary spiral during the rest of Islamic history. The Buyid versions, like the earlier Hamdanid ones, were all compounded with *dawlah* ("state") like 'Izz al-Dawlah ("Strength of the State") or 'Adud al-Dawlah ("Support of the State"). When the Sunni Seljuqs replaced the Shi'ite Buyids in the counsels of the Caliph, the *laqabs* were pointedly changed into compounds of *din* ("religion")–Rukn al-Din ("Pillar of Religion"). At a somewhat later date similar honorifics were given out to scholars as well as Iranian and Turkish warlords.

Mu'izz al-Dawlah was probably neither better nor worse an overlord than Ibn Ra'iq or Tuzun. His titles and privileges, including the mention of his name along with the Caliph's in the Friday prayers, were no more than had been accorded to earlier *amirs*, nor was he the first Shi'ite to appear in high government circles in Baghdad. The Hamdanids were Shi'ites, and both Ibn al-Furat and Mu'nis were of Shi'ite inclinations, a fact that neither drove them into a mutual alliance nor ruined the Sunni Caliphate. The Buyids too, though they held their pensioned Caliphs under a tight surveillance, made no move to dissolve the line or the office that gave them their own legitimacy. Notably, however, they preferred to rule from Shiraz, not from Baghdad.

The Buyid *amirs*, Mu'izz al-Dawlah, his brothers Rukn al-Dawlah Hasan and 'Imad al-Dawlah 'Ali, and their successors down to 1055 were not barbarians. They rose to power on the arms of their soldiery but ruled, during the rare intervals of peace in those troubled times, in the Islamic and even the Arab tradition. At first barely capable of speaking that language, the Buyids developed into willing patrons of Arabic literature and the arts. The greatest of their line, 'Adud al-Dawlah, not only supported poets—Mutanabbi for one—but turned his own hand to Arabic verse. Either by their own initiative or that of their enlightened viziers, like Muhallabi under Mu'izz al-Dawlah (945–967), Ibn al-'Amid under Rukn al-Dawlah (947–977) at Rayy, Ibn al-'Abbad under Mu'ayyad (977–983) and Fakhr al-Dawlah (983–997) at Isfahan, Ibn Sa'dan under Samsam al-Dawlah (983–987) at Baghdad, and the most famous of the Buyid viziers, Ibn Sina under Shams al-Dawlah (997–1021) at Isfahan, the Buyid *amirs* presided over a still flourishing intellectual establishment.

Literary men were well served by the Buyid princes in their new provincial capitals of Shiraz, Rayy and Isfahan. There was patronage to be had in all those cities and access to the kind of magnificently equipped libraries apparent behind Isfahani's monumental *Book of Songs*, Ibn al-Nadim's *Catalogue*, the *Reformation of Morals* by Miskawayh, and the enormously sophisticated editorial work that was done on the Arabic versions of the Greek philosophers in Baghdad during the seventy-five years between Yahya ibn 'Adi (d. 974) and Ibn al-Tayyib (d. 1043). The latter was the last fine fruit of Hellenic scholarship in Islam, the product, generally, of the Christian community of the capital of the Muslim Caliphs.

Under the Buyids Baghdad was the official seat of the Nestorian Catholicus who had his residence and cathedral, the latter constructed sometime about 950, across the Tigris from the Caliph's Round City.[48] In pre-Islamic days the Catholicus had taken up quarters in the Sasanian capital of Seleucia-Ctesiphon, and before coming to Baghdad at the end of the ninth century he had his residence at various times in Mosul, Kufah and Wasit. Shortly after the Catholicus' arrival there the Melchite Bishop of Baghdad was forced to leave the city, and then in 1003 the chief eastern prelate of the Jacobite Monophysites, or Maphrian, as he was called, was likewise obliged by the Caliph to make his headquarters outside the capital. In the latter case, and probably in the former one as well, the decree was the Caliph's but the motivation almost certainly came from the Catholicus.

If it was the intention of the Nestorians to constitute themselves the sole accredited representatives of Christianity at the heart of the Caliphate, they succeeded,[49] though not solely by their own efforts and by paying, in the end, a considerable price: the Catholicus had to be recognized by the Caliph, and more often than not in the late tenth and early eleventh centuries he owed his elevation to that office to the intervention, for a princely sum, of the Buyid *amir*.

The Nestorians throve under Islam. Since the reign of Harun they stood close to the intellectual center of the community. They were the Caliphs' physicians and bankers, and as translators and scholars they received generous patronage. In the ninth and tenth centuries Nestorian secretaries rivaled the Iranian *mawali* not only in the Caliphs' *diwans* but in the administrative apparatus of the Amirates, like those of the Buyids, Hamdanids and 'Uqaylids, where, in addition to their other recommendations, they had the advantage of possessing no vested interest in the contests between Sunni and Shi'ite.

---

48. In the quarter known as the *Dar al-Rum,* or "abode of the Greeks," so called because al-Mahdi had settled his Byzantine prisoners there.
49. Literally so in 1138, when the Caliph Muqtafi II (1136–1160) promulgated a decree naming the Catholicus as the sole official spokesman for the Christians within his realms.

There were dangers for the Christians, to be sure, from sources within Islam and without. In the minds of some Muslims, the Christians living in their midst had an inevitable connection with the Christian Byzantine Empire across the frontier,[50] and what the Byzantines did in Anatolia had its effects upon the Christians of Syria and, by extension, those of Iraq. The Nestorians, who had earlier been regarded with mistrust by the Shahs for much the same motives, were generally successful in divorcing themselves from the policies of the Byzantine Empire. For the Jacobites, on the other hand, whose numerical strength was greatest in the frontier provinces and who were doctrinally linked with the Christian Church of Armenia, the imagined connections with the Byzantines often led to repressive measures by the Muslim authorities.[51]

The presence of Nestorians in high places in Islam did not always preserve their coreligionists from occasional fanatic outbursts from the Muslims. Shortly after 1000 there were frequent assaults on the Christians, Nestorians and Jacobites alike. The worst of them occurred in 1013, when the publicly celebrated wedding of a high Nestorian official in Baghdad outraged Muslim sensibilities and led to wholesale burning and looting of Christian property, including the cathedral and the episcopal residence. The promoters of at least some of these disturbances may have been Shi'ites, and at such moments the Christians not unnaturally fled to the protection of the stanchly Sunni Turkish soldiery of the capital.

Despite the occasionally uncertain attitudes of Islamic officialdom toward their religion, the Christian intelligentsia continued to play their part in the literary history of the *Dar al-Islam.* Initially this was almost exclusively in the Christian vernaculars of Coptic and Syriac. The first was restricted in its use to the

---

50. A suspicion amply documented by the pro-Byzantine attitudes displayed by both the Nestorians and Monophysites of Iraq when Heraclius invaded the Sasanian Empire between 628 and 630.

51. And by the Byzantines as well. The Byzantines considered the Jacobites as Monophysite heretics, and the Byzantine reconquest of Jacobite centers in Mesopotamia often led to a cruel repression of the local clergy.

Christians of Egypt and interested itself in little more than a parochial hagiography. Syriac was, however, a true Christian lingua franca and boasted a deeply rooted intellectual tradition of its own which ran back into Greek philosophical and scientific sources and eventually produced the bilingual cadre of scholars who served the 'Abbasid Caliphs as mentors and translators.

Most of the scholars patronized by the 'Abbasids were Nestorians; the considerable number of Jacobites within the Egyptian and Syrian provinces of the *Dar al-Islam* had more often to struggle for their survival in the face of oppressive government restrictions or their own inclination toward internecine warfare. The Jacobite hierarchies of Syria and Egypt were often at odds, and the first modest era of Jacobite unity was as much the work of Ma'mun and Mu'tasim as it was of the Jacobites themselves. Between 818 and 825 the Jacobite Patriarch was Dionysius of Tell Mahre, a former monk of Qenneshre, and it was chiefly through him—and the Caliph's support of his position—that the violent schisms in Syria were healed and cooperative action was instituted between the Jacobite Patriarchates of Antioch and Alexandria.

Dionysius, whose own literary efforts were devoted chiefly to history,[52] brought peace to the Monophysites and so encouraged a mild literary and scholarly renaissance that reached its climax in Moses bar Kepha.[53] All the scholars connected with it wrote in Syriac—which meant, already in the mid-ninth century, to address oneself to a solely Christian audience of narrowing dimensions. During the next two centuries Arabic rapidly replaced Syriac as the *koine* of Eastern Christendom under Islam, a substitution that appears to have occurred earlier among the Monophysites than among the Nestorians. The Jacobites' close connection with Hellenic centers like Antioch had transformed their Syriac into a purely learned language, while the more vernacular Aramaic of the Nestorians, who even before the

---

52. His Syriac history, which is preserved only in part, began with the accession of the Emperor Maurice in 582 and ended with the death of Theophilus in 842.

53. See Chap. IV, pp. 324–325.

coming of Islam were cut off from the contemporary sources of Hellenism in the Near East, held its ground for a somewhat longer period against Arabic.

Coptic succumbed early to Arabic in Egypt, where Christianity had none of the prestige conferred upon it by the first generations of 'Abbasids in Iraq, and by the tenth century Egyptian churchmen were tracing the history of their own ecclesiastical wars in Arabic.[54] Among the Syrians of Iraq the tradition of scholarly bilingualism begun in the days of Harun continued in the late tenth century to produce men like Yahya ibn 'Adi and Ibn al-Tayyib, for whom Arabic was, however, the preferred medium for philosophy, while for other Christians the new ecumenical tongue of the *Dar al-Islam* was the appropriate vehicle, as it had been for Theodore abu Qurrah, for the theological instruction and refutation of their Muslim contemporaries.

The bibliography of Elias bar Shinaya (975–1049) is instructive in this regard. A monk of Mosul and later Metropolitan of Nisibis, Elias composed a bilingual work on ecclesiastical history and a Syro-Arabic grammar and dictionary. He conducted his voluminous correspondence in both Syriac and Arabic, and it was only when writing on purely Christian subjects like the liturgy that he resorted to Syriac alone. The appearance of his early Syro-Arabic lexicon suggests too that many Christians were already passing into an Arabic monolingualism, and Christian grammarians, who had once used for their own purposes a Syriac translation of the Greek grammar of Dionysius Thrax, now began to prepare Syriac grammars based on Arabic models.[55]

The majority of the Nestorian literary figures under Islam were educated in higher monastic schools, which from the time of the migration of the theological faculty from Edessa[56] were

---

54. So the history of the Councils written in Arabic by the Melchite Patriarch Sa'id ibn al-Bitriq (d. 940) and its rejoinder from the Monophysite side composed in 987 by Abu Bishr ibn al-Muqaffa'.
55. The first preserved example is that written by Elias I, Nestorian Catholicus between 1028 and 1049.
56. See Chap. IV, pp. 316–317.

the chief centers of the Christian intellectual life in Mesopotamia and Iraq. In an earlier day Nisibis and the patriarchal complex in Seleucia were the most notable theological schools, while Jundishapur was the focus of scientific studies. There was also a school in the monastery of Mar Mari at Dayr Qunna, south of the site of Baghdad in pre-Islamic times, and by the mid-tenth century it had attained a position of preeminence. From it issued not merely numbers of eminent theologians and the Nestorian hierarchy in Iraq, but also the skilled Christian secretaries who served in the Baghdad *diwans*. There were several only somewhat less important schools around Mosul and in the highly Christian milieu in which Mansur chose to found his capital city.[57]

The Jacobites too may have been educated in cloisters, but not, it would seem, to any great purpose. Since the death of Moses bar Kepha in 903, Monophysite prestige rested almost uniquely upon the work of Yahya ibn 'Adi. Under pressure from the Byzantines and from their coreligionists, the Nestorians who could bring the Muslim authorities to bear on occasion, the Jacobites' energies were directed more toward survival than toward scholarship and its rewards. Further, the morale of the Jacobite Church received a shattering blow in 1016 when the Maphrian Ignatius bar Qiqi, stung by his clergy's charge of concubinage, defected to Islam.

The Peripatetic scholars who flourished in Baghdad under the Buyids were not, despite the predominance of Christians among them, products of Nestorian convent schools. There was a tradition of purely secular Aristotelianism in Baghdad from 900, a tradition that owed more to the defunct Alexandrian academy than to the modest Aristotelianism of the Syrian cloisters.[58] Christians and Muslims alike were educated in that tradition, including al-Farabi himself. Yahya ibn 'Adi and Ibn al-Tayyib were accomplished Christian theologians and canon lawyers. In addition to his editions of Aristotle, Yahya's preserved works include two important works of polemic, one directed against the

---

57. Oddly, one of the chief sources for the Christian monasteries in Iraq during this period is the work not of a Christian but of a Muslim author, al-Shabusti's (d. 1008) *Book of Monasteries.*

58. See Chap. IV, pp. 328–329.

attack upon the major Christian sects by the ex-Mu'tazilite Abu 'Isa al-Warraq[59] and another against al-Kindi's philosophical objections to the Trinity, the latter answered in turn by the Mu'tazilite al-Rummani (d. 996). In the humanistic strain associated with the Baghdad "school" Yahya also composed a *Reformation of Morals* similar in content and purpose to the identically titled work by another Muslim philosopher also connected with the Baghdad circle, Miskawayh. Abu al-Faraj ibn al-Tayyib, who was a philosopher, lawyer, secretary to the Catholicus, and physician—he lectured at the 'Adudi hospital in Baghdad—was responsible for the Arabic version of the collected canons of the Nestorian Church called *The Christian Law.*

While Yahya appears to have been the mentor of the Baghdad philosophers after the departure of al-Farabi into Syria, the most visible and influential member of that group was the Muslim Abu Sulayman al-Sijistani (d. 990).[60] Most of what we know of him comes from the impressions recorded by one of his literary admirers, al-Tawhidi, and in general his interests were more humanistic than philosophical. At least one of Abu Sulayman's works is preserved, if only in various abridgments, a history of Greek and Islamic philosophy entitled *The Garden of Wisdom.* The *Garden* is perhaps more anecdote than history, but it was heavily drawn on by later authors, and it provides, in what was probably a work of sophisticated vulgarization, an example of the images and impressions that an educated Muslim reader of the tenth century had to draw on for his knowledge of the Hellenic past.

The Buyids themselves were not notoriously devoted to philosophy, but they had an evident concern for history, literature and medicine, interests which brought to their attention not only Abu Sulayman but his student the *littérateur* and lawyer Abu Hayyan al-Tawhidi (d. 1023). Tawhidi was still clearly an *adib* rather than a professional philosopher. His early training in and

---

59. See Chap. II, p. 202.
60. Abu Sulayman was also the chief link to Buyid court circles through his friendship with the vizier Ibn al-'Abbad. Ibn al-'Abbad was himself a philosopher of parts and his commentary on the Aristotelian logic was recommended by al-Tawhidi to Miskawayh.

around Baghdad was properly Islamic, and though professionally a scribe, Tawhidi consorted with most of the intelligentsia of Buyid Baghdad. His first contact with philosophy was through the Christian Yahya ibn 'Adi about 971, and then, some ten years later, he began attending the philosophical salon of Abu Sulayman. Between times he drifted in and out of vizieral circles, earning his living as a scribe and working on some of the popular *adab* themes, much in the style of Jahiz, whom he openly admired.

Tawhidi's work was not steady. He fell afoul of his first patrons, the viziers Ibn al-'Amid and Ibn al-'Abbad, whom he later attacked in print. From about 980 to 985 he was patronized by the Buyid eminence Ibn Sa'dan, but when the latter fell from grace Tawhidi's living once again became precarious. We do not know how long or how well he survived—probably to 1023 and surely in straitened circumstances—but the literary record of his more successful days has survived in the form of *Pleasure and Conviviality* and the *Adaptations*.

Both works are essentially dialogues in which Tawhidi provided a literary recreation of the personages and talk in the literary salons of Baghdad around 980. Abu Sulayman is the central figure, and though the talk is chiefly philosophical, it ranged over the entire broad domain of letters. Tawhidi's works illustrate better than any other document the range and vitality of Hellenic-inspired *adab* in the tenth century. And scarcely since the days of Plato had philosophy found such engaging company or worn such distinguished literary apparel.

Among those with whom Tawhidi became acquainted was the historian and ethician Miskawayh (d. 1030), who had a parallel, if more successful, career in the service of the Buyid *amirs* of Rayy and Baghdad. Like Tawhidi, Miskawayh came to his learning through the enlarged *adab* culture of the tenth century. When scarcely twenty he was engaged as secretary by Muhallabi, the vizier of the Buyid Mu'izz al-Dawlah in Baghdad. Miskawayh remained at the post for twelve years (951–963). By day he worked in the Buyid chancery and by night shared in the brilliant salon life so vividly described by Tawhidi. We know that during this period he studied the *History* of Tabari, but if he did any writing of his own, it received little or no attention.

Muhallabi, the patron of the arts and, in Miskawayh's own words, "one who brought back to life forgotten sciences," died in 963, and Miskawayh then took service with Ibn al-'Amid, Rukn al-Dawlah's vizier in his native city of Rayy. If Muhallabi patronized the arts, Ibn al-'Amid practiced them. A contemporary poet described him as "an Arab in speech, a philosopher in his judgments, and a Persian in his manners," a characterization that might apply with equal justice to Miskawayh, and particularly after his seven-year association with Ibn al-'Amid as tutor to the vizier's son and as chief librarian.

It was in the vizier's library at Rayy that Miskawayh discovered the Hellenic past and its reworking at the hands of the Muslim *falasifah* Kindi, Razi and Farabi. Its exact contents are unknown,[61] but the breadth of Miskawayh's reading is evident in his own works, including the brief tract on the classification of the sciences entitled *The Levels of Happiness,* which dates from this time and was composed at the direct request of Ibn al-'Amid. It was, in the tradition of Farabi and of Greek rationalism, the ordering of human wisdom toward the achievement of the ultimate human felicity. The *Levels* is, however, a theoretical work; only later did Miskawayh devote himself to the question of moral activity.

The vizier died in 970 and was succeeded by his son, and Miskawayh's pupil, Abu al-Fath. Miskawayh stayed on at Rayy, but the son's interests and abilities were far different from his father's, and Miskawayh's later judgments on the young man were severe. Both Abu al-Fath and Rukn al-Dawlah died in 976, and 'Adud al-Dawlah succeeded to the Buyid Amirate. Miskawayh and the new *amir* were known to each other through Ibn al-'Amid, and so, soon after 'Adud's accession Miskawayh was invited once more to Baghdad to join the court as the *amir's* "table companion," or *nadim.* Earlier at Rayy his attention had been drawn to alchemy, and now at a court filled with Muslim and Christian physicians from 'Adud al-Dawlah's new *bimaristan,*[62] Miskawayh took up the serious study of medicine. He may have written some medical books during this period, but they

---

61. By one report it required a hundred camels to move its contents.
62. See Chap. V, p. 390.

have been overshadowed by the beginning of one of Miskawayh's major projects, the *Experiences of Nations,* a world history from the Flood down to his own times. The work was dedicated to 'Adud al-Dawlah and may also have been commissioned by him, since the *amir* requested another member of the court, the Sabian Abu Ishaq Ibrahim ibn Hilal, to compose the official history of his house.

The Sabians of Baghdad had already produced an eminent chronicler in Thabit ibn Sinan,[63] but Ibrahim's talents lay more toward mathematics and a kind of prose-poetry whose elegance, it was thought, would enhance history. The results can be read in his *Crown,* and they are rather like those that followed upon the first Greek attempts at marrying rhetoric and history, a combination well adapted to flattery but somewhat less suited to honest reportage. An obviously embarrassed Ibrahim later admitted that his *Crown* was hardly the whole story on the Buyids.

The *Experiences of Nations* is very different from *The Crown.* It is not perhaps very satisfying as a universal history—he indifferently followed Tabari down to the end of the latter's *History* and thereafter used Thabit ibn Sinan—but from the time in 945 when the Buyid Amirate began, Miskawayh reveals his true talents as a historian. The *Experiences* had a severely pragmatic purpose: not to reveal the ways of God to man or even to chronicle the events of an ecumenical *Dar al-Islam,* but to extract from the deeds of men a moral lesson that might be useful to all men with ethical concerns and, more specifically, those charged with the governance of the state.

Tabari's *History* was, in conformity with the author's theological perspectives, an account of the Prophet of God and his Successors, and its method was that of a tradition collector. Miskawayh had an equal lack of concern for the theology of history and the *hadith* method. Even where he was obviously following Tabari he rationalized the account—the Prophet's miracles were omitted—and ignored the *isnads.* The *Experiences*

63. The author of a lost *History* that covered the years between 902 and 973 and apparently was rich in information on the Baghdad intellectuals of the day. Thabit's chronicle was continued by the grandson of Ibrahim ibn Hilal, Hilal ibn al-Muhassin, and this work *is* preserved.

is a court history of the Buyids written by one who was intimately involved in the workings of that level of society. The players are *amirs*, viziers, and the under-officialdom of the chanceries, and though Miskawayh was an excellent and generally unbiased reporter, his real interest was in ethical analysis.

There was abundant material for such, and earlier students of *adab* had filled their books of "Table Talk," "Culture of the Vizier," and related subjects with richly moral anecdotes about the great and near-great in Islamic government circles. The stuff of Miskawayh's own history was not so much anecdotes as richly detailed reports, his own or those of other eyewitnesses, and incisive moral judgments. By bringing together the *ta'rikh* and *adab* techniques in composition, Miskawayh rendered both of them more genuinely historical. Against the traditionalists' atomistic approach to history Miskawayh argued the historian's responsibility to provide organic causal explanations for events. *Adab* history, on the other hand, lacked precision, rigor, and a detached view of its subject. Miskawayh successfully supplied all three, controlled by his own point of view. He did not possess, as Ibn Khaldun did, a philosophy of history, but he was the first Muslim successfully to locate history *within* philosophy.

Miskawayh's philosophical education must have been largely literary, the epitomes of Plato, the entire range of Aristotelian translations and commentaries, the writings of Kindi, Farabi and Yahya ibn 'Adi. And though none of them was his teacher in a formal sense, Miskawayh had close personal dealings with many of the philosophers who graced the Buyid salons in Baghdad and Rayy, chief among them Abu Sulayman and al-Tawhidi. Tawhidi and Miskawayh must have been thrown together on many occasions, sometimes as friends, sometimes as rivals. The two men were in effect literary collaborators: *Those Loosed and Those Penned* is a series of philosophical queries posed by Tawhidi to Miskawayh, together with the latter's responses.

We do not know whether Tawhidi found satisfaction in the answers, but in his *Pleasure and Conviviality*, written not long after 'Adud al-Dawlah's death in 983, he expressed the judgment that Miskawayh was somewhat superficially instructed in philosophy and that he had, in any event, ruined his mind by studying alchemy and devoting too much time to Jabir ibn Hayyan and

Razi and too little to Abu Sulayman. Abu Sulayman's own judgment was more favorable. He knew Miskawayh's works on logic, the sciences, alchemy, *adab*, history and ethics: "They are widely read and studied under the personal instruction of the author on the days when he holds courses." Abu Sulayman found their style interesting, but what struck him most forcibly about Miskawayh was the moral earnestness of his life.

Abu Sulayman may have been referring to the Miskawayh of the period after the death of 'Adud al-Dawlah. With his sponsor gone, Miskawayh left public service. He was still to be found in the conferences and discussion groups in Baghdad and Rayy after that date, particularly in 983–985, when Ibn Sa'dan was the Buyid vizier and Tawhidi was writing his *Conviviality*, but never again in the employ of the great. How he lived we cannot be certain—possibly he had some kind of pension—but he appears to have withdrawn from employment by design rather than necessity. Tawhidi has preserved a document in which Miskawayh set out a series of resolutions for the emendment and guidance of his life. The sentiments are somewhat too redolent of the careful frigidity of Roman Stoicism to justify speaking of Miskawayh's "conversion," but they did perhaps signal a decision to leave the court and take up the life of a private citizen.

The decision once taken was never rescinded, at least as far as the externals can be judged. Miskawayh did not return to government circles during the nearly half-century of life left to him. He did not become a recluse, however, and the ascetical possibilities of the Sufi life apparently did not appeal to him. Rather, he continued to write. He finished the *Experiences of Nations* and then took up two projects that were the chief fruits of his "retirement." The earlier, his *Reformation of Morals*, is a major work of ethical theory, and the second, *Eternal Wisdom* (also called in some manuscripts *The Culture of the Arabs and the Persians*), written sometime after 995, is an anthology of human wisdom gathered from the books of the Iranians, Greeks, Arabs and Indians.

The *Reformation of Morals* is the first systematic rethinking of a humanistic ethic since the Stoics left off that task in the second Christian century. Both ethics and politics disappeared from the curriculum and interests of the Neoplatonic schoolmen of late antiquity. Indeed, we would not even have been aware that both Porphyry and Themistius had worked on the *Nicomachean Ethics* except that the Arabs had both those works. Themistius' may have been part of his standard paraphrase of the Aristotelian corpus, but Porphyry's was apparently a more ambitious commentary. This was all there was by way of exegetical help; for the rest, the Arabs had an integral translation of the *Nicomachean Ethics,* an anonymous "Alexandrian" summary of the text, an epitome by the first-century Peripatetic Nicolaus of Damascus, some Aristotelian pseudepigraphs under the cover of "Letters" directed to Alexander, and the spurious *On the Virtues and Vices* translated by Miskawayh's Christian contemporary Ibn al-Tayyib.

The sum of this material did not make the Arabs pure Aristotelians when it came to ethics. They had another view of the soul and of human felicity in Plato and in Galen's *On Moral Dispositions,* and out of this they syncretized their own views. The very first of the *falasifah,* al-Kindi, took up the serious study of Hellenic ethics without prejudice to his Muslim faith. Farabi wrote a commentary on the *Nicomachean Ethics*—unfortunately it is not preserved—and two Christian scholars of the tenth century likewise wrote on ethics, Qusta ibn Luqa in his *Causes of Moral Differences Between Men* and Yahya ibn 'Adi's *Reformation of Morals.*

This obvious Islamic interest in a discipline that the Greek Neoplatonists chose, or were forced, to ignore points once again to the fact that the Hellenic scientific tradition in Islam drew much of its immediate inspiration from the "middle" Platonism of the Roman Empire when ethical speculation was not as yet overwhelmed by an occult *gnosis* or intimidated by Christianity's announcement of a spiritual vocation for man.

Muhammad too preached a supernatural end for God's creatures, but he laid no claim to sacramentalize the present. There was no redemptive act in Islam and so the Muslim, like the Jew, had to struggle toward his supernatural end through a revealed but naturalistic Law. The Muslim mystic found his own way of echoing Paul's "Now not I live, but Christ lives in me" by meditating, almost in the face of the Law, an immediate and supernaturalizing experience of God, but most Muslims took their ethical instruction not from Sufis but from earthbound lawyers and scholars of *hadith*.

Not so the philosophers. They invoked the transcendent world of the Intelligences for the higher processes of intellection, prophecy among them; but, in addressing themselves to the question of what is the end of man and how is it to be achieved, they resorted to the naturalistic tradition of Platonic and Aristotelian ethics. Miskawayh's *Reformation of Morals* is the most fully fashioned product of that effort.

Miskawayh had no temptation toward the withdrawal from society advocated by the Christian and Muslim forms of asceticism; he asserted with Aristotle, but with a genuine Islamic conviction as well, that man is a *polis* animal, a citizen whose felicity was somehow associated with the "virtuous city." His object, then, is both ethical and social, to understand what constitutes virtue by studying the soul and its faculties, and to examine how virtue is achieved by virtuous practice and habit and in the more social process known as "education."[64] It is in connection with this latter consideration that the Law enters into Miskawayh's theories: it is the function of the Law to educate men by inculcating habits of moral behavior.

The guardians of the Law and, so, the educators of their fellow men are in the first instance parents, and then, in the larger context of society, the leaders of the community, its *Imams*. The *Imam* must insure that the prescriptions of the Law are observed, not for its own sake but because of the social goods which were associated with it from the beginning. Men have a natural sociability, and in Miskawayh's eyes not the least of Muhammad's motives in promulgating the *shari'ah* was to encourage that instinct of nature.[65] Thus it is the responsibility of the *Imam*, the "head of the city," to enforce the observance of the Law.

By connecting political governance with a religious law Mis-

---

64. Literally, "acculturation," "the acquisition of *adab*" (*ta'dib*).
65. To support this reading of the origins of the *shari'ah* Miskawayh cited the obligations to come together for the Friday prayer and to make the pilgrimage.

kawayh had subtly changed his accent from a Hellenic to an Iranian one, a point he made no effort to conceal. His authority was no less than the "wise man and king of the Persians Ardashir" who said, "Religion and the king are twin brothers; neither can exist without the other." He did not tarry overlong with Ardashir I, however. For Miskawayh the *Imam* was a teacher as well as the guardian of the "right religion," and the subject of his and of all moral instruction was the hierarchy of Hellenic sciences that Miskawayh had already laid out in the *Levels of Happiness*. The *Reformation* did not recover that ground but concentrated on an elaborate analysis of the virtues of the soul. The models here are Aristotle and Galen, and there is a recurring insistence on the composite nature of man, that he is a union of soul *and* body, and so his virtues and in the end his happiness must flow from that dual nature.

Miskawayh wrote the *Reformation* for neither the foreordained saint, the man who from birth manifests signs of divine favor, nor the men whose virtues are imposed by others, by the Law, for example, or the teaching of the philosophers. He was speaking rather to the man who must *become* good, and by his own efforts. And though Miskawayh's position is not without its ambiguities, it does appear that the philosopher who studies and practices virtue may aspire to the same high degree of perfection as the saint sanctified in the womb. This perfection Miskawayh describes as "being illumined by an emanation from the divine light." It is indeed a Neoplatonist's vision of felicity, but Miskawayh, who knew the "Theology of Aristotle" and believed, like his predecessors, that it was genuine, considered it an Aristotelian vision as well.

Miskawayh did not devote much attention to this illuminative wisdom in the *Reformation;* it was, after all, a tract on ethics and not on epistemology. Further, it distracted from his proper Aristotelian and naturalistic purpose to formulate an ethical system that, if it was not specifically Islamic, would conduct the Muslim to his final happiness as certainly as it had done for the pagan Greek. Miskawayh certainly believed that a revelation had been given to Muhammad and that the Law that issued from such a prophetic revelation was a sure guide to the kind of moral activity appropriate to men.[66] But he also held that the philosopher's vision of reality was no different from the prophet's, and that, if the prophet's Law is the guide to action, the teaching of the philosophers is the guide to understanding. Miskawayh was as little inclined as either Farabi or Ibn Sina to make a case for the unique prophetic mission of Muhammad.[67]

Miskawayh's ethical theories are substantially Greek, and whatever religious coloring they do possess is as easily attributable to Neoplatonism as to his own doubtless sincere adherence to Islam. He acknowledged as easily as his Greek predecessors the presence of God in his ethical considerations, but he found man's end in the perfection of what he was. If man had a supernatural vocation, it was simply by virtue of being a man.

A reading of the *Levels of Happiness* and the *Reformation of Morals* might lead one to think that if wisdom was human, it was also exclusively Greek. Miskawayh did not think so. Greek theory did indeed provide him with the model for his analysis; as for the substance of wisdom, it was a genuine *philosophia perennis*, the possession of all men at all times. That appears to be the intention of his *Eternal Wisdom*, though its effect is not improbably just the opposite. The material brought together by Miskawayh from Greek, Iranian, Indian and Arab sources is the popular stuff of an aphoristic, vaguely hortatory morality and a far cry from the scientific ethics of the *Reformation of Morals*.

The Arabs were great fanciers of proverbs, and if the Greek and Iranian material in Miskawayh's anthology is somewhat more sophisticated in its content, it clearly belongs to the same genre. The Greek *gnomai* are for the most part apocryphal, like the *Golden Sayings* attributed to Pythagoras and the *Letters* of

---

66. The Prophet's transmission of his vision was not restricted to the promulgation of a public religious law. Muhammad communicated his teachings in a more immediate manner to appropriate parties. For the Shi'ite Miskawayh the appropriate parties are not dubious types like Abu Hurayrah (see Chap. III, p. 243) and others among the Companions but rather his son-in-law 'Ali.

67. An attitude eloquently testified to by Miskawayh's removal of the miracles in his account of the Prophet's career in the *Experiences of Nations*.

Aristotle, and the Iranian preachments have equally little claim to have come forth from the mouths to which they are ascribed. The *handarz,* or "royal counsels," was a popular literary recreation in Sasanian times, and even though Miskawayh specifies Ma'mun's vizier Hasan ibn Sahl as the translator of this material from Pahlevi into Arabic, the Pahlevi "originals" of the *handarz* that we now possess may very well date from Islamic rather than Sasanian times.

The banal and obviously spurious quality of much of what was collected in Miskawayh's *Eternal Wisdom* did not discourage Muslim authors from the pursuit of gnomonology. Earlier there had been Hunayn ibn Ishaq's *Opinions of the Philosophers,* a mixture of biography, philosophical positions and *gnomai,* and as already has been noted, Abu Sulayman's *Garden of Wisdom* and its *Continuation* by al-Bayhaqi were very similar works. Contemporary with Miskawayh, Ibn Hindu (d. 1029), who was also connected with Baghdad philosophical circles, put together his *Spiritual Aphorisms,* and only a few years later, in 1048, appeared the *Choicest Maxims* of al-Mubashshir ibn Fatik, a bibliophile, physician and philosopher who worked chiefly in Fatimid Cairo. In the thirteenth century al-Mubashshir's *Maxims* and Abu Sulayman's *Garden* were both taken up, epitomized, and continued into Islamic times by al-Shahrazuri in his *Garden of Festivities,* where the biographies and *gnomai* are chiefly those of eastern, Iranian savants.

Not everything in Miskawayh's *Eternal Wisdom* is spurious. The Arab material includes quotes from Hasan al-Basri, Farabi and Abu Hasan al-'Amiri (d. 996). An easterner from Khurasan, 'Amiri had, nonetheless, connections with the Baghdadis. They must have been brief, however, since the morals of Baghdad quickly drove him back to eastern Iran. The ancient bibliographies credit him with a number of commentaries on the Aristotelian logic and psychology, and we know that he was involved in a philosophical correspondence with Ibn Sina. Al-'Amiri shared with Farabi an interest in political philosophy and so in Plato, but his ethical theory, as expressed in his *On Seeking and Causing Happiness,* was distinctly Aristotelian.

'Amiri understood that the intellectualist approach to moral good had raised opposition in Islam, particularly among the traditionalists, and he attempted in his *Notice on the Glories of Islam* to defend the usefulness of Greek philosophy in a way that Miskawayh had never felt called on to do. Its methods served, 'Amiri pointed out, to develop man's potential for virtue, since understanding leads to control. Understanding of the world and its working likewise demonstrates the power and wisdom of the Creator. Finally, philosophy is the invincible defense against the acceptance of blind reliance on authority.

'Amiri's convictions about the usefulness of the rational arguments of the philosopher did not inhibit his use of other, more traditional forms of discourse. And not everywhere in the *Glories of Islam* was he speaking to a Muslim reader. Some unspecified antagonists of Islam were alleging that the Muslim was an adherent of a religion of violence that was spread by the sword and whose own partisans disagreed among themselves to the point of slaughter. The *Qur'an*, they went on, was an inadequate instrument for determining the truth—witness its use by every Islamic sect to justify its own position—and as far as the Muslim claim that Muhammad was foreshadowed in the earlier books of revelation, the partisans of those revelations, the Jews and the Christians, categorically denied it.

In the statement of his own case 'Amiri often argued dialectically, but he did not hesitate to cite the *Qur'an* as a proof text at times. He saw no contradiction in this. For 'Amiri faith was a matter of rational assent and not, as certain of the Muslims would have it, a mere adherence to authority, whether of the *Qur'an* or an *Imam*. Islam was a rational religion, and so there was no inherent contradiction between the correct rational approach and the correct understanding of Allah's revelation.

Al-'Amiri served the same Buyid vizier as Miskawayh, Ibn al-'Amid at Rayy, and it is likely that the two philosophers were personally acquainted. Not well enough to please some, however. Tawhidi complained that during the five years that al-'Amiri was at Rayy, Miskawayh never learned anything from him.[68] Tawhidi was referring to Miskawayh's work as a *faylasuf*, and indeed 'Amiri appears to have been a more considerable, if also a more

68. It has been suggested that al-'Amiri's presence in the *Eternal Wisdom* may have been Miskawayh's retort to that particular charge.

defensive, philosopher than Miskawayh. What the two men shared, and expressed in analogous but different ways, was a deep-seated ethical concern that could be satisfied only by turning to the philosophical ethics of the Greeks. Miskawayh certainly knew the Iranian moral tradition as well, but for him no less than for 'Amiri it was Hellenic theory rather than Iranian aphorisms that represented the ideal, both for himself and for Islam.

The figures of the tenth-century philosopher-humanists like Abu Sulayman, Tawhidi, Miskawayh and 'Amiri debating in the salons of Buyid Baghdad are attractive exemplars of what a Muslim gentleman could be. The old Bedouin virtues of generosity, graciousness and eloquence were still part of the portrait, now urbanized by their contact with Iran and given solid intellectual foundations by Hellenic ethics. More bookish than the Greeks, far more elegant and sophisticated than the contemporary European Christian, the tenth-century Muslim intellectual could still shuttle gracefully between pen and sword, between mosque and cup, without notable signs of guilt or self-doubt.

Not everyone was enchanted, of course. On the streets outside the splendid salons were Hanbalites who read only blasphemies in the books of the Greeks and the humanistic ethics of Miskawayh. Many of Miskawayh's own Shi'ite brethren would have been equally impatient with his path to happiness. It is possible to read Shi'ism into the *Reformation of Morals*, but the virtuous cities of both Farabi and Miskawayh were distant utopian idyls when measured against the ambitious political plans that had already unfolded in the camp cities of the Qarmatians and Fatimids.

Miskawayh's vision of human felicity was an uncompromisingly intellectualistic one. With an equal hand he thrust aside the finely calibrated legalisms of the jurisprudents and the enraptured flights of the mystics and put in their place the older ideal of the Hellenic sage caught up in the difficult task of self-knowledge. Even in the more homogenized Greek culture the latter remained a fugitive ideal, and in the thin soil of philosophical *adab* so carefully cultivated in the Buyid salons its chances of growth, or even of survival, were negligible.

And yet it did survive. Miskawayh's understanding of the good life was only superficially Islamic. It acknowledged a supernatural vocation for man, but it was a calling out of the pages of

Plotinus and Aristotle and not those of the *Qur'an.* A specifically Islamic humanism was a more difficult project and one that could never perhaps be realized by a *faylasuf*. It was not, at any rate, a *faylasuf* who brought Hellenic ethics and the teachings of the Prophet into a coherent union. When a Muslim ethic was proposed a century after Miskawayh by Ghazali in his *Revitalization of the Sciences of Religion*,[69] it was the product not merely of the meditation of the *Nicomachean Ethics* but of a more fruitful experience of that "other" Islam, which held so little attraction for the *hellénisants* of Baghdad, jurisprudence, theology and the increasingly fervid visions of the Sufis.

---

69. See Chap. IX, p. 709.

VIII
ISLAM TRANSCENDENT

The normal ambiguities of Muhammad's teachings, the stunning and rapid success of a conquest that helped to convert Islam into an empire, the community's "trial" in a civil war, all contributed to the conversion of the original coherent *ummah* into a body riven with sectarianism. Some of the sects were mere jurisprudential flotsam, the offspring of men who took a wrong turning along the winding path of orthodoxy and were rewarded by being consigned to a heresiographical pigeon-hole. But other partisan groups were giving voice, from a variety of motives, to their own understanding of what Islam should be.

In 850, as in 650, it was the Caliph who stood at the center; from the outset he possessed the political power. But what the events of even the early years demonstrated was that power could be understood in more ways than the control of armies and the purse. In a religious society, orthodoxy also represented power, and once some gauge of orthodoxy could be constructed, as it was in the *shari'ah,* it was turned with lethal effect against the Umayyads. In 'Abbasid times the Caliphs wielded power both in the more primitive sense of political control and in the form of the new weapon of orthodoxy.

One could contest that first power, and the dissolution of the *Dar al-Islam* into petty principalities is the tale of the rise of new men with their own armies and their own purses. As for the second, the power of orthodoxy, it too could be challenged. The

Caliph's connection with the Law was never organic, as was the Byzantine emperor's and as Ibn al-Muqaffa' suggested to al-Mansur it should be in Islam.[1] Rather, it was an alliance that could be contested and dissolved. It never was dissolved—the lawyers remained faithful to the Caliphs to the end—and those who would have Islam different from what it was had necessarily to resort to other devices—to attacking, for example, the very presumption that the sole criterion of orthodoxy was the *shari'ah* of the lawyers.

The struggle to prevent the conversion of Islam into a talmudic society manifested itself in a variety of ways, but its partisans shared a common tactic, somehow to break the suffocating hold of the "tradition," that body of *hadith* that since Shafi'i's day put in the hands of the lawyers the sole and self-serving instrument for interpreting the *Qur'an.* The philosopher, the Sufi and the Shi'ite, all appealed to an alternate form of exegesis and, behind it, to a higher dimension of reality. If the lawyers appropriated the ground of history through the *hadith* and their chains of *isnads,* those others chose to invoke metahistory.

In the traditionalists' view, Islam was a historic community founded upon a unique historical revelation; for the challengers, the *Dar al-Islam* extended out of the sensible dimension of history into the transcendental cosmos. It was narrower at its worldly base than the traditionalists would have it—not everyone who recited the *shahadah* was privy to the secrets of transcendental Islam—but it broadened out in its upper reaches to embrace, in a cosmic landscape unknown to the lawyer, a veritable communion of saints, what the Sufis called "the friends of God."

The Illumined Path

For the earliest Sufis the "friend of God" was none other than the man who observed the *shari'ah* with well-intentioned scrupulosity and spoke to God in prayer. He possessed no special gifts, nor could he, at least in Muhasibi's view, press any claim to a particular knowledge of God save that given by Allah to his "friends" at the Judgment. There were, as has been seen, counter-

---

1. See Chap. III, p. 247.

vailing views; the development of the notion of a Gnostic wisdom, of private revelation and of divine illumination, all converged on the separation of the mystic, the man who had experienced God, from the simple ascetic by assigning to the former, as either goal or achievement, a state different from that of other Muslims.

Rabi'ah's meditations on the lover's longing for the beloved, with its focus on a personal and essentially private relationship between the creature and his God, perhaps contributed to the same end. She wished, she said, for the veil to be removed so that she might look upon the Beloved. For some, however, looking was not enough. Abu Yazid (d. 875) of Bistam in Tabaristan, who was separated by but one generation from the Zoroastrianism of his grandfather, was initiated into the mystical tradition of a certain Abu 'Ali, the "Indian" (*al-Sindi*), who was apparently himself a recent arrival in Islam, since at the time of his coming to Bistam he knew not even enough Arabic to negotiate the *Qur'an.* Al-Bistami taught him Arabic and the *shari'ah,* and received from Abu 'Ali in return instruction on the "realities" and "extinction of self in the unity of God."

There is no more of Abu 'Ali; thereafter it is only the voice of Bistami himself that is heard, captured solely in what he called "paradoxical utterances," vivid and excited exclamations in his native Persian. Through their subjective fervor shines a fundamental shift in the mystic's approach to God. Earlier Sufis' visionary meditations had striven to render present the distant perspectives of the Judgment. Bistami could not wait for the *eschaton;* he cast himself headlong into the ecstatic position already granted to the Prophet. The *Qur'an* described (81:19–25; 53:1–12) visions vouchsafed to Muhammad by heavenly messengers, and early on tradition had combined them with another famous passage (17:1), wherein the Prophet is spoken of as making a journey by night "from the sacred place of worship to the further place of worship," so that Allah might reveal to him some of his signs. Thus the Prophet's "night journey" became connected with an ascent (*mi'raj*) into the highest heavens, where he was shown the truths of revelation[2] and so

2. The conflation of the two narratives was not impeded by the identification, probably first made in Umayyad times, of the "further place

provided Bistami with a setting for his own ascension to the throne of God.

It is not easy to arrange Bistami's "utterances" in sequential order, but some of them at least appear to give an overview of his efforts toward spiritual perfection. For many years, he said, he had cultivated nothing but his own self. Then, with the suddenness of an illumination, he saw all of creation in a new light. It became corpselike in his eyes, and once he put off his own self, "like a serpent stripping himself of his skin," Bistami began his personal experience of the "heavenly ascent." Carried before Allah, he begged to be invested with God's Unity and Selfhood and Oneness. It was granted. As Bistami himself described it, he was clothed in the divine attributes—"I became a bird whose body was Oneness and whose wings were Eternity . . ."

There followed, if our understanding of the sequence of Bistami's "utterances" is correct, the final experience of "extinction in the unity of God." He arrived at the point of nonbeing, and after resting there for ten years, Bistami passed "from the Not to the Not by way of the Not." Stripped of his own personality, the mystic stood before God in His Essence, and from his lips came the most startling of his paradoxes: "Glory be to Me! How great is My Majesty!" Then he added: "Enough of myself! Enough!"

The reading of these remarkable sentiments has raised disputes from Bistami's own day to this. His appropriation of the Qur'anic *mi'raj* as a vehicle for his own experiences brought on a temporary banishment from his native town, while some of his mystical successors regretted that on the very threshold of the Unitive Way Bistami had halted and cried "Enough!" That is no longer the issue, of course. The current question is, How did Bistami come to make these extraordinary statements? Was he drawing, perhaps with the help of his shadowy "Indian" teacher, from

---

of worship" (*al-masjid al-aqsa*) with Jerusalem. The heavenly ascent was normally described as occurring after the Prophet's nightly translation from Mecca to Jerusalem, and already in the early ninth century Muslims were being shown the Prophet's footprint there, much as Christian pilgrims had Jesus' footprint pointed out to them on the Mount of the Ascension.

contemporary Hindu mysticism or was Bistami's urgent breaking in upon Allah merely the climax of a search begun at the very beginnings of Islam?

There is no easy resolution to the question. Taken without context the expression "extinction in the unity of God" will yield many meanings, from the annihilation of the human essence and its reabsorption in the all-embracing Divine Essence to the loss of man's human attributes in the face of a similarly denuded One. In Bistami the context is poetical and personal, and it is chiefly the presence of Abu 'Ali, who knew so little of the *Qur'an* and the *shari'ah,* but who nonetheless served as Bistami's instructor on the mystical union, that makes one think of Hinduism and not Islam. Neither Muhasibi nor any of the earlier Sufis at Baghdad or Basrah professed a knowledge of "unification" in the mystical sense or of any transcendental "realities" save those revealed in the *eschaton.* Bistami experienced both. Had Abu 'Ali already done so in some religious context other than Islam?

Bistami's transports apparently had an effect on his attitude toward the traditional Muslim *shari'ah.* The Malamatiyah of Khurasan were at that very time driving their radical asceticism beyond the bounds of the Law.[3] Theirs was, however, purely a moral experiment; Bistami had transcended both asceticism and the Law. He had experienced the unity of Allah or, on another interpretation, had *become*—"Glory be to Me!"—Allah. The Law was revealed for those who would never have such an experience, the "commoners" or "laymen" of later Sufism, and Bistami no longer had any need of it.

Reports of Bistami and his experiments with "extinction" and the mystical union traveled rapidly to Baghdad, where the reigning authority was Abu al-Qasim al-Junayd, one of Muhasibi's disciples.[4] Junayd (d. 910) read the "Glory be to Me" in a prudential sense that acquitted Bistami of blasphemy, but it is clear enough that he accepted the possibility of what Bistami had described, a mystical union with God. According to Junayd's

---

3. See Chap. VI, p. 426.
4. Junayd's *Healing of Spirits* draws heavily on Muhasibi. Most of his other writings are in the form of letters addressed to his fellow Sufis.

own formula, this state of union (*tawhid*) was achieved "by separating the Eternal from what has been created in time."

Perhaps this is already a degree of abstract conceptualization alien to Bistami, but Junayd had, in addition, a theory of why and how men may aspire to this extraordinary possibility of union with God. It arose from Junayd's meditation on that passage in the *Qur'an* (7:172) where God summons before himself the still-uncreated sons of Adam and has them bear witness that Allah is their Lord. Others read this famous "covenant" as a type of precreation revelation; Junayd, however, saw it as a clear testimony to a special kind of existence possessed by souls before their creation in time and a pledge to those souls of the possibility of reestablishing such a spiritual existence "in Him."

Before the mystic could advance to this state of primordial spiritual existence he had first to labor for that "self-extinction" (*fana'*) already explored by Bistami. Junayd's version of *fana'* is well within the Qur'anic usage of that term, namely, a divesting of the worldly self, but when he came to its complement, *baqa'*, or continued subsistence in Allah,[5] he was invoking his own somewhat philosophical understanding of man's preexistence, which was suggested and confirmed by his exegesis of the "covenant" passage, as a thought in the mind of God. The goal proposed to the mystic by Junayd was, then, a return to man's original spiritual roots. The enormity of reclining on the bosom of God must have been substantially diminished by the realization that before his temporal existence began, man was created in that very same posture.

Subsistence-in-God was by no means the end of the process. Junayd knew that the mystic had inevitably to return to his temporal state and reassume his individual personality. He has undergone a change, however, both internally and externally. The mystic who has experienced the glories of divine unity now sees the world in a new light, with the clarity of sobriety, accord-

---

5. The notion of *baqa'* may have come to Junayd from a contemporary Sufi, al-Kharraz (d. 899), whom Junayd knew in Baghdad before the publication of *The Secret* caused al-Kharraz to be banished to Bukhara.

ing to Junayd, and "his actions in the world become a pattern for his fellow men." Bistami had emerged from his transports in a state of high intoxication; Junayd's mystic in a cold and even sad sobriety, condemned to live in the world with the remembrance of his briefly restored state of preexistential innocence.

The preexistence of souls, though a familiar feature in Platonic thought, was hardly a staple in early Islam. In Baghdad Junayd, like his master Muhasibi, had ample opportunity to instruct himself on Hellenic thought, but we have no direct evidence that either man was doing so. Our suspicions are somewhat stronger in the case of one of Junayd's contemporaries, however. It is not certain whether al-Tirmidhi, who was surnamed al-Hakim, "the Sage," died just before or just after Junayd. What is known is that he was born in Tirmidh in Iran, was "converted" to Sufism from the traditional sciences at the age of twenty-eight, and took up residence at Nishapur when his orthodoxy became suspect in his native town.

Tirmidhi is represented by an extensive bibliography, most of it still unpublished, but his most important works were *The Reasons behind the Canonical Acts*, which may have been one of the earliest ripostes to the Qarmatians' esoteric undermining of the Islamic Law by showing that the *shari'ah* was grounded in reason, and his *Seal of the Saints*, a somewhat disjointed work composed of more than one hundred and fifty *questiones disputatae* in the Sufi tradition. The *Seal of the Saints* is a dense tract, but its ideological base is clearly exposed. The Muslim tradition is based on an understanding of the phenomenon of prophecy, whose finest achievement was in Muhammad. Tirmidhi set down next to prophecy another grade of being, that of "sainthood." In its widest acceptance sainthood embraced the entire Muslim community by reason of their profession of faith. There is, however, a more particular and elite "saint" who shares in an illuminative understanding given by God and who stands higher in the spiritual ranks than the prophet. Thus, in the same way that Muhammad was the "Seal of the Prophets," so Jesus was the "Seal of the Saints."

Tirmidhi's exaltation of the saint over the prophet had its antecedents—Muhasibi's meditation on Paradise likewise ranked the "friends of God" above the prophets and martyrs, and there was even a *hadith* to that effect which was accepted by traditionalists like Ahmad ibn Hanbal—but Tirmidhi's position was based on ideology, not tradition. The prophet as a lawgiver—and Tirmidhi understood that not all prophets were such—was by that very qualification constituted a "commoner," a notion that ran counter to Tirmidhi's elitist spirituality whereby higher truths are communicated by inspiration or, to use his own figure, by the diffusion of spiritual "lights."[6]

Muhasibi, following in the footsteps of Hasan al-Basri, was the first to spiritualize the moral insights of a still-nascent Sufism, while Tirmidhi, for his part, was engaged in laying down philosophical foundations for the even more novel currents of Islamic mysticism. The Islamic saint now stood upon a psychological base that extended far beyond the *Qur'an*'s own spiritual horizons. Muhasibi's saint won his place in Paradise by reason of his enlightened observance of the Islamic Law; Tirmidhi's by his enlightenment alone. God, it appeared, did not end his activity in this world with the revelation of the Law. He had been experienced by Bistami, an experience that Tirmidhi demonstrated was a proper characteristic of an entire class of "saints."

There is a metaphysics here, in Tirmidhi, if not in the more experimental Bistami. Sufism had progressed from its early exclusive concern with what the Christian tradition called the Purgative Way—in Muslim terms, "renunciation"—to an immediate experience of God, and now, finally, to a world view that verified and explained that experience. Muhasibi pondered his own and others' experiences along the Purgative Way and elicited from them both the notion of *self* as the focus of man's selfish drives for gratification and that of *understanding*, a God-given faculty for distinguishing between good and evil. Both notions belong to ethics and were useful psychological insights for the doing of good and the avoidance of evil. By Tirmidhi's day, on the other hand, soul, understanding and spirit were all part of an elaborate metaphysical structure that far exceeded the bounds of ethics.

In the late eighth century the thought of certain Sufis was invaded by a metaphysics of light that colored their cosmology,

---

6. Junayd too spoke of the spiritual man "whose heart is set ablaze by the light of Allah's essence."

their anthropology, and their view of the spiritual lives of both God and man. Put in its simplest form, the new metaphysics affirmed, contrary to the Islamic tradition, the consubstantiality of God and the spiritual element in man: the Light that is God's essence has descended through a series of emanations, the last of which is the human spirit.

Thus stated, the thesis is no different from what was commonly understood by later Platonism or from the version of the theory propagated by the Muslim representatives of the Platonic tradition. There were, however, somewhat different versions of that metaphysics, including the Sufis' own, which point toward sources other than purely philosophical ones. The mystical Sufis did not subscribe, for example, to the belief that the divine light in man was entirely a natural disposition on the basis of which any man might aspire to union with its metaphysical source. The Sufi version was elitist in its conviction that the substantial radiation from God was a gift limited to the "privileged" and that the knowledge founded upon it was not merely an exalted form of natural intellection (Gr. *episteme;* Ar. *'ilm*) but a special knowledge (Gr. *gnosis;* Ar. *ma'rifah* or *hikmah*) granted to the "saints."

The Muslim mystic was, in short, a Gnostic. How he came to his beliefs is not immediately apparent. He was in a sense surrounded by possibilities: translations of Greek works like the "Theology of Aristotle" or some piece of Hermetica; contacts with one or another of the group of Gnostic attitudes within the *Dar al-Islam,* like the Sabians of Harran, the Manichaeans or the Daysaniyah; or with some Islamic sect that itself had already accepted a Gnostic view of reality, the Isma'ili Shi'ites, for example.[7] The latter is, perhaps, the most attractive possibility. The Neoplatonist Plotinus was not, after all, a genuine Gnostic, while those others like the Sabians were wrapped in a complex cosmic mythology and shared a worldly pessimism that had no counterpart among the Sufis of the tenth and eleventh centuries.

A primary characteristic of the Sufis' view was their belief in the ongoing nature of revelation, their bringing into partnership, much to the advantage of the latter, the prophet and the saint as

---

7. See pp. 600–602.

dual repositories of the divine truths. Thus in its earliest form, that put forward by Bistami, for example, the Sufi merely claimed for himself a share in the extraordinary experience given to Muhammad. In its later versions Muhammad and the Sufi are existential equals in the class of the "privileged,"[8] with the difference that Muhammad typifies the class of prophets whose union with God is "frozen" in the public revelation that follows, while the Sufi is the beneficiary of an ongoing revelation.

This is not very different from what was being asserted by some of the Shi'ites of the circle of Ja'far al-Sadiq; the *Imams* were just such repositories of ongoing revelation by reason of their special connection with the divine source of that revelation. To the extent that the experience of the "Realities" was limited to a single *Imam* descended from the family of Muhammad and 'Ali, to that extent would the Sufi presumably quarrel with the Shi'ite view. The Shi'ites were arguing for a spiritual elite of the very narrowest dimensions and one based upon a dynastic and thus a political consideration; the Sufi mystic opened the experience of God to an entire class of spiritual aristocrats.

As long as Shi'ism was a political and social movement and Sufism was essentially an association of ascetics, there were Shi'ites who bore the title of "Sufi." But when both Sufi and Shi'ite turned to ideology, a Gnostic ideology, the separation of the two groups becomes apparent. The traditionalists may have considered the mystic al-Hallaj a Qarmatian, but only because the Qarmatians had transcended, as the Sufis themselves had, the Shi'ites' lingering connection with history in the person of an 'Alid *Imam*. Sufis and Shi'ites were competitors, not allies, from the mid-eighth to the twelfth century, when Sufism had its next enlarging encounter with Gnosticism.

Part of the complex of ideas shared by Sufism and Shi'ism even at this early stage was the concept of the preexistence of Muhammad. Plotinus had criticized the Gnostics of his own day for multiplying the spiritual emanations produced by the First Cause, and the cosmos of pre-Islamic Gnosticism does indeed appear to be filled with a bewildering array of Intellects and Aions that

---

8. On the similar reduction practiced by the philosophers, see Chap. VII, p. 520.

inhabit the upper World of Light. Among these hypostases was one called simply "Man." According to one Hermetic account, God produced a Primordial Man who was incorporeal, immaterial and impeccable. There was already a hint of this in Plotinus, and whoever converted the passages in the *Enneads* into the "Theology of Aristotle" altered that hint into an unmistakably Gnostic version of the "First Man." Even earlier Philo too had postulated the creation of a spiritual archetype of man possessed of exactly these same qualities and identified with Adam.[9]

The closure of all of these themes, the Primal Man of Gnosticism, the Intelligible Man of Philo, the preexistent Jesus of Hellenic Christianity and even, perhaps, the Gayomart of Iran,[10] in the Muslim theory of a "Muhammad of Light" is an immensely complex historical problem, whose full implications do not unfold until both Sufism and Shi'ism had become far more theosophical than they were in the tenth century. Tirmidhi had already grasped the essentials, however.

Tirmidhi was among the earliest Sufis to assert it, but the preexistence of Muhammad very likely goes back further in the history of Islam, either as an appendage to the doctrine of the heavenly eternal prototype of the *Qur'an* or by way of a union of 'Alid claims to a spiritual Imamate with some type of Gnostic theology. There was some speculation among the Shi'ite theologians of the mid-eighth century on the subject of transmigration, not as a possibility open to (or imposed upon) all souls for moral ends, but in the more restricted sense of the transmission of a supernatural and spiritual power from one generation to the next.[11] This was the theory of the Kaysaniyah and the Khur-

---

9. The creation of the mortal, material Adam comes later in the account.

10. Gayomart is the Primal Man, a creation of Ohrmazd who is destroyed by the evil Ahriman, but from whose purified remains the first human couple is fashioned. Gayomart ("mortal life") has distinct cosmic affinities. He is fashioned by Ohrmazd from the "endless form," the macrocosm that is the sky, to serve as its microcosm. Some of the correspondences are purely physical—Gayomart's veins correspond, for example, to the rivers–but in at least one account dating from Islamic times Gayomart's members have planetary affinities.

11. See Chap. I, p. 131.

ramiyah and of the "veiled prophet" Muqanna'. The origins of this divine power lay before creation, when Allah fashioned from his own substance the "Muhammad of Light." The Sunnis accepted this theory, but in their view the diffusion of the Light ceased with the appearance of the historical Muhammad, while for the later Shi'ites it continued to descend generation after generation through the line of the *Imams*.

Much of this can already be read in Hakim al-Tirmidhi's *Seal of the Saints*, but he was by no means the only metaphysician of his generation of mystics. Sahl al-Tustari (d. 896), though not represented by the same kind of literary evidence, interested himself in the same psychological problems and Gnostic solutions as Tirmidhi. He too argued for an elite "community of saints" who, by sharing in the primordial light, are privy to the "mysteries of the Godhead." This may have been part of the saint's inheritance from all eternity, somewhat in the manner that Junayd understood the precreation "covenant" between Allah and the children of Adam. So it appears, at any rate, in the "school" that claimed Sahl as its founder, the Salimiyah.[12]

The Salimiyah were treated by the polemicists of their time as a school of dogmatic theologians, the abortive beginnings of a moderate theological wing among the Malikite lawyers perhaps, not unlike the Karramiyah and the eventually successful infiltration of the other law schools by the Ash'arite and Maturidite versions of *kalam*. If it was such, it proved attractive to Sufis as well. In it they found ample ground for their exploration of the "mystery of the Godhead" as an existential ground for their own mystical experience of and union with God.

Sahl's most famous pupil was, by all accounts, Husayn ibn Mansur al-Hallaj, who at the very beginning of his own career studied with Sahl and followed him into exile at Basrah in 874. Hallaj, a native of Fars, an Iranian by birth, and, like Bistami, but one generation removed from Zorastrianism, soon deserted his mentor for the Baghdad Sufis, among them Junayd. He stayed there for somewhat more than twenty years, living a life of austere retirement. It was, however, only a prelude. Hallaj broke

---

12. Their eponym, Abu 'Abdallah ibn Salim (d. 909), was both an editor and a disciple of Sahl.

with his Baghdad masters over what had become a cardinal tenet of Sufism, that the "realities" were the esoteric property of a spiritual elite.

As a result of his disagreement, Hallaj left Baghdad and took up a life of public preaching, now no longer dressed as a Sufi, in Khurasan and Fars. This first public ministry lasted for five years, after which he returned briefly to Baghdad and then resumed his travels in an even wider arc that took him through Turkestan and parts of India. In the course of his journeys Hallaj made perhaps fatal contacts with the revolutionary Qarmatians[13] and the notorious heretic philosopher-physician Muhammad ibn Zakariya al-Razi.[14]

Upon his return to Baghdad in 910 Hallaj began to experience some of the political and theological repercussions of what he had done and said. He held, as others had before him, that the canonical obligations of the Muslim Law could be replaced by other, more spiritual activities, and more generally he rendered mysticism part of the public domain by displaying his own miraculous powers and by asserting for all to hear that the union of the soul of the saint with the spirit of God was a reality achieved by love and not a metaphor. "I am the Truth," Hallaj openly avowed, appropriating to himself one of the names of Allah. A true union between the two, the mortal man and his transcendent God, could only be achieved by an identification of the two substances, something that was anathema to Islam but had, the theologians asserted, ample precedence in Manichaeism, where the human soul was a fallen spark of the Divine Light.

Hallaj was formally accused of *zandaqah* on the basis of a judgment rendered against him by the lawyer Ibn Dawud. There was an attempt to arrest him in 913. He escaped, was pursued and was captured. A trial was held in 915 before the vizier 'Ali ibn 'Isa at which the political charge of being a Qarmatian propagandist was added to that of *zandaqah*. Hallaj was convicted and jailed for eight years. The issue was not settled, however. He was tried again, convicted once again, and in March of 922 Hallaj was scourged, mutilated, suspended on a gibbet, and finally decapi-

---

13. See p. 596.
14. See Chap. VI, pp. 440–445.

tated. His body was burned and the ashes thrown into the Tigris.

There is little in Hallaj that cannot be paralleled in Bistami, Tirmidhi, Tustari and Junayd,[15] the first three of whom suffered exile for their teachings. He was not profoundly respectful of the letter of the *shari'ah*, an attitude that had unfortunate political resonances in a Baghdad terrified by the Qarmatian threat of anarchy. Also, Hallaj was more outspoken than his predecessors on the theme of the infusion of divinity into the mortal soul as the basis of a mystical union. Tirmidhi and Tustari tempered their thoughts with a quasi-Gnostic intellectualism; Hallaj cast his in the more dangerous language of love.

The execution of Hallaj did not solve the problem of Sufism in Islam. It may have served, however, to sharpen the issue and in so doing to provide the ground for an eventual resolution. Sufism was strengthened by its first martyr, but it had received a sober warning as well. The language of intoxication with God was not the currency of the *Dar al-Islam,* and there were few after Hallaj who were so imprudent as to think so. The joys of the mystical union were concealed in the metaphors of poetry, the convolutions of Qur'anic exegesis, or the dense pages of speculative theory. And here too lay the means of *détente* with orthodoxy.

Something has already been said of the attempts of Sahl al-Tustari's followers among the Salimiyah to find places for themselves in the Malikite school of law. In the mid-tenth century the Shafi'ite *madhhab* also lay open, but here the lines of approach were somewhat more complex, since they led into *kalam* as well, specifically the *kalam* of al-Ash'ari. The first Sufi to explore that approach was Ibn al-Khafif (d. 981) who attended Ash'ari's lectures and knew Hallaj during the years of his imprisonment.

The *kalam* of Ash'ari had few inclinations toward the Gnostic illuminationism of Tustari and what could be read as Hallaj's identification of the human spirit and God's own essence, and so Ibn al-Khafif's movement into that camp, if it did not shelter Sufism from the attacks of the traditionalists, did effectively

15. In addition to the various anecdotes from and about him and a *diwan* of his poetry, Hallaj's major preserved work is a collection known as *Ta and Sin* after the two letters prefixed to *Surah* 27 of the *Qur'an.*

separate one version of it from both the Salimiyah with their search for the "mysteries of the Godhead" and from the notorious antinomianism of the Malamatiyah.

In the tenth century Sufism found its voice. At first its tones were chiefly hagiographical, collections of anecdotes and the sayings of those men and women who had won a reputation for piety in Islam. Two of the earliest experimenters in the genre were al-Khuldi (d. 959), whose *Tales of the Saints* supplied most of the material on Sufism in Ibn al-Nadim's *Catalogue*, and Abu Sa'id ibn al-A'rabi (d. 952), like Khuldi a disciple of Junayd and the author of *Classes of the Pious*. Both works are lost, but on the basis of what can be reconstructed from later citations, they showed a new concern for orthodoxy, though it was expressed in a familiar way: both authors provided *isnads* for their material in the way that lawyers long since had done for theirs. Thus the validation of Sufi teachings was made to reach back, principally by way of Junayd and Hasan al-Basri, to the generation of the Companions and not permitted to rest solely upon the private illuminations of individual Sufis.

After the work of those two pioneers there is preserved a whole series of treatises, some biographical and anecdotal like the *Classes of Sufis* of al-Sulami (d. 1021)[16] and the monumental *Embellishment of the Saints* of Abu Nu'aym al-Isfahani (d. 1038)[17] which between them tell us much of what we know about the early history of Sufism, a "history" that in the authors' perspective reached back to the era of the "Pious Caliphs." Others were more explanatory. Sulami and Abu Nu'aym were more concerned with asceticism than with the purely mystical side of Sufism, but there is ample testimony to the latter in al-Sarraj's (d. 998) *Book of Radiances*, Abu Talib al-Makki's (d. 996) *Food for the Heart*, al-Kalabadhi's (d. c. 1000) *The Acknowledged Doctrines of the Sufis*, and then in the next century

---

16. Sulami also wrote one of the earliest preserved works of Sufi exegesis on the *Qur'an*, the *Truths of Exegesis*.

17. Another *Classes of Sufis* is attributed to their contemporary al-Naqqash (d. 1023). The work is lost, but it was apparently the first traditionalist—al-Naqqash was a Hanbalite—attempt at the genre.

in al-Hujwiri's (d. 1057) *The Unveiling of What Is Concealed*, the first treatment of Sufism in Persian, and in what eventually became the classic statment of Sufi theory, the *Epistle* of Abu al-Qasim al-Qushayri (d. 1072).

The works just enumerated differ among themselves in scope and emphasis—al-Makki addressed himself to the problems of Sufism and *kalam*, while both Sulami and Qushayri took particular pains to show the difference between the true Sufis and the antinomian adherents of the Malamatiyah—but they shared a common understanding of the purpose and methods of Sufism: to experience the "unity of God" at the term of a series of highly articulated stages of personal striving, marked at its more advanced levels by the dispensation of certain equally well-defined graces from God. From these authors one can elicit a kind of *communis opinio* about the structure of the Sufi "Way," as it had come to be called. The treatment is rarely theoretical, however, since the works in question generally illustrate their points rather than argue or explain them. Despite the authors' conviction that in Sufism they were dealing with a phenomenon that had its historical origins at the very beginnings of Islam, the actual practice of Sufism is displayed in the words and deeds of the Sufis themselves, chiefly those between Hasan al-Basri in the eighth century and Junayd and Hallaj in the tenth.[18]

The path to perfection began, of course, with a "conversion," a turning through repentance from the ways of the world toward a consciousness of God. This was, by common consent, the first of the "stations" (*maqamat*), and it was followed by a series of similar stages: scrupulosity of conscience with regard to moral action, self-restraint from even legitimate pleasures, voluntary poverty,[19] patience, abandonment to God and, finally, the most perfect "station," that of divine complaisance.

---

18. The ambivalence of the historical argument with its implication of *isnad* and that resting upon the *ipse dixit* of the holy man is apparent in the circulation of *hadith* without *isnad* that immediately invoke the authority either of Muhammad (or some other of the Prophets) or of Allah himself.

19. *Faqr*—from which derives the word *faqir*, "mendicant," frequently applied to the ascetic.

These "stations" are the fruits of the mystic's own strivings, but once they are achieved his further progress depends not so much upon personal effort as upon the benevolent and gracious mercy of Allah, who bestows the various "states" (*ahwal*) upon the soul. Here too the terrain was elaborately charted. The Sufi theoreticians distinguished between the "states" of love, fear, hope, longing, intimacy, tranquillity, contemplation and certainty. These were by their very nature transitory, as was the culmination of the Sufi's striving and the terminus of the "Way," unification with God.

The boundary line between the "stations" and the "states" marks precisely a great turning in the history of morality. The "stations" echo, with many mutations and refinements, the traditional Greek view of virtue. For Plato, Aristotle and the Stoics, virtue was a habit of the soul; it was acquired by an *askesis* of one type or another and depended on the continuous efforts of man. By the first and second Christian centuries that notion had been joined by another, quite different one, that virtue was a gift of God, a "grace," as the Muslim would put it. In the Sufi works of the tenth century these two very different sets of virtues have been arranged in a continuous series, now separated only by the passage from "station" to "state."

The same conjunction had already been accomplished by the Christian mystics of the seventh century. Christianity too knew a tradition of virtue as an acquired habit. This method of "action" (*praxis*), as it was called, owed nothing to Hellenic ethics. Rather, the Christian view of virtue as *praxis* grew, like its Muslim counterpart in the "stations," from a meditation on the teachings of Scripture and the example of the Founder. But because early Christian asceticism manifested itself in the monastic life, the "practical" virtues of the Christian holy man found their principal statement in the monastic "rules" that appeared in the Near East from the fourth century onward. Islam, which prized asceticism but did not valorize it in monasticism, knew no such rules until the appearance of the first Sufi "orders" in the thirteenth century.

Christian *praxis*, with its emphasis on the training of the will and its ideal of the imitation of Christ, was soon joined by another view. In the writings of Evagrius of Pontus (d. 399) the training of the will yielded ground to the illumination of the intellect, and ascetical *praxis* became merely the preparation for the higher stages of what Evagrius called *theoria*, which corresponds to the Muslim "states." *Praxis* is the ascetical effort at purifying the soul by the acquisition of virtues. The highest of them is love, and with its achievement the ascetic passes into the realm of *theoria*. At first this is characterized by a series of insights into man's relationship with God and the world, but it finally comes to term in a true *theologia*, where God manifests his own essence and his own light in the purified and unified intellect of the mystic.

There were modifications and adaptations of this system; Dionysius the Areopagite, the pseudonym of an unknown author of the early sixth century deeply influenced by Neoplatonism,[20] introduced a far more Platonized version of the *theoria* in which the passage of God's illumination was mediated through both a celestial and an ecclesiastical hierarchy. Evagrius' combination of the ascetical *praxis* and the mystical *theoria* remained, nonetheless, the standard Christian teaching down to the coming of Islam.

Nor was it limited to Hellenic Christianity. Evagrius' works were translated into Syriac, as was the famous *Book of the Ladder* of John Climacus (d. c. 680), the monk of Sinai who popularized Evagrian spirituality in the ascetically oriented cloisters of Syria and Palestine. Among the Syrians farther east Isaac, the Nestorian bishop of Nineveh and a contemporary of John Climacus, likewise used Evagrian teachings in his own Syriac writings on the spiritual life.

For the Muslim no less than the Christian, progress through the "stations" began as a *jihad*, a struggle against one's worldly inclinations that reflected the ascetical tradition of the earliest Sufism. The conditions and tactics of that spiritual warfare were all clearly defined by the tenth century. The "convert" to Sufism was regarded as a mere novice and was placed under the direction of a *shaykh* already accomplished in the spiritual life.[21] The

---

20. And whose works were available in Syriac in the translation of Sergius of Reshayna; see Chap. IV, p. 321.

21. At a later stage of its development Sufism regarded the *shaykh* not so much as an experienced guide, but rather as the unique medium for the passage of spiritual blessings and powers from God to the adept.

shaykh led him through the "stations" by means of exercises like the examination of conscience, meditation, and the constant repetition of the name of God.[22] Obedience was expected to be prompt and total.

For pre-Islamic partisans of the view that virtue was a gift rather than an acquisition, Hermeticists and Christians among them, the ultimate expression of divine grace was that "state" in which God was fully present in the soul of the adept. This was not the temporary "seizure" common among the Hellenes of all ages, but an identification in fact based on a prior identification of substance: the soul of man is divine in origin and by this "illumination" it is, on God's initiative, once again identified with God.[23]

By reason of this "indwelling" or "illumination" the pagan mystic was saved[24] and so was above and beyond the demands of traditional morality. The Sufi did not speak much of "salva-

---

The tenth-century Sufi was already aware of the premises of that later view in the existence of an elaborate hierarchy of cosmic "saints" descended from a unique "pole star" (*qutb*) whose merits in each generation contribute to the preservation of the universe. The notion of the *qutb* and his "representatives" is obviously similar to the Shi'ite belief in a succession of unique *Imams* and *their* representatives, and Ibn Khaldun (d. 1406), for one, thought that Sufism had borrowed this complex from its Shi'ite contemporaries of the eighth and ninth centuries. Christianity too, in its passage from a Scriptural asceticism to Evagrian mysticism, converted the earlier monastic superior into a *pneumatikos pater*, a "spiritual father" who enjoyed charismatic perfection and was the possessor of a variety of spiritual gifts, among them the ability to read men's souls.

22. *Dhikr*. Already in the fifth century the Christian ascetics of Palestine were practicing the technique of the "Jesus prayer," the constant and rhythmical repetition of the name of Jesus used as a device to achieve the mystical union. John Climacus too, whose works were available in Syriac, was a strong advocate of its use.

23. And in this life. The unification of the soul with its divine source after death—that is, after its separation from the body—was a commonplace in late Greek philosophical speculation.

24. His Christian counterpart was "redeemed," but perhaps not "saved." The Christian, who at baptism could say "I live, now not I, but Christ lives in me," had still to fear the possibility of Hell.

tion"—he was largely exempt from the cosmic or Adamic "fall" that made salvation necessary—but the antinomian consequences of unification with God did suggest themselves to him, and one of the great struggles within Sufism was precisely over the Sufi's relationship with the *shari'ah*. Muhasibi and most of the tenth-century theoreticians confessed their obligation, but Bistami, Hallaj and the Malamatiyah made public issue of their moral indifferentism. The Sufi might conceal his more esoteric visions under silence or metaphor, but his observance or nonobservance of the Law was there for all to see.

A case in point, and an illuminating contrast to a careful and orthodox theoretician like Qushayri, is one of the latter's contemporaries at Nishapur, Abu Sa'id ibn abi al-Khayr (d. 1049). He was born in eastern Khurasan, and though he studied the traditional subjects, his father early exposed him to the "intoxicated" Sufism of his native town of Mayhana. So prepared, Abu Sa'id's "conversion" was not long in coming. Under the guidance of a spiritual director in Sarakhs, where he was studying, he exchanged the life as a student for one of protracted and terrible austerity.

At some point after his fortieth year, sometime about 1009, and when he had achieved "perfect illumination," Abu Sa'id took up residence in a convent for ascetics at Nishapur, and shortly the private ascetic became the publicly celebrated holy man, a director of consciences and the performer of wonders.[25] No longer was a regular austerity the rule—the Purgative Way had reached its term—but an arbitrarily suggestive alternation from constant prayer to none, from severe fasting to sumptuous banqueting. The occasion for the latter was a Sufi manifestation that Abu Sa'id had often witnessed as a boy and that now became an increasingly important part of his spiritual life, the spiritual concert, or *sama'*, where three hundred or more adepts celebrated the unity of God with music and song. On such occasions Abu

---

25. The Muslim normally distinguished between the wonderworking of saints "by the grace of Allah," and the probative miracles of the Prophet, a perhaps overly neat distinction that did not, at any rate, save Hallaj from the charge of miracle making.

Sa'id played the lavish host, a practice that drove him and his heirs deeply into debt.

His creditors hounded the holy man—his pneumatic power to read men's minds was helpful here—but there was more serious opposition. His achievement of illumination had liberated Abu Sa'id from the jurists' view of the Islamic Law. In his eyes the *sama'* was as efficacious as the canonical prayers. "Why don't I go on pilgrimage?" he is reported to have said. "It is no great matter to travel a thousand miles to visit a stone house," and he counseled his disciples to make their *hajj* not to Mecca but to the tomb of his own spiritual director at Sarakhs. When told on another occasion that one of his disciples was lying dead-drunk in the middle of the highway, he commented: "Thank God he is still on the Road at least."

Abu Sa'id had traversed the Sufi "Road" to its end, an ecstatic union with God, but there were some who thought he had strayed from the path of Islam in his journey. When Qushayri encountered him in Nishapur, he was not much taken by this eccentric man who could read people's minds and who spent a great deal of time and money on poetical song fests. The Nishapur Karramites were more active in their opposition. They charged Abu Sa'id before the Sultan Mahmud of Ghazna,[26] and though Abu Sa'id escaped serious blame, it is clear enough that he was treading on most dangerous ground.

By the lifetime of Abu Sa'id Sufism had joined issue with the traditionalists' view of Islam. The Sufi was by then a commonplace figure in the *Dar al-Islam* who stood not at the fringes of the community but ever closer to its intellectual center. Abu Sa'id had given up jurisprudence for Sufism, but there were others like Qushayri who simultaneously pursued the careers of *Sufi* and *faqih* without embarrassment. There was no essential conflict between asceticism and the Law, and Sufis could be found even among the Hanbalite preachers and lawyers of Baghdad. It was beyond asceticism, however, that lay more dangerous vistas, and not merely those associated with the question of the mystical union.

---

26. This was at a time when the Karramiyah still stood high in Mahmud's regard. See Chap. IX, p. 682.

In the *credo* drawn up by the Hanbalite Ibn Batta (d. 997) the line between legitimate asceticism and heretical innovation is drawn with firm clarity. Renouncement of the world is well within the Hanbalite tradition, and Ibn Batta cites with approval, just as Ibn Hanbal himself had done, the Khurasanian holy man Ibn al-Mubarak (d. 797), whose *Book of Asceticism* was a collection of Prophetic traditions justifying various practices of self-denial. But Ibn Batta will grant no indulgence to those Muslims who faint at the mention of the name of Allah, who share Abu Sa'id's reckless indulgence in "spiritual concerts," who "dance, clap their hands or tear their clothes," or who have private visions of God or the saints. Heretical too are those who "pretend to have achieved the love of God."

This was fundamentally the doctrine of Ibn Hanbal, and so too was Ibn Batta's affirmation of the vision of God by the elect on the Day of Judgment. Beyond that no man, save Moses and Muhammad himself, has seen God in this life. Thus in the ninth and tenth centuries, the lifetime of Bistami, Junayd and Hallaj, the Unitive Way was barred to the Hanbalite Sufi. For him Sufism was merely the path to the observance of the Law and not a royal road to union with God.

In a slightly different context Ibn Batta invoked Ibn al-Mubarak once again: "Whoever pursues *kalam* is a *zindiq*." The Hanbalite tradition, both before and after Ibn Batta, was opposed to *kalam;* but already in Ibn Hanbal's own day he had to deal with still another dangerous possibility, the alliance of Sufism and *kalam* in someone like al-Muhasibi. Muhasibi was a moderate in both those areas, but it did not shelter him from the reproaches of Ahmad ibn Hanbal. In the eleventh century the combination was current once again: there were Shafi'ite lawyers committed to the Ash'arite *kalam*, and some of them were Sufis as well.

How dangerous that particular configuration was appears in the case of Ibn 'Aqil (d. 1119), the Baghdad Hanbalite who in 1072 was forced to issue a public statement denouncing his own published works on the subject of *kalam* as well as the achievement of al-Hallaj. We do not possess the latter work, but according to a later Hanbalite it attempted to justify Hallaj's teachings by giving them an allegorical interpretation. Ibn 'Aqil failed, it appears, as was perhaps inevitable in the highly charged atmosphere of Seljuq Baghdad, but another of his younger contemporaries was somewhat more successful in carving out a modest place for mystical Sufism within the Hanbalite tradition.

Al-Ansari (d. 1089) of Herat had his own problems with the Seljuqs, though not through the agency of his fellow Hanbalites. He was as stanch as they in his rejection of *kalam.*[27] His alternative was not, however, the study of the Law. Instead, Ansari advocated by his life and teaching the Sufi Way—the "science of unification" (*'ilm al-tawhid*), as he called it. Ansari's embrace of Sufism came early in life, and it received its strongest impulse from a chance meeting in 1033 with Abu al-Hasan al-Kharaqani, an ancient disciple of Bistami who was then in the last year of his life. "Had I never met Kharaqani," Ansari later remarked, "I would never have known Reality."[28]

The nature of that "Reality" (*haqiqah*) is explored in one of the earliest of Ansari's works, the Persian *Hundred Terrains*,[29] a hundred chapters on the various stages of the spiritual life. The seventy-seventh of them is "Reality" and is distinguished by Ansari into three grades. The highest consists in the objects of the knowledge possessed by God; the second is the object of the knowledge denied even to Moses but taught to Khadir and concealed beneath certain passages in the *Qur'an;*[30] finally, the "Realities" are what certain spiritually gifted men know by the

---

27. See Chap. IX, pp. 685–686.
28. On this same journey, which was actually an unsuccessful attempt at making a pilgrimage to Mecca, Ansari met Abu Sa'id ibn abi al-Khayr at Nishapur. The young man did have some reservations about what he saw, but Abu Sa'id took it with typically good spirits and gave Ansari his own turban and other gifts.
29. Like most of the works preserved under Ansari's name, the *Hundred Terrains* is a *reportatio* by one of his disciples present during a course of lectures delivered at Herat in 1056.
30. Khadir, or Khidr, is the standard Muslim identification of the mysterious person "to whom divine wisdom has been granted" in *Surah* 18:60–82 and who figures in an equally mysterious story there about a certain "Moses," probably, though by no means certainly, the Jewish prophet. Khadir had an elaborate history in Muslim legend, but for the Sufis, as possibly for Ansari here, he was the alleged source of much of their mystical doctrine.

grace of God, "who reveals what he wishes, to the extent that he wishes, and to whom he wishes."

"Reality" appears again in Ansari in his *Stages of the Travelers Toward God*, which he dictated in his convent (*khanqah*) at Herat in 1081–1082. Like the *Terrains*, the *Stages* is structured according to the traditional ladderlike ascent along the Sufi Way. In the later work the going is far more complicated, however. The chapter on "Reality" leads to the final achievement of "unification" (*tawhid*), and here the Ḥanbalite Ansari develops his own careful version of the mystical experience based, to a large degree, on Tirmidhi. Unification, we are told, is of three types. The first is nothing more or less than the *shahadah*, the Muslim's overt (*zahir*) declaration that there is no God but Allah. The second type proceeds from contingent externals toward the "Realities" and consists in a contemplation of God in his attributes; it is reserved for the few. The third and highest degree of unification is that in which God assumes the initiative and manifests his transcendent Unity within the adept and thus causes him to pass from the dimension of time to that of eternity.

In another work composed in Persian about the same time, the *Classes of Sufis*, Ansari returns to the theme. *Tawhid* proceeds from a study of the *Qur'an* and the *sunnah* to a concentration on God alone at the expense of everything that is not God, and finally to leaving aside his attributes and all talk (*kalam*) about "substances, accidents, nature, body and first matter, which is the science of the first *zindiqs*." To strive for unification with God is, in a sense, a waste of time. Man by his own powers can never attain that state. In the end it is Allah who in his mercy causes the revelation of himself in the heart of the mystic.

Ansari's language is controlled, and his judgments are careful or, failing that, ambiguous. Hallaj is a case in point. In the *Classes of Sufis* Ansari, who is obviously sympathetic to his eminent predecessor, recommends suspending judgment on Hallaj. Where Hallaj was clearly at fault, however, was in speaking out publicly on the "secrets of God" and so imposing upon the generality of men an impossible burden of comprehension. On Ansari's own testimony he himself had spoken even more forcibly than Hallaj, but no one had charged him with blasphemy because the common people had heard but did not understand.

The later Sufis' publicly advertised secrecy is a commonplace in the literature. Even the highly orthodox Ansari affirmed the existence of that other world of "realities" never dreamed of in the philosophy of the ordinary Muslim, who was condemned to a literal understanding of the *Qur'an* and a literal observance of the Law. For the Sufi the cosmos of the "realities" remained a private vision, and its geography was still, despite Tirmidhi's efforts at broadening the perspectives, largely uncharted.

But the Sufi was not the only one to have a vision of the beyond. The Neoplatonic *faylasuf* knew its furthest reaches, not so much by reason of a personal vision as by the fact that the transcendental cosmos, the intelligible universe of the Platonists, had long been in the public domain. Farabi and Ibn Sina vindicated the philosopher's right to enjoy prophetic privileges, and a mere reading of the "Theology of Aristotle" was as valid a passport to the "realities" as more visionary transports.

There were other guides, not so public as the *theologica* of the philosophers and less well known to us. The Gnostics too had meditated the transcendentals, but they kept their knowledge secret or wrapped it in metaphor and symbol. These occult geographers of the beyond also came into Islam as part of a sophisticated literary tradition. The visible edges of that tradition are scientific; its religious application, which is obvious enough in its Greek prototypes, is, however, concealed. But, as already has been observed, early Islamic occultism is connected, in ways we do not always understand, with men who figure in the religious as well as the scientific tradition of Islam: Jabir ibn Hayyan, the "Sufi"; Dhu al-Nun, alchemist and mystic; and the Shi'ite Imam Ja'far al-Sadiq.

The theology of developed Shi'ism was transcendentalist; it recognized that other dimension of the "realities," and far more quickly than Sufism it revealed its content. Unlike the tenth-century Sufi who bore only a personal and unique witness to what he had experienced in the world beyond, the Shi'ite spoke from other convictions. The cosmic "realities" might be hidden from most men, but the Shi'ite received his instruction from a spiritual mediator who stood athwart both worlds, the *Imam* who in the course of the early tenth century finally surrendered his claims as a political pretender to the Caliphate to lay hold of something far more extraordinary, the role of infallible teacher and Islam's unique guide to salvation.

The Evolution of Shi'ism

There is a profound mystery surrounding the *Shi'at 'Ali* during the ninth century. For most of that period there were two major branches of the movement, the Rafidites and the Zaydis. They had various differences, but substantially they parted company on the question of the Imamate, the leadership of the community, not, however, as a political consideration, but as a historical and legal one. In the Rafidite reading of history Muhammad had designated 'Ali as his successor, and he in turn was succeeded by designated members of his family. The Zaydis admitted the preeminence of 'Ali among the Companions of the Prophet, but in the face of the historical reality of the Caliphates of the first three *Rashidun*, they conceded the possibility of a "lesser Imamate," the rule by *Imams* who fell short of the ideal. They appear not to have debated contemporary claims to the Caliphate. There were, to be sure, many such, put forward by one 'Alid or another, each with a small body of supporters among the Shi'ah.

After 750 the majority of such claims to the Imamate came from the descendants of Husayn ibn 'Ali, and it may have been the crumbling of Umayyad power that tempted Husayn's grandson Muhammad al-Baqir (d. 731) and particularly the latter's son, Ja'far al-Sadiq (d. 765), into more public claim to the rule of the *ummah*. That expectation was disappointed, as has been seen, and none of the 'Alids—Hasanid or Husaynid—received much encouragement from the early 'Abbasids; indeed, Ja'far's son Musa al-Kazim spent most of his Imamate in confinement and died in prison in 799. Then came Ma'mun's abortive attempt to nominate Ja'far's grandson 'Ali al-Rida (d. 818) as his successor. Nothing came of the plan, but 'Ali al-Rida's son Muhammad al-Jawad (d. 835) continued to live at the Caliphal court until his own death shortly after Ma'mun's. The next two Husaynids of the line, 'Ali al-Hadi (d. 868) and his son Hasan al-'Askari (d. 874), were kept under surveillance by the anti-Shi'ite Mutawakkil and his successors, though apparently without a great deal of fear that they

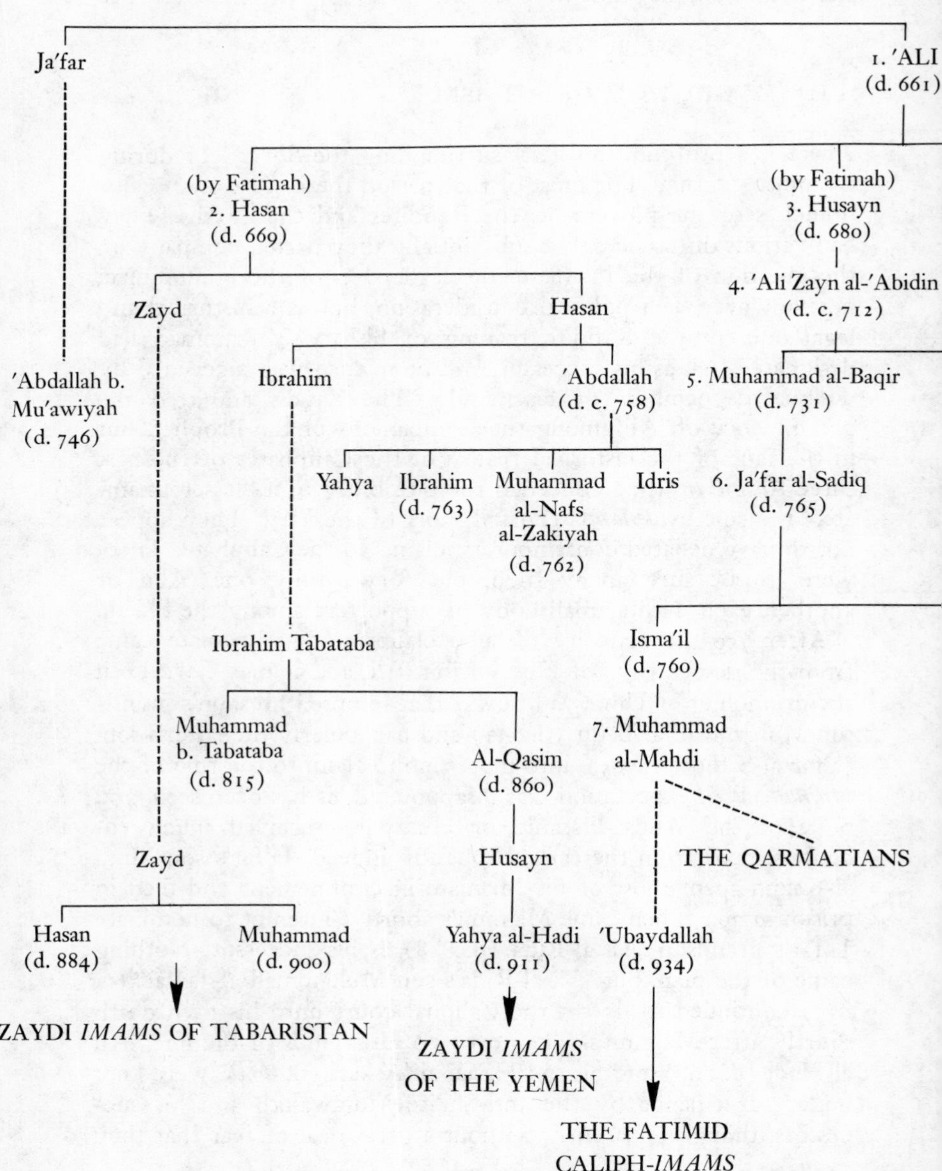
THE HOUSE
Ja'far
1. 'ALI
(d. 661)
(by Fatimah)
2. Hasan
(d. 669)
(by Fatimah)
3. Husayn
(d. 680)
4. 'Ali Zayn al-'Abidin
(d. c. 712)
Zayd
Hasan
'Abdallah b.
Mu'awiyah
(d. 746)
Ibrahim
'Abdallah
(d. c. 758)
5. Muhammad al-Baqir
(d. 731)
Yahya
Ibrahim
(d. 763)
Muhammad
al-Nafs
al-Zakiyah
(d. 762)
Idris
6. Ja'far al-Sadiq
(d. 765)
Ibrahim Tabataba
Isma'il
(d. 760)
Muhammad
b. Tabataba
(d. 815)
Al-Qasim
(d. 860)
7. Muhammad
al-Mahdi
Zayd
Husayn
THE QARMATIANS
Hasan
(d. 884)
Muhammad
(d. 900)
Yahya al-Hadi
(d. 911)
'Ubaydallah
(d. 934)
ZAYDI *IMAMS* OF TABARISTAN
ZAYDI *IMAMS*
OF THE YEMEN
THE FATIMID
CALIPH-*IMAMS*

F 'ALI

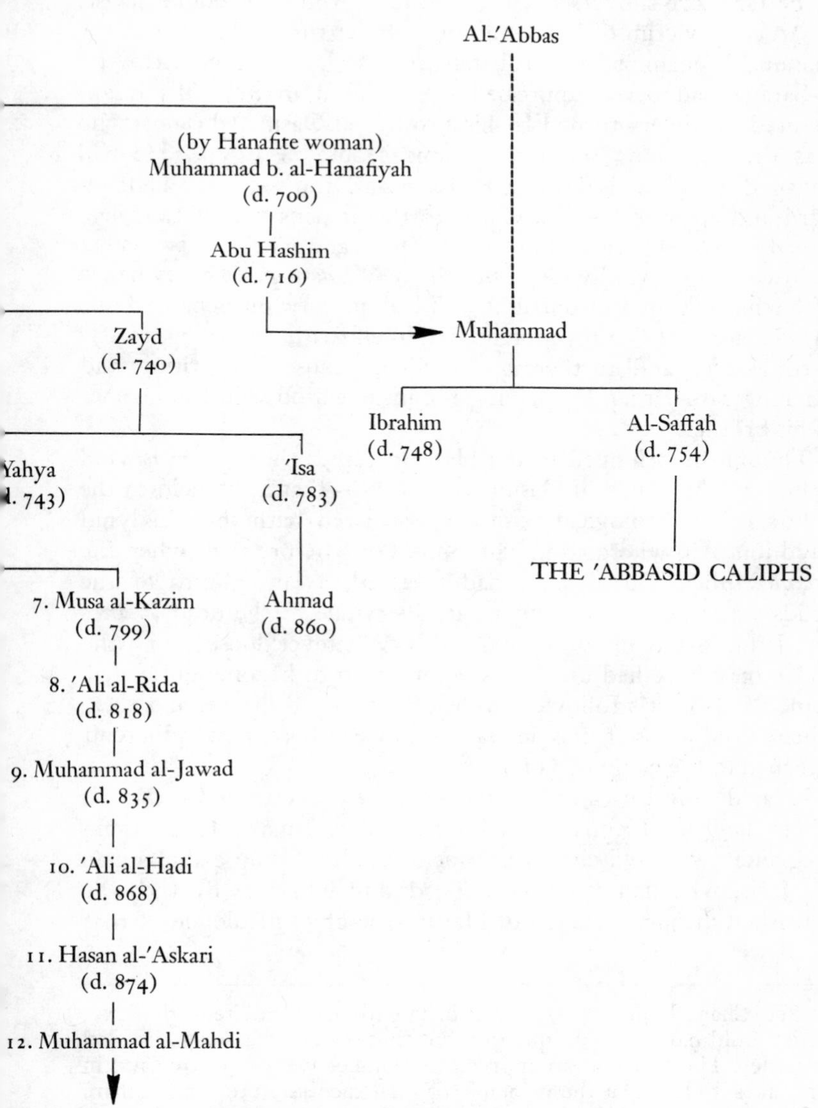

Al-'Abbas
(by Hanafite woman)
Muhammad b. al-Hanafiyah
(d. 700)
Abu Hashim
(d. 716)
Muhammad
Zayd
(d. 740)
Ibrahim
(d. 748)
Al-Saffah
(d. 754)
Yahya
l. 743)
'Isa
(d. 783)
THE 'ABBASID CALIPHS
7. Musa al-Kazim
(d. 799)
Ahmad
(d. 860)
8. 'Ali al-Rida
(d. 818)
9. Muhammad al-Jawad
(d. 835)
10. 'Ali al-Hadi
(d. 868)
11. Hasan al-'Askari
(d. 874)
12. Muhammad al-Mahdi
THE "TWELVER" OR IMAMI SHI'ITES

might be politically dangerous. Indeed, they were not, but behind them was being constructed a theory that would prove in the end to be far more subversive than anything 'Alid arms could devise.

An early victim of 'Alid ambitions under the 'Abbasids was the Hasanid Muhammad ibn Tabataba, whose joint action with Abu al-Saraya had been suppressed by Ma'mun in 815. His disappointed followers turned to his brother al-Qasim (d. 860) who was then a young scholar of some repute in Egypt. He had engaged in *kalam* discussions there, with Dirar's student Hafs al-Fard and apparently with Christian theologians as well, and had already written a refutation of *zandaqah* and Christianity. What followed is not wholly clear, but the new *Imam* gives no evidence of having engaged in outright political activity on behalf of the 'Alid cause. Al-Qasim contented himself with returning to the Medina area and furthering the Shi'ite cause by writing and teaching rather than by playing the insurrectionist in the manner of his brother.

Though he belonged to the Hasanid rather than the Husaynid branch of the 'Alids, al-Qasim was a Zaydi—that is, he held to the political and theological positions associated with the Husaynid Zayd ibn 'Ali, who died in 740. Nine years before that, when the *Imam* Muhammad al-Baqir had perished, a large body of the 'Alids was torn between giving its allegiance to the dead *Imam's* son Ja'far or to his brother Zayd.[31] Whatever loose unity the Shi'ah may have had up to this point began to become unraveled. Some of al-Baqir's followers went over to Zayd in 731, and then, when Zayd himself fell in 740, some of those new adherents returned to the camp of Ja'far.

Ja'far died in turn in 765, predeceased by five years by the son whom he had designated as his successor, Isma'il. Once again allegiances were switched, this time to the leadership of Sulayman ibn Jarir, who had remained a Zaydi and who was by then—he flourished during the reign of Harun—the chief ideologue of that

31. See Chap. I, pp. 124–125. According to later Shi'ite orthodoxy, there should have been no question but that the *Imam's* son succeeded his father. The fact that an appreciable number went over to Zayd in 731 makes it clear that the principle of filial succession to the Imamate was by no means well established in the early eighth century.

branch of the movement. Seventy-five years of shuttling back and forth between rival Shi'ite camps had taken their toll. Doctrinal lines had hardened and by Sulayman's day there were two distinct Shi'ite "schools," those under Sulayman who identified themselves by their original support of Zayd ibn 'Ali and those on the other side who stood firm with Ja'far and are identified in our sources as Rafidites.

Those same sources present Sulayman as a *mutakallim*, and so he appears to have been. In his debates with his Rafidite opposite number, Hisham ibn al-Hakam, he espoused positions not very different from those of Ibn Kullab. He opposed Hisham's somewhat crude anthropomorphism and, in a more direct fashion, the Rafidite denial of the Caliphate to Abu Bakr and 'Umar. Sulayman was by no means a Mu'tazilite; he could not accept the Mu'tazilite theories on either human freedom or the created *Qur'an*. There was, however, a connection: both Sulayman and the Baghdad Mu'tazilite scholarch Bishr ibn al-Mu'tamir recognized the Imamate proclaimed under Zaydi auspices in Daylam in 791 by the Hasanid Yahya ibn 'Abdallah.

There was, then, about 800 a Rafidite theology and a Zaydi theology set against the background of a great number of 'Alid *Imams*, some political and some not. Al-Qasim was not; like Sulayman ibn Jarir, he was a *mutakallim*, albeit a somewhat primitive one. Nor was he a Mu'tazilite. But al-Qasim's enemies and those of the Mu'tazilites were the same: dualists and *zindiqs;* the conservative Hanbalites and the anthropomorphic Rafidites among the Shi'ah; and that constellation of adversaries carried al-Qasim closer to the Mu'tazilah. The unity and justice of God were the foundation stone of his theology as they were of the Mu'tazilah, and it was on the second point, which still separated Sulayman from the Mu'tazilites of his day, that al-Qasim took the decisive step: God is not responsible for the evil in this world; man is responsible and so, of necessity, free. Al-Qasim's treatment of the theme was cautious and not always consistent, but the essential denial of predestination was uttered, and in terms close to the Mu'tazilite understanding of it.

Politically, the Zaydi point of view had some success. In 864, a few years after the death of al-Qasim, there came into existence a Zaydi state in Tabaristan. The regime lasted only thirty years, and the main body of the Zaydis were not particularly enthusiastic for that northern Imamate. For their part the Tabaristan *Imams* Hasan ibn Zayd (d. 884) and his brother Muhammad (d. 900) showed a marked sympathy for the Mu'tazilites, and for a time a later scholarch of the Baghdad Mu'tazilah served as Muhammad ibn Zayd's secretary. Even after their fall, Zaydi sentiments continued to find a sympathetic ear in the lands south of the Caspian, and with them at least some aspects of Mu'tazilite *kalam*.

In the meantime, another Zaydi principality had come into existence in the Yemen where al-Qasim's grandson Yahya ibn al-Husayn al-Hadi (d. 911) was acknowledged as *Imam*. On most theological questions al-Hadi was an out-and-out Mu'tazilite, and his successors remained such. The prestige of the Yemeni Zaydis eventually had its effect in Daylam and Tabaristan as well, and two of the most famous of the Zaydi *Imams*, Abu 'Abdallah al-Mahdi (d. 970) and al-Mu'ayyad (d. 1028), studied *kalam* with the leading Mu'tazilites of their day, the first with Abu Hashim's student Abu 'Abdallah al-Basri (d. 977) and the second with Abu 'Abdallah's most reputed disciple, the Mu'tazilite *qadi* of Rayy, 'Abd al-Jabbar (d. 1025).[32]

Ironically it was the moderate Zaydis who achieved some modest political success against the 'Abbasids, while before 900 the more fundamentally revolutionary theses of the Rafidites generated nothing but theory. Hisham ibn al-Hakam had evolved a metaphysics of sorts, but it differs only in sophistication from what the contemporary Mu'tazilites and even Sulayman ibn Jarir were doing considerably better. Where the Rafidites aimed their most devastating blow, however, was at the foundations of the *shari'ah*. Their denial of the Caliphate to Abu Bakr and 'Umar, who had been acknowledged by the Companions and the entire community, meant that neither the testimony of those Companions nor the consensus of the community was an adequate basis for the Islamic Law. The Rafidites' own theoretical base for the *shari'ah* was explicated in the circle of the *Imam* Muhammad al-

32. Whose works were preserved virtually unknown in Zaydi libraries in the Yemen until their recent rediscovery.

Baqir or, at the very latest, of Ja'far al-Sadiq. In their substance the Shi'ite traditions were grounded in these two men and could be transmitted, according to the Rafidites, by the *Imams* alone, that is, by the descendants of Hasan and Husayn.

Some of the early Zaydis appear to have taken a similar position, probably those who had come over to Zayd after the death of Muhammad al-Baqir. But there was another, older tradition among the Zaydis, and one that may well antedate Zayd himself. The partisans of this latter tradition, moderates who accepted Abu Bakr and 'Umar as legitimate Caliphs, traced their legal traditions back to members of the community other than the *Imams*, and some of them even admitted the possibility that someone who was not an 'Alid could, by reason of his outstanding virtue, be chosen as the *Imam*.

The moderate branch of the Zaydis did not long survive; its views and adherents were in the end absorbed into Sunni Islam. But the scholarly *Imam* al-Qasim was moving toward his own distinctive theory of the Imamate. According to his view, the Prophet had brought the Law, but an *Imam* was likewise necessary for the direction of the community in the ways of that Law. The *Imam*, like the Prophet, is recognized by certain signs, and these are, according to al-Qasim, a family relationship to the Prophet and perfect wisdom. The legitimacy of the *Imam* does not, however, depend on his recognition; he is sent by God, not chosen by men. The Rafidites were willing, as al-Qasim perceived it, to go quite a bit further. For these latter the *Imams* were the equal, or even the superior, of the Prophet, the possessors in infancy of a wisdom that the Prophet acquired only in his maturity.

Al-Qasim is the first Zaydi teacher whose work presents anything like a detailed picture; on the other *Imams*, and particularly the line descended from Ja'far and later recognized as canonical by the main body of the Shi'ah, it is far more difficult to render a judgment. Their literary legacy is in the form of *hadith*, traditions transmitted in their name and collected for the first time in the early tenth century by al-Kulini and others. Like their Sunni counterparts, the Shi'ite *hadith* do not inspire a great deal of critical confidence, and the reconstruction of the theological positions of such *Imams* as Muhammad al-Baqir and Ja'far al-

Sadiq, on whom most of the traditions converge, depends precisely on the authenticity of those Shi'ite *hadith*.

Rafidite theology, 'Alid politics and the Shi'ite Imamate appear not to have coalesced until near the end of the ninth century, when there appeared the first signs of what was to become the "Twelver" (*Ithna 'Ashariyah*) Shi'ah. We cannot be altogether certain how this occurred, but sometime about 900 the Rafidite theologians had become "Imamites," a term in little use before that date, and a large body of the *Shi'at 'Ali* had accepted the fact that not only had Muhammad designated 'Ali as his successor but that after 'Ali there was a line of "designated" *Imams* from (2) Hasan to (3) Husayn, thence to the line of his descendants: (4) 'Ali Zayn al-'Abidin (d. c. 712); (5) Muhammad al-Baqir (d. 731); (6) Ja'far al-Sadiq (d. 765); (7) Musa al-Kazim (d. 799); (8) 'Ali al-Rida (d. 868); (9) Muhammad al-Jawad (d. 835); (10) 'Ali al-Hadi (d. 868); (11) Hasan al-'Askari (d. 874), and finally (12) Muhammad, called al-Mahdi, who some years after his father's death in Samarra vanished from the world and so became the "hidden" *Imam* who will return on the Last Day.

The "occultation" of Muhammad al-Mahdi was achieved in two stages. During his first or "lesser" concealment the direction of Shi'ite policies was placed in the hands of the *Imam's* envoy. There were four such in the years after 874, and at the death of the last of them, Ibn Rawh al-Nawbakhti, in 941 the "lesser" was succeeded by the "greater" concealment and the direct link between the *Imam* and the community of believers was broken until the time of his eschatological return.

Two things are remarkable about this complex of ideas; first, the retroactive claim that these were the only legitimate 'Alid *Imams*, and second, the acceptance by a large body of the *Shi'at 'Ali* of the proposition that the Imamate had deserted history for eschatology. 'Alid history up to 900 witnessed a whole series of claimants to the Imamate, and from all three branches of the House: Hasanid, Husaynid and the descendants of Muhammad ibn al-Hanafiyah. Some were rebels against the Umayyads or 'Abbasids and paid with their lives; some vanished into jails; others stuck to their prayers. Some few even disappeared into the eschatological future, to return, in due time, as a Messianic *Mahdi*.

The notion of a *Mahdi* ("guided one") had been circulating in Islam almost from the beginning. In its original understanding, however, it had no demonstrable connection with Messianism or with 'Isa (Jesus), whose return to earth was generally understood to signal the inception of the end-time. Rather, the title *Mahdi* was applied to someone like Abraham, or even 'Umar II, who by God's grace possessed a special guidance, and it was only in the last years of the seventh century that it began to acquire its eschatological echoes. The followers of al-Mukhtar and his 'Alid token Muhammad ibn al-Hanafiyah, the so-called Kaysaniyah,[33] believed that their 'Alid *Imam* was the *Mahdi* in an eschatological sense, and that he had not died in 700 as reported, but was merely "concealed" during the interval until his final return.

That the Muhammad ibn al-Hanafiyah was regarded for some time as an eschatological *Mahdi* is reasonably well attested, as are similar beliefs among the later Kaysaniyah concerning the *Imam* 'Abdallah ibn Mu'awiyah, who led an insurrection at Kufah in 744, and among the Khurramiyah of Khurasan who venerated Abu Muslim and various of his descendants as *Mahdis*. The Kaysaniyah and Khurramiyah had common origins, and out of the same complex the 'Abbasids constructed their own claim to the Imamate. But once the 'Abbasids came to power they put down their roots in the historical present and had little need of or interest in Messiahs. Most of the 'Alids down to 900 were no more interested in eschatology than the 'Abbasids and they commonly wrote off such longings among some few of their coreligionists as the fantasies of "extremists" (*ghulat*).

There were a number of extremist centers flourishing in the disturbed political climate that marked the last days of the Umayyads. In addition to Abu Muslim's sectaries in Khurasan, the *ghulat* of Kufah made and unmade a number of *Imams* in the years after 716. 'Abdallah ibn Mu'awiyah announced his own divine and prophetic powers to the excitable Kufans, and even in the more restrained circle that surrounded the *Imam* Ja'far al-Sadiq in the Hejaz there were discernibly *ghulat* theologians. One of the most important of these latter was a certain Abu al-

33. See Chap. I, p. 131.

Khattab (d. c. 762) who had some interesting, if obscure, ideas on a spiritual hierarchy and who apparently was preaching some kind of private revelation for all believers. That each man was his own *Imam* ran counter, however, to another theory gaining currency among the Rafidite Shi'ah, and sometime about 755 Ja'far repudiated Abu al-Khattab in favor of an idea that eventually converted the Rafidites into Imamites, that there was but one current *Imam* and that he held his position neither by contract, as the Sunnis maintained, nor as a randomly dispensed spiritual gift, but by reason of a formal designation at the hands of his predecessor.

Despite Ja'far's misfortune in designating for the Imamate a son who predeceased him, the notion of a single designated *Imam* prevailed over the Zaydi theory that it was wisdom and not designation that made an *Imam* and that there could be more than one such. The Zaydis went their own way within the Shi'ah, but Ja'far's teachings may have drawn the Rafidites into a new cohesiveness. The results were not at first remarkable; Ja'far's own successors in the Imamate were neither politicians nor theologians of note, and when Hasan al-'Askari died in 874 the prospects of the Husaynid branch of the 'Alids must have seemed exceedingly dim. The Rafidite theologians, who had an ideology but no visible political program, ignored 'Ali al-Rida and his successors in the Imamate.

But between the time al-Khayyat wrote his *Book of Triumph*, sometime after the death of Jahiz in 869, and the composition of Ash'ari's *Views of the Muslims*, in the second decade of the next century, an important change had taken place in Shi'ite fortunes. The eleven "designated" *Imams* from Hasan al-'Askari back to 'Ali were accepted, to the exclusion of all others, as a standard feature of Shi'ite orthodoxy, as was the belief that the twelfth *Imam*, Muhammad al-Mahdi, was in "concealment" and would one day return to restore the true Islam.

Why this happened, or how, we have no certain information. Speculation has centered on the activities of a family known as the Nawbakhti. One of them, Ibn Rawh, has already been mentioned as the last of those who served as "delegates" for the *Imam* during his "lesser" concealment, and a number of other contemporary members of the Banu Nawbakht appear to stand at the very center of Shi'ite speculation in the early tenth century. Though we cannot always separate their work, two of them, Abu Sahl Isma'il (d. 932) and his nephew Hasan ibn Musa (d. 912), were considerable *mutakallimun* on a Mu'tazilite model not previously seen in Shi'ite circles. A number of obviously philosophical titles are attributed to Hasan, and an important heresiography, *The Sects of the Shi'ites*, has been preserved under his name.[34] The life of a third member of the family, Abu Ishaq Ibrahim, is almost a complete mystery, but he too is credited with a preserved work of Shi'ite *kalam*, *The Sapphire*, which was reputedly composed about 950. If the ascription is correct, which is highly uncertain at this point, the treatise would be the earliest known example of a *kalam* work from a Shi'ite author.

This, then, was the context in which the transformation of the Rafidites into Imamites took place. Nothing new or startling was introduced into the complex of Shi'ite ideas; almost all the motifs were present in one or another group of Shi'ites from the beginning: the adulation of 'Ali, the conviction that the Imamate was somehow connected with an 'Alid genealogy,[35] and last of all perhaps, the twin themes of the *Imam* as a teacher, already much in evidence among the early Zaydis, and of the *Imam* as the restorer not so much of 'Alid fortunes as of a true Islam. Crucial to this latter was the acceptance of the once scorned view of the "extremists" that the last *Imam* was also the *Mahdi*, who would surely return.

The consequences of all of this were enormous. At a stroke the Shi'ite premise undercut both the claims of the speculative theologians and the authority of the lawyers. For the first, it substituted recourse to the authority (*taqlid*) of the *Imam* or his surrogate as the only source of authentic teaching. And in law the Shi'ah denied in effect the entire structure of *hadith* that rested upon the simple witness of the Companions of the Prophet, men whose authority was compromised in Shi'ite eyes by their failure to recognize the Imamate of 'Ali. The Shi'ites were not

---

34. See Chap. II, p. 195.

35. Though not necessarily, as in the later Shi'ah, by descent from 'Ali and Fatimah. The recognition given to Muhammid ibn al-Hanafiyah and 'Abdallah ibn Mu'awiyah speaks for itself.

denying that *hadith* was the source of the *shari'ah;* they were insisting that all valid *hadith* went back through the infallible Husaynid *Imams*.

The most important occurrence at the turn into the tenth century was the disengagement of Shi'ite ideology from the failing 'Alid politics. As rebels and revolutionaries the 'Alid leaders had been able to accomplish very little; as *Imams*, either long dead or, in the case of Muhammad al-Mahdi, in concealment in the transcendental future, they were far more effective. The conversion of politics into ideology was a brilliantly successful coup and presented the 'Abbasids with a new and subversive form of metapolitics.

The Mu'tazilites had no share in this. Though they were associated with the 'Alid and Shi'ite point of view in their early days and still had very close connections with the Zaydi Shi'ah, the Mu'tazilites had no visible lines into the Rafidite, now Imamite, theology. The Rafidite Hisham ibn al-Hakam was among their earliest adversaries, and the defection first of Abu 'Isa al-Warraq and then of Ibn al-Rewandi, both of whom had serious flirtations with the Rafidites en route to *zandaqah*, drove the wedge between Mu'tazilites and Rafidites even deeper.

The Caliphs for their part were of two minds about the *Shi'at 'Ali*. Mutawakkil was violently anti 'Alid, but al-Muntasir (861–862) reopened negotiation with the objects of his father's aversion. Mu'tazz reverted to Mutawakkil's policy, and it was during his reign and those of his immediate successors, Muhtadi (869) and Mu'tamid (870–892), that the tenth, eleventh and possibly twelfth Shi'ite *Imams* met their end, either in prison or under the surveillance of the Caliphs. These measures must have appeared well justified when the Qarmatians began to make their presence felt in Iraq.[36] Mu'tadid reacted vigorously both in the field and on the more treacherous terrain of ideology. Early in his reign he forbade the sale and reading of books on *falsafah* and *kalam*. In 899 this was followed by a more personally revealing act, the imprisonment and execution of his long-time tutor and boon companion al-Sarakhsi, a student of al-Kindi and an intellectual with known connections with Mu'tazilitism.

36. See p. 602.

And yet Mu'tadid was not simply another version of Mutawakkil. In 897 the Caliph was only with difficulty dissuaded from his project of a public *damnatio memoriae* of Mu'awiyah, an act far dearer to Shi'ite desires than to the Hanbalites'; indeed, Ma'mun had once had the same intention. And at the same time that he interdicted *falsafah* and *kalam*, the Caliph banned from the public ways the inflammatory popular preachers, most of them Hanbalites, who kept passions aroused at Baghdad and elsewhere.

The doubts and ambivalences of the ninth century gave way to the more passionate certainties of the tenth. Extremist Shi'ites of the type of al-Shalmaghani were pursued by the Caliphs, but the more moderate Imamite Shi'ah, who had ostensibly surrendered all political hopes with the "occultation" of their *Imam*, rose to positions of power in Baghdad and even, in the case of Ibn al-Furat, to the vizierate itself. In foreign policy the Caliphs could make a similar distinction: they could, when it suited their interests, cooperate with Shi'ite regimes like the Hamdanids while simultaneously resisting the obviously subversive political intentions of the Fatimids and other Isma'ilis.

The Imamites for their part showed restraint with respect to the Caliphate. Nominally the Buyids ruled by grace of the 'Abbasid Caliph, and they did nothing to tamper with that relationship. Indeed, 'Adud al-Dawlah apparently sought to strengthen his own legitimacy by contriving a marriage between himself and the daughter of the Caliph al-Ta'i (974–991). The Buyids were, nonetheless, Shi'ites, a fact they neither dissembled nor denied. Public Shi'ite festivals were instituted at Baghdad and elsewhere; the 'Alid grave sites were enriched and enhanced; and, most importantly, a school of higher studies was founded sometime about 993 by the vizier Sabur ibn Ardashir, an institution modeled perhaps on the recently inaugurated al-Azhar in Fatimid Cairo.[37]

Shi'ite theoreticians had been pursuing their speculations since the time of the *Imam* Ja'far in the early eighth century, and there were, as has been seen, Shi'ite propagandists active in Baghdad

---

37. See Chap. IV, p. 330. Sabur's "House of Science" burned down during the fighting in Baghdad in 1059.

before the Buyids arrived there. The Buyid tenancy of Iraq and the parallel rise in Syria and Mesopotamia of other dynasties sympathetic to the 'Alids did, however, encourage the public flowering of Shi'ite letters and scholarship. The poet and anthologist Isfahani gave to the Shi'ites in 925 their first martyrology in his *Martyrs of the House of 'Ali*, and, if the work is truly his, the *Establishment of the Executive Office of 'Ali* attributed to Mas'udi (d. 956) is the earliest formal history of the Shi'ite Imamate.[38] The Sharif al-Radi (d. 1015), the head of the 'Alid aristocracy in Baghdad, commemorated the discourses of 'Ali in his *Path of Eloquence*.[39]

The Buyid entry into Iraq likewise coincided with the appearance of the first generation of Shi'ite lawyers and theologians. Al-Kulini (d. 939), a native of Rayy who spent the final years of his life in Baghdad, edited the basic collection of 16,000 Shi'ite *hadith* in his *Book of Sufficiency on the Science of Religion* and so provided the groundwork for all subsequent Shi'ite jurisprudence. Ibn Babuyah was the scion of an eminent family from the Shi'ite stronghold of Qumm; he migrated to Baghdad in 966 and became part of the entourage of Rukn al-Dawlah. Before his death in 991 he turned out more than three hundred works on Shi'ite law, theology and polemic. His successor as head of the Baghdad Shi'ites was al-Mufid, another lawyer and polemicist—his targets included Jews and Christians as well as the mandatory Mu'tazilites and Hanbalites—and an associate of 'Adud al-Dawlah.

At al-Mufid's death in 1022 the funeral services were conducted by another Shi'ite eminence of Baghdad, al-Murtada (d. 1044), a descendant of Jaf'ar al-Sadiq, who succeeded his brother al-Radi as official dean (*naqib*) of the 'Alids. The bulk of his preserved work is in the form of *responsa* to questions submitted

---

38. Mas'udi's personal Shi'ism appears to be beyond reasonable doubt. His presentation of the history of the Caliphate in the *Golden Meadows* (see Chap. V, p. 348) gave a prominent place to 'Ali and his descendants, and the references to his own (lost) works point in the same direction. The *Establishment*, on the other hand, which was allegedly composed in 943, is attested to only by considerably later authors.

39. See Chap. III, pp. 234–235.

to him from across the *Dar al-Islam*, but al-Murtada was also a theologian of some note and possessed a knowledge of the speculative *kalam* that was just beginning to engage the interest of the Shi'ites. The last of the Baghdad Shi'ites of the period was Abu Ja'far al-Tusi, the student of both al-Mufid and al-Murtada, who came to the capital in 1017 but wisely left before the arrival of the Seljuqs in 1055. Al-Tusi was the most scholastic of the group, commenting on and systematizing the work of his teachers as well as putting together the valuable *Catalogue of Shi'ite Books.*

The two earliest men in this group, Kulini and Ibn Babuyah, were unmistakably lawyers, and their approach to Shi'ism was through *hadith*. They differed from their Sunni contemporaries chiefly in their obviously straitened view of the "sources of the Law," as this important question was called. Sunni and Shi'ite agreed that the true foundations of the Islamic Law lay in the *Qur'an* and the *sunnah*, the latter contained in the great body of "traditions" going back to the Prophet. In the Sunni view the *hadith* are guaranteed by the Companions, that first, well-nigh infallible generation of Muslims who had direct experience of the Prophet. The Shi'ite "traditions," on the other hand, find their validity in the testimony, or better, the authoritative teaching of the *Imams*.[40]

Regarding the other "sources" admitted by the Sunni jurists since the middle of the eighth century—the consensus of the community and the use of analogous reasoning—the Shi'ites were strenuous in their objections. Consensus was nothing more than the universal recognition of something already taught by an *Imam*. Analogical reasoning was likewise resisted by the Shi'ites, perhaps as early as the time of Shafi'i himself, and from Kulini to al-Murtada the notion of an independent use of reasoning, with its implication of a defect in the teaching of the *Imams*, was cast from among the "sources of the Law."

Despite these obviously radical differences on the very foundations of jurisprudence, Shi'ite legal prescriptions differed very

40. Chiefly the sixth *Imam* Ja'far al-Sadiq (d. 765), who is the guarantor of over half the *hadith* cited in the standard Shi'ite collections, a fact that once again points to the generation of Ja'far as the critical one in the formulation of Shi'ite ideology.

little from the codes of the four Sunni schools. Where the two bodies of Muslim believers effectively parted company was in dogmatic theology. For the Shi'ite no less than for the conservative Sunni, the understanding of the nature of God and the economy of salvation rested upon the *Qur'an* and the same body of *hadith* from which the Law was derived. Kulini, Ibn Babuyah and their successors were, then, theologians as well as jurists.

There were theologians among the Rafidites before 900—Hisham ibn al-Hakam was one of them—but it was not until after that date that the Shi'ites began to interest themselves in the *kalam* model of theology that had first been elaborated by the Mu'tazilites. The closure with Mu'tazilitism, an event associated with various members of the Nawbakhti family, proved, however, as little agreeable to most Shi'ites as contemporary Mu'tazilitism was to the Sunni adherents of Ahmad ibn Hanbal.

The earliest Shi'ite spokesman against the *kalam* was Ibn Babuyah, who energetically attacked the new dialectic in his dogmatic writings, *The Beliefs of the Imamites* and *The Book of the Unity of God*. His weapons were, of course, the transmitted teachings of the *Imams*, themselves not completely free of Mu'tazilite influences.[41] Thus, while Ibn Babuyah was occasionally betrayed by history into agreeing with certain positions of the Mu'tazilites against the more literalist reading of the *Qur'an*, he was opposed in principle to the method of *kalam* and argued strongly against its use.

Ibn Babuyah's position on *kalam* was not very different, perhaps, from that of a contemporary Hanbalite. Al-Mufid, on the other hand, saw the value of *kalam* as precisely the defensive weapon it was intended to be. In his commentary on Ibn Babuyah's *Beliefs*, pointedly entitled *The Correction*, he accused his predecessor of adopting a reactionary position. For al-Mufid rational discussions served a useful purpose—his works contain descriptions of a number of such, including one with the Ash'arite *mutakallim* Baqillani—and in his *Fundamental Views* he

---

41. Ibn Babuyah was deeply interested, for example, in the eighth *Imam*, 'Ali al-Rida (d. 818), the protégé of Ma'mun (see Chap. II, pp. 166–167), and he collected the traditions relating to him and proceeding from him in his *Sources of Information on al-Rida*.

did not hesitate to elaborate on questions of *kalam* for which there was no precedent in the received teachings of the Shi'ite *Imams.*

Al-Mufid returned, in effect, to a stance closer to the Nawbakhtis' in the preceding century. His differences with the Mut'azilites on specific points ran very deep, but elsewhere he was not embarrassed to agree with them and even to see some value in their methods. His student al-Murtada went even further. He had studied with the most eminent Mu'tazilite of his day, 'Abd al-Jabbar (d. 1025), and the effect of the Mu'tazilite's thinly disguised rationalism is apparent from the outset in al-Murtada's approach to theology. The fundamental truths of religion are derived in the first resort from reason alone, and to rely for our knowledge of them exclusively upon authoritative teaching (*taqlid*) is indefensible. No Mu'tazilite could have put it more clearly or more forcibly.

The Buyids never reaped this important Shi'ite elaboration of the faith; it passed instead into the hands of a later generation of Iranian Shi'ites under the dynasty of the Safavids (1501–1732). The Buyids encouraged Shi'ism of this moderate sort, but they never sought to establish it in any political sense of the word. To honor the 'Alid past and to rule in the 'Abbasid present was apparently enough.

It was in the changing political circumstances of a Fatimid Cairo and a Buyid Baghdad that Hanbalite virtue stood revealed. The Hanbalite opposition to Shi'ism and their solicitude for the "*sunnah* and community" were, in effect, a defense of the 'Abbasid house. This surely was not the intent of the Hanbalites; their primary interest was in the *shari'ah* and not the 'Abbasids, and they contested with the Mu'tazilites and Ash'arites as fiercely as they did with the Shi'ah. The context was inevitably legal, and the issue, equally inevitably, was *kalam.*

The tenth century is not particularly luminous in *kalam.* The chief Baghdad Hanbalite of the time, Ibn Batta (d. 997), has been published and studied,[42] but the links between al-Ash'ari or the

---

42. Ibn Batta's chief work was, as might be expected of a Hanbalite, a profession of faith, the *Exposition of the Sources of Sunnah and of Religion.*

Mu'tazilite Abu Hashim and the eminent *mutakallimun* writing about the year 1000 are little more than names: Ash'ari's disciple al-Bahili, a convert from Shi'ism and the teacher of Baqillani; and Abu Hashim's student Abu 'Abdallah al-Basri, who instructed the *qadi* 'Abd al-Jabbar.

On the testimony of the Ash'arites themselves, their founder's attempt at finding a "middle way" between traditionalism and *kalam* was not crowned with success—or not, at any rate, until the time of al-Baqillani (d. 1013). Baqillani was one of a triad of Ash'arites at the end of the tenth century—Ibn Furaq (d. 1015) and Abu Ishaq al-Isfara'ini (d. 1027) were the others—who saved the feeble Ash'arism from extinction at the hands of the Baghdad Hanbalites. The teachings of al-Ash'ari received little or no hearing at Baghdad itself, but farther east, at Nishapur, for example, some shallow roots were put down. Ibn Furaq and al-Isfara'ini each had his own law school (*madrasah*) at Nishapur. The subject of their instruction was doubtless jurisprudence—a chair in *kalam* was unheard of—but the point was that Ash'arism had gained a modest foothold within Shafi'ite legal circles and so had taken its first step toward orthodoxy.

Al-Baqillani's task at Baghdad was considerably more difficult. Resistance to *kalam* ran deep among the Hanbalites, who dominated the law schools there during the first half of the eleventh century. The partisans of Ash'arism had to struggle long and earnestly to retort to the long list of traditions attributed to everyone from the Prophet to al-Shafi'i—whose presence in the list was particularly embarrassing—to the effect that speculative theology was the next thing to *zandaqah*. Nor was Baqillani's work rendered any easier by the fact that he and his two Ash'arite contemporaries were clearly reverting to something close to Mu'tazilite rationalism.

Most of what we know of Ibn Furaq must be reconstructed out of the polemics of his Mu'tazilite contemporary at Rayy, 'Abd al-Jabbar, but for al-Baqillani at least there is a substantial body of preserved work,[43] including the first Ash'arite *summa*, his *Preparation for the Refutation of Worthless Atheism*. The *Preparation* is still part polemical and part systematic, and a good

43. For his *Inimitability of the Qur'an*, see Chap. III, p. 234.

deal of it is taken up with replying to some familiar adversaries: the dualists, Brahmins, Dahriyah, Daysaniyah, Christians, Jews and, finally, the Shi'ite and Kharijite theories of the Imamate. At the beginning, however, the reader is presented with a systematic prolegomenon whose structure is not unlike that of later developed *kalam* works, and here Baqillani set out the crucial issues. He had once publicly disputed with the Mu'tazilites, before 'Adud al-Dawlah in Shiraz, but the fact is that their problems are also his, and their method of solving them, the essential *kalam*, is likewise his.

Baqillani was as strongly convinced of the necessity of speculative knowledge as any Mu'tazilite. Mu'tazilite atomism shored up his positions as surely as it had Ash'ari's,[44] though the later Mu'tazilite efforts at toning down its occasionalist implications by introducing the quasi-causal notion of "generation" met with little approval from Baqillani. The Ash'arites were generally content to rest unembarrassed upon their occasionalism, but here too Baqillani may have reached into the Mu'tazilite armory for a small palliative. Al-Ka'bi had opposed the general Mu'tazilite drift toward a natural secondary causality on the Greek model. For it he substituted the notion of a "customary sequence" in God's creative activity. God creates every body, atom and accident "at every moment," as the Ash'arites put it; according to Ka'bi, the pattern of this creative activity settles into certain habitual configurations which man, for his part, mistakenly infers are the indicators of a causal sequence. This is Baqillani's view too, and it became in time the standard one among the Ash'arites. And like much else in Baqillani it suggestively echoes contemporary Mu'tazilitism.

A considerable part of the *Preparation* is given over to a question of consuming practical and theoretical interest in the tenth century, that of the Imamate. Baqillani came to it in normal Sunni fashion, as a juridical problem. The Shi'ites based their claim to that office on a number of *hadith*, which Baqillani took up and subjected to criticism. The alleged designation of 'Ali

---

44. Baqillani went somewhat further on one point: he accepted, as Ash'ari did not, Abu Hashim's theory of "modes." See Chap. VI, p. 457.

by the Prophet himself, for example, is guaranteed by the testimony of 'Ali alone, and Baqillani raised all the standard legal arguments against the class of *hadith* resting upon a single witness.

Nowhere will Baqillani concede that the Imamate is a supernatural or charismatic office. For him, as for all the Sunni jurists, the Imamate is no other than the Caliphate, a temporal office bestowed by contract by a body of qualified Muslims. The qualities of the *Imam* are those of the Caliph: a Quraysh, though not necessarily of the Banu Hashim as the Shi'ites maintained, a man of mature judgment and of sufficient moral and physical vigor to redress wrongs and conduct wars against the enemies of Islam. Nowhere is it a question of transcendental power or of infallibility.

The Muslim (and Ash'arite) account of the success of Ash'arite *kalam* assigned a prominent role to Baqillani, and for reasons that are no longer quite clear to us. His contributions may have been systematic rather than substantial, however, and their acceptance may have depended as much upon political circumstances as Baqillani's accomplishments as a *mutakallim.* The fate of the school was not, in any event, being decided in Baghdad but in the East, where Ibn Furaq, al-Isfara'ini and the latter's student 'Abd al-Qahir al-Baghdadi (d. 1037) were teaching. Nothing of Isfara'ini's work has survived, but from al-Baghdadi we have two important books, the systematic *Roots of Religion* and his heresiography, *The Sects.* Other of Baghdadi's tracts against Abu al-Hudhayl and Ibn Karram, whose followers al-Baghdadi debated at Ghazna and who were still an important influence in the East, are lost.

During the lifetime of these scholars the Turkish Ghaznavids became the paramount political power in the eastern lands of the Caliphate. The Ghaznavid Sultans were themselves theological eclectics, or perhaps simply political opportunists. They were Shafi'ites at law and at first supported the *kalam* of Ibn Karram, a fact that in 1015 led to the execution of Ibn Furaq, a Hanafite at law and an Ash'arite *mutakallim.* More importantly, the Ghaznavids remained Sunnis and were committed foes of both the *Shi'at 'Ali* in its new virulent form and of the waning Mu'tazilah whose last great representative, the *qadi* 'Abd al-Jabbar, died in

1025, eight years after the Sultan Mahmud and the Caliph al-Qadir came to terms on the subject of religious orthodoxy.

Mahmud had dismembered the neighboring principality of the Samanids in the name of Caliphal legitimacy, and thereafter the growing rapport between 'Abbasid Caliph and Ghaznavid Sultan had bracing effects on both sides. Mahmud used his leverage at Baghdad to exclude his rivals from Caliphal favor; he was insistent in his demands that all the Caliph's dealings with the Qarakhanids and, to a lesser extent, with the Khwarazmshahs pass through him. Al-Qadir (991–1031), on the other hand, had found a counterweight against the failing Buyids. Political action against these latter was out of the question, but in 1017, and again a year later, the Caliph promulgated statements of faith specifically directed against the Mu'tazilites and Shi'ites and called for a public repudiation of both sects, a suggestion that Mahmud promptly put into effect in his own realms.

The Shi'ite Buyids appear not to have reacted; indeed, the quality of their Shi'ism is very difficult to determine. The very first of them to rule in Baghdad, Mu'izz al-Dawlah, instituted a public celebration of the major Shi'ite holy day, the *'Ashura'*, in commemoration of Husayn's bloody death at Karbala' in 680. It was, in effect, a public provocation, but there was no political sequel save an almost halfhearted attempt on the part of Baha' al-Dawlah to have a Shi'ite appointed Chief Qadi and director of the pilgrimage to Mecca. The 'Abbasid Caliph was left to rule, however, if only in name, over his empire. The Caliphs for their part made no overt protest against their masters until al-Qadir's professions of faith in 1017 and 1018. The presence of Mahmud may have done much to stiffen the Caliph's determination on that occasion, but he had other allies, and much closer to home.

The Shi'ite festivals provoked an extraordinary state of unrest among the Sunni population of Iraq, and there was more than one request to the Buyid *amir* to reconsider. The Baghdad Shi'ites, who were likely as confused about Buyid intentions as we are, further inflamed the situation by loudly recognizing what seemed to be a far more potent and committed ally, the Fatimid Caliph of Cairo. The public outcry came to a climax in 1016–1017 with arson and rioting at Husayn's tomb at Karbala', in Samarra,

Baghdad, Mecca and Medina. Circumstances had provided al-Qadir his opportunity to speak out.

Al-Qadir's resort to a statement of orthodoxy had not been attempted by the 'Abbasids since Ma'mun promulgated his Mu'tazilite theses and instituted the *mihnah* to assure compliance. In that instance the target was the Hanbalites and other traditionalists, but now, two centuries later, the former targets had become the instigators. Since Mutawakkil's acknowledgment of Ahmad ibn Hanbal, the Baghdad Hanbalites were the chief defenders of "the *sunnah* and the community" against the rising influence of the Shi'ites, and a review of Hanbalite creeds from those of Ibn Hanbal through the later statements of Barbahari and Ibn Batta reveals their fierce and selective resistance to two movements, the Mu'tazilites and the *Shi'at 'Ali,* once allies but now gone their separate ways.

The tenth-century Hanbalites treated both groups with an evenhanded condemnation, but al-Qadir, who had to deal with political realities, was far more concerned with the Shi'ites.[45] And the Baghdad Hanbalites were his natural allies; the professions of faith promulgated by al-Qadir and his son al-Qa'im (1031–1075) echo almost exactly the *Exposition* of the chief Hanbalite of the former generation, Ibn Batta (d. 997). During al-Qadir's own day the Baghdad Hanbalites were under the intellectual leadership of Abu Ya'la Ibn al-Farra' (d. 1066), who had refused the post of Chief Qadi under al-Qadir but accepted it under his successor. In addition to playing Ibn abi Du'ad to al-Qa'im's Wathiq, Abu Ya'la, by his own efforts and those of his peripatetic students,[46] converted the doctrine of the founder and his immediate disciples from a legal point of view into a formal school.

The chief preserved work of Abu Ya'la, his *Trustworthy*

---

45. There were some measures taken against the Mu'tazilites under both al-Qadir and his son al-Qa'im, and there were occasional outbreaks of violence against the Mu'tazilah of Baghdad as late as 1067.
46. Among them Abu al-Faraj al-Shirazi (d. 1094), the propagator of Hanbalism in Syria, and Abu Ja'far al-Hashimi (d. 1077), who carried on the struggle for the Hanbalite point of view under the early Seljuqs; see Chap. IX, p. 686.

Book, shows that the polemical landscape had not greatly changed from what it had been earlier. Though the Karramiyah were promoted to a new prominence, the issues were still the divine attributes, free will and the Imamate, and the adversaries remained the Rafidite Shi'ites, the Mu'tazilites and, with a new and perhaps urgent emphasis, the Ash'arites, whose influence was growing a century after Ash'ari's own death. On the question of the Imamate, Abu Ya'la was an 'Abbasid legitimist and he stoutly defended the right of any of the Quraysh to possess the Caliphate in the face of Shi'ite claims that it belonged by right only to the descendants of 'Ali and Fatimah.

Mahmud was not, then, the only 'Abbasid legitimist in the Caliph's troubled empire. The Ghaznavid Sultan and the Baghdad Hanbalites had, perhaps, little else in common. Mahmud was, in his own changeable way, a fancier of *kalam*—not the Mu'tazilite variety, to be sure, but the somewhat more orthodox version circulated under the name of Ibn Karram. The dialogue was lively at Ghazna, and at least one eminent Ash'arite, Ibn Furaq, lost his life as well as the debate against the Karramiyah. But no more than two years later, in 1017, when the word came from al-Qadir, Mahmud included the Karramites under the prohibition against the Ash'arite and Mu'tazilite *mutakallimun*. The long Hanbalite arm was clearly capable of reaching from Baghdad to Ghazna.

At 'Abd al-Jabbar's death in 1025 the issue of *kalam* was still unresolved. The Mu'tazilites' attempts at carving out a separate domain for theology were unsuccessful, condemned as much by their guilty association with Shi'ism as by their apparent competition with what had been devised by the lawyers as Muslim orthodoxy. Some Mu'tazilite theses were far too sophisticated to arouse any but the very learned, but in some areas they had openly sinned against Qur'anic sensibilities. Everyone could understand the proposition that the *Qur'an* was a "created" document, even if they could not savor the metaphysic that justified it. The noisy heretics Abu 'Isa al-Warraq and Ibn al-Rewandi, both former Mu'tazilites, stirred up additional controversy. And above all there was the repudiated 'Alid policy of Ma'mun, a policy in which the Mu'tazilites were inextricably entangled.

Kalam was not, however, a dead issue. It could not be sustained as an autonomous discipline, but the methods of the *mutakallimun* could find a place, as Ash'ari and others perceived, within the legal schools. Ash'arism was, then, a kind of Shafi'ite method at this point, or aspired to be such. Other *mutakallimun* had similar aspirations, and both the later Mu'tazilites and the Karramiyah, followed by the Maturidites, struggled for possession of the Hanafite "school." Ibn Hanbal's followers resisted *kalam* on all these fronts, aided at the turn into the tenth century by events that shook the Caliphate to its foundations. The new and dangerous turnings of Shi'ism contributed more to the Sunni posture of orthodox Islam and the compromise triumph of Ash'arism than any Caliph, theologian or lawyer.

The Failed Revolution: The Isma'ilis

According to a story circulating among the orthodox toward the end of the tenth century,[47] the origins of the revolutionary Shi'ite sect known as the Isma'iliyah were to be sought among the companions of the sixth Shi'ite *Imam,* Ja'far al-Sadiq (d. 765). As has been seen, Ja'far was himself one of the chief ideologues of Imamite Shi'ism, that branch of the *Shi'at 'Ali* that acknowledged a line of designated and divinely guided *Imams.* Ja'far was the sixth in that line, and the great mass of the Imamite Shi'ah cast their allegiance to Ja'far's son Musa al-Kazim and his descendants down to the "concealment" of the twelth *Imam* sometime after 874.

Not everyone followed Musa, however. Ja'far had earlier designated an older son, Isma'il, as his successor, but Isma'il died before his father and it became a matter of dispute among Ja'far's followers whether the Imamate had passed on the designation principle to Musa al-Kazim or on the dynastic principle to Isma'il's son Muhammad. The debate led to schism and eventually to the appearance of the Isma'iliyah or "Sevener" Shi'ites.

What had occurred among Ja'far's followers was more than a

---

47. Its first known narrator was a certain Ibn Rizam, who lived about 950. From him it found its way into Ibn al-Nadim and then to a large number of historians.

dynastic quarrel; there was ideology involved, and the tale told among the orthodox centered not so much on the *Imams* as on their ideologues. The first of them was Abu al-Khattab (d. c. 762), who has already been noted for the extremist teachings that led Ja'far in the end to repudiate him. Earlier, among Muhammad al-Baqir's followers there had been another such teacher, Maymun al-Qaddah (d. c. 796), and his son 'Abdallah ibn Maymun (d. 825) was similarly active in Ja'far's circle. According to the story, these three men were the true founders of Isma'ilism: they had supported the Imamate of Isma'il and were as well the creators of the peculiar teachings that characterized the Isma'ili Shi'ah.

The key to that teaching was the doctrine that there were two meanings to Scripture and so also to Islam: a plain or surface meaning (*zahir*) and a deeper reading (*batin*) that revealed the true spiritual reality behind the text. To elicit the spiritual sense, the "reality" (*haqiqah*) of Scripture, Abu al-Khattab wielded the supple instrument of allegorical exegesis whereby the images and even the very letters of the *Qur'an* were forced to yield up their truths. Maymun's own contribution is unclear, except that he was called, by hostile witnesses, it is true, a Daysanite; that is, an adherent of any one of the complex pattern of beliefs associated with that Christian sect. His son 'Abdallah, we are told, claimed prophetic powers for himself down to his death at Salamiyah in Syria in 825.

After the death of 'Abdallah ibn Maymun little is heard of the new Isma'ili wing of the Shi'ah. They must have been active, however, since between 850 and 875 Isma'ili missionaries or "summoners" (*da'i;* pl. *du'at*) spread from Salamiyah all over the 'Abbasid empire. They were particularly strong in Iraq, the Yemen, Syria and Iran. In this latter area we can see something of their methods: they concentrated on areas with strong Shi'ite affinities like Rayy, Qumm and the lands south of the Caspian Sea. In Iraq, which was still recovering from the social and economic shocks of the war of the Zanj, propaganda was aimed primarily at the lower classes of agricultural peasants and Bedouin, while in Iran efforts were made to convert the local governors to the Isma'ili persuasion.

What that persuasion was in the late ninth century was a hope in the imminent return of the *Mahdi*, Ja'far's grandson Muhammad ibn Isma'il. This was the expectation to which Husayn al-Ahwazi, the *da'i* of Iraq, won a man named Hamdan Qarmat in 875; and though Hamdan's own field of activity continued to be Iraq, where he eventually became chief of the Isma'ili apparatus, there were doubtless lines running back to what had become the center for planned political activity against the 'Abbasids, Salamiyah in Syria.

Hamdan and his chief associate, his brother-in-law 'Abdan, concentrated their energies in the vicinity of Wasit and Kufah. In 890 Hamdan founded near that latter city his "retreat house" whence the "call" (*da'wah*) went out all through the cultivated lands of southern Iraq, a call to a revolutionary eschatology initiated by the immediately expected return of the *Imam* Muhammad ibn Isma'il. The Islamic Law was abrogated, it was announced, and the resurrection was near at hand.

This expectation revealed in turn an elaborate view of prophetic history, a view that was already present, perhaps, in the teachings of Abu al-Khattab but is known to us from one of the few pieces of early Isma'ili literature preserved, *The True Direction and Right Course* by the Yemeni *da'i* Husayn al-Hawsab. History, we are told, has shown a succession of six Prophet-Speakers, each of whom has revealed a Law. This is the exoteric revelation (*zahir*), but its true inner significance (*batin*) depends on each Prophet's Executor, who follows him and gives instruction on the essential allegorical exegesis of the revealed Law. Each Executor in turn is the foundation of a line of seven successive *Imams*, and each of the latter is concerned with a combined exoteric-esoteric understanding of the Law.

At this point in history all six of the Prophets have made their appearance: Adam, Noah, Abraham, Moses, Jesus and Muhammad, each followed by his appropriate Executor, in Muhammad's case 'Ali, and a succession of *Imams*. All that remained, according to the Isma'ilis, was for the cycle to draw to a close with the *parousia* of the seventh Prophet who combines within himself the function of both Speaker and Executor. He is the *Mahdi*, the "*Imam* of the Resurrection," and his name is Muhammad. For Hamdan and his followers there could be no doubt: the *Mahdi* was Muhammad ibn Isma'il, the "concealed" grandson of Ja'far al-Sadiq.

The message of the Isma'ili *da'i* and his energetic assistant stirred expectations and a sense of joyful release among the oppressed Aramaeans of Iraq and the Bedouin of the nearby steppe. The area had been in turmoil since the upheavals of the Zanj and complete government control had never been effectively reestablished. Baghdad was eventually made aware of what was going on around Kufah and Wasit, where the economic patterns of life were being disrupted in the name of an eschatological *anomie*. Nothing was done, however.

While Hamdan was preaching his message, the Isma'iliyah made an important and effective convert in Iraq, the Yemenite Abu 'Abdallah. After his conversion Abu 'Abdallah was sent for his training to the *da'i* of the Yemen, Husayn al-Hawsab, and then in 892–893 began his own missionary endeavors by accompanying a group of Berber pilgrims on their way home to Ifriqiyah. At first he made little headway there against the determined opposition of the Aghlabids, but a foothold was finally gained on the strength of Berber dissatisfaction with their Arab masters. The hold was secure enough, at any rate, to draw the true leader of the Isma'iliyah, 'Ubaydallah, from the obscurity of Salamiyah into the light of history.

'Ubaydallah may have been an assumed name—according to later Sunni detractors, his real name was Sa'id—but he was reputed to be the descendant of Ja'far's grandson Muhammad. According to 'Ubaydallah's official biographers, the *Imam* Muhammad ibn Isma'il did not disappear, as many thought, into an eschatological future, but both he and his descendants 'Abdallah, Ahmad and Husayn went into and remained in seclusion. It was the son of this latter Husayn, 'Ubaydallah, who now emerged from concealment and made public claim to the Imamate on the ground prepared in Ifriqiyah by his *da'i* Abu 'Abdallah.

The Sunnis furiously contested this version of 'Ubaydallah's genealogy. The 'Abdallah who appeared in the family tree as 'Ubaydallah's great-grandfather was not, they maintained, the son of the *Imam* Muhammad ibn Isma'il but the son of Maymun al-Qaddah. The 'Abbasids would grant their rivals their ideology but not their impeccable 'Alid genealogy, which remained, quite obviously, a potent weapon in the struggle for legitimacy. The very name assumed by 'Ubaydallah's descendants, the Fatimids, pointed this weapon against the 'Abbasids: the *Imams* soon to become established in Egypt were the scions of 'Ali and Fatimah, the daughter of the Prophet, while the best the 'Abbasids could do was to raise their tenuous connection with 'Ali's other, non-Fatimid son, Muhammad ibn al-Hanafiyah.

In 899, before 'Ubaydallah joined his *da'i* in Ifriqiyah, the Isma'ili movement was convulsed by a major disagreement, possibly provoked by 'Ubaydallah's announced claim of the Imamate for himself rather than for the "concealed" Muhammad ibn Isma'il. This is pure speculation based in the main on the execution, apparently at the instigation of 'Ubaydallah's agents, of 'Abdan—the *da'i* Hamdan barely managed to escape a fate that was intended for him as well—and the later refusal of their followers, the so-called Qarmatians, to accept the Imamate of the Fatimids.

From 899 onward there were, then, two branches of the Isma'iliyah: those who accepted the historical Imamate of 'Ubaydallah and eventually held sway in Egypt as the Fatimid dynasty; and the Qarmatians, who clung to their expectation of the *Imam* Muhammad ibn Isma'il. These latter were to be found chiefly in Iraq and some even in Baghdad, where in 925 the vizier al-Khaqani had to take measures against some Messianic-minded Isma'ilis. Qarmatianism was Hamdan's version of the *da'wah*, and his former jurisdiction in Iraq was for a time under the direction of 'Abdan's nephew.

From southern Iraq the Isma'ili "call" spread among the Bedouin of the Syrian steppe. The *da'i* there was Zikrawayh, who was sent out in the first instance to replace Hamdan and 'Abdan in 899,[48] but was now, together with his sons, at the head of a spreading revolutionary movement of impressive force. By 903 Damascus was under a state of Qarmatian siege, and later in that same year the marauding Bedouin broke into Salamiyah and massacred among others the family of 'Ubaydallah. But the self-

---

48. It may have been Zikrawayh's supporters who were responsible for 'Abdan's death and Hamdan's flight.

declared *Imam*, who was already regarded as a usurper by the Iraqi wing of the Isma'iliyah, had made his escape to Egypt and thence to North Africa. The violent beginnings in Syria could not be sustained, however. The Qarmatian leaders were captured, and with Zikrawayh's death in 906 the Syrian Isma'iliyah lost its energy.

There was a more permanent Qarmatian success in the towns around Bahrayn on the Persian Gulf. Before the events of 899, Hamdan had sent one of his agents there, Abu Sa'id al-Jannabi, and by the time of 'Abdan's murder Abu Sa'id had gained political control of Bahrayn and established the first Isma'ili state. As a direct result of that murder the new rulers of Bahrayn did not recognize the Imamate of 'Ubaydallah or of his Fatimid successors, but adhered instead to the original eschatological form of Isma'ilism preached by Hamdan.

'Ubaydallah's own fortunes progressed slowly at first. From a small beginning among the Berbers on the western borders of Ifriqiyah, Abu 'Abdallah preached the Isma'ili message tirelessly. The province itself was filled with dissidents; the Kharijite Berbers, their own Arab troops and the lawyers of Qayrawan were all unhappy with the Aghlabids' outwardly successful rule. The last of the dynasty's great *amirs*, Ibrahim II (875–902), was forced, by 'Abbasid pressure applied from the unlikely distance of Baghdad, to resign.

Despite serious setbacks suffered by Abu 'Abdallah at the hands of government troops, 'Ubaydallah chose to escape the increasingly threatening situation in Syria and join his energetic missionary in Ifriqiyah. He never made contact with his *da'i* but wandered west and south of the Atlas until he was taken and interned in the distant Kharijite city of Sijilmassah. Oddly, 'Ubaydallah's arrest coincided with the first major Isma'ili victory. The pious Aghlabid *amir* 'Abdallah II (902–903) was murdered by his worthless son Ziyadat Allah III (903–909), and thereafter Abu 'Abdallah and his troops suffered no serious military reverses. City after city fell to the Isma'ilis between 906 and 909, when the last Aghlabid prince deserted his capital at Raqqadah south of Qayrawan and fled to 'Abbasid protection in Egypt. Abu 'Abdallah occupied his prize in March of 909. A column was sent off to release 'Ubaydallah from Sijilmassah, and at the beginning of the new year the Fatimid *Imam* took possession of his earthly kingdom.

'Ubaydallah's triumphant enthronement in Raqqadah marked the successful conclusion of years of effort on Abu 'Abdallah's part and then, almost immediately, the beginnings of new doubts. 'Ubaydallah had been announced to his devotees as the *Mahdi*. He brought in his wake, however, politics and not the Resurrection. The faith of some began to waver, Abu 'Abdallah among them, as their expectations were disappointed. 'Ubaydallah must have judged that he had little choice but to do away with his once faithful *da'i*. It was done in 911, and in an effort to bolster his regime, he announced in the following year that the succession to the Imamate belonged to his son Abu al-Qasim, who immediately assumed the Messianic title of al-Qa'im, "The *Imam* of the Resurrection."

After 912 al-Qa'im dominates the propaganda and activities of the Fatimid Isma'ilis. Their later Sunni adversaries read in this a clear confession on 'Ubaydallah's part that his genealogical pretensions were not credited in Ifriqiyah and that as a result he had tried to pawn off al-Qa'im, who was not really his son, as a more likely descendant of Isma'il ibn Ja'far. We will never, perhaps, know the truth of these allegations; what we do know, however, is that neither 'Ubaydallah nor al-Qa'im did in fact announce the "Resurrection" (*qiyamah*) as it was understood in Iraq by the Qarmatians. The end-time was once again postponed, and the Fatimids ruled as Caliph-*Imams* rather than as eschatological *Mahdis*. The *shari'ah* was not abrogated.

What, then, was the position of the Fatimids? Since they had not ushered in the end-time, as the early Isma'ilis had expected and as 'Ubaydallah had perhaps at first promised, what was their claim to either temporal or spiritual leadership in Islam? An answer was forthcoming in the reign of the Fatimid Caliph al-Mu'izz (953–975). By his own writings and those of his spokesmen, Mu'izz attempted to dampen down some of the revolutionary eschatology of the Isma'iliyah. The failure of expectations had plagued 'Ubaydallah early on in Ifriqiyah and was even then breeding a similar disenchantment among the Isma'ilis of Iran. To check the disease, Mu'izz invoked a new understanding of history.

Neither side in the developing controversy, the pragmatic Fatimids or the revolutionary Qarmatians, was willing to deny that the first coming of Imam Muhammad ibn Isma'il had ended the era of the Prophet Muhammad; they merely drew different conclusions about the operation of the new dispensation. The Fatimids, whom history had raised to rule in Egypt, were willing to embrace a historical Caliphate between the First and Second Coming; the Qarmatians, to whom history denied its rewards, abrogated the historical *shari'ah*.

The debate between the two camps was exceedingly subtle, resting as it did upon a complex "spiritual" reading of history. The Prophet Muhammad had introduced the notion of a sacred history into Islam by locating his own mission in the succession of Judaeo-Christian Prophets. But he had also brought the prophetic phase of that sacred history to an end by declaring himself the "Seal of the Prophets." Thereafter the *ummah* might have its history, but prophetism was a closed book. For the Shi'ites in general and the Isma'ilis in particular, the book was not closed. The fundamental ambiguity of the office of "successor" (*khalifah*) to the Prophet of Islam and their own exaltation of 'Ali combined to reopen the prophetic line to the Shi'ites and to suggest to the Isma'ilis, at the same time, its final closure.

In the end the Isma'ilis rewrote the whole of prophetic history from Adam to 'Ali and his successors. By omitting, on the basis of the original Rafidite premise, the second, third and fourth Caliphs from their considerations, they had perforce to explain the special relationship that existed between Muhammad and 'Ali and that overrode all other claims to the Imamate. 'Ali's investiture was not merely defensible or desirable in Isma'ili eyes; it was inevitable, because it conformed to the pattern of sacred history. Each Prophet had, as has been seen, his "Executor": Adam had Seth, Moses had Aaron, and Jesus had Simon Peter. That was the divine plan. But each Executor was, like the Prophet he followed, mortal, and when he died there was an interval before the appearance of the next Prophet in the cycle. Here the Isma'ilis postulated the institution of the Imamate, a succession of leaders who continued the teaching of the Executor until the coming of the next Prophet.

The motives at work in the construction of this theory were

manifold: the Isma'ilis' desire to justify their claim to the Imamate by their 'Alid descent and not merely by their Quraysh connections; the Shi'ites' early and persistent magnification, though not the divinization,[49] of 'Ali to defend him against the obvious historical reality of an Abu Bakr or an 'Umar; and, finally, the distinction, perhaps first formulated among the followers of Ja'far al-Sadiq, between the "apparent" and the "concealed" reality of things. Muhammad and his revelation were the tokens of the first; the *Imams* who succeeded him were the guardians of the *batin*.

Most of this could doubtless be extrapolated from a "reading" of sacred history nuanced by political ambitions. Even the distinction between the "apparent" and the "concealed" nature of reality is intelligible in terms of the dissimulation forced upon the Shi'ah by their singular and persistent failure to achieve political power. But nothing that was happening in the eighth and ninth centuries explains the larger cosmic pattern upon which this microcosmic sacred history was displayed. The Isma'ili *batin* opened to reveal not merely an allegorical reading of the *Qur'an* but a cosmic panorama that transcended and explained human history.

The Isma'ilis called this macrocosmic view "the truth" (*haqiqah*), or better, "the realities" (*haqa'iq*), and it was, quite simply, an Islamicized version of Gnosticism. Where it came from or through whose hands it passed is unknown. Abu al-Khattab (d. 762) may have been drawing upon it, and so too those still mysterious "extremists" who litter the dead ends of the earliest Shi'ism. And it was central to the Isma'ili understanding of history, the universe's, Islam's, and their own.

In its most general terms,[50] Gnosticism is an elitist understand-

---

49. One of the generally agreed-upon characteristics of the extremists (*ghulat*) among the Shi'ah was their divinization of 'Ali. There may have been such *ghulat* among the Isma'ilis, but they do not come into view until the time of al-Hakim; see Chap. IX, p. 640.

50. "Gnosticism" is used here and throughout to describe the generalized pattern of beliefs and practices visible throughout the Mediterranean world from the second century onward. The relationship of that complex to the specific Christian heresy also called "Gnosticism" is not in question here.

ing (Gr. *gnosis;* among the Muslims frequently *hikmah*) that brings salvation. For the Isma'ilis it was the "call" (*da'wah*), which was revealed in stages to the convert. The substance of this revelation was the body of spiritual realities concealed beneath the material and literal appearances. And in all its forms, Muslim as well as others, the "realities" included the narrative of the great cosmic drama that produced our universe, man's fallen state, and, in the end, his salvation.

The "realities" reveal a world of two, and then, on somewhat closer inspection, three dimensions. The first is that called by the Greek Gnostics the *pleroma,* the upper world of light and the totality of spiritual beings, a Plotinian landscape where there emanates from the supreme One, the God beyond being and description, a chain of spiritual hypostases. In Plotinus there were only two such, Universal Intelligence and Universal Soul, but he knew and disapproved of contemporary Gnostics who multiplied these hypostases beyond measure. The Isma'ili version knew ten such emanations or Intelligences proceeding from the First Cause. The first two are identical with Plotinus': Universal Intelligence and Universal Soul. Then follows a spiritual version of Adam and seven lower Intelligences, sometimes angelic and sometimes planetary, the whole not very different from the model current among the Platonizing Aristotelians who had given themselves over to *falsafah.*

To this point the Isma'ili cosmology might very well be a not unfamiliar version of a Greek emanationist schema concealed under Arabic terminology: the One unconsciously "initiated" the Universal Intelligence which in turn becomes its conscious instrument, its Word, in the production of all the rest. In Plotinus that "rest" descends by a gradual diminution of energy into the production of material beings, and it is at that point that Gnosticism made its break with Hellenism. For the Gnostic our world is not the result, as it was in Plotinus, of a natural diminution of powers but of a cosmic flaw, an unseemly event in the *pleroma* that leads directly to the production of our imperfect material world.

There was no Adam among the hypostases of Plotinus, but the Egyptian Gnostics did include a Primal Man among theirs, and Adam as both a spiritual reality and a historical man was much discussed in Rabbinical Judaism.[51] That line of thought comes to full flower in Islam within Sufi circles, as already has been seen, and in the Gnostic speculations of Isma'ilism. The third Intelligence in the series beneath the One is the Universal Man, the Spiritual Adam. But, for all his glory, he is heedless of the "call" whereby the First Intelligence reveals the truth of the One to the *pleroma*. Adam mistakenly thinks that the First Intelligence is God and for his sin he is cashiered to the position of tenth and last Intelligence.

Adam was not alone in the *pleroma* in misreading the *da'wah*. The angelic Intelligences, who now stood above him, likewise shared his doubt. Their doubt turned to panic and that in turn agitated the *pleroma* into those kinds of antic motion that result in the production of this material cosmos, the planets by the agitation of the angelic Intelligences and the moon by the agency of the Spiritual Adam. Finally, at the dense center of the system appeared the earth, and upon it the earthly Adam.

Most Gnostic systems made the cosmos evil from its origins, and even though the Isma'ilis saw the material universe as the direct result of a sin in the *pleroma*, they did attempt to do justice to the Biblical narrative. In their eyes the earthly Adam, who first appears in the terrestrial paradise of Ceylon, is not identical with the Prophet Adam. He knows not sin but, somewhat in the manner of the Iranian Gayomart, leads a utopian existence on earth in obedience to the tenth Intelligence, the Spiritual Adam.

The presence of the terrestrial Adam and the later arrival of the Prophet-Speaker Adam raised important questions for the Isma'ilis, since their cyclic view of history suggested that the end of the last era, the period after the coming of the *Mahdi*, would be similar to the time preceding the coming of the first Prophet-Speaker. For eschatologists like the Qarmatians the coming of the *Mahdi* meant the dissolution of the *shari'ah* into a perfect under-

---

51. The rabbis took their point of departure, much as Philo had done earlier (see p. 554), from the presence in *Genesis* of a duplicated Creation narrative wherein everything, including Adam, might be construed to have been created twice.

standing, and so they argued that before Adam's revelation there was also a perfect understanding of the "realities," an ideal period of cosmic history that corresponded with the era of the terrestrial Adam. One of the eastern Isma'ilis with a profound interest in philosophy even introduced the cosmological argument at this point: according to Abu Ya'qub al-Sijistani, the unity of God, the central truth among the "realities," could be read in the order and arrangement of the world.[52]

This matter of the abrogation of the Law was obviously of considerable importance to the Fatimids, who were politically committed to history and the theological *status quo*. One of their chief ideologues, al-Kirmani (d. after 1021), answered Abu Ya'qub's argument. He admitted the resemblance of the pre-Prophetic and post-*Mahdi* eras, but he denied that men who lived before the coming of the Prophet Adam had a complete understanding of the "realities." Why else, he asked, did Allah send Adam to reveal a *shari'ah* except that there was misunderstanding? In just the same manner, the period after the return of the *Mahdi* still had need of the guidance of a (Fatimid) *Imam* to explain and administer the Law.

Our Adam was, in any event, the initiator of a debased time when men see the spiritual realities only dimly through the *zahir* of the Law. Adam was a Prophet-Speaker who came with a material revelation whose spiritual sense must be explicated by his Executor, Seth. Thus began once again the "call" to the "realities" that is carried in the sequel through six successive Prophets, each assisted by his Executor and each followed by a cycle of seven *Imams*.

This cycle of Prophets-Executors-*Imams* came to an end with the appearance of the last *Imam* in the cycle begun by the Prophet Muhammad and his Executor 'Ali. Muhammad ibn

---

52. In another obvious retort to what was being discussed among the contemporary *mutakallimun*, Abu Ya'qub insisted that the coming of the *Mahdi* would abrogate only the purely positive prescriptions of the *shari'ah*, like those binding to prayer and almsgiving. The other, "rational" prescriptions are founded on man's nature and so can never be abrogated; see Chap. VI, p. 455.

Isma'il was the *Mahdi-Imam* of the Muslim cycle of prophecy. In the Fatimid view, his first coming did not, however, signal the abrogation of the Muslim *shari'ah* but rather the fulfillment of that Law and those of all the previous Prophets back to Adam. This was, in short, the fullness of time but not yet the Resurrection. Muhammad ibn Isma'il was currently in concealment, but during his temporary absence he appointed a series of Caliphs, or successors, to serve as guides until his final coming, not again in the flesh, as the Qarmatians and others believed, but in the spirit. The Fatimid ruler was the Caliph of the *Mahdi-Imam* Muhammad ibn Isma'il.

This theory, whether al-Mu'izz's or that of one of his theologians, was an ingeniously wrought compromise with the Qarmatian wing of the Isma'ilis, who had all along insisted that Muhammad ibn Isma'il was the *Mahdi*. They were apparently unwilling to accept the Imamate of 'Ubaydallah or his successors, but they might be persuaded to accept the Fatimid claim to being a somewhat vaguer "successor" or "guide." Mu'izz's doctrine may also have reassured the Sunnis by toning down the revolutionary resonances of the Qarmatian version. The Fatimids could now claim that nothing was changed in Islam but its understanding.

The Isma'ilis might concede Islam, but they were not about to compromise on the Caliphate. In the absence of the *Mahdi* the world had one ruler, the *Mahdi's* appointed Caliph or, to be more precise and more political, the Fatimid Caliph. It was from him that the "call" went forth, and it was he who in theory, if not always in practice, stood at the head of the Isma'ili apparatus that spread its propaganda network over the face of the *Dar al-Islam*.

We know something of the idealized structure of that apparatus but very little about how it operated. The prototype of the *da'wah* was to be found in the *pleroma*, and the degrees and grades of the cosmic Intelligences provided the pattern for the hierarchy that had the responsibility of disseminating the "call" here below. From the very first cycle, when Adam sent his representatives abroad, the earth has been divided into twelve districts. Into each of them the *da'wah* has gone forth, sent not by the *Imam* himself but by his divinely guided alter ego, his "Portal" (*Bab*). The *Bab* instructs and directs each of the district leaders who are called "Proofs" (*Hujjah*). Under the *Hujjah* in each district are the "Summoners" (*Du'at*) and the lesser degrees down to the simple initiate.

The organizational chart of the Isma'ili hierarchy has an impressive order to it. The order comes, of course, from its correspondence with the untroubled grades postulated among the Intelligences of the *pleroma*. Information on their fleshly counterparts is thin, however. What is certain is that not all of those in the apparatus who did the actual legwork, the "Summoners," took their marching orders from Qayrawan. In the early tenth century the Fatimids were merely the most successful branch of the Isma'iliyah, not its sole master. And in the years after 909, Fatimid ambitions were still too modest to reach into Iraq or Iran.

'Ubaydallah's ambitions did, however, extend beyond the walls of Qayrawan and even of Ifriqiyah itself. In 912–913 an army was fitted out and the newly designated *Mahdi* al-Qa'im led it eastward in an assault on Tripoli. In 914 there was a second raid toward the east. This time Barqa fell and then Alexandria, which al-Qa'im occupied in November, 914. The city could not be held, however, and al-Qa'im withdrew to the new Fatimid capital of Ifriqiyah at Mahdiyah.

The next Fatimid attempt against Egypt took place in 919. Once again Alexandria was occupied; but while al-Qa'im marched south and plundered the rich land of the Fayyum, the 'Abbasid Caliph took action. The general Mu'nis was dispatched with troops to Egypt. He arrived there toward the end of 920, and after a year of hard fighting al-Qa'im and his Berbers were forced once more to take the road back to Mahdiyah. Between 921 and 936 there were only desultory raids against Egypt. In the meantime 'Ubaydallah had died (934) and his son al-Qa'im (934–946) had succeeded him as head of the house; in Egypt the Caliph appointed a new governor, the Turkish captain Muhammad ibn Tughj (935–946), also known by his Central Asian title of *Ikhshid*.

Ibn Tughj was more than a match for the Fatimids. In 936 another of al-Qa'im's armies approached, once again took Alexandria, and once again was driven out by the Ikhshid's troops within a few months. The Fatimids did not return with any real success for nearly thirty years. Part of the credit belongs to Ibn

Tughj and his extraordinary Nubian slave Kafur,[53] but the Isma'ili *Imams* had their own distractions at home. In 943 there was a major Kharijite uprising in Ifriqiyah and within a year its leader, the schoolmaster Abu Yazid, entered Qayrawan and proclaimed its liberation from the Fatimid *Imam*.

There were many in Qayrawan who received the news with pleasure. As they later failed to convert the population of Egypt to their own version of Shi'ism, so the Fatimids ruled Ifriqiyah in a position of isolation between the Sunni Arabs, who included most of the intelligentsia, and the predominantly Kharijite Berbers. They held Mahdiyah in force, however, and if Abu Yazid was to succeed he had to take the Fatimids' capital. His Berbers besieged the city for ten months in 944–945, and then in an admission of failure withdrew westward to Qayrawan. Now the end was plain. Al-Qa'im died in 946 and later in that same year his son and successor al-Mansur (946–953) came up to Qayrawan in pursuit of Abu Yazid. The Kharijites' support was melting back into the mountains and the *Imam* inflicted a painful and decisive defeat on Abu Yazid's forces. The leader himself was tracked down and killed in the following year.

In 953 al-Mansur died and the new *Imam* was his son al-Mu'izz (953–975). The interrupted drive beyond the borders of Ifriqiyah was resumed and its direction was placed in the hands of Jawhar, a former Christian slave taken in Sicily. For ten years between 958 and 968 Fatimid arms were carried from Qayrawan to the Atlantic. Then Mu'izz turned to the Fatimids' earliest target, the 'Abbasid province of Egypt. The time was most opportune. The 'Abbasids of Iraq were in the grip of their new Shi'ite overlords, the Buyids, and in Egypt Kafur, the hand that had guided the state for the last twenty years, was dead.

In the beginning of 969 the Fatimid armies took the eastward routes traveled by al-Qa'im on many different occasions a half a century before. This time there was no turning back, and by August Jawhar was in Fustat, where he took possession of the

53. Kafur served as regent for Ibn Tughj's two sons from 946 to the death of the second of them in 966. Thereafter he ruled Egypt in his own name until his death in 968.

entire land of Egypt in the name of the Fatimid *Imam.* Almost immediately he laid out to the north of Fustat the new Fatimid capital in Egypt, al-Qahirah, "The Victorious."[54] Fustat, the city that had served the Muslims as their capital since the days of their arrival along the Nile, lingered on unchanged for another two centuries,[55] but it had neither hope nor expectation in the face of the glittering palace-city set down on its northern limits by Jawhar. In the summer of 972 al-Mu'izz arrived in state from Ifriqiyah to take up residence in his new domain, just a few months after Cairo had received and repulsed its first armed attack. The attackers were fellow Isma'ilis from Arabia.

There were Isma'ilis in Bahrayn from the opening years of the tenth century, and in addition to those Qarmatians there were other, less distinct Isma'ili groups scattered through Iraq, Iran and Syria. The latter are politically and ideologically obscure. The 'Abbasids appear to have repressed the original Isma'ilis of Syria during the first decade of the tenth century. There was activity around the edges of the Syrian steppe after that; it came not from Syria itself, however, but from raiders operating under the auspices of the Qarmatians of Bahrayn.

The founder of the Bahrayn line, Abu Sa'id al-Jannabi, died in 913 at the hands of one of his slaves. Some of his followers thought he would return, but the control of the political empire that was spreading from Bahrayn across Arabia and onto the adjacent steppe passed nonetheless into the hands of his brothers and some kind of advisory council of elders. For about ten years relations with the 'Abbasid Caliphate remained peaceful, perhaps, as some said, because of the vizier 'Ali ibn 'Isa's willingness to compromise with the Qarmatian menace. How menacing it indeed was appeared somewhat more clearly in 923 when one of Abu Sa'id's younger brothers, Abu Tahir, emerged as a military leader of the Qarmatians and boldly seized Basrah. Soon he

54. Or, according to another story that looked more to the astrological omens, "Mars," also, in Arabic, al-Qahirah.

55. It was burned down in 1169 by its governor to prevent the city's falling into the hands of the approaching Crusaders. Fustat was later rebuilt but never really revitalized.

demanded from the Caliph the city's legal cession to the Qarmatians, a demand that provoked the fall of 'Ali ibn 'Isa in Baghdad.

There was far worse to come. There were annual raids into Iraq and a Qarmatian army mounted the Euphrates and reached as far as Anbar in the vicinity of Baghdad. The capital was saved by the energy of Mu'nis, the police commandant of Baghdad, but the Qarmatians continued northward and plundered their way through upper Mesopotamia as far as Sinjar and Nisibis. In 930 Abu Tahir struck in another direction. For years the Qarmatians had been preying on the rich pilgrim trade between Iraq and Mecca; now Abu Tahir took and sacked the Holy City itself and carried off to Bahrayn the fetish of an outmoded and abrogated Islam, the black stone of the Ka'bah. It was a stunning gesture, but more to the point was the fact that the Qarmatians were in almost total control of southern Iraq and were a real and constant threat to Baghdad itself.

The Caliphate received an unexpected respite, however. Sometime around 930—the exact date is unknown—there appeared at Bahrayn a young man of Isfahan who claimed that he was the returned *Mahdi* Muhammad ibn Isma'il. The incident suggests that the house of Abu Sa'id al-Jannabi had remained true to Hamdan Qarmat's original teaching and had not claimed the Imamate for themselves, but that Abu Tahir at least had contented himself with some lesser title like "Companion" or "Proof" of the *Mahdi*. Now with the advent of the young Iranian, who somehow convinced Abu Tahir of the validity of his claims, the Qarmatians of Bahrayn embraced the total dialectic of the *parousia*.[56] There were serious consequences. The new *Mahdi* obviously had plans of his own, and they apparently did not include some of the old leadership; an unknown number of the chief men were executed at the *Mahdi's* command.

This curious messianic interval did not last very long. The new

---

56. There were still traces of the original, pre-Bahrayn Qarmatianism in Iraq. At the beginning of the tenth century it was under the leadership of 'Abdan's nephew 'Isa ibn Musa and in some manner cooperated with Abu Tahir's forays into central Iraq. It was likely 'Isa who was responsible for the Isma'ili works that later circulated under the name of 'Abdan.

Mahdi disappeared as abruptly as he had come, and the Qarmatians reverted to their hope of a Future Coming. The 'Abbasids meanwhile opened negotiations. Dealing and quarreling went on in alternating bursts, interrupted in 944 by the death of Abu Tahir. The sources do not agree on who succeeded him, and the custom of conciliar rule may well have created problems within the dynasty as Abu Tahir's brothers and sons struggled to possess themselves of the power he had accumulated. One of the brothers, Abu Mansur, appears to have succeeded, and it is likely he who agreed in 951 to return the black stone to Mecca.

Much of the credit for that restoration went to the contemporary Fatimid Caliph al-Mansur, largely because it was generally believed that the Qarmatians were part of a larger Isma'iliyah directed by the Fatimids. There is little evidence that such was the case, at least not since the persecution of Hamdan and 'Abdan by 'Ubaydallah's agents. It was more likely a huge ransom paid by Baghdad that got the stone back to Mecca. The Fatimids, of course, claimed the credit, while the Qarmatians, whose ideology had no place for stones, took the cash.

In the following decades there were sporadic Qarmatian assaults all around the Fertile Crescent and against the cities of Syria and Egypt. A Qarmatian force routed the Ikhshidid governor of Syria in 968 and he was forced to flee to Egypt. There was no safety there, since the Fatimids were already on the road to Fustat. The Ikhshid apparently felt that the Qarmatians were somewhat safer allies than the Fatimids; he returned to Syria and persuaded the Qarmatians to join him in a rough kind of alliance. The precaution was well advised. The Fatimid general Jawhar overran Fustat, and his advance detachments proceeded directly into Syria, where a combined force of Ikhshidid government troops and Qarmatians attempted, unsuccessfully, to halt the Fatimid advance upon Damascus.

After the Fatimid *Imam* al-Mu'izz established himself in his new capital of Cairo he almost immediately sent a letter of explanation and appeal to the new leader of the Qarmatians, Abu Mansur's son Hasan al-A'samm, to return to what the Fatimid conceived of as Isma'ili orthodoxy. In it Mu'izz made the case for his own divine Imamate and then followed it with the charge that Hasan had departed from the traditions of Abu Sa'id and Abu

Tahir. There is no sign that either of those men had in fact accepted the Fatimid Imamate. Hasan was not, at any rate, convinced and publicly denounced the Fatimid overture. The degree of its failure may be measured by the fact that from 978 onward, when the 'Abbasids' Turkish commander was driven from Damascus, the Fatimids paid the Qarmatians an annual tribute to keep them clear of what was left to the Egyptians in Syria.

The 'Abbasids for their part sensed that the Qarmatians' military threat to Iraq had passed, perhaps as early as 950, and concerned themselves chiefly with those other Isma'ilis, the Fatimids. The two sides fought through their seconds, the Fatimids by means of the *du'at,* who spread Isma'ili propaganda through the 'Abbasid realms, and the 'Abbasids through their own historians, who attacked whatever they knew of Qarmatian or Fatimid history and of Isma'ili ideology. Most of what they did know of the Qarmatians came from Ibn Rizam who wrote his exposé sometime about 950. Somewhat later, in 983, something more substantial was available when Akhu Muhsin, an 'Alid of Damascus, published his refutation of Fatimid pretensions. And in it he gave Sunni Islam its first glimpse of a piece of Isma'ili esoterica.

None of the medieval Sunni authors ever saw the original work described by Akhu Muhsin as *The Book of Governance*, nor have we.[57] From our clues it was apparently explicit in its instructions on the means by which the Muslim might be drawn to Isma'ili beliefs and the subsequent degrees of initiation for the new convert. We are, however, somewhat better off than the 'Abbasid polemicists in other respects. We do have genuine Isma'ili works from the tenth and eleventh centuries.

The preserved body of early Isma'ili work comes from two quite different milieus. Some of it reflects the evolving dogmas of Fatimid orthodoxy, while another substantial group of treatises

---

57. Akhu Muhsin's own work has disappeared and must be reconstructed from the many Sunni polemicists who drew on it for their attacks upon the Fatimids. Among their number were the Ash'arite *mutakallimun* Baqillani and Baghdadi and the Mu'tazilite 'Abd al-Jabbar.

are the products of eastern Isma'ilism, whose authors were essentially missionaries *in partibus infidelium.* The Fatimid *Imams* interested themselves in theory, and the preserved letters of 'Ubaydallah (909–934) and particularly of Mu'izz (953–975) show the direction in which the Fatimid understanding of the Imamate was moving. And both *Imams* had astute lawyers to assist them in drawing up their case, Ja'far ibn Mansur, surnamed "the Yemenite," and the *qadi* al-Nu'man.

Little is known of Ja'far's life except that both he and his father, who died in 914, were part of the Isma'ili apparatus in the Yemen before they came to Ifriqiyah under Mansur (946–953). Ja'far held no official office but devoted himself to the work of allegorical exegesis that was fundamental to the Isma'ili program, efforts that are preserved in his tract called *The Unveiling* and in a number of still unpublished works. Al-Nu'man (d. 974) was a native of Qayrawan. Though he had studied history and philosophy, his proper field was the law, and al-Qa'im appointed him *qadi.*[58] Most of his literary activity took place under Mu'izz, who frequently used the lawyer as his ideological spokesman. Al-Nu'man is represented by a considerable number of extant treatises, most of them still in manuscript. His *Pillars of Islam* was the premier law book of the realm, and the traditions bearing on the important subject of the Imamate were collected in his *Commentary on the Narratives Concerning the Virtues of the Prophet.*

The eastern branches of the Isma'ili mission antedated the Fatimids' rise to power and during most of the tenth century showed an independence of the revisionist theories being proposed by Mu'izz in Cairo. There were two centers in the east, the region around Rayy whence the *da'wah* spread into the neighboring Caspian states, and the provinces of Khurasan and Transoxania. The Isma'ilis arrived in Rayy in 'Abdallah ibn Maymun's

---

58. The pragmatic office of *qadi* had, of course, no place in the cosmic hierarchy of the Isma'iliyah, but eschatology was already yielding to politics among the Fatimids, and there is evidence that during this period at least the office of the chief *da'i*, the *bab*, was combined with that of *qadi.*

time about the beginning of the ninth century. There were some gains as well as persecutions at the hands of the Sunnis. Zeal slackened as the appearance of the immediately expected *Mahdi* receded into the future, and the movement was probably saved from oblivion in Iran by the fourth or fifth *da'i* of Rayy, Abu Hatim al-Razi (d. 934).

Abu Hatim sent missionaries off into Tabaristan, Azarbayjan and Jurjan, and the climax of his own efforts was the conversion of the Samanid governor of Rayy, Ahmad ibn 'Ali (919–924). It was a brief triumph. A new 'Abbasid *amir* was sent out from Baghdad to oust the Samanid. He took Rayy in 924 and put its Isma'ili ruler to the sword. Abu Hatim fled his former headquarters and took refuge in Tabaristan, where another kind of struggle was taking place. The Daylamis were in rebellion against the Zaydi *Imams* who had ruled them since 864. Abu Hatim joined the Daylamite faction and apparently had some influence over their early leader Mardawij. But here too reverses followed success. Caught up in 933–934 in a war against the neighboring Samanids, Mardawij turned savagely against the Isma'ilis. Abu Hatim once again had to flee, and he died shortly after. And when the Daylamis later took over the reins of power in Baghdad under the banner of the Buyid house, they ruled not as revolutionary Isma'ilis with a sister branch in Cairo but as moderate Shi'ites who regarded the Fatimids as rivals and not allies.

Abu Hatim was a dialectician rather than a systematizer. His preserved treatise *The Ornament* is a combined lexicon of technical terms and a heresiography, while his two other known works, *The Signs of Prophecy* and *The Correction*, are pure polemic, the first a record of a public debate held with the philosopher-physician Muhammad ibn Zakariya al-Razi, and the latter directed against a fellow Isma'ili from Khurasan named al-Nasafi. The quarrel between the two *du'at* was on a point of considerable interest to the Fatimids, whether the coming of the *Mahdi* had abrogated the Law. The Fatimids now argued strenuously that it had not and that the Fatimid *Imams* represented the fulfillment of the *shari'ah* through its spiritualization. Without recognizing the Imamate of the Fatimids, Abu Hatim took a somewhat similar position. Like al-Nasafi he was waiting for the return of the *Mahdi* Huhammad ibn Isma'il, but he did not believe, as al-Nasafi apparently did, that the end-time had already broken in and that the *shari'ah* was canceled.

Abu Hatim's *Mahdi* did not appear, and his followers became discouraged. Further confusion arose among the Isma'iliyah when the Bahrayn Qarmatians announced sometime about 930 that Muhammad had returned to their midst in the person of a young man from Isfahan. Not many believed the claim, but after the death of Abu Hatim most of the eastern Isma'ilis were in some disarray. Abu Hatim was succeeded at Rayy by an Abu Ya'qub, perhaps the same man who later appeared in Khurasan as the successor of al-Nasafi as *da'i* in that province. Al-Nasafi too had converted a Samanid prince, Nasr II (914–943), but his successor as Amir of Khurasan, Nuh I (943–954), took a different view of things, and immediately after he took power he had al-Nasafi executed. It was the effective end of the *da'wah* in Khurasan. Abu Ya'qub ended his own career in Sijistan, where sometime toward the end of the tenth century he was captured and executed by the Saffarids.

The three eastern *du'at* Abu Hatim, al-Nasafi and Abu Ya'qub were engaged in a lively intermural debate on the nature of the Imamate, and from it comes our earliest substantial view of Isma'ili literature. All three authors stood somewhat apart from the Fatimids—it is not even certain whether any of them in fact recognized the Fatimid Imamate—but what is most remarkable is the presence in all of them, and particularly in al-Nasafi, who wrote in the opening years of the tenth century, of the kind of detailed Gnostic system familiar from Hellenic antiquity. Eleventh-century authors like Hamid al-Din al-Kirmani and Nasir-i Khusraw provide a far more detailed version of the grades of the *pleroma* and of the cyclic history that unfolds from it, but the entire system was essentially in place more than a century earlier in Nasafi and Abu Ya'qub al-Sijistani.

Another tenth-century version of the Gnostic "realities" may be read in the *Epistles* of the so-called "Brethren of Purity" (*Ikhwan al-safa*). The collection of fifty-two treatises was probably put together at Basrah sometime toward the end of the century. The identity of the Brethren has baffled scholars since their first appearance, but the intent of these tracts arranged in the form of a Hellenic-style encyclopedia is clear enough, to purify Islamic Law by a massive infusion of "wisdom" (*hikmah*), in this case chiefly Greek *hikmah*. The orientation is both philosophical and political, and the project is not unlike that contemplated by the later Isma'ili convert Nasir-i Khusraw in his *Conjunction of the Two Wisdoms*.

When the *Epistles* were submitted to the Baghdad *faylasuf* Abu Sulayman al-Sijistani, he recognized them for what they were, an attempt to subvert the *shari'ah* by substituting, under the cover of allegorical exegesis, the truths of philosophy for the truths of revelation. Nor was the philosophy itself innocent of religious overtones. A great deal of what can be found in the *Epistles* is Hermetic in its origins and nature. This may, indeed, have been the point of Abu Sulayman's critique, that one was dealing with occultists rather than with true philosophers.

The charge is only partially true. The main body of the Brethren's philosophy and science derives from the usual scholastic sources of antiquity, Plato, Aristotle, Plotinus, Euclid and Ptolemy. The occultism, on the other hand, comes, by their own admission, from the Sabians of Harran, who, again according to the Brethren, were the teachers of the Greeks and a link in the chain of wisdom that began in Egypt and Babylon and ended in their own teachings. How the Sabians could have passed on to the early Isma'ilis a substantial body of Greek learning our sources, which are concerned chiefly with the scholastic *falsafah* tradition, do not suggest.

For their part the Brethren were exceedingly sparing in their citations of Greek philosophers, particularly the later ones. If the *Epistles* were composed in the second half of the tenth century, as the few names supplied by contemporaries like al-Tawhidi seem to suggest, the Brethren already had available to their purposes the greater part of the Greek science and philosophy that would eventually pass into Arabic. If, however, the nucleus of the collection goes back to the earliest *Imams*, as the Isma'ili tradition insisted it did—to 'Abdallah ibn Maymun, for example, who flourished early in the second half of the eighth century—then it would antedate most of the translation activity from Greek into

Arabic and the possibility of a Sabian intermediary would be far more appealing.

There were grounds for the Brethren to dissemble their immediate associations with the Sabians of Harran, but their silence on their Greek sources may have arisen from a more genuine ignorance; they had perhaps inherited a synthesis rather than created one. The Proclan Neoplatonism of the body of work associated with the name of Dionysius the Areopagite and available in Syriac was one such and the Greek *Corpus Hermeticum* was another. In neither case were the editors willing to reveal either themselves or their sources. Like their predecessors, the *Epistles* of the Brethren disclosed a perennial wisdom.

For all that there is a great deal of both Plotinus and Aristotle in the *Epistles;* they are, nonetheless, far more than the simple reproduction of some late-antique school curriculum with its standard combination of Platonic theology and Aristotelian physics. The sensibility that informed the *Epistles* was Gnostic and occultist. The Isma'ili distinction between the literal (*zahir*) and the concealed (*batin*) significance of truths is everywhere affirmed; the understanding of the heavens and their effect on terrestrial life is an astrologer's; and the approach to mathematics owes as much to the numerological metaphysics of Nicomachus of Gerasa—as the Brethren freely admitted—as to the "secular" mathematics of Euclid.

The Brethren, whatever their immediate connection with the Isma'ili movement, were part of that Gnostic elite which in many times and many cultures has bent its efforts toward recovering the secret truths necessary for salvation. They recognized many prophets—far more than the orthodox Muslim tradition would admit—and many revelations. Revelations are, however, essentially vulgar, and none more so than the Islamic one addressed to untutored and unsophisticated Arabs. The ordinary Muslim might take the *Qur'an*'s vivid eschatology literally, for example, but the Brethren and their readers were not deceived. They knew that the joys of Paradise had nothing to do with houris; it was assimilation to the One, and man need not wait upon death to attain it.

The *Epistles* are the way to that bliss, a king's highway which takes the novice step by step, from lower science to higher science, and eventually to a knowledge of the "realities" (*haqa'iq*). All of the knowledge of the ancients, now the property of Islam, has been incorporated as stages along the journey that the adept is invited to begin. But not without direction. The guidance of the *Imam* is necessary, and though the *Epistles* are preserved for us in the form of a book, it is virtually certain that they were intended as material for discussion in séances (*majalis*) conducted by more experienced adepts.

The *Epistles* are a more learned and more politicized version of the world view given to his readers a century earlier by Tirmidhi. Tirmidhi's "communion of saints" was replaced by a secret society of searchers after truth. Specifics on that society are presented in the *Epistles*, but more in the vein of Plato's sketch of an ideal society in the *Republic* than a description of an actually existing organization, Isma'ili or otherwise. The novice was to begin his study of the moral and intellectual virtues at the age of fifteen and then proceed upward to the rank of leader and eventually king, who at the age of forty is granted the assistance of the Divine Law. The goal of his striving is the grade of prophet or angel, the state wherein one is in direct communication with the Truth. The prophets are instructed by angelic Intelligences above them, and thus they can serve as infallible guides when purely human speculation fails. Here the prophetic tradition ran together with the philosophical in a manner unknown to Tirmidhi: Jesus and Muhammad have witnessed the Truth, but so too have Hermes and Aristotle.

The *Epistles* of the Brethren of Purity constitute an extraordinarily eclectic document which, together with the works of Tirmidhi and Jabir ibn Hayyan, richly illustrates how little we know about late antiquity and the channels whereby its attitudes and speculations passed into Islam. The *Epistles* unmistakably transcend Islam and belong to the literary history of Gnosticism. Not one but many forms of that latter had come into Islam, where they became the common property of Sufis and Shi'ites alike. Many Muslims resisted the *gnosis* on the ground that such speculation was contrary to Islam; for some few others its secret discourse and infallible authorities violated the basic assumptions of human inquiry. For these latter, the true progeny of Hellenism in Islam, only philosophy openly pursued and scientifically demonstrated could bring men to the truth.

The Intentions of the Philosophers: Ibn Sina

The Muslim did not much favor autobiography as a means of literary self-expression. One of the rare attempts at the genre was made by the *faylasuf* Abu 'Ali al-Husayn ibn 'Abdallah ibn Sina, who dictated to his student Juzjani a brief account of his life from his birth in 980 down to 1013. That was the year in which Juzjani joined him as a disciple, and thereafter, from 1013 to Ibn Sina's death in 1037, the narrative is supplied by Juzjani's own recollections of his master.

Ibn Sina's father, an Iranian of Balkh, was employed in the Samanid civil service and was serving as an official in a village near Bukhara when Ibn Sina was born. Very early in his life the family moved to Bukhara itself, and thus Ibn Sina had the advantage of an education in one of the premier intellectual centers of the Muslim East. That education was at the outset the traditional one of instruction based on the *Qur'an* and then, somewhat later, jurisprudence. It soon moved into more esoteric areas, however. Ibn Sina's father and brother were both won over to Isma'ilism, and it was through them, or rather, by reason of their desire to convert him to Isma'ili beliefs that Ibn Sina was introduced to Greek philosophy and science and eventually to the professional study of medicine. By the age of sixteen he was a practicing physician.

This prodigy of learning did have teachers. His instructor in philosophy was a certain al-Natili, with whom the very young Ibn Sina read Porphyry's *Eisagoge*. The tutelage did not continue for long. They made it through the logic together, but beyond that Ibn Sina had no need for al-Natili, since "he had no knowledge of the subtler points." Taking the books into his own hands Ibn Sina plunged forward alone into physics and metaphysics. At that point he could have been no more than fourteen years of age.

Ibn Sina's somewhat graceless dismissal of his teacher marks an important difference between his education and that known to his Baghdad predecessors and contemporaries. The Baghdad philosophers were all academics and, like Farabi, were all trained on texts by recognized masters within a defined school tradition. Ibn Sina's education was literary but not textual. He read hungrily in the surprisingly fine libraries of late-tenth-century Iran, one of which, that belonging to the Samanid *amir* of Bukhara Nuh ibn Mansur (976–997), Ibn Sina later described in excited terms: "I entered a house with many rooms and in each room there were chests of books piled one upon the other . . . I saw books whose names were as yet unknown to many."

Among the books used by the seventeen-year-old Ibn Sina for his self-instruction was Aristotle's *Metaphysics*. By his own admission he read the Arabic version—again, unlike some at least of his Baghdad contemporaries, he knew no Greek—forty times without understanding it. It is, perhaps, the only concession to modesty in the entire autobiography, and the defect was soon remedied. He chanced upon a copy of Farabi's *The Intentions of Aristotle in the Metaphysics*, read it immediately, and the scales fell from his eyes. There are no further hints as to what he read in philosophy, but in the end he must have gone through most of the Arabic Aristotle, including the "Theology." He must also have remembered everything he read, or so it appears when he came to synthesize it more than twenty years later.

For the first twenty-one years of his life Ibn Sina lived in his father's house and pursued his intellectual interests wherever they chanced to lead. He already had a local reputation in Bukhara as a prodigally gifted student and as the young physician who had successfully treated the *amir* Nuh. But with the death of his father in 1001 a new life had to be fashioned. Over the next fifteen years he found employment in the service of the Khwarazm Shah 'Ali ibn Ma'mun (997–1009) and other petty Iranian dynasts across the towns of the northeast frontier of the *Dar al-Islam*.

Juzjani joined Ibn Sina in Jurjan in 1013 and reported that he had found him lecturing on Ptolemy's *Almagest* and the Aristotelian logic. He had also begun writing an immense medical encyclopedia, *The Canon*. The times were unsettled, however; the attention of the Turkish Ghaznavids was being drawn more closely to Khwarazm in the second decade of the eleventh century.[59] Fortunately Ibn Sina's reputation had by then reached the ears of the Buyids farther west, and rather than follow his fellow scientist Biruni into a Turkish "exile,"[60] he hastily accepted an invitation to join the court of Majd al-Dawlah (997–1029) at Rayy. His duties there are not clear—he cured the *amir* of melancholy—and there was no stability in his position. The sojourn at Rayy was succeeded by another at Qazwin, and then finally he came to the court of Shams al-Dawlah (997–1021), the Buyid *amir* of Hamadhan and Isfahan in Jibal. Here at least we know that Ibn Sina served as vizier, and though there were internal difficulties—the (Turkish?) military at one point conspired against him and contrived to have him imprisoned—it was the most productive period in Ibn Sina's career.

Reconstructions of Ibn Sina's bibliography list more than two hundred and fifty titles, principally in Arabic but including some Persian prose and poetry as well. We can read only a fraction of that total, and even the treatises that have been preserved raise serious problems of interpretation. Ibn Sina the scientist is there plain for the reading;[61] it is the *faylasuf* who eludes capture, even though we have in our possession his most ambitious philosophical project as well as a rich surrounding body of interpretive comment.

Farabi was a commentator in the style of the Alexandrian Neoplatonists and their Baghdad successors of the tenth century; Ibn Sina preferred glosses and paraphrases, and in the end produced something totally new in the philosophical tradition, an Aristotelian encyclopedia. While they were in residence at Hamadhan Juzjani asked his teacher to compose a commentary on Aristotle. The request may have been for something in the Farabian vein, but Ibn Sina at any rate understood it as a systematic work of investigation on disputed points in philosophy and science. He pleaded that he had no time for such an undertaking —he was at the time both vizier and personal physician to Shams

---

59. Mahmud finally occupied Khwarazm in 1017; see Chap. IX, p. 652.
60. See Chap. V, pp. 349–350.
61. See Chap. V, pp. 391–392.

al-Dawlah—but he proposed to provide instead an exposition of philosophy that would be complete but would concentrate upon generally agreed positions and not deal with points of controversy. The work was ten years in the writing (c. 1020–1030) and the result was the *Healing of the Soul*, an encyclopedia of the "foreign sciences."

The *Healing* is structured almost exactly on the lines of the various "divisions of the sciences" familiar to the Alexandrian scholastics and earlier represented in Islam by the *Enumeration of the Sciences* of Farabi: logic, physics, the mathematical sciences, metaphysics and the moral sciences of politics and ethics. Ibn Sina had himself written just such a programmatic work, *On the Division of the Sciences*, but the *Healing* is far more. It is a true philosophical summa composed by a single man who was deeply engaged in matters of state and without access to the normal research materials. According to Juzjani, the *Healing* was composed at night after the completion of Ibn Sina's official duties and at the same time that he was working on his medical encyclopedia. And each night's labors were capped, we are told, by a round of drinking and entertainment.

There is nothing like the *Healing* in the philosophical literature, Greek, Syriac or Arabic, before Ibn Sina, and we have no idea what inspired him to the novel form. There was, of course, a considerable tradition of encyclopedism in the medical tradition, and his own *Canon*, which was begun before the *Healing*, may have suggested to him a treatment of philosophy on a similar scale and ordered along the lines of the already familiar "division of the sciences." Whatever its inspiration, the *Healing* is an impressive monument to the depth and tenacity of Ibn Sina's self-education in the libraries of the East. Most of it was written from a recollection of and reflection on things that he had read twenty years before and were now, between the author's fortieth and fiftieth years, inserted piecemeal into a formally planned outline.

The death of Shams al-Dawlah in 1021 brought an end to Ibn Sina's security. There were protestations from the *amir*'s son that he should stay on at Hamadhan, but prudence apparently dictated otherwise. Hidden away in the house of a friendly druggist, Ibn Sina negotiated by letter with the Kakuyid *amir* 'Ala' al-Dawlah (1008–1041) for renewed patronage while he continued with his work on the *Healing*. News of his correspondence with 'Ala' al-Dawlah, who was then enlarging his holdings in western Iran at the expense of the failing Buyids, leaked out in Hamadhan and as a result Ibn Sina was ferreted out and imprisoned. It did not, however, interrupt his writing.

Eventually Ibn Sina escaped in disguise to Isfahan and the safety of 'Ala' al-Dawlah's court, where he spent the rest of his life. It was at Isfahan that the *Healing* was finally completed and there was much more besides. He composed two considerably briefer versions of the same material that he had used in the *Healing*, the Arabic *Salvation of the Soul* and the Persian *Book of Science*, which was dedicated to his patron. In his introduction to the *Healing* Ibn Sina noted down some of his own future projects. The *Healing* was to be followed by a continuing series of "appendices" in which he would gloss the same material treated summarily in the *Healing*.[62] In the same passage Ibn Sina touched upon yet another project, his *Oriental Philosophy*, "in which I have set out a philosophy in the way it naturally is and right reason dictates." It is a work, he explained, in which he would not fear to express opinions different from those of his philosophical colleagues.

Related to the *Healing* and the *Oriental Philosophy* is another work discussed by Ibn Sina, his *Book of Arbitration*, where he proposed to gloss the works of Aristotle. The work was completed—we do not know when—but it was destroyed when Mas'ud and the Ghaznavids fell upon Isfahan in 1034. Ibn Sina escaped, but his baggage was left behind; in it was the *Book of Arbitration*. In a letter written somewhat later he promised to redo the treatise, and some at least of that second version was completed before his death in 1037, his glosses on the "Theology of Aristotle," *On the Soul* and Book Lambda of the *Metaphysics*.

By his own remarks Ibn Sina has raised perplexing questions about his personal philosophical views. Are they represented by the professed *communis opinio* of the *Healing?* Are the gloss works investigations, revisions or retractions? Is there an esoteric Avicennism concealed in the *Oriental Philosophy* or in the last of

62. These notes are preserved, though they are mixed with a great deal of material from other hands.

his major works, the *Book of Remarks and Admonitions?* Was he a Platonizing Aristotelian or the adept of an older Iranian wisdom?

The answers to most of these questions may never be known, but some ground at least has been cleared. In the *Healing* there are set forth a great number of philosophical positions which Ibn Sina never repudiated in any of his published work. It is clear that he did not agree with all his philosophical contemporaries; it is equally clear that this disagreement, whatever its dimensions, never led to a total rejection of the world view to which both they and he were devoting their attention and energies. That world view was the Neoplatonic Aristotelianism inherited from the Alexandrians of late antiquity and reproduced in the *Healing*. Ibn Sina brought his own important modifications to the system in both metaphysics and psychology, and in the latter discipline his differences may have been radical. But the system as a whole stood.

The *Healing* is divided into four major parts, or "summas," which correspond to the Hellenic curricular distinctions of logic, physics, mathematics and metaphysics. Each is in turn divided into "books" which are analogous, where appropriate, to the Aristotelian treatises on the subject. Thus in the "summa" on logic there are "books" devoted to the *Eisagoge* of Porphyry and to each of the treatises of the Peripatetic *Organon* from the *Categories* to the *Poetics*. The Aristotelian correspondences of the second major division "On Natures" are somewhat less exact. The *Physics*, *On the Heavens*, *On Generation and Corruption*,[63] the *Meteorology* and the various books *On Animals* are all represented, as well as a treatise "On Plants" and another "On Minerals." The sixth book of the Avicennan *summa de naturalibus* is given over to Ibn Sina's version of the Aristotelian psychology.

The third "summa" takes up the mathematical sciences, an area little cultivated by Aristotle and the Peripatetics. Here Ibn Sina turned to other sources, to Euclid for his treatment of geometry and to Ptolemy for the book on astronomy. The final "summa" of the *Healing* is devoted to metaphysics or theology (*ilahiyat*),

63. The fourth "book" extends Aristotle's treatment to "Agents and Patients."

and though they hold the place reserved for Aristotle's *Metaphysics* in the idealized Peripatetic curriculum, the ten books of the *Ilahiyat* are a signal Avicennan contribution to an evolving philosophical tradition that owed as much to the *Timaeus* and the *Enneads* as it did to Aristotle.

Ibn Sina did not hesitate to reorganize the *Metaphysics* in the construction of his own "Theology" in the *Healing*. The first book connects metaphysics with the other sciences, whence Ibn Sina proceeds in the second book to an investigation of substance, which he understands in its primary Aristotelian sense as the union of matter and form. The three following books study the same questions of potency and act, genus, species and difference raised by Aristotle in Books Theta, Iota and Zeta of the *Metaphysics*. Then in the sixth book of the "Theology" we hear, far more distinctly than before, the voice of Ibn Sina himself. And it is, understandably, if somewhat unexpectedly, a Muslim voice.

All through the "Theology" Ibn Sina had been touching upon something new in the *falsafah* tradition, but it is not until the sixth book that its full implications are set forth. It is here that we are introduced to the distinction between the essence or "whatness" of a thing and its actual existence. The latter, according to Ibn Sina's formulation, is something that is added to the essence. If it were part of the essence of a man to exist, one could not comprehend man without first affirming that he existed. An individual man may, indeed, exist, but there are other essences of which one can conceive—the void, for example—and which have no real existence outside the mind. Existence, then, is an accident that is added to certain possible essences.

Ibn Sina was not the first to make the distinction in that form. Al-Farabi had already discussed it in a logical context when he questioned whether, in the proposition "man exists," "exists" is a predicate. Farabi held that from a strictly logical point of view "exists" might qualify as a predicate, but that realistically it adds nothing to the essence "man" and so cannot serve as a predicate in the ontological sense.[64] Even earlier Aristotle himself had touched upon the problem, and it is clear from passages in the

---

64. Ibn Sina disagreed with this view. For him "exists" is a predicate, but an accidental and not an essential one.

Posterior Analytics that he too regarded the essence of man and the fact that a man exists as two different things; the first was a matter of definition, the latter one of demonstration.

In the same passage Aristotle comments that "being is not the essence of anything," a view that necessarily excludes "being" in this sense—that is, existence—from consideration in the science of metaphysics. For Aristotle, no less than Plato, the First Philosophy is a science of essential forms that are both finite and determined. They are determined, however, from within, and there is no hint in Aristotle that there is an efficient cause operating among the separated forms which are the proper object of metaphysics.

The exclusion from the suprasensible world of an efficient causality whereby an agent brings existence to another entity rendered the Aristotelian metaphysics highly inappropriate to either an emanationist creation of the Neoplatonic type or the willed creation in time accepted as revealed truth by Jews, Christians and Muslims. For a willed creation an entirely new metaphysics had to be constructed, and Ibn Sina was its somewhat hesitant architect.

"The physicists," Ibn Sina commented at the beginning of Book VI of the "Theology," "interested themselves in the agent as the cause of motion; the philosopher, on the other hand, is concerned with a beginning in being and the agent of this bestowal, the Creator, for example, with regard to the universe." From that principle of the agent as the cause of existence proceeds the structure of the entire second half of the "Theology" (Books VI–X) of *The Healing*. The world exists, but it is contingent; it requires, in short, a cause of existence outside itself. Given the contingent but actual existence of the universe, there must exist a cause that is both actual and necessary, that is, an agent whose existence depends on no other but itself. That cause is God, the Creator of the universe and the unique Necessary Existent.

Ibn Sina's finished portrait of the First Cause is set out in the eighth book of the "Theology." He is unmistakably Aristotle's self-thinking Intellect who contemplates his own essence. That essence is, as we have already been instructed, to exist, and so the contemplation of his own necessary existence includes the possibility of all other existences. Thus, Plato's transcendental Forms, which once constituted the "really real," are reduced to possibilities,[65] and a tension begins to develop between the Aristotelian and Platonic viewpoints inherent in Ibn Sina's philosophizing.

In the Peripatetic model for Ibn Sina's noetic there was an intimate connection between sense knowledge and intellection. The intelligible forms of things existed prior to our knowledge of them, that is, prior to their becoming intelligized. They subsisted within material things, whence they came, via sensation, into the human intellectual faculty. It was here that they were converted under the action of the Agent Intellect into actually intelligized forms. Ibn Sina all but swept away that sensist base of intellection. In his view the intelligible forms are *given* to the human intellect by the tenth and last divine Intellect and the human knower merely reflects them, "as in a mirror."

Ibn Sina had predecessors in this approach to intelligibility. Middle Platonism had long since converted the ontological reality of Plato's transcendental Forms into something considerably more noetic by installing them as the thoughts of God. Aristotle's God could not possibly have had such thoughts; their presence in the Divine Mind would have introduced plurality into the First Cause. But for the Platonists the issue was no longer crucial, since the Divine Intellect was no longer *the* High God but a lower being in whom the presence of the multiple intelligible Forms was no longer theologically repugnant.

For later Platonism, to exist was, in all save the transcendental One, to be known. Ibn Sina must parcel out his reality from above; the Agent Intellect, the "Giver of Forms" as he called it, imparts them to both sensible beings as their ontological principle and to human intellects as their intelligible principle. And it was here that a difficult problem arose. The second giving, that of the forms into the human intellect, was not ontological. The forms

---

65. Even earlier, before 900, the Mu'tazilites, who were operating within a materialistic system that took its point of departure in the identification of "thing" and "existence," had begun to distinguish modes of existence precisely to grant some degree of reality to God's knowledge of "things" before their creation in time; see Chap. VI, p. 456.

were simply "reflected" in the human intellect; the Agent Intellect "illuminated" them. Hence it was impossible to embrace a corollary of Aristotle's noetic, that the knower "becomes" the thing known. For Aristotle the union between the knower and the known was an intentional one, but these new Platonic-style forms were totally constituted in all their ontological fullness within the Agent Intellect. Their presence within the human knower as anything but a "reflection" would, indeed, destroy the being of the knower.

Ibn Sina returns to the problem in his *Book of Remarks* where he rejects the possibility of an ontological union between knower and known. He has read, he reports, another theory, which he identifies as Porphyry's, in which the knower becomes not the intelligible form of the thing known but identical with the Agent Intellect itself. We know of nothing like this in Porphyry, but Ibn Sina may well have confused Porphyry with another Aristotelian commentator who had to face the problem of two kinds of knowledge implicit in two sets of forms, those immanent in matter and those now located within a Divine Intellect. To grasp the former, Alexander of Aphrodisias could rely upon the normal Aristotelian process of sensible abstraction, but for the latter he was forced to have recourse to a more extraordinary form of knowing, that accomplished by men through an intellect that operated, as Aristotle himself suggested, "from outside" and was identified by Alexander with the First Cause. The Arab translators of Alexander seized the point; the Agent Intellect was freely turned into an "acquired intellect" and so constituted a link between the Divine Intellect and its "divinized" human counterpart.

Whether from Alexander, as seems likely, or from Porphyry, Ibn Sina was as unwilling to accept the theory as Farabi had been previously.[66] For Ibn Sina such a view would seem to introduce a division into the Agent Intellect: one part would remain transcendent, while the other would descend into the human soul, a

66. Farabi was very clear on the difference between the Agent Intellect and the "acquired intellect." The latter is an emanation from the former; they are not identical.

clear impossibility. But once having rejected an ontological union between the Agent Intellect and its human counterpart, Ibn Sina was not freed from the anomalies of his hybrid psychology. The language of Book Six of the "Physics" in the *Healing*, Ibn Sina's formal treatment of psychology, is unabashedly Aristotelian, but his understanding of the true nature of the soul owes far more to Plato than to Aristotle.

For the Muslim, as for Plato, the human soul is a substance.[67] It may have an initial need of a material principle to effect its actualization and individualization—Ibn Sina did not accept the Platonic commonplaces of the preexistence and transmigration of souls—but that is the end of its dependence. Its intellectual activity is not rooted in a sense-derived knowledge, but in outside powers, and its survival after death is likewise independent of matter. But if the soul depended on matter as its principle of individuation, how could it survive as an individual after its separation from matter at death? Ibn Sina recognized the problem but confessed that he had no solution. As a Muslim he affirmed the immortality of the individual human soul, but as a philosopher caught up in Plato's soul-as-substance and Aristotle's soul-as-perfection he was at a loss to explain how it was achieved. And the problem was unique to man. All the other intellectual souls in the cosmos, those of the heavenly bodies, were conjoined to incorruptible bodies and so knew neither death nor dissolution.

Ibn Sina's universe is not unlike that of Farabi or the Platonists of late antiquity. The cosmos flowed forth from the superabundant goodness of the Creator in a descending series of caused Intellects. But according to Farabi's theory of emanation, each caused Intellect produces a twofold effect, another Intellect and a heavenly body. For Ibn Sina, on the other hand, causality proceeds through triads; each Intellect produces another Intellect, a celestial soul, and a celestial body. It is then clear, as it was not in

---

67. One of Ibn Sina's most striking proofs that the soul is a fully constituted substance is its *immediate* awareness of its own existence. He asked his reader to imagine himself in a state of suspension so perfect that all the senses are immobilized. Even in this state, deprived of all sensual stimuli, a man would harbor no doubt about his own existence.

Farabi, how each of the nine celestial spheres is moved—by the desire of the soul immanent in each sphere for the perfection of that Divine Intellect associated with it but separated from it.

In assuming this stance Ibn Sina had apparently resolved for himself a major problem in the interpretation of Aristotle. Aristotle, who shared Plato's belief that the heavenly bodies were alive and so ensouled,[68] did not rely upon the activities of an immanent soul to explain the motion of the heavenly bodies but preferred a theory of the natural motion of the elements, in this case the natural circular motion of the fifth element, the *aither*. This was Aristotle's position in the treatise *On the Heavens,* but in Chapter Eight of Book Lambda of the *Metaphysics* another theory was proposed: each celestial sphere is moved by an Intellect that stands outside it and is its final cause, the object of its love.

Although Aristotle nowhere spoke of planetary souls in this connection, his interpreter Alexander of Aphrodisias did, and his explanation of the relationship between mover and moved in the heavens is almost exactly that of Ibn Sina: the heavenly bodies move by virtue of their souls and they move in their perfect spherical movement by reason of their souls' desire for the object of their love. At that point in the *Metaphysics* astronomy intervened. The observed movement of the heavens is irregular. Since this is philosophically untenable, the apparently irregular movements had to be explained by a composition of regular spherical movements. The decomposition of the movements of the planets was the work of astronomers, and Aristotle followed their findings: there were fifty-six movers for the fifty-six spheres necessary to explain the observed motion of the seven planets and the mass of the fixed stars.

Ibn Sina knew of this theory and thought it might be a consequence of relying too exclusively upon an external final cause. If one were willing to permit some internal control of its motions to the soul of the planet, then the number of external movers might be reduced to ten: one for the First Heaven,[69] the fixed stars, the seven planets, and a final agent to "move" the souls of

68. Expressed most explicitly in his early dialogue *On Philosophy*.
69. See Chap. VII, p. 505, n. 32.

men. Ibn Sina permitted just such an internal principle of motion. The heavenly bodies possessed immanent Souls with faculties of intelligence and will, and it was the will of the celestial Soul that is the efficient cause of the motion of its body. The final cause remains what it was for Aristotle, the disembodied Intellect, one for each heavenly body, which is known by the celestial Soul as its good, and around which each celestial Soul revolves.

In Ibn Sina's world view the descending series of Intellects are identified with the angelic Cherubim of the Judaeo-Christian tradition, and the tenth of them, the Agent Intellect or Holy Spirit, with Gabriel, the archangel who was Allah's instrument in revealing the *Qur'an* to Muhammad. The Souls animating the heavenly bodies are likewise angels, though of a lesser perfection since they are embodied in the spheres. Both grades, the Cherubim and the secondary celestial angels, are gifted with intelligence and will, and those in a more perfect degree than given to man.

There is an elaborate, if obscure, angelology in the *Qur'an*, but it betrays features very different from the Neoplatonic design put forward by Ibn Sina. The Qur'anic angels are, like men, God's creatures, created before men but unmistakably subject to men.[70] They are described there as "messengers with two- and three-form wings," instruments of Allah's will toward men rather than ontological intermediaries between God and lesser orders of being. For Ibn Sina, on the other hand, the Intellect-Angels were what they had been for Plotinus and almost every other Platonist back to Philo, pure spirits who had their own reason of being, a being superior to man's own, and were at the same time intermediaries of the emanationist creation and the executors of High God's providence.

The angels as executors of providence are a favorite Qur'anic motif. But where man is the soteriological focus of creation, Allah's instruments are of decidedly secondary importance. Among the *falasifah* the sense of a special providence directed toward man is only dimly realized. Man depends rather on the

---

70. The Qur'anic proof texts are passages like 2:34 and 18:50, where the angels are bidden by Allah to prostrate themselves to Adam.

higher Intellects for his natural functioning as an intelligent being in the same sense that all effects are oriented to their immediate higher cause. The Plotinian universe is suffused with an ontologically necessary "giving," but it is not peopled, in the manner of the Books of Revelation, with a crowd of special messengers.

The *faylasuf* was also a Muslim, however, and so unlike Plotinus he had to find a significant place in his hierarchically ordered universe for those irregular communications called prophecy and revelation. Here too there were ample Greek precedents, Plutarch for one, for providing a philosophical explanation for extraordinary forms of divine communication with men. For the Hellenes one or another of the *daimones* served as intermediary; for Ibn Sina, one of the Angelic Intellects.

From a purely cognitive point of view, the Avicennan prophet is nothing more than a highly gifted philosopher whose intuitive grasp of the intelligibles and whose purity of intellect permit him to come in contact with the Agent Intellect without recourse to the sensible forms with which most men begin their ascent to the intelligible. Further, the intellect of the prophet receives the intelligibles from the "Giver of forms" as a unified whole and not serially or discretely as they occur in the intellects of other men.

The prophet, with his immediate and universal possession of the intelligible forms of reality, is placed in extraordinary contact with the Agent Intellect. An angelic power flows into his soul and the cognitive figure of mirror and image is banished; the prophetic intellect *becomes* the Agent Intellect. In his supernatural state he does not reflect but rather he knows in that same genuine sense shared by the Higher Intellects.

This is how the prophet knows. In his description of how he reveals that intuitively grasped knowledge, Ibn Sina followed the lead of Farabi. The prophet is characterized by a highly developed imaginative faculty which, though it plays no part in the cognitive processes of the prophet, does provide the instrument whereby his knowledge is converted into a public revelation. It transforms the intelligibles into the material symbols and images capable of moving the hearts of men to action.

Once again the conclusion that Muslim orthodoxy found so repugnant had to be drawn: the revelation of the *Qur'an* and the religion (*millah*) of Islam had a claim to neither uniqueness nor universal validity. Truth and reality were one, but both revelation and religion suffered the participation of matter. Islam might argue the superiority of its symbolism, but it was, after all, symbol and not reality. "Where," asked Ibn Sina, "does the *Qur'an* give a clear account of the unity of God?" Theology does provide such, but Ibn Sina was quick to concede that such formulations are far beyond the comprehension of most men and so of little use in leading them to happiness or salvation.

Ibn Sina exalted the prophet but degraded, as the Brethren of Purity did, the prophet's historical revelation to the level of symbol. The truth was surely in the *Qur'an,* but only an allegorical exegesis could convert its symbolic expression back to the purer stuff of the First Philosophy. Such an attitude, which is not very different from Farabi's own, confesses the Platonist's disdain for the phenomena of history. The *Qur'an* was a document of history and so, like the *Timaeus*, a "likely account," tailored in this case to the imperfections of its intended audience.

The prophet was not the only visionary recognized by Islam; among Ibn Sina's own Muslim contemporaries there were Sufis who laid claim to private visions of God. Ibn Sina was not himself a Sufi, but he knew the phenomenon and attempted, as he did with prophecy, to integrate it into his philosophy. Sufism and its attendant mysticism play no part in the great encyclopedias, but in another work composed near the end of his life, the *Book of Remarks and Admonitions*, the Sufi route from asceticism to a mystical knowledge (*ma'rifah*) is extended into Ibn Sina's epistemology to join that of the prophet.

According to the *Remarks*, the holy man proceeds from asceticism to piety and finally to *ma'rifah,* or its cognate *'irfan,* one or the other signifying the intuitive experience of God proper to the mystic. Ascetic practices have as their end the freeing of the saint's body from concupiscence and the distractions of the body until he is brought to that point of "conjunction" which is the object of his striving and which in the accomplished mystic becomes habitual to the point where he can summon it at will.

Thus far Ibn Sina had done little more than report standard Sufi doctrine. With his explanation of the modalities of this mystical "conjunction" he returned, however, to the Neoplatonic landscape of separated Intellects. The mystic, like the prophet, knows things hidden to most men, the future, for example. The cause, according to Ibn Sina, resides in the very same Intellects and celestial Souls whose activities govern the normal processes of human intellection.

The Cherubim and the Angelic Souls know future events because they are privy to an understanding of the causes of those events. The Intellects know the future in a general and universal manner; the celestial Souls in its particulars, since these latter possess particularized impressions that affect both their reason and their will.[71] When the mystic becomes capable of closing off his soul from the stimuli of the senses, which is the goal of the Sufi's ascetical practices, he is brought into contact with the divine celestial Souls and their particularized images of future events.

The human intellect is capable of receiving from above a great variety of communications that Ibn Sina's elaborate theorizing does not always succeed in distinguishing: awake or asleep, through intellect or imagination, under the form of universals or particulars, accompanied by images and sounds or as purely intellectualized phenomena, the soul of the philosopher, the mystic and the prophet can savor that "conjunction" with the world of Angelic Intellects and Souls above him.

The *Book of Remarks* has been adduced as part of the evidence for Ibn Sina's "Oriental philosophy" by some of those who maintain that his own personal philosophy was not the current mélange of Aristotelianism and Platonism but a more intuitive and perhaps even Gnostic form of wisdom. The identity of the "Orientals" (*mashriqiyun*) with whom Ibn Sina claimed kinship may never be known, as has been said, but the "Occidentals" (*mahgribiyun*) with whom he contrasted his own positions must surely have been neither Plato nor Aristotle but those Christian Peripatetics of Baghdad who claimed, no less than he, to be followers of the "First Master."

Nowhere in his work does Ibn Sina repudiate either Plato or

---

71. And eventually the movement of their bodies—that is, the celestial spheres to which the Angelic Souls are united "by a kind of bond, similar to the one that links our souls to our bodies." For their effects on terrestrial bodies, see Chap. V, pp. 359–360.

Aristotle. His most severe censures are reserved rather for Porphyry. In the *Book of Remarks* the question at issue is the ontological identification of the human soul and the Agent Intellect in the act of intellection. There were doubtless other differences, the individuation and survival of the soul after death, for example, but on all the evidence Ibn Sina proposed no radical departure from the Hellenic-type synthesis of his predecessors. There is nothing in the *Book of Remarks*, or in the *Oriental Philosophy* for that matter, that cannot be paralleled from the later adepts of a Platonic mysticism, and the equation of "Oriental" with either "Iranian" or "Zoroastrian" in the case of Ibn Sina is to credit some of his Muslim successors with a somewhat firmer grasp of the history of philosophy than they actually possessed.[72]

Ibn Sina was not the last *faylasuf* in Islam; the work of Ibn Rushd (d. 1198) in Spain postdated his own by a century and a half. He was, however, the last man to speak on philosophy with the voice of a philosopher to a wide audience in the *Dar al-Islam*.[73] For most of his readers, Ibn Sina's voice was the authentic one of the ancient tradition, or at least that branch of it that Ghazali later called "theism." The judgment is correct, though not perhaps in the sense that the medieval Muslim intended it. Ibn Sina spoke for a rationalized version of the Hellenic philosophical tradition in its final, syncretized stages. He reflected neither Plato nor Aristotle, but a combination of both, and in almost exactly the proportions that served the Platonists of Alexandria: an Aristotelian logic and physics crowned by a Platonic theology.

Though the adherent of a revealed religion, Ibn Sina was more rationalistic than many of his Greek predecessors. Hermeticism, occultism, and Gnosticism play no important part in his thought,

---

72. An Iranian theosophy passing from Zoroaster via the Sasanians into the twelfth century is a mirage. No Sasanian had ever heard of it, nor is there any other trace of such until its appearance in the writings of Suhrawardi (d. 1191), who derived his understanding of the evolution of human wisdom from some Hermetic source; see Chap. IV, pp. 277–278. The Pahlevi *handarz* and Miskawayh testify to the same fact: Iranian "wisdom" was gnomic, not Gnostic.

73. The impact of Ibn Rushd's writings was chiefly on the Christian Scholastics of Europe, who read them in Latin translation.

and there is no real evidence that the "Oriental philosophy" of which he so tantalizingly spoke would have altered that judgment. His Islamic beliefs led him to make room in his system for the possibilities of both prophethood and a mystical union with the divine, though here too his understanding of Muhammad and Sufism differed from that of his more traditional Muslim contemporaries.

In the end Ibn Sina's *falsafah* was too rare and too rationalized to be accepted as a legitimate part of the Muslim intellectual's experience. Ghazali, who contributed more than any other individual to the finished portrait of a rational yet authentically Islamic understanding of the Prophet and his revelation, was educated by Ibn Sina as surely as he was by Shafi'i and Ash'ari. After Ghazali no Muslim with a care for orthodoxy could be an explicit Avicennan;[74] he could, however, be a Ghazalian, and by affirming his allegiance to Ghazali he was affirming as well a view of man and God that ran deeply back into Hellenic rationalism through the pages of Ibn Sina.

---

74. For Ghazali's attack on Ibn Sina, see Chap. IX, pp. 692–695.

IX

ORTHODOXY REDEEMED

In the third quarter of the tenth century the future of the Sunni Caliphate as either a political or a religious institution did not appear promising. Earlier Caliphs had squandered the political credit of the office, and now in the tenth century partisans of a powerful counterview of Islam were making headway among those who still acknowledged the legitimacy of the 'Abbasid in Baghdad. The Shi'ite Buyids controlled western Iran and Iraq and sat as *amirs* in Baghdad itself. There were other Shi'ite principalities in the Yemen and south of the Caspian Sea. And if the Caliphs did manage to scotch the Qarmatians' immediate ambitions against the capital, another branch of the Isma'ili movement was firmly entrenched across North Africa. From their new capital in Cairo the Fatimid Caliph-*Imams* pushed their advance bases into Syria and had a network of missionaries across Mesopotamia, Iraq and Iran. From the Maghrib to Damascus and Arabia it was the Fatimid Mu'izz (953–975) whose name was invoked from the pulpits of mosques during the Friday prayers.[1]

1. And, under his successor, in Constantinople as well. According to a treaty concluded between 'Aziz and Basil II in 987, the Fatimid Caliph was named in the Friday prayers of the mosque in Constantinople. In 1049, when the vision of Tughril Beg loomed large in their minds, the Byzantines decided that a more beneficial invocation might be made in the name of the 'Abbasid Caliph. When the news reached Cairo the Fatimid Caliph Mustansir retaliated by confiscating the treasury of the Holy Sepulcher in Jerusalem.

The Fatimids had serious problems of their own, however. In Syria they were a weak third party between the Byzantines and the Hamdanids, the latter themselves Shi'ites, and though their propagandists caused political anxiety abroad, Egypt remained stanchly Sunni in the face of its Isma'ili masters. Isma'ilism's only bastion in its home province was the palace-city of Cairo. Within its walls lived the Fatimid princes and their large "families," their generals, more and more of them Turkish, and the retainers, bureaucrats and intriguers who made up the Fatimid establishment. On the outside lived the Egyptians, the former Sunni residents of Fustat and whoever else thought he might profit by attendance on the new masters of Egypt. The walled enclosure, a half mile square, was bordered fairly closely on the west by the old Red Sea canal,[2] and on the east by the steeply rising cliffs of the Muqattam hills. The axis of the city ran roughly north and south, and the two northern quarters were dominated by the two Fatimid palaces, the original one of Mu'izz east of the axis and the one built by 'Aziz on the west. Just south and east of Mu'izz's palace lay another of Jawhar's creations, the cathedral mosque of al-Azhar.

It is uncertain when instruction began to be given at the Azhar, but it seems to be associated with the reign of 'Aziz (975–996) and the designs of the vizier Ibn Killis. Al-Nu'man's son 'Ali, likewise a *qadi* and the chief of the Cairo Court of Appeals, taught Isma'ili *fiqh* there sometime after 975, and very soon there was the later familiar apparatus of endowed professorships in *fiqh* and the *hadith* sciences as well as student burses. It is highly unlikely that the "foreign sciences" were taught in this purely Islamic setting, but most of the Neoplatonic *gnosis* that constituted the Isma'ili "realities" was embedded within the allegorical exegesis of *hadith*, and so the professors at the Azhar probably felt little constrained by the traditional curriculum.

Jawhar had time to do little more than lay out the general design of Cairo, and Mu'izz was barely settled in before his death.

---

2. The original cut from the Nile to the Red Sea was made in Pharaonic times, but the one that was used by the Fatimids was the result of a redredging under the Roman Trajan in the second century. It emptied into the Nile opposite Roda Island.

The city's first real builder was 'Aziz, a lavish ruler who was saved from extravagance by the careful management of his viziers and ministers, chief among them the first, Ibn Killis, and the last, a Christian, 'Isa ibn Nastur (Nestorius). The presence of a Christian in such a high position was not unusual under the generally tolerant and affable 'Aziz. His wife, and the mother of his son and successor al-Hakim, was one, and her two brothers became, not entirely unexpectedly, the Patriarch of Alexandria and the bishop of the new Metropolitan See of Cairo.

Most of 'Aziz's political and military attention was directed to Syria, which was controlled as far north as Damascus by his new Turkish mercenaries. Beyond Damascus, however, there were other powers, the Arab Hamdanids of Aleppo and the newly aggressive Byzantines, who intervened at will to prevent the Fatimids from taking northern Syria.[3] The Fatimids for their part showed little appetite for engaging the Byzantines in a *jihad*. Their religious energies were reserved for the 'Abbasids of Baghdad, beyond reach but never far from the *Imams*' thoughts.

Persians and Turks in Islam

The Fatimids had temptations but very few real hopes in Baghdad. There were two major Shi'ite powers in and around the 'Abbasids' holdings, the Hamdanids in Syria and northern Mesopotamia and the Buyids in Iraq itself, as well as a number of Arab Shi'ite principalities around the Fertile Crescent. None of these dynasties showed themselves sympathetic to the Fatimids or to the general Isma'ili cause. The Baghdad Caliphs had, moreover, powerful Sunni allies farther east, the Ghaznavids in Afghanistan and Khurasan and the newly powerful Seljuq Turks, who were beginning to overrun the eastern frontier. But for all the feebleness of the Fatimids' military expectations, the Isma'ili propaganda apparatus was in good health in Iraq, if the number of treatises directed by Sunni authors against the "Batinites" is any indication. Their fear of the methods and ideas of the Isma'iliyah

3. See Chap. VII, p. 496.

brought Hanbalites, Ash'arites and Mu'tazilites together in a common caue.

The chief Isma'ili *da'i* in Iraq in the early eleventh century was Hamid al-Din al-Kirmani, who was summoned to Cairo in 1014 or 1015 to take part in affairs of greater internal consequence than the mission to Baghdad, the crisis provoked by the erratic aspirations of the new *Imam* al-Hakim (996–1021) and his followers. 'Aziz had died in 996 leaving behind an eleven-year-old son who, by the rigors of the Isma'ili succession, had to be acknowledged as the divinely designated *Imam.* The realities of politics did not, however, entirely cede to the "reality" of the Imamate, and there was a scramble for power. Berber lords rose and fell in Cairo and Damascus, while on the frontier Fatimid diplomats tried desperately to buy off the dangerous Basil II, who, from his accession in 976, kept a relentless pressure on the Fatimids' Syrian province.

The affairs of the state were for the most part under the care of a eunuch who had long served the family of 'Aziz, but in 999 the fourteen-year-old Hakim had this minister murdered and began to rule in his own right. It was an extraordinary time. The portrait we possess of the adolescent *Imam* comes from highly unsympathetic sources, and he is made to appear to be in the grip of a crazed megalomania. Perhaps he was mad, but the Isma'ili view of history was mad in almost the same sense, and al-Hakim took more seriously than any of his predecessors the role of *Imam* in the Isma'ili dispensation. Earlier *Imams* had tolerated and even favored Christians and Jews; in 1005 Hakim reversed that policy: the infidels were persecuted and their churches destroyed, including one of the holiest shrines in Christendom, the Church of the Holy Sepulcher in Jerusalem. Three years later followed a complementary move, the recognition of Sunnism at the side of Shi'ism as an acceptable form of Islam. Islam was, after all, the religion of another era.

In the years that followed, Hakim instituted a regime of severe and puritanical justice. Games and wine drinking were forbidden, and women were confined indoors. To insure observance, al-Hakim appointed a Hanbalite as his chief *qadi*, though *not* to the formerly simultaneous office of *bab*. All of these actions are accompanied in our narratives by bloodcurdling tales of cruelty and self-indulgence reminiscent of Nero. There may have been some program behind them, some attempt at putting down the mighty, redistributing property, and alleviating taxes. We cannot know for certain; the witnesses are too hostile.

Not all his acts were mad. During al-Hakim's reign and under his patronage, Egypt was the home of the greatest astronomer of his day, 'Ali ibn Yunus (d. 1009), Islam's premier physicist, Ibn al-Haytham (d. 1038), as well as a number of eminent physicians. The magnet may have been the subsidized amenities of the Caliph's "Hall of Wisdom," a research-and-study complex that Hakim had constructed near the palace in 1005. 'Ali ibn Yunus, who worked there, was not a Hermeticist, nor was Ibn al-Haytham, but "wisdom" (*hikmah*) was a usefully vague term that could apply equally well to Greek science and to its Gnostic or Hermetic counterparts. It was so used by the Isma'ilis in their propaganda, and such seems to have been the case here. The "Hall of Wisdom" was under the direction of the chief *da'i*, and the subjects studied and discussed there ranged from the relatively secularized Greek medicine, through the Islamic sciences, to the Isma'ili Hermetic *hikmah*.

The architect of this eclectic academic approach to Isma'ilism may have been 'Aziz's vizier Ibn Killis, who in his home held conferences (*majalis*) that were attended by scholars in the various disciplines. Al-Hakim showed himself far more interested in public propaganda, however. Under the Caliph's auspices al-Nu'man's son Muhammad and his grandson 'Abd al-'Aziz both gave heavily attended public lectures on Isma'ili doctrine.

Despite his zeal for the *da'wah*, al-Hakim's policies may have been having an adverse effect on the larger fortunes of the Isma'iliyah. From an early date the Fatimids had been converting their eschatological revolution into a kind of transcendental theology. The social drama so eagerly awaited in Iraq in the last quarter of the ninth century was converted into a cosmic drama played out in the *pleroma*. As Mu'izz had promised, the resurrection would be a spiritual one. Most of the Fatimids' theologians subscribed to that view, and the result was that the Isma'iliyah was in fact a sect that differed from the main body of Islam merely by its possession of a baroque metaphysic. Despite all the talk of cosmic Intelligences, the *Imam* in Cairo was little different from the Caliph in Baghdad.

At the outset, however, the Isma'iliyah had promised something more, and there were still some—few in number perhaps—who shared the expectation of that promise. In 1017 they set about, possibly with the connivance of al-Hakim, realizing their revolutionary aims by proclaiming the divinely inspired character of the *Imam*. That was, as has been seen, an old "extremist" premise, the exaltation of 'Ali over Muhammad and, in this case, the attribution of 'Ali's supernatural qualities to his successor, al-Hakim. It was not what then passed as regular Isma'ili doctrine by any means, and when it was publicly preached by a certain al-Darazi in 1017, there was serious opposition from the main body of Isma'ilis. Al-Hakim read the signs correctly and abandoned the apostle of his own divinized person to popular hostility and to his death.

Though the *Imam* ostentatiously disavowed the new cultus, this was not the end of the matter. Another of the Caliph's devotees, Hamzah ibn 'Ali, who followed al-Darazi in the leadership of the Hakim cult, proposed something far more radical, that al-Hakim was not merely divinized by divine infusion, but that he was himself God, the Isma'ili One, while he, Hamzah, was the *Imam*. This notion was unveiled in public in 1020 and once again there were public outcries, and far more serious ones than earlier. Then one night in February, 1021, al-Hakim rode off into the Muqattam hills and was never seen again. With the abrupt disappearance of the *Imam* this extraordinary cult was doomed; Hamzah was killed, either immediately or shortly thereafter.

It is not easy to read Hamzah's motives in this or to discern Hakim's own self-view. What is clear is the ideology. Hamzah was proposing the dismantling of Mu'izz's carefully wrought distinction between the spiritual yonder and the historical here. All the grades of the Isma'ili hierarchy were asserted not to reflect those of the cosmic hierarchy but to be identical with them. For the Christian Jesus, the cosmic *Kyrios*, had burst into history by his incarnation; al-Hakim, it was now revealed, was not the divine *Logos* made flesh—which was something approaching al-Darazi's view perhaps—but was God the Father.

Zahir and *batin* were one; symbol and *shari'ah* were swept away, together with the whole structure of the Gnostic myth, in favor of a revelation that was reality.

It may have been this profound ideological crisis that brought the *da'i* al-Kirmani of Iraq to Cairo in 1015. A great many of his writings have been preserved, including a number of treatises directed specifically against this new view of al-Hakim. Kirmani's own attitudes toward the Imamate were the traditional ones of Mu'izz, Ja'far ibn Mansur, and al-Nu'man; the new cult was heresy and blasphemy. And if one turns from the polemics to the systematic statement of Kirmani's *The Mind's Repose*, one finds the traditional cosmology of the *pleroma* undisturbed, while its fulfillment has once again receded into the eschatological future.

The affairs of the Fatimids appear to have been in good order when the Shi'ite traveler and poet Nasir-i Khusraw arrived in Cairo about a quarter of a century after al-Hakim's disappearance. The Divine One had been succeeded by his son al-Zahir (1021–1036) and immediately the pragmatic *status quo* was restored in Egypt. Crushing taxes and the gay life were rehabilitated in Cairo, and the devotees of the missing Caliph's divinity were relentlessly pursued and prosecuted. Hamzah ibn 'Ali's successor al-Muqtana went into hiding in Alexandria, where he was brought the news that despite the strong repressive measures taken in Egypt, the new cult of al-Hakim had raised peasant revolts in Fatimid Syria. They too were crushed in time, all save scattered communities in the hill country, where as "Druzes" they have awaited the return of al-Hakim from 1021 into modern times.[4]

Al-Zahir died in 1036 and once again Egypt was faced with the succession of a minor *Imam,* in this instance the eight-months-old Mustansir (1036–1094). This time, however, there was no crisis in either politics or religion. The government was in the hands of regents, the new Caliph's Sudanese mother and, from 1050, the vizier al-Yazuri. Yazuri deliberately sacrificed the Fatimids' western holdings on Libya and Tunisia, but with them he bought

4. They apparently took their name from al-Darazi, though almost certainly the instigator and chief shaper of the movement was Hamzah.

peace in Egypt itself.[5] That peace was very much in evidence when Nasir-i Khusraw arrived in Cairo in 1047. The city had grown enormously since Jawhar's day, and to the Iranian traveler it looked like a glittering mountain with its tall, well-built private houses and palaces and its public displays of power and affluence. The memory of the divinity of al-Hakim was buried under the pomp of al-Mustansir.

Nasir has left a firsthand account of his visit in his Persian *Travel Book.* He was born and educated in the region of Merv and was later known locally as a Persian lyricist in the popular hedonistic style. By his own account he had a vision in 1045 with a warning to mend his ways and to take the road to salvation, which lay, in his case, in the direction of Mecca. There is a somewhat worldlier explanation for his departure: a Shi'ite poet was not a very negotiable quantity in Ghaznavid Khurasan. By 1047 Nasir was in Cairo, where he underwent his second "conversion," this time to the Isma'ili *da'wah.* He was back in the East in 1052, but an Isma'ili *da'i* was even less welcome to the Seljuqs than a Shi'ite poet had been to the Ghaznavids, and after further wanderings Nasir came to rest in the obscure valley of Yamgan high in the mountains east of Balkh, where he died sometime between 1072 and 1077.

In addition to the *Travel Book* and the poetry, a number of Nasir's speculative treatises have been preserved, written, like all his work, in Persian. Some of them may have been reworked by later, more orthodox hands, and in others the Isma'ili attitudes are skillfully concealed within an opaque *batin.* One of the earliest, written in 1053, is the *Book of Illumination,* a didactic ethical poem that combines the usual ethical themes with a Greek-style metaphysics. His *Provender for Travelers* is encyclopedic in the

5. Sometime before 1050 two immense Bedouin confederacies, the Banu Hilal and the Banu Sulaym, passed from Arabia into Upper Egypt, where they were ruining the countryside. In an attempt to buy their departure, Yazuri "gave" them Libya and Tunisia, provinces from which the Fatimids' grip was already slipping. The Bedouin leaders accepted, took the free passage through Egypt and trekked westward, destroying en route the economy of many of the North African principalities.

manner and to the point of the *Epistles* of the Brethren of Purity. The *Face of Faith* betrays the clearest influence of the Cairo years, since parts of it appear to have been lifted straight out of Ja'far ibn Mansur. There is no trace of al-Hakim there, however; like the early Fatimids, Nasir was convinced that the final coming of the *Mahdi* was in the remote future.

The best-known of Nasir's speculative works is one of his last. *The Conjunction of the Two Wisdoms*, which is in the form of a commentary on a *qasidah* by the (Isma'ili?) poet Abu al-Haytham al-Jurjani, was written in 1070 for the *amir* of the remote province where he spent his final years. The project which Nasir set for himself was to unite the wisdom of religion—that is, Islam, "which is the product of the Holy Spirit"—with the science of creation, "which is an appanage of philosophy." What followed was a fascinating exercise in allegorical exegesis in which Nasir's somewhat ill-assorted Greek learning in cosmology and physics was brought to bear on the solution of some equally dubious problems. The *Qur'an* and the *hadith* are kept well in the background; when they are glossed the interpretation is almost inevitably Gnostic.

This kind of energetically argued *esoterica* apparently made little impression upon the intellectuals of the 'Abbasids' capital; the chief Isma'ili propaganda successes were in northern and western Iran. The *Epistles* of the Brethren were known and discussed in Baghdad, to be sure, but the philosophers there, many of them Christians, did not appear to take them or other Isma'ili writings seriously either as cosmology or as a blueprint for revolution.

The chief intellectual monument of Buyid Baghdad, the *Catalogue* of Ibn al-Nadim, is not innocent of the esoteric and the occult. But the author, himself a Shi'ite, was the partisan of a public wisdom publicly propagated. The Isma'ilis and the occultists traced their complex learning back through a narrowing tradition to a single divine source; Ibn al-Nadim held for the pluralistic origins of human culture, and in the pages of the *Catalogue* the collected treasures from the intellectual traditions of the Arabs, Iranians and Greeks are laid out in dazzling display, set off by rarer and more exotic pieces from India and China.

There are dark corners too. Greek literature was largely unknown to the Muslim, even to the highly educated Ibn al-Nadim, and Greek history had no meaning for him. Where a sketch of the latter is offered—by Mas'udi for example—it is thin and impressionistic, a shadow without substance from some lost Greco-Roman handbook. Where the Arabs approached most closely to the Hellenic *paideia* was in their reception of Greek ethical literature of the type collected by Miskawayh and others. From Iran, on the other hand, came a rich tradition in which ethics and history were still united within the compass of the Iranian epic and supported by the reviving voice of the Persian language. The Greeks addressed Islam only through the medium of translation; in the tenth century the Iranians began to speak once again in their native dialect.

Early in 'Abbasid days savants who were Iranian in origin but wrote in the ecumenical Arabic of the day undertook to instruct their Muslim contemporaries on the traditions of their own people—Ibn al-Muqaffa' on the literary style of the Sasanian court; Abu Sahl ibn al-Nawbakht on the history of eastern wisdom; and then, somewhat later, Ibn Qutaybah and al-Dinawari on the history of Iran. And once Muslim historiography had extended its horizons beyond the raids of the Prophet and the Arab conquest, much of this Iranian historical material began to be drawn upon by classical Arab historians like Tabari and his successors.

The earliest and most important of these Iranian scholars working in the service of an Arab Islam, Ibn al-Muqaffa' (d. 757), was a translator as well as a *littérateur*, and it is from him, by way of Ibn al-Nadim's *Catalogue*, that we get one of our earliest and most detailed pieces of information on the linguistic geography of Iran. His remarks appear to refer to late Sasanian times when, according to Ibn al-Muqaffa', the languages in use within the empire included the following: "Pahlevi," by which he meant the historical dialect of the Parthians commonly associated with Isfahan, Rayy, Hamadhan, Mah Nihavand and Azarbayjan; *dari,* the everyday spoken language of the court at Seleucia-Ctesiphon; *parsi,* here the literary language of the Sasanian intelligentsia; *khuzi* a local Iranian dialect of Khuzistan; and finally *suryani,* or Syriac, the language of the Aramaeans of the empire.

Ibn al-Muqaffa' 's terminology did not remain the standard one for later Muslim authors. His "Pahlevi," which reflects the historical and geographical origins of the dialect, the area known as "the land of the Parthians," in Persian *Pahla,* came to be applied generally to the literary language of the Sasanian Empire. There were probably very few Iranians who could still read and understand Pahlevi by the mid-tenth century, and they were restricted to the feeble remnant of the Zoroastrian clergy. Those Iranians who still spoke Persian (*farsi*) in preference to Arabic (*'arabiyah*) used what Ibn al-Muqaffa' here calls *dari,* the spoken language of the court, which even in Sasanian times was on the way to becoming a kind of vernacular *koine* of the empire and which, again according to Ibn al-Muqaffa', was developing into something considerably more elegant among the Iranians of Khurasan and particularly at Balkh.

It was also in eastern Iran that the powerful pre-Islamic squires, or *dihqans*, began to reassert themselves in the political life of Islam in the ninth century. Chief among them were the Samanids, whose eponymous ancestor Saman, a *dihqan* from the area around Balkh, was converted to Islam under the Umayyads. Very little is heard of his son, but in 820 Ma'mun granted extensive powers to four of Saman's grandsons in Transoxania in return for their services in putting down an insurrection there. It was likewise Ma'mun who appointed the *mawla* Tahir as *amir* of all of Khurasan (and of its dependency Transoxania) and allowed those lands to be ruled almost autonomously by Tahir and his descendants.[6] With the collapse of Tahirid control of Khurasan in 873 the Samanid Isma'il marched upon and took Bukhara and the season of Samanid ascendancy was at hand.

In 873 the Oxus was the southern boundary of the lands to which Isma'il could press his claims. Beyond that, in Khurasan, the Saffarids were in firm, if temporary, control. The ineffectual Caliph Mu'tadid (892–902) dispensed charters to the Amirate in both directions, but in the end the issue of Khurasan was settled by the principals themselves. In 900 the Saffarid 'Amr and the Samanid Isma'il clashed near Balkh. 'Amr was taken and dis-

---

6. See Chap. II, p. 168.

patched to Baghdad; in return Isma'il received the Amirate of Khurasan, an office which his descendants held, in name if not always in fact, down to 1005.

The Samanids represented a new order in eastern Iran, or rather, the rebirth of an old one. Before Islam the Sasanians were the nominal sovereigns of those lands, but the local government rested firmly in the hands of the *dihqan* class. The Samanids were from that class, and their early successes depended on the continued prosperity of the small landowners. But now they ruled over an increasingly Islamicized Khurasan and Transoxania in the name of a Muslim Caliph; they governed from Bukhara through a bureaucracy which was a diminished image of the one in Baghdad. Like the Caliph, they were protected by Turkish guards and like him, they embraced Sunni Islam. The language of the *diwans* was, of course, Arabic, but that of most of the population was, despite the growing Arabization of the province, the same Iranian *dari* to which Ibn al-Maqaffa' had already directed attention.[7]

By all appearances *dari* was already well advanced along the path of self-promotion from a vernacular to a literary tongue. Arabic supplied some additional impetus from its own by now sophisticated vocabulary and by making available a new script. It was precisely the use of the Arabic script—awkward perhaps for an Indo-European language, but infinitely superior to the defective Pahlevi manner of writing—which contributed the crucial element to the literary resurrection of the language that had never ceased being spoken in Iran.

Though there are earlier traces of poetry in the new literary *dari*, the first major figure whose work is preserved in Persian is the poet and musician Rudaki, who was drawn to the court of the Samanid *amir* Nasr II (914–943). It was a stormy time in Bukhara. Shi'ite and Isma'ili pressure was strong on the *amir*, to the point that in the last year of his life Nasr embraced Isma'ilism and declared his allegiance to the Fatimid Caliph al-Qa'im. It was a politically injudicious act and raised against the *amir* the opposition of both the *'ulama'* and the Turkish slave-mercenaries to

7. That is, some form of western Iranian. The lingua franca of eastern Iran, Sogdian, was still being used, but it was probably well into its decline during the Samanid period.

whom the Samanids were already beholden. Nasr quickly recanted.

By that time Rudaki was already dead, but even earlier there had been Shi'ite troubles that somewhat obscurely led to the fall of the Samanid vizier Abu al-Fadl Bal'ami, troubles in which Rudaki was implicated. Whether the poet was himself an Isma'ili is not certain; if so, his treason was against the Sunni Caliph and not the *amir* since what is left of his once immense poetical outpouring is filled with *qasidah*-style panegyrics of his princely patron. There are as well erotic *ghazal;* in Rudaki's lyrics the language and sensibilities may be Persian, but the forms are still Arab.

Rudaki took up other themes already familiar to the Arabs and the Iranians. Earlier a collection of fables attributed to a certain Bidpai had come into Pahlevi from Indian sources. Ibn al-Muqaffa' had translated them into Arabic prose as the *Kalilah and Dimnah,* and now Rudaki reworked them in the epic verse of the new literary *dari.* He did the same for the tales of Sinbad, another borrowing from the Indian via Pahlevi. Here too there were Arab antecedents, the Arab poet al-Lahiqi (d. c. 815), who had worked both the Bidpai and the Sinbad themes in the rhyming epic couplet.

The Arab influences on Rudaki are not remarkable. There was a Persian poetry before Islam, and the Parthian minstrel tradition was much cultivated by the Sasanians. Its themes were, however, epic rather than lyrical, while the Arabic poetic had long been producing attractive and sophisticated results in the *qasidah* and the *ghazal.* And it was there that Rudaki turned to learn form and metrics. His is the glamour of a pioneer, an Ennius rather than a Vergil. His successor in Persian letters, Abu 'Ali Muhammad Bal'ami, the son of Nasr's vizier, was more like a Livius Andronicus.

The young Bal'ami served the Samanid 'Abd al-Malik (954–961) in the same capacity as that in which his father had served, considerably more aggressively, Nasr II. In 963 the *amir* commissioned his vizier to perform a task that was probably far more to his liking than the administration of a principality, the translation into Persian of the *History* of al-Tabari. Bal'ami shortened the original to a great extent by removing the chains of oral transmission and the alternate versions of events cited by Tabari, but he made no attempt at extending the chronicle down to his own day. It ended where the Arabic original ended, in 842, with the result that Bal'ami's version, the first major prose work in the new literary *dari*, is a recounting of Islamic history during the great age of the 'Abbasids, an Arab dynasty. Thus the fate of Iran was linked by the Samanids with that of Islam.

After Bal'ami's pioneer work, the Persian prose tradition continued to flourish under Samanid auspices side by side with the earlier poetry. Tabari's commentary on the *Qur'an* was given an abridged translation into Persian shortly after the *History*, but even where authors attempted something more than a mere translation from the Arabic, the themes and treatments remained close to Arabic prototypes: al-Muwaffaq's work on drugs;[8] the *Introduction to Astronomy* composed by Abu Nasr al-Qummi in 975; the anonymous *Boundaries of the World*, a geographical treatise written in 982; and finally, the *Wonders of the Lands*, a work composed for Ibn Sina's patron Nuh II by Abu al-Mu'ayyad al-Balkhi, the bilingual author who also reworked part of the Iranian epic cycle.

The Samanids encouraged these projects by their famous libraries and by patronizing, out of their considerable commercial wealth,[9] the artists and scholars who produced them. Arabic too was promoted, as in the case of the Samanids' principal historian, al-Narshakhi, whose *History of Bukhara* was written for Nuh I in 943,[10] Ibn Sina, who enjoyed the patronage of Nuh II (976–997),[11] the geographer Abu Zayd al-Balkhi,[12] and the two Khwarazmians, Muhammad al-Khwarizmi[13] and Biruni. That the

---

8. See Chap. V, p. 392.
9. The Samanid oasis cities were important way stations on the traditional "silk route" between Iran and China, but they also had a share in the important trade that ran northward into Russia.
10. The Arabic original is lost, but an abridgment of a Persian translation done in 1128 is preserved.
11. Ibn Sina's major prose work in Persian, the compact encyclopedia called *The Book of Knowledge*, was written not for a Samanid but for the Kakuyid dynast of Isfahan, 'Ala' al-Dawlah (1108–1141).
12. See Chap. V, pp. 349–351.
13. See Chap. V, p. 333.

arts and sciences flourished as they so manifestly did at Bukhara, Nishapur, Balkh and elsewhere in the East in the tenth century is largely the work of the Samanids. But they are important in the history of Islam not merely for their patronage but because they presided over a crucial turn in the fortunes of the *Dar al-Islam.* For the first time under the Samanids large numbers of Turks were integrated into the domains of the Caliphs in the East. And it was under those same Samanid auspices that the Turks were converted to Islam.

When the Arabs first advanced into the lands beyond the Oxus they found there Turkic peoples who had already replaced the Iranians on the steppes of Central Asia. Such, for example, were the Türgish, who between 724 and 737 threatened the fragile Arab hold on Samarqand. The Türgish were merely the westernmost of the great bands of Turks that stretched from the Oxus back to the borders of China. Now and again they were joined into a substantial federation, as when the Uighurs put together a tribal empire in the middle of the eighth century and so dominated the steppe for nearly a hundred years.[14] The breakup of the Uighur confederation in 840 had as one of its results the coming into prominence in northeastern Iran of the Turkish Qarluq, and during the latter half of the ninth century they and the Samanids struggled for advantage in Transoxania and north of the Jaxartes frontier.

Beyond the Jaxartes was the domain of the nomads, but Turks had been settling into the commercial oases and cultivated land of Sogdia as well. Not all of them came into the *Dar al-Islam* of their own will. With the increased Islamicization of the central domains of the Caliphate the need for slaves had to be satisfied elsewhere—Islamic Law forbade one Muslim to enslave another —and the Caliphs turned to their frontier provinces in the Caucasus and Transoxania. In the latter region the Turks soon became highly prized for their martial qualities and their loyalty, and the Tahirids, Saffarids and Samanids did a brisk business in shipping back to Baghdad the valuable Turkish soldier-slaves (*ghulams*) to protect the Caliphs.

---

14. See Chap. II, pp. 153–154.

The Samanids themselves were not immune to the lure of letting their enslaved Turks do their fighting, and there as elsewhere the Turkish captains rose swiftly to power and ended by controlling their masters. At Bukhara this occurred during the reign of the *amir* 'Abd al-Malik (954–961), and thereafter the provincial governorship and effective control of Khurasan were in the hands of one or another of the Samanids' Turkish *ghulams*.

It was on the Samanid governor of Khurasan that rested the defense of the realm against the growing strength of the Buyids. Through their Turkish seconds the Shi'ite Buyids and the Sunni Samanids contested for western Iran and the Caspian states throughout the middle decades of the tenth century. Neither side was strong enough to dominate the other. The Buyid princes ruled over a divided empire—only 'Adud al-Dawlah (949–983) had the benefit of a unified Buyid inheritance—and were seriously threatened by the power and propaganda of the Fatimids. The Samanids, for their part, were increasingly the pawns of their Turkish guards.

In 988 the chief of one of the most powerful of the Turkish families, Abu 'Ali-Simjuri, forced the *amir* Nuh II (976–997) to declare him viceroy of all the Samanid holdings south of the Oxus. What occurred in Nuh's own lands on the northern side of the river was apparently of little concern to Simjuri, and sometime before 992 he is alleged to have arranged by secret treaty to hand Transoxania over to the *khan* of the Qarakhanids poised on the other side of the Jaxartes.

The Qarakhanids were a tribal confederation of Turkish nomads descended from the ruling house of the Qarluq. There were Islamic missionaries carrying the Sunni beliefs of the Samanids among the steppe people, and sometime about 950 the *khan* of the Qarakhanids, Satuq Bughra Khan, accepted Islam under the name of 'Abd al-Karim. It was his grandson, Harun Bughra Khan, with whom Abu 'Ali Simjuri made his reported pact, and accordingly in 992 the Qarakhanids occupied Samarqand and Bukhara with the support of rebels within Sogdia. The Qarakhanids had not come to stay on this occasion, and Nuh quickly returned from his headlong flight. But it was evident to all concerned that unless help were to come the Samanid Amirate would fall to the Turks.

Nuh turned for assistance to one of his former captains. The Turk Alptegin had come to military prominence in Khurasan with the younger Bal'ami. He attempted to manipulate the Samanid succession in 961, failed, and was forced to withdraw with his dependents southward to Ghazna in modern Afghanistan, where his troops deposed the local ruler and set up an independent state under the nominal sovereignty of Bukhara.

Among the intimates of Alptegin who took the road to Ghazna was Sebuktegin, another Turkish *ghulam* who had traveled the classic route upward from slavery to military eminence and eventually political power. In 977 Sebuktegin, by now the son-in-law of his former patron, wrested the control of Ghazna from the last of Alptegin's successors, and it was he and his son Mahmud who responded to Nuh's call for help in the years after 992.

Nuh and Sebuktegin both died in 997. The succession was troubled in Ghazna as well as in Bukhara, but Mahmud quickly disposed of his elder brother Isma'il, and once master of his own house, he cast his regards on that of his enfeebled sovereigns, the Samanids. The armies of Ghazna overran Khurasan in 999, but there also came uninvited to the feast the Qarakhanids, who in that same year crossed the Jaxartes and again occupied Bukhara and Samarqand.

The Ghaznavids and Qarakhanids composed their ambitions and shared the booty—they agreed that the Oxus should mark the border between them—and the official recognition of Baghdad. When Mahmud marched into Khurasan in 999 he came as the champion of Caliphal legitimacy against the Samanids, who had allegedly failed to recognize the accession of the Caliph al-Qadir in 991. For his newly discovered loyalty to the Caliph Mahmud was granted a charter to the possession of Khurasan and showered with a clutch of honors and titles, including that of "Right Hand of the State," which he liked, and "*Mawla* of the Commander of the Faithful," which he did not.

His growing prestige in Baghdad and the successes of his armies in India[15] did not exempt Mahmud from the less benevo-

---

15. Sebuktegin had begun the enterprise of raiding into India, and Mahmud continued the practice. His armies ranged across northern

lent attentions of the Qarakhanids lodged across the Oxus. Whenever the Ghaznavid armies disappeared over the mountains into India there was Qarakhanid raiding in Khurasan. Mahmud returned suddenly in 1008 and crushed the intruders.

Mahmud's only other rival in the eastern Caliphate was the principality of Khwarazm in the delta of the Oxus. The Khwarazmians, who had lived in relative political isolation since their inclusion in the *Dar al-Islam* early in the eighth century, were nominal dependents of the Samanids, but in 1014 Mahmud asserted his claim to have his name publicly commemorated in the Friday prayers as sovereign of Khwarazm. The local ruler, Ma'mun, who was Mahmud's brother-in-law, was in an extremely delicate position, and the negotiation between the two parties was put into the hands of one of the principality's most illustrious sons, al-Biruni. He failed, however, to avert an ultimatum from Mahmud. Its immediate effect was the death of Ma'mun at the hands of his own people. Mahmud delayed just long enough to retrieve his sister and then in 1017 marched into Khwarazm on the pretext of avenging his slain brother-in-law. The resistance was spirited, but in vain. Mahmud installed his man Altuntash as the new ruler and carried off al-Biruni to Ghazna.

Biruni joined a distinguished literary colony that was already coming to maturity in Ghazna. Biruni was doubtless the most spectacular catch of the lot, and Mahmud and his successors took some pains to remain on good terms with their resident astronomer-historian.[16] Things did not proceed quite so smoothly with another, sometimes reluctant, admirer, the poet Firdawsi. Biruni's professional language was Arabic, though his native tongue was the Iranian dialect of Khwarazm, and he could write in the new literary Persian as well. Firdawsi belonged, however, entirely within the Iranian tradition, and there, in part, lay his difficulty with Mahmud.

India no fewer than seventeen times between 1001 and 1027, chiefly from his base at Lahore in the Punjab. The Islamicization of the northern Indus valley was the work of Mahmud and it won him the title and reputation of *ghazi* or "warrior for the faith."

16. On Biruni's scientific career, see Chap. V, pp. 349–351.

The life of Firdawsi is filled with obscurity and legend. He was born near Tus sometime after 940, the son of a *dihqan* and so independent enough to pursue the career of poetry from his youth. For nearly a quarter of a century he labored on his *Book of Kings*, an adaptation and continuation of an earlier epic by Daqiqi. Daqiqi, who was a poet in the Samanid courts of Khurasan under Nuh II, had taken up the Iranian epic tradition and attempted to fashion a poetical version of it in the new literary Persian. The historical epic, which in its finished form dated back to late Sasanian times, was very much alive in tenth-century Khurasan. Daqiqi had at least two almost contemporary versions of it to draw on. Abu Mansur ibn 'Abd al-Razzaq, the feudal lord of Tus in Firdawsi's native district, had set a commission of four scholars to turn the Pahlevi *Book of Kings*, presumably the same one translated earlier into Arabic by Ibn al-Muqaffa', into Persian prose. They finished their work in 957, and it was used by Firdawsi and perhaps Daqiqi as well. Again in Khurasan, and under the same Nuh II, Abu al-Mu'ayyad al-Balkhi, already cited as the author of a Persian *Wonders of the Lands*, composed his prose *Book of Garshap*, which dealt with one popular part of the epic cycle.

Whatever sources he was relying upon, written or oral, Daqiqi completed about ten thousand verses of his own Persian *Book of Kings* before his death sometime after 976. It was at this point that Firdawsi took up the task—Daqiqi is reported to have appeared to him in a dream and urged him to complete the work—and integrated into it a thousand lines of his predecessor's version. A few years before 1000 this great epic of Iran's past was presented by the author to Mahmud of Ghazna, at the time, perhaps, when he was still struggling with the Turkish Qarakhanids for the possession of Iranian Khurasan. Firdawsi's work describes just such a conflict between Iran and Turan, and if the poem seems somehow more appropriate to the Samanids, to whom, some have suggested, it was originally dedicated, the Iranicized Turk Mahmud must have seemed a likely enough alternate during the eclipse of the Samanids in Iran.

Mahmud was, however, only a sometime standard-bearer of Iranian nationalism, and after 1010 the Ghaznavid *amir* found it more to his profit to draw closer to the 'Abbasid Caliph in Baghdad and to present himself in Sunni Arab weeds rather than the Iranian vestments of the Samanids, which had, one notes, a distinct, if occasional, whiff of Isma'ilism about them. According to tradition, Mahmud was lukewarm about the *Book of Kings* and recognized its value only after the poet's death back in Tus, perhaps in 1020 or 1025. The alleged reason for Mahmud's lack of enthusiasm was Firdawsi's Shi'ism. This is not at all unlikely, particularly when viewed against Mahmud's own shifting politics, which made something that he himself called "the history of the Persians" a somewhat embarrassing gift.

The *Book of Kings* was precisely that, a history of the Persians traced out from the earliest times down to the fall of the Sasanians. It knew nothing of Islam, or even of the Samanids—they may have been edited out for the dedication to Mahmud—and true to its Sasanian orientations, it paid little attention to the Parthian dynasty of the Arsacids. The entire poem, about fifty thousand lines in our manuscripts, is an unashamed rhapsody to feudal Iran, its heroes and their chivalrous values, portrayed in idealized terms. In one sense the *Book of Kings* is remote from history in its mythologizing of the past; in another it is, like the *Iliad* of the Hellenes, the most realistic description of that Iranian past as it existed before the coming of Islam.

If Mahmud's attitude toward Firdawsi's glowing Iranian nationalism was ambivalent, he showed more enthusiasm for the straightforward panegyrics of the Arab-style *qasidah,* which in Baghdad had long been the favored vehicle for the praise of princes. Among the other literary luminaries who adorned the court at Ghazna, the poet al-'Unsuri (d. 1039) was singled out for special honors. Mahmud appointed him "King of the Poets," and in his position as Ghaznavid laureate 'Unsuri presided over a poetical establishment of hundreds of versifiers, all bent, doubtless, on rivaling the "king's" praises of the Right Hand of the State. Like his model, Rudaki, 'Unsuri wrote both lyrics and adaptations of the romantic epic, but it is chiefly the panegyric *qasidahs*, gracefully adapted to a Persian form, that are still preserved. They are markedly more rhetorical and sophisticated than Rudaki's pioneering attempts at the genre. The best-known of his colleagues is al-Farrukhi (d. 1037), whose considerable later reputation came not so much from his panegyrics as from the *ghazals*, where the erotic and hedonistic themes favored by the Persian poets of the following centuries are already fully and artistically displayed.

The Ghaznavids had their prose panegyricists as well. Both the Buyids of Iraq and the Samanids of Khurasan had supported official historians, and the Ghaznavids continued the profitable custom. Mahmud was the subject of a full-scale biography in Arabic by Muhammad ibn 'Abd al-Jabbar al-'Utbi (d. 1035),[17] the descendant of a family of Samanid viziers and himself a *diwan* official under Mahmud. 'Utbi's connection with the *diwans* is fairly clear from the attitudes and judgments expressed in his *The Right Hand of the State*, as well as from the overblown chancery style of rhymed prose, the latter in imitation of Ibrahim ibn Hilal's official history of the Daylami Buyids.

The eastern provinces of the *Dar al-Islam* were the subject of a lively tradition of local history. Much of this came to rest in al-Gardizi's *Adornment of Narratives*, a Persian continuation for the years 955 to 1041 of earlier Arab chronicles, with a distinct emphasis on Khurasan and the eastern provinces and on the Muslims' eastern neighbors like the Indians and Turks. The underpinning of a local historiography can also be detected in the major historical work devoted to the Ghaznavids, the Persian *History of the House of Sebuktegin* by Abu al-Fadl al-Bayhaqi (d. 1077). The original design of the work was apparently to cover the entire dynasty, though we are not absolutely certain where it began—perhaps in 1018—or where it ended. What is preserved is most of the six volumes devoted to the career of Mas'ud ibn Mahmud (1030–1041). Even this admittedly truncated portion is an important testimony on the Ghaznavids. Bayhaqi was a subordinate in, and finally head of, the diplomatic ministry of the Ghaznavids for twenty years. And if Bayhaqi had to rely on his literary predecessors for the events of early

17. Later, in 1025, translated into Persian. From that point onward 'Utbi's version of Mahmud's career became a standard part of the Persian chronicle tradition.

Ghaznavid history, he had access to a great deal of official correspondence covering the period of Mas'ud's reign, and his work reflects this unusual view from within.[18]

In 1025 the glories of Mahmud's well-reported career were approaching a climax. In that year he conducted an expedition in force across the Oxus and intervened in the quarrels of the Qarakhanid chieftains there. The political and social waters of Transoxania were further roiled by a new Turkish presence more recently come in from the Kirgiz steppe north of the Caspian and Aral seas. Tribes of this great Oghuz confederation, which were called Turkoman after their conversion to Islam, were now serving the Qarakhanids as their military arm, though not always to their own satisfaction. The restless and destructive nomads were barred from the cities of Transoxania and had little to look forward to in either victory or defeat.

One family, which was by no means the most powerful, can be distinguished within the great Oghuz confederacy, that of Seljuq, the eponymous founder of the later Seljuq dynasty. His sons Arslan Isra'il, Musa and Mikha'il, and the latter's sons Tughril and Chaghri, were all deeply involved in the political strife across the Oxus, and one of them, Arslan Isra'il, who was eventually captured and executed by Mahmud, had so alienated his own tribesmen that they petitioned Mahmud for permission to cross the Oxus and pasture in the lands on the fringe of Khurasan. They were followed by other Turkoman tribes during the succeeding years, and within a decade Mahmud's son and successor Mas'ud was no longer capable of containing them.

One final triumph was reserved for the Ghaznavids, however. The Buyid line in Jibal had split into two branches after the death in 977 of Rukn al-Dawlah Hasan, the last of the three brothers who had founded the dynasty. One branch ruled in Rayy and the other in Hamadhan and Isfahan, where both Ibn 'Abbad and Ibn Sina once served as viziers. After 1008 the latter two cities were under the effective control of a related Daylami

---

18. Some of the details of the author's life are known from another al-Bayhaqi (d. 1169), also a historian, who wrote a history of his native town in Persian as well as an Arabic continuation of the *Garden of Wisdom* of Abu Sulayman al-Sijistani; see Chap. VII, p. 540.

family, that of 'Ala' al-Dawlah ibn Kakuya and his offspring. Mahmud, who had never had a direct confrontation with the Buyids in western Iran, was finally invited into their midst in 1029 by the Buyids of Rayy in the suicidal hope that he would resolve their quarrels. He did resolve them, and in precisely the way that might have been anticipated: Mahmud deposed the Buyids and installed his own governors in Rayy and Jibal. At the same time Ibn Kakuya had to accept Ghaznavid sovereignty over Isfahan and Hamadhan.

Mahmud died in 1030 and the glories of even the recent past were soon forgotten. He preferred a younger son as his successor, but by treachery Mas'ud, the elder, prevailed, only to be granted ten scant years before the structure of his father's empire came crashing down around him. From the outset Mas'ud could not pretend to control the marches of Khurasan where the Seljuqs and their nomadic Turkomans were crossing the Oxus in increasing numbers. Khwarazm was still a nominal vassal of Ghazna, but Altuntash and his sons Harun (1032–1034) and Isma'il (1034–1041) had far more to fear from the Oghuz tribes clustered on the lower Jaxartes.

Khurasan was on the edge of disaster between 1035 and 1040 as the rampaging Turkomans swept through the open land around the cities while the inhabitants cowered and starved within the walls. Pressured from all sides—some of his father's western vassals were in revolt—Mas'ud decided to face the Seljuqs' redoubtable Turkoman troops. The encounter between Mas'ud's modern but dispirited army and the Seljuqs' nomads took place at Dandanqan between Sarakhs and Merv in 1040. This time Ghaznavid arms and elephants did not prevail; Mas'ud was deprived of his richest province and, shortly, of his throne. He was deposed in the following year, and his successors ruled only in eastern Afghanistan and northern India.

Farther west the collapse of the Khurasanian buffer was felt soon after 1040. The crumbling remains of 'Adud al-Dawlah's empire in Iraq and western Iran had been ruled uncertainly after 1025 by two of his descendants—'Imad al-Din Abu Kalijar was lord of Fars, Khuzistan and Kirman, while his uncle Jalal al-Dawlah Shirzil was the *amir* of Baghdad and most of Iraq. The two men lived under an uneasy truce imposed by the fear of greater dangers from outside their realms, but when Jalal al-Dawlah died in 1044 his nephew deposed the intended successor in Iraq and possessed himself of the whole of Buyid territory.

Judged by the only standard applicable in the middle of the eleventh century, the rule of both Jalal al-Dawlah and Abu Kalijar was successful; they held at bay the westward approaching tide of Turkomans and their Seljuq masters. The latter's control was not very effective, and the rather aimless wandering of the nomads eventually brought great numbers of them into the province of Azarbayjan fronting on the territory of Christian Armenia and Byzantium.

It seems doubtful that Tughril and the other Seljuq *khans* were as drawn by the prospect of fresh pasturage and a *jihad* against the Christians as were their tribal compatriots. The grandsons of Seljuq were rapidly learning about politics during their trek across the top of Iran. For them, power meant control over at least part of the Turkoman horde. They acted in concert at Dandanqan and were rewarded by a stunning victory over the best army in the East. After that battle they had divided their conquests: Tughril was to have the Khanate of Iraq and western Iran, while Chaghri, assisted by his son Alp Arslan, had control of Khurasan. Tughril, at the cutting edge of the Turkoman advance, had the difficult task of directing the wildest of his *ghazis* into Azarbayjan, where they could discharge their enthusiasms against the Christians, and at the same time work out some arrangement with the Buyids in Iraq.

The Buyids for their part were prepared to deal with the now more reasonable Tughril. A *modus vivendi* began to emerge, fashioned out of a defensive posture,[19] dynastic marriages and political compromise. Shi'ism and Sunnism had, on the face of it, very little to do with it. But with Abu Kalijar's death in 1048 his successor found it impossible to maintain the dangerous equilibrium.

Al-Malik al-Rahim (1048–1055), Abu Kalijar's son and successor, had to contend not only with the ambitions of his

---

19. Including the walling of cities. The Turks, who would one day take the most strongly fortified position in the world, Constantinople, were still quite incapable of taking a walled city by siege.

disgruntled brother but with the reviving power of the 'Abbasid Caliphate. From the days of al-Qadir, or, more accurately, from the days when Mahmud of Ghazna first appeared as a political counterweight to the Buyids, the Caliph's hand can be seen somewhat more surely in the delicate counterplay of force and diplomacy in the eastern provinces. Now with al-Qa'im, who assumed the Caliphate in 1031 and would hold it until 1075, a greater trial of strength was in the making, conducted, on the Caliph's side by the vizier Ibn al-Muslimah and the constitutional lawyer al-Mawardi.

Al-Mawardi was a lawyer who served as *qadi* under both al-Qadir and al-Qa'im until his death at the age of eighty in 1058. His role in al-Qa'im's growing assertiveness must have been a delicate one: he represented the Caliph's displeasure to Jalal al-Dawlah in 1037 when the Buyid *amir*, who ruled by virtue of an office conferred upon him by the Caliph, assumed the old—and autonomous—Sasanian title of *Shahanshah*. Again, in 1043, he was entrusted with the mission of demanding justice from Tughril after his troops' devastation of Rayy.

The date of Mawardi's major work, *The Ordinances of Government*, is not known, but it must have been written when Mahmud was still flourishing in Ghazna, since the presence of a powerful Sunni *amir*, and one who had displayed his loyalty to the Caliph and his zeal for the faith, goes far to explain the thinly veiled threats against the Buyids that can be read in its pages. The *Ordinances* is superficially a theoretical treatment of the Caliphate as a political office, the earliest such work preserved in Islam—there were of course a great many *legal* treatments of the theme under the rubric "On the Imamate"—but the circumstances under which it was composed cast that theory in a peculiar light. There are arguments on the nature and function of the Caliphate directed against not only the theoretical speculations of the Mu'tazilah but also the more pressing Shi'ite claims that the Imamate passed from *Imam* to *Imam* by infallible designation rather than by the Sunni method of election.

The latter was very much a practical question in 1030. The Imamite Shi'ah had, it is true, very few political expectations at this point, but in Cairo there existed a Fatimid anti-Caliph whose plans for ruling Baghdad had nothing of fantasy about them.

Mawardi firmly rejected the possibility that there could be more than one Caliph at a time, but he did explore the unpleasant possibility of a Fatimid army's coming to Baghdad and deposing the 'Abbasid Caliph.

The most significant element in the *Ordinances* is Mawardi's—and al-Qa'im's—refusal to relegate the Caliphate to simply a religious office, certainly the direction it was heading under the powerful early Buyids. The Caliph, it was asserted, was still the chief executive of the Islamic *ummah*, with responsibilities for civil and political order. He may delegate his powers, but they cannot be usurped. In the event they are seized and the Caliph becomes a captive, possibly the present situation in Baghdad, then all depends on the disposition of the captors. If they govern in the spirit of the *shari'ah*, then the circumstances may be tolerated; if not, then the Caliph may summon others to his aid.

If those "others" included Mahmud of Ghazna before 1030, then the hope had vanished ten years later. After 1040 the Ghaznavids possessed little power either in Iraq or in Iran. Their troops were not, in any event, summoned to Baghdad, and the Seljuq pressures continued to converge on the capital of al-Qa'im and his fading Buyid custodian-*amir* al-Malik al-Rahim. The city itself was close to anarchy. Despite the thriving intellectual life and the Buyids' sporadic attempts at a public-works program, the social and economic fabric of the city was unraveling. The western Shi'ite quarter of Karkh was flourishing, but elsewhere ruin had set in. The city had shrunk considerably in size from its days of glory under al-Muqtadir (908–932). The Turkish garrison was troublesome, and the Shi'ite festivals decreed by the Buyids brought a new element of tension to an already disturbed populace. Bloody fights between Shi'ites and their orthodox and conservative opponents, particularly the Hanbalites, were common and destructive, while other commotions lacked even the veneer of theological dispute. For decades before the coming of the Seljuqs the streets of Baghdad gave the appearance of being under the control of paramilitary bands of "vagabonds" (*'ayyarun*), who struck out against Baghdad officialdom in the name of justice and terrorized the rich on behalf of the suffering poor. Against them and the other forces of dissolution the Turkish military commandant al-Basasiri could do nothing.

The issues and physiognomy of these disturbances remain obscure. The *'ayyarun* who show up in Baghdad early in the Buyid occupation appear to have analogues in the contemporary groups of young men in the cities of Syria. These latter had, however, some official standing as a kind of local urban militia who served for pay under a commander. Not infrequently they were involved in heated imbroglios with the political authorities, who more often than not were the representatives of a foreign power. The *'ayyarun* had, however, no vestige of legality about them and appear to have arisen out of economic and social unrest. In Baghdad they belonged on both sides of the political fence, pro-'Alid and pro-'Abbasid, but on the religious issue of Shi'ite versus Hanbalite they must have been chiefly in the camp of the latter.

In December of 1055 Tughril and his Turkoman troops entered Baghdad amidst a swirl of political plots and counterplots. The Caliph al-Qa'im, who was keeping his own counsel, did not meet his new *amir*. The helpless al-Malik al-Rahim was arrested shortly after, and the Buyid line came to a quiet and inglorious end. Tughril was not in Baghdad to stay, however; he had clearly announced his intentions of passing on to the west to Syria and Egypt and to the eventual chastisement of the Fatimids. The Caliph there was already alerted to what had occurred by a request for aid from al-Basasiri, the Turkish commandant in Baghdad, and Tughril's announced intentions against Egypt guaranteed that the request fell upon attentive if not enthusiastic ears.

The intermediary in the negotiations between Cairo and its somewhat unsteady partisans in Baghdad was the notorious Fatimid missionary al-Mu'ayyad fi al-Din, who had even earlier made a convert to Isma'ilism of Abu Kalijar and who now in 1056 brought back troops, money and supplies from Egypt to Iraq. Tughril meanwhile was faced with a revolt within his own family and was forced to leave Baghdad. Basasiri took advantage of the opportunity by reoccupying Baghdad at the end of 1058. Al-Qa'im, who had not fled at the approach of Tughril, now read the omens differently and escaped the city before Basasiri's troops reached the palace.

In January of 1059 al-Basasiri, who was now for the first time the undisputed master of Baghdad, officially proclaimed the Caliphate of the Fatimid al-Mustansir and sent the official paraphernalia to Cairo. Al-Mustansir, who had expected al-Qa'im as well as the turban and cloak of the Prophet, grew disenchanted with his Turkish agent, and when Tughril returned to Baghdad at the end of that same year, there was no help for Basasiri from any quarter. Basasiri fled at Tughril's approach but was captured and killed in January of 1060. Al-Qa'im was restored to Baghdad to rule as *khalifah* for another fifteen years, but now for the first time in over a century the 'Abbasid Caliph had a Sunni protector.

The missed opportunity in Baghdad signaled changes in Cairo as well. The Fatimid vizier Yazuri was dismissed for his mismanagement of the Basasiri affair, and not long afterward there were grave disorders in Egypt itself. A series of crop failures struck the land, and the merchants, who had in the past been kept under tight control by Yazuri, were now free to exploit the disaster in their own interests. Berber troops from the early days of Fatimid glory, the Turkish mercenaries imported by 'Aziz, and the Sudanese and Nubians who had supported Mustansir's mother fell upon each other with chaotic abandon.

It was the Turks who finally triumphed in Cairo, but they succeeded merely in driving the Berbers and Sudanese into the countryside, where they plundered and destroyed. Plague and famine followed while the Turks ran riot in the capital. The treasures of Mustansir were despoiled, confiscated, or simply scattered. 'Aziz's library of 200,000 volumes was destroyed. The country was near collapse, and when the Seljuqs marched into Syria in 1071 and took possession of that former Fatimid province, there was little or no effective resistance.

It was the end of the Fatimids. In 1074 Mustansir found an Armenian vizier, Badr al-Jamali, who restored order to Cairo and the countryside, and the dynasty stumbled on for another century under a succession of ineffective Caliphs. But its rulers were incapable of dealing with either the Seljuqs or the European Franks. The Fatimid version of the Isma'ili crusade was all but over, worn out in Egypt and stifled by Seljuq orthodoxy in the East. In the end it rested upon an ideology with a political program. Isma'ili ideas appeared dangerous in Baghdad, but it was Berber arms and not their own ideology that had carried the Fatimids to power. And once established in Egypt, they ruled, with the exception of al-Hakim, little differently from the 'Abbasids. When Salah al-Din restored Sunni orthodoxy to Egypt in 1171 there was scarcely a murmur of protest.

The Custodians of the Caliphate

The tension between Iran and Turan, the settled agriculturists of the plateau and the Turkish nomads of the steppe, is echoed in the Iranian tradition from Firdawsi and Ibn Sina as far back as Zoroaster. The view from the outpost of Balkh northeast across Sogdia was always a troubled one, and never more so than in the opening decades of the eleventh century, when the Iranicized Turkish dynasty of the Ghaznavids were cast in the role of defenders of the plateau by reason of their possession of Khurasan, a position and a function that brought little ease to either Ibn Sina or Firdawsi.

In the end the Ghaznavids were unsuccessful, not merely by reason of the military disaster visited upon Mas'ud at Dandanqan in 1040, but because their tenure of Khurasan was ineffectively despotic. The poet and the philosopher were not the only ones who sensed that eastern Iran was in the hands of rapacious opportunists whose real interests lay not in the stability of agricultural Khurasan but in the flashier spoils of India and the possibility of usurping the Caliphate. Khurasan was, for all that, a rich province, and the Ghaznavids fought with the enthusiasm of property owners to defend it against the relentless pressures of the Qarakhanids and the Oghuz.

The sons and grandsons of Seljuq were merely one family among the mass of Turkoman nomads, now mostly Muslims, who even before 1040 were swarming across the frontier of the Oxus, and their almost unique reaping of the rewards of Dandanqan has something fortuitous about it, an extravagant chance seized by political ambition. Over the next decades the Seljuq chiefs identified the paths to power within the Caliphate and learned, under the expert tutelage of their viziers, to govern territories rather than tribes, but for the greater part of their Turkoman followers the military windfall was an invitation to plunder rather than rule. While their Seljuq leaders turned south to Baghdad and the prize of the Caliphate, the Turkoman nomads trekked along the northern edge of the plateau, and it was only when they reached Azarbayjan that their predatory energies, already crossed with the *ghazi* mentality of the northeastern frontier whence they had come, were cast into new channels. There on the borders of the Christian kingdoms of Armenia and Georgia the zealous Turkomans were drawn into the century-old roil of a Holy War.

In Baghdad the new Seljuq masters of Iraq and Iran, and now custodians of the Caliph as well, Sultans ("rulers"), as the Caliphs permitted them to call themselves, were plunged into the considerably more complex struggle of Muslim against Muslim. The Seljuqs were as authentically orthodox as the Ghaznavids, a circumstance that may have given some hope to al-Qa'im, up to that point the prey of the Shi'ite ambitions of Basasiri, of his Fatimid paymasters in Egypt, and of the scores of Isma'ili agents who roamed the Caliphal domains. Tughril did indeed thwart the Fatimids' attempt at a coup in Baghdad in the wake of the Buyid collapse there, but in so doing he promoted a complex series of events that altered, to some extent permanently, the religious complexion of the *Dar al-Islam.*

Tughril and his successors knew well enough how to deal forcibly with the various Shi'ite principalities. The Shi'ite Arab domains in Mesopotamia and their Iranian counterparts south of the Caspian Sea all had to yield in the end to the advancing Seljuqs. Turkoman bands under Seljuq leadership entered Syria in the seventies and all but thrust the Fatimids back into Egypt. In matters political and theological they relied, however, on their viziers, Turks and Iranians as aggressively Sunni as themselves.

Tughril's premier vizier was al-Kunduri, a Khurasanian Sunni and an enthusiastic partisan of the Hanafite school of law. Once in Baghdad it was he who was given the delicate task of introducing the Caliph al-Qa'im (1031–1075) into the new order of things. Among the first items of business was a series of political marriages, and though al-Qa'im was not unwilling to marry a Seljuq princess, as circumstances seemed to dictate, the prospect of giving over his only daughter to the steppe sensibilities of the seventy-year-old Tughril was apparently an unwelcome one. Kunduri had to apply considerable pressure—the Caliphs, for all their decline from temporal power, still valued their property—

and al-Qa'im eventually yielded. Tughril barely saw the lady; he died shortly after the ceremony in 1063.

The Caliph had no choice but to yield. The details of the constitutional relationship between Caliph and Sultan had still to be explored by theoreticians like Nizam al-Mulk and Ghazali, but from the outset it must have been clear that this was no mere continuation of the purely pragmatic arrangement that existed between the Caliphs and the Buyids. The Seljuqs brought to the Caliphate a religious and constitutional security long denied it, but they brought severity as well. They secured the Caliph's place and kept him firmly within it. Many of the weapons that the Caliphs-in-opposition could raise against the Buyids were rudely denied them by the Seljuqs.

As has already been noted, the Seljuqs compacted among themselves the division of their new holdings even before they left Khurasan. Tughril was to rule Iraq and western Iran, while his brother Chaghri in Merv had suzerainty over Khurasan and the East—and with it, of course, the difficult task of blocking passage into his realms by the Turkish tribes on the steppe behind him, where the Qarakhanids ruled, generally as Seljuq vassals, and of dealing with the Ghaznavids in Afghanistan to the south.[20] Other members of the family received lesser shares in the spoils, though not to everyone's satisfaction. Ibrahim Inal, Tughril's half brother, was twice taken into custody on charges of treason, and on the second occasion, in 1059, there was an open revolt to convict him. He was executed and his followers were dispersed.

Tughril died without a male heir in 1063, three years after his brother Chaghri in Khurasan. The latter had been succeeded by his son Alp Arslan and now it appeared likely that, contrary to

---

20. The Seljuqs and Ghaznavids struggled without issue for Sijistan, and the successors of Mahmud of Ghazna held on to their possession of Afghanistan and northern India for another century. Their principal heirs were the Ghurids, a tribe of central Afghanistan whom the Ghaznavids had never really subdued and were still trying to convert to Islam in the mid-eleventh century. The Ghurid 'Ala' al-Din Husayn (1149–1161) finally took and sacked the once splendid Ghazna in 1150.

the custom of the steppe, there would be a single unified Sultanate fashioned from the family's territories. Tughril had not intended that there be such and there was some brief resistance from Kunduri, who had his own more flexible candidate for the Sultanate of Baghdad,[21] but the will of Alp Arslan prevailed and with it that of his vizier, Nizam al-Mulk. Kunduri paid for his opposition with his death.

The thirty-year reigns of Alp Arslan and his son Malik Shah spanned the height of Seljuq glory in the *Dar al-Islam.* They marked as well the rapid transition of the Seljuqs from marauders to rulers on the pattern familiar in the Caliphate since the mid-ninth century. Not all the Turkoman tribesmen were willing to accept Alp Arslan; by ancient tribal right of seniority the rule belonged to his uncle Qutlumush, who in 1064 placed himself at the head of rampaging Turkoman bands and signaled his insurrection by devastating the land round about Rayy. It was a display of the kind of energy that brought the Seljuqs to power, but now, after twenty years of identifying the welfare of the *Dar al-Islam* with their own, the Seljuq chiefs judged it anarchy. Alp Arslan turned his professional soldiers against his former tribesmen and Qutlumush was destroyed.

Turkoman nomads might be useful for breaching frontiers or even for resisting insurrection; they would not serve, however, as the military arm of the state. Early in their career in the Caliphate the Seljuqs reverted to a standing professional army made up of slaves (*ghulams* or *mamluks*) and freedmen trained in the formal arts of war and reared in a tradition of loyalty to the Sultan. This is what the Buyids had done before them, and now the Seljuqs recruited their own Turks, Daylamites and Caucasians, though on what appears to have been a much larger scale than their predecessors.

With military might came both security and increased difficulty in meeting the payroll. It was once suggested to Malik Shah that he cut expenses by mustering out part of his large army, a

---

21. Earlier Kunduri had tried a similar maneuver against Tughril himself. During the Sultan's absence from Baghdad in 1058, Kunduri sought unsuccessfully to raise support in Caliphal circles for the replacement of Tughril by his stepson Anushirvan.

notion strongly resisted by the vizier Nizam al-Mulk on the grounds that in so doing the Sultan would be simultaneously diminishing the glory of his realm and raising up unemployed soldiers as his potential rivals. The vizier's comment was born of hindsight, but he did, it seems, address himself to the problem of paying the troops. Though the custom had a fairly venerable history in Islam, Nizam al-Mulk's name is connected with an extension of the system of land grants (*iqta'*) whereby the Sultan undertook to pay his military commanders, and some of the bureaucracy as well, by giving them title to the *income* of fixed parcels of land. They were not given free title to the land itself, which was, in theory at least, the inalienable property of the community, but the grant holder did have a right to its income (after taxes, either the tithe or the land tax, as circumstances dictated) in lieu of salary.

Under the Seljuqs, not merely soldiers but princes and *amirs* were beneficiaries of these grants, in the hope, perhaps, that the holders might interest themselves in the prosperity of the land. Nizam al-Mulk warned the beneficiaries that they did not in fact possess any rights over either the land or the peasants on it, but it is difficult to believe that the possessor of an *iqta'*, particularly an administrative one where the services rendered were precisely the governing of the territory in question, did not consider himself its master.

Among those who received an *iqta'* as a matter of course was the *atabeg*, an official whom the Turks brought into the *Dar al-Islam* from their earlier history on the steppe. In one of his functions the *atabeg* behaved little differently from the tutor-viziers favored by the early 'Abbasids; he supervised the education of one of the young princes of the house. But there was more. The *atabeg*, who at his appointment not infrequently took the boy's mother to wife, supervised the politics of the prince as well as his reading matter, or, to put it more bluntly, he ensured his loyalty to the Sultan, by force of arms if necessary. It was, in short, a military office and as such eventually lost its original connotation. After Malik Shah the *atabeg* was simply a powerful *amir* who was granted this honorary title but who possessed in fact the authority once vested in his young charge.

With the passage of time the granting of *iqta'* privileges and their abuse led to the creation of a feudal class whom the Seljuqs found increasingly difficult to control, but in the beginning it was their own tribal past that frustrated the Sultans' attempts at consolidating their own power. Resistance came from within their own family, from an Ibrahim Inal in the days of Tughril, from his uncle Qutlumush and his half brother Qavurt against Alp Arslan. From as early as 1042 Qavurt and his followers had carved out an independent Amirate in Kirman. When Alp Arslan first came to the Sultanate he thought to dislodge his brother by force, but when this proved impossible Alp Arslan bowed to some acceptable form of the inevitable and recognized Qavurt's special privileges in Kirman. Those special privileges did not, of course, include any claim upon the Sultanate of the Seljuqs. Or so it seemed for the present.

The affairs of Qutlumush and Qavurt were painful but minor blemishes upon the Sultanate of Alp Arslan (1063–1072), the apogee of whose glory came in 1071, when near the town of Manzikert (or Malazgird) north of Lake Van in Armenia he defeated a large Byzantine army and captured in the field the reigning Byzantine Emperor, Romanus Diogenes.[22] Neither man was new to the conflict in Anatolia. The Seljuqs had been sending Turkoman troops into Anatolia for years. Tughril had fought there, and Qutlumush had made his reputation by taking Malatya (Melitene) in 1058. Alp Arslan too was in the field soon after his accession to the Sultanate in 1063, and his target was the almost defenseless kingdom of Armenia. The last king there, Gagik II, had been enticed to Constantinople in 1045 by Constantine X and threatened into abdication. The Byzantine Empire thus gained a large territory filled with hostile subjects whom it was almost perfectly incapable of protecting against the menace of the Turks. Alp Arslan, accompanied by his son Malik Shah and his

---

22. The last time that feat had been accomplished was almost precisely eight centuries earlier, when the Sasanian Shah Shapur captured the Emperor Valerian. Though it is doubtful that Alp Arslan's historical interests ranged that far afield, the earlier event was commemorated in bold relief near the main road running from the Sultan's capital at Isfahan to Shiraz; see Introduction, p. 16.

vizier Nizam al-Mulk, marched north from Azarbayjan in 1064 and captured the Armenian capital of Ani.

The Seljuqs now held the Byzantines' eastern flank and threatened Anatolia to the west and isolated the Christian kingdom of Georgia to the north. Alp Arslan immediately made his intentions clear. He attacked Georgia in 1064 and again in 1068 and placed a Muslim *amir* in Tiflis. Thereafter the going was less easy. The inept Constantine X died in 1067, and his widow married a soldier, Romanus Diogenes, and so secured for him the throne. At that very moment Turkoman armies only nominally under the control of the Sultan were sacking Kayseri (Caesarea) and Amorium. Romanus had fierce political troubles at home, but he judged that his first obligation was to the frontier, and in 1068 he came to northern Syria and Mesopotamia to display his arms before Antioch, Edessa, and the rest of the Byzantine holdings there. He probably represented no threat to the bulk of Arab Syria, which had once been in the uneasy possession of the Fatimids of Egypt but was now left to its own violent devices as the Fatimid Caliphs struggled against plague and anarchy at home.

Whatever the inclination of the Turkoman *ghazis* in Anatolia, Alp Arslan himself was far more interested in the tottering Fatimids than he was in driving the Byzantines from Anatolia. With the obvious expectation of turning to Syria the Sultan concluded a treaty with Romanus in 1070 and was establishing his writ in Syria when the news came that the Emperor had mustered a large army at Erzerum in despite of the treaty and was moving to the reconquest of Armenia. That was the prelude and occasion of Manzikert, after which the Sultan somewhat unexpectedly ransomed his royal captive with the understanding that Antioch and Edessa would be restored to the *Dar al-Islam.*

In the sequel Alp Arslan was cheated of both Syria and his expectations from the Romans. The Byzantines had, even before his release, replaced Romanus with Michael VII Ducas. For the politicians at Constantinople, the returned Romanus was merely an embarrassment. To make sure that he would not rule again he was handed over to be blinded, but the job was bungled and the unfortunate Romanus died of the cure. Thus for the Byzantines, who had no intention of honoring Romanus' promises, the price for Manzikert was remarkably light. The Sultan, it is clear, did not covet Anatolia for himself, though it must have been equally clear that there was at this point no Byzantine authority capable of denying it to the other Turkomans whom either fanaticism or gain was driving on toward Constantinople.

Nor was Alp Arslan to add Syria to his territories. The Arab tribes continued to fall upon the Fatimid garrisons there, as they had done for years. There were few avenues of help open to the Fatimids, and the Fatimid governor of Acre, the redoubtable Badr al-Jamali, who later assumed control of Egypt as Grand Vizier, chose one of the more dangerous among them: he summoned to his aid the Turkoman Atsiz, who arrived in 1071 and promptly took and despoiled Jerusalem for his own profit. Nor did it end there. Within a few short years Atsiz had annexed a major part of Palestine and southern Syria.

Atsiz later made a display of recognizing the Seljuqs as his overlords rather than the Fatimids; it was not for the benefit of Alp Arslan, however, but that of his son. In 1072, the year after Manzikert, the Sultan was far from Syria in eastern Khurasan preparing to march against his fractious Qarakhanid allies. Alp Arslan had fought on that eastern frontier on more than one occasion and had sent his sons there to rule as his *amirs*. He himself married a Qarakhanid princess, as his son Malik Shah was to do, but those alliances by marriage were accompanied by a ceaseless vigilance against the ambitions of the Qarakhanids of Sogdia and Ferghana, a vigilance that prompted the expedition of 1072 when the Sultan was stabbed to death shortly after crossing the Oxus into Qarakhanid territory.

Malik Shah (1073–1092) was formally designated his father's successor in 1066, and he had long been involved in the business of rule both at Isfahan and on campaign. Neither fact secured for him unanimous acceptance as Great Sultan. The Turkish claim on seniority died slowly before the dynastic ambitions of the Seljuqs. Alp Arslan's half brother Qavurt, long established in his own principality of Kirman, once again put forward his claims and managed to take and hold Isfahan for a brief season in 1073. Malik Shah marched against the pretender and defeated him near Hamadhan. This time Qavurt received no leniency—he was executed on the advice of Nizam al-Mulk it was said—but in the following year the new Sultan restored Kirman to Qavurt's sons, to rule in his name.

It was not the Sultan's last problem with his family. As was customary his brother Tekish was given Balkh as his *iqta'* with authority over Khurasan. This was in 1073, shortly after Malik Shah completed the work interrupted by his father's murder and reduced the Qarakhanids across the Oxus to a somewhat more respectful vassalage. For a time Khurasan was quiet, but in 1081 Malik Shah did precisely what his vizier told him was poor policy ten years after the fact: he discharged from his army some seven thousand mercenaries, who proceeded to Khurasan, where their presence prompted Tekish to think that the opportunity was at hand for unseating his brother. It was not. Malik Shah put down Tekish and his mercenaries without difficulty and even pardoned his brother. In 1084 Tekish made yet another attempt at insurrection while Malik Shah was engaged in Mesopotamia. This was no more successful, nor was there any forgiveness. Tekish was executed.

The Sultan's presence in Mesopotamia in 1084 was dictated by the extraordinary complex of events there and in Syria. By the time Malik Shah came to the throne the Fatimids had lost even their ports of Acre and Tyre, and the rest of Syria-Palestine was rapidly falling under the control of Atsiz, who had occupied both Jerusalem and Damascus. He now recognized Malik Shah as his sovereign, while the Fatimids, his first patrons there, turned to other allies, to the sons of Qutlumush. They apparently caused little concern to Atsiz, who marched against Egypt itself in 1076. It was an unsuccessful attempt. Badr al-Jamali was by then fully in control of Egypt. He met and defeated Atsiz and in the following year pursued the *amir* back into Syria. It was the end of Atsiz's "empire"; rather than surrender it to Badr, the *amir* turned it over to a brother of the Sultan, Tutush, who was given Syria as an appanage in 1079 and who confirmed the event by putting Atsiz to death.

Thus, from 1079 the Seljuqs were a major political presence in Syria. The power of the Fatimids was broken—they did recover the ports of Acre and Tyre in 1089—and if the Sultan had any real rivals it was in the Arab dynasts, the Marwanids of Diyarbakr and the 'Uqaylids of Aleppo. The first were suppressed in a campaign fought in 1084 by Malik Shah's *ghulam* commanders in concert with the Caliph's ambitious vizier, Ibn Jahir.[23]

The 'Uqaylids had once been allies of a strange political power established at Antioch and Edessa in the Christian enclave carved out by the Byzantines in the mid-tenth century.[24] Philaretus Vahram was an Armenian general of Romanus Diogenes who refused to accept the new Emperor Michael VII, and in the decade after Manzikert he put together for himself a principality from among the inhabitants of "Lesser Armenia." These new Armenians of Cilicia and northern Syria were likewise products of Manzikert. With the loss of all hope for a Christian Armenia, many of the notables there migrated across the Turkoman bands wandering through Anatolia and settled in what appeared to be the last secure Byzantine and Christian strongholds in Cilicia and around Edessa. It was they and the Christians of Antioch who either invited or accepted the lordship of Philaretus in the seventies.

The Antiochene branch of Philaretus' realm lasted until 1084, when it was taken over by another Turkoman adventurer, Sulayman, the son of Qutlumush, who had been among the chief beneficiaries of the battle of Manzikert. Most of the Turkoman *ghazis* of Anatolia acknowledged him as their chief, and at their head he had swept across the Anatolian plateau against what must have been only token Byzantine resistance. By 1080 Sulayman was already well established in Iznik (Nicaea), almost in sight of the Bosporus. Then suddenly in 1084 Sulayman was occupying Antioch from Philaretus, perhaps, as has been suggested, as the agent of the new Byzantine Emperor Alexius Comnenus (1081–1118), who used the lure of Antioch to distract the Turkoman from Constantinople.

The arrival of Sulayman almost immediately provoked a breach between himself and the 'Uqaylid Muslim ibn Quraysh of

23. Ibn Jahir held the post from 1058 under al-Qa'im, and his two sons succeeded him in office until 1113.
24. See Chap. VII, pp. 495–496.

Aleppo. Muslim appealed to Malik Shah, who sent Tutush. In the fighting of 1085–1086 both Sulayman and Muslim ibn Quraysh perished. Malik Shah then came to take hold of his new possessions from Mosul westward to Antioch. That they were his prizes and not Tutush's was made evident from the outset; Tutush was left with Damascus, while the Sultan installed his own *ghulam* governors in Antioch, Aleppo and Edessa.[25]

The Great Sultan had reached the pinnacle of his achievements. He ruled from the Mediterranean to the Himalayas, from Georgia and the Caspian to the Persian Gulf. It may have been Nizam al-Mulk's plan that the final triumph would be celebrated in Baghdad. Alp Arslan had never visited that city or even seen the Caliph. Nor had his son entered Baghdad up to this point; like his father and his uncle Tughril, Malik Shah ruled from Isfahan or the mobile court that accompanied him on campaign. Now at the age of thirty-two he came to the center of the Caliphate for a dual purpose, for his own investiture at the hands of the Caliph with the supreme temporal power in the *Dar al-Islam* and to attend the marriage of al-Qa'im's son, the Caliph al-Muqtadi (1075–1094), to his daughter. The betrothal had been worked out five years before between Nizam al-Mulk and the Caliph's vizier Ibn Jahir, and now in 1087 it was celebrated on a truly lavish scale. Nizam al-Mulk, whose domestic policy it was to bring the Caliph and the Sultan into closer harmony, was delighted. And so, for the moment, was Malik Shah.

It is not recorded how Muqtadi reacted to the occasion. Not long after, however, he dismissed Ibn Jahir's son from the vizierate. The move angered Nizam al-Mulk, who thought for a brief moment of abolishing the Caliphate. Then in 1089 the bride returned to her father alleging neglect on the Caliph's part. With her was her two-year-old son Ja'far.

Though obviously outraged, the Sultan did nothing for the moment. Because of religious complaints against the Qarakhanid chief Ahmad Khan, Malik Shah crossed the Oxus and occupied

---

25. Among the prizes was Sulayman's son Kilij Arslan, whom the Sultan took into custody. After Malik Shah's death Kilij escaped to return to his patrimony in Anatolia.

Samarqand and Bukhara. Ahmad's problems are obscure, but he may have been slipping toward Isma'ilism,[26] and elsewhere there were disquieting signs that the Isma'ilis, who were present but politically quiescent in the Caliphate during the early Seljuq years, were planning a concerted assault. In 1090 a force of Qarmatian Bedouin sacked Basrah, and in that same year there were Isma'ili uprisings in Daylam and Kuhistan. It was also in 1090 that the Isma'ili *da'i* of Daylam, Hasan ibn al-Sabbah, recently returned there from training in Egypt, seized the fortress of Alamut in the Elburz mountains south of the Caspian Sea.

Malik Shah was well aware of this and sent out some ineffective forces against the revolutionaries. But for the present he appears to have been more concerned about his relations with the Caliph. These were strained from 1088 or 1089 onward, and by the time he revisited Baghdad in 1091 the Sultan had resolved to send Muqtadi into exile, perhaps into the Hejaz, and to set up in his place his own infant son Ja'far. Sultan father and Caliph son would both rule from Baghdad.

Nothing came of the plan. In 1092 Nizam al-Mulk was struck down on the road from Isfahan to Baghdad. His assailant was, as all the sources agree, a young Isma'ili from Alamut. There is an almost equally strong tradition that the deed was done in collusion with the Grand Vizier's enemies at court, including the Sultan himself, whose motive may have been no more complicated than greed. Three months later Malik Shah too was dead, aged thirty-seven, of a fever.

In somewhat fewer than forty years the Seljuqs had come into the lands of the Baghdad Caliphate as simple marauders from the steppe and proceeded to restore to those lands the kind of political and religious unity they had not enjoyed for centuries. The Fatimids in Egypt were still beyond the Sultans' reach, and the Ghaznavids clung to central Afghanistan and their Indian provinces, but elsewhere local dynasts and princes, many of them Shi'ite in their sympathies, had all to accept Seljuq suzerainty and with it recognition of the Sunni Caliph. The Oxus frontier was apparently secure, and on that other frontier in Anatolia, where

---

26. He was in fact murdered by the orthodox of Samarqand in 1095 on precisely that charge.

the armies of Islam had been stalled, sometimes inexplicably, by the Byzantine resistance, the Seljuqs achieved the decisive encounter that had eluded their predecessors.

The glory of the Seljuqs was only doubtfully the glory of the Caliphs, however. Since the ninth century the Caliphate had been a pawn in the hands of others, Turkish soldiers and powerful viziers, and it was at base only the shadowy prestige of the office and the Caliph's power to depose that enabled him to survive. Lately Caliphs like Qadir and Qa'im had begun to explore the use of new weapons—the issue of orthodoxy, for example—to be exploited against the Shi'ite Buyids. The Seljuqs undermined this modest renaissance of Caliphal power by making the issue their own. From their beginnings as Muslims the Turks were as piously orthodox as the Sunni merchants and popular preachers who accomplished their conversion on the steppe, and the Caliphs could have no quarrel with the religious convictions of their new protectors, who restored their name to honor in the Friday prayers and who zealously took up the struggle against the Isma'ilis within the *Dar al-Islam* and the infidels without.

When the Seljuqs took up their position as the orthodox defenders of al-Qa'im they had but to assume, like the 'Abbasids in the mid-eighth century, a place already prepared for them. They rode into Baghdad on a rising tide of traditionalist sentiment, which was provoked, in the first instance, by the Buyids' not unnatural patronage of Shi'ism. In 1017 the Caliph al-Qadir published a profession of faith that was in essence a statement of Hanbalite orthodoxy. This Hanbalite credo was reaffirmed by al-Qa'im and his viziers in 1038 and again in 1053, but on these latter occasions it was broadened to include other figures who had no ostensible connection with Shi'ism but who troubled the Hanbalites of Baghdad every whit as much as the Isma'ilis themselves, the new Ash'arite theologians.

For the Seljuq Sultans this was probably no issue at all, this rarefied debate within the orthodox schools on speculative theology and the premises of knowledge. But for their considerably more sophisticated viziers, who could understand both the theology and the political dangers involved, the opinions of the outspoken Hanbalite lawyers of Baghdad were important indeed.

At first it appeared that the Seljuqs would be powerful allies in this struggle of the Hanbalites against the Ash'arite *kalam* that was making inroads in the Shafi'ite school. It was not to be so. The beginnings of the affair are obscure, but sometime about 1045, no more than five years after Tughril had settled into Nishapur, accusations began to be leveled against the orthodoxy of the Ash'arites of that city. The defense was taken up by the Sufi Abu al-Qasim al-Qushayri[27] and another rather conservative Ash'arite, Abu Bakr al-Bayhaqi (d. 1066). Both men addressed a series of open letters to Tughril's vizier al-Kunduri in which they insisted on the orthodoxy of Ash'ari and of his teaching.

They apparently had little effect. Between 1045 and his own imprisonment and death in 1063, Kunduri, whose motives may have been no more complicated than his fanatical devotion to the Hanafite *madhhab*, systematically undercut the Shafi'ites by concentrating his fire against the Ash'arite *kalam* that was associated with legal Shafi'ism in Nishapur. Eminent Ash'arites were banned from public preaching in the mosques and eventually forced into exile, among them Qushayri, Bayhaqi and the rising Ash'arite eminence in Khurasan, Abu al-Ma'ali al-Juwayni (d. 1085).

The Ash'arites had enemies enough in Khurasan. Kunduri could count on the support of various Mu'tazilites, Shi'ites and Karramiyah in his efforts to discredit Ash'arism. The ironic effect may have been to push the Asha'rites, albeit only temporarily, closer to the Hanbalite traditionalists. Such at least appears to be the thrust of Bayhaqi's *The Names and Attributes of Allah*, written at the height of the troubles in 1057. It was frankly intended for *mutakallimun* whose grasp of the traditional *hadith* arguments for the positions was not entirely firm. Bayhaqi was perfectly competent and willing to invoke the *kalam* arguments, but for each divine name and attribute he took pains to locate the question in a deep Scriptural context.

Kunduri's attacks on Ash'arism in Khurasan came to nothing in the end. With the accession of Alp Arslan the Hanafite vizier lost his political footing and was replaced by the aggressive Shafi'ite Nizam al-Mulk who, for the next thirty years, was the most powerful force in shaping the internal policy of the Seljuqs.

The Iranian Nizam al-Mulk, the son of the Ghaznavids' tax

---

27. See Chap. VIII, p. 559.

collector in Khurasan, began his own career as a minor functionary in Ghazna and then entered the service of Chaghri and Alp Arslan. When the latter rose to the Sultanate, Nizam al-Mulk was promoted to the Grand Vizierate, a post he held all during the reigns of Alp Arslan and Malik Shah. Under the latter, whose *atabeg* he had been, he was unquestionably the most powerful man in the Seljuq empire. He controlled the entire apparatus of the Sultan's *diwan*[28] and its subordinate ministries of the chancery, military affairs, taxation and intelligence. His relatives and retainers held important staff positions there. The vizier himself possessed what amounted to a small private army and he was, like the Barmacids, immensely wealthy.

Nizam, the Khurasanian, was as much a Sunni as the Turks in his religious convictions. Reared in stanchly Sunni Khurasan and trained under the Ghaznavids, the Seljuqs' premier vizier found in his Sunnism and in the ancient Iranian tradition, religious as well as political, an identity of purpose. "What a king needs most," he wrote, echoing the words of Zoroaster seventeen hundred years earlier, "is right religion." "Right religion," in his case Sunnism, meant order and stability; "evil religion" brings in its train religious innovation and political insurrection.

Zoroaster's "evil religion" referred to the anarchical nomads of the steppe beyond Balkh, but what the vizier had in mind was a purely Islamic phenomenon, the Isma'ilism radiating from Fatimid Cairo. He caught perfectly the political implication of Shi'ism and its threat to a powerful monarchy. In Nizam's view the Sultan was merely a military appanage of the Caliph himself. The Caliph was the legitimate head of Islam, and the Sultan was his authorized delegate charged with the maintenance of good order, the defender of the "right religion" in the external forum. And for the Seljuqs and their vizier that religion was Sunni Islam.

Much of Nizam al-Mulk's thinking on the subject can be read in his *Book of Governance*, a traditional Iranian "Mirror for Princes," written in Persian for Malik Shah shortly before the death of both men in 1092. The work is not a treatise on theory–the bulk of it is aphoristic and anecdotal–but its main

---

28. The Caliph had his own vizier and *diwan*, as did the various Seljuq princes and *amirs*.

themes are clear enough: a strongly autocratic rule committed to justice and based on the *shari'ah*. It is no other than the Iranian ideal of rule informed by the religious sensibilities of Islam.

By tradition the Turkish Seljuqs were unpromising candidates for the role of ideal Shah. Among the Turks, rule was shared within the family, was consultative rather than autocratic, and generally fell far short of the absolutism demanded by their vizier in the name of an Iranian tradition. And yet both Alp Arslan and Malik Shah, and even Tughril without the benefit of Nizam al-Mulk, adapted themselves to the pattern, and that despite the sometimes violent opposition of their Turkoman constituents. They had, it is true, the example of the Ghaznavids before them, and with their professional standing armies and their elaborate *diwan* organization they passed, tolerably, for the Shahs their vizier would have them be.

The *diwan* was not, however, the only instrument of the Sultan's rule. He had, in addition, his own court (*dargah*) composed of the members of his household and, even more prominently, the various military officials who presided over the affairs of the Seljuq Sultanate. Nizam al-Mulk, whose immense influence over the Sultan was at its weakest in the court, had a great deal to say about the proper conduct of the *dargah* in his *Book of Governance* and very little about the *diwans* over which he himself exercised immediate control. The court was far too informal for his liking, offering, as it did, direct access to the Sultan for the vizier's rivals and potential foes.

In practice the Sultan's power was exercised through his local agents. The Seljuqs did not rely on urban police or militia but garrisoned the cities of their empire, and it was the chief of the military garrison, the *shahnah*, who was in effect the military governor of the city and the Sultan's chief "secular" representative there. The *shahnah* was expected to keep peace and order, but his soldiers were used for other purposes as well, notably to put muscle into the arm of the Sultan's tax collector (*'amil*). The religious counterparts of the *shahnah* in the community were the *qadi*, likewise an agent of the Sultan, and his executive, the *muhtasib*, or market inspector,[29] whose mandate to enjoin good

---

29. See Chap. III, p. 236.

and forbid evil covered a wide range of activities from the proper conduct of religious minorities to the supervision of weights and measures.

These four men, the *shahnah*, *'amil*, *qadi* and *muhtasib*, were the Sultan's face and voice on the local level. For their part the local population approached these officials through a complex and still obscure system of associations. The followers of the various law schools, the 'Alids, the *dhimmis*, town merchants and craftsmen, the growing communities of ascetics and, apparently, even bands of the footloose were all organized into some kind of appropriate body under its own head who represented it vis-à-vis the Sultan's delegates. These were not guilds on the model of either the voluntary and autonomous associations of medieval Europe or the state-organized and state-controlled corporation of the Byzantine Empire. Islam did not foster corporate identity, with the result that the medieval Muslim worked out his social salvation within his own extended family or clan. For most urban Muslims between the clan and the ecumenical *ummah* stood only their own city quarter, in many instances little more than a neighborhood, as a locus for community of purpose and action.

The Sultan had perforce to share his powers over these various officials and institutions with the Grand Vizier, whose control of the *diwans* put his hands firmly on the purse strings of the empire, but it was to the Sultan alone that the administration of justice belonged in that conjunction of religion and politics sanctioned by Nizam al-Mulk himself. The link between the two, the "good religion" and the well-ordered state, was justice. The exaltation of justice had deep roots in the Iranian tradition, but in the present dispensation it continued to be administered by a purely Islamic officer, the *qadi*, according to the prescriptions of the *shari'ah*. Nizm al-Mulk drew the *qadis* closely within the protection and patronage of the Sultan, who appointed and sustained them and had the ultimate responsibility of executing their decisions.

The Sultan had his own justice as well. He or his deputy presided over the special court of complaints (*mazalim*), where grievances, chiefly contractual, were settled not by the procedures set down in the *shari'ah* but on the basis of custom or even governmental decree. The *mazalim* courts, which go back to the time of the early 'Abbasids, may also have had their origins in Iranian practice and the ideal of the Shah as the paramount dispenser of justice. In Nizam al-Mulk's scheme of things they were placed firmly within the jurisdiction of the Sultan, who, the Grand Vizier clearly intended, should function like the Shahs of old, with the Islamic Caliph reduced to a purely spiritual authority.

Religious functionaries who, like the *qadi*, once served the will of the Caliph now found themselves beholden to the Sultan, not merely as a matter of practical patronage but by reason of a new theory of the state which made the Sultan the chief executor, political and religious, of the Caliph. Such an arrangement was obviously implausible under the Shi'ite Buyids, but the publicly proclaimed orthodoxy of the Seljuq Sultans allowed a new appreciation of political power and its disposition in the *Dar al-Islam.*

The Grand Vizier did more than promote this view in theory. He found, it appears, an effective instrument for welding together the two great domains of religion and politics. The *qadis* and lawyers of the courts and the *katibs* of the *diwans,* who from the mid-eighth century represented different and often contradictory ideals in Islam, would be educated side by side in a new educational institution that, if Nizam al-Mulk was not its originator, owed its great subsequent popularity in Sunni circles to him.

Instruction in the traditional sciences of Islam was normally given within the confines of a mosque, either the cathedral-mosque (*jami'*), which was primarily a place in which the congregational Friday prayer took place and secondarily a place of instruction in the *Qur'an*-related sciences like *hadith,* exegesis or jurisprudence, or a mosque-college (*masjid*), a mosque in which prayer was offered but whose primary function was to serve as a school for the specialized study of one of the Islamic sciences, and particularly of jurisprudence. Similar to both the *jami'* and the *masjid* was the shrine-college (*mashad*), an oratory erected over the tomb of a holy man and in which instruction was also given. Finally, there was the *madrasah,* or law school proper, neither a mosque nor an oratory, but an institution whose sole function was to provide advanced instruction in jurisprudence.

The construction of most of these institutions, particularly the mosque-college, took place through the generosity of wealthy and pious patrons who also undertook to endow chairs for professors with life tenure and to establish scholarships for students.[30] Like their founders' bequests, these institutions were private, and, except for the cathedral-mosque, where all the legal systems might be represented by professors, the *masjid*, *mashad* and *madrasah* were intended for and devoted to an education in the legal system of a single school.

So it was that in 1065, not long after the accession of Alp Arslan and his own rise to power, Nizam al-Mulk ordered the construction at his own expense of a *madrasah* in the eastern quarter of Baghdad for the exclusive training of Shafi'ite lawyers. Two years later the building was completed and the first professor of Shafi'ite law, Abu Ishaq al-Shirazi (d. 1083), began to give public instruction.[31] The endowment for building, professor and students came from the pocket of the wealthy vizier, and it was he and his descendants after him who controlled the institution in a manner impossible in other schools.

Nizam al-Mulk was not the first to build a *madrasah*, and his foundation certainly was not the first school in Baghdad for the exclusive use of one legal system; there was a famous *mashad* that was constructed there in honor of Abu Hanifah at almost exactly the same time as the Nizamiyah *madrasah*. And yet almost all the medieval historians judged the vizier's institution to be of considerable importance, as a wedge for Ash'arism against the predominant Hanbalism of the capital, as some have thought, or as a buffer for Sunnism against the intellectual pressures from Isma'ili Shi'ism, according to others.

It is unlikely that Nizam al-Mulk acted out of simple piety. He was one of the most politically aware men of the time; in addition, the existence of a network of such institutions suggests

---

30. The *madrasah* provided living accommodations for students; the *masjid* did not.

31. He had some hesitation about accepting the post. When he finally decided to accept the vizier's offer, an earlier appointment had abruptly to be canceled. Nizam's *madrasah* appears to have been remarkable for the frequent violation of what elsewhere was lifetime tenure of an endowed chair.

purpose—there were other Nizamiyahs at Nishapur, Merv, Balkh, Herat, Amul, Isfahan, Basrah and Mosul. The first four were in Khurasan; indeed, there was a tradition of *madrasahs* in Khurasan going back to the previous century, and the leading Ash'arite *mutakallim* of al-Qadir's day, Abu Ishaq al-Isfara'ini (d. 1027), held a chair in just such an institution in Nishapur.

We know that before Kunduri's violent, if temporary, scattering of the Ash'arites from the province Khurasan was a stronghold not merely of Sunnism but of the new Ash'arite *kalam* and of its rival form among the Karramiyah. The strength of the latter was well established in Khurasan since the days of the sect's founder, Ibn Karram (d. 869), and had survived the crisis of the defection of Mahmud of Ghazna, a former supporter, to the ranks of the traditionalists to serve the political ends of the Caliph al-Qadir. Attacked by the traditionalists for their sympathy with *kalam* and by more liberal theologians for their apparent adherence to anthropomorphism and a simplistic view of the act of faith, the Karramiyah had, like the earlier followers of Ibn Kullab and of Ash'ari himself, the uncomfortable task of attempting to mediate between the partisans of a traditional and a rationalized view of Islam.

In the end the Ash'arites were successful, and they seasoned their triumph by condemning their earlier rivals along the "middle way." Much of what is known of the Karramiyah comes from the ungracious pages of the Ash'arite al-Baghdadi's *Sects* and from the only-somewhat-less polemical controversies that Fakhr al-Din al-Razi (d. 1209), who had little respect for Baghdadi's *Sects*, sustained against the Karramiyah in Ghurid court circles at Ghazna in the 1190's. But in addition to the polemic there may have been borrowing between the two factions as well. Early traditions attribute to Ibn Karram or to his immediate disciples the foundation of spiritual centers where the Karramiyah not only pursued their pious exercises but were engaged in some form of public instruction. The evidence here is obscure, but the Ash'arites may very well have had Karramiyah precedents in mind in installing themselves in *madrasahs* in Khurasan and in Nizam al-Mulk's famous foundation in Baghdad.

Kunduri's purge of the Ash'arites in Khurasan quickly ran its course with Nizam al-Mulk's promotion to the Grand Vizierate.

The victims of the Ash'arite ban returned to Khurasan, among them Abu al-Ma'ali al-Juwayni, who was able to end his enforced four-year exile in Mecca and Medina[32] and come once again to Nishapur where he accepted a chair in Shafi'ite law at the *madrasah* founded for him by the Grand Vizier.

Juwayni's earlier training at Nishapur was a traditional one in *hadith* and Shafi'ite legal theory, and it was conducted chiefly by his father, Abu Muhammad, an eminent Shafi'ite lawyer who had joined with Qushayri in protesting Kunduri's repression of the Ash'arites. Despite his youth—he was only nineteen at the time—the younger Juwayni succeeded to his father's academic position at Abu Muhammad's death in 1046.

Juwayni's brilliant career as a lawyer and *mutakallim* was seriously interrupted by the Hanafite-Shafi'ite eruptions in Nishapur, but after 1063 he had a secure place in the Nizamiyah *madrasah*, and it is probably from this period that most of his literary work dates. A considerable part of it was devoted to law, and it is on works like his *Most Profound Questions in Law*, which Ghazali summarized while he was Juwayni's student at Nishapur, that Juwayni's reputation rests. But he was also a *mutakallim*, and these were the years in which he made his own considerable contribution to Ash'arite *kalam: The Common Book on the Roots of Religion*, *Spiritual Guidance to the Decisive Proofs on the Roots of Belief*, *Illumination of the Beliefs of the Partisans of the Sunnah and the Community*, and finally *The Nizamiyah Creed*.[33]

All of Juwayni's *kalam* works, save the *Common Book*, which may, however, be only partially preserved, betray the same scholastic organization already visible in the earlier treatises of Baqillani and Baghdadi. That scheme is essentially the one introduced by the Mu'tazilites: the existence of God, his attributes, human acts and their consequences, prophetology, eschatology and the Imamate, the whole now preceded among the Ash'arite

---

32. Where his teaching activity won him the honorific title of "Imam of the Two Holy Cities" (*Imam al-Haramayn*).

33. This last work has apparently been transmitted by Juwayni's student Ghazali, a fact that has led on occasion to its being listed among Ghazali's treatises.

mutakallimun by an elaborate treatment of the foundations of knowledge.

Whatever the Ash'arite *kalam* may have owed to the Mu'tazilites—and Juwayni's own debt was considerable—the latter were still ranked among the adversaries. No less than his predecessors, Juwayni was attempting to steer the narrow course between the non-Scriptural rationalizing of the Mu'tazilites and those others who, by their literal acceptance of the language of the *Qur'an*, appeared to posit a "resemblance" (*tashbih*) between God and man. *Tashbih*, as practiced by the Karramites, for example, was anthropomorphism, but the Mu'tazilites, by separating themselves from Scriptural evidence or by resorting to an extreme "allegorizing" of the *Qur'an*, were equally reprehensible in Ash'arite eyes.

In choosing the middle way Juwayni more often conceded the Mu'tazilite position than that of their more literalist-minded opponents.[34] He could not, and did not, agree with the Mu'tazilite denial of a real existence to the attributes of God, but Juwayni had at hand a palliative in the theory of "modes" put forward by the Mu'tazilite Abu Hashim (d. 933).[35] The "mode" was an attribute of which neither existence nor nonexistence could be predicated, and so to affirm them of God was to satisfy the Mu'tazilite demand for a transcendental God without the limitation of "attributes" and the traditionalist insistence that justice be done to the names given to God in the *Qur'an*.

The theologians' untroubled embrace of both allegorical exegesis and, in the broader context, *kalam* itself, shows how far Ash'arism had progressed—or deviated—from its original desire to ally itself with traditionalist Hanbalism against Ash'ari's former mentors, the Mu'tazilites. But Juwayni went even further than his immediate predecessors Baqillani and Baghdadi. According to a later report, Ghazali studied *falsafah* with Juwayni

---

34. Placed in a similar position between the two, Ibn Furaq (d. 1015), the earliest of the Khurasanian Ash'arites (see Chap. VIII, p. 586), did not hesitate to use allegorical exegesis against the Karramiyah of his day.

35. See Chap. VI, p. 437, and for Baqillani's acceptance of the same position, Chap. VIII, p. 587.

during his student days at Nishapur and, indeed, the *Common Book* does show a developed acquaintance with the philosophers' approach to questions of substance, accidents and bodies. Even more strikingly, Juwayni was concerned with introducing into the standard *kalam* arguments a philosophical rigor they had never known. Dialectical reasoning might suffice for the lawyers and an earlier generation of *mutakallimun*, but for a theologian plying his trade in the generation after Ibn Sina it would no longer do, and first Juwayni, and then his student Ghazali attempted to introduce into *kalam* the apodictic methods long insisted upon by the partisans of Hellenic *falsafah*.

Nizam al-Mulk's public support of Ash'arism and of scholars like Juwayni in Khurasan was not entirely typical, however. The Grand Vizier was personally committed to Ash'arism, but not at the expense of political peace. At the same time that he was restoring Ash'arites to Nishapur he was restraining them in Baghdad, and his treatment of the most famous mystic of the day, 'Abdallah al-Ansari (d. 1089), gives equally impressive evidence that Nizam al-Mulk was far from being the uninhibited Ash'arite champion that some of his contemporaries may have expected him to be.

Ansari, who was born and raised in Herat in Khurasan, was both a Hanbalite traditionalist and a mystic.[36] His reputation for learning and piety was widespread and uncontested, but in an area outspoken in its Ash'arite sympathies and where Mu'tazilitism too still had its supporters, Ansari acquired enemies as well as admirers. The accession of the Seljuqs, and particularly Nizam al-Mulk, presented these latter with an opportunity to undermine Ansari. Alp Arslan and his vizier passed through Herat in 1066, and a discussion was provoked with Ansari in their presence. Nothing came of it for the moment, but Ansari must have caught the drift, since he published a series of vigorous tracts in defense of his Hanbalism, pamphlets which found their final expression in his *Condemnation of Kalam and Its Partisans*, a work based on traditional arguments—it is little more than a collection of *hadith* —and directed against the Mu'tazilites and Ash'arites.

Ansari's aggressive defense of his own position may have en-

---

36. See Chap. VIII, pp. 566–568.

couraged his opponents among the *mutakallimun* to increase their pressure on the vizier, who finally signed an order forbidding Ansari to teach and remanding him to Balkh. The prohibition did not last very long. The vizier was prevailed upon to reverse himself, and Ansari was back in Herat before the end of 1066. Alp Arslan was also in the city in 1067, and once again an attempt was made to trip Ansari in a public disputation. "Why," he was asked in the presence of the Sultan and the vizier, "do you condemn al-Ash'ari?" "Ash'ari I do not know," was the answer, and Ansari then proceeded to express his unequivocal condemnation of some of the contemporary Ash'arite positions—that the *Qur'an*, for example, the eternal heavenly Book, is not "present" in its actual exemplars in the hands of men. Nizam al-Mulk, far from being scandalized, was apparently delighted by the answer.

There were other attempts after this—his enemies even went to the ludicrous extent of planting an idol in his prayer rug—but Ansari was clearly in no danger from either the Sultan or Nizam al-Mulk. The situation at Baghdad was, however, of far greater delicacy. The head of the Hanbalite community there was Abu Ja'far al-Hashimi (d. 1077), a vigilant and outspoken defender of traditionalism. The primary targets of his wrath were the Mu'tazilites, notably Ibn al-Walid (d. 1086), the student of 'Abd al-Jabbar, who generally confined his teaching, which may have included *falsafah* as well as *kalam*, to his own house in the more hospitable Shi'ite quarter of Karkh, but who was twice attacked for publicly propagating the doctrines of the Mu'tazilites. On the second occasion, in 1067, it was Abu Ja'far who was in the van, and it was also he who detected subtle pro-Mu'tazilite tendencies among the Hanbalites themselves. The prime offender here was Ibn 'Aqil (d. 1119), who was accused by Abu Ja'far of holding the theses of Mu'tazilite *kalam* and of being a follower of the executed mystic al-Hallaj.[37] His actual offense may have been somewhat less serious, his succession to a professorial chair that Abu Ja'far had ambitioned for himself, but he had, at any rate, to issue a degrading public retraction in 1072.

Whether intended to or not, the Nizamiyah *madrasah* did provide the Ash'arites with a base and a refuge in strongly tradi-

---

37. See Chap. VIII, pp. 555–557.

tionalist Baghdad. Earlier, in 1053, when Tughril and his vizier Kunduri had moved the public condemnation of Ash'arism in Nishapur, the defense of the founder was taken up there, unsuccessfully it appears, by the Sufi Abu al-Qasim al-Qushayri (d. 1072).[38] A quarter of a century later, under the new circumstances of the vizierate of Nizam al-Mulk, it was his son Abu Nasr (d. 1130), a student of Juwayni, who carried the attack directly to Baghdad. He came to the capital in 1077, with at least the implicit approval of Nizam al-Mulk, to deliver a course of public sermons at the Nizamiyah.[39] Their message was unmistakably Ash'arite, and lest there be any misunderstanding, Abu Nasr added a ringing denunciation of the Hanbalites as anthropomorphists.

There were, predictably, public outcries against this attack on the traditionalist theology. The head of the Baghdad Hanbalites became involved, then, from the other side, Nizam al-Mulk, and finally the Caliph Muqtadi and his vizier Ibn Jahir. The two factions took to raiding each other's schools in the manner of warring armies, and some of the Ash'arites from the Nizamiyah were even heard invoking the name of the Fatimid Caliph. Nizam al-Mulk wrote from Nishapur to express his displeasure at what was being done to his *madrasah*. It was only when the leader of the Hanbalites was restrained by the Caliph and Nizam al-Mulk was persuaded to recall Abu Nasr al-Qushayri to Nishapur that the violence slowly died away, not entirely to the liking of the beleaguered Baghdad Ash'arites who thought that Nizam al-Mulk, so energetic an Ash'arite in Nishapur, should have taken a stronger hand against the Hanbalites of Baghdad.

In a letter written to his first appointee to the chair of jurisprudence at the Baghdad Nizamiyah, Abu Ishaq al-Shirazi, who was a Shafi'ite but whose own commitment to Ash'arism was somewhat dubious, the vizier explained his position. As far as the

---

38. Like a number of others, he had to flee Nishapur for Baghdad. He returned to Khurasan ten years later.

39. *Kalam*, whether Ash'arite or any other, was nowhere part of the curriculum of the *madrasah*. There were, however, preachers on the staff, and it was generally their public pronouncement that set off the theological scuffling.

law schools were concerned, it was not the function of either the Sultan or his vizier to favor one of the orthodox schools over the others. Baghdad was obviously Hanbalite in its sympathies and there was nothing for Abu Ishaq to do but accept it. As for Abu Nasr al-Qushayri, he would have been better advised to show prudence in his public utterances in the capital.

The vizier was being politic but not a little disingenuous. The quarrel was not between Shafi'ites and Hanbalites as competing schools of law, but it arose from the fact that certain Shafi'ite lawyers like the Qushayris and Juwayni were either supporting or had adopted the new Ash'arite *kalam*. The Hanbalites reacted precisely because they themselves were more than a law school. They represented a certain way of looking at Islam, while *kalam* had another, radically different way. Hanbalite "theology" was merely an extension of Hanbalite jurisprudence and its study of the "sources of the Law," while *kalam* grew up out of a soil that was apparently alien to the Islamic Law, either al-Shafi'i's version or any other.

The Hanbalites would find God only in the pages of the *Qur'an* and the *sunnah*, a position that the earlier lawyers in Islam had succeeded in defining as orthodoxy. Now, however, there were other lawyers who had learned to theologize, and their understanding of the *Qur'an*, which was broadened by an increasingly sophisticated dialectic and a taste for the prudent allegorizing of texts, clashed with that earlier definition. Both sides took the issue to the streets of Nishapur and Baghdad.

Some Muslims, however, had surrendered the study of jurisprudence and *hadith* for quite different pursuits, though for professedly similar ends. The partisans of Hellenic *falsafah* argued that the philosopher too was a prophet, that he had access to the same truths as those revealed in the *Qur'an*. The study of philosophy was not the same naturalistic activity it had been for Plato and Aristotle, of course, and the Muslim version of *falsafah* was true to its immediate antecedents in late antiquity in presenting itself as a quasi-religious enterprise that couched its absolutist claims in terms of some sort of "union" with a higher divinized Intelligence.

All of this could be read in Ibn Sina, as indeed it was by many Muslims since the *falasifah* wrote in an open book unprotected by either allegory or esotericism. Not so the Gnostics in Islam, the increasing numbers of Sufis, Imamites and Isma'ilis, whose paths to God lay, like the philosophers' own, around and above the *Qur'an*, but whose thoughts were concealed from the "commonalty."

"Truth" was the great shibboleth of eleventh-century Islam. The philosophers maintained that it could be achieved by man's rational faculty without apparent benefit of the *Qur'an*. The Sufi claimed to have seen the Truth that is God, and even though his "Way" invoked the need of God's grace for its fulfillment, it stood in no such need of either the *Qur'an* to come to God or the *shari'ah* to serve Him. The Sufi and the *faylasuf* understood the "truths of reality," because each in his own way had striven to attain them. For the Isma'ilis, on the other hand, the "realities" were the matter of initiation, the sum of cosmic reality taught here on earth by the infallible *Imams* and their representatives sent forth from Cairo and Alamut. There was plentiful talk of the *Qur'an* in Isma'ili circles, not the "open" (*zahir*) *Qur'an* of the traditionalists, to be sure, but a more arcane (*batin*) document the key to whose esoteric understanding rested with the *Imams* and no other persons.

A public or a private Islam was one issue confronting the Caliphate in the eleventh century, and its complement, the choice of a legal or a spiritual Islam, was the other. And the issues had become dangerously polarized. The principal model for a public Islam was the talmudic one of the lawyers and the traditionalists, while the advocates of spiritualizing Muhammad's legacy were locked within elitist premises that served only the rationalist, the politically ambitious, or the idiosyncratic mystic, and raised doubts in the minds of most others.

The Caliph was impotent to resolve the issue, even had he wished to. His predecessors in the Caliphate had cast their lot with the lawyers, and the holders of that office under the Seljuqs showed no disposition to change the arrangement. The unique concern of the Caliph was to prevent his own replacement by a Shi'ite *Imam* of one persuasion or another. The lawyers of the Sunni establishment were equally resolved that it should not be so, and so too were the Seljuq Sultans and their viziers.

It was the most famous of those viziers, Nizam al-Mulk, who

cast out the seeds of a solution to the ideological strife by strengthening the hands of the moderate lawyers among the *'ulama'*. Within the Shafi'ite school there was room, it appeared, for both a rationalized and spiritualized Islam of a public type. No one man created it—its outlines were already present in the work of Hasan al-Basri, Muhasibi, Baqillani, Miskawayh, Ansari and Juwayni—but one man gave it shape, voice and the benefit of his own immense prestige, Juwayni's student and Nizam al-Mulk's protégé, the "proof of Islam" and its "centenary reformer," Abu Hamid al-Ghazali.

The Revitalization of the Sciences of Religion

Al-Ghazali died, at age fifty-three, in semiretirement in his native Tus in 1111. Some few years before his death he produced a kind of spiritual testament entitled *The Deliverer from Error*, and in it he undertook to describe his own passage from skepticism and spiritual restlessness to the higher certitude of a consuming love of God.[40] It is, to be sure, a highly schematized landscape traveled by Ghazali, and it is not always easy to distinguish the literary *topoi* from the ground of history. But Ghazali does profess to trace his spiritual progress against a background of times and places, and so the *Deliverer* must serve, within limits, as autobiography.

Later Muslims generally took Ghazali's account at its face value, though they added some precisions to his own scanty indications of when and where he lived and worked. Ghazali was born in Tus in 1058 and almost immediately showed promise as a student. He was set to study the traditional jurisprudence, first in his native town and then successively in Jurjan and Nishapur, where he was the student of Juwayni until the latter's death in

---

40. A similar exercise was performed by Muhasibi almost two centuries earlier; see Chap. VI, p. 422. On his own information, Ghazali had studied the earlier theologian, and the coincidences between his own *Deliverer* and passages in Muhasibi's *Faithful Counsels* may have been quite deliberate on Ghazali's part.

1085. One of Ghazali's disciples, al-Farisi, further informs us that during those early days he studied Sufism too under the direction of the eminent master Faramdhi. It was not, according to the same source, a very satisfying experience. The tutelage of Juwayni was little better, despite the young Ghazali's dazzling and continuing success as a student, and his studies in Nishapur led to the crisis of certitude with which the *Deliverer* opens, a bout of skepticism which, on Ghazali's own testimony, lasted no more than two months.

Farisi is explicit on the causes of Ghazali's self-doubt, the well-known problem of "the equivalence of proofs." Ghazali studied *fiqh*, *falsafah* and *kalam* at Nishapur with Juwayni, and all these disciplines were troubled by the fact that equally persuasive proofs could be presented for absolutely opposed propositions. Indeed Ansari, who like Ghazali found relief in mysticism, told his readers that Ash'ari had died in just such a state of dialectical ambivalence. Ghazali had done his best to ward off his doubts. In the *Deliverer* he tells how he investigated the writings of the theologians, the "esotericists" (*batiniyah*), the philosophers, and the Sufis. In the end it was only the last who offered rest to the heart.

When did all this occur? While he was studying with Juwayni at Nishapur before 1085 or immediately before his notorious disappearance from the Baghdad Nizamiyah ten years later? The earlier period appears more likely. We have it on good authority that at Juwayni's death Ghazali sought out Nizam al-Mulk at the latter's mobile camp-court, and after winning the esteem of the Grand Vizier he was appointed to the chair of Shafi'ite law at the Baghdad Nizamiyah. This was in 1091, and the new professor, now thirty-three, won an immediate success.

Success was not enough. Nizam al-Mulk fell to an Isma'ili assassin in 1092 and the Sultan Malik Shah's death followed in the same year. Shortly thereafter Ghazali began to experience what appears from the *Deliverer* to be a new crisis, not one of intellectual skepticism but a more genuinely religious fear for his own salvation provoked by a continued reading of the mystics. This time the crisis was resolved by flight. Giving it out that he was going off on pilgrimage, Ghazali went secretly to Damascus, "where I stayed for two years."

Ghazali says that he finally departed Baghdad in 1095 after a number of false starts, and another source dates his first qualms to 1093, a date close enough to Nizam al-Mulk's assassination to suggest to some that it was not for his salvation that Ghazali feared, but for his own life, now apparently threatened by the Isma'ilis. This does not agree with what we know of Ghazali's activities up to his "flight" in 1095, and the earlier date may well be incorrect. But even if it be granted that Ghazali suddenly decided to leave Baghdad in 1095, it does not clarify the mysterious circumstances under which he chose to cloud his departure.

The period of his professorship at Baghdad was the richest in Ghazali's highly productive career. At Nishapur most of his published work was on jurisprudence, but after 1091, and presumably after his first brief period of skepticism, Ghazali ranged far more widely in the rational sciences. During his four-year stay in Baghdad he wrote his *Intentions of the Philosophers,* a summary of the systems of Farabi and Ibn Sina, the best Muslim interpreters of the philosophy of a group Ghazali called "theists" and in which he included Socrates, Plato and Aristotle. In the *Deliverer,* Ghazali states that his own study of *falsafah* was accomplished in his spare time in Baghdad when he was engaged in instructing three hundred students in the *shari'ah.* After two such years of private study, probably 1092–1093, he devoted an additional year (1094) to critical reflection on what he had learned. The result was the *Incoherence of the Philosophers,* which was completed early in 1095.

Ghazali was well aware of both the strengths and the dangers of philosophy. Parts of the ancient tradition he rejected out of hand, the theories of groups he characterized as "materialists" and "naturalists," but the current version of Aristotelianism, that popularized in Islam by Farabi and Ibn Sina, was more perplexing. These people were, after all, theists (*ilahiyun*), and the latter-day proponents of Aristotelianism even made a show of professing Islam and addressing themselves to some of its problems, while others, like the Brethren of Purity, unscrupulously mixed into their philosophizing bits and pieces of the genuine Prophetic tradition.

Ghazali, who was concerned from the outset of his own intellectual development with the problem of certitude, recognized that the Hellenic claim to have achieved true and certain knowledge was to some extent justified. The proofs of Greek mathematics, for example, brought absolute conviction, and the Muslim must resist the temptation to embrace, on that basis, everything the mathematicians say or to mindlessly condemn their discipline without being able to refute it. Logic posed the same kind of problem. Its demonstrations are verifiably scientific, and if they lead to conclusions repugnant to the Muslim, it is not by reason of logic itself, but because of its incorrect use. Aristotelian theology is a case in point—the premises and methods of the *falasifah* are correct; they are mistaken in the conclusions they draw from these premises.

Ghazali's opinion—and there is no evidence that he ever departed from it—is that truth is not the unique property of Islam, and so it is neither unlikely nor scandalous that he and Aristotle might say the same thing, and in identical words. The Hellenes were not, on the other hand, infallible. The Muslim must, then, discern, on the basis of the two criteria available to him, where the truth lies. One "touchstone" is precisely the scientific method of logic; the other is divine revelation. And there is, Ghazali insists, no contradiction between them.

There are two groups against whom the touchstone of revelation is of only limited value, the philosophers who had to deny its validity, and those Muslims whose interpretation of the *Qur'an* served merely to cloak another reputed access to the truth, the infallible teaching of the *Imam*. In both instances Ghazali was forced back upon his first touchstone, the scientific method of logic. Thus, in the case of the philosophers Ghazali was operating on their own ground in attempting to convict them of error out of their own mouths. But if his methods were those of a *faylasuf*, his conslusions were those of a lawyer. The *Intentions of the Philosophers* was little more than an exposition of the system of the theistic *falasifah* in logic, theology and physics,[41] but in the *Incoherence* their theses were subjected to a scientific—that is,

---

41. The translation of the purely expository *Intentions* into Latin without its explanatory preface and without the critique of the *Incoherence* led the Western Scholastics to place "Algazel" among the *falasifah*.

logical—criticism. The conclusion was not simply the philosophical conviction of truth or error but a juridical one; some of the theses of the philosophers were transparently heresy, or, better, irreligion (*kufr*), while others were redolent of temerarious innovation (*bid'ah*).

The distance between philosophical error and judicial heresy is precisely the *Qur'an*, which, though not absolutely essential for knowledge, defines what is needful for salvation. Philosophical error need not jeopardize one's salvation, but where that error has to do with one of the essentials of belief as enunciated in the *Qur'an* and the *sunnah*, it then qualifies as heresy, and the person holding it can no longer be considered a Muslim.

Ghazali did not make the charge against the philosophers lightly. In one of his works, *The Distinctive Difference Between Islam and Irreligion,* he showed nothing but scorn for the impulsive quickness with which some Muslims were willing to read out of the Islamic community those who disagreed with them. *Kufr* was a terrible condemnation, but it was unfortunately separated only by degree from "innovation." All innovation was blameworthy in Islam in that it departed from precedent, the all-authoritative *sunnah* whereby the community attempted to govern its life, and the line that separated the blameworthy but tolerable *bid'ah* from the extreme and intolerable *kufr* must indeed have been difficult to draw.

According to Ghazali, the three juridically heretical theses of the *falasifah* were their denial of the resurrection of the body and its sharing in the punishments and rewards of the Judgment, their denial that God possesses knowledge of particulars as well as universals, and, finally, their denial of the creation of the world in time. The other seventeen propositions taken up in the *Incoherence* are the innovative ones, the denial of God's attributes, for example, and the philosophers' affirmation of a series of secondary causes operating in the universe. These were positions long held by the Mu'tazilites, as Ghazali was well aware, but the Mu'tazilites were not by that fact constituted infidels. Ghazali might disagree with them, but he was not yet ready to burn them.

Sixteen of the twenty questions in the *Incoherence* are "theological" questions—that is, theses pertaining to God, his attributes, and his activities—and the remaining four are "physical" questions having to do with secondary causality and the body-soul relationship in man. The questions are not treated in equal detail. A great deal of attention is given to the very first question, that of the creation of the universe in time, while only a page or two is given over to discussing the movement of the heavens.[42] The logic of the *Intentions* does not, however, play any part in the *Incoherence*, since logic is not a branch of philosophy in the sense that it arrives at its own proper conclusions.

Despite its professed aims, the *Incoherence* does not meet the philosophers head on, since it is the retort, after all, not of a *faylasuf* but of a *mutakallim*, who differs from his predecessors chiefly by reason of his infinitely more sophisticated logic. The world view of the philosophers rested, for example, on the affirmation of a true causal sequence at work in the universe. Ghazali, no less than Ash'ari before him, was unwilling to accept such a hypothesis. For him, as for the *mutakallimun*, Allah was the only creator and so the only true agent in the universe or out of it, and what men interpret as causality is nothing more than a customary sequence of events.[43]

His *kalam*-begotten atomism and his occasionalist view of causality pressed Ghazali into devising, here and elsewhere, arguments that differed widely from the philosophers' own. The classical Aristotelian analysis of change into potentiality and actuality and the consequent necessity of an unmoved First Mover will not do for the occasionalist Ghazali, and so when he came to setting out his own proofs for the existence of God he had to resort not to a First Mover—there are no secondary "movers" in his system—but to a First Will who makes the

---

42. The same order and roughly the same emphases are found in the philosophers' best-known rejoinder to the *Incoherence*, the *Incoherence of the Incoherence* written by the Spanish *faylasuf* Ibn Rushd (d. 1198). Though Ibn Rushd as a practicing Muslim in a lawyer-ridden society had to be personally concerned with the charge of *kufr*, his response was philosophical and not juridical. "The aim of this book," he wrote, "is to show the different degrees of assent and conviction attained by the assertions in the *Incoherence of the Philosophers*, and so to prove that most of them are neither evident nor true."
43. See Chap. VIII, p. 587.

"choice" that brings this world, out of all possible worlds, into existence.

This is a *kalam* argument and not a philosophical one, and we have it on the testimony of the Christian Yahya ibn 'Adi that he found the *mutakallimun* method of arguing meaningless and as a consequence refused to debate with them. It was essential for Ghazali's purposes to prove, for example, that the world had a beginning in time before he proceeded to his demonstration of the existence of God, and Maimonides (d. 1204), who offered an elaborate critique of the *mutakallimun* in his *Guide of the Perplexed,* identified this approach as the common property of *kalam.* Maimonides also thought he knew whence it came, from the Christian Greeks and Syrians who attempted to defend their faith from the theories of the Hellenic philosophers.

We cannot gloss that text of the *Guide* with any great certainty, but surely one of the "Greeks" in question was John Philoponus, the Alexandrian Christian who took up arms against the common philosophical arguments for the eternity of the world. John's arguments were well known in Islam,[44] by the "Syrians" Yahya ibn 'Adi and his student Ibn Suwar among others, and it may have been they whom Maimonides had in mind. If so, a series of major adjustments had been imposed on Philoponus' arguments to make them applicable to the atomic physics of *kalam.*[45] This was done long before Ghazali's day, and if it was chiefly the Philoponus tradition to which Maimonides was referring, its assimilation into *kalam* must have begun in the earliest Mu'tazilite circles.

It is, however, a long way from the first articulation of *kalam* by the Mu'tazilites of the late eighth century to Ghazali's more highly polished version three centuries later. In the *Deliverer* Ghazali professed to have taken up *kalam* only to reject it in his quest for certitude. But if it did not provide him with rest for his

---

44. See Chap. IV, pp. 297–298.

45. One of Philoponus' proofs has to do, for example, with the procession of forms across matter: what is apt to receive many forms is destructible and, so, generated as well. In all the *kalam* versions of this argument, including Ghazali's own, the progression of "accidents" across bodies is substituted for the Aristotelian "forms."

mind, *kalam* gave to Ghazali his view of the universe and its workings. It offered as well a rationally defensible alternative to the philosophers' vision of God as a featureless One engaged in an eternal and necessary emanation and of a hierarchically arranged series of causes and effects bound together in what appeared to Ghazali as a relentlessly imposed determinism. The God of *kalam* was not a metaphor but a "true agent," Ghazali insisted; he created the world in a moment of time by an act of his will and he omnipotently sustains each and every one of his creatures by continuous acts of creation. He does as he wills and intervenes when and where he wills.[46]

The God of the *mutakallimun*, and particularly of the Ash'arite *mutakallimun*, was closer to the Allah of the *Qur'an* than the severely rationalized God of the *falasifah* who ruled remotely and indirectly from the apex of the universe. The Hanbalite traditionalists would have him closer still, but for those Muslims who had come to accept the need of a theology, that proposed by Ghazali and ably utilized by him in the defense of orthodoxy against the *falasifah* must have appeared amply satisfactory.

The chief effect of the *Incoherence* may have been that it instructed the *mutakallimun* on how to deal with heterodox *topoi* of the philosophical tradition in a far more rigorous fashion than had previously been the case. Whether it provoked anyone to abandon philosophy may be doubted. Ibn Sina continued to be read by Muslim intellectuals, *mutakallimun* among them; and if his immediate disciples in the East were somewhat less than notable, Ibn Sina and the Neoplatonism he so brilliantly synthesized in the *Healing* and elsewhere had an immense effect on the evolving forms of speculative theology in Islam, and particularly on the mystical theology that was at the same time Hellenic, Iranian and Gnostic, and that surely would have found little favor with the more severely scholastic Ghazali.

---

46. God's power knows only one limitation, it appears: He is bound by the law of contradiction. In conceding this, Ghazali could save the entire structure of logical necessity from the kind of dissolution visited upon ontological necessity and the laws of nature by his denial of secondary causality.

Even before he finished the *Incoherence* Ghazali had embarked upon another literary project, *The Ignominies of the Esotericists and the Virtues of the Partisans of the Caliph al-Mustazhir.*[47] The work was commissioned by the Caliph, who appealed not to one of the traditionalists but to an Ash'arite *mutakallim* to take up weapons against the newly revived threat of Isma'ilism. Earlier the 'Abbasids and their partisans had been content to attack the historical claims of the Isma'ilis to the Caliphate—the pretended descent of 'Ubaydallah from 'Ali, for example[48]—but now, in the final decade of the eleventh century, Isma'ili pretensions had taken on a new and different urgency with their seizure of strong points in the Caspian region and the diffusion from those centers of aggressive missionaries who were now, for the first time, openly preaching an Isma'ili theology.

The origins of the Isma'ili movement are surrounded with an almost impenetrable obscurity, but its second founder, Hasan ibn al-Sabbah, stands somewhat more plainly in the light of history. The Iranian Hasan was raised in the tradition of Imamite Shi'ism, and it was only after a near-fatal illness that he became a convinced Isma'ili. He became part of the apparatus of the *da'i* of Isfahan, 'Abd al-Malik ibn 'Attash,[49] and in 1078 was sent to Isma'ili headquarters in Cairo. The current Fatimid Caliph-*Imam* was al-Mustansir (1036–1094), but the real power in the state rested with his Armenian vizier, Badr al-Jamali, whose chief concern was with the stability of Egypt itself. Talk of subverting the 'Abbasids, who now had the potent protection of the Seljuqs, was muted in Egypt in the seventies and eighties of the eleventh century.

Hasan may have been ill received in Cairo (or the stories of his stay there are colored with hindsight) but his position in the major schism that affected the Isma'ilis at Mustansir's death in 1094 is equally explicable in terms of strict Isma'ili orthodoxy.

---

47. The 'Abbasid Caliph in question, al-Mustazhir, came to power in February, 1094, and reigned until 1118.

48. See Chap. VIII, p. 595.

49. Isfahan was a Sunni stronghold under the Seljuqs, but it was also the administrative capital of their empire and so the logical, if dangerous, center for the *da'i's* activities. Ibn 'Attash's jurisdiction appears to have extended throughout western Iran from Azarbayjan to Fars.

Mustansir was said to have early designated his elder son, Nizar, as his successor. He was not, however, the choice of either Badr or of Afdal, his son and successor as vizier, who favored a younger son, Must'ali. With this powerful support Must'ali (1094–1101) was duly promoted to the Caliphate at the death of his father. And since his legitimacy as *Imam* depended on a formal designation, it was given out that Mustansir had chosen upon his deathbed to reverse himself and had named Must'ali as his heir.

Afdal's authority guaranteed acceptance of Must'ali in Egypt, but for the Isma'ilis abroad the circumstances of the succession were portentously similar to those surrounding the heirs of Ja'far al-Sadiq.[50] On that occasion they had followed the dead Isma'il into schism, and now in 1094 they were prepared to support Nizar on the same grounds. Nizar was not available to his followers—he died, or was killed, in Cairo—nor was there, despite later rumors of a son of his in Iran, any Nizarid heir to serve as *Imam.*

By reason of their support of the dead Nizar, the Iranian Isma'ilis became, in effect, independent of the Isma'ili establishment at Cairo, where an impotent Caliph and his conservative vizier had surrendered all hope of revolution. Hasan, who was now perhaps the undisputed head of the Isma'ili "call" in Iran, could give free rein to his own plans and ambitions. Or so we surmise, since the exact *political* relationship between Cairo and its Isma'ili missionaries abroad remains unclear.

Politically Hasan was favored by events in the 'Abbasid Caliphate after the death of Malik Shah in 1092. The parties of the Seljuq empire struggled to seat one or another of the dead Sultan's sons, and it was only with the help of Nizam al-Mulk's vast and still-powerful family that the twelve-year-old Berk-Yaruq was uneasily seated. His rivals were formidable: Malik Shah's wife Terken Khatun and her infant son, Muhammad, and the new Sultan's uncles, Arslan Arghun and Tekish in the East and Tutush in Syria. Terken Khatun and her son died in 1094, and Tekish was deposed of in the same year. Arslan Arghun was killed by one of his own men in 1097. Tutush came to Baghdad

---

50. See Chap. VIII, pp. 572–573.

with a large army almost immediately after Malik Shah's death, but there was a falling-out between himself and the other military commanders in Syria, and when Berk-Yaruq's army finally joined the issue with Tutush's forces near Rayy in 1095, it was once again an assassination, this time of Tutush by one of his lieutenant's men, that tipped the balance in favor of the young Sultan.

In 1095, after the death of Tutush, Berk-Yaruq was received in Baghdad for the first time as Sultan. It was also the moment of Ghazali's sudden decamping from his post at the Nizamiyah there, an event he ascribed in the *Deliverer* to a spiritual crisis but which may have had considerable political provocation as well. Ghazali was interested in political theory, and he wrote at some length on both the Caliphate and the Sultanate. A year before his departure from Baghdad he composed his *Ignominies of the Esotericists* in defense of the legitimacy of the 'Abbasid Mustazhir vis-à-vis his Fatimid rival in Cairo, and his dogmatic works include the usual section on the question of the Imamate.[51] There is also ascribed to him a "Mirror for Princes" entitled *The Book of Counsel for Kings* and addressed to Sanjar, the Seljuq *amir* of Khurasan after 1097.

In all his political writings Ghazali affirmed the close relationship between Caliph and Sultan. The two were bound together by the joint need of a spiritual head for the Islamic community and of a ruler with sufficient power and authority to insure that government would in fact be carried out in accordance with the *shari'ah*. Ghazali allowed for the designation of the Caliph, within certain juridical limits, by the Sultan, who in turn had to legitimize his own position by swearing an oath of allegiance to the Caliph.

If this was Ghazali's theory of the functioning of the Islamic polity, the reality was far different.[52] He left Baghdad in 1095 with the resolve to have no more traffic with Sultans, an attitude

---

51. Which was not, in Ghazali's view, the subject of metaphysical speculation, as the Isma'ilis would have it, but a purely legal question to be settled on the usual juridical grounds. On Baqillani's similar sentiments, see Chap. VIII, pp. 587–588.

52. Much of it described for us in Ghazali's letters in Persian.

that bespeaks something more than spiritual anxiety. That the Sultan was then Berk-Yaruq and that Ghazali had supported his infant half brother may have had much to do with both his resolve and his sudden departure for Damascus, where Berk-Yaruq's arm did not as yet reach.[53]

The death of his uncles brought neither peace nor security to the new Sultan. From 1097 until his death in 1105, during the years of Ghazali's "retirement" in Syria and Khurasan, Berk-Yaruq had to fight almost uninterruptedly to hold his place in the face of the claims of his half brother Muhammad Tapar. In the end he was unsuccessful. After five exhausting but inconclusive battles Berk-Yaruq died of illness at the age of twenty-five and was succeeded as Great Sultan by his persistent rival, Muhammad Tapar (1105–1118). The true victors were the Isma'ilis, who from their bases in Daylam extended their control over large areas in Kuhistan and Fars; and where they did not gain overt control, the Isma'ilis emerged for the first time as active and public elements in the life of the cities of the Caliphate.

At first the Seljuqs, and particularly Berk-Yaruq, ignored the Isma'ilis in the name of their own self-preservation. Isma'ili contingents even appeared in the Sultan's army. In 1101 there was a reversal as all the Seljuq princes from Syria to Khurasan joined in a violent public disavowal of the Isma'ili movement. Straightway serious countermeasures began to be taken against the Isma'ilis both in the field and in cities like Baghdad and Isfahan. In 1107 the purge netted its most notorious victim, the son of 'Abd al-Malik ibn 'Attash.

The Seljuq counteroffensive of the years after 1101 never reached Hasan ibn al-Sabbah, who was secure in the major Isma'ili fortress of Alamut in the mountains of Daylam. He directed the movement by remote control—he never left Alamut—and provided for his *da'is* a new theological ground on which to offer combat to what he saw as the legalistic and highly uncertain premises of traditional Islam. Hasan's works perished in the destruction of the Alamut library by the Mongols in 1256, but the Ash'arite *mutakallim* al-Shahrastani (d. 1153) had access to

53. Ghazali returned to teaching, as will be seen, in the year following Berk-Yaruq's death in 1105.

what appears to have been Hasan's most important theoretical treatise, *The Four Points*, a work originally composed in Persian but available to us only in an Arabic summary in Shahrastani's heresiographical *Book of Creeds and Sects*.

In the Sunni view of Isma'ilism, Hasan ibn al-Sabbah was credited with issuing a "new call," not in the sense of introducing new doctrines among the Isma'ilis but in that of bringing into relief a thesis that struck tellingly at both Sunnism and his own Imamite rivals among the *Shi'at 'Ali*. Ghazali characterized his opponents not as Isma'ilis but rather as "esotericists" (*batiniyah*) or "partisans of *ta'lim*," and it is precisely the doctrine of *ta'lim*, or absolutely authoritative teaching, that Hasan leveled against traditional Islam in *The Four Points*. By a series of dilemmas he showed that absolute certitude is impossible without the authoritative teaching of a divinely certified *Imam*, since in every other case the believer is left at the mercy of conflicting assertions and arguments, each apparently persuasive in itself, with no means of choosing between them.

The first two of Hasan's four points asserted against the philosophers and Muslim theologians the same principle of the equivalence of proofs that had plunged Ghazali into skepticism. Nor were the Shi'ites themselves immune, as Hasan demonstrated in his third point, since to have an *Imam* but to be uncertain of his identity, as the Imamite Shi'ites were since the time of the "occultation," was to be no better off than the *mutakallimun* or the traditionalists. Only the Isma'ilis with their designated *Imam* were guaranteed a certain knowledge of the truth.[54]

In the last of his points Hasan undertook to provide a more rigorous proof for the existence of an authoritatively teaching

---

54. The Iranian Isma'ilis were seemingly not embarrassed by the nonaccessibility of a Nizarid as *Imam* since the responsibility for the "teaching" was transferred, by implication at least, to Hasan ibn al-Sabbah. This transference, and with it the rupture of all ideological connections with Cairo, was not explicitly promulgated until 1164, when Hasan's third successor at Alamut, Hasan II, publicly read a letter from the *Imam* in which he, Hasan, was named as his representative with full powers. There is little doubt, however, that Hasan ibn al-Sabbah himself functioned as "Proof of the *Imam*," that is, his authoritative spokesman.

Imam. Just as the necessary existence of God is demonstrated from the contingency of all other existents, so man's strongly felt and unfulfilled need for certitude is the ultimate proof of the existence of an *Imam* and his infallible *ta'lim.* He needs neither demonstration nor miracle to certify his necessity; from necessity he is.

In 1094 Ghazali was summoned to the task of providing an answer to the "new call," and in both the *Ignominies* and in other works written at a somewhat later period he confronted the Isma'ilis with a substantial theological refutation and not, as his predecessors had done, with a historical polemic. The Isma'ilis were, for his purposes, a sect, the *batiniyah* or the *ta'limiyah*, and not a political movement, and he treated them accordingly. The new approach was not to everyone's liking, however, and in the *Deliverer* Ghazali later mused on the opposition of some of his fellow Ash'arites who thought that he had made a serious mistake in consenting to study Batinite documents, a charge that Ghazali compared to Ahmad ibn Hanbal's reproaches to al-Muhasibi when the latter took up dialectical weapons against the Mu'tazilites.[55]

Ghazali cited a variety of arguments against *ta'lim*, but his basic position is stated succinctly in the *Deliverer.* Islam has an infallible *Imam*, the Prophet, who left his teaching in the *Qur'an* and the *sunnah.* For the rest, man must rely on the personal exercise of his God-given reason. This is, of course, nothing more than the standard Shafi'ite position on the *shari'ah*, except that Ghazali had a far different view on the fourth of Shafi'i's "roots of the law," analogy, where the personal exercise of reason came into play. For Ghazali mere analogy and the dialectical arguments of *kalam* no longer sufficed as modes of proof; what was needed was strict syllogistic demonstration.

The point is made most precisely by Ghazali in his *Right Balance*, whose exact date of composition is not known but which was written sometime after the *Ignominies* and before the *De-*

---

55. The writing of the *Ignominies* in 1094 is not the work of someone who had begun to fear for his safety in 1093, but the opposition that that work raised among the Baghdad Ash'arites, Ghazali's natural constituency, may have helped his decision to leave in 1095.

liverer. The tract is in the form of a dialogue between a Sunni and an Isma'ili, and in it Ghazali attempted to elicit the Aristotelian rules for demonstration from the text of the *Qur'an* itself. The project was not, perhaps, a happy one,[56] but Ghazali's more general concern to introduce syllogistic rigor into Islamic discourse met with broad success. From its beginnings among the Mu'tazilites, *kalam*, like Islamic jurisprudence, had contented itself with rhetorical forms of argument.[57] But now that the apodictic demonstration had become a commonplace in the writings of the Islamic philosophers, as it had long since been in those of the Christian theologians,[58] analogy and its congeners would not serve. Ash'arite theologians before Ghazali had already come to that understanding—Juwayni had made some modest efforts in the direction of introducing Aristotelian logic into *kalam*—but to Ghazali belongs the credit for establishing it beyond question and so of having initiated what later Muslims understood as a new phase in the history of *kalam*.

Ghazali's own major work on dogmatics, *The Just Course in Matters of Belief*, was promised in the *Incoherence* and may well have been written in the last year before Ghazali's abrupt departure from Baghdad. In it Ghazali invoked the well-worn *topos* of *kalam* as a defensive weapon to repel rationalistic and skeptical attacks upon Islam. He did not advocate that it be taught to everyone; the study of speculative theology was merely a communal not an individual obligation. In Ghazali's view it made no difference whether a Muslim came to his faith by means of demonstrative proof or by accepting the authority of another. But for those on whom the obligation to speculate does rest, the *mutakallimun*, arguments must be drawn correctly, that is, deductively.

Ghazali set down these preliminary considerations on the

---

56. Earlier Farabi had tried something similar by collecting Prophetic *hadith* on the subject of logic. The work is not preserved, and so it is impossible to judge the results.

57. See Chap. II, pp. 190–191.

58. Though here too there was opposition. Yahya ibn 'Adi's student Ibn Zur'ah (d. 1008) still felt the need to write on *The Innocence of Those Who Inquire into Philosophy and Logic*.

nature and method of *kalam* in what had become by his day the obligatory introduction to treatises on theology. From Baqillani to Ghazali the scholastic structure of *kalam* tracts becomes increasingly apparent: methodological preliminaries; the existence of God; his essence and attributes; his acts, often studied under the guise of a theodicy; and finally a section on "traditional" questions like prophetology and the Imamate. The subjects do not change so much as the rigor of the proofs. Later critics found fault with the demonstrations of some of the eleventh-century *mutakallimun*, but then only because Ghazali had pointed out the route to the *via moderna* in *kalam*, the Aristotelian syllogism.

Then, suddenly, Ghazali bade farewell to Baghdad and, though purportedly going on pilgrimage to the Hejaz, made his way to Damascus, Jerusalem, Hebron, and perhaps even Egypt.[59] The chronology of his self-imposed exile is as obscure as the motives that prompted it. One witness claims to have met him teaching again in Baghdad as early as 1097. This too may be a mistake. All we know for certain is that at some point Ghazali left off his traveling in the Arab lands and returned to his native Tus, where he remained in quasi retirement until 1105.

Ghazali mentions in his *Deliverer* that he spent two years of his "exile" in Damascus, and tradition names that city as the place where he composed the work upon which his great fame in Islam ultimately rests, *The Revitalization of the Sciences of Religion.* The appreciation granted to Ghazali by Western scholarship has centered upon his *Incoherence* and its place in the history of philosophy in Islam. The Muslim view is quite different. If the attention of later scribes and commentators is taken as the criterion, it is not the *Incoherence*, but the *Revitalization*, that won Ghazali his place in the first rank of Muslim thinkers. *Falsafah* was at best a rarefied and peripheral issue in Islam, and both the *Intentions* and the *Incoherence* were written in a milieu and in circumstances that ceased to interest Ghazali in his maturity. He

---

59. The genuineness of both the sojourn in Egypt and the work Ghazali allegedly wrote there, *An Appropriate Refutation of the Divinity of Jesus by Way of Commentary on the Gospels*, with its unmistakable references to Coptic Christianity, has been severely questioned.

never repudiated either *falsafah* or *kalam;* it is merely that his concerns became more personal and at the same time more ecumenical in the years after 1095.

The *Revitalization* is Ghazali's contribution to ecumenical Islam. It is aimed directly at orthopraxy, and in it Ghazali manifests his position in the mainstream of Islamic ethics, which from the beginning addressed itself more urgently to action than it did to questions of orthodoxy. Ghazali was by no means an ethical primitive, however. His view of the good life for man is constructed upon a base of philosophical ethics derived, largely by way of Ibn Sina, from the *Nicomachean Ethics* of Aristotle. Like that of his Hellenic and Hellenized predecessors, Ghazali's schematization of virtue depends upon an analysis of the soul and its faculties that is at root Aristotelian and lays claim to being scientific in the Greek understanding of that word.

For the Greeks, scientific knowledge was that capable of strict apodictic demonstration. Aristotle had shown the way in his *Analytics*, and the *falasifah* had little trouble in accepting either the methods or the conclusions of the *Organon.* Ghazali was willing to go down the same path. In his *Standard of Knowledge*, written not very long after the *Incoherence*, Ghazali attempted to set out his reasons for accepting the methods of the Hellenic-style logic, including its notion of certain undemonstrable premises that underlie the science of ethics. Somewhat later he returned to the same question in his *Criterion of Action*, wherein his efforts were directed toward applying the premises elicited in the *Standard of Knowledge* to action—to construct, in short, a humanistic ethics.

In the very act of construction Ghazali betrayed his other, very non-Greek concerns. A rational science like ethics neither describes nor regulates the human condition in an adequate manner. Man has also received a divine revelation embodying a code of conduct, and so at the side of the rational sciences consideration must also be given to the religious sciences that have their origins in that revelation. Further, man's ultimate happiness is not achieved in this world, as the Hellenic tradition believed, but in the next, and at this point Ghazali added a new distinction between the "this-worldly" and the "other-worldly" sciences.

All of this occurs in the *Criterion of Action*, written probably in Baghdad after Ghazali's study of Greek philosophy and *kalam* but before the notorious crisis of 1095 that turned his attention to other modes of thought and other ways to salvation. Indeed, the seeds of that crisis may already be present in the *Criterion*. The introduction of the "other-worldly sciences," which are, in effect, the sciences of the mystic, betrays an interest in an area only imperfectly explored by the philosophers and the theologians.

The monumental *Revitalization* is a treatise on neither *falsafah* nor *kalam;* it is an elaborate attempt at spiritualizing the Law for the practicing Muslim.[60] His object was to bring understanding to action, and precisely to that action which links man to God. There is, according to Ghazali, a "science of revelation" which deals with knowledge alone and so plays no part in the *Revitalization.* His subject was rather the "science of activity," a science that embraces both knowledge and action and can be considered in both its internal aspects—that is, the virtues and dispositions of the soul, and externally, insofar as those dispositions overflow into deeds, whether they are directed toward God alone or have as their object one's fellow men.

This highly scholastic schema provided Ghazali with the general organization of the *Revitalization* into four "quarters" in which he considered the true spiritual "refinement" (*adab*) of the Muslim as it pertains to (1) the ritual Muslim acts like prayers, fasting, et cetera; (2) his moral relations with other men; (3) the interior dispositions of the soul; and (4) the "qualities of salvation."

For Ghazali, salvation begins quite simply with the five "pillars of Islam." The first of them, the *shahadah,* is more than a simple declaration of faith; it includes an understanding of the articles of faith, which range from Creation to the Last Things. From there Ghazali takes his reader through the fundamental acts of worship prescribed by Islam, stressing in each case the interiorization of the act through different levels of spiritual understanding. It was not Ghazali's intention to reduce Islamic ritual to a dumb show

60. Here too Ghazali had an exemplar in Muhasibi, and a somewhat similar intention lay behind al-Tirmidhi's *Reasons for the Performance of the Canonical Acts;* see Chap. VIII, p. 550.

concealing an elaborate esoteric symbolism. He affirmed the reality of the act, while at the same time transmitting to the reader his conviction that the perfection of the act depends upon the spiritual states that accompany it.

The direction of Ghazali's thoughts is revealed by his ignoring the *jihad* in his treatment of the "pillars." Instead, he concludes the first "quarter" of the *Revitalization* with a lengthy discussion of the practice of reciting the *Qur'an* and of the Sufi device of "invoking the name of Allah," two forms of liturgy that were, in Ghazali's mind, the highest forms of worship.

All through the *Revitalization* the voice of Ghazali echoes with the rich polyphony of a Muslim educated in the Law, *kalam, falsafah* and Sufism. In the first "quarter" there is a visible effort at suppressing the speech of the lawyer, since it deals only with external acts, something which professedly did not interest Ghazali in this context. His task in the second "quarter" was even more complex. The *Qur'an* is filled with prescriptions regulating the conduct of one man toward another. Many of these relationships are contractual—marriage, for example—and provided Islamic lawyers with ample scope for their subtle and elaborate techniques. Here too Ghazali's concern was to retrieve such acts for the moralist.

The object in this second "quarter" was not, of course, to construct a humanistic code of conduct—these are after all acts specifically prescribed by divine command—but to elicit the moral quality of such prescribed acts. This "quarter" of the *Revitalization* examines in turn the appropriate spiritual "refinement" with respect to food, marriage, commercial transactions, "things permitted and forbidden," social acts and those more appropriate to solitude, travel and singing.[61] The "quarter" ends with Ghazali's reflections on the essential moral imperative "to do good and prohibit evil" and on the character of the Prophet as a paradigm for human morality.

The third "quarter" of the *Revitalization* opens with a tract on "an explanation of the wonders of the heart," and here Ghazali

---

61. Here too, as in the earlier section on "invoking the name of Allah" (*dhikr;* see Chap. VIII, p. 562, n. 22), there is an obvious reflection of Ghazali's Sufi interests.

passes over from the realm of act into that of the virtues of the soul. First the appropriate distinctions are drawn between "rational" and "religious" science, between the this-worldly and the other-worldly sciences, and between those acquired by instruction or speculation and those that come into the heart through some form of inspiration.

The third and fourth "quarters" of the work represent the center of Ghazali's ethical theory, an elaboration of the program sketched out in the *Criterion of Action.* They embrace, as he himself describes it, a series of tracts devoted to the "reformation of character," a task already undertaken for the Muslim community by Miskawayh. And, like his predecessor, Ghazali drew heavily on the Hellenic ethical tradition, not directly but through Ibn Sina. His analysis of the faculties of the soul into deliberative, concupiscent, and irascible is pure Aristotle, and so too are the four cardinal virtues—wisdom, courage, temperance and justice—that proceed from a training of those faculties. Equally Greek is his notion of virtue as a mean.[62] There are explicit references to the Hellenic medical theory of health as the middle ground between excess and defect, and it is only when he introduces a spiritual physician, a Sufi *shaykh,* to cure the disease that Ghazali moves beyond his Hellenic predecessors onto fully Islamic ground.

Ghazali agreed with the Greeks that the ultimate end of man is happiness. For the Muslim, however, or for those Muslims unaffected or unconcerned by the *falsafah* tradition, happiness was, in the last resort, a gift of God, from whom all things proceed. Thus, at the very least God must cooperate in the achievement of human happiness or, according to others, bestow it in its totality upon man. Ghazali stood close to the latter end of that spectrum of opinion: the various goods of body and soul are impossible without the accompaniment of what he calls "the virtues of divine cooperation," specifically Allah's guidance, or the knowledge of the distinction between good and evil, His direction toward the good and his removal of obstacles toward that end, and finally His support. Without them, man's efforts at achieving virtue, and so happiness, would be in vain.

---

62. There was, of course, an appropriate *hadith* on the subject.

There is nothing remotely resembling this within the humanistic confines of Miskawayh's *Reformation of Morals*. Nor is there anything in that earlier work corresponding to the fourth "quarter" of the *Revitalization*, wherein Ghazali gives his explanation of the "qualities of salvation." These are, in Ghazali's view, the virtues of the few. All men are obliged to the cultivation of the cardinal virtues, whether derived by the rational method of investigation or given by a public revelation. Some few men go further, however. By means of private inspiration they penetrate into the "hidden" virtues.

This spiritual elite is the mystics, the Sufis whose wisdom had effected his "conversion" in 1095, and Ghazali proposed to give a theoretical account of their teachings in the fourth and longest part of the *Revitalization*. He drew heavily on the mystics themselves, notably on the most orthodox and analytical of them, al-Muhasibi and al-Makki, passages of whose *Food of the Heart* are extensively reproduced in the *Revitalization*. Ghazali was not interested in describing the spiritual experiences of the mystics, which were far too personal for his own essentially literary purposes. His intention was rather to construct an ethics of mysticism, and so Makki's careful analysis of the various "states" and "stations" of the mystical way were admirably suited to Ghazali's own theoretical bent.

There is little difference beween Ghazali's presentation of the "stations" from repentance to love of God and that given by al-Makki and others, save that Ghazali had integrated his material into his ethical theory—the mystics' "stations" are, in effect, virtues, permanent dispositions of the soul based on understanding and practice.

The last and most perfect of the "stations"—and, so, the highest virtue that can be achieved by man—is the love of God, and Ghazali's treatment of it in the *Revitalization* is an illustration of both the tensions implicit in Ghazali's thought and the complex use of his intellectual antecedents to resolve them. The love of God was introduced into Muslim pietist circles by mystics like Rabi'ah and never set easily with the traditionalists, whose strongly held sentiments about the "otherness" of Allah were violated by the possibilities of such a relationship. Indeed Aristotle himself, for whom friendship or love (*philia*) implied an equality of terms, had difficulty in positing a similar relationship between God and man.

Despite his exclusion of God as an object of *philia*, Aristotle did devote a considerable analysis to that quality in Books Eight and Nine of the *Nicomachean Ethics*, and Ghazali's own detailed study of love appears to owe a great deal to his Greek predecessor, even though his conclusions are quite different. According to Aristotle, we love what is good or pleasurable or useful, but it is only the first that grounds perfect friendship. Ghazali permits a more elaborate motivation by incorporating into his analysis the Stoic theory of self-love or self-preservation[63] and by introducing a notion only touched on by Aristotle, a relationship based on spiritual affinity. Some people, Aristotle remarks, define *philia* as a kind of likeness, and for Ghazali that likeness lies at the heart of man's love of God. It is a hidden, spiritual affinity that is related to revelation and, so, all but ineffable.

Consistent with his rationalizing approach to the traditional virtues of the mystic, Ghazali founded the love of God on a prior knowledge of him—not the speculative knowledge (*'ilm*) of the philosopher but the intuitive knowledge (*ma'rifah*) granted to some few men who have freed themselves from worldly passions and desires. Knowing God, they love him and, so, achieve for themselves the highest virtue in this life and a claim to the ultimate happiness, the beatific vision, in the next.

On that note of the vision of God the *Revitalization of the Sciences of Religion* ended what Aristotle had begun in the *Nicomachean Ethics* by defining happiness as action of the soul over a lifetime in accordance with virtue. For Ghazali not even a lifetime was sufficient for gaining happiness. It lay beyond life, in another, supernatural dimension. Happiness, for Ghazali, was not action in accordance with virtue but the reward for such action. Nor were the natural virtues alone adequate to achieve it. God has revealed a code of conduct and guides men to an understanding of the spiritual refinement that underlies that code. Thus, to Aristotle's "rational" virtues Ghazali added a new scale of "reli-

---

63. The subject does appear in the *Nicomachean Ethics*, but not in the prominent position later bestowed upon it by the Stoics.

gious" (*shari'iyah*) virtues derived from a meditation on the Book of Revelation.

A life in accordance with the rational and religious virtues wins Paradise, and Ghazali described its pleasures in the last book of the *Revitalization*. But Ghazali had discovered more. Beyond the rational ethics of the Greeks and the religious ethics of the theologians is the ethic of the mystic, that ultimate refinement of soul whose premises are revealed by God to the saint and whose reward lies beyond Paradise in a vision of God Himself.

The Ghazali who put those sentiments onto paper in Damascus may or may not have been lecturing on them publicly—though certainly not in the Nizamiyah—in Baghdad in 1097 before resettling into a life of private devotion in his native Tus. In 1106 he was prevailed upon by Nizam al-Mulk's son, Fakhr al-Mulk, then serving as vizier to Sanjar, the *amir* of Khurasan, to return to active teaching in the Nizamiyah *madrasah* in Nishapur. This he did, and he wrote the *Deliverer from Error* during the year he served as professor there. At the assassination of Fakhr al-Mulk in 1107, Ghazali once again gave up public teaching and retired to Tus, where he gave private instruction, pursued his devotions and studied *hadith*. He died at Tus in 1111, only shortly after finishing his final work, *On Restraining the Common People from the Study of Theology*.

Talk of his "conversion" and perhaps Ghazali's own description of his spiritual evolution in the highly schematic passages of the *Deliverer* have given rise to the false impression of a man passing through various stages of conviction, shedding one before embracing the next, and of a seeker after truth who found it in Sufism alone. Whatever his views on the most effective means of salvation, Ghazali remained a Shafi'ite lawyer and an Ash'arite theologian to the end of his life. He never professed to be a *faylasuf*, though there is a broad streak of rationalism running through most of his writings. One could believe without understanding, in Ghazali's view, but the perfection of human character demanded understanding. Similarly, one could understand without savoring. Paradise was prepared for those who understood, but those who savored in this life could look forward to the beatific vision in the next.

Ghazali was not the first theologian to turn to mysticism.

Muhasibi was early in the field, and as has already been noted, Sufism of the temperate sort represented by the great theoreticians of the tenth century was fully domesticated within the various orthodox law schools well before Ghazali wrote his *Revitalization* or his own personal testament to Sufism in the *Deliverer from Error*. Sufism had no need of being "saved" by Ghazali; it was, despite the occasional misgivings of a Hanbalite traditionalist, an accepted and orthodox part of the Islamic experience. Where the true danger to Sufism lay was in the resemblances between the casual attitudes toward the Law of adepts like Ibn abi al-Khayr or the Malamatiyah and what the traditional Muslim imagined were the teachings of the Isma'ilis.

By its general structure the *Revitalization* is addressed to that problem. The Sufis were an elite, men privy to a special knowledge denied to the mass of believers—Ghazali made no effort to deny it—but the *Revitalization* revealed that their virtues were continuous with the religious obligations of all Muslims. More, Ghazali distilled what had earlier been expressed by Sufi authors in terms of individual and idiosyncratic experiences into a general theory. The material lay ready at hand—in Makki for example—but it first had to pass through Ghazali's own sensibilities, which were and remained those of an intellectualizing theologian.

The evidence for it appears elsewhere than in the *Revitalization*. In a series of works whose exact chronology is uncertain but which probably date from the final years of his life, Ghazali took up the question of mysticism as such and without the broad context he provided for it in the *Revitalization*. The Persian *Alchemy of Happiness* and his Arabic treatises *Niche of Lights*[64] and *Mystical Epistle* are Ghazali's mature attempt at supplying Sufism with a metaphysics. His predecessors had described the mystical experience in detail, and the theoreticians among them had charted the human perspectives of the "stations" and "states" that lead thither, Ghazali gave his own understanding of the landscape on the other side of the divide.

Ghazali trod carefully on the dangerous topic of "annihilation

---

64. So called because of its being a commentary upon the famous verse in the *Qur'an* (24:34) in which Allah is described as a light "which is like a niche in which there is a lamp."

of self," the *fana'* of Bistami and Junayd. Those who come to that point, by discursive reasoning, he pointed out, as well as by "savoring," do indeed have the experience that nothing, neither themselves nor the world, exists save God, and so in a sense all appears to be God. They gave voice to that experience by their intoxicated utterances, "I am the Truth," and "Glory be to Me," but when their drunkenness abates and they return to their normal state, that wherein the "touchstone" of reason operates, the Sufis once again come to understand that they are other than God. Unity *with* God (*ittihad*) is no more than a metaphor; what the Sufi has actually experienced is the unity *of* God (*tawhid*).

But not that alone. Ghazali was willing to concede the experience of a Bistami or a Hallaj; subjectively the mystic may feel at the moment of his ecstasy that "All is Allah and apart from him there is nothing." But when he himself comes to describe what lies beyond that, Ghazali peers into the *pleroma* not with the eyes of Hallaj but with those of Ibn Sina. Above the world of sense lies that of the "kingdom of the spirit" (*malakut*), where dwell the souls of the celestial spheres and, in its upper reaches, a veritable Plotinian hierarchy of transcendental beings: Allah, the One, and his two primordial emanations, Universal Intellect understood in the sense of the Qur'anic "command" whereby God created the world, and Universal Soul.

For Ghazali as for the Neoplatonists, the Supreme Being was incapable of serving as a creator of the universe in any sense save that as the source of an eternal and necessary emanation. For the Neoplatonists emanationism was an adequate explanation for the existence of the universe, but for the Muslim Ghazali, who accepted the *Qur'an*'s description of the world as coming into being through a willed command, "Be!" emanationism alone could not suffice. The command, then, which is God's eternally emanated "Word," is hypostatized as Universal Intelligence and identified in the *Mystical Epistle* with that transcendental "Muhammad of Light" earlier meditated on by the Sufis.[65] Allah,

---

65. Ghazali's own version of the "Muhammad of Light" is rendered somewhat more complex by his description of him as "the Obeyed One," a phrase used in the *Qur'an* (81:21) and traditionally interpreted as referring to Gabriel.

who could not will the creation of the world in the obviously Neoplatonic sensibilities of Ghazali, had to surrender the task of serving as Prime Mover to the "Muhammad of Light."

The mystic achieves his sense of *tawhid* only in his experience of the One, but in achieving it he comes to understand the "kingdom of spirit," a Neoplatonic and Avicennist landscape that had escaped the notice of Bistami, Junayd and Hallaj. Ghazali, who resisted many of its implications in the *Incoherence of the Philosophers,* openly embraced that vision of the world in the *Mystical Epistle.* In the earlier work he had come to it as a scholastic critic of Aristotelian physics and metaphysics, but here at the end of his life Ghazali had discovered behind the arguments of Ibn Sina's *Healing,* of Simplicius, Philoponus and Aristotle, the spiritual perspectives of Plotinus that lay concealed within the "Theology of Aristotle," and the final chapters of Ibn Sina's *Book of Remarks.*

There was to be more of Plotinus in Islam, though his paternity was never acknowledged. The Muslim Neoplatonists of the twelfth and following centuries in Iran preferred to invoke their own Hermetic vision of history, which linked Plato, Pythagoras and Zoroaster in the cause of an "Oriental wisdom" that was in fact an elaborately Gnostic version of Plotinus. It is not at all certain whether those later theosophists ever read Plato, much less Zoroaster or the nonexistent sages of Sasanian Iran. For them, as for Ghazali, *falsafah* was represented by Ibn Sina and not by his own masters, Aristotle and Plotinus.

Ghazali, part *mutakallim,* part *faylasuf* and part Sufi, opened what may have been a fatal fissure in Islam. From very different motives the Sufi and the Isma'ili had long argued for an intellectual and spiritual double standard for Muslims. The faith of the ordinary Muslim was driven into crabbed and unbecoming quarters, where it would rest, despite Ghazali's best efforts to the contrary in the *Revitalization,* as the sole purview of traditionalist lawyers. The "realities" were reserved, in the Sufi and Batinite views, for the adept. Ghazali had no sympathy for the Batinite version of this dichotomy, but he was willing to subscribe to it in its Sufi form, and in the end he permitted to the esoteric Sufi the *falsafah* that he so strenuously denied to the exoteric Muslim.

Islam was not denied its "age of enlightenment," but it came in precisely the form heralded here by Ghazali, as an "age of illumination" celebrated by theosophists. The possibilities of that other "enlightenment" of rational and publicly conducted discourse on the nature and quality of Islam that was so brilliantly begun by Farabi, Abu Sulayman, Miskawayh and Ibn Sina received no further hearing. The only rivals to the Sufi and the theosophist, who guided private enthusiasms and secret visions of the truth, were the guardians of public morality, the traditionalist and the lawyer.

The lawyers' powerful grip on public Islam is clearly demonstrated by the willingness of the Isma'ilis and other Shi'ites to surrender the struggle in that corner of the arena—their version of the *shari'ah* was little different from that of the Sunni traditionalists—and to confine their attempts at reforming Islam to an elaborate charting of the transcendentals. Miskawayh and even Ghazali had far more daring plans for reforming the *praxis* of the Muslim than any Shi'ite. Their reforms were a reflex of the Hellenism on which they both had fed, an authentic Hellenism that regarded morality as a function of human history and not a flight from it into another dimension where no Sunni Caliph or Turkish *amir*, no Islamic lawyer or Hellenic sage, and in the end no one of the "commonalty" of Muslims could possibly follow.

CHRONOLOGY: THE NEAR EAST FROM THE BIRTH OF MUHAMMAD TO THE DEATH OF AL-GHAZALI

570	Traditional date of birth of Muhammad; Abraha's unsuccessful attack upon Mecca
575	Brief Sasanian protectorate in Yemen
578	Death of Muhammad's grandfather 'Abd al-Muttalib
582–602	MAURICE Emperor at Constantinople
584	Dismemberment of Ghassanid phylarchate by Maurice
590–628	KHUSRAW II PARVEZ Shah of Iran
595	Marriage of Muhammad and Khadijah
602–610	PHOCAS Emperor at Constantinople
603	Sasanians invade Byzantine Empire
604	End of Lakhmid phylarchate
605	Confederation of Arabs defeats Sasanians at Dhu al-Qar
610–641	HERACLIUS Emperor at Constantinople
610	First revelations to Muhammad on Mt. Hira
614	Fall of Jerusalem to Sasanians
615	Migration of Muslims to Abyssinia
618	Civil war at Medina
619	Sasanians enter Alexandria; death of Muhammad's wife and uncle
620	Muhammad's first encounter with Medinese
622	*Hijrah* of Muhammad and Emigrants from Mecca to Medina; beginning of Muslim era; Byzantines begin counteroffensive against Sasanians

624 Battle of Badr; Muhammad changes orientation of Muslim prayer
625 Battle of Mt. Uhud
627 Battle of the Ditch
628 Death of Khusraw II; Sasanians sue for peace; Muhammad's *détente* with Quraysh near Mecca; capture of oasis of Khaybar
629 Civil and political anarchy in Iran; Muslims raid Mu'tah
630 Heraclius restores True Cross to Jerusalem; Muhammad returns in triumph to Mecca; defeats nomad confederation; raid on Tabuk
631 Abu Bakr leads *hajj*
632–651 YAZDIGIRD III Shah of Iran
632 Death of Muhammad

632–661 RASHIDUN CALIPHS AT MEDINA

632–634 ABU BAKR Caliph at Medina
632–633 Wars of *Riddah*
633 Heraclius discontinues stipend to Sinai Bedouin; Muslims and Banu Bakr capture Hirah
634 Heraclius orders conversion of all Jews in empire; Muslims successfully penetrate Sinai, defeat Byzantines at Ajnadayn in Palestine
634–644 'UMAR Caliph at Medina
635 Damascus falls
636 Battle of the Yarmuk
637 Sasanians defeated at Qadisiyah; founding of Basrah
638 Jerusalem and Antioch fall to Muslims; founding of Kufah
641 Death of Heraclius and regency of Martina; 'Umar has first *diwan* roll drawn up
642–668 CONSTANS II Emperor at Constantinople
642 'Amr founds Fustat in Egypt; final defeat of Sasanians at Nihawand north of Hamadhan
643 Muslims in Tripoli
644–656 'UTHMAN Caliph at Medina
644–646 Muslim conquest of Armenia
645 Byzantine fleet temporarily regains Alexandria
649 Muslim fleet attacks Cyprus
650 Muslims occupy Fars

651 Death of Yazdigird III, end of Sasanian line; Muslims in Khurasan

652 Muslims take Herat and Balkh; death of al-Ghifari, early ascetic and Companion

c. 653 'Uthman's recension of the *Qur'an;* death of al-'Abbas

656–661 'ALI Caliph at Medina and Kufah

656 Battle of the Camel: 'Ali defeats Talhah and al-Zubayr, sequesters 'A'ishah; revolt of Mu'awiyah in Syria

657 Battle of 'Ali and Mu'awiyah at Siffin; death of early ascetic and Companion Hudhayfah

658 Preliminary arbitration; rejection by Kharijites; 'Ali crushes them at Nahrawan

659 Final arbitration

661 Assassination of 'Ali; proclamation of Caliphate of Hasan at Kufah

661–750 UMAYYAD CALIPHATE AT DAMASCUS

661–680 MU'AWIYAH Caliph at Damascus

662 Death of historian Ka'b al-Ahbar

663–668 Constans moves Byzantine government to Italy and Sicily

665 Mu'awiyah appoints Ziyad governor of Basrah

667 Death of Christian scholar Severus Sebokht

668–685 CONSTANTINE IV POGONATUS Emperor at Constantinople

669 Arabs besiege Constantinople; death of Hasan

670 Foundation of Qayrawan in Ifriqiyah; the mosque there (670–675); Muslims reach Oxus

674 Muslims cross Oxus and occupy Bukhara

677 Muslims lift siege of Constantinople

678 Death of Companion Abu Hurayrah

680–683 YAZID I Caliph at Damascus

680 Death of 'Ali's son Husayn, proclaimed Caliph at Mecca and destroyed by Ziyad's son 'Ubaydallah at Karbala'

683 Insurrection of 'Abdallah ibn al-Zubayr at Mecca; Yazid's response aborted by his death

683– MU'AWIYAH II Caliph at Damascus

684–685 MARWAN I Caliph at Damascus; puts down revolt of Qays

685–705	'ABD AL-MALIK Caliph at Damascus
685–695	JUSTINIAN II Emperor at Constantinople
685	Pro-'Alid insurrection by al-Mukhtar at Kufah; joined by *mawali;* death of genealogist Daghfil
686	Mukhtar defeats 'Ubaydallah and Syrian army
687–691	Dome of Rock in Jerusalem
687	Mukhtar destroyed in Kufah by Mus'ab, brother of Ibn al-Zubayr; death of Qur'anic commentator Ibn al-'Abbas
692	Final defeat of revolt of Ibn al-Zubayr in Mecca; Chinese occupy Tarim basin
694	Al-Hajjaj crushes opposition to Umayyads in Iraq
695–698	LEONTIUS Emperor at Constantinople
695–698	Muslims and Byzantines struggle for Carthage; first Muslim gold coins struck
698–705	TIBERIUS III Emperor at Constantinople
700	Death of 'Ali's son Muhammad ibn al-Hanafiyah
702	Founding of Wasit by Hajjaj
705–715	WALID Caliph at Damascus
705–711	JUSTINIAN II regains throne in Constantinople
705	Qutaybah appointed governor of Khurasan, begins conquest of Transoxania; Great Mosque at Damascus
708	Death of Christian scholar Jacob of Edessa
710	Death of 'Ali ibn Husayn, fourth Shi'ite *Imam;* about this time death of Umayyad poets al-Akhtal, Ibn al-Rabi'ah, Jamil and "Majnun"
711–713	PHILIPPICUS Emperor at Constantinople
711–713	Muslim conquest of Spain and Sind; Qutaybah takes Samarqand
713–715	ANASTASIUS II Emperor at Constantinople
713	Death of Ibn al-Zubayr, early biographer of Prophet
714	Qutaybah repulsed from Tashkent by Chinese; death of al-Hajjaj
715–717	SULAYMAN Caliph at Damascus
715–717	THEODOSIUS II Emperor at Constantinople
716–717	Muslims advance to Constantinople under Sulayman's brother Maslamah; death of Abu Hashim, son of 'Alid Muhammad ibn al-Hanafiyah
717–741	LEO III the Isaurian, Emperor at Constantinople
717–720	'UMAR II Caliph at Damascus; transfer of school of Alexandria to Antioch

717–718	Leo defeats Muslims before Constantinople and raises siege
c. 718	Muhammad the 'Abbasid begins laying claim to Caliphate
720–724	YAZID II Caliph at Damascus
723	Caliph orders destruction of Christian images
724–743	HISHAM Caliph at Damascus
724–737	Turks drive Arabs from Transoxania
724	Death of George, Metropolitan bishop of Arabs
725	Muslim armies in southern France
726	First Iconoclastic edict of Leo III
728	Death of Hasan al-Basri, theologian and ascetic
731	Death of fifth Shi'ite *Imam*, Muhammad al-Baqir, and of poet Dhu al-Rummah
732	Charles Martel repulses Arabs at Poitiers; death of poets Farazdaq and Jarir and of historian Wahb ibn Munabbih
737	Charles Martel again defeats Muslims near Narbonne; death of Mughirah ibn Sa'id, Shi'ite occultist
740	Leo III defeats Arab army in central Anatolia; revolt and death of Zayd, the *Imam* of the Zaydi Shi'ites; Berber revolts in Ifriqiyah
741–745	CONSTANTINE V Emperor at Constantinople
742	Death of jurist al-Zuhri
743–744	WALID II Caliph at Damascus
743	Execution of Ghaylan al-Dimashqi; death of Muhammad the 'Abbasid
744–750	MARWAN II Caliph at Damascus
744	Revolt of 'Alid 'Abdallah ibn Mu'awiyah at Kufah
745	Resurgence of Kharijites in East
746	Constantine V invades Syria; death of Jahm ibn Safwan
747	Revolt of Abu Muslim in Khurasan
748	Death of theologian Wasil ibn 'Ata'; execution by Marwan of Ibrahim, son of Muhammad the 'Abbasid
749	Ibrahim's brother Abu al-'Abbas proclaimed Caliph by Abu Muslim and his troops; Abu Muslim disposes of Bih'afrid
750	Battle of Great Zab; defeat and death of Marwan II at hands of 'Abbasid forces; death of John of Damascus

750–1258 'ABBASID CALIPHATE AT BAGHDAD

750–754	Abu al-'Abbas al-Saffah Caliph
751	Muslims turn back Chinese advance in Central Asia at Talas River
754–775	Al-Mansur Caliph at Baghdad; contested by his uncle 'Abdallah, who is defeated at Nisibis by Abu Muslim; Khalid ibn Barmak minister
754	Mansur engineers murder of Abu Muslim
757	Execution of Ibn al-Muqaffa'
758	Death of Hasanid 'Abdallah and of *maghazi* editor Musa ibn 'Uqbah
760	Death or disappearance of Isma'il, son of Ja'far al-Sadiq; organization of first *khanqah* in Palestine
761	Death of 'Amr ibn 'Ubayd
762	Founding of new 'Abbasid capital of Baghdad
762–763	Hasanids Muhammad and Ibrahim raise unsuccessful revolt in Medina and Basrah
c. 762	Death of Shi'ite theologian Abu al-Khattab
765	Jurjis ibn Bukhtishu' summoned from Jundishapur to serve as physician for Mansur; death of sixth Shi'ite *Imam,* Ja'far al-Sadiq
767	Death of jurist Abu Hanifah and the Prophet's biographer Ibn Ishaq
770	Death of Abu 'Amr ibn al-'Ala', Qur'anic expert
771	Death of Hammad al-Rawiyah, collector of *qasidahs*
775–785	Al-Mahdi Caliph at Baghdad
775–780	Leo IV, the Khazar, Emperor at Constantinople
776	Insurrection of al-Muqanna' in Khurasan; death of Ibrahim ibn Adham, first ascetic of Khurasan
777	Kharijite uprisings in eastern Iran
778	Leo IV invades Syria
780–797	Constantine VI Emperor at Constantinople
781	Nestorian inscription of Sian-fu; death of Khalid ibn Barmak
782	Muslims break Byzantine army and advance to Chrysopolis
783	Al-Muqanna' brought down; al-Mahdi begins inquisition
784	Death of poet Bashshar
785	Death of Christian scholar Theophilus of Edessa
785–786	Al-Hadi Caliph at Baghdad

786–809	HARUN AL-RASHID Caliph at Baghdad
786–803	Vizierate of Yahya the Barmacid
786	Death of al-Khalid, lexicographer
790	Death of Queen Mother Khayzuran
793	Death of ascetic 'Abd al-Wahid ibn Zayd
795	Death of jurist Malik ibn Anas and of Shi'ite theologian Hisham ibn al-Hakam
796	Death of poetry collector Khalaf al-Ahmar, the mystic Rabah ibn 'Amr, and Shi'ite theologian Maymun al-Qaddah
797	Irene blinds and deposes Constantine VI and proclaims herself sole Empress
797–802	IRENE Empress at Constantinople
797	Death of ascetic Ibn al-Mubarak
798	Irene contracts to pay tribute to Arabs
798	Death of Chief Qadi Abu Yusuf
799	Death of seventh Shi'ite *Imam*, Musa al-Kazim
800	Ibrahim ibn al-Aghlab, semiautonomous *amir* of Ifriqiyah; activity of theologian Dirar ibn 'Amr in Baghdad; death of grammarian Sibawayh and of Christian scholar Yahya ibn al-Bitriq
801	Death of mystic Rabi'ah
802–811	NICEPHORUS I Emperor at Constantinople
802	Harun determines the succession of his sons
803	The fall of the Barmacids
804	Death of al-Kisa'i, grammarian and tutor of Crown Princes Amin and Ma'mun
805	Jibril ibn Bukhtishu' appointed Caliphal physician; death of jurist al-Shaybani
806	Harun invades Anatolia
809–813	AL-AMIN Caliph at Baghdad
810	Death of poet Abu Nuwas and of mystic Shaqiq
811–	STAURICIUS Emperor at Constantinople
811–813	MICHAEL I Emperor at Constantinople
813–820	LEO VI Emperor at Constantinople
813–833	MA'MUN Caliph at Baghdad
813–816	Ma'mun's civil war with his brother Amin
814	Death of Christian scholar Job of Edessa
815	Revolt of Abu al-Saraya and of Hasanid Muhammad ibn Tabataba; death of al-Fadl ibn Nawbakht, translator from Pahlevi, of astrologer Masha'allah and of Jabir ibn Hayyan

816	Revolt of Babak in Azarbayjan
817	Ma'mun announces that his successor will be the 'Alid 'Ali al-Rida
818	Revolts against Ma'mun in Baghdad; death of eighth Shi'ite *Imam,* 'Ali al-Rida
818–825	Dionysius of Tell Mahre Jacobite Patriarch
820	Grandsons of Saman-Khuda appointed *amirs* of Samarqand and Herat; death of jurist Shafi'i and of Christian theologian Theodore Abu Qurrah

820–1005 SAMANID DYNASTY IN KHURASAN AND TRANSOXANIA

820–823	Thomas the Slav revolts against Byzantines
821	Tahir ibn al-Husayn Ma'mun's *amir* in Nishapur

821–873 TAHIRID DYNASTY IN KHURASAN

822–829	Talha Tahirid *amir* at Nishapur
823	Death of Nestorian Catholicus Timotheus, of traditionalist al-Waqidi, and of Shi'ite theologian and propagandist 'Abdallah ibn Maymun
825	Muslims capture Crete; death of philologist Abu 'Ubaydah
827	Ma'mun proclaims dogma of uncreated *Qur'an;* Byzantine rebel summons Aghlabids to Sicily
828	Death of Mu'tazilite Thumamah and of philologist al-Asma'i
829–845	'Abdallah Tahirid *amir* at Nishapur
829–842	THEOPHILUS Emperor at Constantinople
830	Muslims take Palermo
832	Ma'mun founds "House of Wisdom" in Baghdad
833	Ma'mun's persecution of heresy (*mihnah*); imprisonment of Ahmad ibn Hanbal
833–842	MU'TASIM Caliph at Baghdad and Samarra
834	Death of Ibn Hisham, editor of *Sirah*
835	Caliph moves against Babak in Azarbayjan; death of ninth Shi'ite *Imam,* Muhammad al-Jawad
836	Foundation of Samarra, 'Abbasid capital until 892
837	Death of al-Azraqi, historian of Mecca
838	Muslim invasion of Anatolia
840	Collapse of Uighur confederation in Central Asia
841	Death of Mu'tazilite Abu al-Hudhayl

842–867	MICHAEL III Emperor at Constantinople
842–847	AL-WATHIQ Caliph at Samarra
843	Defeat of Byzantine expedition against Crete
845	Death of Ibn Sa'd
846	Death of poet Abu Tammam; composition of Ibn Khurdadhbih's *Routes and Kingdoms*
847–861	AL-MUTAWAKKIL Caliph at Samarra
848	Mutawakkil disavows Mu'tazilite and 'Alid policies of Ma'mun
850	'Ali al-Tabari's *Paradise of Wisdom;* death of mathematician al-Khwarizmi
853	Byzantine expedition against Egypt
854	Death of theologian Ibn Kullab and of Mu'tazilite *qadi* Ibn Du'ad
855	Death of Ibn Hanbal and al-Nazzam
857	Death of Ibn Masawayh and the mystic Muhasibi
858	Hallaj begins his journeys to India and Turkestan
860	Mathematical activity of Banu Musa; death of Zaydi *Imam* al-Qasim
861–862	AL-MUNTASIR Caliph at Samarra
861	Death of mystic and occultist Dhu al-Nun
862–866	AL-MUSTA'IN Caliph at Samarra
862	Ascendancy of Ya'qub al-Saffar in Sijistan
864	Establishment of Zaydi Shi'ite state in Tabaristan
866	Al-Musta'in besieged in Baghdad by Mu'tazz
866–869	AL-MU'TAZZ Caliph at Samarra
866	Oldest Arabic paper manuscript
867–886	BASIL I Emperor at Constantinople

867–c. 1495 SAFFARID DYNASTY IN SIJISTAN AND KHURASAN

867	Ya'qub al-Saffar occupies Kabul

868–905 TULUNID DYNASTY IN EGYPT

868–884	Ahmad ibn Tulun independent *amir* in Egypt
868	Outbreak of *zanj* revolt in southern Iraq; death of Khurasanian theologian Ibn Karram and of tenth Shi'ite *Imam,* 'Ali al-Hadi
869–870	AL-MUHTADI Caliph at Samarra
869	Death of al-Jahiz

870–892	AL-MU'TAMID Caliph at Baghdad; effective rule in hands of his brother al-Muwaffaq
870	Death of Bukhari, collector of traditions, and, at about the same time, of *faylasuf* al-Kindi
871	Death of Ibn 'Abdalhakam, historian of conquest of Egypt
872	Construction of first hospital in Egypt
873	Saffarids dislodge Tahirids from Khurasan; death of physician and translator Hunayn ibn Ishaq
874	Death of eleventh Shi'ite *Imam*, Hasan al-Askari; "lesser concealment" of his son Muhammad al-Mahdi; Saffarids repulsed from Baghdad
875	Samanid Nasr I made *amir* of all of Transoxania; Hamdan al-Qarmat converted to Isma'ilism; death of traditionalist Muslim and mystic Abu Yazid Bistami
878	Dispute between Muwaffaq and Ibn Tulun
879–901	'Amr Saffarid *amir* in Sijistan
883	Death of Dawud ibn Khalaf, founder of Zahirite legal school; Muwaffaq crushes *zanj* revolt
884–896	Khumarawayh *amir* in Egypt
886	Death of traditionalist Ibn Maja and astronomer Abu Ma'shar
886–913	LEO VI Emperor at Constantinople
888	Death of traditionalist Abu Dawud
889	Death of philologist and historian Ibn Qutaybah
890	Organization of Qarmatian movement; rise of Hamdanids
892–902	AL-MU'TADID Caliph at Baghdad
892	Capital returned to Baghdad; death of historian Baladhuri and of traditionalist Tirmidhi; Abu 'Abdallah Isma'ili *da'i* in Ifriqiyah
893	Death of historian Ahmad ibn abi Tahir
895	Death of historian Dinawari
896	Death of poet Ibn al-Rumi and Sufi Tustari
897	Establishment of Zaydi Shi'ite state in Yemen; death of poet Buhturi and historian Ya'qubi
899	Schism between Hamdan and "Qarmatians" and the Isma'ilis of Syria
901	Death of Sabian scientist Thabit ibn Qurrah
902–908	AL-MUKTAFI Caliph at Baghdad
902	Muslims complete conquest of Sicily

903 Defeat of Qarmatians in Syria; death of Christian scholar Moses bar Kepha and of Ibn Hanbal's son and editor 'Abdallah

905 'Abbasids depose Tulunids in Egypt and reassert sovereignty; death of Bahshal, historian of Wasit

907–914 Ahmad II Samanid *amir* of Bukhara

908– IBN AL-MU'TAZZ Caliph at Baghdad

908–932 AL-MUQTADIR Caliph at Baghdad

909–1171 FATIMID CALIPHATE IN NORTH AFRICA AND EGYPT

909–934 'UBAYDALLAH Fatimid Caliph in Ifriqiyah

910 Death of translator Ishaq ibn Hunayn, of heretic Ibn al-Rewandi and of mystic Junayd

911 'Ubaydallah has Abu 'Abdallah assassinated; death of Zaydi *Imam* of Yemen, Yahya al-Hadi

912 'Ubaydallah takes Cyrenaica and proclaims his son al-Qa'im as *Mahdi;* Ash'ari repudiates Mu'tazilitism; death of Qusta ibn Luqa and Shi'ite Hasan ibn Musa al-Nawbakhti

913–959 CONSTANTINE VII PORPHYROGENITUS Emperor at Constantinople

913–917 First vizierate of 'Ali ibn'Isa at Baghdad

913 Death of Abu Sa'id al-Janabi, head of Qarmatians of Bahrayn

914–943 Nasr II Samanid *amir* of Bukhara

914 End of Tabari's *History;* appointment of translator Abu 'Uthman al-Dimashqi head of Baghdad physicians

915 First trial of al-Hallaj; death of Mu'tazilite al-Jubba'i

919–944 ROMANUS I LECAPENUS associated with Constantine VII as Emperor at Constantinople

920 Morocco falls to Fatimids

921–922 Ibn Fadlan's journey to Volga Bulgars

922 Crucifixion of al-Hallaj in Baghdad

923 Qarmatians under Abu Tahir seize Basrah; death of Hanbalite al-Khallal and Shi'ite Abu Sahl Isma'il al-Nawbakhti

924 Qarmatians attack pilgrimage caravan; rise of Turkish captain Mu'nis at Baghdad

925 Death of *faylasuf* al-Razi
929 Death of mathematician al-Battani
930 Qarmatians attack Mecca, remove black stone; death of al-Kulini, collector of Shi'ite *hadith*
931 Death of Mu'tazilite al-Ka'bi
932–934 AL-QAHIR Caliph at Baghdad
933 Death of Mu'tazilite Abu Hashim; rise to prominence of Byzantine general John Curcuas
934–940 AL-RADI Caliph at Baghdad
934–946 AL-QA'IM Fatimid Caliph in Ifriqiyah
934 Deaths of Shi'ite "extremist" al-Shalmaghani, Isma'ili *da'i* Abu Hatim al-Razi and geographer Abu Zayd al-Balkhi

935–969 IKHSHIDID DYNASTY IN EGYPT

935–946 Muhammad ibn Tughj Ikhshid *amir* of Egypt
935 Death of theologian al-Ash'ari and of Mardawij, Daylami rebel
936 Ibn Ra'iq appointed Grand *Amir* in Baghdad
939 Ibn Ra'iq resists Ikhshidid advance into Syria
940–944 AL-MUTAQI Caliph at Baghdad
940 Death of Persian poet Rudaqi and of Christian scholar Abu Bishr Matta
941 "Greater concealment" of Shi'ite Imam Muhammad al-Mahdi
942 Byzantines on offensive in Mesopotamia; al-Farabi leaves Baghdad for Damascus; death of Sinan ibn Thabit and al-Jahshiyari; Hamdanids restore Caliph to Baghdad; death of Ibn Ra'iq; Abu Dulaf's journey to China
943–954 Nuh I Samanid *amir* at Bukhara
944–946 AL-MUSTAKFI Caliph at Baghdad
944 Romanus deposed by his sons at Constantinople; John Curcuas captures Edessa; death of theologian Maturidi, Qarmatian leader Abu Tahir, and of last head of Sabians of Baghdad; Hamdanid Sayf al-Dawlah occupies northern Syria

945–1004 HAMDANIDS OF ALEPPO

945–967 Sayf al-Dawlah Hamdanid ruler in Aleppo; Ikhshidids lose grasp on Syria

945–1055 BUYID *AMIRS* OF IRAQ AND WESTERN IRAN

945	Buyids acknowledged as *amirs* by Caliph
946–974	AL-MUTI' Caliph at Baghdad
946–953	AL-MANSUR Fatimid Caliph in Ifriqiyah
946–951	Unujur Ikhshidid *amir* in Egypt under regency of Kafur
948	Poet Mutanabbi joins court of Sayf al-Dawlah
950	Death of *faylasuf* al-Farabi; Ibn Rizam's writings on Isma'ilis; conversion of Turks to Islam
951	Death of Shi'ite Ahmad ibn al-Zayyat; Qarmatians return black stone to Mecca
952	Death of Persian poet Daqiqi and Sufi Ibn al-A'rabi
953–975	AL-MU'IZZ Fatimid Caliph in Ifriqiyah and Egypt
954–961	'Abd al-Malik Samanid *amir* of Bukhara
955	Nicephorus Phocas replaces his father, Bardas, as Byzantine commander in Anatolia
956	Death of historian Mas'udi
957	Byzantines on offensive in Anatolia; completion of prose version of Persian *Book of Kings*
959–963	ROMANUS II Emperor at Constantinople
959	Death of Sufi al-Khuldi
960	Nicephorus recaptures Crete from Muslims; Sayf al-Dawlah defeated by Byzantines in Anatolia
961–966	'Ali Ikhshidid ruler in Egypt under regency of Kafur
961–976	Mansur Samanid *amir* of Bukhara; Alptegin, his Turkish commander, attempts coup, is thwarted and withdraws to Ghazna
961	End of Hamzah al-Isfahani's chronicle
963–969	NICEPHORUS PHOCAS Emperor at Constantinople
963	Vizier Bal'ami begins translation of Tabari's *History;* death of Muhallabi, Buyid vizier at Baghdad
965	Death of poet Mutanabbi
966–968	Kafur, former regent in Egypt, now ruler in his own name
966	Composition of al-Maqdisi's *Book of Creation*
967–991	Sa'd al-Dawlah Hamdanid ruler of Aleppo
967–978	'Izz al-Dawlah Buyid *amir* in Iraq
967	Death of anthologist Isfahani
968–969	Ahmad, last Ikhshidid ruler of Egypt

969	Fatimid general Jawhar takes Fustat, and Egypt falls; founding of Cairo; invasion of Syria begun
969–976	JOHN TZIMISCES Emperor at Constantinople
970	Death of Ibn al-'Amid, Buyid vizier at Rayy
973	Cairo becomes capital of Fatimids
974–991	AL-TA'I' Caliph at Baghdad
974	Fatimids capture Damascus; death of Christian theologian Yahya ibn 'Adi, of anthologist Tanukhi, and of Fatimid Qadi Nu'man
975–996	AL-'AZIZ Fatimid Caliph at Cairo
975	Byzantine counterattack reaches Caesarea in Palestine; formal instruction begun at al-Azhar under direction of vizier Ibn Killis; composition of al-Qummi's *Introduction to Astronomy;* death of Thabit ibn Sinan
976–997	Nuh II Samanid *amir* of Bukhara
976	Death of Qur'anic scholar Ibn al-Mujahid and of Persian poet Daqiqi; composition of al-Khwarizimi's *Keys of the Sciences*

977–1186 GHAZNAVID DYNASTY OF AFGHANISTAN

977–997	Sebuktegin *amir* at Ghazna
978–983	'Adud al-Dawlah succeeds to united Buyid empire
978–1012	Qabus Ziyarid *amir* in Tabaristan
981	Death of Ash'arite mystic Ibn al-Khafif
982	Composition of Persian *Boundaries of the World*
983	Akhu Muhsin's writings on Isma'ilis; death of 'Adud al-Dawlah
985	Composition of Muqaddasi's *Best Division*
987	Composition of Ibn al-Nadim's *Catalogue* and Ibn Juljul's *Classes of Physicians*
988	The Turk Simjuri declared Samanid viceroy in Khurasan; death of the Sufi al-Sarraj
c. 990	Death of *faylasuf* Abu Sulayman al-Sijistani
991–1031	AL-QADIR Caliph at Baghdad
991	Death of Shi'ite lawyer Ibn Babuya
992	Qarakhanid Turks occupy Bukhara
993	Buyid vizier Shapur ibn Ardashir organizes his "House of Science" in Baghdad
994	First edition of Firdawsi's *Book of Kings*

995	Death of Ibn al-Nadim and Buyid historian and stylist Ibrahim ibn Hilal; Basil thwarts Fatimid advance on Antioch
996–1021	AL-HAKIM Fatimid Caliph at Cairo
996	Death of mystic al-Makki, rhetorician al-Rummani, and *faylasuf* al-'Amiri
997	Ibn Sina joins court at Bukhara shortly before the death of Nuh II
997–999	Mansur II Samanid *amir* of Bukhara
998	Second edition of Firdawsi's *Book of Kings*
998–1030	Mahmud Sultan of Ghazna
999–1000	'Abd al-Malik Samanid *amir* of Bukhara
999	Mahmud invades Khurasan
1000–1005	Isma'il II Samanid *amir* in Bukhara
1001	Ten-year truce between Fatimids and Byzantines
1004	Hamdanids of Aleppo overthrown by slave general Lu'lu; Fatimids in possession of Syria; death of rhetorician al-'Askari
1005	Death of last Samanid *amir*, Isma'il al-Muntasir, division of Samanid holdings between Qarakhanids and Ghaznavids; al-Hakim founds his "Hall of Science" in Cairo
1007	Death of lexicographer al-Jawhari
1008	Mahmud defeats Qarakhanids in Khurasan; death of Christian physician and editor Ibn Zur'ah
1009	Al-Hakim orders destruction of Church of Holy Sepulcher in Jerusalem; death of astronomer 'Ali ibn Yunus
1013	Death of Ash'arite theologian al-Baqillani; completion of al-Hakim's mosque in Cairo
1015	Ibn Sina takes up post of vizier to Buyid *amir* of Hamadhan, begins *Healing;* arrival of Kirmani in Cairo; death of theologian Ibn Furaq and 'Alid al-Sharif al-Radi
1016–1017	Anti-Shi'ite and anti-Mu'tazilite demonstrations in Baghdad
1017	Al-Qadir's public indictment of Shi'ites; al-Hakim's apotheosis announced by al-Darazi in Cairo; Mahmud occupies Khwarazm, Biruni joins court; death of Christian scholar Ibn Suwar
1018	Death of Sufi biographer al-Sulami

1020	Hamzah ibn 'Ali proclaims new Hakim cult
1021	Disappearance of al-Hakim; death of Kirmani; Ibn Sina joins court of 'Ala' al-Dawlah at Isfahan
1021–1035	AL-ZAHIR Fatimid Caliph at Cairo
1022	Death of Shi'ite al-Mufid
1024	Mahmud crushes Hindu confederation
1025–1028	CONSTANTINE VIII Emperor at Constantinople
1025	Death of Mu'tazilite *oadi* 'Abd al-Jabbar
1027	Death of Ash'arite theologian Isfara'ini
1028–1034	ROMANUS III Emperor at Constantinople
1029	Death of Ibn Hindu
1030	Completion of Biruni's *History of India;* death of ethician Miskawayh
1031–1075	AL-QA'IM Caliph at Baghdad
1031–1041	Mas'ud ibn Mahmud Sultan of Ghazna
1034–1041	MICHAEL IV Emperor at Constantinople
1035–1094	AL-MUSTANSIR Fatimid Caliph at Cairo; ascendancy of viziers Yazuri and Badr al-Jamali
1035	Death of Ghaznavid historian 'Utbi
1036	Treaty between Byzantines and Fatimids acknowledging former as protectors of Christians of Jerusalem
1037	Seljuqs take Nishapur from Ghaznavids; death of Ibn Sina and Ash'arite theologian al-Baghdadi
1038	Death of physicist Ibn al-Haytham, anthologist al-Tha'alibi, and Sufi biographer Abu Nu'aym al-Isfahani
1039	Tughril, Seljuq chief, proclaims himself Sultan in Nishapur; death of Ghaznavid court poet 'Unsuri
1040	Seljuqs' Turkomans defeat Ghaznavids at Dandanqan
1041–1042	MICHAEL V Emperor at Constantinople
1041	Seljuqs occupy Khwarazm; end of Gardizi's Persian history
1042–	ZOE and THEODORA Empresses at Constantinople
1042–1055	CONSTANTINE IX Emperor at Constantinople
1043	Death of Christian theologian Ibn al-Tayyib
1044	Death of Shi'ite al-Murtada
1045	Tughril's vizier Kunduri begins persecution of Ash'arites in Khurasan
1045–1052	Nasir-i Khusraw's journey through Near East
1049–1090	Kay Ka'us Ziyarid *amir* in Tabaristan

1049 Composition of al-Mubashshir's *Epitome of Wisdom;* death of Christian scholar Elias bar Shinaya and mystic Ibn abi al-Khayr

1050 Death of al-Biruni; debate in Cairo between Ibn Butlan and 'Ali ibn Ridwan; literary activity of "Pseudo-Majriti"

1055–1194 SELJUQ SULTANS OF IRAQ

1055 Tughril enters Baghdad; title as Sultan confirmed

1055– THEODORA Empress at Constantinople

1056–1057 MICHAEL VI Emperor at Constantinople

1057–1059 ISAAC I COMNENUS Emperor at Constantinople

1057 Death of Sufi al-Hujwiri

1058 Basasiri and Turks occupy Baghdad in name of Fatimids in Tughril's absence; death of Abu Sa'id 'Ubaydallah of Bakhtishu' family

1059–1067 CONSTANTINE X DUCAS Emperor at Constantinople

1060 Normans begin reconquest of Sicily; Seljuqs in Syria, take Aleppo; death of eastern Sultan Chaghri, succeeded by son Alp Arslan

1063 Death of western Sultan Tughril, succeeded by Alp Arslan; death of vizier Kunduri

1063–1072 Alp Arslan Great Sultan of Seljuqs; Nizam al-Mulk vizier (to 1092)

1064 Seljuqs take Ani, capital of Byzantine Armenia; death of Spanish heresiographer and poet Ibn Hazm

1065 Foundation of Nizamiyah *madrasah* in Baghdad

1066 Famine and disorders in Egypt

1067 Death of Spanish cultural historian Sa'id al-Andalusi

1068–1071 ROMANUS IV DIOGENES Emperor at Constantinople

1069 Seljuqs take Konya in Anatolia

1071 Seljuqs defeat Byzantines at Manzikert in Armenia, capture Romanus IV; death of historian al-Khatib al-Baghdadi

1071–1078 MICHAEL VIII Emperor at Constantinople

1071 The Turkoman Atsiz begins occupying Fatimid strong points in Palestine

1072 Death of Ash'arite Sufi al-Qushayri

1073–1092 Malik Shah Great Sultan of Seljuqs

1074–1080 Armenian migration under Seljuq pressure to Cilicia

1074 Badr al-Jamali restores order in Egypt; Malik Shah's observatory and revision of calendar; death of Nasir-i Khusraw

1075–1094 AL-MUQTADI Caliph at Baghdad

1076 Atsiz marches against Egypt, repulsed

1077–1307 SELJUQ SULTANS OF RUM AT KONYA

1077 Sulayman ibn Qutlumush raises independent Seljuq Sultanate at Konya (to 1086); Ghazali student of Juwayni at Nizamiyah *madrasah* at Nishapur; death of Ghaznavid historian al-Fadl al-Bayhaqi and of Hanbalite Abu Ja'far al-Hashimi

1078–1081 NICEPHORUS III Emperor at Constantinople

1078 Death of 'Abd al-Qahir al-Jurjani; Seljuq Tutush occupies Syria

1079 Syria and Palestine granted to Tutush by Malik Shah

1081 Nicephorus forced to yield Cyzicus and Nicaea (Iznik) to Seljuqs

1081–1118 ALEXIUS I COMNENUS Emperor at Constantinople

1082 The *Book of Qabus* of Kay Ka'us

1083 Death of al-Shantamari, final collector of *diwans* of early Arab poets

1085 Antioch falls to Seljuqs

1086 Tutush meets and destroys Rum Sultan Sulayman; construction of cathedral-mosque of Isfahan

1089 Death of Hanbalite mystic al-Ansari

1090 Isma'ilis under Hasan ibn al-Sabbah seize fortress of Alamut; interregnum of Danishmend (or his son) in Anatolia

1091 Ghazali lecturer at Nizamiyah *madrasah* in Baghdad

1092 Assassination of Nizam al-Mulk and death of Malik Shah; Qilich Arslan restores Sultanate of Rum

1092–1105 Berk-Yaruq Great Sultan at Baghdad

1093 Death of Badr al-Jamali, Fatimid vizier

1094–1118 AL-MUSTAZHIR Caliph at Baghdad

1094 Death of Fatimid Caliph-*Imam* Mustansir in Cairo; eastern Isma'ilis declare for his son al-Nizar, while younger Must'ali seated in Cairo

1094–1101 AL-MUST'ALI Fatimid Caliph at Cairo

1095 Council of Clermont and preaching of First Crusade; Ghazali withdraws from teaching and leaves Baghdad; Berk-Yaruq defeats his uncle Tutush near Rayy

1097–1098	Crusaders and Byzantines meet and defeat Seljuqs in Anatolia
1098	Crusaders take Antioch
1099	Crusaders take Jerusalem; Ghazali in retirement at Tus
1101–1130	AL-AMIR Fatimid Caliph at Cairo
1101	Concerted Seljuq purge of Isma'ilis
1102	Crusaders defeat Fatimids at Ramallah and take Caesarea
1105–1118	Malik Shah II, then Muhammad Tapar Seljuq Sultans at Baghdad; Ghazali resumes lecturing at Nishapur
1111	Death of Ghazali in retirement

GLOSSARY OF TECHNICAL TERMS

The terms defined below appear as well in the General Index, where specific page references may be found. Stressed syllable is indicated by diacritical mark.

Ádab: culture, in the first instance a literary culture, but the concept came to embrace both the more specialized style of the vizier, secretary, et cetera, and the spiritual refinement that was the goal of the intellectualizing Sufis; hence *adíb*, the man of culture or refinement.

Ahl (or *asháb*) *al-hadíth:* traditionalists, those who took a conservative view of the Law and rejected all forms of personal investigation (*ijtihad*) connected with rationalist speculation (*nazar*).

Ahl al-kitáb: "People of the Book"; the Jews, Christians, Sabians and, latterly, the Zoroastrians who had received a Scriptural revelation thought to be parallel with the *Qur'an* and so eligible for the protected legal status of *dhimmis*.

Ahl al-súnnah wa al-jamá'ah: partisans of precedent and the community; originally those willing to support the Umayyads for the sake of legitimacy and the unity of the *ummah;* political "unitarians" opposed to the "sectarianism" of the *Shi'at 'Ali;* the Sunnis.

Akhláq (pl.): ethics, either in a generalized sense close to *adab* or more particularly the humanistic and philosophical ethic based upon Hellenic *hikmah*.

'Álim (pl. *'ulamá'*): a learned man, one who possesses *'ilm;* particularly one learned in the Islamic sciences as distinguished from one learned in the "foreign" sciences, the *hakim*.

'Ámil: tax collector.

Amír (pl. *umará'*): the delegate of the Caliph who possessed full executive, judicial, financial and military powers in the territory of his jurisdiction; the provincial governor.

Amír al-Mu'minín: "Commander of the Faithful," the Caliph in his function of Commander in Chief.

Ansár (pl.): the "Helpers"; those Medinese who accepted Islam and aided Muhammad and the Meccan Emigrants (*Muhajirun*) who came to Medina in 622.

'Aql: the rational faculty; the intellect as opposed to both the body and the lower faculties of the soul; the mind as opposed to the egoistic "self" (*nafs*).

'Áqli: knowledge derived from speculation (*nazar*) and not merely from report or on the authority of another; "rational" sciences as opposed to those "traditioned" (*naqli*).

'Arabíyah: the pure Arabic tongue; the art-speech of the Bedouin poets.

'Asabíyah: a sense of group solidarity, possessed in its highest degree, according to Ibn Khaldun, by the Bedouin.

Átabeg: originally the tutor of a Seljuq prince, later his military supervisor, and eventually the all but autonomous governor of the prince's putative province.

áyah (pl. *ayát*): signs; hence (1) individual verses or rhythmical units of the *Qur'an*, and (2) the natural signs whereby Allah manifests his power and intentions in the universe.

Ayyám al-'Árab: mixed accounts in poetry and prose of the "battle days of the Arabs" during the pre-Islamic period.

'Ayyárun: "vagabonds"; one of a number of designations given to paramilitary groups with vaguely social purposes who appear in urban contexts in the tenth century.

Bádi': a new style of poetical diction; embellishment; hence *'ilm al-badi'*, the science of poetical diction.

Balághah: eloquence; the study of the tropes and figures thought to constitute the essence of style in Arabic.

Baqá': subsistence in God; the new mode of existence granted to the mystic in the experience of the unity (*tawhid*) of Allah.

Bátin: the hidden sense of things, particularly of Scripture; the hidden "realities" (*haqa'iq*); hence *al-Batiniyah*, sects like the Isma'ilis, whose point of departure was the dichotomy between the *zahir* and the *batin*.

Bid'ah: innovation, departure from the *sunnah;* hence, heresy (*kufr*).

Bimáristan: hospital, the Greek *nosokomeion.*

Burhán: the demonstrative and apodictic proof by the syllogistic method described by Aristotle in the *Analytics* and thought to be the chief characteristic of scientific knowledge (*'ilm*).

Dá'i (pl. *du'áh*): "summoner"; the Isma'ili missionary or propagandist.

Dar al-Islám: "the abode of Islam"; the lands under the immediate control of the Muslim *ummah;* the jurisdiction of the Caliph; opposed to the "abode of war" (*Dar al-Harb*), the territory of the infidel.

Dárghah: the militarized court of the Seljuq Sultans.

Dá'wah: the "call" first issued in the *pleroma* and repeated here on earth to summon men to an acknowledgment of the "realities" (*haqa'iq*); the Isma'ili movement.

Dáwlah: a turning; the *Dar-al-Islam* regarded as a political entity; the empire of the 'Abbasids.

Dhikr: the continuous and rhythmical repetition of the name of Allah, a technique current among Sufis.

Dhímmah: the covenant of protection entered into by the Muslim community with the "People of the Book" (*Ahl al-kitab*), whereby the latter are guaranteed the practice of their religion in return for the assumption of certain legal and financial constraints; the *dhímmi* is one who lives in the *Dar al-Islam* under such a covenant.

Dihqán: the lesser landed aristocrat in the Sasanian empire.

Diwán: the military registry of the *muqatilah;* hence, the ministry charged with keeping such; chancery, divan; a collection of poetry.

Fálsafah: the tradition of Greek philosophy introduced into Islam through Arabic translations and characterized by a Hellenic organization of the sciences, rationalistic premises, a scientific methodology based on demonstrative proof (*burhan*), and a synthesis of Plato and Aristotle.

Faná': annihilation of self; the Sufi state that precedes the experience of the unity of God (*tawhid*).

Faqíh (pl. *fuqahá'*): the jurisprudent; man learned in *fiqh*.

Faqr: voluntary poverty—hence, *faqír*, the Sufi mendicant.

Fátwa: a legal opinion, or *responsum*, delivered by a qualified jurisprudent on an issue of law as opposed to a judgment rendered by a *qadi* on a case in litigation.

Faylasúf (pl. *falásifah*): philosopher; an adherent of the *falsafah* tradition.

Fiqh: jurisprudence; the study of the *shari'ah* in its sources and its positive precepts.

Gházal: a short, subjective lyric developed from the longer and more stylized *qasidah*.

Ghâzi: a frontier warrior against the infidel.

Ghulât (pl.): "extremists"; specifically those Shi'ites who embraced positions, like transmigration and the divinization of 'Ali, that were considered alien to Muslim beliefs.

Hadîth: a tradition that reports, generally on the authority of one of the Companions, the sayings and deeds of the Prophet; the collective vehicle for the transmission of the *sunnah* of the Prophet.

Hajj: pilgrimage; the canonically prescribed pilgrimage to Mecca and its attendant rites.

Hakîm (pl. *hukamâ'*): the man of *hikmah;* one skilled in the "foreign" sciences, as distinguished from the *'alim,* the scholar in the traditional Islamic sciences.

Hal (pl. *ahwâl*): state, particularly the state between being and non-being; the condition of the soul granted by God to the Sufi on his progress toward the mystical union.

Hándarz: collections of Sasanian aphoristic wisdom.

Haníf: one who had recognized the rights of Allah even before the formal revelation of Islam; Abraham, for example, who antedated all the Scriptural revelations.

Haqíqah (pl. *haqâ'iq*): truth, reality; frequently in the plural referring to the transcendental "realities" of the Gnostic *pleroma;* the matter of both the occult sciences and of the "teaching" (*ta'lim*) of the *Imams.*

Híjrah: flight, migration; the Prophet's migration from Mecca to Medina in 622 and the beginning of the Muslim era.

Híkmah: wisdom, particularly the wisdom of the "foreign" sciences and so not much different from *falsafah; gnosis,* or revealed or occult knowledge, as opposed to the purely rational procedures of *'ilm.*

I'jáz: inimitability, particularly of the *Qur'an;* the miraculous quality that validates the divine origin of the Book.

Ijtihád: the exercise of personal effort (*jihad*) or discretion, and so in jurisprudence the extension of the Law by such means.

'Ilm: knowledge; like the Greek *episteme,* either a unified and organized body of knowledge on a single subject, thus *'ilm al-lúghah,* the science of language; or a kind of knowledge characterized by the method of demonstration (*burhan*) and opposed to a knowledge based on dialectic (*jadal*) or intuitive knowledge (*ma'rifah*) or occult Gnostic wisdom (*hikmah*).

'Ilm iláhi: the divine science, theology; speculative theology as opposed to *kalam,* dialectical theology.

Imám: the head of the Islamic *ummah,* either in the simple sense of one who leads the community's prayers or in the sense of Caliph;

also the leadership of the *ummah* understood as a spiritual office; in the latter, Shi'ite view, the descendants and successors of 'Ali.

Imán: faith, the quality or act, like the *shahadah*, that makes one a Muslim.

Iqtá': a grant of revenues from state land in compensation for services rendered.

Islám: submission; submission to the will of Allah.

Isnád: the chain of transmitters' names attached to a *hadith* and on whose authority the *hadith* is transmitted.

Jádal: dialectic; a manner of discourse wherein the arguments are developed by nonrigorous—i.e., nonsyllogistic—methods like analogy (*qiyas*); the characteristic method of *kalam*.

Jafr: divination; the sum of the secret knowledge allegedly given to 'Ali and his descendants whereby they can predict the future, particularly through the "reading" of numbers and letters.

Jahilíyah: the "time of ignorance," the Muslim characterization of the period before the coming of Islam.

Jámi': the cathedral or Friday mosque where the common Friday prayer is authorized to be held in each community.

Jihád: striving; hence (1) the personal striving along the path of holiness; (2) personal discretion in the explication of the Law; and (3) the Holy War of the Muslim against the infidels of the *Dar al-Harb*.

Jinn (pl.): personified forces of nature, frequently malevolent.

Jízyah: the poll or head tax levied on the *dhimmis* resident within the *Dar al-Islam*.

Kalám: dialectical theology; an explication, based on Scriptural texts but invoking a dialectical method (*jadal*) of reasoning, in defense of the Islamic faith; *jadal* was rejected as illegitimate by the *ahl al-hadith* and as unscientific by the *falasifah*.

Kátib (pl. *kuttáb*): scribe, secretary; clerical civil servant in the *diwan*.

Khábar (pl. *akhbár*): a prose narrative with historical content.

Khalífah: successor; Successor of the Apostle, the head of the Islamic *ummah*, the Caliph.

Kharáj: the land tax paid by the *dhimmis* within the *Dar al-Islam;* the rate was normally determined by the original treaty of submission.

Khitábah: rhetoric; the art and practice of eloquent and persuasive speech.

Khútbah: the discourse delivered during the Friday congregational prayers. (Omission of the reigning Caliph's name from the *khutbah* was tantamount to a declaration of political independence or a switch in political allegiance.)

Kufr: infidelity; giving assent to a proposition that is fundamentally opposed to Islam; to give a partner to Allah, for example, to deny that Muhammad was an Apostle, or to hold for the eternity of the world—hence, *kafír:* an unbeliever, an infidel.

Mádhhab (pl. *madháhib*): an orthodox Muslim school of jurisprudence; the body of coherent views on the sources of the *shari'ah* and its positive prescriptions collected under the name of a single eighth- or ninth-century jurist who was regarded as its founder; thus, the *madhhab* of Malik ibn Anas or the Hanbalite school.

Mádrasah: a law school, an institution whose primary purpose was to give instruction in *fiqh* and the related sciences according to the methods of one of the legal *madhahib.*

Magházi (pl.): the raids of the Bedouin Arabs and the literary works in which they were described.

Máhdi: the "guided one"; the divine or glorified figure whose return to the world signals the restoration of the faith of Islam or the *eschaton.*

Májlis (pl. *majális*): seance, discussion group.

Malakút: the "kingdom"; the world of universal spiritual essences above the world of sense.

Maqámah (pl. *maqamát*): "station"; the conditions of the soul achieved by the Sufi's own striving (*jihad*) toward union with God; the Greek *praxis.*

Má'rifah: the intuitive, nondiscursive knowledge of the mystic as opposed to the speculative knowledge (*'ilm, nazar*) of the *faylasuf.*

Márzuban: a district governor under the Sasanians.

Máshad: the shrine, mosque or oratory erected at the tomb of a holy or learned man.

Másjid: the mosque college where prayer was offered but whose primary function was to offer instruction in jurisprudence.

Matn: the text of a *hadith,* as distinguished from its *isnad.*

Mawálid (pl.): nativities, the Greek *genethliaka,* the subject of horoscopic predictions.

Máwla (pl. *mawáli*): client; adopted member of a tribal society; a non-Arab convert to Islam.

Mazálim (pl.): complaint courts where contractual cases could be raised and judgments rendered outside the framework of the *shari'ah.*

Míhnah: a scrutiny of orthodoxy according to a defined standard; thus, the *mihnah* instituted by Ma'mun on the subject of the created *Qur'an.*

Mi'ráj: the ascent of Muhammad into heaven, a concept that was later expropriated by the Sufis to explain their own mystical experiences.

Misr (pl. *amsár*): the military encampments constructed for garrisoning the *muqatilah* in the early days of the Muslim conquests; the administrative centers for the new provinces.

Móbadh (pl. *mobadhán*): a member of the Zoroastrian clergy; *mobadhan mobadh:* the chief priest.

Muhajirún (pl.): the "Emigrants"; those who accompanied Muhammad on his migration (*hijrah*) from Mecca to Medina in 622.

Muhásabah: the Sufi technique of examination of conscience.

Muhtásib: the market inspector, but actually an official with far greater police powers.

Muqátilah: warriors; those who shared in the early conquests of Islam and were inscribed in the army musters of the *diwan.*

Múslim (pl. *muslimún*): one who has submitted to the will of Allah; one who had embraced Islam.

Mutakállim (pl. *mutakallimún*): the dialectical theologian; the practitioner of *kalam.*

Nábi: the prophet; the medium of revelation.

Nafs: the soul as opposed to the body; the Greek *psyche;* the "self" as opposed to the rational faculty (*'aql*); *'ilm al-nafs:* psychology.

Náqli: "traditioned" information or knowledge as opposed to "rational" (*'aqli*) knowledge derived by one's own speculative resources (*nazar*).

Názar: speculative investigation; discursive reasoning as opposed to intuitive knowledge (*ma'rifah*) or acceptance on authority (*taqlid*).

Qádi: judge; the Caliph or *amir's* delegated representative with powers to adjudicate, on the basis of the *shari'ah*, cases at law.

Qasídah: the classical Arabic ode.

Qíblah: the physical orientation of prayer; the direction of the Muslim's prayer toward Mecca.

Qiyámah: resurrection or restoration; the *eschaton* signaled either by the absolute Judgment or, in the Isma'ili view, the arrival of the *Mahdi.*

Qiyás: analogical reasoning; in jurisprudence, the extension of the Law by comparative methods; in *kalam*, a parallel method that is dialectical (*jadal*) rather than rigorously syllogistic (*burhan*).

Qur'án: "recitation"; *al-Qur'an:* the book containing the revelations of Allah to Muhammad.

Rashidún (pl.): the "right-directed ones," an epithet applied to the first four Caliphs to distinguish them from and contrast them with the Umayyads who followed.

Rasúl: one who is sent; an apostle or messenger.

Sahábah: collectively, the Companions of the Prophet; those Muslims who on chronological or geographical grounds could have been eyewitnesses of the Prophet and who thus constitute the authorities on his customary behavior (*sunnah*).

Sahíh: "sound," a judgment rendered upon valid and integral *hadith*, which are, consequently, binding in law.

Saj': rhymed prose and the style characterized by its use.

Salát: prayer; the canonical prayers obligatory for all Muslims.

Shahádah: a "witnessing"; the Muslim profession of faith—"There is no God but Allah, and Muhammad is His Prophet."

Sháhnah: the military commandant of a city or district under the Seljuqs.

Sharí'ah: the positive Islamic Law; the body of prescriptions extracted from the *Qur'an* and the *sunnah* of the Prophet.

Shu'ubíyah: the movement that challenged the social ascendancy of the Arabs in Islam by asserting the cultural claims of other peoples, particularly the Iranians.

Siná'ah: an art; the Greek *techne*, when contrasted with *'ilm* (*episteme*); *al-sina'ah:* "The Art," alchemy.

Siyásah: governance, political science.

Súnnah: precedent, the customary mode of action; hence, "the *sunnah* of the Prophet," the words and deeds of Muhammad as recorded in the *hadith* and used as a legal criterion.

Súrah: a group of Qur'anic verses (*ayat*) collected under a single title; one of the 114 "chapters" of the *Qur'an.*

Tabaqát (pl.): "classes," or "layers"; biographies collected and arranged according to generations, beginning with the generation of the Companions of the Prophet (*sahabah*).

Tadbír al-mánzil: administration of the household; "economics," in the Greek sense of the word.

Ta'lím: "teaching," particularly the teaching of the infallible *Imams*, which included the *haqa'iq* and the matter of the *batin.*

Taqlíd: The acceptance of a truth on the authority of another—of the teaching (*ta'lim*) of an *Imam*, for example, simply because he is an *Imam.*

Ta'ríkh: an era; hence, an "era work," a collection of historical narratives (*akhbar*) arranged on the annalistic principle; a history.

Tashbíh: anthropomorphism, the attribution of human qualities to Allah.

Tawhíd: unity; hence (1) the unity and simplicity of Allah in the context of the dispute concerning the divine attributes; and (2) unity *with* Allah, the state of mystical union.

Thanawiyah: dualism; the belief in dual principles of good and evil, a characteristic belief of both Manichaeism and its derivative *zandaqah*.

Tibb: medicine; hence, *'ilm al-tibb:* the science of medicine; *tabíb:* physician; and *tibb al-nabi:* Prophetic medicine, the advice on medical matters given by Muhammad and preserved in the *hadith*.

Úmmah: the community of all Muslims.

Waqf: an inalienable bequest whose usufruct is directed toward the support of some pious purpose specified by the donor.

Wazír "helper"; hence, the chief secretary of the ruler and eventually his chief civil minister and the head of the chancery; the vizier.

Záhir: the external, literal sense of things, particularly of Scripture, as opposed to their concealed (*batin*) significance.

Zakát: the alms tax or tithe obligatory for all Muslims.

Zándaqah: a body of beliefs which, while superficially Islamic, was considered tainted with dualism or some other aspect of Manichaeism or Zoroastrianism; hence, *zindiq*, one who holds such.

Zij: a table of planetary and stellar appearances.

A GUIDE TO SOME FURTHER READING

General

The notes that follow are, quite obviously, an exercise in selection. Where there are good general treatments I have mentioned them, but otherwise I have not refrained from detailed studies, even some highly technical ones, where they appear essential to understanding. Nor is it possible to rely solely upon books in English for a true appreciation of the work currently being done on Islam. So I have chosen widely from the old and the new, the general and the specific, the familiar and the dense, secure in the knowledge that there is no lack of bibliographical substitutes for my own private preferences.

The reader has only to turn, for example, to either the *Cambridge History of Islam* (2 vols., Cambridge, 1970) or *The Encyclopaedia of Islam* (new edition in progress, Leiden, 1960; 1st ed., Leiden, 1913–1942; compare the *Shorter Encyclopaedia of Islam*, Leiden, 1953) for both general and detailed studies as well as elaborate bibliographies. Since most of the topics treated in this book are represented by articles in one or another edition of *The Encyclopaedia of Islam*, I have generally refrained from citing such here. The reader should note, however, that topics are treated in the *Encyclopaedia* under their Arabic rubric; thus philosophy will be found under "falsafa" and theology under "kalam."

The current periodical literature concerning Islam is listed in J. D. Pearson, *Index Islamicus 1906–1955* (Cambridge, 1958) with *Supplements* for 1956–1960 (Cambridge, 1962) and 1961–1965 (Cambridge,

1966). Another method of finding one's way into further reading is C. Cahen's reediting of Jean Sauvaget's *Introduction to the History of the Muslim East* (tr. Berkeley and Los Angeles, 1965). There are a number of excellent atlases for the area, including R. Roolvink, *Historical Atlas of the Muslim Peoples* (Cambridge, Mass., 1958); and G. LeStrange, *The Lands of the Eastern Caliphate* (rp. London, 1966) is still extremely useful.

There are two major bio-bibliographical repertoires of authors writing in Arabic during the period under discussion: C. Brockelmann, *Geschichte der arabischen Literatur*, 2 vols. (2nd ed. Leiden, 1945–1949) and 3 supplementary volumes (Leiden, 1937–1942), an extremely cumbersome work which is, moreover, considerably out of date; the work is being done anew on a more rational plan by F. Sezgin, *Geschichte des arabischen Schrifttums,* 3 vols. to date (Leiden, 1967–1971). Since both works (abbreviated *GAL* and *GAS*) contain all the pertinent information about texts and translations, that information will not be repeated here. There is, in addition, a similar work for Christian Arabic literature, G. Graf, *Geschichte der christlichen-arabischen Literatur* in 5 vols. (Vatican City, 1944–1953) of which the first two are relevant here, and for the authors writing in Syriac, A. Baumstark, *Geschichte der syrischen Literatur* (Bonn, 1922).

The equivalent work on authors writing in Persian is C. Storey, *Persian Literature, a Bio-Bibliographical Survey* of which only three parts, those on Qur'anic studies, history and biography, and the mathematical sciences, have been published (London, 1927–1958). The work will probably be redone and completed under different auspices; see Y. Borschevsky and Y. Bregel, "The Preparation of a Bio-Bibliographical Survey of Persian Literature," *International Journal of Middle East Studies* 3 (1972), 169–186. In the meantime the reader may be better served by J. Tavadia, *Die mittelpersische Sprache und Literatur der Zarathustrier* (Leipzig, 1956) and J. Rypka, *History of Iranian Literature* (tr. Dordrecht, 1968).

The Near East Before Islam

The history and culture of the Near East from Alexander to the reign of Theodosius is surveyed in F. E. Peters, *The Harvest of Hellenism* (New York, 1971), and A. H. M. Jones, *The Cities of The Eastern Roman Provinces* (2nd ed., Oxford, 1971) is instructive on the Hellenic urban culture of the area. For the following centuries on the Byzantine side of the frontier there are the general works by G. Ostrogorsky, *A History of the Byzantine State* (3rd ed., tr. New Brunswick,

1969) and A. H. M. Jones, *The Later Roman Empire 284–602* (3 vols., Oxford, 1964) and the new edition of *The Cambridge Medieval History*, IV, *The Byzantine Empire* (Cambridge, 1966) with elaborate bibliographies. For the Sasanians, A. Christensen, *L'Iran sous les Sassanides* (2nd ed., Copenhagen, 1944) is still standard, though there are interesting and important additions signaled in R. Frye, *The Heritage of Persia* (pb. New York, 1966) and J. Neusner, *A History of the Jews in Babylonia* (5 vols., Leiden, 1966–1970).

The religious situation in the fifth and sixth centuries is described in Vols. IV and V of A. Fliche and V. Martin, *Histoire de l'Église* (Paris, 1947, 1948) and the consequences of Chalcedon are laid out in rich detail in A. Grillmeier and H. Bacht, *Das Konzil von Chalkedon. Geschichte und Gegenwart* (3 vols., Würzburg, 1951), and W. H. C. Frend, *The Rise of the Monophysite Movement* (Cambridge, 1972), the latter a clear and informative guide to the Near East on the eve of Islam.

I. Shahid, who has devoted a number of studies to the Ghassanids, is preparing a general history of the Arabs before Islam, but in the meantime there is his sketch "Pre-Islamic Arabia" in *The Cambridge History of Islam* I, pp. 3–29 with a bibliography of the older works on the Ghassanids, Kindah and Lakhmids by Nöldeke, Olinder and Rothstein, to which should be added S. Smith, "Events in Arabia in the Sixth Century A.D.," *Bulletin of the School of Oriental and African Studies* (1954), 425–468. On the religious situation among the tribes there see, with caution, F. Nau, *Les Arabes chrétiens de Mesopotamie et de Syrie du VIIe au VIIIe siècle* (Paris, 1933) and H. Charles, *Le Christianisme des arabes nomades sur le Limes et dans le désert syro-mesopotamien aux alentours de l'Hégire* (Paris, 1936). For Muhammad's own environment there is H. Lammens, *Le Berceau de l'Islam* (Rome, 1914) and *L'Arabie occidentale avant l'Hégire* (Beirut, 1928), as well as the preliminary chapters of the studies of Muhammad cited below.

Muhammad and the Qur'an

There are many translations of the *Qur'an*, and here it is merely a question of some recent ones in English. R. Bell's *The Qur'an. Translated with a critical re-arrangement of the Surahs* (2 vols., Edinburgh, 1937, 1939) is, as the title suggests, more than a simple translation but embodies an extensive resifting of the material. Since Bell there have appeared the versions of M. Pickthall, *The Meaning of the Glorious Koran* (pb. New York, 1953), of N. J. Dawood, *The Koran* (pb. Baltimore, 1956) and of A. J. Arberry, *The Koran Interpreted* (pb. New York, 1970).

Bell's research on the *Qur'an* is conveniently summarized in his *Introduction to the Qur'an* (Edinburgh, 1953), which was extensively revised and enlarged by W. M. Watt as *Bell's Introduction to the Qur'an* (Edinburgh, 1970) and is the best introduction to that subject available in English. The standard of Qur'anic scholarship remains, however, the monumental *Geschichte des Qorans* begun by T. Nöldeke in 1860 and subsequently revised in a three-volume second edition (Leipzig, 1909–1938) by F. Schwally, G. Bergsträsser and O. Pretzl.

The history of Qur'anic exegesis at Muslim hands is set out by I. Goldziher, *Die Richtungen der islamischen Koranauslegung* (Leipzig, 1920; rp. 1952), and J. Baljon, *Modern Muslim Koran Interpretation 1880–1960* (Leiden, 1961), but Western scholars have preferred very different approaches. They have undertaken, for example, an intense investigation of the Jewish and Christian influences present at the birth of Islam, either through an analysis of the loanwords in the *Qur'an*, as in A. Jeffery, *Foreign Vocabulary of the Qur'an* (Baroda, 1938), or in wider literary contexts, as in Bell's *The Origin of Islam in Its Christian Environment* (London, 1926); T. Andrae, *Les Origines de l'Islam et le Christianisme* (tr. Paris, 1955); J. Jomier, *The Bible and the Koran* (tr. pb. New York, 1964); and A. Katsh, *Judaism and the Koran* (pb. New York, 1962).

The possibility of writing a biography of the Prophet rests upon just such research, but it must face as well the difficult question of the historicity of the *hadith* tradition concerning Muhammad, and particularly as it is found in the *Life* by Ibn Ishaq. The Jesuit scholar H. Lammens took a skeptical view in his "Qoran et tradition; comment fut composée la vie de Mohamet," *Recherches de science religieuse* (1910) and in a number of other publications (cf. K. Salibi, "Islam and Syria in the Writings of Henri Lammens" in B. Lewis and P. Holt, *Historians of the Middle East* [London, 1962], pp. 330–342), but the *Life* has found its defenders and the project of a biography has gone forward. F. Buhl's *Das Leben Muhammads* (2nd ed. Heidelberg, 1955) is probably the most firmly based and convincing account, but there are other, somewhat more partisan approaches that are equally instructive. Social and economic factors are in the foreground in M. Rodinson, *Mohammed* (2nd ed. tr. Cambridge, 1971) and W. Watt, *Muhammad at Mecca* (London, 1953) and *Muhammad at Medina* (London, 1956), both summarized in his *Muhammad, Prophet and Statesman* (pb. London, 1965), while the religious background is emphasized in T. Andrae, *Mohammed, the Man and His Faith* (tr. pb. New York, 1960). For a Muslim's point of view see M. Hamidullah, *Le Prophet de l'Islam, Sa Vie, Son Oeuvre* (Paris, 1959).

The Conquests and the Rashidun

There is a brief but interesting survey of the various conquests by F. Gabrieli, *Muhammad and the Conquests of Islam* (tr. pb. New York, 1968). A more popular account is J. B. Glubb, *The Great Arab Conquests* (London, 1963), which does have the merit of attending to the military aspects of the campaigns and some clear cartography. The older works are still important: A. Butler, *The Arab Conquest of Egypt and the Last Thirty Years of the Roman Dominion* (Oxford, 1902); M. J. de Goeje, *Mémoire sur la conquête de la Syrie* (2nd ed. Leiden, 1900); and H. A. R. Gibb, *The Arab Conquests in Central Asia* (London, 1923).

The financial consequences of the conquests are explored by F. Løkkegard, *Islamic Taxation in the Classic Period* (Copenhagen, 1950) and D. C. Dennett, *Conversion and Poll Tax in Early Islam* (Cambridge, Mass., 1950), and their effect upon the conquered peoples by A. S. Tritton in *The Caliphs and Their Non-Muslim Subjects. A Critical Study of the Covenant of 'Umar* (London, 1930). The early sections of E. Tyan's *Histoire de l'organisation judiciaire en pays de l'Islam* (2 vols., Paris, 1938–1945) are also pertinent here, as is the same author's *Institutions du droit publique musulman*, I, *Le Califat* (Paris, 1954).

History and historiography are both the subject of E. L. Petersen's *'Ali and Mu'awiya in Early Arabic Tradition* (Copenhagen, 1964) and " 'Ali and Mu'awiya: The Rise of the Umayyad Caliphate," *Acta Orientalia* 23 (1959), 157–196. Important new sources are examined by L. Veccia Vaglieri, "Il conflitto 'Ali-Mu'awiya e la successione kharigita riesaminati alla luce di fonti ibadite" in *Annali di Instit. Orient. di Napoli* n.s. 4 (1952), 1–94, and 5 (1953), 1–98, and the further history of the Kharijites by W. M. Watt, "Kharijite Thought in the Umayyad Period," *Der Islam* 36 (1961), 215–231 and L. Veccia Vaglieri, "Le Vicende del Kharigismo in epoca abbaside," *Revista degli Studi Orientali* 24 (1949), 31–44.

The Umayyads

As has been noted in the text, the Umayyads represent a difficult historiographical problem. They have been given a sympathetic hearing by H. Lammens in his *Études sur la régne du calife omaiyade Mo'awiya Ier* (Paris, 1908), *Le Califat de Yazid Ier* (Beirut, 1910–1921), and *Études sur le siècle des Omayyades* (Beirut, 1930). H. A. R. Gibb has given his own reflections on the period in a series of studies now reprinted in *Studies on the Civilization of Islam* (pb. Boston, 1968). The classic treatment was, and to some extent remains, J. Wellhausen, *The Arab Kingdom and Its Fall* (tr. Calcutta, 1927; rp. Beirut, 1964). His interpretation was not the only one, of course (see C. Cahen, "Points de vue sur la 'revolution abbaside'," *Revue historique* [1963], 295–338), and recently Wellhausen's conclusions have been critically reexamined by M. A. Shaban, *The 'Abbasid Revolution* (Cambridge, 1970). The two regimes, the Umayyad and the 'Abbasid, were compared by G. Wiet, "L'Empire néo-byzantin des Omayyades et l'Empire néo-sassanide des 'Abbasides," *Journal of World History* 1 (1953), 63–70.

Early Sectarianism

The study of early sectarianism, where direct sources are notoriously lacking, is largely an exercise in reconstructing the positions behind heresiographies. The genre itself has been surveyed by H. Ritter, "Muhammadanische Häresiographien," *Der Islam* 28 (1929), 34–55; and H. Laoust, "L'Hérésiographie musulmane sous les Abbasides," *Cahiers de Civilization Medievale* (1967), 157–178; and some idea of how the material is laid out within them may be seen in I. Friedländer, "The Heterodoxies of the Shi'ites," *Journal of the American Oriental Society* 28 (1908), 1–80, 29 (1909), 1–183; and H. Laoust, "Classification des sectes dans le *Farq* d'al-Baghdadi," *Revue des Etudes Islamiques* 29 (1961); and the latter author has constructed his own "heresiography" in *Les Schismes dans l'Islam* (Paris, 1965). On the important new Shi'ite heresiographical sources see W. Madelung, "Bemerkungen zur imamitischen *Firaq*-Literatur," *Der Islam* 43 (1967), 37–52; and for the nature of heresy itself there is B. Lewis, "Some Observations on the Nature of Heresy in the History of Islam," *Studia Islamica* 5 (1953), 43–63; and M. Talbi, "Les *Bida'*," *ibid.* 12 (1960), 43–78.

The early struggle over free will and its political and legal consequences are surveyed by A. S. Tritton, *Muslim Theology* (London, 1948), and W. M. Watt, *Free Will and Predestination in Early Islam* (London, 1948); and A. J. Wensinck, *The Muslim Creed* (Cambridge, 1932) has traced the evolution of the Muslim *credo*. For the Murji'ites there is J. Schacht, "An Early Murji'ite Treatise," *Oriens* 17 (1964),

96–117, and W. M. Watt, "The Concept of *Iman* in Islamic Theology," *Der Islam* 43 (1967), 1–10. Jahm ibn Safwan's very different concerns have been analyzed by R. M. Frank, "The Neoplatonism of Jahm ibn Safwan," *Le Muséon* 78 (1965), 395–424, and the position of those later identified, not always carefully, as his followers by J. van Ess, "Dirar b. 'Amr und die Cahmiya," *Der Islam* 43 (1967), 241–279, 44 (1968), 1–70.

A number of attempts have been made to relate the early evolution of *kalam* to its contact with Christian theology. Among them the most influential has been C. H. Becker, "Christliche Polemik und islamische Dogmenbildung," reprinted in his *Islamstudien*, I (Leipzig, 1924), pp. 432–449. The material on both sides is now somewhat better understood by reason of studies like A. D. Khoury's *Théologiens byzantins et l'Islam. Textes et auteurs. VIIIe–XIIIe siècles* (Louvain-Paris, 1969), and M. S. Seale's *Muslim Theology: A Study of Origins in Reference to the Church Fathers* (London, 1964).

The 'Abbasid Empire

Four broadly ranging works with a great deal of detailed information on the workings of the medieval *Dar al-Islam* are T. Arnold, *The Caliphate* (rp. London, 1965), A. Mez, *The Renaissance of Islam* (tr. London, 1937), R. Levy, *The Social Structure of Islam* (rp. pb. Cambridge, 1965), and M. Gaudefroy-Demombynes, *Muslim Institutions* (tr. London, 1950). The papers by S. Goitein collected in his *Studies in Islamic History and Institutions* (Leiden, 1966) are likewise rich in detail and insights, particularly on the subject of the origins of the vizierate. That latter office has now received its definitive treatment by D. Sourdel, *Le Vizirat 'Abbaside de 749 à 936* (2 vols., Damascus, 1959–1960).

The studies by E. Tyan cited above in connection with the conquests are also pertinent here, as is the article by A. K. Lambton, "Quis Custodiet Custodes?," *Studia Islamica* 5–6 (1956). B. Spuler, *Iran in früh-islamischer Zeit* (Wiesbaden, 1952), includes details on the administration of the eastern provinces of the empire, and further information will be found in the works cited below in connection with the various provincial dynasties.

C. Cahen has been one of the chief contributors to an understanding of the social and economic life of medieval Islam, and so the reader will find an excellent guide into that complex subject in Cahen's revision of Jean Sauvaget's *Introduction to the History of the Muslim East* (tr. Berkeley and Los Angeles, 1965), pp. 86–94.

Mu'tazilitism

There is no good general study of Mu'tazilitism; A. Nader, *Le système philosophique des Mu'tazila* (Beirut, 1956), is barely adequate. There is still far more to be learned from older studies like O. Pretzl, "Die frühislamische Atomenlehre," *Der Islam* 19 (1931), 117–130; *idem, Die frühislamische Attributenlehre* (Munich, 1940); and S. Pines, *Beiträge zur islamischen Atomenlehre* (Berlin, 1936); and from more specialized treatments like the opening chapter of W. Madelung, *Der Imam al-Qasim ibn Ibrahim und die Glaubenslehre der Zaiditen* (Berlin, 1965), and the two studies by R. M. Frank, *The Metaphysics of Created Being According to Abu al-Hudhayl* (Istanbul, 1966), and "The Divine Attributes According to the Teaching of Abu al-Hudhayl al-'Allaf," *Le Muséon* 82 (1969), 451–506.

On the state of affairs at the time of Ma'mun the article "Ahmad ibn Hanbal" by H. Laoust in the new *Encyclopaedia of Islam* is important, as is D. Sourdel, "La politique religieuse du Calife 'Abbaside al-Ma'mun," *Revue des Etudes Islamiques* 30 (1962), 27–48, but the older work by W. Patton, *Ahmad ibn Hanbal and the Mihna* (Leiden, 1897), is still extremely useful. J. van Ess, "Ibn Kullab and the Mihna," *Oriens* 18–19 (1965–1966), 92–142 is a pioneer study of the other, non-Mu'tazilite *kalam* of the period and leads into the question of the Karramiyah taken up by E. Bosworth, "The Rise of the Karramiyya in Khurasan," *Muslim World* 50 (1960), 5–14.

The People of the Book

On the legal status of the religious minorities in Islam the reader should consult A. S. Tritton, *The Caliphs and Their Non-Muslim Subjects* (London, 1930); A. Fattal, *Le statut légal des non-musulmans en pays d'Islam* (Beirut, 1958); and the article "Dhimma" by C. Cahen in the new *Encyclopaedia of Islam*. The reality was, of course, quite different at times and some sense of the difference may be gotten on the Christian side from W. Hage, *Die syrische-jakobitische Kirche in frühislamischer Zeit* (Wiesbaden, 1966), J. M. Fiey, *Assyrie chrétienne. Contribution à l'étude de l'histoire et de la géographie ecclésiastique du Nord de l'Iraq* (2 vols., Beirut, 1965), and M. Allard, "Les Chrétiens à Baghdad," *Arabica* 9 (1962), 375–388; and from the Jewish side, W. J. Fischel, *Jews in the Economic and Political Life of Medieval Islam* (rp. London, 1968), S. Goitein, *A Mediterranean Society: The Jewish Community of the Arab World as*

Portrayed in the Documents of the Cairo Geniza, I, *Economic Foundations* (Berkeley and Los Angeles, 1967), and G. Vajda, "Le milieu juif à Baghdad," *Arabica* 9 (1962), 389–393.

The Islamic Sciences

Some pertinent material has already been cited in connection with the *Qur'an*, above, and there is much additional information on the Islamic sciences in Vol. I of Sezgin, *GAS*. Its broader context can be studied in the provocative papers collected by R. Brunschvig and G. von Grunebaum, *Classicisme et déclin culturel dans l'histoire de l'Islam* (Paris, 1957), and the interesting study by F. Rosenthal, *The Technique and Approach of Muslim Scholarship* (Rome, 1947). On Muslim education there is A. S. Tritton, *Materials on Muslim Education in the Middle Ages* (London, 1957), the article "Madrasa" by J. Pedersen in the *Shorter Encyclopaedia of Islam*, and the important study of G. Makdisi, "Muslim institutions of learning in eleventh century Baghdad," *Bulletin of the School of Oriental and African Studies* 24 (1961), 1–56.

The investigation of the Arab grammarians goes back to G. Flügel's *Die grammatischen Schulen der Araber* (Leipzig, 1862), and the most recent historical work on the subject has been done in connection with Khalil: W. Reuschel, *Al-Khalil ibn Ahmad, der Lehrer Sibawaihs, als Grammatiker* (Berlin, 1959). For lexicography there is J. Kraemer, "Studien zur altarabischen Lexicographie," *Oriens* 6 (1953), 201–238, and the survey by J. A. Haywood, *Arabic Lexicography* (2nd ed. Leiden, 1965).

Arabic literary criticism was the special preserve of the late G. von Grunebaum; see particularly his *Kritik und Dichtkunst* (Wiesbaden, 1955), *A Tenth Century Document of Arabic Literary Theory and Criticism* (Chicago, 1950), and the wealth of insights in his *Medieval Islam* (2nd ed. pb. Chicago, 1953). There are in addition the rich introductions by H. Ritter to 'Abd al-Qahir's *Asrar al-balaghah* (Istanbul, 1954) and by S. A. Bonebakker to Qudamah ibn Ja'far's *Naqd al-shi'r* (London, 1956).

The best works on the *sunnah* sciences remain the studies by I. Goldziher collected in his *Vorlesungen über den Islam* (2nd ed. Heidelberg, 1925) and the second volume of his newly translated *Muslim Studies* (tr. London, 1971), to which should be compared Sezgin, *GAS* I, pp. 53–84. On Goldziher's foundations J. Schacht constructed his classic *The Origins of Muhammadan Jurisprudence* (Oxford,

1953). Two general studies of Muslim law and jurisprudence are J. Schacht, *An Introduction to Islamic Law* (Oxford, 1964), and N. J. Coulson, *A History of Islamic Law* (Edinburgh, 1964).

The best brief introduction to Muslim historiography is probably H. A. R. Gibb's article "Ta'rikh," originally written for the *Encyclopaedia of Islam* and now reprinted in *Studies on the Civilization of Islam* (pb. Boston, 1968). F. Rosenthal, *A History of Muslim Historiography* (2nd ed. Leiden, 1968), is not quite that but is interesting nonetheless. There are a number of good essays collected by B. Lewis and P. M. Holt, *Historians of the Middle East* (London, 1962), to which should be added W. Caskel, "Aiyam al-'Arab," *Islamica* 3 (1931), 1–99; R. Paret, *Die legendäre Maghazi-Literatur* (Tübingen, 1930); R. Sellheim, "Prophet, Calif und Geschichte, die Muhammad-Biographie des Ibn Ishaq," *Oriens* 18–19 (1965–1966), 31–91; F. Rosenthal, "Die arabische Autobiographie," *Analecta Orientalia* 14 (1937), 1–40; and M. S. Khan, "Miskawayh and Arabic Historiography," *Journal of the American Oriental Society* 89 (1969), 710–730.

The Reception of Hellenism

A major contributor to the study of the transmission of Greek thought into Islam has been R. Walzer. A number of his most important articles have been collected in *Greek into Arabic* (Cambridge, Mass., 1962) and he has been responsible for most of the pertinent entries ("Aflatun," "Aristutalis," "Baruklus," etc.) in the new *Encyclopaedia of Islam.* The modern pioneer of the study was M. Steinschneider, and his *Die arabischen Übersetzungen aus dem griechischen* (rp. Graz, 1960) is still important, as is M. Meyerhof's "Von Alexandrien nach Baghdad: Ein Beitrag zur Geschichte des philosophischen und medizinischen Unterrichts bei den Arabern," *Sitz. Ak. Wiss. Berlin* 23 (1930), 388–429. More recently there has been F. E. Peters, *Aristotle and the Arabs* (New York, 1969), A. Badawi, *La transmission de la philosophie grecque au monde arabe* (Paris, 1968), and the two bibliographical surveys by R. Paret in *Byzantion* 29–30 (1959–1960), 387–446, and J. van Ess in *Parousia: Festgabe für Johannes Hirschberger* (Frankfurt, 1965), pp. 333–350.

The Foreign Sciences

There is no general treatment of this subject, but one can get some sense of the terrain from S. H. Nasr, *Science and Civilization in Islam* (Cambridge, Mass., 1966), and the brief excerpts offered in translation in F. Rosenthal, *Das Fortleben der Antike im Islam* (Zurich-Stuttgart,

1965). The works of the scientists appear, of course, in both *GAL* and *GAS*, and there are other bibliographical treatments of individual authors in A. Mieli, *La Science Arabe* (2nd ed. Leiden, 1966), an extremely uneven work, and in G. Sarton, *An Introduction to the History of Science* (3 vols. in 5, Baltimore, 1927–1947).

For the mathematical sciences one may begin generally with Carra de Vaux's "Astronomy and Mathematics" in *The Legacy of Islam* (Oxford, 1931), pp. 376–398. The most fundamental work is still H. Suter, *Die Mathematiker und Astronomen der Araber und ihre Werke* (Leipzig, 1900), with the additions and corrections of H. Renaud in *Isis* 18 (1932), 166–183, and the reviews of newer work by P. Luckey, "Beiträge zur Erforschung der islamischen Mathematik," *Orientalia* n.s. 17 (1948), 490–510; n.s. 22 (1953), 166–189. The most recent research in Islamic astronomy has taken as one of its focuses the Sasanian antecedents; see, for example, D. Pingree, "Historical Horoscopes," *Journal of the American Oriental Society* 82 (1962), 487–502, and "Astronomy and Astrology in India and Iran," *Isis* 54 (1963), 229–246. Pingree's book, *The Thousands of Abu Ma'shar* (London, 1968), also looks back to Sasanian times. There is a good history of the observatory in A. Sayili, *The Observatory in Islam and Its Place in the General History of the Observatory* (Ankara, 1960).

Treatments of geography in Arabic have been mostly of the descriptive branch of the science, as is apparent from the article "Djughrafiya" by S. M. Ahmad in the new *Encyclopaedia of Islam* and that on "Geography and Commerce" by J. H. Kramers in *The Legacy of Islam* (Oxford, 1931), pp. 79–107. For a more detailed presentation there is the introduction by W. Barthold to V. Minorsky's edition of the *Hudud al-'alam* (London, 1937).

Fundamental to any understanding of the occult sciences in Islam is A. J. Festugière's *La Révélation d'Hermès Trismégiste*, particularly Vol. I, *L'Astrologie et les Sciences Occultes* (Paris, 1950) with the appendix by L. Massignon, "L'Hermetisme Arabe," pp. 384–400. The Arab *Hermetica* have also been considered by M. Plessner, "Hermes Trismegistus and Arab Science," *Studia Islamica* 2 (1954), 45–59, and A. Affifi, "The Influence of Hermetic Literature on Muslim Thought," *Bulletin of the School of Oriental and African Studies* 13 (1951), 840–855. H. Ritter's study of Majriti is also instructive on occultism in general: "Picatrix, ein arabisches Handbuch hellenistischer Magie," *Vorträge, Bibliothek Warburg* (1921–1922), 94–124. Finally there is Manfred Ullmann's *Die Natur- und Geheimwissenschaften im Islam* (Leiden, 1972), the most recent and by all accounts the best treatment of occultism in Islam.

Vol. IV of Sezgin, *GAS* (Leiden, 1971), is given over to alchemy, and there are briefer treatments of that subject from very different points of view in E. J. Holmyard, *Alchemy* (pb. Harmondsworth, 1957), and T. Burckhardt, *Alchemy* (tr. pb. Baltimore, 1971). Sezgin has reopened the question of Jabir ibn Hayyan and has directed attention once again to the rich collection of occult material in P. Kraus, *Jabir ibn Hayyan. Contribution à l'histoire des idées scientifiques dans l'Islam* (2 vols., Cairo, 1942).

Medicine is the subject of Vol. III of Sezgin, *GAS* (Leiden, 1970), which has, unfortunately, its *Doppelgänger* in M. Ullmann, *Die Medizin im Islam* (Leiden, 1970). These two, taken with S. Hamarneh, *Bibliography on Medicine and Pharmacy in Medieval Islam* (Stuttgart, 1964), cover every conceivable angle of the field, but for a more general orientation there is M. Meyerhof, "Science and Medicine," in *The Legacy of Islam* (Oxford, 1931), pp. 311–355.

FALSAFAH

Philosophy in Islam has been well studied for over a century, and the reader will find a convenient review of the most recent work on the subject by G. Anawati, "Bibliographie de la philosophie médiévale en terre de l'Islam pour les années 1959–1969," *Bulletin de Philosophie Médiévale* 10–12 (1968–1970), 316–369. Attention is drawn here merely to three recent general works: W. M. Watt, *Islamic Philosophy and Theology* (Edinburgh, 1962); H. Corbin, *Histoire de la Philosophie Islamique* I (Paris, 1964); and M. Fakhry, *A History of Islamic Philosophy* (New York, 1970).

KALAM

Theologians have their place in both *GAL* and the first volume of *GAS*, and the general histories of philosophy by Watt, Corbin and Fakhry devote some attention to theology as well, but *kalam* has clearly not interested Western scholars to the same degree as *falsafah*. The pioneer study by L. Gardet and G. Anawati, *Introduction à la théologie musulmane, Essai de théologie comparée* (Paris, 1948), has not had many sequels, and one of the best recent surveys of *kalam* is not a history at all but an interpretive and heavily commented translation of the propaedeutic chapters of a work of *kalam* by the later scholastic al-Iji (d. 1355): J. van Ess, *Die Erkenntnislehre des 'Adudaddin al-Ici. Übersetzung des ersten Buches seiner Mawaqif* (Wiesbaden, 1966).

For the fortunes of Ash'arism there is G. Makdisi, "Ash'ari and the

Ash'arites in Islamic Religious History," *Studia Islamica* 17 (1962), 37–80, 18 (1963), 19–39; D. Sourdel, "La politique religieuse des successeurs d'al-Mutawakkil," *Studia Islamica* 18 (1960), 5–21, and, more generally, M. Allard, *Le Probleme des attributes divins dans la doctrine d'al-Ash'ari et ses premiers grands disciples* (Beirut, 1965).

In another article, "En quoi consiste l'opposition faite à al-Ash'ari par ses contemporains hanbalites," *Revue des Études Islamiques* 28 (1960), 93 ff., Allard has attempted to do justice to the Hanbalite position, but there are fuller treatments by H. Laoust, *La Profession de Foi d'Ibn Batta* (Damascus, 1958) and G. Makdisi, *Ibn 'Aqil et la résurgence d'Islam traditionaliste au XIe siècle* (Damascus, 1963), as well as in the survey by H. Laoust, "Le hanbalisme sous le califat de Bagdad," *Revue des Études Islamiques* 27 (1959), 67–128.

Sufism

The most profound study of early Sufism and still the point of departure of much of what follows is L. Massignon, *Essai sur les origines du lexique technique de la mystique musulmane* (2nd ed. Paris, 1954), and the same author's article "Tasawwuf" in the *Shorter Encyclopaedia of Islam* is an excellent introduction to the subject. Among other general treatments are R. A. Nicholson, *Studies in Islamic Mysticism* (rp. Cambridge, 1967); M. Smith, *Studies in Early Mysticism in the Near and Middle East* (London, 1931); G. Anawati and L. Gardet, *Mystique musulmane* (Paris, 1961); and A. J. Arberry, *Sufism: An Account of the Mystics of Islam* (2nd ed. pb. New York, 1970). On the difficult question of Indian influences the positions pro and con are put forth in R. Zaehner, *Hindu and Muslim Mysticism* (pb. New York, 1969), and M. Moreno, "Mistica musulmana e mistica indiana," *Annales Lateranensi* 10 (1946), 103–212.

Some few of the Muslim mystics have received individual treatments of a critical nature, but attention is drawn here to only two by reason of the wider issues raised by them: L. Massignon, *La Passion d'al-Hallaj, martyr mystique de l'Islam* (Paris, 1922), and J. van Ess, *Die Gedankenwelt des Harith al-Muhasibi* (Bonn, 1961).

Shi'ism

Much remains obscure in the early history of the movement. M. Hodgson, "How Did the Early Shi'a Become Sectarian?" *Journal of the American Oriental Society* 75 (1955), 1–13, is important, and there is, in addition, W. M. Watt, "Shi'ism Under the Umayyads," *Journal of the Royal Asiatic Society* (1960), 158–172; S. Moscati, "Per una storia dell'antica Shi'a," *Revista degli Studi Orientali* 30 (1955), 251–267; and, for a political and economic interpretation, M. Hinds, "Kufan Political Alignments and Their Background in the Mid-Seventh Century," *International Journal of Middle East Studies* 2 (1971), 346–367. The Zaydi situation is much clearer thanks to W. Madelung, *Der Imam al-Qasim ibn Ibrahim und die Glaubenslehre der Zaiditen* (Berlin, 1965), which is important for the history of Mu'tazilitism as well.

Various Shi'ite authors are taken up in Vol. I of Sezgin, *GAS*, but the reader may perhaps get a better perspective on recent work from the symposium papers edited by T. Fahd, *Le Shi'isme Imamite* (Paris, 1970) and the at times overengaged pages of H. Corbin, *En Islam iranien: Aspects spirituels et philosophiques*, I, *Le shi'isme duodécimain* (Paris, 1971).

The Isma'ilis and Qarmatians pose special problems. There have been a number of studies of the former, as W. Ivanov, *A Brief Survey of the Origins of Isma'ilism* (Bombay, 1952), and B. Lewis, *The Origins of Isma'ilism* (Cambridge, 1940), and the later phases of Isma'ili history have been investigated by S. M. Stern, "The Early Isma'ili Missionaries in North-West Persia and in Khurasan and Transoxania," *Bulletin of the School of Oriental and African Studies* 23 (1960), 59–90; B. Lewis, *The Assassins* (London, 1967); and M. Hodgson, *The Order of Assassins* (The Hague, 1955). Hodgson also contributed the chapter on "The Isma'ili State" to *The Cambridge History of Iran*, V, *The Saljuq and Mongol Periods* (Cambridge, 1968), pp. 422–482. The issues are by no means settled, however. So much is clear from two recent studies by W. Madelung, "Fatimiden and Bahrainqarmaten," *Der Islam* 34 (1959), 34–88, and "Das Imamat in der frühen ismailitischen Lehre," *ibid.* 35 (1960), 43–135. On the Druzes there is M. Hodgson, "Al-Darazi and Hamza in the Origin of the Druze Religion," *Journal of the American Oriental Society* 82 (1962), 5–20.

The Dynasties

A convenient chronological approach to the various Muslim dynasties is through C. E. Bosworth, *The Islamic Dynasties* (Edinburgh, 1967). Egypt is well served by G. Wiet, *L'Égypte arabe* (Paris, 1937), Z. M. Hassan, *Les Tulunides: étude de l'Égypte musulmane à la fin du IXe siècle* (Paris, 1933), and M. Canard, *Les Institutions des Fatimides en Égypte* (Algiers, 1957); and the Syrian dynasties by H. Lammens, *La Syrie, précis historique* (Beirut, 1921), C. Cahen, *La Syrie du Nord à l'époque des croisades* (Paris, 1940), and M. Canard, *Histoire de la dynastie des Hamdanides de Jazira et de Syrie* (Paris, 1953).

For the Buyids there is now the major study of H. Busse, *Chalif und Grosskönig: Die Buyiden im Iraq* (Beirut, 1969), to add to V. Minorsky's earlier *La Domination des Dailamites* (Paris, 1932), and for the Ghaznavids, C. E. Bosworth, *The Ghaznavids. Their Empire in Afghanistan and Eastern Iran* (Edinburgh, 1963), both books with extensive bibliographies. For the lesser dynasties in the East one may turn more conveniently perhaps to somewhat more general works: B. Spuler, *Iran in früh-islamischer Zeit* (Wiesbaden, 1952), W. Barthold, *Turkestan Down to the Mongol Invasion* (3rd ed. tr. London, 1968), and J. A. Boyle (ed.), *The Cambridge History of Iran*, V, *The Saljuq and Mongol Periods* (Cambridge, 1968).

The Seljuqs are treated in detail in that latter volume, to which should be compared C. Cahen's *Pre-Ottoman Turkey* (tr. London, 1968), for their activities other than in Iran. There is, finally, H. Horst, *Die Staatsverwaltung der Grosseljuqen und Khwarazmshahs* (Wiesbaden, 1964); and H. Laoust, *La Politique de Ghazali* (Paris, 1970) casts considerable light upon the policies of the Seljuqs as well as on Ghazali.

INDEX